International Conferences ICT, Society, and Human Beings (ICT2020); Connected Smart Cities (CSC2020); and Web Based Communities and Social Media (WBC2020)

Held at MCCSIS 2020 (Held online due to COVID-19)

Lisbon, Portugal
21 - 25 July 2020

ISBN: 978-1-7138-2276-9

Printed from e-media with permission by:

Curran Associates, Inc.
57 Morehouse Lane
Red Hook, NY 12571

Some format issues inherent in the e-media version may also appear in this print version.

Printed with permission by Curran Associates, Inc. (2021)

International Association for Development of the Information Society (IADIS)
Rua Sao Sebastiao Da Pedreira
No. 100, 30, 1050-209
Lisbon, Portugal

Phone: 351 21 3151373
Fax: 351 21 3151244

secretariat@iadis.org

Additional copies of this publication are available from:

Curran Associates, Inc.
57 Morehouse Lane
Red Hook, NY 12571 USA
Phone: 845-758-0400
Fax: 845-758-2633
Email: curran@proceedings.com
Web: www.proceedings.com

TABLE OF CONTENTS

MANAGING MILLENNIALS AS OUTSOURCED INFORMATION TECHNOLOGY PROFESSIONALS: A SYSTEMATIC REVIEW

Tiago Jacob Fernandes França[1], Henrique São Mamede[2] and Vítor Duarte dos Santos[3]
[1]*Instituto Superior Técnico, Universidade Aberta, 1250-100 Lisboa, Portugal*
[2]*Universidade Aberta, INESC TEC, 1269-001 Lisboa, Portugal*
[3]*Universidade Nova – IMS, 1070-312 Lisboa, Portugal*

ABSTRACT

The Information Technology Outsourcing (ITO) model has been a trend in recent decades, becoming the dominant trend in contemporary outsourcing scenario. Millennials will soon, globally, be the majority of the workforce, having a particular way of relating to organizations and to work itself as no previous generation did. Information technologies continue to employ more and more human resources, having an increasing demand and a shortage of competent resources. It is therefore important to rethink current Human Resources Management (HRM) models and design a new strategic and appropriate model to accommodate and anticipate the needs of managers and monitor the development of this generation as Information Technology (IT) professionals. The intersection and analysis of the Information and Communications Technologies (ICT), millennials, Human Resource Management, outsourcing and organizations is the objective of this study, to identify the most relevant articles regarding millennials as outsourced IT professionals.

KEYWORDS

Organizations, ICT, Outsourcing, HRM, Millennials, ITO

1. INTRODUCTION

A systematic review was performed based on a search of the literature where a total of 22 articles were retrieved. The combined articles report the context of millennials as IT professionals thus contributing to enhance our knowledge of the subject, especially being such a specific perspective, adding new insights on the matter. The following five dimensions, as seen in figure 1, forms an interconnected structure, essential to understand the specific context of millennials as outsourced Information Technology (IT) professionals. The five dimensions are born from Organizations, including the Information and Communications Technology (ICT), which often uses the Outsourcing model, where the Human Resources Management (HRM) plays a fundamental role, especially in Millennials, the target group of this study.

As providers of opportunities and managers of both professional and social development of their human resources, organizations are considered to be the first dimension, encompassing the other four dimensions, where millennials are so different from those of one and two generations ago (Thompson and Gregory, 2012). The second dimension, the ICT, an area in constant development and increasingly strategic for any organization that wants to evolve and obtain a competitive advantage (Deloitte, 2019). Outsourcing is the third dimension, increasingly valued and used, especially in the area of information technologies (Deloitte, 2019). HRM, the fourth dimension, is fundamental to the management and development process of millennials. "Working with the human being means developing it" (Drucker, 1986). Finally, millennials themselves, the target population of this study, are considered the fifth dimension.

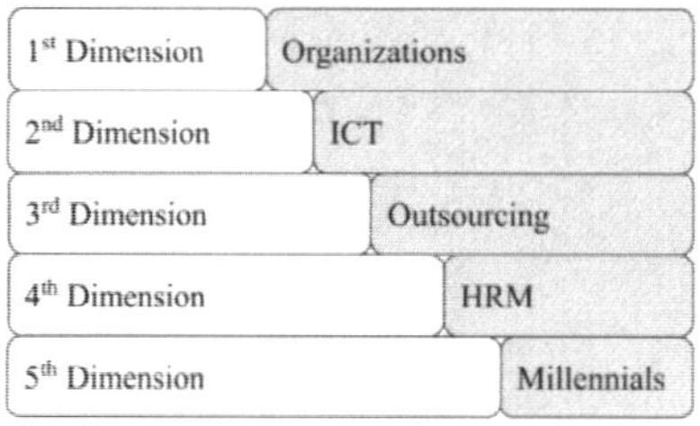

Figure 1. The five dimensions

The reason for this study is due to the urgency of the generation, for being current and because it will soon be the largest workforce in the world. Therefore, it is urgent to understand them, within organizations, and in a context in constant evolution and mutation such as ICT, where the hiring models - due to the growth and the particularities of the area - are very permeable to subcontract or outsource services. The convergence of digital transformation and the impact of changes in the technological, sociological, psychological and management dimensions merge in the millennials, shaping them by their relationship with technology (Elmore and Cathy, 2009), where everything is relational, of associated intelligence and collective, with effectively global behaviors.

The Information Technology Outsourcing (ITO) model in organizations is becoming a constant (Deloitte, 2019) and has been a trend in recent decades, becoming the dominant trend in the contemporary outsourcing scenario. Inserting themselves in the transition to the new century, highly technological and global, millennials are the first truly digital generation, not only are they interested in technology, they are also specialists (Holt, 2012).

According to Schawbel (2012) millennials will soon, globally, be the majority of the workforce. Thus, to accommodate and anticipate the needs of managers and monitor the management of millennials as outsourced IT professionals, it is understood that it is necessary to rethink current HRM processes and design new ones, as the psychological and sociological needs of millennials are very specific and different from previous generations, to which organizations are accustomed. As such, organizations must evolve and follow the reality of this generation, considering the relevant dimensions which require an increasingly strategic attention, in order to be successful in this organizational dynamic.

We intend to obtain a selection of articles related to outsourcing, organizational management, human resources management, millennials and the area of information technologies, so it is needed to understand the state of the art with regard to these themes, relating the information where it is relevant. The target population of this study are millennials as outsourced IT professionals, considering the processes that address specific questions about the management of human resources. The results must be related to the factors of importance for outsourcing in the areas of information technology and the context will be the management of human resources of information technologies, specifically regarding millennials. The research question was "What is the management process of millennials as outsourced information technology professionals?". The following chapters will describe the literature review, method, results and conclusions.

2. LITERATURE REVIEW

This Systematic Literature Review was carried out following the proposal by Kitchenham (2004) aiming to present a correct assessment on the research topic using a reliable, rigorous and auditable methodology. The first step when developing a Review Protocol is to define the query string that will be used to search the defined data sources, in order to find the maximum number of studies on the subject in question. Several attempts were made with different query strings until finding a more suitable one, according to the keywords used in table 1. The defined query string was: ("millennials" OR "Generation Y") AND ("human resources management" OR "HRM") AND ("information technology outsourcing" OR "ITO").

Table 1. Keywords and synonyms

Keyword	Synonyms
Human Resources Management	HRM
Information Technology Outsourcing	ITO
Millennials	Generation Y

The search process was based on a digital search, accessing the information sources listed in table 2.

Table 2. Information sources

Information Sources	Address
Crossref	https://www.crossref.org
Google Scholar	https://scholar.google.com
Scopus	https://www.scopus.com

Inclusion and exclusion criteria were defined and listed in table 3, in order to be applied to collected documents based on the previous step.

Table 3. Inclusion and exclusion criteria

Inclusion Criteria	Exclusion Criteria
Scientific Documents	Incomplete articles; Duplicate articles; Publications prior to 2000; Lack of access to the article; Languages different from English or Portuguese.
Thesis	Themes not relevant to this investigation.
Reference Consultant Publications	Themes not relevant to this investigation.

Although there were no intentions for the study to be biased in any way, it should be mentioned that it has limitations, specifically over the dependency on the selected keywords, the selected databases and in the fact that literature and publications written in other languages than English and Portuguese were excluded. Also, the inclusion and exclusion criteria have a relevant impact on the chosen articles and therefore on the included articles in this study. The exclusion criteria for publications prior to 2000 was based on the fact that this study is centered on millennials, so, studies from the year in which millennials begin their professional career were considered to be more relevant.

Only three databases were used, and for that reason we may be excluding relevant articles, but we believe that among these sources we are searching the vast majority of the relevant documents. These sources provide a simple way to search extensively over academic literature, articles, thesis, books, abstracts, academic editors, professional societies, online repositories and universities, where it is possible to search across different disciplines. In addition to the collected articles through this protocol, other relevant documents were also identified, either because they are references used in the researched documents or because they are the result of separate research on the topics in question, documents that are however included in this study and that are an integral part of the bibliographic reference.

2.1 Method

In this section we describe the review, in which we select primary studies and extract data using the review protocol developed in the previous step. After applying the defined query string, a total of 559 results were obtained. The records identified by data source are distributed as follows: Scopus (n = 104), Google Scholar (n = 222) and Crossref (n = 233), as shown in figure 2.

After applying the criteria defined in the previous section, the number of documents was reduced to a set of 35. In addition, a quality assessment was carried out on them, consisting of the following questions, which helped selecting the articles to include in this study:

- Is the article relevant to answer the research question?
- Does the article focus on millennials as the subject of the study?
- Does the article refer to information systems (technology, people and processes)?
- Does the article refer to ITO as a research objective, motivation or question?
- Does the article refer to how organizations manage human resources in order to provide the information needed to achieve their goals?

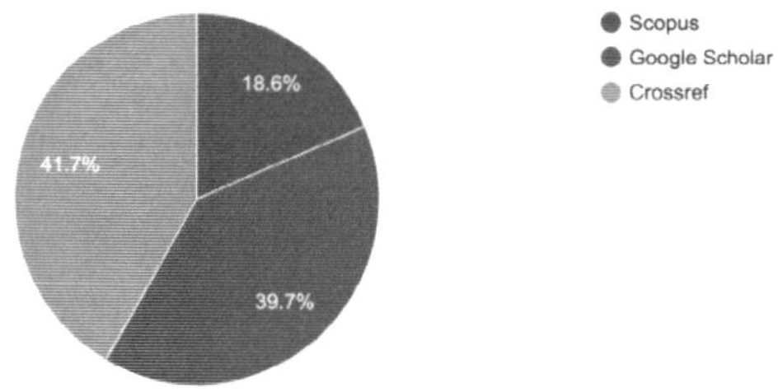

Figure 2. Article distribution by information sources

Table 4 shows the possible answers and respective scores for the quality assessment questions. The answers were limited to "Yes", "Partially" and "No", and for each one, a score was assigned, determining the definitive inclusion or exclusion of articles in the study.

Table 4. Answer score for quality assessment questions

Answer	Score
Yes	1.0
Partially	0.75
No	0

The maximum score is 5.0, a calculation based on the number of possible answers with the highest score, while the minimum score for electing an article was set at 2.5. There are articles in which the content does not answer all the proposed questions, but it is relevant enough to be included in the study, therefore, when defining the minimum eligibility score, it will be necessary to have at least one answer whose result is "Yes" and two answers with "Partially".

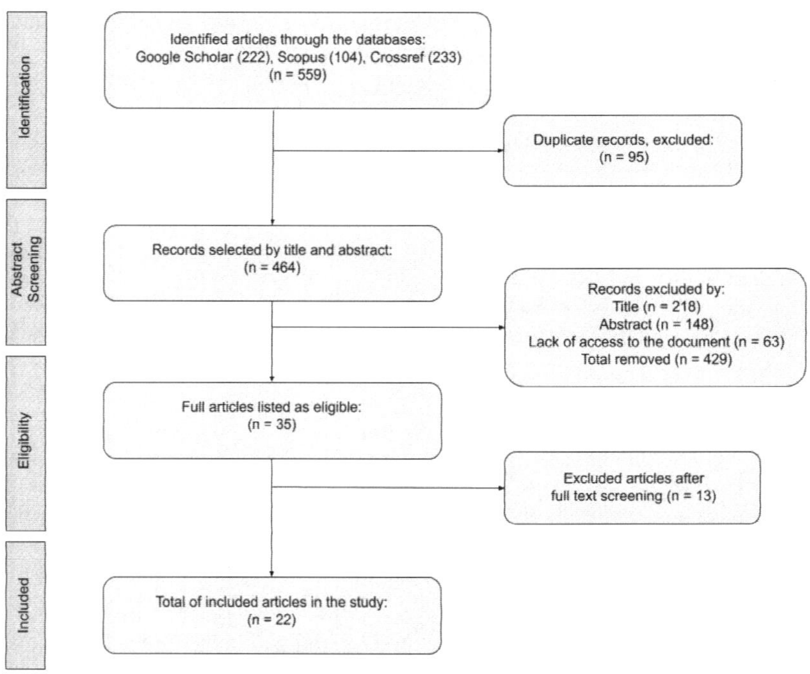

Figure 3. Article selection flowchart

The total number of records identified were (n=559), and were removed (n=95) identified as duplicates. Of the remaining articles (n=464), several articles were excluded by title and abstract, in the following proportion: excluded by Title (n=218), excluded by Abstract (n=148). It was not possible to access some of the articles, due to unavailability of the source or because they had limited access, which excluded them (n=63). A total of (n=429) articles were removed.

There were (n=39) articles eligible to be included in the investigation. After reading these articles in full and scoring according to the quality assessment answers, some articles were still excluded (n=13). The total articles included in the investigation are (n=22) as seen in figure 3.

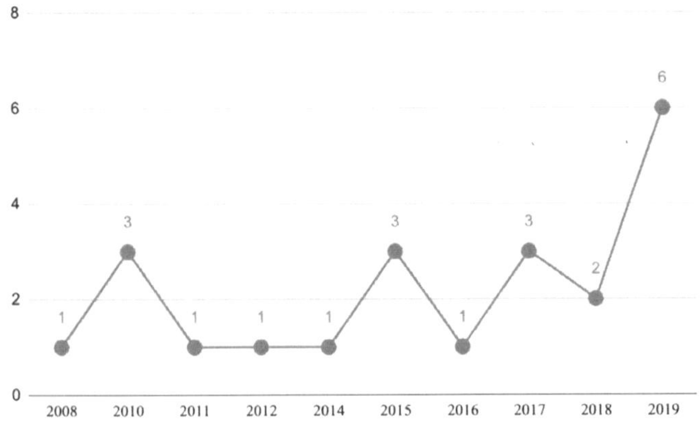

Figure 4. Number of included articles by year of publication

The selected articles were published between 2008 and 2019, as shown in figure 4. Table 5 shows the article's authors, the dimension to which it relates to, the year of publication and the score obtained. The included articles were annotated in order to show its relevance, from a critical perspective and in the light of the research question.

Table 5. Selected articles list

Author	Dimension	Year	Score
Conde, S. R.	Outsourcing | Organization	2019	4.0
Soares, L. P. M	Millennials | HRM	2019	3.0
Azmi, F.	HRM | ICT	2019	3.25
Hassan, M. *et al.*	Millennials | HRM	2019	3.5
Solomon, C., & Van Coller-Peter, S.	Millennials | Organization | HRM	2019	3.0
Thite, M.	HRM | ICT	2018	3.25
Souto, C.P.	Millennials | Organization | HRM	2018	3.25
Lioliou, E., & Willcocks, L. P.	ICT | Outsourcing	2018	2.75
Nasir, S. Z.	HRM | ICT	2017	2.75
Cassell, S. K.	Millennials | HRM	2017	3.5
Bartz, D. *et al.*	Millennials | Organization | HRM	2017	2.5
Marler, J. H., & Parry, E.	HRM | ICT	2016	3.0
Galetić, L.	Millennials | HRM	2015	2.5
Özçelik, G.	Millennials | Organization	2015	3.0
Valente, A. & Correia, I.	ICT	2015	4.0
Jerome, A. *et al.*	Millennials | Organization	2014	2.5
Thompson, C., & Gregory, J.	Millennials | Organization	2012	3.25
Smyrl, B. J.	Millennials | HRM	2011	2.75
Hershatter, A., & Epstein, M.	Millennials | Organization	2010	3.0
Myers, K. K., & Sadaghiani, K.	Millennials | Organization	2010	3.0
Levenson, A. R.	Millennials | Organization	2010	2.75
Westlund, S.	Organization | ICT	2008	3.0

2.2 Results

Organizations that do not attract a vital core of millennial employees will be lacking in competitive vigor (Jerome, 2014) so, in order for organizations to attract millennials, it is necessary to understand their expectations and contribution to the success of organizations.

There is a lack of hundreds of thousands of qualified professionals in the digital area (Valente and Correia, 2015) suggesting that education and training entities, having the scope for adaptation and innovation, should connect with organizations in the sector renewing training references, providing internships, ensuring access to business training.

The strengths and opportunities of using human resources outsourcing services outweighs the weaknesses and threats (Conde, 2019) sustaining the fact that outsourcing is clearly beneficial for organizations as it allows bringing specialized knowledge. According to Lioliou and Willcocks (2018) selective outsourcing carried out by different suppliers with short-term contracts is the scenario most likely to generate positive results, as it has been the trend for the past 25 years for organizations to outsource through different suppliers, becoming the dominant trend in the contemporary outsourcing scenario.

The retention of young employees has become an increasing and global problem and remains unresolved, so it is necessary for organizations to focus on leadership, to promote innovation, to recognize employees as an important factor in the organization (Hassan, 2019) and with a leadership capable of promoting the balance between personal and professional life.

Perhaps the most important factor for millennials is to feel valued and supported by their direct supervisor (Cassell, 2017) revealing that the main elements identified for creating feelings of support are organizational policies that promote development opportunities, flexible options for work and balance between professional and personal life. Bartz (2017) speaks of an environment for millennials in which they can be and give their best, through processes of feedback and coaching, supported by their supervisors.

According to Solomon and Van Coller-Peter (2019) coaching is a viable strategy for organizations to involve and retain their millennial professionals, particularly with regard to career development, as millennials highly value the balance between professional and personal life. Human resource managers started designing complex strategies for the organization, including finding balance between personal and professional life (Nasir, 2017) and Soares (2019) verified the positive impact of performance evaluation on the career of millennial professionals, namely in the search for knowledge, in the development of skills, in the knowledge of new technologies, in self-evaluation and in influencing decision making.

According to Westlund (2008) organizations should develop cultures that stimulate creativity, autonomy, motivation and organizational commitment, progressively challenging and creating opportunities so its employees can learn new technologies and recognize the achievements of the teams. Souto (2018) concluded that the work values most valued by millennials are those of development, where they intend to have the opportunity to develop their skills, have adequate training and be able to work on motivating projects. They also value the opportunity to be part of a team, to have a manager who gives constructive feedback, where the work environment is dynamic, fun and allows for constant social interaction.

Galetić (2015) reveals that millennials give more importance to non-material rewards and shows that millennials are not necessarily a homogeneous group, recommending that human resource managers should adapt reward strategies to individual characteristics, emphasizing that young millennials with work experience greatly favor job training, teamwork and participation in decision-making.

For Thite (2018) the focus of digital human resource management must be on a digital workforce, agile and focused on innovation, in a digital workplace characterized by a learning mentality. Both the digital transformation and the human resource managers generate a circular impact in the strategic role of the HRM over the organization (Marler and Parry, 2015), also Azmi (2019) explains how the interaction between information technologies and HR brought a new culture of information, through instantaneity, interactivity, informality and intangibility where organizations take advantage of the experiences created by social networks using their power to effectively manage human resources for the acquisition, management and retention of talent. Ozcelik (2015) states that employees must receive value propositions through effective communication, especially millennials who develop feelings of loyalty through the opportunity to work from home or have flexible hours.

Thompson and Gregory (2012) refer that organizations consider common stereotypes of millennial employees in the educational, political, economic and social contexts present in their formative years suggesting that management style can be the key to successfully leveraging the talents of millennials in organizations. Hershatter and Epstein (2010) say millennials are concerned with authenticity and institutional values because they rely on work to promote change, where their skills with technology allow them to access information easily and creatively and to think and function in a world without borders, being oriented to people and organizations, thus facilitating the process of involvement and acculturation.

Smyrl (2011) describes millennial's main values as optimistic, reliable, civic and achievement oriented and according to Myers and Sadaghiani (2010) millennials work well as a team, are motivated to create an impact on their organizations, favor open and frequent communication with their supervisors and are at ease with information technologies. Real change is probably much more incremental and gradual from one generation to the next so organizations should be aware whether this change is significant as a characteristic that defines an entire generation knowing when a gradual change becomes a turning point (Levenson, 2010).

3. CONCLUSION

There are a growing number of studies concerning millennials and their profile definition is consistent. Millennials now make up a large percentage of the global workforce and will soon be the majority. We know that millennials have a particular way of relating to organizations and to work itself, as no previous generation has done. ICT continues to employ even more human resources, but there is an increasing demand and a shortage of competent resources while the ITO model has become the dominant trend in the contemporary outsourcing scenario.

It is understood that people management will represent one of the greatest challenges for organizations, not only due to multigenerational issues, where organizations will have to find the best practices to simultaneously maintain different generations with different satisfaction factors, but also to learn how to understand these generational groups and enabling them to do their best, together and in line with the organization's strategy. Technology, globalization, demographics and other factors influence organizational structures and cultures. Nowadays organizations deal with the reality of the scarcity of competent resources, managing people through change, in an attempt to create an effective workforce.

We know that millennial professionals are attracted to organizations by a distinct set of advantages, valuing the organization's culture and flexibility in determining their own ways of working and showing their views through open communication channels. After joining the organization, they seek support and guidance through mentors and to keep them in the organization they demand balance between personal and professional life, they want to be constantly learning and to strengthen their knowledge.

Any processes suitable for millennials management will have to respond to their needs and integrate them with the needs and reality of the organizations. The author believes this study findings contribute to add knowledge mainly to organizations and human resources management, as we can perceive millennial's profile as outsourced IT professionals allowing organizations to better adapt to them.

Further research should be taken in order to create new or enhance existing organizational management processes highlighting millennials as outsourced IT professionals, considering all the environment it relates to, like multigenerational issues, incorporating technology in the professional relation with millennials and considering new work habits like remote working.

REFERENCES

Azmi, F. (2019). Technology and HRM. In Strategic Human Resource Management: Text and Cases (pp. 80-108). Cambridge: Cambridge University Press. doi:10.1017/9781108687058.004

Bartz, D. *et al.* (2017). Maximizing the Human Capital of Millennials Through Supervisors Using Performance Management. International Journal of Management, Business, and Administration, Vol.20(No.1).

Cassell, S. K. (2017). HRM Solutions for Retaining Millennials in Western Societies. Mediterranean Journal of Social Sciences, Vol.8(No.5).

Conde, S. R. (2019). Outsourcing Human Resources: a Practical View. https://hdl.handle.net/10216/123277

Deloitte. (2019). Outsourcing and Shared Services 2019-2023. http://outsourcing-outlook.com/assets/pdf/Deloitte-DOC-Whitepaper_outsourcing-and-shared-services2019-2023.pdf

Drucker, P. F. (1986). The Frontiers of Management (1st ed.). New York, EUA: Dutton Adult.

Elmore, T., & Cathy, D. (2009). Generation iY: Our Last Chance to Save Their Future. Atlanta, GA: Poet Gardener Publishing.

Galetić, L. (2015). Adapting reward strategies to millennials pay preferences. http://bib.irb.hr/datoteka/790664.Adapting_reward_strategies_to_millennials_pay_preferences.pdf

Hassan, M. *et al.* (2019). Redesigning the retention strategy against the emerging turnover of generation Y: Revisiting the long-standing problems from the 20th to the 21st century. International Journal of Entrepreneurship, Vol.23(No.2).

Hershatter, A., & Epstein, M. (2010). Millennials and the World of Work: An Organization and Management Perspective. Journal of Business and Psychology, Vol.25(No.2), 211-223. https://doi.org/10.1007/s10869-010-9160-y

Holt, S. *et al.* (2012). Bracing for the Millennial Workforce: Looking for Ways to Inspire Generation Y. Journal of Leadership, Accountability and Ethics, Vol.9(No.6), 81–93. http://www.na-businesspress.com/JLAE/MarquesJ_Web9_6_.pdf

Jerome, A. *et al.* (2014). Millennials in the Workforce: Gen Y Workplace Strategies for the Next Century. E-Journal of Social & Behavioral Research in Business, Vol. 5(No.1), 1–12.

Kitchenham, B. (2004). Procedures for Performing Systematic Reviews (Keele University Technical Report TR/SE-0401).

Levenson, A. R. (2010). Millennials and the World of Work: An Economist's Perspective. Journal of Business and Psychology, Vol.25(No.2), 257–264. https://doi.org/10.1007/s10869-010-9170-9

Lioliou, E., & Willcocks, L. P. (2018). The Study of Information Technology Outsourcing. Global Outsourcing Discourse, 21–57. https://doi.org/10.1007/978-3-319-74045-4_2

Marler, J. H., & Parry, E. (2015). Human resource management, strategic involvement and e-HRM technology. The International Journal of Human Resource Management, Vol.27(No.19), 2233–2253. https://doi.org/10.1080/09585192.2015.1091980

Myers, K. K., & Sadaghiani, K. (2010). Millennials in the Workplace: A Communication Perspective on Millennials' Organizational Relationships and Performance. Journal of Business and Psychology, Vol.25(No.2), 225–238. https://doi.org/10.1007/s10869-010-9172-7

Nasir, S. Z. (2017). Emerging Challenges of HRM in the 21st Century: A Theoretical Analysis. International Journal of Academic Research in Business and Social Sciences, Vol.7(No.3). https://doi.org/10.6007/IJARBSS/v7-i3/2727

Ozcelik, G. (2015). Engagement and Retention of the Millennial Generation in the Workplace through Internal Branding. International Journal of Business and Management, Vol.10(No.3). https://doi.org/10.5539/ijbm.v10n3p99

Schawbel, D. (2012). Millennials vs. Baby Boomers: Who Would You Rather Hire? Accessed on February 2, 2020, https://business.time.com/2012/03/29/millennials-vs-baby-boomers-who-would-you-rather-hire/

Smyrl, B. J. (2011). Leading a Multi-Generational Workforce: Understanding Generational Differences for Effective Communication. College of Professional Studies Professional Projects. Paper 28.

Soares, L. P. M. (2019). O impacto da avaliação de desempenho na carreira profissional da geração Y. http://hdl.handle.net/1822/61103

Solomon, C., & Van Coller-Peter, S. (2019). How coaching aligns the psychological contract between the young millennial professional and the organisation. SA Journal of Human Resource Management, 17. https://doi.org/10.4102/sajhrm.v17i0.1146

Souto, C. P. (2018). Employer Branding: A Importância dos Work Values na atração de colaboradores da Geração Y. https://hdl.handle.net/10216/116794

Thite, M. (2018). Electronic/Digital HRM: A Primer. (M. Thite, Ed.) (1st ed.). London: Routledge.

Thompson, C., & Gregory, J. (2012). Managing Millennials: A framework for improving attraction, motivation, and retention. The Psychologist-Manager Journal, Vol.15(No.4), 237–246. https://doi.org/10.1080/10887156.2012.730444

Valente, A., & Correia, I. (2015). Mapeamento da Oferta de Educação e Formação em TICE em Portugal. Portugal: Fundação para Ciência e Tecnologia (FCT) e Fundação Calouste Gulbenkian (FCG).

Westlund, S. (2008). Retaining talent: Assessing job satisfaction facets most significantly related to software developer turnover intentions. International Journal of Information Technology and Management - IJITM. 19.

ESTIMATION OF SOCIAL CAPITAL BASED ON USER BEHAVIOR INFORMATION ON REGIONAL ELECTRONIC COUPON

Toshiomi Moriki[1], Hiroki Satoh[1], Hideyuki Maki[1] and Norihisa Komoda[2]
[1]*Research & Development Group, Hitachi, Ltd., 1-280, Higashi-koigakubo Kokubunji, Tokyo 185-8601, Japan*
[2]*Code Solutions, Co.,Ltd., Daidoseimei south building 9th floor, 1-2-11 Edobori Nishi-ku,Osaka, Osaka 550-0022, Japan*

ABSTRACT

The relationship between the usage information of electronic coupons at regional food and beverage events and the index of the state of accumulation of the social capital of users is clarified. In order to vitalize the local economy, "Machi-Bars" – street bar events are designed to invite local residents and commuters to visit multiple shops, to discover new shops that they do not usually visit, and to attract potential customers. From the analysis of the usage data of such events, it is found that the index indicating the degree of accumulation of social capital advocated by the OECD is related to the purchase and the usage of the coupon tickets. By using this knowledge, the amount of the social capital can be estimated without high costly questionnaires.

KEYWORDS

Electronic Currency, Electronic Coupon, Social Capital, Regional Vitalization, Street Bar Event

1. INTRODUCTION

The social capital is a concept that focuses on interpersonal relationships such as trust between people, norms of reciprocity, and networks (Yodo, M. and Yano, M., 2017). For modern people, the social capital is an important factor that can greatly influence the quality of their life (level of happiness), and it has been attracting attentions. For this reason, four types of clarification have been proposed by the OECD (Scrivens, K. and C. Smith, 2013.) In Japan, a movement to incorporate social capital into policy making has been started since the 2000s, and (Cabinet Office of Japan, 2006), (Ministry of Agriculture, Forestry and Fisheries of Japan, 2006), and (Ministry of Education, Culture, Sports, Science and Technology of Japan, 2011) have been conducting surveys and studies.

Typically, the social capital is measured by questionnaires on paper or via the Internet (World Wide Web) to the survey respondents. Therefore, the cost of measurement is high because it requires the distribution, collection, and the tabulation of the questionnaire by the researchers and the answers by the respondents.

On the other hand, people's consumption behavior patterns in the region are expected to reflect people-to-people relationships and people-to-community relationships, which can be used to measure social capital. In particular, in advance ticketed drinking and eating events - hereinafter referred to as "street bar events" - (Shimizu, Y. and Nakayama, T., 2014) and (Kurita, K. et al, 2012) aimed at vitalizing local shopping districts, participants purchase local coupons to drink and walk around multiple shops. In recent years, electronic coupons have begun to replace paper coupons which have a high administrative burden and are suitable for collecting local people's purchase and usage data at low cost. Therefore, we consider the use of this behavior data from the street bar events to measure the social capital.

In this paper, we analyze the relationship between the usage history of the electronic coupons and the social capital measured by a questionnaire survey based on the OECD framework, and examine the possibility of measuring the social capital from the behavior history of the electronic coupons at a street bar event "Bunji Bar 2019" held in Kokubunji, Tokyo, Japan.

2. SOCIAL CAPITAL

2.1 Overview of Social Capital

There are various aspects of the social capital, and its definition has been debated mainly by sociologists. Although the role of the social capital differs depending on how it is understood, it generally focuses on the relationship between people and the benefits it brings, and can be said to be a concept that refers to trust, norms, and networks. A number of attempts to quantitatively model the social capital and to apply it to economic policymaking have been made in many countries (Siegler, V., 2014) (Ministry of Land, Infrastructure, Transport and Tourism of Japan, 2008).

In the process of its formation, the investment behavior similar to that of ordinary capital can be observed. Previous study to model the accumulation process, points out that individual attributes such as age, the local economic and social environment are factors that influence the formation of the social capital among individuals (Healy, T. and Cote, S., 2001).

The OECD subdivides the social capital into four categories shown in Table 1. This is based on two assessment axes: "whether the activity or outcome is individual or collective" and "whether the activity or the resource produced by the network structure or the activity to maintain it".

(1) Personal Relationships are the degree of connection with others that increases the likelihood of receiving the intrinsic value and support that comes from the feeling of being connected to a person.

(2) Social Network Support is a resource available to individuals through their personal networks, and refers to the depth of business placements, information, and spiritual and financial support available to them.

(3) Civic Engagement is the degree of participation in activities that contribute to civic and community life.

(4) Trust and Cooperative Norms are trust, social fundamentals, and shared values that allow for mutually beneficial cooperation.

Table 1. Four Types of Social Capital

	Network Structure and Activities	Productive Resources
Individual	(1) Personal Relationships	(2) Social Network Support
Collective	(3) Civic Engagement	(4) Trust and Cooperative Norms

In the quantification of the social capital, according to previous study (Yodo, M. and Yano, M., 2017), the questionnaires according to the four OECD classifications shown in Table 1 are defined as shown in Table 2, according to the questions used to create the index of social capital, respectively (Cabinet Office of Japan, 2006) (The Japan Research Institute, Limited, 2008.)

Table 2. Questionnaires for Social Capital

(1) Personal Relationships	
Q1.	How often do you communicate with your neighbors? (frequency of neighbor communication)
Q2.	How many neighbors do you communicate with? (numbers of neighbor communication)
Q3.	How often do you communicate with your friends and acquaintances? (frequency of friends communication)
Q4.	How often do you communicate with your relatives? (frequency of communication with relatives)
(2) Social Network Support	
Q5.	Do you have a person or organization to consult or rely on for daily life problems or concerns? (trust in the neighborhood)
Q6.	Do you have a person or organization to consult or rely on for daily life problems or concerns? (trust in the friends and acquaintances)
Q7.	Do you have a person or organization to consult or rely on for daily life problems or concerns? (trust in the relatives)
(3) Civic Engagement	
Q8.	Have you taken part in any local group activities? (ex. residents' associations, neighborhood associations, women's associations, elderly associations, youth groups, children's associations, etc.)
Q9.	Have you taken part in any sports / hobby / entertainment activities? (ex. sports, arts and cultural activities, lifelong learning, etc.)
Q10.	Have you given any unpaid help to any groups, clubs or organizations in any of the ways? These could include non-political organizations and citizen activities (ex. city planning, welfare for the elderly and persons with disabilities and child care, sports guidance, beautification, crime prevention / disaster prevention, environment, international cooperation, proposal activities, etc.)
Q11.	How much cash or in-kind did you donate during the past year?
(4) Trust and Cooperative Norms	
Q12.	Generally speaking, would you say that most people can be trusted or that you can't be too careful dealing with people?
Q13.	Generally speaking, would you say that most people can be trusted where you are unfamiliar or on-travel?

2.2 Hypothesis on the Relationship between Social Capital and Individual Behavior of Food and Drink Event Participants

Recently, food tourism (Hall, C. Michael, et al., 2004) has been attracting attention for the development of the regional economy. In Japan, the food and drink events have been held frequently since the 2000s, which targeted in this paper are generally called "Machi-Bar." Its name is derived from the Spanish restaurant name "Bar." In the bar, light snacks such as pinches and alcoholic beverages are served. And bar visitors enjoy conversing with the owner and other customers while wandering through several restaurants. Accordingly, it is positioned as a regional vitalizing event in which visitors visit several shops in a relatively narrow area around a specific station or nearby shopping street.

The "Machi-Bar" has adopted a fixed-price food and beverage coupon system that can be used only at that event. From the visitor's point of view, the coupons offer the advantage of exploiting local restaurants that are different from the ones they usually use within the scope of the coupons, as well as special menus and value-added food and drink experiences that are limited to the period of the event. On the other hand, from the point of view of restaurants, it is possible to advertise efficiently by planning joint events in the same shopping street, and to attract potential customers who do not usually visit through word of mouth, etc. In other words, there are mutual benefits for both the guest visitors and the host shop owners.

Not only residents of the surrounding area who are related to each other, but also commuters and students from remote areas and many other people come to the event. Therefore, it is thought that there is a gap in the temperature of the visitors' feelings and attitudes toward the community, and it is possible to infer whether they have more or less social capital by observing their behavior in the street bar event. Based on this hypothesis, in this paper, an estimation method of the amount of the social capital of the participants based on the coupon purchase and usage behavior data in the bar event is proposed.

3. ANALYSIS OF THE BEHAVIOR OF PARTICIPANTS IN FOOD AND DRINK EVENT IN THE KOKUBUNJI AREA

3.1 Summary of the Street Bar Event

Bunji Bar is a street bar event that is jointly organized by the merchant associations in the shopping district near the north exit of Kokubunji Station, located in the western part of Tokyo, Japan. It has been held 9th times from 2013. Table 3 shows an overview of the latest "9th Bunji Bar 2019".

Table 3. Summary of the event, "Bunji Bar 2019"

Name	Description
Event period	During 25th to 31st Aug. 2019
Place	Around Kokubunji Station, Tokyo, Japan
Format of food/ drink coupons	Paper-based or electronic coupons provided. (400 JPY x 7 / set)
Num. of shops	49 shops. (22 shops: e-coupon ready)
Number of visitors	Approx. 500 visitors (51: e-coupon users, 24: answers of questionnaire)
Types of shops	Bar and Izakaya (Japanese style pub): 22 shops (45%) Restaurant: 16 shops (33%) Café and coffee: 6 shops (12%) Others: 5 shops (10%)

An electronic coupon system (Sato, H, et al., 2020) has been introduced at Bunji Bar 2019, accessible through visitors' smartphones. A conceptual diagram of the electronic coupon system is shown in Figure 1. Participants pay cash to the business owner (the "Marchant association" in the figure) and receive an electronic coupon. This electronic coupon can only be used at regional shops participating in the Bunji Bar 2019 event. It is classified as a gift certificate or a local coupon.

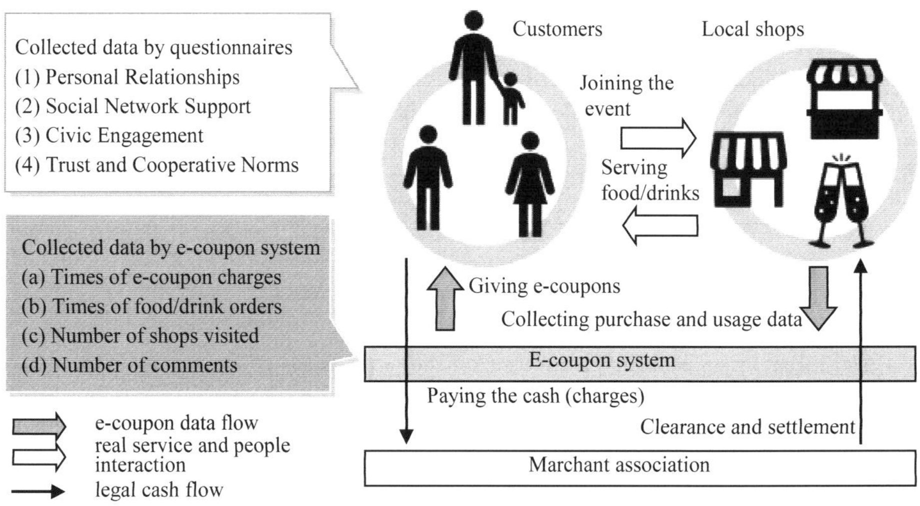

Figure 1. Summary of the e-coupon system

The electronic coupon system is organized around a mobile website, and if participant has a smartphone and an e-mail address, he/she can use the service on the same day without downloading application. In addition, business owners can monitor the participants' usage of bar events at any time via the electronic coupon system.

3.2 Participant Survey

A web-based pre- and post-survey has been administered to electronic coupon users. The objectives of the questionnaire are (i) impressions and expectations before participating in Bunji Bar 2019, (ii) satisfaction after the experience of Bunji Bar 2019, (iii) survey of social capital (listed in Table 2). Table 4 shows a comparison of the questionnaire items.

Table 4. Questionnaires for E-coupon Users

(i) Impressions and expectations before participating in Bunjibar 2019	
	Preliminary expectations: What are your expectations for Bunjibar 2019 and electronic coupons? (Multiple answers possible: Because I like Kokubunji's streets and shops / I want to eat an event-limited menu / it looks fun / I can find new shops and menus / I hope to meet new people and build connections)
(ii) Feelings and satisfactions after experiencing Bunjibar 2019	
	Would you tell me your gender? (Male / Female)
	Would you tell me your age group? (10year increments)
	Do you live in Kokubunji? (Yes / No)
	Totally are you satisfied? (10 levels)
	Post-event satisfactions: Please tell us what was good. (Multiple answers possible: Because I like Kokubunji's streets and shops / Because I could eat a bar-limited menu / Because I enjoyed eating / I found new shops and menus / I met new people and formed a network)
(iii) Survey of social capital	
	Same as the questionnaires in Table 2.

Respondents' demographics and expectations of Bunji Bar were obtained from the results of questionnaire items (i) and (ii). About 80% of the respondents were male and their age group was mainly in their 40s. More than 80% of the respondents were living outside the city, and some of them were commuting to work in Kokubunji City.

3.3 Coupon Usage History and Social Capital Accumulation Indicators

Table 5 shows the data items obtained from the e-coupon system. The data items that allow us to understand the user's purchasing behavior in a straightforward manner are (a) the number of charges, (b) the number of meals ordered, (c) number of shops visited during the bar event period (excluding duplicates), and (d) the number of comments written.

Table 5. Summary of Purchase and Usage Data (N=24)

e-coupon usage	Avg.	SD.	Min.	Max.
(a) Times of e-coupon charges	1.79	1.41	1	5
(b) Times of food/ drink orders	5.38	3.98	1	16
(c) Number of shops visited	2.67	1.88	1	9
(d) Number of comments	1.67	1.83	0	7

Avg: Average, SD.: Standard Deviation, Min: Minimum, Max: Maximum

Table 6 shows the results of the analysis of social capital obtained from the questionnaires of the participants of the Bunji Bar 2019 (N=24.) The data analyzed are compared to the data in the previous research (Yodo, M. and Yano, M., 2017), which were studied more extensively with the same questions. The results show almost the same trend.

Table 6. Summary of Social Capital Data (N=24)

Social capital indicators	Avg.	SD.	Min.	Max.	Med.
(1) Personal Relationships	11.1	2.7	5	18	11.0
Q1. Frequency of neighbor communication	2.4	0.8	1	4	2.0
Q2. Numbers of neighbor communication	2.5	0.9	1	4	2.5
Q3. Frequency of friends communication	3.5	1.0	1	5	3.5
Q4. Frequency of relatives communication	2.7	0.9	1	5	3.0
(2) Social Network Support	9.5	2.6	5	14	9.5
Q5. Trust in the neighborhood	2.6	1.1	1	4	3.0
Q6. Trust in friends and acquittances	3.0	1.3	1	5	3.0
Q7. Trust in relatives	3.8	1.0	2	5	4.0
(3) Civic Engagement	11.6	4.6	5	22	11.0
Q8. Local group activities	2.0	1.4	1	5	1.0
Q9. Sports or cultural activities	4.1	1.8	1	7	4.5
Q10. Unpaid helps	1.9	1.3	1	6	1.5
Q11. Donations for others	3.6	2.5	1	8	3.0
(4) Trust and Cooperative Norms	11.5	3.7	4	18	11.5
Q12. Generalized trust for others	6.2	2.2	2	10	6.5
Q13. Generalized trust for unknown people	5.3	2.3	2	9	5.5

Avg: Average, SD.: Standard Deviation, Min: Minimum, Max: Maximum, Med: Median

4. ESTIMATION OF SOCIAL CAPITAL BASED ON PURCHASE AND USAGE DATA

4.1 Aims and Estimation Methods

The higher the level of social capital accumulated by users (the higher user group), the more likely they are to be interested in the activities of local organizations such as merchant associations. It is expected that users have a high level of understanding about those activities.

For this reason, it seems good to invite additional benefit events and distribute benefit coupons to the higher user groups for efficient regional vitalization. In this section, the participants of Bunji Bar 2019 were asked to answer the following questions on each of the indicators (1) to (4) of social capital with the median as the threshold, we aim to detect a group of users above the threshold.

We use an SVM, Support Vector Machine (J.A.K. Suykens and J. Vandewalle, 1999) to construct the discriminator. The input explanatory variables include information on purchase and usage data in the electronic coupon system (a) to (d), as well as Age group information is used, which has acquired by user questionnaires shown in table 4. The reason why we add age is because a previous study (Glaeser, E. et al, 2002) pointed out the relationship between age and social capital. In addition, a preprocessing is performed for inputting the data, (b) the number of food and beverage menu orders less than or equal to one. It is considered to be a one-off behavior that does not sufficiently capture the purchasing trend in the region. We exclude them (total of three) for this reason and discriminate against all 21 user's valid coupon purchase and usage data.

The SVM configuration parameters used in this estimation are listed in Table 7. We try to optimize the cost parameter C and the kernel parameter Gamma within the scope of the table. In the optimization, we use the precision rate (Precision rate: the ratio of cases judged truly to be high-level users) and false-positive rate (False-Positive rate: the ratio of cases judged faulty to be higher users.) The policy of optimization is to maximize the difference between precision-rate and false-positive rate.

Table 7. Configuration Parameters of SVM

Parameter	Adapted value
Library used	Scikit-Learn (ver 0.20.4)
Kernel type	RBF (Gaussian Kernel)
C(Cost parameter)	Optimized between (0.01 – 10000)
Gamma	Optimized between (0.0001 – 100)

4.2 Evaluation of Estimation Method

The cross-validation test was used as a method for evaluating the performance of the estimator described in section 4.1. The cross-validation test is one of the supervised learning methods. The dataset consisted on k data is divided into the (k-1) training data used training and one remained data for test data. The all selections of the k data set are tested. The cross-validation test is used to avoid reliance on specific combinations of training data.

In this evaluation, for all 21 valid coupon purchasing data, 20 are used as teacher data and the last one is used as test data. The SVM detector is trained by teacher data and used to estimation for the remaining one if the estimate result is correct or wrong. A total of 21 estimations are performed with different combinations of training and test data set and we evaluate the probability of its estimation.

Table 8 shows the detection results for the top groups of social capital. We achieve a goodness of fit ratio of more than 0.5 on all indicators, which may allow us to estimate the target efficiently. In addition, the false positive rate is lower than the fit rate described above, and the false positive rate is relatively low.

Table 8. Cross Validation Results of SVM

Probability	Precision rate	False-Positive rate
(1) Personal Relationships	0.50	0.40
(2) Social Network Support	0.50	0.36
(3) Civic Engagement	0.69	0.63
(4) Trust and Cooperative Norms	0.80	0.09

def. Precision rate = TP / (TP+FN), False-Positive rate = FP / (TN+FP),
TP: True-Positive, FP: False-Positive, FN: False-Negative

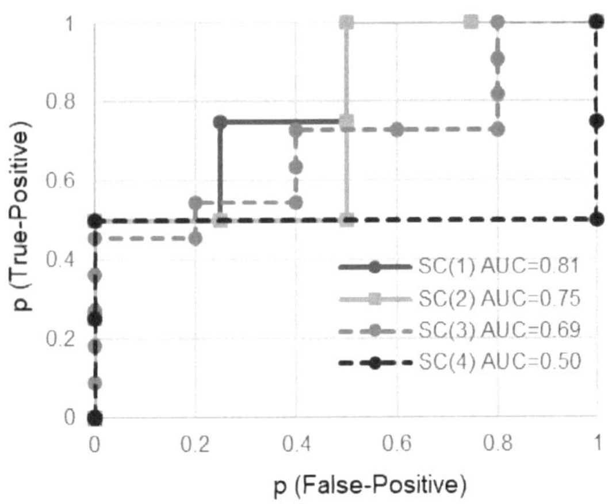

Figure 2. ROC analysis results

Figure 2 shows the discrimination performance of this discriminator for the social capital in terms of ROC - Receiver Operating Characteristic Curve – analysis (Huang, J. and C. X. Ling, 2005). This curve represents the performance of detecting the higher user group of the social capital, with true-positive rate on the vertical axis and false-positive on the horizontal axis, in order to plot the SVMs in the order of probability. The area under the ROC curve is called the AUC (Area under the ROC Curve). Its area is in the range from 0 to 1. Generally, the higher the AUC is, the better the performance of the detector is.

In this study, we have constructed a detector using the purchase and usage data of Bunji Bar 2019 event. We have achieved AUC = 0.50 or higher on each of the indicators of the social capital. The figure 2 shows the highest AUC = 0.81 of the estimation for (1) personal network, and (2) (3) and (4) following in that order. From this evaluation, the usefulness of the proposed method is confirmed.

5. CONCLUSION

As an alternative to questionnaires with a high survey burden, we proposed an SVM-based detector with input data from the purchase and usage history of local coupons. Our proposed method has achieved the precision rate of 0.5 or higher for detection higher user group for all 4 types of the social capital. We have demonstrated the possibility of a new method for estimating the index of the social capital.

REFERENCES

Cabinet Office of Japan, 2006. Social Capital: Seeking Rich Human Relations and a Virtuous Cycle of Citizenship, [online] Available at: https://www.npo-homepage.go.jp/toukei/2009izen-chousa/2009izen-sonota/2002social-capital [Accessed 7 Jun. 2020]. (in Japanese)

Glaeser, E. et al, 2002. An Economic Approach to Social Capital, *The Economic Journal*, 112(483), F437-F458.

Hall, C. Michael, et al. eds., 2004, Consuming places: the role of food, wine and tourism in regional development, *Food tourism around the world.* Routledge.

Huang, J. and C. X. Ling, 2005. Using AUC and accuracy in evaluating learning algorithms., *IEEE Transactions on knowledge and Data Engineering* 17.3, pp.299-310.

Healy, T. and Cote, S., 2001. *The Well-Being of Nations: The Role of Human and Social Capital. Education and Skills.* Organisation for Economic Cooperation and Development, 2 rue Andre Pascal, F-75775 Paris Cedex 16, France.

Japan Research Institute, Limited, 2008. *Japan's Social Capital and Policy: Report of the 2007 National Survey of Japan*, [online] Available at http://www.jipps.org/scarchive/sc/file/report01.pdf [Accessed 7 Jun. 2020].

J.A.K. Suykens and J. Vandewalle, 1999. Least squares support vector machine classifiers, *Neural processing letters,* 9.3, pp.293-300.

Kurita, K. et al, 2012. CC Coupon Circulation and Shopkeepers' Behavior: A Case Study of the City of Musashino, Tokyo, Japan, *International Journal of Community Currency Research*. Vol. 14 Issue 1, pp.136-145.

Ministry of Agriculture, Forestry and Fisheries of Japan, 2006. Rural Social Capital Study Group, [online] Available at: http://www.maff.go.jp/j/nousin/noukei/social_capital.html [Accessed 7 Jun. 2020]. (in Japanese)

Ministry of Education, Culture, Sports, Science and Technology of Japan, 2011. Estimation of the Effect of Educational Investment on Accumulating Social Capital, [online] Available at http://www.mext.go.jp/a_menu/shougai/chousa/1351465.htm [Accessed 7 Jun. 2020]. (in Japanese)

Ministry of Land, Infrastructure, Transport and Tourism of Japan, 2008. Area Management Promotion Manual, [online] Available at https://www.mlit.go.jp/kisha/kisha08/03/030425_.html [Accessed 7 Jun. 2020]. (in Japanese)

Sato, H., et al., 2020. Management System for Regional Electronic Coupon, *Proc. of 22nd International Conference on Enterprise Information System (ICEIS 2020)*, pp.571-578.

Scrivens, K. and C. Smith, 2013, Four Interpretations of Social Capital: An Agenda for Measurement", *OECD Statistics Working Papers*, No. 2013/06, OECD Publishing, Paris,

Shimizu, Y. and Nakayama, T., 2014. Study on the way of continuous shopping street revitalization event, *Architectural Institute of Japan Technical Report* 20.44, pp 285-290. (in Japanese)

Siegler, V., 2014. *Measuring social capital* in the UK, [online] Available at https://www.researchgate.net/publication/281293496_Measuring_Social_Capital_in_the_UK_July_2014_Office_for_National_Statistics [Accessed 7 Jun. 2020].

Yodo, M. and Yano, M., 2017. Household Income and the OECD's Four Types of Social Capital. *Discussion papers, Research Institute of Economy, Trade and Industry (RIETI)*.

CREATION OF A PUBLICLY ACCESSIBLE RESOURCE FOR INCREASING THE VOLUME OF FREELY DISTRIBUTED MEDICAL DATASETS

Artyom Lobantsev, Artyom Beresnev, Mark Tkachenko, Olga Alekseeva, Natalia Gusarova, Aleksandra Vatian and Anatoly Shalyto
ITMO University, Sankt-Petersburg 197101, Russia

ABSTRACT

The lack of data of the required volume and quality is a bottleneck for the widespread use of artificial intelligence technologies in all spheres of human being. This issue is especially acute in medicine. The article discusses the social, motivational and organizational aspects of this problem. As a means to increase the volume of freely distributed medical datasets the creation of a publicly accessible Internet-resource is proposed, which would combine the work of students and young professionals, led by expert radiologists, as well as IT professionals involved in improving markup tools and building datasets. Participating in such kind of work will leverage the motivation of mature specialists and the professional level of young ones. Patients and their attending physicians who wish to promptly receive a second (expert) report on the diagnosis and course of the disease and who agree to use their information anonymously to form datasets will provide the flow of input information. Through an expert survey, we identified the requirements for such a resource. The main business process of such a resource and its system architecture are represented. We conducted experimental studies of the main functionalities of the developed service in terms of meeting the user's requirements as well as a security audit. Quite high estimates were obtained, which allows us to proceed to launch the resource on the platform of the ITMO University (St. Petersburg, Russia).

KEYWORDS

Medical Dataset, Publically Accessible Resource, Radiologist's Motivation

1. INTRODUCTION

The principles of machine learning and, more broadly, artificial intelligence are the basis of most modern high-tech solutions in all spheres of human being. This issue is especially acute in medicine, including such areas as medical diagnostics, data analysis, P4-medicine, drug design, etc. However, the effectiveness of systems based on the principles of machine training is critically dependent on sufficient quantity and quality of data. The problem of lack of data, which is especially acute in the field of medical information systems, is largely due to objective reasons: as a rule, the available data cannot cover the whole variety of clinical manifestations of the studied disease, and even the available data for the most part remain unused, since their markup is very resource-intensive procedure.

For example, for diseases associated with the occurrence of neoplasms, the most valuable medical data are extracted from high-tech medical images, primarily CT and MRI images. However, the nomenclature of such diseases is very wide, and, accordingly, clinical cases for each of them are not enough to form a complete dataset for training the neural network. In addition, manual segmentation is extremely slow and tedious, and an expert physician can make mistakes due to fatigue. Noise, parameter variations, and artifacts of the equipment on which the image is formed introduce additional difficulties in this process.

To solve the indicated problem, different approaches are proposed, including:

- the use of neural networks such as U-Net [Ronneberger], focused on processing small datasets;
- problem-oriented data augmentation;
- creation of synthetic datasets, for example, parametric modeling of high-tech medical images through generative adversarial networks (GAN) [Han, Jin];

- the simultaneous use of multimodal medical data having a different nature and presentation format, but complementing each other in essence, like MRI-image and radiologist report compiled from it [Lahat, Rajalingam].

However, all of the above approaches remain alleviative to some extent, since they cannot completely replace datasets collected in real clinical conditions and marked up by professional radiologists. The lack of data of the required volume and quality is a bottleneck for the widespread use of artificial intelligence technologies. It must be emphasized that this problem is not of narrow medical, but of a complex nature and affects such aspects of ICT and modern society interactions as medicine, especially in the diagnosis of neoplasms. The open datasets such as BraTS, LIDC-IDRI, CheXpert, etc. are in great shortage.

In addition, in most cases, open datasets cannot be a panacea. They are created mainly for academic purposes – for example, to assess the quality of models, for research, hypothesis testing, but not for final development. In general, it rarely happens that a dataset not assembled for a specific task is completely representative.

Thus, the creation of means for the formation of freely distributed medical datasets of proper volume and quality is an urgent problem. It must be emphasized that this problem is not of narrow medical, but of a complex nature and affects many aspects of ICT and modern society interactions. From the point of view of radiologists, these are motivation, skills and competencies as well as quality of working life. From the point of view of patients, these are trust, security and privacy of data provided. In terms of their interaction, that is creating of virtual community. Finally, from the point of view of society as a whole, it is improving of health and quality of life.

The article discusses the possibility of creating an Internet resource that integrates all of the above aspects, which we will consider on the example of an important problem – forming freely distributed datasets of high-tech medical images supporting ICT-diagnostics of different types of lung and brain neoplasms. Technological, organizational and educational aspects of such a resource, as well as data privacy issues are considered.

2. BACKGROUND AND RELATED WORKS

According to [Kumar, Norouzi], the markup of the medical image for the dataset comprises identifying region of interest, in particular, the separation of healthy and pathological areas (locating tumor, lesion and other abnormalities). In addition, it is highly desirable to accompany each image with a detailed textual radiologist's report.

When creating a means to support the markup of high-tech medical images a number of interrelated questions arise: who performs the markup, what tools are used for it, where do source data come from. Substantially, these questions correspond to three groups of requirements, which can be identified as follows: community aspect (physical and virtual) – **C**; labour market aspect (outsourcing, integration, mobility) – **L**; security aspect (trust – security – privacy) – **S**. Note that the brief notation will be used in table 1.

Regarding the first question, a shortage of qualified radiologists has become a serious worldwide problem nowadays [Allyn, Clinical, Orenstein]. For example, according to the report [Clinical], hospitals in United Kingdom are short of at least 1,104 radiologist to keep up with the demand for diagnostic and interventional radiological care. In developing countries, the situation is even worse [Fornell]. According to the World Health Organization, over half the people in the world are without access to diagnostic and interventional radiology services [Improving]. In these conditions, large hospitals widely use outsourcing, overtime and locum cover, primarily for urgent and interventional radiology, thereby further reducing the circle of specialists who are ready to engage in marking up datasets.

The answer to these challenges is commercial teleradiology, which allows the patient to get an opinion on his medical image from a remote radiologist [Orenstein]. For example, in China teleradiology helps alleviate some of the drawbacks associated with practicing in rural areas [Allyn]. However, as practice shows, teleradiology has so far been developed only in the most advanced countries. In Russia, for example, there are no such services.

In the literature, the problems of motivation of young radiologists, especially students and clinical residents, are widely studied [Goldman, Taylor, Yen]. The work [Taylor] shows declining medical student interest in radiology. As demotivating factors, students note the lack of practice, the inability to get enough experience with real medical images, the lack of contact with practicing radiologists. Among the motivating factors, young radiologists, along with the level of salary, note influence of a mentor, perceived job satisfaction, intellectual stimulation and competitiveness of the process [Goldman], as well as competitiveness and professional growth [Yen]. However, the existing worldwide training schemes for young radiologists use these factors very little (see, for example, [Pool]).

As mentioned in [Sunshine], increased productivity is the predominant way to ease the radiologist shortage. Therefore, the organization of the workspace and tools is especially important. The classic workplace of the radiologist is a stationary hardware-software complex, aggregating visualization tools for every kind of medical images, as well as means of communication, storage, etc. [Rugerio]. For marking a specific type of medical image (only CT and MRI images), this equipment is clearly redundant, moreover, it deprives the radiologist of the necessary mobility. That's why, in recent years, more and more portable solutions for the operational support of the work of a radiologist appear in clinical practice (see, for example, [Horos, Mechtash]). A detailed review of such solutions can be found in the work of the authors of present article [Boitsov]. Their development follows the path of maximally simplifying the work of radiologists while maintaining their personal context and marking accuracy; for this, machine-learning technologies are widely used. For example, the toolkit developed by the authors of present article [Boitsov] provides the radiologist with the opportunity of his choice to work in an interactive (semi-automated) or non-interactive (automated) mode. This achieves marking accuracy, measured in Dice coefficient, up to 0.9104 and 0.8333 respectively, along with a high working speed (approx. 15 s in interactive mode and 5.8 ms in non-interactive mode).

The last but not least point is where source data come from. The most interesting for the formation of the dataset are real and operatively obtained images of patients with specific diseases, accompanied by a detailed description of the course of the disease, which would allow the radiologist to draw the most accurate report. However, such information falls under a number of laws on the protection of personal data, medical information, etc. For example, the main document concerning the basics of protecting the health of citizens in the Russian Federation is [Federal]. In accordance with this law, the patient's data can be used for telemedicine purposes, for making a decision on the need for face-to-face admission or for treatment correction, but subject to a previously defined diagnosis and a course of treatment prescribed at the face-to-face appointment. Thus, the patient or his attending physician has the right to use the services of teleradiology to obtain a second (expert) opinion on the disease, and ensuring the security of the data when sending it becomes the main problem.

As world practice shows, a promising way to solve this problem in medicine is to use blockchain technology [Vazirany]. Blockchain allows you to create a distributed secure registry of medical records. Given the delicacy of information, access to records can be limited: if the patient and his attending physician agree to show the information to another specialist, they will digitally sign and the system will open access to the specified person.

Combining all of the above, we can conclude that an effective way for increasing the volume of freely distributed medical datasets can be the creation of a publicly accessible Internet resource that works on the principle of teleradiology. The resource will combine the work of students and young professionals, led by expert radiologists, as well as IT professionals involved in improving markup tools and building datasets. Participating in such kind of work will leverage the motivation of mature specialists and the professional level of young ones. Patients and their attending physicians who wish to promptly receive a second (expert) report on the diagnosis and course of the disease and who agree to use their information anonymously to form datasets will provide the flow of input information. The commercialization of such a resource should become a separately discussed topic, but it is clear that by attracting students and young specialists, the price of services for patients will be significantly lower than when contacting a large teleradiological company.

As far as the authors know, resources of this type in developing countries, in particular, in Russia, are not yet available, and this gap should be filled.

Thus, the authors of this article set themselves the following tasks:

1. to identify the applications requirements for Internet resource of such kind;
2. to develop the main business process of such a resource and its system architecture;
3. to conduct experimental studies of the main functionalities of the developed service in terms of meeting the user's requirements.

3. REVEALING OF RESOURCE REQUIREMENTS

To create a list of requirements for the resource under consideration, we conducted an analysis of development practices of medicine resources of analogous types. Besides, we interviewed expert radiologists, students and clinical residents, each of whom independently described his own vision of business process supported by the resourse under consideration as well as it's desirable usability characteristics. The total number of respondents was 15 people, the average work experience of 6.3 years with a range from 0 to 21 years.

Identified requirements are presented in table. 1. In addition, it also shows what enlarged aspects of creating a resource (see section 2) each of them corresponds to.

Table 1. Resourse requirements

Aspect	Reguirement
S	1. Compliance with legislation on the protection of personal data.
S	2. Unhindered access of the patient to his own medical data to eliminate the obstacle for patients to receive copies of their medical records or transfer them to another health care provider.
S	3. The integrity and lack of bias of medical data. At any stage, the system must ensure the integrity of the data, versioning and unambiguous authorship of the data itself and its changes. At the same time, it is necessary to ensure that the medical data has not been discreetly changed by anyone, including doctors and the patients themselves.
L, S	4. For the system owner - receiving a marked-up quality dataset, with multi-parameter additional attribute attribution.
C, L	5. Minimum requirements for the user to start using the resource (without installing special client software and with the possibility of using common, including mobile, platforms).
C, L	6. Lack of strict regulation on the format of the input data (the patient can present data in a variety of graphic formats).
C	7. Lack of requirements for the level of medical knowledge for patient users (maximum use of data entry wizards, refusal of medical terminology in patient interfaces, nevertheless maintaining its availability in the form of hints).
C, L, S	8. For rediologists-experts - ease of use of the service, the ability to develop their professional level and professional impact.
C, L	9. Support for a professional community, maintaining a rating of experts on consensus assessment.
C, L	10. For students and clinical residents - easy access to real anonymous data and the result of evaluations of practicing experts.

4. BUSINESS PROCESS AND SYSTEM ARCHITECTURE

An analysis of the requirements presented in Table 1 shows that the most suitable architecture option for the developed resource is the implementation of a modular Web service, with data storage in the form of a private block chain.

Figure 1 shows a use case diagram describing the capabilities of a resource. The main actors include: the patient, an expert doctor, trainee (medical student or clinical resident) and the owner of the portal. Consider the goals of using the portal and the key cases for these actors.

Patient. The patient's goal is to obtain a qualified, accessible consultation in the form of decoding of an MRI or CT scan from several specialists. Before starting work, the Patient performs registration, places his pictures in an accessible format, and fills out a medical history, thereby forming a request. The patient's personal data is entered into the system anonymously, that is, the full name, exact date and place of birth, as well as document numbers, are not stored. We note, however, that the architecture of the system will allow a transparent transition, if necessary, to the storage of such data. After processing the images by expert doctors, the Patient can get access to all reports on his images from all the experts who processed the images, and the rating of experts and their portfolio is available to the patient.

Expert doctor. The purpose of using the portal for an expert doctor is to create a personal portfolio, expand medical practice, present your skills and level of expertise, indirectly evaluate your skills and level of expertise, discuss complex cases in the professional community, train medical students and clinical residents.

Before starting work, an expert doctor can register in the system, fill out an expert questionnaire, optionally indicating his name, academic degree, publication list, his contacts, etc. After that, the expert will have access to a list of patient applications with selection by fields of history, area of images, etc. An expert doctor, working in the system, carries out the markup of images, gives his report. For each report, assessments of other experts on this application and indicators of the degree of consensus of experts are available to him. The doctor can repeat the analysis of the application by creating its new edition. Relevant and accessible to other experts is the latest version of report. In addition, an expert doctor can create applications for the analysis of images in order to obtain the opinions of other experts. If the expert doctor is a mentor, then he can form sets of applications for his students to implement various pedagogical tasks.

Trainee. Actor trainee is a medicine student or intern (clinical resident). His purpose is the acquisition or development of competencies in the field of radiology. This actor has access to registration, assignment to a mentor (with his consent), study of reports for familiarization with the selection according to the fields of anamnesis and training sessions when Trainee receives an application, either independently or from a mentor, and performs its analysis with automatic comparison of results with expert estimates through consensus evaluation algorithms.

Portal owner. The owner of the portal, in addition to the humanistic goal of expanding access to qualified medical care, aims to create a high-quality dataset with marked MRI and CT images. The value and difference of this dataset is in additional attribution, namely in the presence of a connection with the anamnesis, the availability of the author rating report, the availability of data on the author report and data on the consensus assessment of experts. The generated dataset can be used for scientific research, as well as to improve the quality of existing diagnostic tools based on machine learning.

Separately, we note that gaining full access to the dataset is possible only for this role. No roles are available to delete report. Also outside the scope of the article are issues of managing electronic digital certificates. In the system, they are solved by using an external PKI.

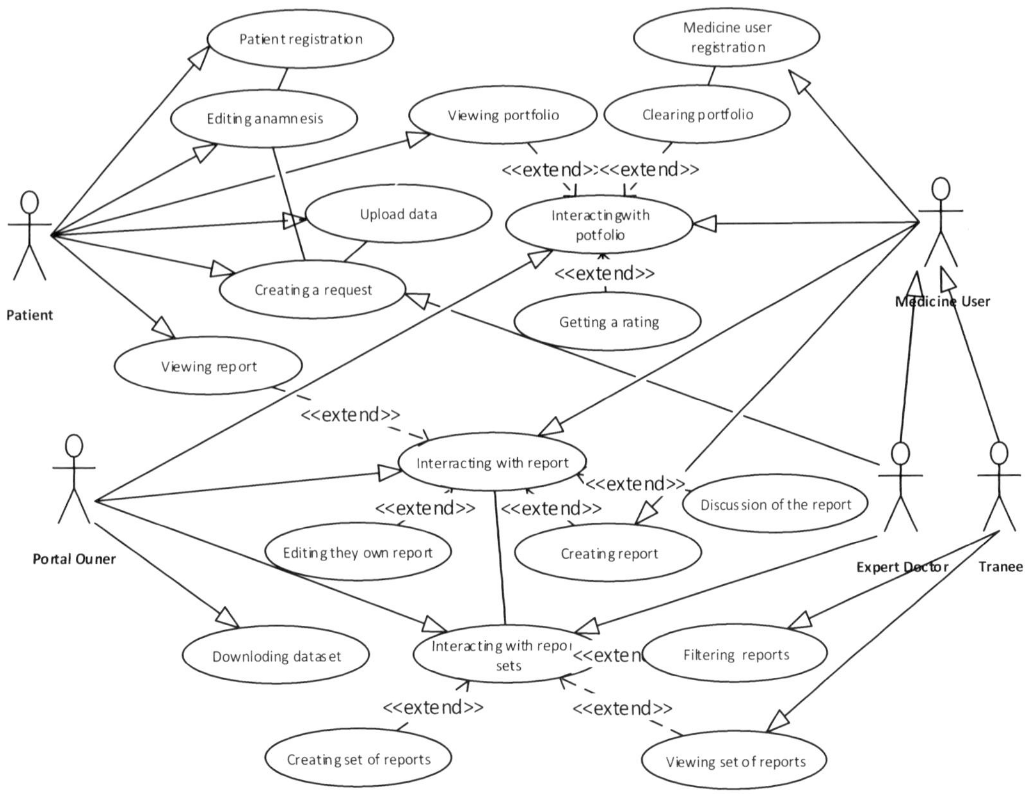

Figure 1. Use Case diagram

The system architecture of the resource is shown in Figure 2. The client application runs in the browser. The server part of the resource has a modular structure. The Information Resource Interaction Service, deployed on a separate platform, interacts directly with the client. This is a key component of the system through which all the other components, as well as the external PKI service, work. The Information Resource Interaction Service component performs authentication, authorization, interaction with the user interface, as well as the processing of all data coming from other components of the system. The DataConvertation module is functioning on the same physical node, which is designed to automatically bring the data downloaded by the patient to prepare images for marking by an expert. Currently, most raster formats, PDF, DOC \ DOCX, RTF and the specialized DICOM format are accepted. The remaining components of the system are hosted on a virtualization platform on separate Linux virtual machines.

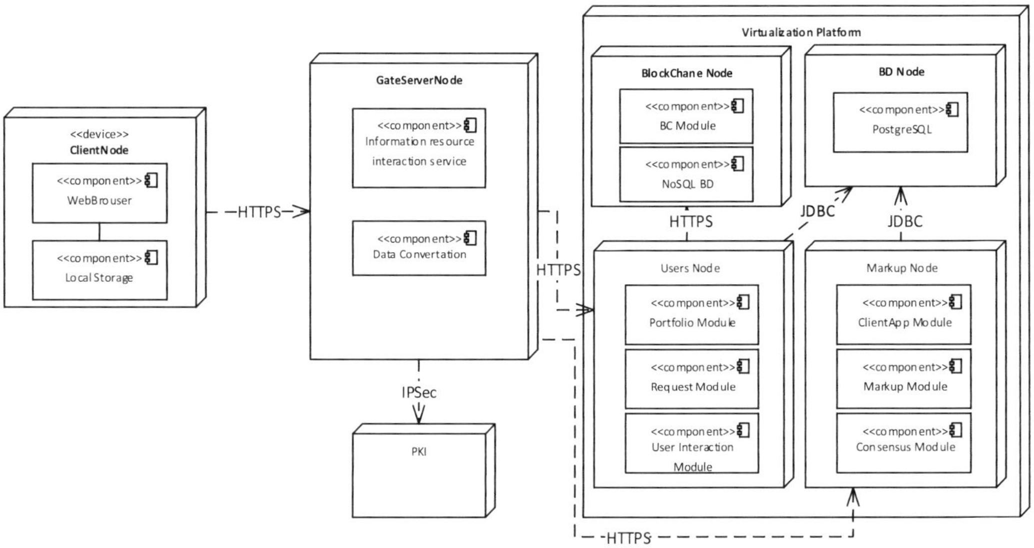

Figure 2. System architecture of the resource

The Users Node node contains modules for the work of patients (Request Module), a module for the work of physicians (Portfolio Module), and a module for user communication within the resource. The Markup Module node contains components for marking up images and comparative processing of reports to compile an expert rating. The rating calculation is based on direct and indirect parameters. The former includes the degree of coincidence of each markup with the markups of other experts, the latter - data on publications, academic degrees, work experience.

In order to fulfill the requirements for security, integrity, non-repudiation, accessibility (privacy, data integrity, signature, non-repudiation), blockchain technology elements are used to organize the storage of requests and reports. A private blockchain with a single node has been implemented with a full copy of the blockchain or full node (see BlockChain Node in Figure 2). This eliminated the fork problem in distributed storage. Both requests and responses are stored in a similar way. The first link in the chain is the request sent by the patient; if the expert takes the request into work, the next block is formed. If an expert decided to edit his report, a new block is formed in the same chain. For another expert, the reporting chain will be different, but with one start - initial request. A time stamp is added to each block, and the author's signature and author rating in the system existing at the time the report was created.

To implement the signing mechanism, a certificate is created for each user on an external PKI. The certificate is stored in a keychain protected by BlockChain Node. For patients, export of certificates is not provided. In the future, it is planned to implement certificate export or use of a user's personal certificate for medical experts.

The system architecture does not allow all actors except the Portal Owner to intervene in the blockchain (he can theoretically modify the blockchain due to the storage of certificates inside the resource), but even a modification by the Portal Owner can be detected due to time stamps. The blockchain stores data that cannot be deleted by users by end user agreement. Other data, such as user attributes in the portfolio, can be cleared. To store the rest of the data, a relational DBMS is used.

5. RESOURCE TESTING

Currently, the developed resource is being prepared for launch on the platform of the ITMO University (St. Petersburg, Russia).

To this end, we conducted various types of resource testing. Among others, user testing was conducted using focus groups composed of typical users: an expert doctor (3 persons), medical students (7 persons), patients (10 persons). After working with the resource, the focus group participants were offered questionnaires with qualitative criteria that met the project goals and the formed requirements. We used a five-point scale. Estimates obtained and averaged are presented in Table 2.

Table 2. User Test Results

Criteria (wording shortened)		Focus groups		
		Experts	Students	Patients
1	Convenience of resource navigation	4,7	4,9	4,5
2	Clarity and uniqueness of linguistic support	4,9	4,3	3,7
3	Convenience of posting a request (pictures, medical history)	4,5	-	4,7
4	Convenient image layout and report preparation	4,8	4,8	-
5	Usefulness of a resource for skills formation	4,5	4,9	-
6	Ease of requesting of colleagues ratings	4,8	4,8	-
7	Ease of selecting requests for processing	4,7	4,8	-
8	Ease of finding an expert for patients / mentor for students	4,1	4,4	4,2
9	The feasibility of using the resource for the development of professional qualities	5	5	-

As can be seen from table 2, the resource as a whole received quite high user ratings. The relatively low scores given by patients on question 2 are explained by the fact that the medical history interface uses purely medical terms. Since the resource architecture provides for the use of different interfaces for different actors, this defect will be fixed in the next version of the system.

In addition, we conducted a security audit of the developed resource. The audit revealed problems with the configuration of KeyRings module security and network access to the BlockChain node. Identified deficiencies have been resolved.

6. CONCLUSION

The article addressed the issue of creation of a publicly accessible resource for increasing the volume of freely distributed medical datasets. The tasks set by the author of the article have been successfully fulfilled.

We identified the applications requirements that meet the main aspects for Internet resource of such kind, namely: community aspect (physical and virtual); labour market aspect (outsourcing, integration, mobility); security aspect (trust – security – privacy).

We developed and implemented the resource. The main business process of the resource and its system architecture are presented in the article.

We conducted experimental studies of the main functionalities of the developed service in terms of meeting the user's requirements as well as a security audit. Quite high estimates were obtained, which allows us to proceed to launch the resource on the platform of the ITMO University (St. Petersburg, Russia).

ACKNOWLEDGEMENTS

This work was financially supported by Russian Science Foundation, Grant 19-19-00696.

REFERENCES

Allyn J. International Radiology Societies Tackle Radiologist Shortage. Feb. 20, 2020. https://www.rsna.org/en/news/2020/February/International-Radiology-Societies-And-Shortage

Boitsov V. et al. Software Tools for Manual Segmentation of Tomography Images Supporting Radiologist's Personal Context // Proceedings of the 25th Conference of Open Innovations Association FRUCT - 2019, pp. 64-76

Clinical radiology UK workforce census report 2018. https://www.rcr.ac.uk/publication/clinical-radiology-uk-workforce-census-report-2018

Federal Law of November 21, 2011 No 323-ФЗ (as amended on 04.24.2020). http://www.pravo.gov.ru - 24.04.2020.

Fornell D. A Glimpse into Radiology in the Developing World in Africa. Dec. 08, 2017. https://www.itnonline.com/content/blogs/dave-fornell-itn-editor-rsna/glimpse-radiology-developing-world-africa

Goldman D.et al. Differential Motivations for Pursuing Interventional Radiology: Implications for Residency Recruitment. J Am Coll Radiol . 2019 Jan;16(1):82-88. doi: 10.1016/j.jacr.2018.08.002.

Han C. et al. Synthesizing diverse lung nodules wherever massively: 3D multi-conditional GAN-based CT image augmentation for object detection //2019 International Conference on 3D Vision (3DV). – IEEE, 2019. – C. 729-737.

Horos: Horos Project – Free DICOM Medical Image Viewer https://horosproject.org/

Improving radiology readiness in low-resource countries and regions. September 10, 2019. https://www.carestream.com/blog/2019/09/10/improving-radiology-readiness-in-low-resource-countries-and-regions/

Jin D. et al. CT-realistic lung nodule simulation from 3D conditional generative adversarial networks for robust lung segmentation //International Conference on Medical Image Computing and Computer-Assisted Intervention. – Springer, Cham, 2018. – C. 732-740.

Kumar S. N.et al. A voyage on medical image segmentation algorithms. Biomedical Research 2018; Special Issue: S75-S87

Lahat D., Adalı T., Jutten C. Multimodal Data Fusion: An Overview of Methods, Challenges and Prospects. Proceedings of the IEEE, Vol. 103, Is. 9, 2015

Mehrtash A., Pesteie M., Hetherington J., Behringer P.A., Kapur T., Wells W.M. III, Rohlinga R., Fedorov A., Abolmaesumi P. DeepInfer: Open-Source Deep Learning Deployment Toolkit for Image-Guided Therapy. Proc SPIE Int Soc Opt Eng. 2017 February 11; 10135: . doi:10.1117/12.2256011.

Norouzi A. et al. (2014) Medical Image Segmentation Methods, Algorithms, and Applications, IETE Technical Review, 31:3, 199-213, DOI: 10.1080/02564602.2014.906861

Orenstein B. W. Virtually Indispensable. Radiology Today. Vol. 19 No. 12 P. 18

Pool KJ.L. et al. A Structured Global Health Training Program for Radiology Residents. Journal of the American College of Radiology. February 2018 Volume 15, Issue 2, Pages 334–339

Rajalingam B., Priya R. Multimodality Medical Image Fusion Based on Hybrid Fusion Techniques. International Journal of Engineering and Manufacturing Science. Vol. 7, No. 1 (2017)

Ronneberger O., Fischer P., and Brox T. U-Net: Convolutional Networks for Biomedical Image Segmentation. arXiv:1505.04597v1 [cs.CV] 18 May 2015.

Ruggerio S., Weisser G. Integrating Mac Systems into a Medical IT Infrastructure: Creating an affordable radiology workstation with OsiriX. https://www.osirix-viewer.com/pdf/IntegratingMacSystems.pdf

Taylor C. S. et al. Generating Medical Student Interest in the Field of Radiology. Journal of the American College of Radiology. Journal of the American College of Radiology. February 2018 Volume 15, Issue 2, Pages 340–342

Vazirani A. A., O'Donoghue O., Brindley D. et al. Blockchain vehicles for efficient Medical Record management. npj Digit. Med. 3, 1 (2020). https://doi.org/10.1038/s41746-019-0211-0

Yen A.J. et al. The Stability of Factors Influencing the Choice of Medical Specialty Among Medical Students and Postgraduate Radiology Trainees. J Am Coll Radiol 2018;15: 886-891.

Sunshine J. H., and Meghea C. How Could the Radiologist Shortage Have Eased? American Journal of Roentgenology. Vol.187, Issue 5. 1160-1165. 10.2214/AJR.06.0559

A COLLECTIVE AWARENESS PLATFORM FOR MISSING CHILDREN INVESTIGATION AND RESCUE

Ariadni Michalitsi-Psarrou, Christos Ntanos and John Psarras
National Technical University of Athens, Athens, Greece

ABSTRACT

The plight of missing children is particularly strenuous and sensitive for society at local, national and European levels, cutting across class, race, and age. A quarter million cases of missing children is reported in the EU annually, which are either parental abductions, stranger abductions, runaways, missing unaccompanied migrant minors, and generally lost, injured, or otherwise missing children. The problem of missing children is a complex, multi-faceted phenomenon, comprising legal, psychological and sociological aspects, which are complicated further due to the strong emotions from the close environment of the missing child. This paper presents the challenges missing children investigation and rescue currently faces, and proposes a solution that uses ICT, advanced analytics and collective intelligence, to achieve more rapid and effective resolutions. The proposed methodology leverages the untapped potential of open, social, and linked data to augment the background information of missing children, through multi-layer - personal, psychological, social and activity - profiling and predictive analytics, respecting and protecting privacy, and personal data. Using location-based mobile notifications that spread using geo-fencing, citizens close to the place a missing child was last seen or is more probable to be found become "social sensors" for the investigation, contributing and validating potential pieces of evidence. Through the EU-funded project ChildRescue, the proposed solution is currently at the last phase of its development and aims to be adopted by different voluntary organisations, according to their needs and the readiness of their systems and processes. The project's results are now piloted in missing children cases by organisations responsible for the Amber Alert, and the 116 000 pan-European hotline, as well as unaccompanied minors' cases supported by the Hellenic Red Cross. The resulting collaboration platform and mobile applications will be publicly launched in 2020.

KEYWORDS

Missing Children, Collective Awareness, Profiling, Analytics, Crowdsourcing, Unaccompanied Migrant Minors

1. INTRODUCTION

While the phrase "going missing" regarding a child is generally understood as the occurrence of a situation characterised by a lack of information on the whereabouts of that child, each country tends to adopt its own, nonbinding definition of what constitutes a missing child. These definitions have significant variations to the risk posed, the cause of the disappearance and the existence (or not) of indications that a crime is being or has been committed, leaving it up to the authorities to decide instantly how an individual case should be handled and whether it should be registered as referring to a missing child or not (Best 1987). Such a process often introduces delays in the crucial early stages of a disappearance, especially if an official report should have been filed to declare a disappearance so as to trigger an official alert (Cancedda et al. 2013; Griffin et al. 2007; Sicafuse and Miller 2010).

A special missing children case, that in the recent years has become increasingly and alarmingly pertinent, is that of unaccompanied refugee minors. The lack of family, which is usually, at least geographically, out of reach, as well as the lack of other reliable social networks, renders their position highly insecure and vulnerable. Paradoxically, despite the enormous risks to which unaccompanied refugee children are exposed and the fact that all actions and laws which apply to missing children, in general, equally apply to unaccompanied migrant children, their disappearance is usually underreported, strengthened by the fact that some European countries have employed mechanisms that give these cases an automatic lower priority than other missing children, by imposing, for instance, a mandatory waiting period before filling a missing person report (Cancedda et al. 2013). Research reveals that up to 50% of the unaccompanied children accommodated go missing from reception centres in the European Union, and in many cases, information about the child's whereabouts remains scarce (available at: http://missingchildreneurope.eu/).

Currently, missing children alerts, patterned after the Amber Alert System, have been implemented in many European countries (named either Amber or Child Alert), while more and more EU countries develop similar alert systems. These systems aim to quickly disseminate critical information about particularly worrying child disappearances to the public through a variety of channels, thus increasing the probability of a positive outcome. The idea behind the Amber/Child Alert System is that, by broadcasting and distributing information about a missing child to the community, the public's involvement can trigger critical feedback that would have otherwise been ignored, and which can prove critical in finding the missing child (Griffin 2010). It is launched only in exceptional cases, the reason being that too frequent alerts would lead to lack of interest by the public. It has been claimed that identification times have been reduced for a high number of missing children cases thanks to information provided by citizens aware of the issued amber alerts, leading to an estimated effect of more than 62% of cases resolved based on citizens' tips or discovery of the missing person (Griffin 2010; Kamel Boulos et al. 2011). At the same time, the effectiveness of these systems has been criticised by several researchers, especially on what concerns the claim for high annual numbers of 'saved lives', due to intrinsic difficulties with the evaluation of the effectiveness of these alerts (Griffin et al. 2016; Griffin and Miller 2008; Sicafuse and Miller 2010). It is, indeed, a reasonable consideration that since it would be immoral to form a control group to validate the impact of the Amber Alert, by selecting cases where alerts should have but aren't issued, a scientific measurement for the claim for "saved lives" and the reduction of time needed to locate a missing child becomes very difficult.

2. CHALLENGES AND OPPORTUNITIES

Despite the remarkable efforts at state and European level to effectively address the issue of missing children, several concerns regarding the effectiveness of Amber Alert system are raised and several key challenges remain open. Clues coming from concerned citizens are instrumental to locating missing children, yet most of the information typically originates from recorded phone calls, often without adequate supporting evidence, which may derail the investigation. The ability of people to remember faces from pictures and descriptions and be able to recognise them after just a little while has been questioned by a significant body of research (Frowd, Erickson, and Lampinen 2014; Lampinen, Curry, and Erickson 2016; Sweeney and Lampinen 2012). Limits of people's cognitive functions and memory retrieval errors, such as the "tip-of-the-tongue" phenomenon, may hinder the AMBER Alert System's success, despite a person's intention to remember information from the Amber Alert and his willingness to contribute to the cause (Miller and Clinkinbeard 2006). The development of new systems that offer a real-time, two-way channel, from and to members of the community, that would allow flow of information at any time, could be proven beneficial in minimising these effects.

The lack of a mechanism that makes use and merges all available sources of information is also a challenge faced. While the information received by the relatives and the close social environment of a missing child is always the starting point for an investigation, other sources of information can prove of equal or greater value. This includes information that can be deduced from social media activities and networks of friends, as well as information coming from open data sources, such as the transportation infrastructure, road networks, or land use, which may enrich the information available and improve predictive capabilities regarding the whereabouts of the missing child (Ledoux and Van Oosterom 2013; Yuan, Zheng, and Xie 2012), resulting in an informed behavioural and activity profile of the child. According to current literature and practices (Crosland et al. 2018; Johnson, Rew, and Kouzekanani 2006; Payne 1995), the common approaches to profiling for a missing person are mostly analyses of the person's personal data and psychosocial characteristics by domain experts. The conclusions are drawn from testimonials and interviews and are of a qualitative nature. Therefore, there is no systematic way to apply different profiling techniques for recognising activity patterns of missing persons. The research challenge here is to perform semiautomated behavioural profiling for missing children.

Further to the information sources above, past cases of missing children could also be used to identify correlations and common patterns. This can be performed by applying pattern recognition techniques, already known in other application fields. Finally, since important clues may be coming from multiple witnesses' reports, these can be combined and incorporated into the investigation so as to focus on possible time-sensitive routes, which is only currently done manually, sparsely, and based on human intuition.

Identifying the potential location of a missing person is a very complex task, requiring all sources of related information to be analysed as quickly as possible. The result of this process should be a case-specific prediction of geographic areas where the investigation and/or alerts should focus.

What is more, it is widely acknowledged that time is of the essence in the investigation of missing children, and the first hours after a disappearance are of vital importance. Although the alerts for missing children are currently quickly broadcasted on media, there is no mechanism to focus and intensify the calls for help to part of the community based on its proximity to the point the person was last seen at and other high priority areas. Efficient mobilisation of the local community is therefore usually accomplished by distributing flyers and putting up posters in these areas – a slow process – while SMS messages notifying volunteers based on their registration address are sometimes used, but don't take into account their current location and also do not contain enough details or multimedia content. Propagating localised real-time notifications to citizens (Rahate and Shaikh 2016) according to the output of predictive analytics and profiling for missing persons does not have a precedent in the international research and practice.

Lack of cross-border cooperation between institutions, law enforcement agencies and networks for missing children is also a critical issue, especially in cases of disappearances of unaccompanied migrant minors. Different national legal strategies in dealing with missing unaccompanied migrant minors further reinforce complications in cross-border cases. There is therefore a strong need for tools supporting a fast cross-border exchange of information on missing unaccompanied minors, as well as a reliable way to cross-reference and identify a child that moves from one hosting facility to another, in order to improve migration data and the misallocation of search efforts.

Dealing with these challenges in a unified and effective way requires significant research towards effectively exploiting and guiding the spontaneous network effect, by combining multiple sources of information and applying intelligent data analysis and prediction techniques. Such a novel, well-thought-out process could be considered the key to achieving faster and better conclusions to missing children's investigations.

3. THE CHILDRESCUE SOLUTION

To meet these fundamental challenges, this paper presents the ChildRescue solution, which develops a unique, unified approach and an applicable solution aspiring to have an outstanding impact in missing children's discovery, while also covering one of the greatest issues related to the refugees' crisis, the disappearance of unaccompanied children and the additional difficulties for identifying them. The result is a novel methodology for accelerating and amplifying the network effect and harnessing collective intelligence in the investigation of missing and unaccompanied children by creating an uninterrupted cycle of information flow and communication between all stakeholders, achieved by working on top of social theories and identifying how they can be influenced by novel ICTs towards addressing a critical societal challenge.

The ChildRescue solution aims at effectively and quickly raising collective awareness and instigating instant community action during the investigation of missing children. The phases of the missing person investigation cycle, on which the ChildRescue focus lies, include: (a) Preparation in order to lead the investigation to proper directions from its onset, (b) Coordination, with new models for collaboration among the missing children response organisations, (c) Action in order to motivate society to seamlessly contribute to the research, (d) Archiving of the case in privacy-respectful way.

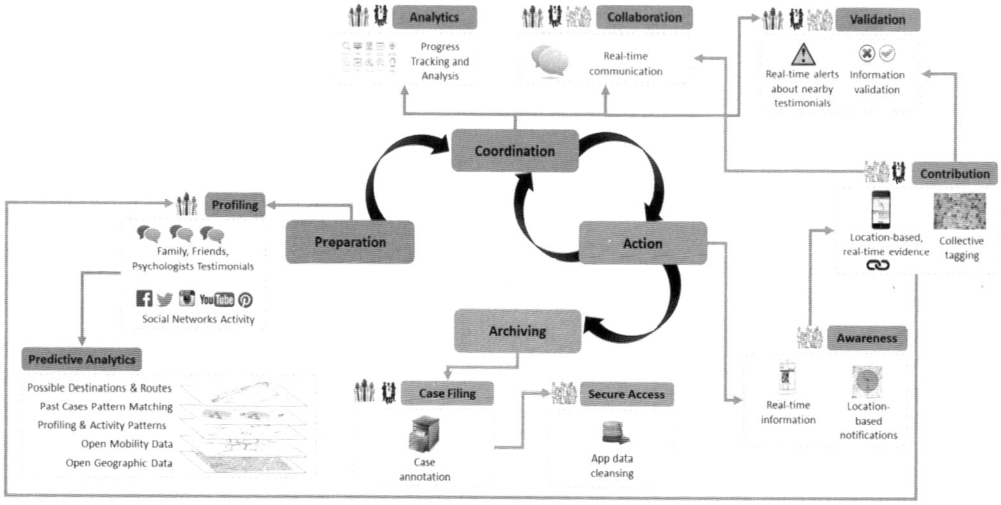

Figure 1. ChildRescue concept

Figure 1 presents the overall ChildRescue concept and solution, which is formed and cultivated around the four aforementioned phases of the missing children investigation cycle. In particular, during the investigation preparation phase, ChildRescue solution augments the information collected by the missing children response organisations by researching and employing advanced profiling methods towards the construction of a multilayer -personal, psychological, social - profile of the missing child or the unaccompanied minor. To accomplish that goal, system theories, such as Activity Theory and Collective Behaviour Theory, are analysed along with methods and scientific fields stemming from the computer science, such as Social Network Analysis and Machine Learning for modelling human behaviour, to construct reliable activity and behaviour profiles of children from both a technological and a sociological perspective. Profiling information of the missing child is then combined with open data, like geographic and transportation data, along with insights and patterns revealed from pattern matching of similar past cases, to deduce potential Points of Interest (POIs) and consequently routes and directions that the investigation should follow, in an evidence-based and scientifically-sound manner, the preliminary findings of which approach can be found in (Michalitsi-Psarrou et al. 2019).

During the coordination phase, the ChildRescue solution allows search and rescue team members to gather and contribute to the investigations under the coordination of the responsible authorities. Through a collaboration space, real-time sharing of information and communication among team members who operate in the same field is offered, in a privacy-aware manner, while an analytics interface is offered to support investigation progress tracking. A real-time interactive map is also provided, showing the location of individuals and teams on the field, allowing for better operation, monitoring, and guidance. The collaboration spaces can help organisations build a team for an investigation quickly, enhance intercommunication and enable case managers to provide guidance and support, having a complete picture of the investigation progress and its updates.

Then, in the investigation action phase, the momentum for collective intelligence in the missing child cause is built through an intuitive mobile application. Real-time and evidence-based mobile alerts and updates are broadcasted to all citizens that have the app installed on their mobile phones, but are shown using geo-fencing techniques (Garg et al. 2017), only to those in areas designated to be close to the place where the child was last seen or in a specified radius from identified POIs stemming from the analysis in the preparation phase. With the advent of time, new POIs can be extracted from the validated pieces of evidence contributed by the citizens, and thus new notifications will be diffused. Any citizen, having the application installed, may send feedback, along with potential evidence (e.g., photo). This feedback is then algorithmically assessed on the credibility of the sender, based on his past behaviour and completeness of his profile, as well as the quality of the evidence they provided. The reliability of the evidence receives an automatic provisional classification by comparing its content, its location and the time that it was captured and sent, to the current case data. Through this process, the consistency of reported information in missing children cases increases and critical information is not only brought to the attention of the responsible authorities, but is also spread almost in real time, through updated geo-fenced alerts.

Finally, in the archiving phase, ChildRescue supports the responsible authorities to handle the case's closure in a secure and privacy-respectful manner. Semantic annotation of the documentation and lessons learnt for each case are kept inside the organisations, in order to support similar cases in the future. Regarding the public mobile app, all data related to a case are completely erased.

From an end-user's perspective and considering the application of the above-presented ChildRescue concept in action, the ChildRescue solution is composed of two main technological elements. Firstly, a user-friendly mobile application is offered to the citizens, who will have a direct communication channel to contribute eyewitness reports. Secondly, a collaboration platform will be at the disposal of the response organisations and the search and rescue teams, offered in the form of intuitive management and coordination interfaces. From a technological perspective, on the other hand, in order to deliver the functionalities envisaged in the ChildRescue concept, the ChildRescue solution consists of several components, such as the "Collaboration Space", mentioned before, allowing all investigators to securely share location-based, multi-media information regarding the investigation in groups with specific access rights, as well as the "Notification Engine", providing a scalable and flexible mechanism for managing and delivering mobile notifications, based on applied rules (e.g., the radius around POIs, duration of notification), and the "Analytics" engine, providing real-time insights to the organisations about each case under investigation. Adopting a modular design approach, each of the components exposes the necessary functionality for its integration in the overall ChildRescue solution under an Application Programming Interface (API) that is built according to state-of-the art practices and standards.

4. APPLICATION

The ChildRescue solution is currently tested against two different use cases and respective scenarios. The first use case examines the emergency response to reported child disappearances and is explored by two different pilot response organisations, one in Greece, coordinated by the Smile of the Child, and the other in Belgium, by Child Focus. Both organisations are the official response organisations for missing children in their respective countries and members of the Missing Children Europe federation. The second use case engages with and supports the registration, tracing, and discovery in case of a disappearance of unaccompanied migrant minors from hosting facilities and is coordinated by the Hellenic Red Cross. The ChildRescue platform aims to be used in parallel to Red Cross's mechanisms contributing to the prevention of disappearance, improving time-management and providing a tool that will reinforce coordination, decision making and information sharing on different organisational levels (e.g., hosting facilities, regional Red Cross Departments).

By now, the first Alpha versions of the ChildRescue platform and mobile app have been released, while a simulation/tabletop exercise has run for all the three organisations. The developed scenarios were based on actual past cases to create a plausible environment, but any personal data related to the children were carefully anonymised. Members and staff of the pilot organisations participated in the exercise, highlighting several benefits, compared to the established processes, most importantly the enhancement of fast information exchange with the alerts and team coordination tools, the simplification of information transfer between hosting facilities, the promotion of public engagement and the easier identification of irrelevant incoming information. The participants' feedback is going to be used for the refinement of the public release of the ChildRescue platform, which is planned for May 2020.

Along the development and testing procedures, a set of interviews with different stakeholders and domain experts has been conducted to enrich technical expertise and research findings. The results of these interviews have exposed the needs of and challenges faced by missing children, both by the experience itself, by being away from their families, and have highlighted the great potential for preventive and intervention strategies. Combining the expertise of heterogeneous parties and creating a mutual understanding of the particularities when designing, implementing and running new processes was, though, challenging and enlightening. Applying the insights from the feedback acquired, enables a more efficient data analytics process, and the building of an enhanced, complete profile of a missing child case, that extends simple case description and attempts to explain also child's social and psychological motivations. Since the project's development and testing is still in progress, valuable feedback and insights are expected to from the field exercises that will take place in the following months, as well as the use of the platform in production afterwards, that we aspire to further validate its effectiveness. On what is more, a robust exploitation plan is being developed, to ensure wide exploitation and utilisation of the ChildRescue solution after its release, building, amongst others, on the Missing Children Europe's (MCE) wide network, being the umbrella organisation of all missing children response organisations in the EU, and its extensive experience in communicating activities.

5. CONCLUSION

This paper investigated the current challenges and opportunities in missing children investigations and rescue efforts, while presenting a possible solution to enabling faster and more effective resolution of missing children cases, including those that relate to the registration, profiling and tracing of unaccompanied migrant minors. The proposed solution builds on top of existing, state of the art social theories and technological solutions and combines them to generate added value for missing children organisations towards creating a market-ready technological offering, that will work in parallel with their existing processes.

Several key take-aways can be elicited at this point. Firstly, given the highly sensitive nature of the data needed to create activity and behaviour profiles for the missing children, data privacy and protection needs to be at the forefront of such a solution's concerns and priorities. For this reason, encryption and anonymisation techniques are employed, and GDPR compliance is ensured. Moreover, the requirement for GDPR compliance has also seriously affected the availability of data, thus restricting the research on human behaviour, mobility and activity analysis, that intrinsically relies upon public personal data. Although it is undoubtedly for the best interest of individuals, a balance between data security and scientific progress is needed, while it is still a period of adjustment. It needs to be stressed, also, that each child is unique, rendering the issue of missing children quite diverse – as highlighted by social workers – a tiny, unpredictable detail may affect a child's current mindset and turn a case towards an erratic course of events. Therefore, a completely automatic process based on analytics insights and computations cannot be a substitute of the expertise of social workers, psychologists, and other trained professionals.

Although there are several private and public organisations all over the world that have developed or adapted systems for designing and managing missing persons cases (e.g., NamUs accessible at https://www.namus.gov/Dashboard, and FASTID accessible at https://www.iosb.fraunhofer.de/servlet/is/19908/), there is no inclusive solution, to the best of our knowledge, for addressing the complexity of missing children issue. The novelty of the proposed solution can be summarised in three axes. The first is the distribution of alerts based on the users' proximity to points of interest for a case, instantly grabbing the attention of several citizens at the same time, and the collection of their feedback for the development of an almost real-time and evidence-based profile of the missing child. The second axis is the facilitation of the information exchange between organisations acting on the field. The final axis is the development of data analytics and machine learning algorithms for the analysis of behavioural profiles, and their inclusion in existing investigative processes for missing children, research on which is currently limited (Blackmore et al. 2005; Lin and Goodrich 2010).

A remaining open research question concerns the validation of the success of such a process, for the same reasons that Amber Alert's success is questioned and difficult to be verified. In that respect, we consider a scientific validation feasible through a realistically simulated environment, taking into account the special characteristics of both the missing children cases and the mobility characteristics and particularities of the citizens of the wider geographical area where the child was last seen, who contribute as social sensors in the investigation,. This would provide the opportunity to run experiments comparing different alerting systems, as well as investigating process methods, in identical experimental cases, by defining baselines and controls. In that view, future work includes the development of such a simulation framework that will serve as evidence of the effectiveness of different alert systems, or lack thereof, and ChildRescue's own methodology.

ACKNOWLEDGEMENT

This work has been co-funded by the European Union's Horizon 2020 Research and Innovation programme under the ChildRescue project, grant agreement No 780938.

REFERENCES

Best, J., 1987. "Rhetoric in Claims-Making: Constructing the Missing Children Problem." *Social Problems* 34(2): 101–21. https://academic.oup.com/socpro/article-lookup/doi/10.2307/800710 (January 22, 2020).

Blackmore, K. et al, 2005. "Data Mining of Missing Persons Data." *In Springer*. Berlin, Heidelberg, 305–14. http://link.springer.com/10.1007/11011620_19 (December 18, 2018).

Cancedda, A. et al, 2013. "Missing Children in the European Union Mapping, Data Collection and Statistics." *Luxembourg:Publications Office of the European Union*: 106.

Crosland, K. et al, 2018. "Why Youth Run: Assessing Run Function to Stabilize Foster Care Placement." *Children and Youth Services Review* 85: 35–42.

Frowd, C. et al, 2014. "Locating Missing Persons Using Age-Progression Images from Forensic Artists." In *Proceedings - 2014 International Conference on Emerging Security Technologies, EST 2014*, Institute of Electrical and Electronics Engineers Inc., 1.

Garg, A. et al, 2017. "Smart Geo-Fencing with Location Sensitive Product Affinity." In *Proceedings of the 25th ACM SIGSPATIAL International Conference on Advances in Geographic Information Systems - SIGSPATIAL '17*, New York, New York, USA: ACM Press, 1–10. http://dl.acm.org/citation.cfm?doid=3139958.3140059 (January 22, 2019).

Griffin, T. and Miller, M., 2008. "Child Abduction, AMBER Alert, and Crime Control Theater." *Criminal Justice Review* 33(2): 159–76. http://journals.sagepub.com/doi/10.1177/0734016808316778 (February 13, 2019).

Griffin, T. et al, 2007. "A Preliminary Examination of AMBER Alert's Effects." *Criminal Justice Policy Review* 18(4): 378–94. http://journals.sagepub.com/doi/10.1177/0887403407302332 (January 22, 2020).

Griffin, T. et al, 2010. "An Empirical Examination of AMBER Alert 'Successes.'" *Journal of Criminal Justice* 38(5): 1053–62.

Griffin, T. et al, 2016. "Does AMBER Alert 'Save Lives'? An Empirical Analysis and Critical Implications." *Journal of Crime and Justice* 39(4): 490–511.

Johnson, R. J. et al, 2006. "Gender Differences in Victimized Homeless Adolescents." *Adolescence* 41(161): 39–53. http://www.ncbi.nlm.nih.gov/pubmed/16689440 (January 28, 2020).

Boulos, M. N. K. et al, 2011. "Crowdsourcing, Citizen Sensing and Sensor Web Technologies for Public and Environmental Health Surveillance and Crisis Management: Trends, OGC Standards and Application Examples." *International Journal of Health Geographics* 10(1): 67. http://www.ij-healthgeographics.com/content/10/1/67.

Lampinen, J. et al, 2016. "Prospective Person Memory: The Role of Self-Efficacy, Personal Interaction, and Multiple Images in Recognition of Wanted Persons." *Journal of Police and Criminal Psychology* 31(1): 59–70.

Ledoux, F. and Van Oosterom, H., 2013. "Transportation Mode-Based Segmentation and Classification of Movement Trajectories)." *International Journal of Geographical Information Science* 27(2): 385–407. http://dx.doi.org/10.1080/13658816.2012.692791 (February 7, 2019).

Lin, L. and Goodrich, M., 2010. "A Bayesian Approach to Modeling Lost Person Behaviors Based on Terrain Features in Wilderness Search and Rescue." *Computational and Mathematical Organization Theory* 16(3): 300–323. http://link.springer.com/10.1007/s10588-010-9066-2 (February 13, 2019).

Michalitsi-Psarrou, A. et al, 2019. "Complementing Amber Alert: Increasing the Social Sensors' Effectiveness through Focused Communication Channels." In *Institute of Electrical and Electronics Engineers (IEEE)*, 1–7.

Miller, M. and Clinkinbeard, S., 2006. "Improving the AMBER Alert System: Psychology Research and Policy Recommendations." *Law & Psychology Review* 30. https://heinonline.org/HOL/Page?handle=hein.journals/lpsyr30&id=5&div=&collection= (February 13, 2019).

Payne, M., 1995. "Understanding 'Going Missing': Issues for Social Work and Social Services." *The British Journal of Social Work* 25(3): 333–48. https://academic.oup.com/bjsw/article/25/3/333/1665718/Understanding-Going-Missing-issues-for-social-work (January 28, 2020).

Rahate, S. and Shaikh, M., 2016. "Geo-Fencing Infrastructure: Location Based Service." *International Research Journal of Engineering and Technology*. www.irjet.net (January 28, 2020).

Sicafuse, L. and Miller, M., 2010. "Social Psychological Influences on the Popularity of Amber Alerts." *Criminal Justice and Behavior* 37(11): 1237–54. http://journals.sagepub.com/doi/10.1177/0093854810379618 (January 22, 2020).

Sweeney, L., and Lampinen, J., 2012. "The Effect of Presenting Multiple Images on Prospective and Retrospective Person Memory for Missing Children." *Journal of Applied Research in Memory and Cognition* 1(4): 235–41.

Yuan, N. J. et al, 2012. "Discovering Regions of Different Functions in a City Using Human Mobility and POIs." *Proceedings of the ACM SIGKDD International Conference on Knowledge Discovery and Data Mining.* pp.186-194.

YOU JUST REMINDED ME – I'M HUMAN!: VIEWING OR INTERACTING WITH ROBOTS INCREASES HUMAN CONFORMITY TO OTHER HUMANS

Julian Welsh[1], Marlena Fraune[1,*] and Yanfen You[2,*]
[1]Department of Psychology, New Mexico State University, Las Cruces, New Mexico, USA
[2]Marketing Department, New Mexico State University, Las Cruces, New Mexico, USA
[*]Dr.

ABSTRACT

As robots become prevalent, merely thinking of their existence may affect how people behave. When interacting with a robot in a game with no objective answers, people conformed to the robot's answers more than to their own initial response (Scassellati ,2018). In this paper, we examined how robots affect conformity to other humans in two studies. In Study 1, an online survey, we primed participants (N = 113) to think of different experiences: Humans (an experience with a human stranger), Robots (an experience with a robot), or Neutral (daily life). We measured if participants conformed to other humans in survey answers. Results indicated that people conformed more when thinking of Humans or Robots than of Neutral events. In Study 2, in the real world, participants (N = 21), interacted with and Agent (human, robot) at a bake sale. Preliminary results indicated that in >90% of cases, groups of participants, rather than individuals, approached the robot while no such effect was observed when the human was at the bake sale. The bake sale was donation-based, and donations depended on whether the Agent was human or robot. In the human condition, participants donated an average of 1.00 dollar to the common cause and 3.00 dollars to the less common cause. Conversely, in the robot condition, participants donated an average of 2.00 dollars to both the more common cause, and an average of 1.00 dollar in the less common cause. The first study indicated that humans and robots have a similar effect on conformity in humans; however the second study suggests that the effects are more complex. Because participants in Study 1 typically imagined machinelike robots, but in Study 2 saw a humanlike robot, we recommend that future studies examine how group effects and anthropomorphism can influence conformity in people when interacting with robots in real-world settings.

KEYWORDS

Human-Robot Interaction, Group Effects, Conformity, Anthropomorphism

1. INTRODUCTION

Robots are becoming increasingly prevalent in today's world (e.g., roombas, vending machines, Walmart self-pilot floor cleaners). Viewing groups of robots has been shown to change how people act at a basic psychological level, possibly even increasing their likelihood to categorize themselves as human (Fraune, et. al, 2015). How people categorize themselves affects their goals and behaviors to be more like the norm for their group (Abrams et. al, 1990). If thinking of robots causes people to categorize themselves as human, they may conform more to other humans, or follow more social norms from humans, when robots are around. This would have implications for expected human behavior in society in the future.

In this paper, we define conformity as individuals changing the way they think or behave to fit group norms. Conformity to robots can be harder to induce than conformity to humans (Brandstetter et. al, 2014). Still, when the robot is considered an expert, is trusted, or the task is ambiguous, people have conformed to robots (Hertz, Wiese, 2014) (Brandstetter et.al, 2017). However, it is not yet studied how robots affect conformity to other humans.

Robot characteristics may influence how robots affect conformity. For example, anthropomorphism of robots (i.e., viewing the robots as humanlike) may affect perceptions of robot similarity to humans (Damiano, Dumouchel, 2018)(Tondu, 2012), which would influence conformity. Further, anthropomorphism of a robot, can increase emotional connection or identification with the robot (Döring, 2019), which is shown to increase conformity to that individual (Haslam, Reicher 2012).

Group size also influences conformity. People conform more to groups of 3-5 people, than just one or two people (Asch, 1951). In the real world, people often interact with robots in groups rather than as individuals (Wikman, 2006) (Fraune, 2019) possibly because people were more likely to accept robots when interacting with them as groups than as individuals (Fraune, 2019). In our Study 2, performed in the real world, it is likely that groups will be more willing to approach the robot than individuals. Therefore, people may conform more to other people in the condition because the robot is there or because they are acting in a group.

Surveys give insight into the thought process and perceptions of items and situations (Wikman, 2006). However, surveys cannot accurately assess how people would respond to robots in the real world (Wikman, 2006). In this paper, we compare survey responses in an online study to behavioral responses in a real-world setting.

We report the results of two studies: an online survey (Study 1) and preliminary results from a real-world study (Study 2). Both studies examine how robots affect human-to-human conformity. In Study 1, we primed participants to think of humans, robots, or a neutral aspect of the daily life, and we measured how much they conformed to other humans. In Study 2, a human researcher, or a humanoid robot (Nao) asked participants to donate to more common or less common causes (Figure 1). We hypothesized that thinking of or interacting with robots would increase human conformity to humans.

2. METHOD

2.1 Study 1

We recruited participants from eight business classes at [location redacted for anonymity]. Participants (N = 113) completed an online 5- to 10-minute survey in Qualtrics. Participants were randomly assigned to between-subjects conditions in which they were asked to "recall and describe, as vividly as possible, two experiences in which you encountered" each different prime: a Human ("someone you had never known before"), Robot ("an experience you can recall having with a robot") , or Neutral event (i.e., "regular things (neither positive nor negative) you did yesterday"). The participants in the robot-prime condition stated the type of robot they interacted with in all accounts. We attempted to control for novelty of robots by asking participants in the Human condition to write about someone with whom they were not familiar.

We created for this study two measures of conformity with other humans: movie conformity (i.e., rating a preference towards a popular movie versus an equally well accredited film festival one) and book club conformity (i.e., preference towards a book club that everyone else was joining versus a book club that would make them stand out). Participants rated their answers on a bipolar scale from 1 (less conformity) to 7 (greater conformity).

Hypothesis 1: We hypothesized that participants in the Robot condition would indicate more conformity on these measures than participants in the Human or Neutral condition.

2.2 Study 2

Next, we ran a study in the real world in the science building at [location redacted for anonymity]. We ran a donation table associated with a psychology honors society (Psi Chi), and anyone who approached the table (came within 6 feet of the table) was considered a participant (N = 21). The table held two donation boxes labeled: "travel" and "general." During each trial, one box was labeled as being "less" or "more" commonly donated to, counterbalanced across hours of the study. This variable behaviorally measured conformity to supposed prior participants. The set up was a bake sale, and participants could also take cookies that were labeled as "home-made" and "factory-made" (though in reality the cookies came from the local grocery store).

In a between-participants design, we manipulated which Agent (Human, Robot) acted as the bake sale host to collect donations and advertise Psi Chi. In the Robot condition, a researcher discretely controlled the humanoid Nao robot from a distance. The Agent interacted with participants in a standard way, reading or reciting from a script (greeting participants, indicating the cause for the donations, and noting which was more popular).

We ran the study for four hours surrounding lunch (10 AM until 2 PM). We ran each condition for one hour, twice, with the box counterbalanced in each. The onset of COVID-19 prevented further data collection for now.

We measured conformity as the total donation to the supposedly more- and less-common causes during each hour of the conditions. We also measured the number of cookies that were homemade, and factory made taken in each condition.

Hypothesis 2: We hypothesized that participants would conform more by donating more to the supposedly more-common cause and less to the supposedly less-common cause in the Robot than Human condition. Hypothesis 3: We also hypothesized that participants would take more homemade cookies in the Robot than Human condition. The latter is a more novel and exploratory hypothesis because it does not measure conformity to prior humans, rather moving toward things that are related to other humans.

3. RESULTS

3.1 Study 1

Data were analyzed in SPSS version 25. We performed between-subjects ANOVAs on the data, using Sidak to correct for multiple comparisons.

Participants showed a marginal difference in conformity across conditions on the movie review measure ($F(2, 133)= 2.576$, $p = .080$; Figure 1). Post hoc tests revealed that participants who were primed to think of robots ($p = .085$), or humans ($p = .035$), showed significantly more conformity to humans than participants who were primed to think of a neutral experience. No significant difference occurred across conditions for the book club measure of conformity ($F(2,113) = .415$. $p= .661$; Figure 2).

In Study 1, when participants were asked to describe their experience they had with a robot, they did not describe anthropomorphic, highly intelligent robots with human-like tendencies, but instead self-piloting floor cleaners from Walmart, Roombas, or automated vending machines. This is probably because most people do not interact extensively with robots on a regular basis.

Figure 1. Robot at bake sale

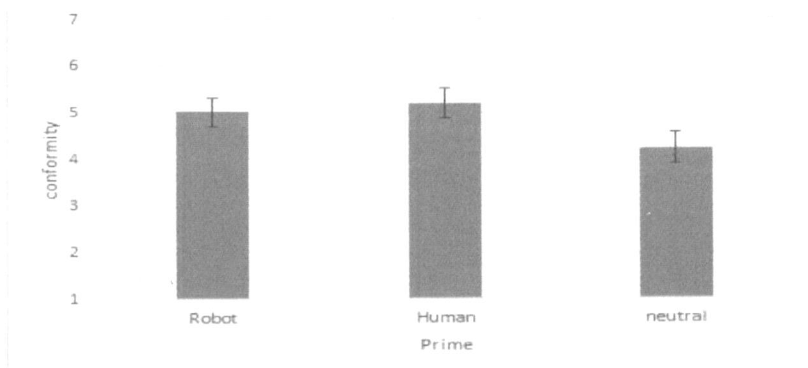

Figure 2. Differences in participant conformity across conditions when rating which movie they would rather watch
Error bars represent standard error

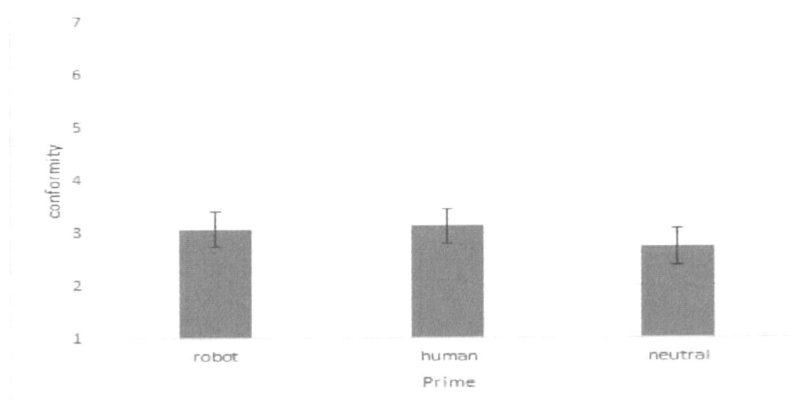

Figure 3. Differences in participant conformity across conditions when rating which book club they would rather attend
Error bars represent standard error

3.2 Study 2

Due to the collection being cut short, there were too few participants in Study 2 to quantitatively analyze data. Instead, we report qualitative assessments.

Homemade/factory. There was no trend in whether participants took more homemade or factory-made cookies, but participants took more cookies in the human than robot condition (31 total cookies taken; 14 total in the homemade condition, with 10 in the human condition and 4 in the robot condition; 17 total in the factory condition, with 14 in the human condition and 3 in the robot condition). There was no observable trend of Agent on which cookies participants took; participants took cookies in roughly equal measure between the factory and homemade conditions.

Donations. We calculated the average number of dollars donated in each condition. Donations to the common or uncommon cause depended on whether the Agent was human or robot. In the human condition, participants donated an average of 1.00 dollar to the common cause and 3.00 dollars to the less common cause. Conversely, in the robot condition, participants donated an average of 2.00 dollars to both the more common cause, and an average of 1.00 dollar in the less common cause. There was no observable main effect of Agent or Cause.

Distinct from hypotheses, in the human condition, experimenters observed participants openly approached the human bake sale host both individually and as groups as one would expect. In the robot condition, the experimenters observed a consistent trend of participants only approaching the NAO robot bake sale host in groups of 3-4 people. Specifically, data collection consisted of three groups of three and one group of two approaching the robot, and many passersby who observed the robot but did not approach the robot. Because it was not the original intent to study individuals or groups approached the robots, we did not collect objective data on the number of cases for which this occurred.

4. DISCUSSION

In this project, we examined participant conformity to humans after thinking of robots on an online survey and interacting with a robot in the real world. In Study 1, we examined participant conformity to other humans after they were primed to think of humans, robots, or a neutral experience. The results partially supported our hypothesis that thinking of robots would increase human conformity to human groups. In Study 2, we examined real-world effects of human-robot interaction on conformity to human groups. Our preliminary data showed evidence of robots affecting participant behavioral conformity. Additionally, we found a general trend of people avoiding the robot and only approaching it when they were in groups, opposed to individual. These results show observable trends, but due to the small sample size and limited data collection possible with the outbreak of COVID-19, need further data to draw solid conclusions.

In Study 1, primes of humans and robots increased conformity on one measure, but not another, partially supporting Hypothesis 1. The difference in significance across measures suggests that the degree to which people conform while thinking of robots (or humans) is contingent on the context. More typical contexts, like seeing movies, may increase likelihood of conformity. Conversely, it may be that participants have not joined many book clubs, and therefore joining a book club is not a good measure of conformity.

Study 2 supported Hypothesis 2, but not Hypothesis 3. Study 2 therefore partially supported the overall hypothesis that robots increased conformity. In Study 1, both humans and robot primes influenced conformity among participants; in Study 2, the robot increased conformity on the common cause measure, while the human decreased conformity. Participants interacted with robots only in groups, as opposed to the mix of individual and group approaches in the human condition. It may be that group conformity affected who approached the robot. The trends from Study 2 suggest that individuals have no issue approaching a table with human bake sale hosts, but avoid approaching robots unless they are in groups of 2-5 people. Another potential reason for the observed increase in conformity may have been because most of our participants already knew each other (classmates heading to and leaving classes walking in groups); groups of people who already know each other also have shown to have greater conformity effects than strangers (McKelvey, Kerr, 1988)(Stallen, 2013). However, future research should examine the effects of social context and group conformity more closely to see if this effect replicates with more data.

4.1 Limitations and Future Directions

The lack of difference in conformity effects in the book club measure is likely not related to viewing the robots as social actors, because participants typically indicated that they were thinking of machinelike robots in the robot condition. Interestingly, this difference occurred even though participants in the human condition often wrote about the first time they met a significant other or best friend. Future researchers should examine differences due to thinking of a familiar human.

Anthropomorphism of robots may affect how similarly robots are perceived to humans (Damiano, Dumouchel, 2018)(Tondu, 2012). This would influence conformity, and conformity could potentially affect the size of the group interacting with the robot (Asch 1951). Future research should directly manipulate robot anthropomorphism and human group size during interaction.

Our future research will continue testing real-world interactions with robots. In Study 2 we used an area that had a modest number of passersby, and consequentially a relatively limited number of potential participants. To increase our sample size in our next study, we plan on using an area between buildings with more traffic. We plan on using a telepresence robot programmed with an array of potential responses to participants instead of a Nao. A follow-up study continuing to examine actual interaction with robots will give us greater insight on the differences in conformity people display when compared to human-human interaction.

This research enhances our understanding of how humans conform in the presence (real or imagined) of robots. This contributes to the psychological and sociological understanding of how humans and robots affect conformity to humans. These results might change for participants who were more familiar with robots. Future research should examine if people conform more if they see robots more regularly, or these results represent the novelty effect. We predict there will be an effect of decreased conformity with increased familiarity (i.e. electrical engineers, technicians, people who interact with machines/robots on a regular basis), as previous research has suggested a negative correlation between familiarity and conformity (Myers & Arenson, 1968).

Results of this type of research can help marketers determine how to optimize and sell robots. For example, if people thinking about robots or humans increases conformity, advertisements about robots might be most effective when appealing to consumers' desire to follow human social norms. A greater variety of results from experimental trials in different real world settings will also help us understand the factors that play into avoidance and group effects of conformity, as well as to whether anthropomorphism plays a role into the strength of conformity effects. This would suggest not only a, but also major implications in business and marketing with the types of robots that will be most popular and therefore have the greatest market demand.

ACKNOWLEDGEMENT

Thank you to Cheyenne Valdespino for assisting our first study. Thank you also to grant number 1849591 from Discovery Scholars of New Mexico State University for partially funding this study.

REFERENCES

Asch SE. (1951). Effects of group pressure upon the modification and distortion of judgments. In H. Guetzkow (Ed.), *Groups, Leadership and Men.* Pittsburg, PA: Carnegie Press.

B. Scassellati, et al. (2018). "Humans conform to robots: Disambiguating trust, truth, and conformity," in *Proceedings of the 2018 ACM/IEEE International Conference on Human-Robot Interaction*, pp. 187-195.

D. Abrams, M. Wetherell, S. Cochrane, M. A. Hogg, and J. C. Turner (1990). "Knowing what to think by knowing who you are: Self-categorization and the nature of norm formation, conformity and group polarization*," *British Journal of Social Psychology,* vol. 29, pp. 97-119,

Damiano L and Dumouchel P (2018) "Anthropomorphism in Human–Robot Co-evolution". *Front. Psychol.* 9:468. doi: 10.3389/fpsyg.2018.00468

David G. Myers & Sidney J. Arenson (1968) Stimulus Factors in Conformity, *The Journal of Social Psychology*, 76:1, 37-41, doi 10.1080/00224545.1968.9919821

Fraune, M. & Šabanović, S. & Kanda, Takayuki. (2019). Human Group Presence, Group Characteristics, and Group Norms Affect Human-Robot Interaction in Naturalistic

Industrial Robot, Vol. 39 No. 6, pp. 609-618. https://doi.org/10.1108/01439911211268840

J. Brandstetter, C. Beckner, E. B. Sandoval, and C. Bartneck (2017), "persistent lexical entrainment in HRI," in *Proceedings of the 2017 ACM/IEEE International Conference on Human-Robot Interaction*, pp. 63-72.

J. Brandstetter, P. Racz, C. Beckner, E. B. Sandoval, J. Hay, and C. Bartneck (2014) "A peer pressure experiment: Recreation of the Asch conformity experiment with robots," in *Intelligent Robots and Systems (IROS 2014), 2014 IEEE/RSJ International Conference on*, pp. 1335-1340.

Lee JM, Baek J and Ju DY (2018) Anthropomorphic Design: Emotional Perception for Deformable Object. *Front. Psychol.* 9:1829. doi: 10.3389/fpsyg.2018.01829

M. R. Fraune, S. Kawakami, S. Šabanović, R. De Silva, and M. Okada (2015). "Three's company, or a crowd?: The effects of robot number and behavior on HRI in Japan and the USA," *Robotics: Science and Systems.*

N. Döring (2019) Psychological access to media and gender: Media psychology and social psychology, *Media and Gender Manual*, 10.1007/978-3-658-20712-0_32-1, (1-15)

N. Hertz and E. Wiese (2016) "Influence of agent type and task ambiguity on conformity in social decision making," in *Proceedings of the Human Factors and Ergonomics Society Annual Meeting*, pp. 313-317.

R. B. Cialdini and M. R. Trost (1998). "Social influence: Social norms, conformity and compliance"

S. A. Haslam and S. D. Reicher (2012). "Contesting the “nature” of conformity: What Milgram and Zimbardo's studies really show," *PLoS biology,* vol. 10, p. e1001426,

S. E. Asch (1956). "Studies of independence and conformity: I. A minority of one against a unanimous majority," *Psychological Monographs: General and Applied,* vol. 70.

SettingsPresentation_1.pdf. Frontiers in Robotics and AI. 6. 10.3389/frobt.2019.00048.

Stallen M, Smidts A and Sanfey AG (2013) Peer influence: neural mechanisms underlying in-group conformity. *Front. Hum. Neurosci.* 7:50. doi: 10.3389/fnhum.2013.00050

Tondu, B. (2012), "Anthropomorphism and service humanoid robots: An ambiguous relationship",

W. McKelvey, Nancy H. Kerr. (1988) Differences in Conformity among Friends and Strangers. Oglethorpe University. https://doi.org/10.2466/pr0.1988.62.3.759

Wikman, A. (2006). Reliability, Validity and True Values in Surveys. *Soc Indic Res* 78, 85.

EMPLOYERS' MIXED SIGNALS TO WOMEN IN IT: UNCOVERING HOW GENDER EQUALITY IDEALS ARE CHALLENGED BY ORGANIZATIONAL CONTEXT

Hilde G. Corneliussen and Gilda Seddighi
Western Norway Research Institute, Box 163, 6851 Sogndal, Norway

ABSTRACT

Digitalization across sectors drives an increasing demand for IT specialists. Women, however, still make up a small part of computing communities, IT education and work – in the US and across Europe. The "gender equality paradox" is a label for women's underrepresentation in STEM disciplines, particularly in IT, that seems to be more extreme in highly gender egalitarian cultures. It has been suggested that the paradox is a result of women's choices in wealthy countries with a high degree of individual freedom. However, our research suggests that there is another side to this paradox, thus demonstrating the importance to recognize how other groups affect women's participation in IT. Our study of attitudes towards women's underrepresentation in IT among IT employers and organizations uncovers mixed signals from these actors, as they both welcome and doubt women in IT. Employers' negotiation of the meaning of women's underrepresentation in IT leaves little space for gender equality actions. While this can have major consequences for women's careers in computing and IT work, it also illustrates a central mechanism of the "gender equality paradox" characterized by a widely accepted norm of gender equality existing alongside employers' skepticism to the goal of gender balance in computing.

KEYWORDS

IT Work, Employers, Gender Equality, Paradox, Discursive Resources

1. INTRODUCTION

Digitalization across sectors drives an increasing demand for IT specialists (EIGE, 2018). Women, however, still make up a small part of computing communities, IT education and work – in the US and across Europe (Bailey & Riley, 2018; EUROSTAT, 2019; Simonsen & Corneliussen, 2020). Women's underrepresentation in IT has often been depicted as a challenge concerning girls and women (Wajcman, 2004). However, it is also important to recognize how other groups affect women's participation in IT. Our study explores *attitudes towards women's underrepresentation in IT among IT employers and organizations*. The research questions guiding this chapter are: How do IT employers and organizations perceive the underrepresentation of women in IT? Do they consider it a goal to increase women's participation in IT, and if so, which strategies or actions do they engage for improving the gender balance in IT work in their own organization?

The analysis uncovers mixed signals from these actors as it shows a tendency for the employers to accept the norm of gender equality, while simultaneously negotiating, and even questioning, the goal of recruiting more women to IT work. This leaves the organizations with little space for gender equality actions. Based on dialogue meetings in 12 IT organizations, this paper analyses these attitudes that work as barriers to gender equality work in the IT sector. While this could be identified as a type of "resistance" towards gender equality, we rather suggest analyzing this through a more productive notion of "discursive resources" that individuals use to make sense of their context (Dick, 2004). Applying a unique wide and cross sectoral perspective on central actors in the field of IT work makes this study able to identify an underlaying mechanism of the gender equality paradox.

1.1 A Gender Equality Paradox

Despite increasing digitalization and exciting job opportunities for IT expertise, the proportion of women is developing slowly, in some places even negatively (National Science Foundation, 2019). Women's underrepresentation in IT is recognized as even more extreme in wealthier and more egalitarian countries such as the Nordic countries in general and Norway in particular (Chow & Charles, 2019; Stoet & Geary, 2018), which is the object of our study.

The strong notion of gender equality in the Nordic countries is reflected in rules and regulations aimed to fight gender discrimination and to secure equal rights and opportunities (Skjeie & Teigen, 2005). In the face of this national gender equality regime, the underrepresentation of women has been narrated as a "gender equality paradox" (Chow & Charles, 2019; Stoet & Geary, 2018). It has been suggested that the phenomenon is caused by the high level of gender equality itself, creating freedom not only from gender discrimination, but also a "right to choose poorly paid female-labeled career paths" (Charles & Bradley, 2006). Other explanations suggest that the national level of wealth makes it less urgent for women in more affluent societies to aim for well-paid jobs (Stoet & Geary, 2018). While such explanations place the responsibility on girls and women, research has demonstrated a perseverance in how masculine cultures of computing (Blum et al., 2007), gender stereotypes associating IT with men (Master et al., 2016) and "the perception of ICT jobs as a playground for men" (EIGE, 2018) have a negative impact on women's entry into IT careers.

Gender equality as a goal and the welfare state as an active force pushing towards this goal characterizes the Nordic countries (Borchorst & Siim, 2008; Hernes, 1987). The widely accepted ideal of gender equality and inclusion of women in working life has become something "we cannot not want" (Brown, 2000), but still it can be difficult to transform into active practices of inclusion (Holli et al., 2005). A political goal of "mainstreaming", making gender equality a general principle in organizations has been criticized for making it everybody's task in a way that makes it nobody's responsibility (Teigen & Eggebø, 2017). Even in a context where the state actively promotes gender equality, like in Norway, there is found little focus on this among employers when there are no incentives for such engagement (Nordberg, 2019). Furthermore, there are no routines for enforcing the employers' statutory duty to secure gender equality in their organizations (Ibid.). It is, however, recognized as vital that the IT sector is involved in work to improve the gender balance in IT, and also, since men hold at least 75% of IT jobs, men must become "advocates", Bailey and Riley emphasize (2018). The first step is to acknowledge that there is a problem so that changes can be made in strategies for recruiting women to IT jobs (Ibid.; Corneliussen & Seddighi, 2019).

A low motivation to engage in gender equality work, as well as outright resistance towards such initiatives, have been recognized in studies of male dominated occupations (Johansson et al., 2019). Meritocratic principles, seeing opportunities and promotion as resting on individual's competence, is often considered to "solve" gender inequality by assuming that participation is based on individuals' efforts rather than being affected by discriminatory processes (Powell et al., 2018). A similar situation can be recognized in IT, where a low proportion of women has been used as a documentation for women's low interest rather than seeing it as a result of discriminatory practices (Corneliussen & Prøitz, 2016). Within such perspectives, positive actions for gender equality can even be perceived as enhancing the problem instead of solving it (Johansson et al., 2019). Contrary to this view, evidence suggests that interventions are necessary to achieve a better gender balance in the most male dominated fields of IT (National Science Foundation, 2019; Simonsen & Corneliussen, 2020; Vabø et al., 2012). Meanwhile, gender stereotypes characterizing women with a weak relationship to IT (Payton & Berki, 2019) continue to have effect. Stereotypes make it difficult to associate women with IT expertise in a culture where they tend to fail the "if-can"-test (Corneliussen et al., 2019). The "if-can"-test, West and Zimmerman (1987) claim, reflects a tendency to identify people as belonging to a certain category *if* they *can* be perceived as belonging to this category. This challenge is of particular relevance to fields like IT which are strongly associated with men (Payton & Berki, 2019), illustrated by our findings showing employers' and organizations' doubts about women's rightful belonging in IT jobs.

The analysis below explores how employers and organizations involved in IT research, development, and innovation perceive and deal with the underrepresentation of women in IT in Norway. The findings illustrate how a national gender equality regime is renegotiated by relevant employers and organizations challenging the meaning of women's underrepresentation as well as the ideal of gender equality in IT.

2. METHODS

2.1 Case Study

Our study included 13 women and 10 men from a total of 12 organizations, private as well as public, with a shared interest in *IT in research, development, and innovation*. "IT" here refers to a wide notion of expertise in fields of information and communication technology including computing and other adjoining disciplines. The study had a cross-sectoral profile, as we observed a growing engagement of IT specialists in new sectors and industries (EUROSTAT, 2019). Some of the participating organizations represented the traditional private IT sector, while others were public bodies, research funders, and research institutes with IT and digitalization as a key area. Thus, together they represent a wide specter of organizations that contribute to shaping IT work. The 23 men and women participating were appointed by the organizations. They were leaders and managers for the organizations, head of IT or HR departments or had other administrative positions, while some represented the professional IT staff. When analyzing the material we found more similarities than differences between the sectors and industries; we therefore only occasionally refer to the sector in the analysis presented below.

The organizations were invited to dialogue meetings to discuss the underrepresentation of women in computing and how to improve the situation. The meetings aimed to explore as well as create dialogue with the organizations to learn from their practices and they loosely followed a focus group design where the aim is to study how meaning is created in a social context (Patton, 2002). Six main questions were presented on a piece of paper on the table to start the discussion, pertaining to the meaning of IT for the organization, gender distribution in the organization and across positions, strategies to recruit women, and gender equality goals and actions.

2.2 Analyzing Contextualized Attitudes as Discursive Resources

The study is based on a theoretical tradition of Feminist Technology Studies (FTS) (Bray, 2007) recognizing both gender and technology as socially constructed and shaping or co-constructing each other (Corneliussen, 2011; Kelan, 2007). The analytical method engaged focusses on the discursive level (Livholts & Tamboukou, 2015) of the dialogue meetings, exploring how meaning of gender and IT are constructed and negotiated. As will be elaborated below, the organizations' responses involved a type of negotiation that could be perceived as a form of *resistance* to gender equality in IT. However, labelling this as resistance involves a risk of misrepresenting how the organizations perceived the situation: they did not consider their response to the situation a rejection of gender equality norms. It is more productive to analyze the mechanisms at play here as productive "discursive resources" that the individual engages to understand and negotiate the question of gender equality in their own organizational context (Corneliussen & Seddighi, 2019; Dick, 2004). This helps to understand the mixed messages from the organizations that simultaneously welcome and doubt women's entry into IT jobs.

The examples discussed below should not be considered the organizations' formal attitudes but rather represent individual voices. However, these voices suggest that the organizations do not have clear guidelines for working with gender equality (Nordberg, 2019).

3. RESULTS: ALTERNATIVE APPROACHES TO WOMEN'S UNDER-REPRESENTATION

In the invitation to the dialogue meetings, we introduced some "fixed points" of departure by recognizing that women are *underrepresented* in computing and it is an ideal to get *more women* into computing, which, in turn, means that *gender equality action* is required. All the organizations initially agreed with the above definitions of the situation and the goal. However, when reflecting on how this goal could be realized in their own organization, other ways of seeing the situation were presented. Thus, during the discussion, alternative approaches were introduced, as shown in the table below, presenting how the meaning of gender equality was negotiated in relation to their organizational context. This involved alternative perceptions of women's underrepresentation, alternative ways of seeing the goal of increasing women's participation, and, consequently, the effect this had on their attitudes towards engaging in gender equality actions.

Table 1. Examples of organizations negotiating the ideal of gender equality in IT

Approaches to gender equality in IT	Organizational context for gender equality	Perception of women's under-representation	Perception of the ideal to increase women's participation	Attitudes towards gender equality action
1. Gender equality is not a challenge	a) "We already have gender balance, but not in IT"	Invisible	Unimportant	Unnecessary
	b) "We employ women in other positions"	Agree	Unimportant	Unnecessary
	c) "We have gender equality"	Agree	Agree	Unnecessary
2. Gender is not a focus	d) "We focus on equality for other groups"	Unimportant	Unimportant	Yielding for other goals
	e) "We avoid focusing on women"	Agree	Agree	Gender neutral (no) strategies
3. Men and women are different	f) "Women have other interests"	Agree	Questioning goal	Do we *need* women?
	g) "Men fit IT work better"	Agree	Questioning goal	Do we *want* women?
	h) "We just want the best"	Agree	Questioning goal	Competence before gender
4. Indifference and passivity	i) "It will pass"	Agree	Agree	Wasted energy
	j) "It is not a requirement"	Agree	Agree	Not required

3.1 Gender Equality is Not Perceived as a Relevant Challenge

Gender imbalance in IT is not necessarily perceived as a relevant identification of gender inequality in an organization. The table shows three examples of "discursive resources" used to argue that gender equality is not a challenge as it is already secured in the organization at large. The first two suggest that the problem is *already solved* by transferring the issue to the overall organization rather than IT.

a) *"We already have gender balance, but not in IT"* is a reaction typically found in public sector organizations that employ many women (SSB, 2018). This approach disguises gender imbalance in IT and renders it unimportant: "*We have many women in different positions and with higher education, so we don't experience it the same way. So, I think that we have not considered it necessary to have more women in IT*". Changing focus from IT workers to the overall organization allows for a claim that gender balance has already been achieved; therefore, it is less important to work towards further changes in IT recruitment.

b) "We employ women in other positions" is a similar logic found in the private sector, some with no women in IT positions: "*Our main initiative to recruit more women is to focus more on roles in HR.*" Their strategy is primarily targeting a better gender balance in the work environment rather than in IT jobs. Having female employees erodes the need for women in IT, another illustrates: "*We have one woman in IT development ... she has other women around in other positions. So that means, perhaps it is not so important to have more women in IT.*" Gender equality in these cases is more about the social environment and less about women working with IT.

c) "We have gender equality" reflects attitudes in an organization with no women in IT positions. They renegotiate what gender equality means, suggesting that it is a matter of how people are *treated*, rather than who works with IT: "*Everybody is treated the same, we don't think much about it. [...] We don't see any difference between our co-workers*". Defining gender equality as something that already exists almost automatically, makes actions aiming at increasing the number of women in IT positions less relevant: women are invited, and they are treated "the same", they are just not coming. Gender researchers have, however, warned that *similar* treatment does not necessarily represent *equality* when the starting point for men and women is one of difference (Kvande & Rasmussen, 1993 (1990)).

The examples above illustrate how the initial claim of women's underrepresentation in IT is renegotiated by identifying the challenge as already solved in their organizations. They do not reject the gender equality ideal as such, but rather engage "discursive resources" to make sense of the ideal within their own organizational context, concluding that it is unnecessary to engage in gender equality actions.

3.2 No Focus on Gender

Gender equality is a difficult topic to address. There are few guidelines for employers, and gender issues compete with other concerns.

d) "We focus on equality for other groups" is a claim that is supposed to justify less focus on gender and more on other groups, for instance ethnic minorities. "*That is where we cannot reach our goals*", one organization explains. Not only the overall organization, rather than IT jobs, but also other types of inclusion and "equality work" takes the focus away from women's underrepresentation in IT.

e) "We avoid focusing on women" illustrates a fear of drawing attention to their failure in hiring women: *"We don't believe in the typical 'women are encouraged to apply'. That is a bad recipe for making women apply."* Their strategy for recruiting women is rather based on a universal "non-gendered" perspective, as they are convinced that targeting women *"will result in the opposite effect"* – despite their lack of success in recruiting women so far.

The examples above illustrate how gender equality often loses out to other, apparently more pressing, matters (Skjeie & Teigen, 2003). It also illustrates the challenges for the organizations that, despite a national gender equality regime, have little knowledge of how to implement a gender equality strategy.

3.3 Men and Women are Different

This approach is based on perceptions of gender as a difference illustrating how gender equality norms are "disarmed", or even rejected, with references to stereotypical perceptions of men's and women's relationships to IT. In the three examples, the organizations' representatives realize that women are underrepresented in IT, however, seeing gender as a difference between men and women in terms of interest, abilities and competences in IT, makes them question the ideal of recruiting more women.

f) "Women have other interests" reflects a perception of gender differences as a cultural product that rather schools and parents need to address: *"Our greatest challenge is something that we cannot change, and that is the fact that we have a society that makes girls do 'girls' things' and boys do 'boys' things'."* Change is out of reach for the organizations, leaving them with the question: *"Do we really need more women in IT?"*

g) "Men fit IT work better" is a related perception, however, this time calling upon "natural" differences between men and women. Using himself as an example, one of the men explains that "*boys are very single-minded and very focused on their interests*", thus building their IT competence already as teenagers. Describing this as boys' advantage over girls who lack this background, makes it all but impossible for girls to compete on this arena.

h) "We just want the best" builds on the attitudes described above and makes gender equality appear to conflict with highly skilled competence in IT. "*The most important thing is to get the right person, and if that happens to be a woman, that is great*". Although women are wanted in IT, expectations of women remain low and gender equality appears to require compromising with the need for competence – as if women and IT qualifications are not expected to exist in pair.

3.4 Indifference and Passivity

The final approach illustrates organizations that agree with the gender equality ideal, they are just not convinced that it is worth the effort.

i) "It will pass" sees the underrepresentation of women as a temporary problem that will solve itself, thus any gender equality action would be wasted energy.

j) "It is not a requirement" and therefore "*it is not an explicit part of our mission now*" reflects that policies and regulations aiming to promote gender equality in employment is followed by few and vague requirements for employers. Also, there are no public sanctions against the absence of such engagement (Nordberg, 2019).

The employers agree that women's situation as underrepresented in IT should be improved, but as they find no reason for active engagement, passivity is their actual response.

4. MIXED MESSAGES OF GENDER EQUALITY IN IT

The analysis above shows how the representatives for the organizations that participated in dialogue meetings, even from public sector organizations with more requirements to gender equality measures and processes, redefined the call for gender equality in IT in ways that made gender equality actions a non-existing feature.

Table 1 illustrates that while only two of the examples (a and d) renegotiate the initial description of women as underrepresented in IT, six renegotiate the need to recruit more women to IT jobs. This demonstrates how many of the employers question the need for increasing women's participation in IT, and furthermore, that none of them embraced the call for gender equality action. The most remarkable feature, however, is that even when agreeing that women are underrepresented and seeing it as a goal to improve the situation, the employers and organizations find little reason to engage in action that may change the situation, some even seem to argue that changes are not really desirable. This is a critical point to observe, because it means that gender equality as a norm is widely accepted, while the organizational contexts undermine the will to deal with women's underrepresentation in IT.

The examples analyzed above are not unique and it is likely that related articulations and renegotiations can be found in other organizations. A more generic description of the mechanisms at play could look like the figure below: the national gender equality regime creates expectations to employers' active work to improve the gender imbalance in IT, reflected in rules and regulations. However, gender balance in IT is not a specific requirement and there are few and vague guidelines for the organizations for engaging in gender equality work in general. The organizations' representatives see the request for gender equality in the context of their organization, introducing internal and external factors that contribute to modifying the understanding of women's underrepresentation and whether or not it is worth changing. This process introduces doubt and alternative ways of perceiving the situation, resulting in limited space for organizations to find motivation to engage in gender equality actions.

Figure 1. A model of renegotiation of the gender equality norm in an organizational context

The mechanism at play illustrates how gender imbalance in IT is simultaneously visible and invisible: it is indeed recognized, but as a result of cultural perceptions and gender stereotypes, it is not necessarily considered worthy of change (Corneliussen & Prøitz, 2016).

Stereotyping women in IT makes it particularly difficult for women to be recognized as IT experts – or to pass the "if-can"-test in IT (Corneliussen et al., 2019). It is vital to recognize that women's participation is not only challenged by the most extreme attitudes, like identifying men with a unique masculine way of achieving IT competence. Even more problematic, many of the employers and organizations did recognize women's underrepresentation, but did not recognize this as a problem, which means that the gender equality norm can co-exist with the very attitudes that undermine the norm. This, we suggest, provides a better explanation to the gender equality paradox: the national gender equality regime promoting gender egalitarian norms and ideals is not disputed, but rather confirmed and simultaneously renegotiated to fit the organizational contexts, yet drained of the potential to spark change.

5. CONCLUSION: CONTEXTUALIZED KNOWLEDGE

We need more knowledge about how employers and organizations hiring IT experts perceive and deal with gender equality in IT, and our study suggests a need to understand the perspectives of the organizations better. Analyzing the alternative approaches presented above as "resistance" to gender equality would probably not have produced knowledge that the organizations could recognize. On the other hand, analyzing the approaches as "discursive resources" increases our understanding of how the organizations proceed when challenged to reflect on inclusion and gender equality in their own organizational context. This contributes to building the knowledge that is necessary for helping these organizations to develop future strategies to tackle the gender imbalance in IT.

ACKNOWLEDGEMENT

This is partly based on and a reworked version of the analysis reported in Corneliussen & Seddighi, 2019, published in Norwegian under the Creative Commons CC-BY-NC 4.0. We want to thank the representatives for IT companies and organizations that participated in dialogue meetings. The work with this article was funded by Nordwit, a Nordic Centre of Excellence, studying women in tech-driven careers in the Nordic countries. Read more about Nordwit: https://nordwit.com/.

REFERENCES

Bailey, M., & Riley, S., 2018. 2018 Women in Tech: Unconscious Bias, Parity, and the Path Forward, https://mailchi.mp/57c92dac9f60/2018-women-in-tech-unconscious-bias-report.

Blum, L., Frieze, C., Hazzan, O., & Dias, M. B., 2007. A Cultural Perspective on Gender Diversity in Computing. In C. J. Burger, E. G. Creamer, & P. S. Meszaros (Eds.), *Reconfiguring the Firewall. Recruiting Women to Information Technology across Cultures and Continents* (109-133), Wellesley, MA: A K Peters, LTD.

Borchorst, A., & Siim, B., 2008. Women-friendly policies and state feminism: Theorizing Scandinavian gender equality. Feminist Theory, 9(2), 207-244.

Bray, F., 2007. Gender and technology. Annual Review of Anthropology, 36, 37-53.

Brown, W., 2000. Suffering rights as paradoxes. Constellations, 7, 208-229. doi:https://doi.org/10.1111/1467-8675.00183

Charles, M., & Bradley, K., 2006. A Matter of Degrees: Female Underrepresentation in Computer Science Programs Cross-Nationally. In J. M. Cohoon & W. Aspray (Eds.), *Women and Information Technology. Research on Underrepresentation* (183-203), Cambridge, Massachusetts, London, England: MIT Press.

Chow, T., & Charles, M., 2019. An Inegalitarian Paradox: On the Uneven Gendering of Computing Work around the World. In C. Frieze & J. L. Quesenberry (Eds.), *Cracking the Digital Ceiling: Women in Computing around the World* (25).

Corneliussen, H. G., 2011. Gender-Technology Relations: Exploring Stability and Change, Basingstoke: Palgrave Macmillan.

Corneliussen, H. G., & Prøitz, L., 2016. Kids Code in a rural village in Norway: could code clubs be a new arena for increasing girls' digital interest and competence? Information, Communication & Society, 19(1 (Special Issue: Understanding Global Digital Cultures)). doi:https://doi.org/10.1080/1369118X.2015.1093529

Corneliussen, H. G., & Seddighi, G., 2019. "Må vi egentlig ha flere kvinner i IKT?" Diskursive forhandlinger om likestilling i IKT-arbeid. Tidsskrift for kjønnsforskning, 43(4), 273-287.

Corneliussen, H. G., Seddighi, G., & Dralega, C. A., 2019. Women's Experience of Role Models in IT: Landmark women, substitutes, and supporters. In Ø. Helgesen, E. Nesset, G. Mustafa, P. Rice, & R. Glavee-Geo (Eds.), *Modeller: Fjordantologien 2019*: Universitetsforlaget.

Dick, P., 2004. Resistance to diversity initiatives. In R. Thomas, A. Mills, & J. H. Mills (Eds.), *Identity politics at work: Resisting gender and gendering resistance* (67-84), Oxfordshire, New York: Routledge.

EIGE, 2018. Women and men in ICT: a chance for better work–life balance - Research note, Luxembourg: EIGE: European Institute for Gender Equality, Publications Office of the European Union.

EUROSTAT, 2019. ICT specialists in employment - Statistics Explained, https://ec.europa.eu/eurostat/statistics-explained/index.php/ICT_specialists_in_employment.

Hernes, H. M., 1987. Welfare state and woman power. Essays in state feminism, Oslo: Norwegian University Press.

Holli, A. M., Magnusson, E., & Rönnblom, M., 2005. Critical studies of Nordic discourses on gender and gender equality. Nordic Journal of Women's Studies, 13(03), 148-152. doi:https://doi.org/10.1080/08038740600590442

Johansson, K., Andersson, E., Johansson, M., & Lidestav, G., 2019. The Discursive Resistance of Men to Gender-equality Interventions: Negotiating "Unjustness" and "Unnecessity" in Swedish Forestry. Men and Masculinities, 177-196. doi:https://doi.org/10.1177%2F1097184X17706400

Kelan, E. K., 2007. TOOLS AND TOYS : Communicating gendered positions towards technology. Information, Communication & Society, 10(3), 358-383. doi:10.1080/13691180701409960

Kvande, E., & Rasmussen, B., 1993 (1990). Nye kvinneliv. Kvinner i menns organisasjoner [New Women's Lives. Women in Men's Organizations], Oslo: Ad Notam.

Livholts, M., & Tamboukou, M., 2015. Discourse and Narrative Methods, Los Angeles: SAGE.

Master, A., Cheryan, S., & Meltzoff, A. N., 2016. Computing whether she belongs: Stereotypes undermine girls' interest and sense of belonging in computer science. Journal of Educational Psychology, 108(3), 424.

National Science Foundation, 2019. Women, Minorities, and Persons with Disabilities in Science and Engineering: https://ncses.nsf.gov/pubs/nsf19304/digest.

Nordberg, T. H., 2019. Arbeidsgivers ansvar for likestilling i arbeidslivet. Tidsskrift for kjønnsforskning, 43(2), 90-107. doi:https://doi.org/10.18261/issn.1891-1781-2019-02-03

Patton, M. Q., 2002. Qualitative research and evaluation methods, Thousand Oakes, London, New Delhi: Sage Publications.

Payton, F. C., & Berki, E., 2019. Countering the negative image of women in computing. Commun. ACM, 62(5), 56–63. doi:10.1145/3319422

Powell, S., Ah-King, M., & Hussénius, A., 2018. 'Are we to become a gender university?' Facets of resistance to a gender equality project. Gender, Work & Organization, 25(2), 127-143. doi:https://doi.org/10.1111/gwao.12204

Simonsen, M., & Corneliussen, H. G., 2020. What Can Statistics Tell About the Gender Divide in ICT? Tracing Men and Women's Participation in the ICT Sector Through Numbers. In D. Kreps, T. Komukai, G. TV, & K. Ishii (Eds.), *Human-Centric Computing in a Data Driven Society*: Springer.

Skjeie, H., & Teigen, M., 2003. Menn imellom. Mannsdominans og likestillingspolitikk, Oslo: Gyldendal akademisk.

Skjeie, H., & Teigen, M., 2005. Political constructions of gender equality: Travelling towards… a gender balanced society? Nordic Journal of Women's Studies, 13(03), 187-197. doi:https://doi.org/10.1080/08038740600590004

SSB, 2018. Women and men in Norway, Satistics Norway.

Stoet, G., & Geary, D. C., 2018. The Gender-Equality Paradox in Science, Technology, Engineering, and Mathematics Education. Psychological Science, 29(4), 581-593. doi:10.1177/0956797617741719

Teigen, M., & Eggebø, H., 2017. Debatt: I politikken har klima samme vikeplikt som likestilling. Kilden: kjønnsforskning.no, http://kjonnsforskning.no/nb/2017/2012/klima-samme-vikeplikt-som-likestilling.

Vabø, A., Gunnes, H., Tømte, C., Bergene, A. C., & Egeland, C., 2012. Kvinner og menns karriereløp i norsk forskning: En tilstandsrapport (8272188201), Rapport 9/2012, NIFU.

Wajcman, J., 2004. TechnoFeminism, Cambridge: Polity Press.

West, C., & Zimmerman, D. H., 1987. Doing Gender. Gender & Society, 1(2), 125-151.

TIME ESTIMATION IMPROVEMENT IN AGILE DEVELOPMENT

Willem van der Feltz[1], Niels van der Pas[2] and Mark van der Pas[3]
[1]*European Center for Machine Learning, Gutenbergstraße 21, 50823 Köln, Germany*
[2]*European Center for Machine Learning, Willem II singel 2, 6041HS, Roermond, The Netherlands*
[3]*European Center for Digital Transformation, Willem II singel 2, 6041HS, Roermond, The Netherlands*

ABSTRACT

Estimating the time needed to execute an IT project has turned out to be a major challenge in daily praxis. Despite high inaccuracies, these estimations are important as they can be used to determine the cost for offering an IT project and in deciding whether to execute it at all. In this study we focused on the estimations for user stories created by a European Software company delivering 100% of their software in an agile way of working. Over a time-span of 10 months, 1738 estimations were created on small user stories (around 5 hours of work on average). Three main conclusions could be drawn from the data. Firstly, it was found that smaller-than-two-hour user stories were over-estimated roughly as frequently as under-estimated. In contrast, estimations for larger-than-two-hour user stories were less balanced and on average too low (under-estimated). Secondly, and surprisingly, we did not see that estimations were better when the estimator was able to execute the task himself versus when he was not. The statistics suggest that estimators who are able to do the task themselves tend to *underestimate* the time needed to deliver the user story. Finally, we found that the accuracy of estimations does not improve over time.

KEYWORDS

IT Projects, IT Portfolio Management, Plan Accuracy, Deadlines, Decision Support

1. INTRODUCTION

Delivering projects on time remains a major challenge. Nowadays, a central part of many big projects is software development. Delays and complications in this field can have big effects on the overall project. Recent examples of time overrun due to software problems come from the London Crossrail delaying the schedule from 2018 to 2021 (Farrel & Topham, 2019) or from the Smart Energy meter pushing its deadline back more than four years into 2024 (Ambrose, 2019). A third example comes from a newly identified software flaw in the grounded Boeing 737 Max (Levin & Schlangenstein, 2020). More recent examples can be found in a new paper by S. Lauesen (Lauesen, 2020).

This challenge, delivering IT projects on time, is not new and it has been monitored for more than two decades by the Standish Group. In their 2015 research, they found that 60% of IT projects are not finished on time (The Standish Group, 2015).

Finishing projects requires the successful execution of hundreds, thousands and sometimes millions of small activities. The time needed for each of these steps can be estimated and those estimations can be compared to the actual time needed. The accuracy of these estimations is likely to go down in case of a large amount of interdependent activities planned with a bias and over multiple years. Developing software in an agile way (e.g. (Hoffmann, et al., 2020)) reduces the need to plan over long time spans as well as the size of the individual activities.

An important part in the flow of a project is making estimations of how long things will take and, very much related, how much they will cost. Part of the above problem could be solved by becoming better at making estimations. Estimation accuracy has been the subject of a lot of research in the past (Boehm, 1984), and still is today (Bilal, et al., 2020).

In this research we focus on time estimations made for smaller IT programming tasks executed within an agile work setting, taking around 5 hours on average. We will use the words *user story* to describe these tasks. We consider two aspects: 1. estimating the time a user story will take and 2. how well the user story is delivered within the estimated/allocated time. We will study the accuracy of time estimations for different categories (or reference classes) of user stories as well as the usage of feedback instruments to improve this accuracy.

This paper discusses the theoretical foundations and associated hypotheses. Then the research method is outlined and results are presented. Finally, the conclusions, limitations and suggestions for future research are presented.

2. THEORY AND HYPOTHESES

Goldratt (Goldratt, 2004) proposes several actions to improve on time (and in budget) deliveries. Amongst others he proposes to:

1. split work into small tasks
2. assure accurate estimations created by experts
3. openly discuss the time needed for a task
4. plan buffer at the end of the critical chain
5. report daily progress
6. protect the critical chain

In this study we focus on the first two topics. User stories can differ significantly in size but can, as compared to complete IT projects, be seen as 'small tasks'. Goldratt suggests splitting a project into small tasks to force the team to list all steps needed. This avoids some tasks being overlooked, helping with the overall estimation accuracy. Splitting up could also help because the estimation accuracy for small user stories could be higher than that of larger user stories: small user stories are easier to oversee. To use a metaphor for this argument: estimating the time needed to travel to the nearest city is probably more accurate than estimating the time needed to travel to Timbuktu, assuming that is not your nearest city. This brings us to our first hypothesis

H1: Plan accuracy of time estimations for smaller-than-two-hour user stories are more accurate than those for larger user stories.

Goldratt suggests that the estimations should be created by an experienced person, preferably a colleague who will execute the task. Expert-based estimation of software development has been investigated quite extensively and is often considered on equal footing with formal, model-based estimations (Mahmood, et al., 2020). To build on the earlier metaphor: in case you know how to travel to the nearest city, then you can more accurately estimate the time needed to do so. On the other hand the 'expert blind spot' (Wiggins & McTighe, 2005) indicates that the expert will underestimate the time as it is complex to correct the estimation for the experience difference between the estimator and the person delivering the work. This blind spot is especially expected when there is a large difference in expertise. As this is more the case in educational settings and expectedly less in professional settings, we come to the second hypothesis.

H2: The plan accuracy of estimations is higher in case the estimator can execute the task himself.

Thirdly, perhaps most straightforwardly, we can look at the time-component of the data and test whether estimators improve accuracy over time. To build on the earlier metaphor: in case you have already estimated time to travel to several cities and received feedback on these estimations, then you can more accurately estimate the time needed to do so the next time.

For estimators to be able to improve, some form of feedback is needed. This can be done by giving estimators basic feedback on the actual time spend as compared to their estimation (Jørgensen, 2004). This feedback can be provided for each estimation separately. As estimators learn over time based on their previous estimations, we expect their accuracy to improve. Even though these improvements are not always present in IT, e.g. in a paper on the predictability of IT investment business value (van der Pas & Furneaux, 2015) it was concluded that estimates of the *value* of projects do not improve over time, we nevertheless expect that:

H3: Plan Accuracy of estimations of an estimator improves over time.

In the next section we present the methods used to test these hypotheses.

3. METHOD

Our research is based on data and experience from an international software organisation with customers in Europe and on-site operations in four European countries. A part of that organization shared estimations for the work they do in an agile Kanban organized structure. In total, 2086 user story estimations were offered for analysis spanning a time frame from June 8th 2019 up to March 15th 2020. In total the organization shared data from three estimators. For our analysis, only data from activities larger than 0.5 hours were considered: the very small user stories hold very large relative deviations and are of less interest to practitioners. Data from 1738 estimations remained.

For the first hypothesis, tasks were split into two categories: the user stories that took more than two hours to complete were considered 'large' tasks, the user stories that took less 'small'. Two hours was selected because the organisation's CEO considers all user stories that can be delivered within 2 hours to be small. For both the small and the large category, a boxplot was made indicating the plan accuracy of the estimations. Plan accuracy is in our case defined as:

$$\text{Plan accuracy} := \left(\frac{estimation}{actual} - 1\right) * 100\%$$

In this we followed the convention of the forecast/actual ratio from a study on the estimation quality of business *value* (Eveleens, et al., 2012). The formula was altered slightly based on practitioners' feedback: the number 1 was subtracted so that a positive percentage means over-estimation and a negative percentage means under-estimation. This turned out to be easier to use and interpret in daily praxis (in the paper on business value, above 1 means over-estimation and below 1 under-estimation).

The boxplots give a more qualitative idea of the difference in estimation precisions and spread. To quantitatively compare both categories, a t-test was used. Independence and normality of data are required for a t-test. Data were assumed to be independent as they were on different user stories requiring new software. Because both categories have big sample sizes (>500), their mean-values could be assumed to be continuous and we also assumed it to follow a normal distribution.

Also the second hypothesis was tested by splitting the data into two categories. The organisation creates software in both SQL as well as in Typescript, and user stories were categorised accordingly. As the estimators in the company do regularly program SQL they are considered as 'experienced' on the user stories delivered using SQL. Since they do not or hardly program Typescript, they are considered not to be experienced on those user stories. For hypothesis 2 the same method will be used as for hypothesis 1 (box plot and a t-test).

Hypothesis three was tested by fitting a linear regression model to the observed data. Two different models were made: one based on the monthly mean, the other on the monthly median. The significance of the fitted regressions were tested using t-tests, where the null hypothesis was zero slope (no regression) and the alternative hypothesis a positive slope (improvement).

4. RESULTS

We begin the section with some overall statistics on the data that was analysed.

The average time spend on a user story was 5.2 hours. 75% of all user stories were delivered within 6.2 hours. The outliers are user stories consuming 69.4, 57.0 and 48.8 hours, and the three largest estimations were 74.0, 40.0 and 24.0 hours.

Accuracy of estimations was calculated as mentioned above using the formula

$$\text{Plan accuracy} := \left(\frac{estimation}{actual} - 1\right) * 100\%$$

The mean of the inaccuracy over the complete dataset is -13.1%, indicating an overall under-estimation. All estimations in the second quartile contain an underestimation of at least -66.7%. The estimations in the third quartile hold an overestimation of up to 5.3%. The borders of the quartiles indicate that the bulk of estimations was too low.

4.1 Results for H1

Comparing small and large user stories for testing H1 resulted in data shown in Figure 1. In the analysis, 644 of the stories were small, the remaining were big.

From the boxplot and the accompanying distribution data, it becomes visible that *big tasks are more commonly under-estimated* than small tasks. The mean estimation error for small tasks was +42.36%, for big tasks it was -37.95%. Therefore, in terms of sample means, there does not seem to be an *absolute* advantage for small tasks. The median for small tasks (6.67%), however, lies much closer to zero than the median for big tasks (-52.38%). This indicates that small tasks are under-estimated roughly as frequently as over-estimated. The spread in estimation errors is bigger for small tasks than for big ones, which can be explained by the fact that small errors in time are still large percentages of the smaller total time. A two-tailed Student's t-test performed on the data resulted in a small p-value, smaller than 0.001 hence there is a statistically significant difference between small and large tasks. We conclude that big tasks are under-estimated more frequently than small tasks, but we cannot accept H1, as we cannot conclude that small tasks are estimated better.

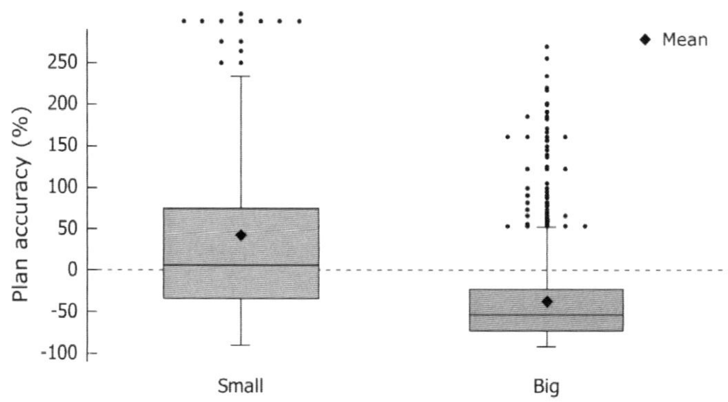

Figure 1. Comparing estimations for small and large user stories

4.2 Results for H2

In the boxplot in Figure 2 we present the difference between experienced and inexperienced estimations. Excluding outliers, we found 1454 User Stories where the estimators had experience in similar tasks, and 284 where they did not. The spread in errors is slightly smaller when the estimators could execute the task themselves. The mean error (-16.65%) is much smaller than the mean error for when they could not deliver the user story (5.69%). A two-tailed Student's t-test performed on the data resulted in a p-value smaller than 0.01, so the difference is statistically significant. Interestingly, it seems that experienced estimations are on average worse. Most of the spread lies *under zero*, meaning under-estimations. This could be explained by the expert's blind spot. We cannot accept H2 that experienced estimations are better. It can be concluded, however, that user stories are more often under-estimated when the estimator could execute them him/herself.

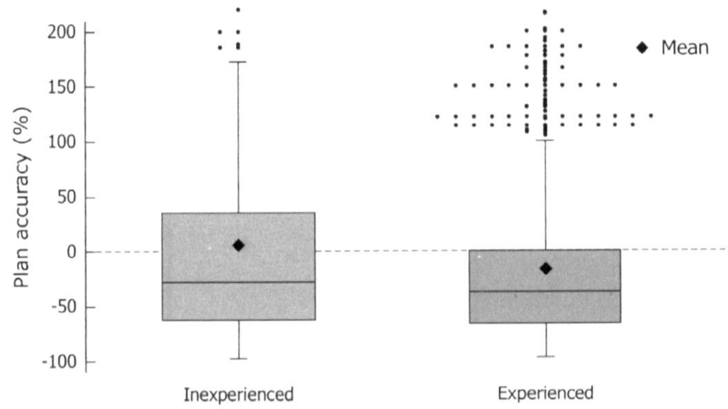

Figure 2. Comparing inexperienced and expert estimations

4.3 Results for H3

The data used for H3 is visualised in Figure 3. The amount of datapoints per month are displayed in Table 1. By eye, estimations seem to improve: averages and medians get closer to zero. The spread in errors does not visibly improve.

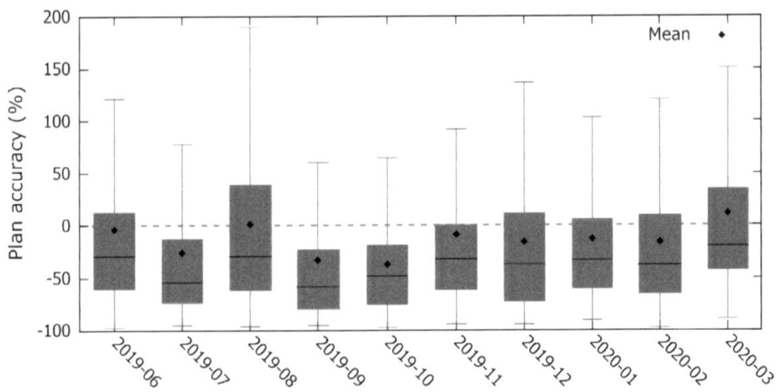

Figure 3. Development of accuracy over time

Table 1. Number of datapoints per month

2019/06:	313	*2019/11:*	161
2019/07:	229	*2019/12:*	106
2019/08:	247	*2020/01:*	148
2019/09:	128	*2020/02:*	186
2019/10:	132	*2020/03:*	88

In order to test for improvement, the daily average plan accuracy was plotted and a linear regression model was fitted. Results are shown below in Figure 4. A slight improvement is visible: the difference between the fitted accuracy and 0 (no error) decreases over time. A t-test was performed to determine the significance of this fit. A p-value of 0.17 was found, meaning the improvement is not significant and also H3 must be rejected.

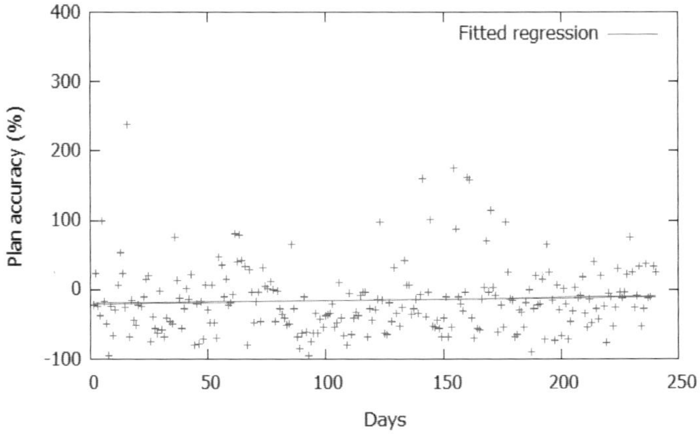

Figure 4. Mean plan accuracy per day

Table 2. Overview of hypotheses and results

H1	**Plan accuracy of time estimations for <2h user stories are more accurate than those for larger user stories.**	Rejected	
H2	**The plan accuracy of estimations is higher in case the estimator can execute the task himself.**	Rejected	
H3	**Plan Accuracy of estimations of an estimator improves over time.**	Rejected	

5. CONCLUSION

The data studied in this paper does not shine a positive light on estimation accuracy: large inaccuracy was found across different types of user-stories. However, statistically significant differences were found between them.

It cannot be concluded that user stories < 2 hours are estimated better than larger user stories. It did become clear, however, that large user stories are more commonly under-estimated, whereas estimations for smaller user stories are more 'balanced'.

It also could not be concluded that experienced estimations were better than inexperienced estimations. However, our analysis showed that experienced estimations were in general too low suggesting that the expert blind spot should not be underestimated in professional environments.

H3 was also rejected, meaning estimators do not improve their estimation accuracy on their own. This suggests more elaborate feedback should be given, a subject for further research.

We do think that the results acquired can be of value for practitioners: they give a more detailed insight into where weaknesses lie in making estimations. Furthermore, we still think it is possible to increase plan accuracy by providing better feedback, for which we make some suggestions in the next section.

To support practitioners, we present in (see for example Van der Pas and Furneaux).

Table 3 the combinations of the H1 and H2 parameters. This model builds four simple reference classes that can be used by practitioners to further improve predictions (see for example Van der Pas and Furneaux (2015)).

Table 3. Effect of different combinations of parameters

	Estimated by non-expert	Estimated by expert
Smaller-than-two-hours user story	Mean: 95.4% Median: 46.4%%	Mean: 28.9% Median: 0%
Larger-than-two-hours user story	Mean: -31.3% Median: -45.5%	Mean: -42.3% Median: -56.5%

Additional instruments for improving the accuracy are described in the next section as suggestions for future research.

6. LIMITATIONS AND SUGGESTIONS FOR FUTURE RESEARCH

This research was focussed on small user stories (5.2 hours on average). The conclusions from this study cannot be projected on the estimation of large-scale IT projects consuming multiple years of effort and millions of Euros of investment.

There is a shortcoming of the used definition of plan accuracy in combination with the many small user stories. The problem with small tasks is that, with the current definition, small deviations result in big percentages. These percentages do not necessarily reflect how humans perceive: for example, in day-to-day tasks the difference between 5 and 6 minutes is considered to be unimportant, while the difference between 5 and 6 hours is seen as significant. Their percentage difference is the same, however. This non-intuitive behaviour should be kept in mind when studying the results.

When starting with this study, the estimators had limited experience in estimating user stories. The experience was cumulated fast with the start of this study in June 2019. The existing experience of the estimators should be taken into account when projecting the findings to other environments.

The current feedback the software company provides on estimations is simply a message showing the time estimated versus the time taken. Besides this case by case feedback, there was no statistical feedback. Feedback could be given by providing personalised, monthly estimation statistics like presented in the boxplot in

Figure *3*, giving a better idea of structural errors. It could also be in the form of a boxplot presenting the actual time written. The latter gives insights to the average, mean as well as the spread of past user stories and could be used by the estimator as a guidance for future estimations. Also adding reference classes describing user stories realised to the plan accuracy feedback could improve the estimators learning curve. For the software organisation this could be reference classes on components they are programming such as 'workflow', 'reporting', 'investment management', 'scorecard', 'product catalogue' or 'agile performance management'.

On top of statistical feedback and reference classes, machine learning could be applied to push estimation quality. E.g. the techniques (van der Pas & van der Pas, 2020) used to predict the likelihood of project cancellation could also be used to calculate an estimation as an output parameter. Input features for this estimation could be the initiator, the person who delivers the user story but also the already present data on the kind of software to be delivered. The machine learning prediction of the estimation could be used as an input parameter for the estimation made by the estimator.

Furthermore, future research could be done around the transparency of the estimation. The software company decided not to open the estimation to the person actually working on the user story. The reason for this is that the estimation could have a self-fulfilling effect on the person delivering the user story. It could make her relaxed in case she thinks that the work can easily be delivered in the estimated time or put pressure when the estimated time seems too little. This is contradictory to Goldratt who expects an open discussion to improve the estimation quality.

Finally, theories from social science can be used to influence the behaviour of estimators. Ajzen (Ajzen, 1991) developed the Theory of Planned Behaviour to predict behaviour of human beings. It was shown (van der Pas & Walczuch, 2018) how, amongst others, intention and subjective norm can be used for this purpose. Asking estimators to confirm their intention on good estimations as well as adding automated plan reminders is likely to push the quality of their estimation (see e.g. Wicaksono, et al., 2019). Likewise, their intention for creating good estimations is likely to improve by increasing the subjective norm. The latter can be done by talking about and explaining the importance of estimations.

ACKNOWLEDGEMENT

The authors wish to thank Dr. Tobias Hartwich for his meaningful contribution towards designing the statistical methods to test the three hypotheses presented in this article.

REFERENCES

Ajzen, I., 1991. The theory of planned behavior. *Organizational behavior and human decision processes,* 50(2), pp. 179-211.

Ambrose, J., 2019. Smart energy meter rollout deadline pushed back to 2024. *The Guardian*, 16 September.

Bilal, K., Khan, W., Arshad, M. & Jan, N., 2020. Software Cost Estimation: Algorithmic and Non-Algorithmic Approaches. *International Journal of Data Science and Advanced Analytics,* Issue 2.2, pp. 1-5.

Boehm, B. W., 1984. Software engineering economics. *IEEE transactions on Software Engineering,* Issue 1, pp. 4-21.

Eveleens, J. L., Van Der Pas, M. & Verhoef, C., 2012. Quantifying forecast quality of IT business value. *Science of Computer Programming,* 77(3), pp. 314-354.

Farrel, S. & Topham, G., 2019. Crossrail faces further delays and will cost more than £18bn. *The Guardian*, 8 November.

Goldratt, E. M., 2004. *The goal : a process of ongoing improvement..* Great Barrington, MA: North River Press.

Hoffmann, D., Ahlemann, F. & Reining, S., 2020. Reconciling alignment, efficiency, and agility in IT project portfolio management: Recommendations based on a revelatory case study. *International Journal of Project Management,* 38(2), pp. 124-136.

Jørgensen, M., 2004. A review of studies on expert estimation of software development effort. *Journal of Systems and Software,* 70(1-2), pp. 37-60.

Lauesen, S., 2020. IT Project Failures, Causes and Cures. *IEEE Access,* Volume 8, pp. 72059-72067.

Levin, A. & Schlangenstein, M., 2020. New Software Flaw Could Further Delay Boeing's 737 Max. *Bloomberg*, 17 January.

Mahmood, Y., Kama, N. & Azmi, A., 2020. A systematic review of studies on use case points and expert-based estimation of software development effort. *Journal of Software: Evolution and Process,* p. 2245.

The Standish Group, 2015. *Chaos Report,* s.l.: The Standish Group International, Inc.

van der Pas, M. & Furneaux, B., 2015. *Improving the predictability of IT investment business value.* Münster, ECIS 2015 Completed Research Papers. Paper 190.

van der Pas, M. & van der Pas, N., 2020. *Improving Gate Decision Making Rationality with Machine Learning.* Cham, Springer.

van der Pas, M. & Walczuch, R., 2018. *Behavior of Organizational Agents on Managing Information Technology.* Cham, Springer, pp. 774-788.

Wicaksono, A., Hendley, R. & Beale, R., 2019. Investigating the Impact of Adding Plan Reminders on Implementation Intentions to Support Behaviour Change. *Interacting with Computers,* 31(2), pp. 177-191.

Wiggins, G. & McTighe, J., 2005. *Understanding by Design.* Expended 2nd edition ed. s.l.:Association for Supervision and Curriculum Development.

DESIGNING FOR TRANSITIONS IN RURAL TRANSPORT

Amela Karahasanović[1], Alma Leora Culén[2], Jan Håvard Skjetne[1] and Geir Hasle[1]
[1]*SINTEF Digital, Norway*
[2]*Department of Informatics, University of Oslo, Norway*

ABSTRACT

Rural areas are less attractive and sustainable for people and businesses alike, partially due to inadequate transport services. In this paper, we address transport-related challenges in rural Norway. The focal aspect of our approach is to define a set of values for the design and mechanisms of transitioning towards more sustainable rural transport making a real-life difference for people living in rural areas. We connect UN sustainability goals and transition design to discuss how these can be operationalized and used throughout the design process seeking to innovate rural transport. Reflecting on how to find the initial 'leverage points' to scaffold the transition to more sustainable transport systems, we explore the possibility of introducing relevant Key Performance Indicators early on in the design process. We report on our experiences and findings regarding the Key Performance Indicators and discuss their role in design-led innovation processes.

KEYWORDS

Sustainable HCI, Transition Design, Leverage Points, Key Performance Indicators, Transportation Systems

1. INTRODUCTION

It has been almost two decades since the field of Human-Computer Interaction (HCI) tried to reconcile its inherent dichotomies between research and design by focusing on designing for values, that is, *"HCI must be objectively systematic and reliable in the pursuit of subjective value. Traditional disciplines have delivered truth. The goal of HCI is to deliver value"* (Cockton, 2004). Although the HCI community has been working toward establishing its sustainability agenda for more than a decade, during the era of fast social, environmental, and technological changes, views forwarding incremental reductions (e.g., in energy consumption, individual changes in behavior patterns) are no longer enough (Bendor, 2018; Fredericks et al., 2019; Light, 2019; Light et al., 2017). The community is now focusing on larger, at scale, systemic solutions toward sustainable development (Fredericks et al., 2019; Knowles et al., 2018; Silberman and Interpreter, 2013). We position the work presented in this paper within this discussion, in which we focus on the mitigation of challenges that rural communities experience with the transport sector.

Good transport systems can contribute to the sustainable development of rural areas and provide people with novel opportunities, such as the freedom to settle where they want and increase wellbeing ("Ta heile Noreg i bruk - Meld. St. 13," 2013). The rapid development of Intelligent Transport Systems, sharing economies and Mobility-as-a-Service (MaaS) concepts (Alliance, 2017), presents a novel set of potentially better solutions within the sector. In particular, the development of MaaS concepts for rural areas is acutely needed ("Developing rural services," 2017). These concepts are considered enablers of combining transport services from different providers through a unique service platform in which transport needs can be custom tailored. At present, MaaS proposals do not cover a spectrum of needs; for example, transport-induced CO_2 emissions are not covered (Alliance, 2017). According to the World Bank, CO_2 emissions are one of the major contributors to climate change, with transport being responsible for more than 20% of the global CO_2 emissions (www.data.worldbank.org/indicator). Furthermore, some services had to be stopped because of high costs despite their high popularity (Skollerud, 2014). The coronavirus pandemic in 2020 unexpectedly allowed the world to directly witness the impact of traffic and industry emissions on air quality (Watts and Kommenda, 2020).

The challenge is to offer an efficient transport system that provides good transport services to everyone and, at the same time, keeps financial and environmental costs low. This is especially difficult to achieve in sparsely populated rural areas, where the distances are considerable and transport resources are limited. Transport systems, being critical centralized infrastructures (Tomlinson et al., 2015), need to move toward decentralization (ibid.), but such transformations cannot be done hastily. They involve multiple stakeholders, sometimes with conflicting interests, require an interdisciplinary approach, and need to continually adapt to changes in regulations, mobility patterns, and technology. Thus, finding an adequate approach to tackle this challenge is crucial and requires a more systemic approach.

Recently, transition design (TD) has been proposed as an approach to lead transitions toward more sustainable futures and is suitable for addressing wicked problems, such as climate change, over-consumption, pollution, and poverty (Escobar, 2018; Irwin, 2018; Tonkinwise, 2015). It is based on a sustainable, multi-perspective (cross-disciplinary), value-based, long-term, forward-looking design and contributes to a better understanding of societal transitions (Zolfagharian et al., 2019). As such, TD aligns well with our problem of looking into appropriate solutions for rural transport systems. It builds on the premises of TD and, in particular, on leverage points that may help initiate and carry out sustainability transitions (Abson et al., 2017).

In this paper, we introduce and discuss sustainable transport Key Performance Indicators (KPIs) as a tool focusing on leverage points, such as CO_2 emissions, to address sustainability in TD processes. Concerned with real-life solutions and visible improvements in rural transport services, we focused on how KPIs could align with both sustainability goals and the TD framework. The motivation to explore KPIs is based on our need to identify and consider performance measures already in the design process and use them as building blocks in a larger innovation project aiming to develop a MaaS solution especially tailored for rural areas in Norway.

In what follows, we first discuss existing frameworks that point toward sustainable futures. We then describe the Sustainable Transport KPIs and report our first practical experiences with a prototype for finding alternative transport routes that help reduce CO_2 emissions.

2. TOWARD SUSTAINABLE FUTURES

Long-term visions for desirable global futures, co-created by the United Nations (UN), were articulated through the UN Sustainable Development Goals (SDGs) ("Sustainable Development Knowledge Platform," 2015). For this work, SDG 9 (*Build resilient infrastructure, promote inclusive and sustainable industrialization, and foster innovation*) is of particular relevance, as it addresses the importance of efficient transport systems and services as the key drivers of economic development. The document (ibid.) defines specific targets related to each goal (e.g., develop quality, reliable, sustainable, and resilient infrastructures, with a focus on affordable and equitable access for all, promote inclusive and sustainable industrialization, increase the access of small-scale industrial and other enterprises), as well as specific indicators that might help reach these targets (e.g., finding out what proportion of the rural population lives within 2 km of an all-season road, number of passengers and freight volumes by mode of transport). The SDGs are not mutually independent. Working with transport systems also relates to other goals, such as SDG 13 (*The Climate Action*), SDG 11 (*Sustainable Cities and Communities*), and SDG 12 (*Responsible Consumption*).

The Doughnut, Kate Raworth's iconic model of an economy that respects both social needs and the ecological boundaries of the planet, is another way of framing sustainable development (Raworth, 2017, 2012). The doughnut represents a developmental space that is safe and just for all, respecting a social well-being boundary that no one should fall below, and an ecological ceiling of planetary pressure that we should not go beyond.

Building on these and on UN and Norwegian policy documents, such as the UN's policy document on sustainable transport ("Mobilizing Sustainable Transport for Development," 2016) and the Norwegian Transport Plan 2018–2029 (Samferdselsdepartementet, 2017), a list of specific transport-related goals is suggested (Samferdselsdepartementet, 2017). These goals highlight the need for reliable and available transport that is accessible for all, shortened travel time, and a good capacity for passengers and goods, and aim to double the global rate of improvement in energy efficiency ("Mobilizing Sustainable Transport for Development," 2016).

Recently, a Norwegian guide for the development of sustainable, productive, and resilient cities and local communities has been introduced to support local and regional authorities, community groups, researchers, entrepreneurs, and other stakeholders (DOGA, 2019). It describes the basic principles for sustainable development, prioritizing climate and the environment and promoting inclusion and co-creation in design processes. Furthermore, the guide proposes the following phases to move from these principles toward smart and sustainable cities and communities: understanding, creating, experimenting, learning, and building. At present, the guide only offers a set of key questions related to each of these phases. Measures, tools, and best practices are to be added as the guide evolves.

In summary, there are considerable design and research activities that aim to lay out alternative paths toward more sustainable futures. Nevertheless, at this moment, the approaches that can demonstrate good results in practice are not many.

The TD community strives to bridge the more abstract principles of sustainable development and concrete, designed outcomes. The approach forwards the following four main areas of research and design activities (Irwin, 2018) that support transitions in a sustainable direction: 1) finding and using the appropriate theories of change that support socio-technological transformations; 2) understanding and developing visions for transitions; 3) working with the mindset and posture, including values, that are appropriate for transitions (e.g., precautionary, explorative, reflexive, critical, participatory, local, situated); and 4) discovering and using new ways to design that lead to impactful, large-scale solutions contributing toward a more sustainable future (Knowles et al., 2018). In contrast to traditional HCI design approaches (including the more systemic ones, such as service design, experience design, and sustainable design), which tend to frame problems within relatively limited spatio-temporal contexts and identify a limited number of stakeholders and potential conflicts of interests, TD calls for a more holistic approach that considers the development of ecological and environmental literacy, takes a long-term perspective, and re-thinks potential solutions beyond financial and commercial interests. The role of design in TD has been further elaborated by Boehnert, Lockton, and Mulder as follows: *"designing for transitions involves designing how transitions are conceived, enacted, governed and managed"* (Boehnert et al., 2018). However, Van Selm and Mulder also point out the lack of case studies with real users to test the TD framework and associated processes and tools (van Selm and Mulder, 2019). Furthermore, the lack of actionable components (Ceschin and Gaziulusoy, 2016) and methods for the phase in which a design intervention is implemented, with one being in the *waiting and observing* phase before the next intervention can take place, has also been identified (van Selm and Mulder, 2019).

Our aim is to understand and fill these gaps when working on making rural transport more sustainable, a case in which we chose the actionable components (KPIs) in work with real users, which might enable designed outcomes with good performance measures in real life.

3. KPIs IN SUSTAINABLE TRANSPORT

KPIs are commonly used to measure the performance of an organization or an activity (Fitz-Gibbon, 1990). They might be quantitative, such as the number of new customers in marketing, or qualitative, such as employee satisfaction in human resource management. Expanding on this idea, we used KPIs to operationalize our design for transitions. We developed sustainable transport KPIs as an instrument to be used throughout the whole lifecycle of the project to scaffold continued focus on sustainability. Within the TD framework, these KPIs offer leverage points that help promote changes through design until a desired outcome is achieved.

A project that we describe here aims to develop tools and services for MaaS specifically tailored for sparsely populated rural areas. The main idea is to create a holistic system for transport planning that dynamically coordinates the transport of people and goods to make the most of transport resources. New services and tools for planning are to include carpooling, car sharing, transport on demand, and use of mini-buses and taxis for transport optimization. The project was driven by the overall goal to *"Develop quality, reliable, sustainable and resilient infrastructure, including regional and trans-border infrastructure, to support economic development and human well-being, with a focus on affordable and equitable access for all,"* which is UN Sustainable Target 9.1 ("Transforming our world: the 2030 Agenda for Sustainable Development," 2015). However, the indicator associated with this target, passenger and freight volumes, is not comprehensive enough. For example, the above-mentioned Norwegian national goals (Samferdselsdepartementet, 2017) include shortened travel time and sustainable transport systems for all, in addition to a good capacity for passengers and goods. Although more specific, the latter set of goals also does not capture the full complexity of transport in rural areas.

4. DATA GATHERED WITH SUSTAINABLE TRANSPORT KPIs

The idea for the project evolved through a dialog between the problem owner (county municipalities' transport section) and the researchers in several meetings and workshops, resulting in a joint research proposal to design MaaS for rural transport. In this initial phase of the work, a list of KPIs was created, starting with the above-described UN and national goals and input from experts in transport planning and HCI. The list was then expanded with additional indicators using a radar chart (see Figure 1) in two workshops with eight experts to assess the importance of KPIs on a scale from 1 (not important) to 3 (very important). The KPIs found to be most relevant for this project were costs (for passengers, transport providers, and the municipalities), travel and waiting times for passengers, distance, utilization of resources, reduced used of private cars measured in kilometers, increased income from ticket sales, impact on the environment, the last mile (distance to the pick-up point), and drivers' workload. The radar chart was designed to show a passenger's perspective (e.g., pick-up at home, travel time, waiting time, ticket price, environment) and a transport provider's perspective (e.g., drivers' workload, operating costs), but it also had an open category (allowing both providers and passengers to add new indicators).

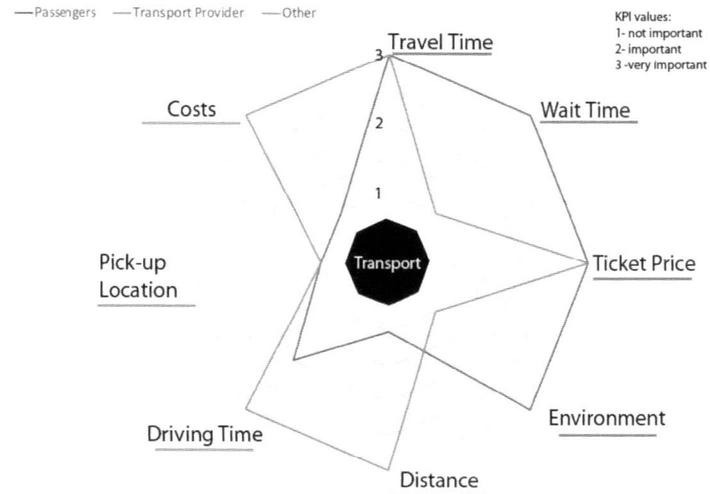

Figure 1. The radar chart was used to elicit the most relevant KPIs for passengers and transport providers

In what follows, we present how sustainable transport KPIs were used, and we give some examples of the insights gained from their usage.

4.1 Relating KPIs to Present Concerns and Future Visions

In the next phase, the project stakeholders engaged in workshops to map the current problems, creating a map of stakeholder concerns, and the relation between these and the visions for transition (Irwin, 2018). The KPIs that emerged as the most significant through this work included passenger and freight volume, monetary and environmental costs, utilization of transport resources, travel time, and waiting time. These were further developed through workshops discussing concerns related to public transport in the rural county participating in the project.

For example, the discussion on the utilization of resources revealed that there are many small entrepreneurs with vans and minibuses that constitute available resources, as their use is not optimized at present. These small entrepreneurs were then included in the list of project stakeholders that should participate in the user studies in later phases of the project.

Furthermore, discussions on passenger/freight volumes and costs revealed the importance of these topics for many stakeholders in rural areas. The core issue here is that in scarcely populated areas, the passenger/freight volumes are low in a range of transport types. One way of keeping costs at an acceptable level is to allow combining different transportation types in future solutions. The need to include a broad range of stakeholders in the TD process surfaced again here. Working actively on expanding the list of stakeholders in the project with new ones who might benefit from joining the project was defined as an important project goal.

In the discussion on travel/waiting time, the issue of motivating citizens to change their transportation habits was raised. One stakeholder framed this issue as follows: *"We transport people from the place they don't want to start their travel to the place they don't want to end it at a time which is not convenient for them. People simply want to go from A to B when they want. And there is already a perfect solution. It is called a private car. The question is how to compete with it. How do we motivate people to use public transport?"* Exploring how to encourage people to engage in more environmentally friendly behaviors became one of the larger project goals.

Sustainable transport KPIs enabled us to be more specific when envisioning the future. They helped us structure our discussion about expectations and tangible, measurable goals for the project. One of the examples we used was a calculation of the expected benefits from considering two KPIs: environmental cost and passenger volume. We calculated the expected benefits for the environment (reduced CO_2 emissions and fuel consumption) and the increased income for transport service providers. The calculations showed that if two persons used public transportation from Folldal to Alvdal/Tynset (two small Norwegian municipalities) instead of their private cars 250 days a year, the reduction in driving distance would be approximately 200 km per day, reducing CO_2 emissions by approximately 6 kg and the fuel consumption by approximately 3,000 L, whereas the public transportation ticket fares would amount to approximately €5,000 in benefits for the public transport provider.

In summary, working explicitly with KPIs at the very start of the project has helped strengthen the research agenda and set a range of practical goals for the project. When working with sustainable transport KPIs, doing concrete exercises and providing examples helped grasp the extent that changes might bring.

4.2 Designing Interventions

The next phase of the process involved *"looking up and down system levels in space, and backward and forward in time"* (Irwin, 2018) and implied understanding how the problems and concerns are amplified or mitigated at different system levels and seen from different time perspectives. We started this phase by collecting users' insights and identifying how the current situation amplified the set of problems. Interviews with project stakeholders were used for the latter. The interviewees had a broad understanding of the needs and problems related to public transport in the rural area we observed. We recruited 13 participants (six females and seven males) from the public sector. Four of them were decision makers in leading municipality positions, and nine were employees working with transport daily, both at the strategic and tactical levels. We conducted 11 individual interviews and one interview with two persons at the same time. Three interviews were conducted over the phone, whereas the remaining ones were done in face-to-face meetings. During the interviews, the participants were asked to envision the public transport of their dreams and then critically reflect on it (i.e., find obstacles to using it). They were also asked to reflect on what is important for them when they use public transport or want to send goods. They were shown the radar chart and asked to explain what is important for them and why. We asked them first to answer these questions as citizens of the county (passengers) and then to answer the same questions from the perspective of their work position. After discussing the KPIs we presented, we asked them if they could think of their own indicators.

The participants first talked about their own experiences when using public transport and what would be needed to motivate them to take a bus or train instead of their own car. We found that the way in which they weighted different KPIs depended on the situation (that is, there was no single answer). For example, when asked about the importance of ticket prices and travel time, one participant said, *"I take the bus to work and for leisure activities. When I have children with me, I take the bus rarely. It has to do with costs. When you have three kids with you, then you drive yourself. It is cheaper. And this is, this is a challenge. It has to do with costs and not to mention time."*

The participants added several new indicators, such as the quality of the driver's service, the quality of real-time information, and the quality of waiting places, and argued for their importance when designing new services. The quality of the driver's service was explained as follows: *"I wrote a 'good driver,' and, by this, I mean more than his driving style. I mean a driver who is pleasant to meet on the bus, a driver who is professional and provides good service. It is these three [indicators] that are very important."*

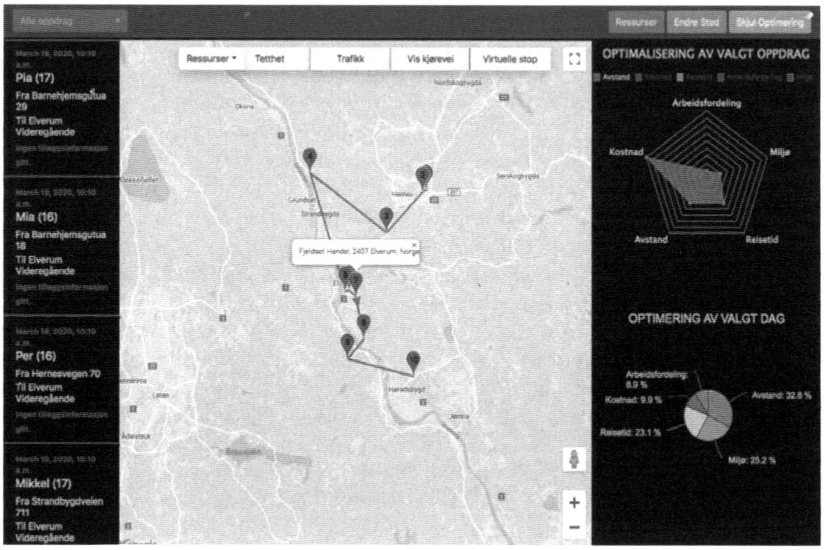

Figure 2. Front-end prototype of a transport planning tool (in Norwegian). The radar chart and the pie chart on the right have five KPIs: drivers' workload, the environment, travel time, distance to the pick-up point, and costs. Incoming orders are listed on the left side of the screen. The map for the proposed route is shown at the center

Discussing environmental KPIs, the participants often considered the problem from a broader perspective. KPIs helped them understand situations that contributed to current environmental problems. Two participants explained how the environmental impact of transport is related not only to the planning of transport services but also to the planning of development. One participant said, *"It is also about how we plan municipality development, where to place the kindergarten in relation to residential areas."* Another participant said, *"We would like to be involved much earlier in the development of new residential areas and roads. When they build an area without a space for the bus to turn, it is too late."* Furthermore, discussing environment KPIs helped identify the importance of collaboration among different stakeholders. One participant explained how their planning of school bus services depended on school plans: *"It does not help to plan being in front of school A at 8:15 a.m. and in front of school B at 8:30 a.m. if school B starts at 8 a.m. We have to negotiate with them or drive one bus to school A and another to school B, which is bad for the environment."*

Insights gained helped us define design goals and engage in prototyping different solutions. For example, the goal to *"motivate the increased use of public transport"* led to some design ideas and suggested solutions. One of the proposed solutions explicitly used sustainable transport KPIs. Figure 2 shows the front-end prototype for a transport planning tool. The envisioned functionality aims to enable operators to work with transport planning and explore the effects of different transport solutions on KPIs. The radar chart in the upper right-hand side allows the operator to prioritize different sustainable transport KPIs for a journey. A user (a passenger, a customer ordering the transport of goods, or an employee at the transport center) can choose priorities for a particular trip using the radar chart; for example, low costs are prioritized over the distance to the pick-up point, travel time, and impact on the environment. An optimization tool that is a part of the system we are developing proposes an optimized solution (a travel route shown at the center of Figure 2) according to the chosen criteria. The pie chart in the lower right corner of the screen summarizes the journeys during a selected day according to KPIs.

In summary, TD methods, tools, and techniques can be used to create design interventions, including prototypes of more sustainable solutions, featuring KPIs as a way to evaluate choices.

5. CONCLUSIONS AND FUTURE WORK

We bring the idea of KPIs from business management into TD. Our first experience showed that sustainable transport KPIs were useful for mapping the problem, mapping stakeholder concerns, envisioning the future, obtaining user insights, identifying the current situations that contribute to the problem, and designing interventions. They enabled us to keep the focus on sustainability and have common themes through the projects. The insights gained through different phases of the project allowed us to work toward sustainable solutions. KPIs and the associated radar charts worked very well to initiate and structure the discussion in workshops and interviews. They worked well for both individual and group interviews and for both online and face-to-face interviews. However, it was easier to follow up on participants' opinions with additional questions during face-to-face interviews. The indicators also made the analysis of the collected data straightforward, as the data collection was already structured around KPIs (e.g., workshops and interviews), or KPIs were used to generate the coding schema (e.g., content analysis of the related projects). This work adds KPIs as an instrument to operationalize design for transitions, fulfilling the need for actionable components and methods (Ceschin and Gaziulusoy, 2016) (van Selm and Mulder, 2019).

Although KPIs showed their usefulness, more studies are needed to further elaborate when and how they could be successfully used. We applied KPIs on a project within the transport sector, and we believe that the same approach might be useful for other domains. As this is ongoing work, we have not yet applied sustainable transport KPIs to evaluate the effect of the interventions introduced by the project. Nevertheless, we believe that sustainable transport KPIs can be beneficial for measuring the short- and long-term effects of TD projects, serving as leverage points that scaffold the transformation from the current situation to a sustainable one. Future work includes further development of this instrument for a better understanding of its role in real-life transitions toward sustainable rural transport.

ACKNOWLEDGEMENT

The project 'Smart Transport in Rural Areas' is funded by the Research Council of Norway, the Transport 2025 program (grant nr. 296639). We thank the project partners Innlandstrafikk, Folldal Municipality, EnTur and Hospital Innlandet for their contribution to this work. Especially, we thank Lasse Jordbru for his insight into challenges of rural traffic and to Ophelia Prillard for prototype implementation.

REFERENCES

Abson, D.J., Fischer, J., Leventon, J., Newig, J., Schomerus, T., Vilsmaier, U., von Wehrden, H., Abernethy, P., Ives, C.D., Jager, N.W., Lang, D.J., 2017. Leverage points for sustainability transformation. Ambio 46, 30–39. https://doi.org/10.1007/s13280-016-0800-y.

Alliance, M., 2017. White Paper: Guidelines & Recommendations to create the foundations for a thriving MaaS Ecosystem. Bruss. MaaS Alliance AISBL.

Bendor, R., 2018. Sustainability, hope, and designerly action in the anthropocene. interactions 25, 82–84.

Boehnert, J., Lockton, D., Mulder, I., 2018. Editorial: Designing for transitions. In Storni, C. et al, Proceedings of the Design Research Society. Published by the Design Research Society, pp. 892–895.

Ceschin, F., Gaziulusoy, I., 2016. Evolution of design for sustainability: From product design to design for system innovations and transitions. Des. Stud. 47, 118–163.

Cockton, G., 2004. Value-centred HCI, in: Proceedings of the Third Nordic Conference on Human-Computer Interaction, NordiCHI '04. Association for Computing Machinery, Tampere, Finland, pp. 149–160. https://doi.org/10.1145/1028014.1028038.

Developing rural services: European Mobility as a Service Roadmap 2025, 2017. Int. VERKEHRSWESEN. URL https://www.internationales-verkehrswesen.de/maas-roadmap-2025/ (accessed 5.3.20).

DOGA, 2019. Roadmap for smart and sustainable cities and communities in Norway.

Escobar, A., 2018. Designs for the Pluriverse: Radical Interdependence, Autonomy, and the Making of Worlds. Duke University Press Books, Durham.

Fitz-Gibbon, C.T., 1990. Performance indicators. Multilingual Matters.

Fredericks, J., Parker, C., Caldwell, G.A., Foth, M., Davis, H., Tomitsch, M., 2019. Designing Smart for Sustainable Communities: Reflecting on the Role of HCI for Addressing the Sustainable Development Goals, in: Proceedings of the 31st Australian Conference on Human-Computer-Interaction. pp. 12–15.

Irwin, T., 2018. The Emerging Transition Design Approach, in: DRS 2018. Presented at the Catalyst, pp. 968–989.

Knowles, B., Bates, O., Maria Håkansson, 2018. This Changes Sustainable HCI, in: Proceedings of the 2018 CHI Conference on Human Factors in Computing Systems. pp. 1–12.

Light, A., 2019. Design and Social Innovation at the Margins: Finding and Making Cultures of Plurality. Des. Cult. 11, 13–35. https://doi.org/10.1080/17547075.2019.1567985.

Light, A., Powell, A., Shklovski, I., 2017. Design for existential crisis in the anthropocene age, in: Proceedings of the 8th International Conference on Communities and Technologies. pp. 270–279.

Mobilizing Sustainable Transport for Development [WWW Document], 2016. UN DESA VOICE. URL https://www.un.org/development/desa/undesavoice/more-from-undesa/2016/11/29738.html (accessed 5. March 20).

Raworth, K., 2017. Doughnut Economics: Seven Ways to Think Like a 21st-Century Economist. Chelsea Green Publishing, White River Junction, Vermont.

Raworth, K., 2012. A safe and just space for humanity: can we live within the doughnut. Oxfam Policy Pract. Clim. Change Resil. 8, 1–26.

Samferdselsdepartementet, 2017. Meld. St. 33 (2016–2017) [WWW Document]. Regjeringen.no. URL https://www.regjeringen.no/no/dokumenter/meld.-st.-33-20162017/id2546287/ (accessed 5. July 20).

Silberman, M.S., Interpreter, F., 2013. Sustainability and structural change: the role of HCI.

Skollerud, K.H., 2014. "Halv på hel" i Tolga. Brukererfaringer og evalueringer (No. 1343/2014).

Sustainable Development Knowledge Platform [WWW Document], 2015. URL https://sustainabledevelopment.un.org/index.html (accessed 7. July 20).

Ta heile Noreg i bruk - Meld. St. 13 [WWW Document], 2013. Regjeringa.no. URL https://www.regjeringen.no/nn/dokumenter/meld-st-13-20122013/id715615/ (accessed 7.8.20).

Tomlinson, B., Nardi, B., Patterson, D.J., Raturi, A., Richardson, D., Saphores, J.-D., Stokols, D., 2015. Toward Alternative Decentralized Infrastructures, in: Proceedings of the 2015 Annual Symposium on Computing for Development, DEV '15. Association for Computing Machinery, London, United Kingdom, pp. 33–40. https://doi.org/10.1145/2830629.2830648

Tonkinwise, C., 2015. Design for Transitions–from and to what? Des. Philos. Pap. 13, 85–92.

Transforming our world: the 2030 Agenda for Sustainable Development [WWW Document], 2015. URL https://sustainabledevelopment.un.org/post2015/transformingourworld (accessed 7. July 20).

van Selm, M., Mulder, I.J., 2019. On transforming transition design: from promise to practice, in: Academy for Design Innovation Management Conference 2019.

Watts, J., Kommenda, N., 2020. The Pandemic Has Led to a Huge, Global Drop in Air Pollution. Wired.

Zolfagharian, M., Walrave, B., Raven, R., Romme, A.G.L., 2019. Studying transitions: Past, present, and future. Res. Policy 48, 103788. https://doi.org/10.1016/j.respol.2019.04.012

ICT FOR DEVELOPMENT, EMPOWERMENT, OR EMANCIPATION? A REFLECTION ON TERMINOLOGY BASED ON CASE STUDIES IN UNDERSERVED COMMUNITIES OF CAPE TOWN

Maria Rosa Lorini and Wallace Chigona
University of Cape Town
Rondebosch, Cape Town, South Africa

ABSTRACT

A University research project sparked, followed, and analysed three processes of social and human development that unfolded in urban underserved communities in Cape Town, South Africa. The processes developed over three years through a flexible approach to outcomes connected with the use of information and communication technologies. A series of final questions drives the analysis of the evaluation of this multiple-case study. What were the processes about? What did the processes do? What did they bring about? What is the legacy of these projects? These questions are analysed through the explanation of the evolution of the case studies presented. The most important question about the intentions of the participants –researcher, external professionals and community members- connects with their philosophical background and assumptions. Seldom stated, occasionally externalised in the approach to interventions, the reasons to participate in a project are the most likely determinants of its outcomes -development and/or empowerment and/or emancipation- and nevertheless the less evaluated. The paper claims that the elucidation of the terminology stimulates the reflection over ideologies and motivations that drive research and activities.

KEYWORDS

Development, Empowerment, Emancipation, ICT4D

1. INTRODUCTION

In academia terminology misuses and abuses are common. This is generally due to simplifications, popularity or convenience, while synthesising complex contexts with unclear boundaries (Castellví, 1998). Occasionally a paragraph or note is added, mentioning the complexity of the term, justifying with space constrains the impossibility to deepen explanation.

In the field of Information and Communication Technology for Development (ICT4D), over the last thirty years, the term 'development' has been used commonly without any reference to its history or its meaning. This, despite the complexity of the term development and the not homogenous use in the different disciplines and amongst practitioners. In the last two decades, a dialectical tension emerged between a macro approach focused on national economic development and the approach that focuses on human development (Ranis et al., 2000). Development does not anymore correspond solely to economic growth and westernization (Mehmet, 2002). In different scenarios of economic, social, political and personal development, studies show how certain issues are cross-border and unite high-GDP countries and lower and middle income countries (LMICs). Inequality growth, rising unemployment, and illiteracy are not limited to the once so-called developing countries (Cingano, 2014). For the sake of better explanations, other terminologies have emerged over time. They are valid in different economic and cultural contexts, and usually, they bear different ideological references. The terms 'emancipation' and 'empowerment' are among the ones primarily used in specific contexts, such as in the feminist debate (Hafkin & Huyer, 2006).

In the context of information systems and technology we observe a generic and sometimes interchangeable use of such terms (Lincoln et al., 2002). In this way, the specificity and possible contribution of the meaning of the words to the phenomenological analysis is therefore compromised. When choosing theoretical frameworks for reference and support, the value and meaning of the words are often underestimated and the choice of a conceptual approach risks to be accomplished without the assessment of the ideology behind it (Denzin and Lincoln, 2013).

In an attempt to elucidate some inevitable assumptions or deficiencies associated with ICT4D, a presentation of a multiple case study will follow focusing on its evaluation. Evaluation was based on the questions developed prior to fieldwork, in particular, 'What kind of contribution can ICT4D projects make'; questions posed throughout the process and related to the specific context; and, finally, following the work carried out: 'What kind of contribution did the projects make for different participants?'

In the research field of ICT4D, the expected contributions are connected with development, which, as stated above, is sometimes referred to as empowerment or emancipation, depending on the framework of reference. We have to consider whether the desired contribution is aimed at economic development, in the classical sense (Ranis & Fei, 1961); or if the research claims to support the integral human development (Alkire, 2010); or if development represents the increased capacities to act and the ability to choose (Sen, 1999); or if it is emancipation from discrimination, constraints and ideological, political and social super-structures (Macdonald, 2015). These questions can be answered from different ontological perspectives and still bring similar results; preliminary questions, on the other hand depend on the participants' philosophical background. While analysing critically specific case studies, this paper reflects on the question that lies behind the ontological and methodological choices and that is often neglected: 'What are the intentions of the participants?' In the case studies, an emergent and flexible approach allowed for receptiveness from all participants' objectives, while continuous reflection on action allowed participants' roles and goals to evolve.

A synthesis of the development terminology in literature highlights potential aims in ICT4D projects. The paper continues with the introduction of embedded case studies representatives of ICT4D projects. The evaluation of the analysis of the findings about the participants' intentions let emerge the importance of the methodology chosen and of the reflective practice approach. The conclusion emphasises the importance of assessing if values and intentions of every participant had been respected, independently of the possible development, empowerment or emancipation goal reached.

2. AN EVOLVING TERMINOLOGY

The word *development* came into being after World War II to formalise a series of conditions of countries with low GNP, limited economic growth with structural changes (Gore, 2000), limited governance systems (dictatorships and possible new coups d'état expected) (Olson, 1993) and limited infrastructure investment (roads, hospitals, schools, etc.) (Agénor, 2010). Already at that time, GNP was considered as insufficient index, due to the lack of income distribution data (Marrama, 1958). From 1990, the United Nations Development Program introduced the Human Development Index to measure the quality of life and the social wellbeing in the countries on the base of the expectations of life, education and income (Sagar & Najam, 1998).

While the terminology connected with the division into first, second, third and fourth worlds was questioned at the end of the eighties with the end of the Cold War, together with the 'underdeveloped countries' concept (Berger, 1994), the new terminology of developed and developing countries emerged. The developing countries were the ones with low and middle income groups, compared to the developed countries with high income groups. The distinction is still used despite a certain disagreement emerging from the LMICs. In the debate, the Wold Bank suggested to interrupt its use (Khokhar & Serajuddin, 2015). Meanwhile, new words gained consensus.

Empowerment is one of those words that in the last two decades gained success (Wilkinson, 1998). While development seemed too complex to envisage as the aim of a short-term project, the empowerment of the participants seemed to be more realistic and affordable. Empowerment becomes a means towards the wider end – development (Parpart, 2002). The terminology, empowerment, reflects a real and tangible improvement in the life of the involved person or in its quality, without assuming an integral approach to the complexity of the context (Friedman, 1992). While development became associated with an economic, social, cultural and political change, empowerment could focalise on the limited uplifting of an individual or a group in a determined context (Perkins & Zimmerman, 1995).

A more limited impact in the recent development literature, had the word *emancipation*. While strongly addressed by the critical social theory as the main desired outcome for any process (Devetak, 1996), it has an historical background and a political flavour that discourage many researchers from adopting it. While development and empowerment seem socially recognised as significant for every person in every country, emancipation seems connected with past realities, when slavery was still in vogue (e.g. in South Africa, Dooling, 2007), and later on when political dissidents and women were fighting for changes (Azmanova, 2009; Dolphyne, 1991). Moving beyond that tradition, emancipation can be interpreted as the reached capability of a person to freely decide on the base of her own values and knowledge and in connection with her community (Steinberg and Kincheloe, 2010).

The terminologies, once explained, instead of being interchangeably, suggest a complementarity: the structural changes of society required to enjoy the freedom that emancipation implies could be achieved through social, economic and political development projects. In turn, empowerment –as the more *ad personam* approach to development- can become the leading instrument to emancipation.

In the ICT4D field, the debate around terminology and intentions created an initial reaction with the possibility to choose whether using the ICTD expression (ICTs in developing countries) or the ICT4D one (ICTs with development aims) (Brown and Grant, 2010). In future, the 'D' may refer to any conditions that need to be improved or modified in any region of the world. This approach will help to dismiss judgement of secondary importance of what comes from the once-called developing countries, such as reverse innovation, products referred to as 'good enough' (Govindarajan & Ramamurti, 2011).

3. CONTEXT AND PARTICIPANTS

The case studies developed in the underserved urban areas of Cape Town, South Africa, specifically in the informal settlements growing inside and around the townships, the once designated areas for non-whites. The groups that participated in the research are based in the poorest sections of the surroundings, where the majority of the population inhabits shacks without running water and formal electrical cables. Philippi, where most of the activities took place, has 44.3% formal dwellings, and with only 26,7% of the homes having piped water (Statistics SA, 2011). The area has a limited number of facilities for pre-school children, whereas schools are usually overcrowded. Hospitals and clinics, another major infrastructural element of development, are unable to serve the growing population coming from the rural areas (Jacobs & Du Plessis, 2016). Unemployment is a national issue that reaches 31.9% of youth at country level and scores 38% in Philippi, where more than half of the population lives under the poverty line surviving with less than 120 euros per month (Statistics SA, 2011). At national level, HIV prevalence is 19.2%, compared to the world 0.8% (WHO, 2017; USAIDS, 2015).

In this context where infrastructural, economic and social development issues are striking and development projects appear to be essential, different networks of people have emerged and succeeded in recreating social ties, in order to cope with the lack of services and in order to support each other (Haddad & Maluccio, 2003). Hundreds of women became part of mass movements that use daily savings and loan practices as a tool for social mobilisation. Through door-to-door collection of small change, communities create flexible, home-grown financial structures that fulfil a critical economic gap and provide a social safety net to ensure the availability of funds for basic survival (Bolnick, 1993). The ritual of daily savings fulfils also a social need, reducing isolation among women and fostering community trust. The groups participating in the study are part of the Women's Network, coordinated largely through community-to-community learning exchanges. These horizontal learning initiatives allow women to see themselves and their peers as experts, thereby reducing isolation, improving confidence, strengthening solidarity and increasing critical mass.

Similar to women, youth living in these underserved communities are trying to organise themselves. In Philippi, where the projects developed, as well as in the neighbouring townships, unemployment and exclusion lead to frustration, lack of income, and 'boredom', making it easy for young people to turn to drug abuse and crime (Wegner et al., 2006). The informal Inyanda Youth Network is a collective of groups, interested in organising edutainment activities (education through entertainment), associated with positive messaging (e.g., on HIV-AIDS through hip-hop or drama). 'Inyanda', in the local Xhosa language, is a bundle of wood. The bundle comprises of various small and bigger pieces of wood found in different places. In the same way, the Youth Network consists of a multitude of groups from different townships intended bring warmth to the townships thanks to the strength of togetherness.

4. CASE STUDIES – EVOLVING PROCESSES

4.1 Women Groups

At the beginning of 2014, six groups of women of the Women's Network took part in the exploratory phase of a research project through interviews and focus groups. At the end of the year, two groups of Mamas, as they are usually called in their communities, participated in the creation of digital storytelling to present their activities and to use new technologies that might support their own groups. The emergent approach chosen supported the possibility to develop an unfolding process that evolved in time, allowing all the participants to reflect and decide on their roles and intentions. As a result of activities and encounters, the women requested training in computer literacy and in the use of several common applications. The training had a long preparatory analysis of the way to introduce novelty and on how to interact. It took place in June 2015, with 10 women from five different groups taking part in the activity. In November, they requested a follow-up to another organisation in order to strengthen their technological knowledge and to improve their skills. At the beginning of 2016, some of the women became co-trainers to support new training on basic computer skills for other women in their community. In May 2016, they presented some of the results of the process at a university seminar. They explained their approach to technology in their own words, showing great understanding and ownership of the process and of skills acquired, as well as great strength and self-esteem in addressing for the first time an academic audience. To this day, the women are still supporting the organisation which helped them mobilising youth to attend training.

4.2 Youth Groups

In 2014, five groups of youth contributed to the research exploratory phase through focus groups and interviews. At the end of the same year, three of the groups participated in the creation of digital storytelling that evolved into a motivational video for youth. In 2015, a series of workshops took place involving different youth groups and a number of professionals, such as web designers and event organisers, in order to evaluate and improve youth skills. In particular, the aim of some workshops was to organise an event where skills, resources and tools of the different groups were analysed to verify the strength of the network and of each group commitment to continue working together, offering a service to the community. At the same time, other workshops for the creation of a website for the network and for the individual groups developed, while several members acquired new skills. In 2016, a follow up analysis of the outcomes of the activities carried out during the previous year, was done. It showed how some groups strengthened their connections and capacities to collaborate, as it was verifiable from the number of events organised in the community and from the number of followers that the groups reached on Facebook. The main projects developed are *Philippi Music Project, The Bridge Experience, Poetics not for the sake of it*, and the re-launch of the network that gathers the different subgroups: the Inyanda Youth Network. In 2016, some youth representatives also participated in the presentation organised at the University where they elaborated on their capabilities and specifically on some of the ICT knowledge they had developed thanks to a series of training, such as the one they attended on applications' creation. Some of the projects are now becoming economically self-sustainable.

4.3 Community Radio Station Group

One of the five youth groups participating in the research at the beginning of 2014 was particularly interested in ICT; its members expressed their desire and dream to create a radio station for the community. Their project was described and presented through a digital storytelling which illustrated the process done by the group from the moment the idea was conceptualised to the creation and opening of a pirate community radio station in July 2014. In 2015, a series of workshops were organised at the request of the radio station founders. A number of people attended the activities: founders, community listeners of the radio, technicians and professionals who wanted to support the team to make a difference. The external experts who participated in the realisation of the workshops were researchers, professional journalists and web designers.

The workshops developed around the theme of ethics in journalism, community activism and, on the technical side, on the creation of a website to reach out to more people, expand the visibility of the station and become more professional.

The team also used the opportunity to start utilising a new application, in order to broadcast from outside the radio station, directly from the community. The project continued evolving in 2016 when the founders of the community radio station decided to request a licence from the government. At the same time, some of the founders decided to register their local organisation in order to continue working with the community and not to lose the momentum created by the radio station activism. That same year, the radio station team presented the results of their activities at a University seminar and used the opportunity to try to develop new contacts and networks. The licensing process required the temporal suspension of the activities, which restarted once the radio became legally registered and economically sustainable.

5. PROCESSES' ACHIEVEMENTS

5.1 Women' Groups

The Women embraced from the beginning of the research the new activities suggested and after a brief exposure to new ICT tools, they requested to strengthen their skills. Their persuasion, commitment and enthusiasm are a testament to their desire to continue their *empowering* path. They used the new opportunity to increase their capacities to support their communities and engage in social activities. In addition to their motivations, the endorsed computer training had an empowering focus on strengthening their capacities, making them feel at ease and secure, and supporting the growth of their self-esteem connected with their ability to develop and apply new skills and to increase their knowledge. The trainers never put pressure on participants but rather worked with them, at their own pace, giving them full attention and ad hoc one-on-one coaching. The follow-up training reinforced a process initiated directly by the women. Their capacity to independently plan, schedule and elaborate it with the participation of a new training organization is further proof of the empowerment gained throughout the process.

This project develops into a fully rounded process of *development*. The main intention driving the women was their desire to keep on supporting their community, and they used an inclusive approach, inviting more members and new groups to participate in the follow up phases. Furthermore, the women evaluated every option available to affect their society without focusing on their individual or group benefit. Thanks to the empowerment of the participants, and thanks to the perspective they maintained to make a difference for their community, this project is still ongoing, still evolving and producing new results.

Concerning the possible progress in women *emancipation* through ICTs activities, in time new skills led to an enhanced perception of self and to a stronger ability to interact with their surroundings and peers through the use of technology. The Women were able to continue the process without the support of external experts. They discussed and agreed on what could be useful, self-determining the follow-up steps. A full emancipation process might require further steps for the development of decision-making capabilities based on the inner values and knowledge.

5.2 Youth Network and Radio Station Group

The workshops the youth decided to engage in allowed them new opportunities. In particular, the participants could gain additional knowledge and further develop plans they were already working on. *Empowerment* was represented here was the possibility to strengthen the network and visualize connections and ties between individual groups digitally. In the long term, the process strengthened their relationship and trust and the feeling of shared social responsibility. The same happened to the radio station process, when the group engaged with community members to discuss further possibilities through a website or smartphone applications.

Development-wise, the youth network aimed to potentiate its capabilities to reach out to more youngsters, capitalising on their skills and expertise. The outcomes of the activities carried out were oriented towards the community, beyond the groups participating. The process of development is evolving, growing and aggregating more youth in the network experience, as proven by social media and events' participation. Concerning the radio station group, its members reinforced ties and commitment to their community through the process of registration of the radio station and of their new organization, founded in order to access more opportunities.

An examination of the *emancipatory* process could be done for the network as well as for the single groups. The growth of the network and the empowerment of the single groups, like the radio station one, allowed an occasion for members to increase the sense making, contemplate their reasons for coming together and for participating, as well as an occasion to ameliorate their collective decision-making system. Their capabilities and reinforced self-assuredness developed in time, strengthening self-consciousness and desire to achieve set objectives. The aims of each group remained separated and connected with their passions and desires. Nevertheless, for all of them, it was possible to analyse and see increased consciousness and determination to reach out personal and community objectives.

6. DISCUSSION

The evaluation of the projects and of their outcomes was based on participant observation, interviews with community members and with development professionals operating in the same context, feedback by external observers indirectly involved in the projects, and social media use analytics. These evaluation tools were used both during the course of the projects, once the same had ended, and a few months after that, in order to validate the analysis' results. The findings present several elements of empowerment, development and emancipation that emerged along the processes. In order to fully evaluate projects outcomes, an in depth analysis of participants intentions and aims is required.

In the cases presented, given also the community-based nature of these action research projects, a grassroots emergent approach more easily supported valorisation and disclosure of participants' values and strengths (Krauss, 2012). The choice of letting processes unfold allowed participants to empower themselves; over the course of the projects, participants developed new skills, deepened their knowledge, took significant decisions and undertook specific responsibilities for their future (Razak, 2009).

To support a path of emancipation, focused on self-consciousness and determination, the projects included context and culture specific approaches during the technical workshops and trainings, that matched and respected participants' cultural background and values. Strengthening the community specific local mechanisms of empowerment and approaching projects with a perspective of mutual respect and mutual learning, allowed participants to shape and pursue their own motivations and goals, disconnected from forms of cultural imperialism (Stahl, 2006). This further allowed not only for ICTs based empowerment, but also for the beginning of emancipatory dynamics.

In the cases presented, an emergent approach was initially used to best establish the focus of the ICTs support interventions. Such emergent approach then allowed to avoid potential risk factors associated with the development of counterproductive solutions (Lin, Kuo & Myers, 2015). An analysis of how groups and individuals operate and cooperate in that particular context, as well as an analysis of their values, best directed the projects. The visualisation of those elements allowed the participants to understand options, choose, and lead the change To fully impact communities and individuals, ICT4D processes require such an analysis, and not only an assessment study.

A reflection over terminology is crucial also in the process of evaluation. What people want to achieve, the reason for the same and their preferred approach are strictly linked on their values and ideology. In every process it is essential to define the intentions and expectations of participant-researcher, external professionals and community members, as well as the overall objective, which in the case studies presented was namely: development, empowerment, emancipation.

7. CONCLUSION

The main concept and contribution the author wished to develop is the importance of the use of specific terminology and the explicit disclosure of ideological and theoretical frameworks adopted. Terminology used reflects choices made and the intentions behind the same. Clarifying intentions underlying the choice to study, analyse, operationalise and evaluate ICT4D projects, supports dialogue with similarly minded researchers, and diminishes possible misunderstandings with or misrepresentation by researchers working from within different theoretical frameworks.

The focus of several ICT4D projects may be on infrastructural or technical aspects; others may focus more closely on developmental aspects of the same. Regardless of such focus, results analysis will be based on the selected philosophical framework and the questions raised, which will justify selected approaches. Likewise, weather the research focus is on human development, economic development, technical development, defining terminology used in research and in presenting analytical results fosters a fuller understanding of the work.

The cases in the long term, generated a number of results, evaluated on the basis of criteria directly derived from initially expressed intentions and newly risen ones. The intentions were discussed with and within the community participants as well as participating external experts, notwithstanding potential difficulties in truthfully establishing each participant's personal and group objectives.

The study underlines the key importance of defining framework, intent, focus and terminology used, in each and every ICT4D research project.

ACKNOWLEDGMENT

The paper is part of the main author PhD dissertation "Collective empowerment through information and communication technologies: co-creation processes in underserved communities in Cape Town" (Lorini, 2018). Faculty of Commerce, Department of Information Systems, University of Cape Town, South Africa. http://hdl.handle.net/11427/30004.

In the thesis, the 'Women Groups' are referred to as 'Mamas groups', as the women referred to each other in their communities. I am grateful I was asked by the participants to address them in that same familiar way, and I am grateful to all the participants for their engagement during the processes.

REFERENCES

Agénor, P. R. (2010). A theory of infrastructure-led development. *Journal of Economic Dynamics and Control*, *34*(5), 932-950.

Alkire S. 2010. Human Development: Definitions, Critiques, and Related Concepts. Human Development Research Paper HDRP/2010/01. New York: United Nations Development Programme.

Azmanova, A. (2009). 1989 and the European Social Model: Transition without emancipation? *Philosophy & Social Criticism*, *35*(9), 1019-1037.

Berger, M. T. (1994). The end of the 'Third World'? *Third World Quarterly*, *15*(2), 257-275.

Bolnick, J. (1993). The People's Dialogue on Land and Shelter: community-driven networking in South Africa's informal settlements. *Environment and Urbanization*, *5*(1), 91-110.

Brown, A. E., & Grant, G. G. (2010). Highlighting the duality of the ICT and development research agenda. *Information Technology for Development*, *16*(2), 96-111.

Castellví, M. T. C. (1998). Do we need an autonomous theory of terms? *Terminology. International Journal of Theoretical and Applied Issues in Specialized communication*, *5*(1), 4-19.

Cingano, F. (2014). Trends in Income Inequality and its Impact on Economic Growth. *OECD Social, Employment, and Migration Working Papers*, (163), 0_1.

Denzin, N. K., & Lincoln, Y. S. (Eds.). (2013). *The landscape of qualitative research: Theories and issues*. Sage.

Devetak, R. (1996). Critical theory. *Theories of international relations*, 145-173.

Dolphyne, F. A. (1991). *The emancipation of women: an African perspective*. Ghana Universities Press, Accra, Ghana.

Dooling, W. (2007). *Slavery, emancipation and colonial rule in South Africa* (Vol. 87). Ohio University Press, Ohio.

Friedman, J. (1992). *Empowerment: The Politics of Alternative Development.* Blackwell, Oxford.

Gore, C. (2000). The rise and fall of the Washington Consensus as a paradigm for developing countries. *World development*, *28*(5), 789-804.

Govindarajan, V., & Ramamurti, R. (2011). Reverse innovation, emerging markets, and global strategy. *Global Strategy Journal*, *1*(3-4), 191-205.

Haddad, L., & Maluccio, J. A. (2003). Trust, membership in groups, and household welfare: Evidence from KwaZulu-Natal, South Africa. *Economic Development and Cultural Change*, *51*(3), 573-601.

Hafkin, N. J., & Huyer, S. (2006). *Cinderella or cyberella?: Empowering women in the knowledge society*. Kumarian Press, Bloomfield, CT.

Jacobs, W., & Du Plessis, D. J. (2016). A Spatial Perspective of the Patterns and Characteristics of Main- and Substream Migration to the Western Cape, South Africa. In *Urban Forum* (Vol. 27, No. 2, pp. 167-185). Springer, Netherlands.

Khokhar, T. & Serajuddin, U. (2015) "Should we continue to use the term "developing world"?", available at: http://blogs.worldbank.org/opendata/should-we-continue-use-term-developing-world (accessed: January 2016).

Kleine, D., & Unwin, T. (2009). Technological Revolution, Evolution and New Dependencies: what's new about ICT4D? *Third World Quarterly*, *30*(5), 1045-1067.

Krauss, K. (2012). Towards self-emancipation in ICT for development research: narratives about respect, traditional leadership and building networks of friendships in rural South Africa. *The African Journal of information systems*, *4*(2),1.

Lin, C. I., Kuo, F. Y., and Myers, M. D. (2015). Extending ICT4D studies: The value of critical research. *Management Information Systems Quarterly*, *39*(3), pp.97-712.

Lincoln, N. D., Travers, C., Ackers, P., & Wilkinson, A. (2002). The meaning of empowerment: The interdisciplinary etymology of a new management concept. *International journal of management reviews*, *4*(3), 271-290.

Macdonald, B. J. (2015). Critical Theory. In *The Encyclopedia of Political Thought*. 1-9, M. T. Gibbons (Ed.). Wiley Blackwell.

Marrama, V. (1958). *Saggio sullo sviluppo economico dei paesi arretrati* (Vol. 23). Edizioni Scientifiche Einaudi, Torino, Italy.

Mehmet, O. (2002). *Westernizing the Third World: The Eurocentricity of economic development theories*. Routledge.

Olson, M. (1993). Dictatorship, Democracy, and Development. *American Political Science Review*, *87*(03), 567-576.

Parpart, J. (2002). Lessons from the field. Rethinking empowerment gender and development from a post-(post-?) development perspective. In: *Feminist post-development thought: rethinking modernity, postcolonialism and representation*, edited by Saunders. 41-56, Zed Books. London, England.

Perkins, D. D., & Zimmerman, M. A. (1995). Empowerment theory, research, and application. *American journal of community psychology*, *23*(5), 569-579.

Ranis, G., & Fei, J. C. (1961). A theory of economic development. *The American economic review*, 533-565.

Ranis, G., Stewart, F., & Ramirez, A. (2000). Economic growth and human development. *World development*, *28*(2), 197-219

Razak, N. A. (2009). Empowering the rural communities via the telecentres. *European Journal of Social Sciences*, *9*(3), 425-432.

Sagar, A. D., & Najam, A. (1998). The human development index: a critical review. *Ecological economics*, *25*(3), 249-264.

Sen, A. (2001). *Development as freedom*. Oxford Paperbacks, Oxford.

Stahl, B. C. (2006). Emancipation in cross-cultural IS research: The fine line between relativism and dictatorship of the intellectual. *Ethics and Information Technology*, *8*(3), 97-108.

Statistics SA (2011). "My settlement: Philippi", Statistics South Africa, available at: http://www.statssa.gov.za/?page_id=4286&id=323 (accessed: January 2017).

Steinberg, S. R., & Kincheloe, J. L. (2010). Power, emancipation, and complexity: Employing critical theory. *Power and Education*, *2*(2), 140-151.

UNAIDS (2015). "HIV and AIDS estimates" (2015), available at: http://www.unaids.org/en/regionscountries/countries/southafrica (accessed: January 2017).

Wegner, L., Flisher, A. J., Muller, M., & Lombard, C. (2006). Leisure boredom and substance use among high school students in South Africa. *Journal of Leisure Research*, *38*(2), 249.

WHO (2017). "HIV-AIDS", available at: http://www.who.int/gho/hiv/en/ (accessed: January 2017).

Wilkinson, A. (1998). "*Empowerment*" in M. Poole, and M. Warner (Eds.). *International Encyclopaedia of Business and Management Handbook of Human Resource Management*, ITB Press, London.

ICTS USAGE AMONG RURAL COMMUNITIES IN THE INFORMATION AGE: A CASE STUDY OF SMALL SCALE FARMERS IN EASTERN CAPE PROVINCE SOUTH AFRICA

Agyei Fosu and Darelle van Greunen
Nelson Mandela University
P O Box 77000, Nelson Mandela University, Port Elizabeth, 6031, South Africa

ABSTRACT

There is a mismatch between research output and farmers' ICT practices. In this case study in the former Transkei and Ciskei Homelands, 48 small-scale farmers were approached to understand the factors that impede ICTs use to access agricultural information. The farmers were found to use and see the usefulness of ICTs basically in terms of social interactions and the most frequent used ICTs by respondents are mobile phone (100%) followed by radio (58.3%), Television (18.8%), Internet (10.4%) and news paper (6.3%). There is a need to do an in-depth research about e-skills of the farmers and other factors that may be causing hindrance to the usage of other recent advances of Internet and ICTs for seeking information.

KEYWORDS

ICTs, Information Age, Development, Small Scale Farmers

1. INTRODUCTION

Development literature is fraught with various perspectives on how to improve living conditions in rural areas. Central to all these perspectives put forward for rural development is the assertion of Chambers and Conway, (1991) that explains the process of rural development to involves a participatory set of activities that must involves local people, the natural environment, outside development practitioners, and other stakeholders such as developmental agencies. In the course of embarking on these set of activities, different forms of knowledge are generated of which access to these knowledge as well as its implementation becomes critical to attaining development for that area. Knowledge and access been crucial for any development and also can make rural development process achievable has been highlighted by Wong, (2010); Bruckmeier and Tovey, (2008). Thus, the achievability of the rural development process and its sustainability relies on availability of information to the rural communities and their ability to access and use the information for improvement of their livelihood is imperative towards the sustainability of the rural development process in the information age (Ali et al., 2015). Information and Communication Technologies (ICTs) can play a significant role in rural sustainability development process by serving as a platform to capture, convert, store and share the knowledge generated during the rural development process activities in the form of Internet and Intranet web portals, digital libraries, blogs, as well as mobile and smart phones, CDs and DVDs, TV and radio broadcasts. If ICTs are appropriately deployed and effectively utilized it can become a powerful tool to address some of the challenges and also can aid the uplifting of the livelihoods of poor people in rural areas in the information age.

Agriculture as an economy sector worldwide in the information age is not spared from the crucial needs of information to increase production, improve marketing and distribution strategies (Oladele, 2006). With information, farmers can be empowered with best farming practices, sources of financial assistances and available market places for their produce. Agriculture is an important sector in most developing countries' economy as majority of their population lives in rural areas and earns their livelihood by agriculture in the form of small scale farming is well documented. With the major challenges such as water shortages, declining soil fertility, effects of climate change, etc., facing small scale farmers day to day, there is continual urgent need for new approaches and technical innovations for small scale farmers to cope with these challenges and to enhance the livelihoods of the rural population. This is where the availability and use of ICTs can make a significant contribution by serving as a medium or platform to deliver useful agricultural information to small scale farmers about crop care, animal husbandry, fertilizer applications, feedstocks, market prices to increase productivity and efficiency as well as sustainability of small scale farming.

1.1 Problem Statement and Background of the Study

The role of ICTs to enhance food security and support rural livelihoods is recognized and was officially endorsed at the World Summit on the Information Society (WSIS) 2005. One of the thoughts behind the use of ICTs that includes radio, TV, mobile phone and Internet in the agricultural sector was to applied these tools to narrow the gap between researchers and farmers by providing channels to convey information between researchers, extension agents and farmers (Nyirenda-Jere, 2010; Musa et al., 2013). However, it has been demonstrated that the linkages between researchers, extension agents and farmers is not effective and that there is a mismatch between research output and on farm practices (Simumba and Koopman, 2011, Musa et al., 2013). Even though Internet access and ICTs devices are becoming more common in South Africa (World Bank, 2008; Goldstuck, 2012), the use of them to enhance farming activities are limited. In view of this, it is important to carry out research on ICTs usage especially among rural farmers to understand the factors that impede its use to access agricultural information.

The research question for the study is: *How can ICTs usage to seek or access agricultural information among small scale farmers support sustainable rural development in the information age?*

Thus, *we hypothesize that the use of ICTs among small scale farmers to access agricultural information can make sustainable rural development goal achievable.*

One is not far from the truth to assert that for rural communities to play a meaningful role in developing countries economy in the information age, access to information is paramount. Hence, it is also critical to check information needs; information practices of the indigenous people in this context the small scale farmers prior to understanding the ICTs usage among them. Maepa (2000) argues that the concept of information needs does not only presuppose the lack of information, but it also means linking the need with the use of that information to solve a problem. Suggesting also that once a person has identified the information needs, then the person is in a better position not only to seek the information but also be able to determine where and means or medium to use to seek the information. The information needs assessment in this study will seek to answer the following questions which are also the specific objectives of the study is to:

1. Specify the information needs of the small scale farmers.

2. Describe conditions for information sharing among the small scale farmers as a community.

3. Specify the type and rate of usage of ICTs to access/seek information needs.

This study examines the case of black small scale farmers in the former Transkei and Ciskei Homelands in the Eastern Cape Province South Africa. The region is typically an area of widespread large rural population with agricultural based rural economy and deep poverty where illiteracy, unemployment and poor access to basic and social services continue to be endemic.

1.2 Research Methodology

The researchers designed a survey questionnaire and purposeful approached a total of 48 black small scale farmers in animal products and field crops from Peddie, Fort Beautfort, Idutywa, Ngqamakhwe, Keiskammahoek, Adelaide, Middledrift to gather quantitative data on their information needs, patterns of seeking information, type and rate of ICTs usage to access their information needs.

According to Bless et al., (2007) quantitative research methods enable a researcher to obtain relevant information from the sample group through a questionnaire with closed and open-ended questions which can be analyzed using descriptive and inferential statistics. The data were analyzed using MS Excel spreadsheet database for conversion into percentages for the descriptive statistics and thematic analysis was used for the open-ended question. The approach was that the researchers first visited the selected towns to identify the farmers, and then arranged a suitable time to meet them individual to administer and assist the farmers to answer the questionnaire. This process helped to overcome misunderstanding and misinterpretation of words or questions on the questionnaire.

1.3 Literature Review

Whilst the limitation of industrial resources, infrastructure in rural areas remains a challenge, but the rapid growth of ICTs and its gadgets have created opportunities for rural communities especially those in developing countries to participate in the21st century global digital and knowledge-based economy (normally called the information age) without the need to experience an industrial shift. For instance, the use of ICTs such as Internet, mobile phone in rural communities can help such areas overcome the physical barrier to access and participate in the global knowledge-based economy activities such as e-commerce, e-health and ecotourism.

There is ample empirical evidence in literature on key factors that influence ICTs usage and adoption among rural communities in Africa and other developing countries across the globe (James, 2010; Jacobs and Herselman, 2006; Meyer, 2003; Okon, 2015; Ramirez, 2001). Findings such as physical access; costs; lack of awareness of the benefits of ICTs; lack of skills; attitudinal barriers; literacy; content, gender and age, etc., have been identified by researchers such as Okon, (2015); Chatterjee et al., (2002); Musa et al., (2005); Cullen, (2001); Rao, (2003); as key factors that prevent rural people globally from reaping the benefits of ICTs and serves as barriers to using technology. In the case of small scale farmers in Africa, similar findings have been echoed in the findings of most studies. The study conducted by Musa et al., (2013) among farmers in Sudan's Gerzira State identified low education levels, low income, cultural inertia, inadequate ICTs skills among researchers and farmers, and the scarcity of relevant content in local languages as hurdles to adoption and use of ICT. Chavula (2013) in his study the role of ICTs in agricultural production in Africa used the 2000-2011 panel data for 34 Africa countries to assess if at all the proliferation of ICTs on the African continent has had any significant impact on agricultural production, found that ICTs play a significant role in enhancing agricultural production. Job et al., (2013) identified with regards to usage of ICTs by small scale farmers in Niger State, Nigeria, language barrier, poverty and illiteracy as challenges. According to the study of Anyan et al., (2018) to investigate into barriers that hinders the effective use of ICTs in farming by small scale farmers in Asuogyaman District in Ghana, found three main barriers namely attitudinal, accessibility and technical skills. Similar findings were identified by the study of Muriithi et al., (2009).

Various researchers writing on small scale farmers in Africa access and utilizing ICTs to increase productivity highlight the following. The study of Kituyi-Kwake et al., (2008) conducted on Kenya rural women farmers to analyze access and ICTs usage among them found that cost of the ICTs services, time, the far away of the ICTs services, computer illiteracy, poor roads and cultural taboos to be some of the constraints to ICTs adoption among the women. Cultural factors in the setting of cultural beliefs, legal frameworks and politics were identified in the study of a cross-tabulation between adoption of ICTs and cultural factors conducted by Musa et al., (2013). Chilimo (2008) reported that most of the small scale farmers who participated in the study of the four rural districts in Tanzania main access to ICTs are radio and mobile cell phones.

2. DATA PRESENTATION AND DISCUSSION

We are in the information age that is the call made by authors such as Castells, (2000); Hughes, (1991) and Friedman (2006) and they further sound the alarm that it is the age where information generation, processing and transformation are critical to societal functioning, change and development as well as it is also the age where ICTs enable the widespread expansion of vital information and networking for development throughout the societal structure. ICTs application in agriculture has become a critical tool due to its potential in improving agricultural productivity by serving as a platform to access vital agricultural information.

As highlighted early, in the information age, without information and the use of ICTs increasing productivity, efficiency and sustainability becomes a tall order. Thus, increasing productivity, efficiency and sustainability among rural small scale farmers certainly requires access and usage of ICTs. The key findings of the present study are presented below:

2.1 Demographic Information of Participants

Studies have revealed that age, gender and educational levels do have influence when it comes to technology adoption and usage (Venkatesh et al., 2003). The age, gender and educational background of respondents are shown in Table 1 below.

Table 1. Demographic information of participants

Age	Frequency	Percentage
25 – 30	3	6.3
31 – 36	2	4.2
37 – 42	3	6.3
43 – 48	7	14.6
49 – 54	9	18.8
55 – 60	13	27.1
Above 61	11	22.9
Gender of respondents		
Male	44	91.7
Female	4	8.3
Educational background of participants		
No formal education	23	47.9
Primary education	6	12.5
Secondary education	10	20.8
Post –secondary education	9	18.8

The findings from Table 1 shows that majority of respondents who took part in this study were aged between 55 – 60 years (27.1%) followed by those above 61 years (22.9%). Approximately 18.8% were aged between 49 – 54 years, 14.6% were aged between 43 – 48 years, 6.3% were aged between 25 – 30 years and 37 – 42 years and the least percentage were aged 31 – 36 years (4.2%). The low number of young people in the study depicts that the youth are not been attracted to take up farming as a career. The findings also showed that there were more males (91.7%) than females (8.3%). This could probably be attributed to the fact that most household have males as breadwinners.

2.2 Information needs and Habitual Source

As asserted by Harris and Dewdney (1994) that people tend to follow the habitual patterns in seeking information, in exploring the information needs of respondents the habitual source of information seeking of the respondents were also explored in an open-end question on the questionnaire and the results are shown in Table 2 in common themes with frequencies and percentages below:

Table 2. Information needs and habitual source

Information needs	Habitual source	Frequency	Percentage
Market prices for farm produce	1)True relations (such as family, friends and other farmers) 2)True social gathering(such as church, drinking bar) 3) local market (such as grocery shops) 4) True ICTs (such as Radio, TV, Internet and Newspaper)	1) 42 respondents 2) 5 respondents 3) 33 respondents 4) 7 respondents	1) 87.5 2) 10.4 3) 68.8 4) 14.6

Prices for agricultural products (such as fertilizers, seeds, etc)	1)True relations especially fellow farmers 2) True local markets 3) True agricultural offices and officers	1)42 respondents 2)30 respondents 3) 15 respondents	1)87.5 2)62.5 3)31.3
Farming practices (such as pests and disease control, fertilizer application, animal care)	1)True relations especially fellow farmers 2)True ICTs especially local radio programs on agriculture 3)True agricultural officers and offices	1)45 respondents 2)13 respondents 3)36 respondents	1)93.8 2)27.1 3)75
Government projects and services (such as financial aid, health, home affairs)	1)True relations 2)True Community leaders 3) True service office	1)34 respondents 2)40 respondents 3) 27 respondents	1)70.8 2)83.3 3)56.3
Politics, local and international news	1)True relations 2)Community leaders 3)ICTs	1)46 respondents 2)38 respondents 3) 36 respondents	1)95.8 2)79.2 3)75

The results from Table 2 clearly indicate that the respondents prefer to seek information from people and familiar places. In hindsight, this is understandably so because of the assertion of Meyer, (2003) that people living in oral cultures prefer to exchange information in ways that are familiar to them and as such people within the community are key source. This will certainly have implications in certain type of ICTs usage such as social media networks, SMS and voice calls of mobile phones commonly used for interpersonal communication then Internet, Intranet portals, blogs, etc., use for searching information. Thus, agricultural extension programmes and policies, researchers need to be cautious about the type of ICTs to be used for disseminating of agricultural information to farmers in rural areas.

2.3 Respondent's Perception of ICTs and its Usefulness to Them

The study also explored the perceptions and usefulness of ICTs to the farmers. As highlighted by Roman and Colle, (2003) that the relevance and sustainability of technologies among rural communities depend most of the times on what they believe it can offer them. The results are shown in Table 3 in common themes with corresponding percentages below:

Table 3. Respondent's perception of ICTS and its usefulness to them

Perception of ICTs	**Frequency**	**Percentage**
Using computer	13	27.1
Tool for sending and receiving message	9	18.8
Use of technology to communicate	10	20.8
Use of modern and new technology to communicate	4	8.3
Don't know	12	25
Usefulness of ICTs to respondents		
Communicate with friends, family and other farmers	48	100
For the purpose of communicating with my customers	43	89.6
Banking purposes	13	27.1
Seeking information	7	14.6

The most obvious result in Table 3 is that the respondents (100%) see the usefulness of ICTs basically in terms of social interactions.

2.4 Type and Pattern of ICTs Usage to access/seek Agricultural Information Needs Regularly

The study sought to determine the most ICTs tool to acquire agricultural information needs regularly. Table 4 gives the results.

Table 4. Type and pattern of ICTs to access/seek agricultural information needs

Type of ICTs	Frequency	Percentage
Mobile phone (mostly as medium to ask information from other farmers)	48	100
Television (To watch agricultural programs)	9	18.8
Radio (To listen to agricultural programs)	28	58.3
Newspaper (To read about agricultural news)	3	6.3
Internet as ICT tool (To search agricultural information)	5	10.4
All of the above	2	4.2

According to the results in Table 4 the regularly used ICT tool was mobile phone (100%) followed by radio (58.3%), TV (18.8%), internet (10.4%) and newspaper (6.3%). The findings of the study confirm the findings of Chilimo (2008) and other past studies. The findings also affirm what Okon (2015) said, that in studying ICTs use in everyday it is critical for one to understand the social networks of people within the community been study way of exchange of information because it does play a key role in how and type of technology that will be used. Therefore it is imperative for developmental agencies task with facilitating rural development agenda when integrating and using ICTs as a tool to reach rural people needs to be cautious of this as well.

3. CONCLUSION AND RECOMMENDATION

According to Diekmann et al., (2009) having information on how farmers as well as medium use to search information is critical for extension educators, agricultural professionals, information specialists and marketers to be able to create effective strategies for disseminating information to the farmers.

The study set out to examine the usage of ICTs among small scale farmers in Eastern Cape Province South Africa. The findings of the study are as follows: majority of the farmers (50%) were above 55 years. If there were more youthful farmers the expectation would have been a relatively more usage of ICTs for the purpose of seeking information as most research studies have demonstrated that the older generation is unfamiliar with recent advances in Internet for seeking information. According to Obinne, (1991) and Venkatesh (2003) education has been shown to be a factor in the adoption of high yielding modern farm practices as well as the adoption and usage of technology. Thus, the low educational levels among the farmers certainly have influence on the type and usage of ICTs to seek information and the source of seeking agricultural information. Again, the finding of the pattern of using human sources and the type of ICTs used in seeking agricultural information will certainly not fully support the achievable sustainable rural developmental goals rather it will hinder the farmers from accessing vital information put on other recent advances in Internet and ICTs for dissemination of information. Hence, the hypothesis of the study cannot be accepted.

As proposed by Hargittai and DiMaggio (2001) that meaningful ICTs usage will only be realized if it fulfills a real purpose for the user and if there is no reason for the user, technology will be quickly discarded as not important. The study recommends programmes be develop to educate rural small scale farmers about the importance and benefits that they will derived from using ICTs to support their farming activities in the information age. There is a need to do an in-depth research about e-skills of the farmers and other factors that may be causing hindrance to the usage of other recent advances of Internet and ICTs for seeking information.

REFERENCES

Ali, L., and Avdic, A. (2015). A frame-work for ICT-based knowledge sharing in sustainable rural development: the case of Gilgit-Baltistan, Pakistan. *Electronic Journal of Knowledge Management,* Vol.13, No.2, pp. 103 -116.

Anyan,F. Y., and Frempong, G. (2018). An Investigation into Barriers that Hinder the Effective Use of ICT in Farming by Small Scale Farmers in Asuogyaman District, Ghana. *International Journal of Humanities Social Sciences and Education (IJHSSE),* vol 5, no. 1, pp. 23-32.

Bless, C., Higson-Smith, C., and Kagee, A. (2007). *Fundamentals of social research methods: An African perspective.* 3rd ed. Kenwyn:Juta.

Bruckmeier, K., and Tovey, H. (2008). Knowledge in sustainable rural development: From forms of knowledge to knowledge processes. *European Society for Rural Sociology,* Vol. 48, pp. 313-329.

Castells, M. (2000). *The information age:Economy, society and culture.* Oxford: Blackwell.

Chatterjee, D., Grewal , R. and Sambamurthy, V. (2002).Shaping up for e-commerce: Institutional enablers of the organizational assimilation of web technologies. *MIS Quarterly,* Vol. 26, No. 2, pp. 65-89.

Chavula, H. K. (2013). The role of ICT in agricultural production in Africa, *journal of development and agricultural economics,* Vol. 6, No. 7, pp. 279-289.

Chambers, R., and Conway, G. (1991). Sustainable rural livelihoods: practical concepts for the 21st century. *IDS Discussion paper*. No. 296, pp. 1-33.

Chilimo, W. L., (2008). Information and communication technologies and sustainable livelihoods: a case of selected rural areas of Tanzania.Unpublished PhD Thesis, University of KwaZulu-Natal, Pietermaritzburg.

Cullen, R. (2001). Addressing the digital divide. *Online Information Review,* Vol. 25, No. 5, pp. 311-320.

Friedman, T. (2006). *The World is flat: The globalized world in the twenty-first century.* London: Penguin Books.

Diekmann, F., Loibl, C. & Batte, M. T. (2009). The Economics of Agricultural Information: Factors Affecting Commercial Farmers' Information Strategies in Ohio. *Review of Agricultural Economics,* Vol. 31, No.4, pp. 853-872.

Goldstuck, A. (2012). *Internet Access in South Africa 2012.* World Wide Worx.

Hargittai, E., and DiMaggio, P. (2001). *From the "digital divide" to "digital inequality": Studying internet use as penetration increases*. Princeton, NJ: Center for Arts and Cultural Policy Studies, Woodrow Wilson School, Princeton University.

Harris, R.M., and Dewdney, P. (1994). Barriers *to information; How formal help system fail battered women.* Westport, CT: Greenwood Press.

Hughes, G. C. (1991). The information age. *Information Development*, Vol. 7, No. 2, pp.72-74.

Jacobs, S.J. and Herselman, M. E. (2006). Information access for development: A case study at a rural community center in South Africa. *Issues in Informing Science and Technology*, Vol. 3, pp.295-306.

Legris, P., Ingram, J., and Collerette, P. (2003). Why do people use information technology? A critical review of the technology acceptance model. *Information and Management*, Vol. 40, No. 3, pp. 191-204.

James, J. (2010). Mechanisms of access to the Internet in rural areas of developing countries. *Telematics and Informatices*, Vol. 27, No. 4, pp. 370-376.

Job N. N., Fatima. A. A., and Halima, S. (2013). Use of ICT in Securing Marketing Information among Small Scale Farmers in Niger State, Nigeria. *International Journal of Trade, Economics and Finance, Vol. 4, No. 2.*

Kituyi-Kwake, A. and Adigun, M. O. (2008). Analyzing ICTS use and access amongst rural women in Kenya, *International Journal of Education and Development using Information and Communication Technology, 4* (4), 127-147.

Maepa, M. E. (2000). *Information needs and information seeking patterns of rural villagers in the Northern Province*. Unpublished Thesis, RAU, Johannesburg.

Meyer, H. W. J.(2003). Information use in rural development. *The New Review of Information Behaviour Research*, Vol. 4, pp.109-126.

Musa, P. F. Meso, P., and Mbarika, V. W.(2005). Towards sustainable adoption of technologies for human development in sub-Saharan Africa: Precursors, diagnostics, and prescriptions. *Communications of the Association for Information Systems*, Vol. 15, No.1, pp. 592-608.

Musa, N. S., Githeko, J. M. & El-siddig, K. (2013). The adoption and use of ICTs by small scale farmers in Gezira State, Sudan, *Research Application Summary,* pp.625 – 633.

Muriithi, A. G., Bett, E. and Ogaleh, S. A. (2009*). Information Technology for Agriculture and Rural Development in Africa: Experiences from Kenya.* Paper presented at the Conference on International Research on Food Security, Natural Resource Management and Rural Development, Tropentag 2009, University of Hamburg, October 6-8, 2009

Nyirenda-Jere, T. (2010). Unlocking the promise of ICTs for transforming agriculture in Africa. NEPAD e-Africa Commission, CSIR, Pretoria, South Africa. Available at: http://knowledge.cta.int/index.php/en/Dossiers/S-T-Issues-in-Perspective/ICT-fortransforming-research-for-agricultural-and-rural-development/Articles/Unlocking-the-Promise-of-ICTs-for-Transforming-Agriculture-in-Africa [Accessed 17/11/2018].

Oladele, O. I. (2006). Multilinguality of farm broadcast and agricultural information access inNigeria. *Nordic J. Afr. Studies,* Vol. *15, No.* 2, pp. 199-205.
Okon,U. A. (2015). ICT for Rural Community Development: Implementing the Communicative Ecology Framework in the Niger Delta Region of Nigeria. *IT for Development, Vol.21*, No.2, pp. 297-321.
Obinne, C.P. (1991). Adoption of improved cassava production technologies by small scale farmers in Bendel State. *Journal of Agriculture, Science and Technology,* Vol. 1, No. 1, pp. 12-15.
Ramirez, R. (2001). A model for rural and remote information and communication technologies: A Canadian exploration. *Telecommunications Policy*, Vol. 25, No. 5, pp. 315-330.
Rao, S. S. (2003). Information systems in Indian rural communities. Journal of Computer Information Systems, 44(1), 48-56.
Roman, R., and Colle, R. (2003). Content creation for ICT development projects: Integrating normative approaches and community demand. Information Technology for development, 10(2), 85-94.
Simumba, D. and Koopman, M. (2011). More effective information flow between researchers, extension officers and farmers in Zambia. Learning Brief, International Institute for Communication and Development (IICD). Livelihood, Zambia, January 2011.
Venkatesh, V., Morris, M. G., Davis, G. B., & Davis, F. D. (2003). User Acceptance of Information Technology: Toward a Unified View. *MIS Quarterly*,Vol. 27, No. 3, pp. 425-478.
World Bank. (2008). *World Data Bank, Africa Infrastructure: National Data.* Available at: http://databank.worldbank.org. [Accessed: 15/05/2018].
Wong, D. M. L. (2010). Knowledge management catalyst for sustainable development. ITSim 2010 (3), pp. 1444-1449.

COMPARATIVE ANALYSIS OF NATIONAL OPEN DATA PORTALS OR WHETHER YOUR PORTAL IS READY TO BRING BENEFITS FROM OPEN DATA

Anastasija Nikiforova
Faculty of Computing, University of Latvia
Rainis Boulevard 19, Riga, LV-1586, Latvia

ABSTRACT

This paper focuses on the analysis of usability of the national open data portals. Open [government] data are considered as one of the most influenceable tool for preventing and reducing corruption and reaching innovative solutions that create added value for society. Thus, it is important to ensure that they are provided in a form that are useful and suitable for the original purpose of the open data. Critical voices and many discussions on whether open government data and national open data portals are of sufficient quality appear more frequently. Therefore, this study deals with this topic and aims to find the main challenges that can negatively impact users' experience through an analysis of usability of 42 open data portals by applying a unified methodology on them allowing their comparative analysis to be carried out. This study highlights the weakest aspects for 42 national open data portals, pointing on both, the most common weakest points, and individual. The analysis carried out also identifies portals that can be considered as leaders and as an example for the less successful open data portals.

KEYWORDS

Open Data, Open Data Government, Open Data Portal, Usability of a Portal

1. INTRODUCTION

Open government data (OGD) initiative is an approach in which external stakeholders can play a greater role in the innovation of government services, providing citizens with new and innovative services, and have the capacity to play a catalytic role in co-creation of new public services (McBride et al., 2018). OGD also becomes the main topic of the 2030 Agenda for Sustainable Development (UNDESA, 2016). However, it is known that open data itself does not play an important role since value is generated by the use of data (Charalabidis et al., 2018). Therefore, barriers should be identified and solved.

According to (McBride et al., 2018), the most of OGD barriers are directly related to the release and publishing of open data, while at the user level, most of the barriers relate to their ability to use OGD, which is related to open data portals and, in particular, their usability. This is also in line with (Janssen et al., 2012), according to which, a sufficiently high-quality and user-friendly open data portal are needed, which allow access to the data for any stakeholder, resulting in the transformation of the data into a value for the society (Faini and Palmirani, 2016). While previous studies deal with quality of open data (Nikiforova, 2019, 2020b), this paper addresses this issue by focusing on the open data portal. One of the most important reasons for initiating such research is critical voices, which appear more frequently, addressing the current issue of the low quality of open data portals, which is a serious risk that can disrupt the open data project (Umbrich et al., 2015).

The aim of the study is to explore 42 national open data portals, by evaluating them from the perspective of the usability in order to understand the current state of national open data portals and compare them, trying to identify (a) key challenges and (b) portals which can be used as an example by other less competitive portals. As for the method used, the preference was given to the framework proposed in (Máchová et al., 2018) as one of the most recent and cited in the last 5 years. Such an assessment can be used to compare different portals, thereby helping governments and citizens to understand where the country is between other countries in the scope of certain aspects. Among other results, this study outlines the progress of national open data portals.

The paper addresses the following issues: a brief overview of the related researches (Section 2), an overview of the current state of national open data portals and rationale for research (Section 3), an analysis of 42 national open data portals, highlighting their main challenges (Section 4), and conclusions (Section 5).

2. RELATED WORKS

Although the popularity of the open data is increasing more rapidly, that is also reflected in the number of studies covering this topic, only a few studies cover the topic of open data portal. According to *Google Scholar* data analysed, despite the increase in popularity of the topics of the OGD and open data portals, the ratio of these researches to the researches dealing with open data does not exceed 7% (Nikiforova, 2020a). The usability of open data portals is being studied even less frequently, since over the last 5 years, only 6% of studies covering open data portal topic at least a little, mention the usability aspect. It also demonstrates the "uniqueness" of the presented research. However, it should be also mentioned that a number of benchmarks and indexes were recently introduced to assess the state of OGD and open data portals (a brief overview in (Nikiforova, 2020a)).

According to (Attard et al., 2015) and the author of this study, many researchers cover their own national OGD initiatives, which in most cases turns to the an assessment of national open data portals, assessing them from different perspectives, including aspects such as data, functionality, features, stakeholder participation, stakeholder feedback. Other studies focus on such aspects as the relevance of the open data sets of a specific portal to the "5-stars" classification (Matheus et al., 2012).

According to (Osagie et al., 2017), most of the studies focus mainly on data delivery and the data environment, considering what data providers have done to facilitate users, but have not actually consulted users. Thus, it appears that most of the frameworks lack a user perspective. In addition, most studies (a) mainly refer to one or just only a few countries without a comprehensive comparison between different initiatives, (b) lack a common methodology that would allow comparisons between studies and portals.

The study that drew the attention of the author of this paper to base the study on, is the framework proposed in (Máchová et al., 2018). This study proposes to evaluate open data portals using three key aspects, divided into 14 sub-aspects: (1) ***open data specification***, *which includes (a) description of data set, (b) publisher of data set, (c) thematic categories and tags, (d) release date and up to date, (e) machine readable formats, (f) open data licence, (g) visualization and analytics tools; (2)* ***open data set feedback***, *which includes (a) documentation and tutorials, (b) forum and contact form, (c) user rating and comments, (d) social media and sharing; (3)* ***open data set request***, *which includes such aspects as (a) request form, (b) list of requests, (c) involvement in the process.* According to the authors and studies underpinning this methodology, these 14 criteria reflect all the functionality of the portal and are typical tasks normally performed by users on the portal. In addition, it complies with the majority principles used or mentioned by other well-known researchers (see (Charalabidis et al., 2018), (Attard et al., 2015), (Zuiderwijk et al., 2015)). This methodology was found to be reasonably appropriate including the fact that it is cited by other researchers, meaning that it is accepted by the public/ researchers. It also considers a user perspective that, according to (Osagie et al., 2017), is one of the key challenges for most solutions. While (Máchová et al., 2018) analysed open data portals of Canada, Australia, India, UK, USA, this paper extends this significantly, by applying the methodology to 42 portals that allows to carry out comprehensive analysis, providing their comparison. Thus, common challenges and "good examples" are identified.

3. OPEN DATA PORTALS AND RATIONALE FOR THE RESEARCH

Nowadays, open data can be considered as a major step towards a digital society (Hansen and Schrøder, 2019). Many countries have established open data portals in order to provide access to open data sets, which allows public sector information to be opened to maximise their re-use by collecting and publishing different data catalogues to a wide audience for their further reuse (Attard et al., 2015). The development of software applications and services through open data provides many benefits to citizens and society as a whole, such as greater transparency, communication, acquisition of trust, innovation, and business value.

However, despite the fact that many countries develop and launch their own open data portals, they received a great deal of criticism from both, society by which is meant users who may not have IT knowledge, and technical experts. In other words, despite the fact that open data portals are intended to benefit and improve the re-use of open data and exploit its potential, the more often they do not achieve these aims and the poor usability of the open data portals is highlighted by complaining that these platforms were not intended for non-technical users ((Osagie et al., 2017), (Tinholt et al., 2013), (Purwanto et al., 2020)). The European Data Portal (Blank, 2019) and (Tinholt, 2013) also indicate that the usability is one of the main aspects of open data portals (among data availability, political leadership, and data portal usability). It follows from all the above that the quality of open data portals and, in particular, their usability are vital. This study deals with this issue. At present, one of the most comprehensive and up-to-date reports on open data portals is the *European Data Portal report* (Blank, 2019), which evaluates EU28+ national open data portals, assessing policy, portal, impact, and quality. As for the portal category, it is divided into 4 groups: feature, usage, data provision and sustainability.

Table 1 summarises the development of open data portals over the years (2016-2019) and ranking evolution ("up" and "down" arrows), based on the annual reports published by the European Data Portal. It shows whether and how fast portals are developing, what are the leading countries and which countries are less successful.

In 2019 (Blank, 2019) analysed 32 national open data portals and, according to Table 1, the best results were demonstrated by France, Spain, and Ireland. In terms of progress, the best progress in one year was demonstrated by Cyprus, which took 24th place in 2017, however came 2nd in 2018, but the most impressive negative result was demonstrated by Germany, which lost 23 positions between 2017 and 2018. Moreover, only four countries improve their positions from year to year – Ireland, Latvia, Italy, and Malta. The most impressive result in terms of continuous development was demonstrated by Latvia, which improves its position from the first appearance in this rating.

Table 1. The maturity of open data portals

Country	*2019*	*2018*	*2017*	*2016*	*Country*	*2019*	*2018*	*2017*	*2016*
France	1 ↑+4	5 ↑+3	8 ↓-5	3	Belgium	17 ↓-2	15 ↑+3	12 ↓-1	11
Spain	2 ↑+6	8 ↓-3	5 ↓-1	4	Estonia	18 ↑+8	26↑+10	16 ↓-14	2
Ireland	3	3	3 ↑+7	10	Denmark	19↑+10	29 ↑+2	27 ↓-10	17
Cyprus	4 ↓-2	2↑+22	24↓-6	18	Norway	20 ↑+2	22 ↓-8	14	14
Finland	5 ↓-4	1 ↑+5	6 ↑+3	9	Bulgaria	21 ↑+3	18	18 ↓-10	8
Slovenia	6 ↑+1	7↑+13	20↓-7	13	UK	22 ↓-6	16 ↓-5	11 ↑+5	16
Austria	7 ↑+3	10↓-1	9 ↓-4	5	Malta	23 ↑+8	31	31 ↑+1	32
Romania	8 ↓-4	4	4↑+11	15	Switzerland	24 ↓-7	17 ↑+8	25 ↓-3	22
Luxembourg	9	9 ↓-8	1	1	Portugal	25 ↓-2	23 ↓-4	19 ↑+1	20
Netherlands	10↑+4	14↓-4	10↓-3	7	Sweden	26 ↓-5	21 ↓-4	17↑+10	27
Latvia	11↑+8	19↑+2	21↑+9	30	Lithuania	27	27 ↑+1	28 ↓-3	25
Poland	12↓-1	11↑+12	23↑+1	24	Czech Republic	28	28 ↓-6	22 ↑+1	23
Italy	13	13	13↑+6	19	Slovakia	29 ↓-15	12 ↑+3	15 ↑+6	21
Germany	14↑+9	25↓-23	2 ↑+4	6	Hungary	30	-	30 ↓-2	28
Greece	15↓-9	6↑+20	26	26	Iceland	31 ↓-1	30 ↓-1	29	29
Croatia	16↑+4	20↓-13	7 ↑+5	12	Liechtenstein	32	-	32 ↓-1	31

↓-n – decrease in rank by n positions compared to the previous year
↑+n – improve in rank by n positions compared to the previous year
ranking (last column) – below EU28 average

As for the given research, a total of 40 users with IT background participated in the experiment, that corresponds to the experiment design proposed in (Máchová et al., 2018). The experiment took place from January to May 2020. This method was also chosen because the expert assessment was found to be one of the most appropriate methods for the OGD and related analyses (Susha et al., 2015).

4. ASSESSMENT OF OPEN DATA PORTALS

As in (Máchová et al., 2018), a three-level Likert scale (fulfilled - 3, partially fulfilled - 2, and unfulfilled – 1), that belongs to the acceptability tasks, was used to measure the usability of 42 national open data portals. Portals were selected by combining all portals addressed in (Blank, 2019), more precisely EU28+, by supplementing this list with portals originally addressed in (Máchová et al., 2018) - Canada, Australia, India, UK, USA, and some other portals on which positive feedback from their users are observed. 40 participants were selected on a voluntary basis to carry out this task, using in-group (between subject) observational method to reduce the potential subjectivity of the results, which cannot be obtained if the total number of participants is less than 30. This also means that if this experiment is replicated, the results may vary slightly, however, such a selection reduces it to a minimum and allows to carry out a comparative analysis, since all portals were assessed by the same group of participants. Each portal was analysed by assessing the fulfilment of 14 criteria representing 3 categories:

1) **open data specification** including such aspects as (**1a**) description of data set, (**1b**) publisher of data set, (**1c**) thematic categories and tags, (**1d**) release date and up to date, (**1e**) machine readable formats, (**1f**) open data licence, (**1g**) visualization and analytics tools;
2) **open data set feedback** including (**2a**) documentation and tutorials, (**2b**) forum and contact form, (**2c**) user rating and comments, (**2d**) social media and sharing;
3) **open data set request** including (**3a**) request form, (**3b**) list of requests, (**3c**) involvement in the process.

Table 2 summarises the results of the analysis, where (a) the 1st column is a portal ranking based on the results of the assessment (7th column "*Total*"), (b) 3rd column contains data regarding available languages, where the language notion corresponds with ISO 639-1 (two-letter codes), (c) 4th – 6th columns represents the score for three categories (*I* for open data specification, *II* for open data set feedback and *III* for open data set request) and 7th column is a total score that can vary from 14 to 42 points for each portal. The last column ("*Rank EDP*") contains the rank of the portal, according to (Blank, 2019) and Table 1.

The overall result of all aspects for all countries is 29.76 out of 42 points. Since the result is far from perfect, and, this applies to all portals, as none of the portals has scored more than 38.17 points (Cyprus), it can be concluded that there is room for improvements for all portals analysed.

The first category, namely "**open data set specification**", appears to be the best among the assessed, since it was assessed on average by 2.38 points out of 3 (total of 16.7 out of 21), while the second – "**open dataset feedback**" - gained only 1.98 points (total of 7.9 out of 12), however, "**open dataset request**" – 1.72 points (total of 5.2 out of 9).

For the first aspect - "*description of dataset*", the positive point is that most open data portals meet this requirement. However, nevertheless, data publishers often do not provide any or sufficiently detailed descriptions, and in many cases only the name of data set is recopied as a description, but in some cases the specification is missing and not even intended to appear that is the case for Malta. For the best results, which ranges between 17.9 and 20.2 point out of 21, they were demonstrated by France, Cyprus, Singapore, Portugal, Austria, Slovenia, Finland, India, Spain. However, the worst results were demonstrated by Malta, Czech Republic, Poland, Croatia, Belgium, Japan, Lithuania and Romania scoring between 12.41 and 15.3 points. As regards the "*publisher of dataset*", this information is mandatory for most open data portals. This is also valid for the majority of the aspects of this category.

For "**open dataset feedback**" category, which includes documentation and tutorials, forums and contact form etc., the most successful portals are Austrian, Finnish, Russian, Taiwanese, Portuguese, Cypriot and Romanian portals, estimated between 11.59 and 10.14 out of 12 points. However, this aspect appears to be very weak for Bulgaria, Sweden, Switzerland, Denmark, Hungary, Iceland, Liechtenstein and Japan, as the overall score is below 6 points.

In scope of the category of "**dataset requests**", the best results were demonstrated by New Zealand, Lithuania, Russia, Colombia, Canada, Spain and Cyprus, with a score of between 8.78 and 7.34 out of 9 points. The Irish portal has to be mentioned here, as it not only allows to request a data set, but also assumes that the request can be commented, and as a result the portal's employees explain to the users whether (and why) the request can or cannot be met, which is a great opportunity because it can create feedback and educate users, especially when users do not understand what data can be opened, that is the case for Latvia (Nikiforova, 2020a).

Table 2. Results of assessment of open data portals

#	*Country*	*Languages*	*I*	*II*	*III*	*TOTAL*	*Rank (EDP)*
1	Cyprus	EL, EN	20,2	10,63	7,34	**38,17**	**4**
2	Russia	RU, EN	16,61	11,39	8,49	**36,49**	N/A
3	France	EN, FR, ES	20,2	9,38	6,59	**35,93**	**1**
4	Spain	ES, CA, GL, EU, EN	17,97	9,58	8,01	**35,56**	**2**
5	Taiwan	EN, TW, CN	17,09	10,84	7,06	**34,99**	N/A
6	Canada	EN, FR	17,57	8,97	8,22	**34,76**	N/A
7	Austria	AU	18,84	11,59	**4,31**	**34,74**	**7**
8	Colombia	ES, EN	17,59	8,36	8,24	**34,19**	N/A
9	New Zealand	EN	17,67	7,26	8,78	**33,71**	N/A
10	Ireland	EN, GA	17,7	8,79	7,09	**33,58**	**3**
11	Portugal	EN, FR, ES, PT	19,01	10,69	**3,65**	**33,35**	25
12	Finland	FI, SV, EN	18,7	10,85	**3,35**	**32,9**	**5**
13	Lithuania	LT, EN	15,27	8,19	8,75	**32,21**	27
14	Slovenia	SL +Google Translate	18,71	9,15	**4,28**	**32,14**	**6**
15	India	EN	18,39	8,16	5,22	**31,77**	N/A
16	Netherlands	NL	15,97	8,41	7,16	**31,54**	10
17	Latvia	LV, EN	16,43	8,28	6,76	**31,47**	11
18	USA	EN	17,54	8,97	**4,63**	**31,14**	N/A
19	Singapore	EN	19,08	6,51	4,90	**30,49**	N/A
20	Estonia	EE, EN	16,81	8,66	4,94	**30,41**	18
21	Slovakia	SK, EN	16,08	9,48	4,58	**30,14**	29
22	Luxembourg	EN, FR	17,17	9,19	**3,61**	**29,97**	9
23	Romania	RO, EN +23 more*	15,29	10,14	**3,03**	**28,46**	8
24	Australia	EN	16,41	**6,25**	5,44	**28,1**	N/A
25	Germany	DE	15,52	8,67	**3,18**	**27,37**	14
26	Norway	NO	16,48	7,52	**3,33**	**27,33**	20
27	Croatia	CR	15,09	6,51	5,72	**27,32**	16
28	Sweden	SW	15,61	**4,94**	6,42	**26,97**	26
29	Greece	GR	16,79	6,9	**3,15**	**26,84**	15
30	Poland	PL, EN	**14,88**	6,61	5,01	**26,5**	12
31	Liechtenstein	EN, FR, PT, ES	15,93	**5,9**	4,63	**26,46**	32
32	Iceland	IS, EN	17,22	**5,7**	**3,23**	**26,15**	31
33	Japan	JP, EN	15,1	**5,96**	4,96	**26,02**	N/A
34	Switzerland	EN	16,63	**5,31**	**4**	**25,94**	24
35	Italy	IT	16,09	6,54	**3,09**	**25,72**	13
36	UK	EN	15,4	6,7	**3,5**	**25,6**	22
37	Belgium	EN, NL, FR, DE	15,1	6,88	**3,47**	**25,45**	17
38	Bulgaria	BG, EN	15,88	**4,89**	**4,29**	**25,06**	21
39	Hungary	HU +37 more*	15,81	**5,7**	3	**24,51**	30
40	Denmark	DA	15,58	**5,48**	**3**	**24,06**	19
41	Czech Republic	CZ, EN	**13,45**	**6,15**	**4,19**	**23,79**	28
42	Malta	EN, MT	**12,41**	**6,18**	**4,03**	**22,62**	23

n – competitive in a specific aspect, should be considered as an example
n – very weak result, improvement needs to be made, it is worth looking at leaders (in green)

The lowest results with 3 to 3.15 points were gained by Denmark, Hungary, Romania, Italy and Greece. It is also important to note that such a low overall assessment of this category is due to the fact that 22 out of 42 open data portals do not have the possibility to request a data set. As a result, it impacts both, the "*list of open datasets requests*" and "*involvement in the process*" aspects. Thereby the average score of this category is the worst among all analysed – only 5.16 out of 9 points.

As for more detailed results, the best aspects gained more than 2.5 out of 3 points are "*thematic categories and tags*" (2.64 points), "*open data licence*" (2.63), "*description of dataset*" (2.58) and "*publisher of dataset*" (2.46). However, even these results are not high enough, since this means that the assessment of these aspects is close to "partly fulfilled".

As regards the licence, which was assessed as one of the best aspects, this result is also relevant with (Máchová et al., 2018), where it was found that all portals assessed met this requirement because open data license is today the key part of each portal and all portals are available in machine-readable formats. However, according to (Janssen et al., 2012), only a few years ago, it was a great challenge. Moreover, even now in 2020, there are portals that either do not provide license information or use multiple licenses, where some of them assign limitations on data sets to be used. This aspect is challenging for Hungary, Czech Republic, Germany, Greece, Luxembourg.

The worst aspects for open data portals are the "*involvement in the process*" (1.54), "*list of open datasets requests*" (1.55), "*user rating and comments*" (1.65), "*visualization and statistics*" (1.77), "*forum and contact form*" (1.94). An important note here is that 4 out of 5 aspects are related (at least partly) to cooperation between data consumers and users that is one of the most important aspects in the case of open data portal. Moreover, in terms of cooperation and feedback – a total of 7 aspects - only 4 countries scored at least 17.5 out of 21 points – Spain (17.59), Canada (17.9), Cyprus (17.97), Russia (19.88), while a one more country scored more than 17 points – Canada (17.19). However, 6 countries scored less than 10 points (Italy, Switzerland, Bulgaria, Iceland, Hungary and Denmark). This means that improvements must be made as regards to these aspects since they are directly related to the main portals' objective.

A few more examples that demonstrate a positive example of involving data users are: (a) Cyprus and the assessment of user satisfaction through the "satisfactory survey" covering different aspects such as website design, organization/ searchability of data, formats of data sets, API, overall state of open data portal, which, in addition to other opportunities covered in the framework, supports the possibility for users to express their opinion by answering specific questions; (b) Spain, which provides an information on a list of events related to open data which facilitates public engagement, and organize so-called "challenges" to attract users; (c) Canada, which suggests "student challenges". These opportunities supply the abovementioned functionality; therefore, these additional aspects highlight these portals among others.

As for "*thematic categories and tags*", the majority of open data portals allocates data sets to different categories that mostly follows the same guidelines in regards of the nature of these categories, and the most portals provides a tags that are separated from categories. However, even this aspect sometimes is challenging. For instance, for the Latvia's open data portal, despite 14 different categories exist, by the end of May 2020 there were 102 data sets not belonging to any category, that is not related to poor design, because the publisher did not specify a category that should be assigned to the specific data set (Nikiforova, 2020a). As a result, the absence of the allocation to the specific category makes it difficult to find data sets if a user studies data sets by category. Some countries solve this challenge by involving the category "*other*" or "*uncategorized*", as in the case of Bulgaria.

As regards *visualisation and statistics* by which in (Máchová et al., 2018) are meant visualization and analytical possibilities for obtaining information about a data set, such as charts or visualizations in maps, this aspect is really weak, since it is assessed by 1.77 points (worst aspect for the 1st category) – sometimes the possibility of visualizing data is provided, but it is often ensured as a preview feature for data sets. The best results belong to Cyprus and Singapore scoring more than 2.8 points.

As for the "*user rating and comments*", this is often not provided, however, there are countries that provide a "good example" to others that should be considered and implemented. These countries are France, Cyprus, Austria, Romania, Canada and Taiwan, since the participants assessed this aspect very high.

As regards multilingualism (4th column in Table 2), that, according to (Zuiderwijk et al., 2015), is one of success factors of the open data initiatives since this facilitates the reuse of data (Attard et al., 2015), 33.33% of the portals analysed are available in only one language and only 42.86% of them are available in English, while other portals are available in only one country language, thereby reducing the number of potential users. In addition, it should also be noted that even if the portal is available in more than one language, only part of its content is sometimes translated, but most of the information is still provided in the main language. For some countries this may not have a serious impact, however, such "big players" as Germany, Denmark, Austria etc., may lose potential users. The worst results in the way of languages supported belong to Germany and Denmark, where portals support only relevant languages and are not suitable for English speakers, thereby limiting the portal's capabilities and the reuse of their data sets. Slovenia could be mentioned here as one of the unusual positive examples, since despite the fact that the portal is provided in only Slovenian, the portal holders provide a built-in *Google Translate* that allows the content of the entire portal to be adapted. In some cases, this option is even better than translation in several languages, since, as demonstrate the Romanian and Hungarian portals, in the case of attempts to provide as many languages as possible (35+), the most part of the content is not translated (e.g., name of data sets, their description, etc.).

One more aspect, that is considered as one of the key success factors for open data portals, is the presence of use-cases or showcases, by which are meant open data based applications published or at least mentioned in portal, thereby enabling users to get an insight of the potential of open data (Zuiderwijk et al., 2015). For the study carried out, 30 out of the 42 open data portals analysed (71.43%) provides showcases, which number may range from 3 (Slovakia) to 2044 (France). In addition, in some cases, such as France, Luxembourg or Portugal, the national portal has a "*use case upload*" feature. Moreover, 18 portals offer a mapping between the use cases and the data sets that these use cases are based on (for instance, Ireland), that should impact an insight of the potential of open data even better, thereby increasing public participation.

To sum up, Cyprus, France, Russia, Spain, Taiwan, Canada, Austria, Colombia, New Zealand, Ireland, Portugal demonstrated the best results, according to the 40 participants, while the portals of Malta, the Czech Republic, Denmark, Hungary, Bulgaria and Belgium are currently less successful in terms of their usability. This is partly in line with (Blank, 2019), however, as shown in Table 2, the results vary significantly for some countries, and this study shows some aspects that are most affected by such assessment. Thereby, their improvement would have an impact on the overall level of satisfaction of these portals, however, possible improvements can be obtained from the positive examples listed.

5. CONCLUSION

The popularity of open [government] data in recent decades has been growing more rapidly. Governments are moving toward e-governments, and OGD aims to facilitate these changes. However, it is well-known fact that open data by itself is not of great importance since value is generated by the use of data. It is therefore important to establish cooperation between data publishers and data consumers, that usually is done through a platform that can provide faster, better and different data usage opportunities. In other words, in order to benefit from the data being released and opened, a sufficiently high-quality and user-friendly open data portal should be provided, allowing access to the data for all stakeholders, which would result in the transformation of the data into value and knowledge for the society. This study addresses one of the most important aspects – the usability of open data portals.

42 national open data portals were analysed by applying to them a single common framework allowing their comparative analysis to be carried out. The analysis carried out demonstrates that there are portals that can be considered as leaders and as an example for the less successful open data portals that were also identified. However, this study demonstrates that even more successful open data portals have the room for improvements. In addition, the study shows that, in cases of less successful portals, certain aspects are sometimes better implemented.

This study highlights the weakest aspects for 42 national open data portals analysed, pointing on both, the most common weakest points, and individual. This should allow national open data portals to improve the usability of their portals, in particular, since 4 out of 5 weakest aspects are related (at least partly) to feedback and cooperation between data consumers and users.

It is intended to extend the results provided to a more detailed coverage of portals and individual aspects in order to provide comprehensive overview of the state of play of the open data portals. In addition, it is recommended that countries analyse their portals in depth, thereby extending this study, since some aspects should be covered by citizens of the country, as demonstrated in (Nikiforova, 2020a), by providing a set of aspects covered by the framework used with additional aspects, as well as by analysing data sets.

ACKNOWLEDGMENT

This work has been supported by University of Latvia Faculty of Computing project AAP2016/B032 "Innovative information technologies". I am also grateful to the participants for taking part in the experiment within my workshop "Open data and data quality", which allowed to collect data and led to such results.

REFERENCES

Attard, J. et al. (2015). A systematic review of open government data initiatives. *Government Information Quarterly*, 32(4), 399-418.

Blank, M. (2019) Open Data Maturity Report 2019, Europeam Data Portal, online: https://www.europeandataportal.eu/sites/default/files/open_data_maturity_report_2019.pdf

Charalabidis, Y. et al. (2018). The Open Data Landscape. In *The World of Open Data* (pp. 1-9). Springer, Cham.

Faini, F. and Palmirani, M. (2016). Italian Open and Big Data Strategy. In *International Conference on Electronic Government and the Information Systems Perspective* (pp. 105-120). Springer, Cham.

Hansen, H. S. and Schrøder, L. (2019). The Societal Benefits of Open Government Data with Particular Emphasis on Geospatial Information. In International Conference on Electronic *Government and the Information Systems Perspective* (pp. 31-44). Springer, Cham.

Janssen, M. et al. (2012). Benefits, adoption barriers and myths of open data and open government. *Information systems management, 29(4)*, 258-268.

Máchová, R. et al. (2018). Usability evaluation of open data portals. *Aslib Journal of Information Management*.

Matheus, R. et al. (2012). Anti-corruption online monitoring systems in Brazil. In *Proceedings of the 6th International Conference on Theory and Practice of Electronic Governance* (pp. 419-425).

McBride, K. et al. (2018). Open Government Data Driven Co-creation: Moving Towards Citizen-Government Collaboration. In *International Conference on Electronic Government* (pp. 184-195). Springer.

Nikiforova, A. (2020a). Assessment of Latvia's Open Data Portal or how Close are We to Gaining Benefits from Open Data (in preparation)

Nikiforova, A. (2020b). Definition and Evaluation of Data Quality: User-oriented Data Object-Driven Approach to Data Quality Assessment. *Baltic Journal of Modern Computing*, *8*(3).

Nikiforova, A. (2019). Analysis of Open Health Data Quality Using Data Object-Driven Approach to Data Quality Evaluation: Insights from a Latvian Context, In *IADIS International Conference e-Health 2019*, pp.119-126, MCCSIS 2019. IADIS.

Osagie, E. et al. (2017). Usability evaluation of an open data platform. In Proceedings of the *18th Annual International Conference on Digital Government Research* (pp. 495-504).

Purwanto, A. et al. (2020). Citizen engagement with open government data. *Transforming Government: People, Process and Policy*.

Susha, I. et al. (2015). Benchmarks for evaluating the progress of open data adoption: Usage, limitations, and lessons learned. *Social Science Computer Review*, 33(5), 613-630.

Tinholt, D. (2013). The Open Data Economy: Unlocking Economic Value by Opening Government and Public Data. *Capgemini Consulting*.

Umbrich, J. et al. (2015). Quality assessment and evolution of open data portals. In 2015 *3rd international conference on future internet of things and cloud* (pp. 404-411). IEEE.

UNDESA, U. (2016). Department of Economic and Social Affairs. United Nations e-government survey 2016: E-government in support of sustainable development.

Zuiderwijk, A. et al. (2015). Open data disclosure and use: Critical factors from a case study. *In CeDEM15: Conference for E-Democracy and Open Government* (Vol. 197). MV-Verlag.

COUNTER TERRORISM FINANCE BY DETECTING MONEY LAUNDERING HIDDEN NETWORKS USING UNSUPERVISED MACHINE LEARNING ALGORITHM

Amr Ehab Muhammed Shokry[1], Mohammed Abo Rizka[2,*] and Nevine Makram Labib[3,*]
[*]*Prof.*
[1]*College of Computing and Information Technology, AASTMT, Cairo, Egypt*
[2]*Dean of College of Computing and Information Technology, AASTMT, Cairo, Egypt*
[3]*Chair of Computer and Information Systems Department, SAMS, Cairo, Egypt*

ABSTRACT

Today's most immediate threat to address is terrorism. Terror organizations use illegal methods to raise their fund, such as scamming banks, fraud, donation, ransom and oil. This illicit money needs be laundered to be used within legal economy through financial institutions (FI). This paper is a complementary to our previous research. And it's proposes an unsupervised machine learning technique for detecting Money Laundering hidden patterns, groups and transactions in a timely manner to counter terrorism finance. Two different algorithms were implemented and performance was measured, compared and summarized. The preliminary experimental results show the effectiveness of the proposed technique. Domain experts confirm that the proposed method has produced efficient accurate results by identifying and detecting similarities, hidden patterns, grouping across all transactions and all the suspicious accounts involved.

KEYWORDS

Terrorism Financing, Money Laundering, Anti-Money Laundering, Machine Learning

1. INTRODUCTION

Considering the rapid growing threat of terrorism, Counter terrorism financing is becoming the most pressing matter for the globe. Terrorism financing even poor flows of money, can have a major impact by playing a part in serious terrorist crimes. Terrorism financing has become a major political issue, especially after the September 11th terrorist attacks in the United States. In the aftermath of these attacks, Financial Action Task Force (FATF) developed a series of Recommendations (FATF, 2006). Later, such recommendations approved officially as an international standard for counter money laundering, terrorism financing and weapons proliferation, issued in 1990, modified in 1996, 2001, 2003 and 2012 to guarantee that these recommendations are up to date and applicable. Terrorism Financing is often closely linked with money laundering, because criminals and terrorism organizations need to use illegally obtained money without drawing attention of law enforcement officials and deposit this money into financial institutions (FI). This can happen only if the money appears to be obtained through legal sources (to be laundered). So that money laundering acts as a mechanism for aiding terrorism financing. “Simply, Money laundering is the process that disguises illegal profits and integrate it with legal financial systems without exposing criminals who wish to benefit from these profits” (FATF, 2009). The amount of money laundered globally in one year is approximately 2-5 percent of global Gross Domestic Product (GDP) (UNODC, 2011).

Criminals use financial institutions (FI) to exploit weakness in the global financial system to blur the trail of illicit funds. FI are delegated by law to actively monitor report and detect suspicious activities to prohibit money laundering, finance of terrorism and corruption. Using all procedures, laws, policies, regulations, pieces of legislation, programs known as “counter financing of terrorism (CFT)” or “Anti money laundering (AML)”.

Money laundering has a three dynamic stage process that requires Placement, Layering and Integration. The placement stage where criminal or launderer moves black money from its illegal sources into financial institution both locally and abroad. The layering stage main purpose is to make it difficult to detect or trace all chaining transactions of black money by making different financial transfers like wire transfers between different accounts (one to many or many to many) various bank to bank transfers and changing the money's currency. The Integration stage for criminals and launderers is the easiest stage as money had entered legitimate financial institutions as if money has come from a legal transaction and it's impossible to detect a launderer with no documentation from the previous stages (Salehi et al, 2017). Detecting suspicious activities is becoming more and more difficult and tricky since the number of suspicious activities is increasing extraordinarily and the rules based systems alone is not enough to monitor those suspicious activities.

More recently, researchers have applied various artificial intelligence and machine learning techniques such as neural networks, genetic algorithms, fuzzy logic, clustering, sequence matching, Bayesian network, support vector machines (SVM), and outlier detection, in order to better detect and prevent suspicious transactions, activities and hidden patterns.

This paper aims at proposing an unsupervised machine learning technique for detecting Money Laundering hidden patterns, groups and transactions in a timely manner to counter terrorism finance. Paper is organized as follows: a literature review that deals with related work of different machine learning approaches and techniques used for money laundering detection, the methodology that describes the proposed model of money laundering detection using unsupervised machine learning approach in detail, and the evaluation and analysis that contains implementation detailed steps, environment and experimental results. The paper ends with a conclusion and future directions.

2. LITERATURE REVIEW

Detecting suspicious activities related to terrorism financing and money laundering is substantial and inevitable since it affects economy, industries, financial institutions and the entire nation. Because of large amount of banking data and enormous number of transactions involved, banks create a convenient environment for money launderers to hide the origins of money laundering and terrorism financing, so that money laundering techniques became more sophisticated and hard to trace. Hence, the solution for detecting money laundering must be balanced between accuracy and the process time. Finding a suitable technique for money laundering detection in financial institutions / banks is the most significant step for the solution, applying a suitable machine learning approach with a perspective of dataset. Money laundering detection approaches and techniques are varied and this makes comparisons difficult. "However, analyzing, reviewing and comparing various methods of money laundering detection is essential to detect money laundering crimes, patterns, unusual behavior and money laundering groups‖" (Labib et al, 2020). In this part, different machine learning approaches, methods and techniques will be introduced. They specifically do not belong to a particular approach of machine learning technique and are a combination of several methods used in pervious works.

Late 1990s statistical methods and sequence matching were implemented for money laundering detection (Phua et al, 2010), and then rule based methods were used. These methods depend on rules and reputation lists that can be implemented without AI expertise‖. However, it has to be permanently updated and it detects the most naive launderers only. Later on, financial institutions began to adopt statistical and machine learning models in their automated AML/CFT programs. Those models are highly challenging, due to the rising number of customer transactions and automated interaction with customers and this made anti money laundering compliance become more difficult. Some recent researches referenced that the large dataset size problem can be handled by applying supervised learning techniques which requires a labeled dataset to learn from, and then model classify new data into different label categories. Therefore, supervised learning models can only detect suspicious activities, transactions and patterns which are similar to training data. Nonetheless, many sophisticated modern day money launderers are still able to get around these Supervised Machine Learning models and fabricate new money laundering techniques, literally every day. (Wang et al, 2007) Validated the use of decision tree to create the detection rules of money laundering risk by customer's profiles of Chinese bank. Based on the rules generated, 12% of 160 thousand current customer profiles are considered high AML risk and need to be further monitored with regard to their future transactions. The study results specified the effectiveness of decision tree in generating anti money laundering rules from company's customer profiles and determining money laundering risks of bank customers. (Lv, L et al, 2008) Provided a new method to detect suspicious transactions using neural networks composed of three layers.

This method can adapt to the changing means of money laundering and used one million transaction records. The RBF neural network model is compared against SVM and outlier detection. The RBF neural network result was promising with a high detection rate and low false positives. (Keyan et al, 2011) Proposed the cross validation method to optimize selection of parameters of the support vector machine (SVM) model so as to improve the identification of suspicious financial transactions. Using 1.2 million transactions records, the results show that training SVM by employing the selection parameters by cross validation method has more effect than employing the randomly selected parameters on enhancing performance and improving detection of suspicious transactions. (Michalak et al, 2011) Presented a graph mining method to detect suspicious transactions and identify sub graphs within a network that closely matches known typologies. Their method is parameterized using fuzzy numbers which represent parameters of transactions and of the transaction sub graphs to be detected with a synthetically generated data set by simulating a mini economy. The study provided greater flexibility than simple studies using fuzzy matching where the sub graphs might deviate from given typology. (Khan et al, 2013) Used a new Bayesian network (BN) based technique to analyze transactions in a financial institution for suspicious behavior detection. Testing was on more than 8.2 million real financial transaction and more than hundred thousand accounts. Research indicate that new transactions will be considered suspicious activities if the activity has considerable variation to the pattern, but this might result a high false positive rate. (Savage et al, 2016) Described money laundering detection system that analyses group behavior, using network analysis and supervised machine learning. Using (AUSTRAC) unpublished data, System indicates that suspicious pattern and activity is detected with a suitable level of accuracy, high precision and a low false positives. Furthermore, other studies suggest applying semi supervised techniques which can learn from both labeled and unlabeled datasets; new data will be counted invalid if their behavior doesn't match with the training set. (Le Khac et al, 2010) Implemented a knowledge based approach that combines data mining and neural networks in bank to detect suspicious transactions or activities of money laundering using K-means clustering, neural network and genetic algorithm for 10 million real transactions records from CE-Bank. The results show that money laundering cases can successfully be detected within the investment activities, and, thus, improves learning process and the performance from current CE bank's solution in terms of running. (Liu et al, 2011) Presented a core decision tree algorithm to identify money laundering activities, apply a combination of decision trees with BRICH and K-means clustering algorithms in order to detect money laundering using unpublished data source. The study has identified suspicious transactions more effectively but it is too dependent on the strong performance of IBM mainframe and did not gain popularity due to the high cost. (Drezewski et al, 2015) Examined an approach applying the social network analysis for detecting money laundering. The system constructs social networks from the bank statements and National Court Register. The assignment of the roles to persons from the network shows that there are true leaders and vulnerabilities inside the network. The dataset is taken from the X banks disk files and web pages. The study showed that the SNA is a reliable and effective technique for money laundering detection. It also made it clear that finding algorithm is always faster than the interconnection analysis.(Shaikh et al, 2018) Proposed a model for identifying association and relationships within accounts and transactions, using Social Networks Analysis (SNA). For groups and gang mafia, those who play a vibrant role in money laundering activities can be identified by using (AUSTRAC) unpublished data. The study has successfully identified specific relations among illegal transactions and suspicious customers, such as businesses, parents, spouses, friends, and siblings.

Moreover, other recent researchers pointed out to apply unsupervised machine learning techniques that try to separate data points into different groups without having labeled datasets, these groups known as clusters, which hold data point's unique characteristics / patterns and are defined by similar member instances. Since financing systems, technologies and operations may vary from time to time, there is a need for new and up to date anti-money laundering systems. Unsupervised machine learning approaches, techniques and models that are more effective and able to detect new money laundering patterns earlier and identify all of the accounts associated with these money laundering groups without knowing what suspicious activity looks like. (Wang et al, 2009) Proposed a new algorithm for money laundering detection using improved minimum spanning tree clustering. The experiment on real 65,001 financial records from X bank shows that the new algorithm has not been affected by noise data, detection of suspicious money laundering transactions; it is complete and effective and has decreased dependency on the parameters. (Cao et al, 2012) Presented an implemented system for money laundering detection in Vietnam's banking industry using CLOPE algorithm for 8,020 transactions records from bank X. The results of the study have proved that CLOPE is a proper algorithm to detect money laundering based on the ability of analysts to provide a criterion for validating clusters after clustering. (Chen et al, 2014) Examined the use of expectation maximization for detecting suspicious financial transaction with 30 million transactions from local X bank in Malaysia. The results show that Expectation Maximization (EM) defeated traditional clustering method k -means for AML in detecting true suspicious transactions with low false positive rate, giving the advantage to EM to be employed in this field. (Paula et al, 2017) Presented results from implementing unsupervised deep learning model for detecting fraud suspects in Brazilian exports, using Auto-Encoder to detect anomalous transactions with regards to the data pattern. The datasets used in this work are 819,990 records from foreign trade of the Secretariat of Federal Revenue of Brazil. The experimental results reduced dimensionalities about twenty times faster, using Deep Learning Auto-Encoder in contrast with PCA proved to be successful detecting suspicious accounts of exporters. The model was able to detect anomalies in at least 20 exporters. (Camino et al, 2017) Presented the use of unsupervised learning methods without the use of ground truth to analyze financial transactions from different sources. The dataset used is from a publicly available data source (Ripple transaction data) and X private company. User ranking results have led to suspicious findings, detected expected anomalies and cases that weren't known before, confirmed that anomaly detection of user behavior is a must in both traditional and modern financing systems.

3. METHODOLOGY

This section describes the proposed model of money laundering detection using unsupervised machine learning approach in detail. The Model starts by reviewing the input dataset which contains banking transactions dataset wherein the researcher considers only cash debit and credit transactions, the pre-processing of the dataset, and the feature extraction, and then searches for anomaly transactions. Anomaly transactions are financial transactions that have common attributes such as similarity in deposit and withdrawal amounts, structuring and time series (transactions have been conducted in the same time window).

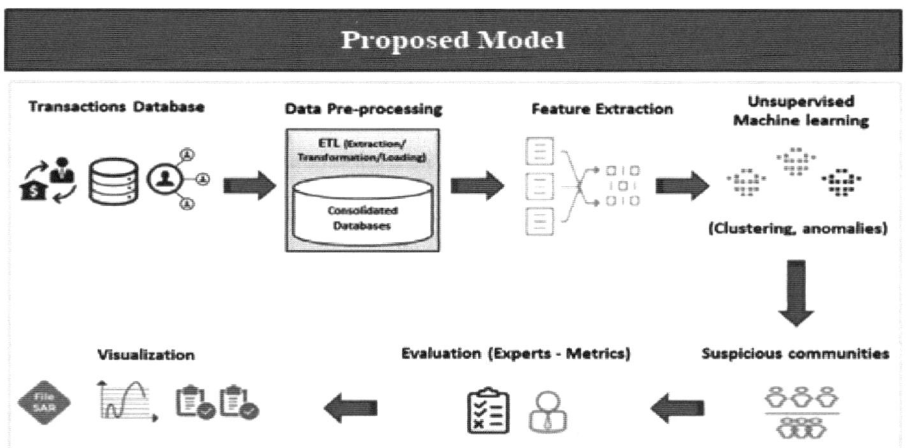

Figure 1. Model

Next, the model then applies an unsupervised machine learning algorithm method to find anomaly transactions and hidden patterns as frequent accounts should not be the only criteria for ending out the suspicious transaction as the case may be when the transaction does not occur frequently but even then they are illegal. With the chaining of accounts, suspicious account which identities the sure relation between these identified model will return then a list containing potential groups of money laundering accounts, Finally, the extracted list of (accounts, groups, and transactions) is rearranged, sorted and visualized to be validated by domain expertise as the output of the framework.

4. EVALUATION AND ANALYSIS

The implementation environment is Windows 10 Pro with 6 GB RAM Intel(R) Core(TM) i7- @ 3777 GHz. Implementation is carried out based on NumPy and mostly on its arrays. The Pandas package builds on the NumPy array object and contains a large number of mathematical functions that can operate on them. And Matplotlib library is a widely used package for Python that allows plotting. The sklearn ensemble includes an implementation of Isolation forest and One Class SVM that was used for this project.

4.1 Dataset and Feature Engineering

One of the difficulties with money laundering domain is the lack of datasets. There is a significant challenge to get realistic data, as real datasets are generally private and hard to get since transaction data and customer profiles are privacy sensitive. In experimentation, the researcher used 118250 transactions with three fraud patterns (Fan-in, Fan-out and Cycle) from a tailored synthetic dataset for an AML problem from (AMLSim) (Weber et al, 2018). As privacy of transaction data and customer profiles is not impacted, conducting and injecting different suspicious activity are controlled and defined by domain expertise. Transactions behave like normal bank account transfer money to other accounts and a small fraction of accounts make suspicious transactions modeled on real world patterns.

Feature engineering was mainly done by domain expertise, not analytically, only four relevant features numerical attributes remained, the input to the algorithm is a set of financial transactions; each transaction has the following four attributes:

- **Source Node Id**: The unique ID of the account sending the funds.
- **Target Node Id**: The unique ID of the account receiving the funds.
- **Amount**: The amount of funds being transferred.
- **Time**: The date and time of when the transfer takes place.

The dataset is comprised of three files containing three different money laundering patterns (Fan-in-Cycle-Fan-out) and normal transactions in CSV (comma separated values) format.

4.2 Experimental Results

The experimental results from implementing two unsupervised outlier detection Isolation Forest and One Class Support Victor machine for the synthetic AML data are generated from (AMLSim). The results and performance of the two algorithms can be seen in the following figures. Figure (2) shows the anomaly score of both algorithms where histogram x axis represents the anomaly score of the dataset and y axis represents the frequency of the transactions. Figure (3) determines the number of fraud and normal transactions in the entire dataset using both algorithms. Figure (4) represents consumed time for training of the two algorithms. Figure (4) represents consumed time for prediction of the two algorithms. Then Domain expertise results and evaluation, detailed results in Table (1). Hence, both algorithms were implemented on Synthetic AML data generated from (AMLSim).

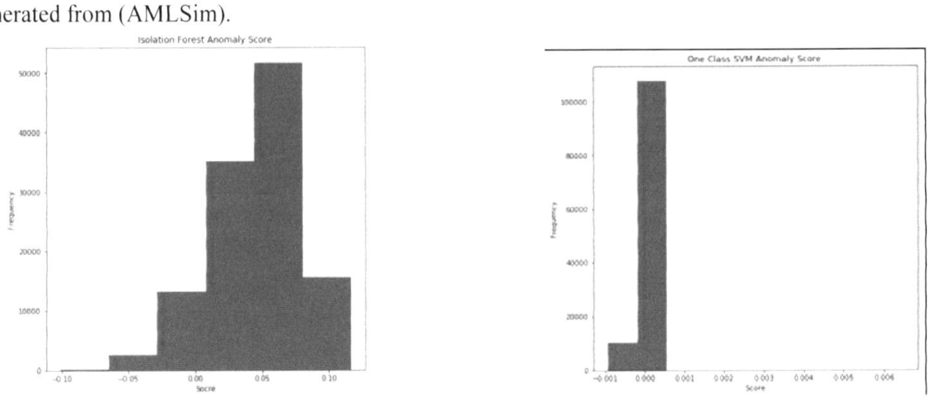

Figure 2. Shows the anomaly score of both algorithms

Figure 2 shows the transactions class distribution of the two algorithms which is to help know the number of fraud and normal transactions. Isolation Forest predicted 106425 transactions as normal transactions and 11825 transactions as suspicious (Fraud) transactions. On the other hand, One Class SVM prediction result was 107028 transactions as normal transaction and 11222 as suspicious (Fraud) transaction.

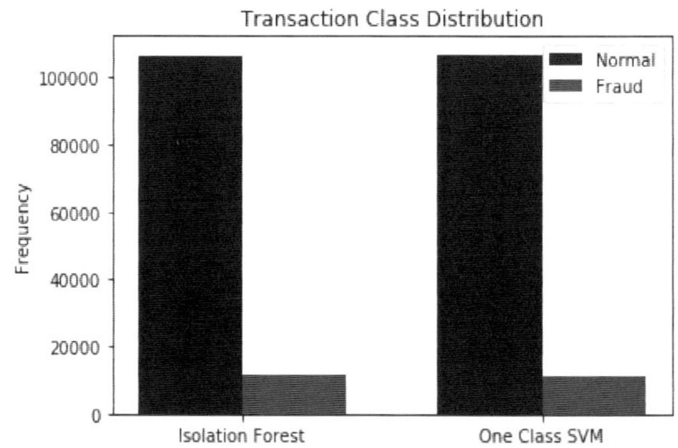

Figure 3. N.O fraud and normal transactions in the dataset

Isolation Forest performed much better than One Class SVM, as Isolation Forest detected 11825 anomalies versus One Class SVM detecting 11222 anomalies. Hence, the overall Isolation Forest method performed much better in determining the fraud cases.

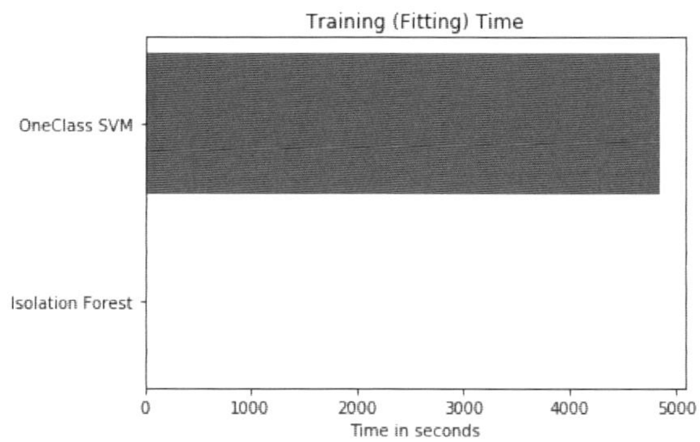

Figure 4. Training time for both algorithms

As discussed above, the One Class SVM algorithm performed badly in the consumed time for training / prediction and memory usage. As a comparison, Figure (4) and Figure (5) are the results of training time parameter where Isolation Forest consumed 7.0073 seconds. On the other hand, One Class SVM consumed 4836.9632. As for the prediction time parameter, Isolation Forest consumed 5.1798 seconds while One Class SVM consumed 911.1394.

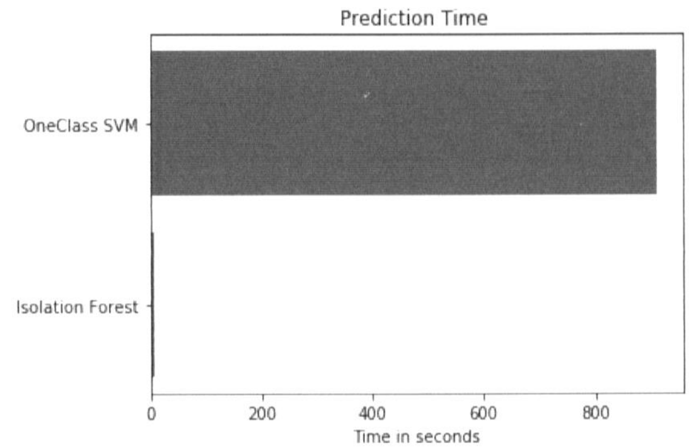

Figure 5. Prediction time for both algorithms

About One Class SVM, it runs fine for somewhere in the 10s of thousands, but 100s of thousands take very long. However, financial institutions have tons of data and do not want to wait for days, and maybe even more for nothing to come of it, and miss the chance of preventing fraud transactions before they take place. Nonetheless, Isolation Forest showed a promising performance, low time complexity and low memory usage, and, thus, it is clear that the Isolation Forest was much better than the One Class SVM algorithm at time complexity and memory usage, as predicted by the theory.

Evaluation was done by domain experts as a sample test of 5000 records and the results of suspicious transactions were analyzed by anti-money laundering analysts and officers. It is important to highlight the investigation results of Isolation Forest implementation and the following aspects are about the analysed cases as a sample test: All cases classified by the system are considered high risk, whereas 50 cases were clearly identified as suspects with a 414 suspicious transaction and 4 Money Laundering groups.

Table 1. Detailed results of domain experts from IF Findings

Procedure	Result
Number of matched transactions	414
Number of Money Laundering nodes identified	50
Number of Money Laundering groups identified	4

5. SYNTHESIS AND DISCUSSION

The method of using Isolation Forests for the anomaly detection in money laundering / terrorism financing detection prevention field is still relatively new. It is no secret that detecting suspicious transactions, patterns and groups has become more challenging as money launderers have become more sophisticated. Advanced outlier detection methods, such as Isolation Forests, are imperative for financial institutions detecting and preventing money laundering / terrorism financing because isolation forest (Liu et al, 2008) is an ensemble regressor and uses concept of isolation to "explain / separate away anomalies, no profiling of normal instances and no point based distance calculation. Instead, isolation forests builds an ensemble of random trees for a given dataset and anomalies are points with the shortest average path length", mainly different from all existing techniques, such as One Class SVM which is different from (Support Vector Machine) a boundary is created around normal data points to separate them from the anomalous ones. It can find nonlinear boundaries with the help of kernel functions, but its accuracy is degraded if too many anomalies are present in the training dataset. However, Isolation Forests exploit subsampling to achieve a small memory requirement, low linear time complexity and to deal with swamping and masking, building it's model using small subsamples of fixed size regardless of dataset size and detects anomalies based on isolation without using density measure. This improves detection rates and reacts in a timely manner to new money laundering / terrorism financing patterns. On the other hand, One Class SVM classifier training time increases exponentially with the size of training data and also prediction time. However, no one has figured out the problem yet. The researcher considers time parameter an issue as it eliminates the chance of detecting and preventing the suspicious transaction before it is completed.

Interpreting the results from an unsupervised learning scheme is a very difficult task; interpreting and evaluating the results from detected suspicious/money laundering transactions have been difficult in this research as well. Isolation Forest showed a great, promising result and should be a better algorithm for the current problem than One Class SVM. As discussed above, both algorithms were good at handling outliers, but Isolation Forest results are easier to interpret. Furthermore, for the consumed training/prediction time and memory usage, there is a huge difference from One Class SVM, achieving low linear time complexity and a small memory requirement, dealing with the effects of swamping and masking effectively, higher transparency and interpretability of the results.

6. CONCLUSION

This paper motivated the challenge of detecting money laundering which is a crucial step and mechanism for countering terrorism financing, encouraged technical research community to help financial institutions and law enforcement harness artificial intelligence technologies to counter terrorism financing. Normal financial activities / transactions behavior is chaotic, but money laundering / terrorism financing activities make patterns, whether criminals recognize it or not. From a theoretical point of view, It is confirmed that unsupervised machine learning approach is a more suitable machine learning approach, than supervised and semi supervised approaches for the current problem due to its ability to detect similarities, hidden patterns, structures or grouping across all transactions without prior training, it detects suspicious activities without knowing what suspicious activity behavior or pattern looks like and this is a huge differentiator from and rule based models, supervised and semi supervised which requires knowledge of suspicious patterns / activities to detect similar ones.

Researcher reviewed current AML methods and provided implementation to two unsupervised approaches (Isolation Forest – One Class SVM) for transaction monitoring using a tailored synthetic dataset for an AML problem (AMLSim).

Isolation Forest was much better than One Class SVM algorithm at time complexity and memory usage. Therefore, Isolation Forest algorithm seems more useful, effective and can detect suspicious transactions in a timely manner before transaction is completed or money gets to criminals' hands in the context of anti-money laundering / counter terrorism financing.

Domain experts confirmed that Isolation Forest has produced higher efficient results and accurate findings, and improved the efficiency of the existing anti money laundering techniques by identifying and detecting similarities, hidden patterns, structures or grouping across all transactions and all chaining suspicious accounts involved.

7. FUTURE DIRECTION

In near future, to better assess the effectiveness and evaluate performance of the proposed model, researcher aims to install the proposed model or conduct experiments on real financial data and real life scenarios from financial institutions which would help in fine tuning the proposed approach. The researcher is planning to focus on the detection of unexpected changes in user's behavior and will extend the analysis methods in order to automatically discover the money laundering patterns in real time.

REFERENCES

Action, F. and Force, T. (2006) "FATF Special Recommendations on Terrorist Financing," *Financing Terrorism*, 2001(February 2008), pp. 131–145. doi: 10.1007/0-306-48044-1_9.

Fatf-gafi.org. (2009). Money Laundering - Financial Action Task Force (FATF). [online] Available at: https://www.fatf-gafi.org/faq/moneylaundering/.

United Nations Office on Drugs and Crime (2011) "Estimating Illicit Financial Flows Resulting from Drug Trafficking and other Transnational Organized Crimes," *United Nations Office on Drugs and Crime*, (October), pp. 1–140.

Salehi, A., Ghazanfari, M. and Fathian, M. (2017) "Data mining techniques for anti money laundering," *International Journal of Applied Engineering Research*, 12(20), pp. 10084–10094.

Labib, N. M. and Rizka, M. A. (2020) "Survey of Machine Learning Approaches of Anti-money Laundering Techniques to Counter Terrorism Finance". Springer Singapore. doi: 10.1007/978-981-15-3075-3.

Phua, C. *et al.* (2010) "A Comprehensive Survey of Data Mining-based Fraud Detection Research." doi: 10.1016/j.chb.2012.01.002.

Wang, S. N. and Yang, J. G. (2007) "A money laundering risk evaluation method based on decision tree," *Proceedings of the Sixth International Conference on Machine Learning and Cybernetics, ICMLC 2007*, 1(August), pp. 283–286. doi: 10.1109/ICMLC.2007.4370155.

Lv, L. T., Ji, N. and Zhang, J. L. (2008) "A RBF neural network model for anti-money laundering," Proceedings of the 2008 International Conference on Wavelet Analysis and Pattern Recognition, ICWAPR, 1(1), pp. 209–215. doi: 10.1109/ICWAPR.2008.4635778.

Keyan, L. and Tingting, Y. (2011) "An improved support-vector network model for anti-money laundering," *Proceedings - 2011 International Conference on Management of e-Commerce and e-Government, ICMeCG 2011*, pp. 193–196. doi: 10.1109/ICMeCG.2011.50.

Michalak, Krzysztof & Korczak, Jerzy. (2011)" Graph Mining Approach to Suspicious Transaction Detection.". Federated Conference on Computer Science and Information Systems, FedCSIS 2011. 69-75.

Khan, N. S. *et al.* (2013) "A bayesian approach for suspicious financial activity reporting," *International Journal of Computers and Applications*, 35(4), pp. 181–187. doi: 10.2316/Journal.202.2013.4.202-3864.

Savage, D. *et al.* (2016) "Detection of money laundering groups using supervised learning in networks," pp. 43–49. Available at: http://arxiv.org/abs/1608.00708.

Le Khac, N. A. and Kechadi, M. T. (2010) "Application of data mining for anti-money laundering detection: A case study," *Proceedings - IEEE International Conference on Data Mining, ICDM*, pp. 577–584. doi: 10.1109/ICDMW.2010.66.

Liu, R. *et al.* (2011) "Research on anti-money laundering based on core decision tree algorithm," *Proceedings of the 2011 Chinese Control and Decision Conference, CCDC 2011*, pp. 4322–4325. doi: 10.1109/CCDC.2011.5968986.

Drezewski, R., Sepielak, J. and Filipkowski, W. (2015) "The application of social network analysis algorithms in a system supporting money laundering detection," *Information Sciences*, 295, pp. 18–32. doi: 10.1016/j.ins.2014.10.015.

Shaikh, K. A. and Nazir, A. (2018) " A Model for Identifying Relationships of Suspicious Customers in Money Laundering using Social Network Functions," *Proceedings of the World Congress on Engineering*, 1, pp. 4–7. Available at: http://www.iaeng.org/publication/WCE2018/WCE2018_pp141-144.pdf.

Wang, X. and Dong, G. (2009) "Research on money laundering detection based on improved minimum spanning tree clustering and its application," *2009 2nd International Symposium on Knowledge Acquisition and Modeling, KAM 2009*. IEEE, 2, pp. 62–64. doi: 10.1109/KAM.2009.221.

Cao, D. K. and Do, P. (2012) "Applying Data Mining in Money Laundering Detection," *Intelligent Information and Database Systems*, pp. 207–216.

Chen, Z. *et al.* (2014) "Exploration of the effectiveness of expectation maximization algorithm for suspicious transaction detection in anti-money laundering," *ICOS 2014 - 2014 IEEE Conference on Open Systems*, pp. 145–149. doi: 10.1109/ICOS.2014.7042645.

Paula, E. L. *et al.* (2017) "Deep learning anomaly detection as suppor fraud investigation in Brazilian exports and anti-money laundering," *Proceedings - 2016 15th IEEE International Conference on Machine Learning and Applications, ICMLA 2016*, pp. 954–960. doi: 10.1109/ICMLA.2016.73.

Camino, R. D. *et al.* (2017) "Finding suspicious activities in financial transactions and distributed ledgers," *IEEE International Conference on Data Mining Workshops, ICDMW*, 2017-November, pp. 787–796. doi: 10.1109/ICDMW.2017.109.

Weber, M. *et al.* (2018) "Scalable Graph Learning for Anti-Money Laundering: A First Look," (1970). Available at: http://arxiv.org/abs/1812.00076.

Liu, F. T., Ting, K. M. and Zhou, Z. H. (2008) "Isolation forest," *Proceedings - IEEE International Conference on Data Mining, ICDM*, (October), pp. 413–422. doi: 10.1109/ICDM.2008.17.

THE ROLE OF SUSTAINABLE TRANSPORTATION IN THE PUBLIC HEALTH IMPROVEMENT

Raed Nayif Alahmadi
Dr., Assistant Professor of Transportation Engineering,Albaha University,Civil Engineering Department Albaha City, Kingdom of Saudi Arabia

ABSTRACT

This paper introduces sustainable transportation and its role in public health improvement. It goes through the effect of Transportation policy and planning decisions in health. It discusses the Sustainable Transportation Area of impact in terms of Traffic Accidents, Pollution Emissions, Physical Activity and Fitness, Mental Health Impacts, Affordability, and Basic Mobility. This paper indicates that public transit improvements and more transit-oriented development can provide largely but often-overlooked health benefits. People who live or add communities with high-quality conveyance tend to drive significantly less and rely more on alternative modes (walking, cycling, and public transit) than they would in more automobile-oriented areas. This reduces traffic crashes and pollution emissions increase physical fitness and mental health, and provides access to medical care and healthy food.

KEYWORDS

Transportation, Health, Traffic, Sustainable

1. INTRODUCTION

Numerous researchers, institutes, and government organizations are working on reducing traffic congestion and building a sustainable transportation system all around the world. The common conclusion for this problem is that it is not feasible to continue to consume resources at current rates and the time is limited to take action. These conclusions cause the thought of sustainable development implementations on transportation systems. "Sustainable development" was defined by the United Nations' Report in 1987 as; "generating a development which meets the needs of the present without compromising the ability of future generations to fulfills their own needs." This definition is often restatement for systems of transportation as ensuring that future generations' need for mobility and transport will not be compromised. Researchers, governors, decision-makers, etc. are still working on building a sustainable world, and sustainable transportation systems, however, the results of these efforts do not indicate significant improvements. The concept of sustainable development is not straightforward since it has various indicators. For instance, transportation affects fuel (petroleum) reserves, global atmosphere, local air quality, sound pollution, level of mobility, congestion rate, and mortality rates (fatalities and crashes). Congestion and level of mobility are directly affected by the increase of VMT and the number of vehicles. Today in most urban areas, traffic congestion is one of the main concerns of residents. Even the local government agencies invest enormous amounts of money to expand roads and reduce congestion; however, the results of these investments do not indicate significant benefits since the existing roads cannot be expanded to the infinity. In addition, congestion is the main reason for low air quality in urban areas, due to vehicle emissions. Traffic crashes are another issue that should be included as a part of sustainable development. According to the World Health Organization (WHO), crashes are responsible for almost 1 million fatalities each year and nearly 70 million injuries (2001) (World Health Organization, 2004). Fortunately, per 100 million VMT mileage death rates are decreased from 2 to 1.25 in the last 10 years in the U.S. This decrease in crash rates can be explained by an increase in enforcement of traffic laws and new traffic regulations by the U.S. Government in last decade. Also, every crash costs a significant amount of money to society. For instance, a moderate injury crash costs $392,000 and where fatality crash costs $4.2M in 2009 dollars (costs converted from the year 2000 to the year 2009 by consumer price index). A template may be a set of designs and page layout settings that determine the looks of a document.

2. SUSTAINABLE TRANSPORTATION

Sustainable transport as a term came into use as a logical follow-on from sustainable development and is used to elucidate modes of transport, and systems of transport planning, which are consistent with wider concerns about sustainability. There are many definitions of sustainable transport, and of the related terms of sustainable transportation and sustainable mobility. One such definition, from the ECU Union Council of Ministers of Transport, defines sustainable transportation together that:

- Allows the essential access and development needs of individuals, companies, and society to be met safely and during a manner according to human and ecosystem health, and promotes equity within and between successive generations.
- Is affordable, operates fairly and efficiently, offers a choice of transport mode, and supports a competitive economy as balanced regional development.
- Limits emissions and waste within the planet's ability to soak up them uses renewable resources at or below their rates of generation and uses non-renewable resources at or below the rates of development of renewable substitutes while minimizing the impact on the utilization of land and therefore the generation of noise.

Sustainability can extend beyond just emissions, efficiency, and operating. A life-cycle assessment involves production, use, and post-use considerations. Cradle-to-cradle design is more important than attention to one factor like energy efficiency. Sustainable transport refers to the broad subject of transport that is sustainable within the sense of social, environmental, and climate impacts. Elements for evaluating sustainability contains the actual vehicles used for road, water, or air transport; the source of energy; and thus the infrastructure wont to accommodate the transport (roads, railways, airways, waterways, canals, and terminals). Transport operations and logistics as transit-oriented development also are involved in the evaluation. Transportation sustainability is essentially being measured by transportation effectiveness and efficiency because of the environmental and climate impacts of the system. Short-term activity often encourages incremental improvement in fuel efficiency and vehicle emissions controls while long-term goals include migrating transportation from fossil-based energy to other alternatives like renewable energy and the use of other renewable resources. The whole life cycle of transport systems is subject to sustainability measurement and optimization. Sustainable transport systems make a positive contribution to the social, environmental, and economic sustainability of the communities they serve. Transport systems exist to supply social and economic connections, and other people quickly take up the opportunities offered by increased mobility, with poor households benefiting greatly from low carbon transport options. The advantages of increased mobility got to be weighed against the environmental, social, and economic costs that transport systems pose.

Transportation may be a tricky thing to research within the context of sustainability. It consists of part of the built environment: the physical infrastructure of roads, runways, airports, bridges, and rail lines that makes it possible for us to get around. It also consists partially of individual choices: what mode we use to urge around (car, bus, bike, plane, etc.), what time of day we travel, what percentage people we travel with, etc. It is also made from institutions: federal and state agencies, oil companies, automobile manufacturers, and transit authorities, all of whom have their own goals and their own ways of shaping the choices we make. Most importantly, transportation is complicated because it is what is called derived demand. With the exception of joyriding or taking a walk or bicycle ride for exercise, very rarely are we traveling just for the sake of moving. We are usually going from Point A to Point B. What those points are home, work, school, shopping and where they are located downtown, in a shopping mall, near a freeway exit influence how fast we need to travel, how much we can spend, what mode we are likely to take, etc. The demand for transportation springs from other, non-transportation activities. To know transportation sustainability, we have to know the spatial relationship between where we are and where we would like to travel, and therefore the infrastructure and vehicles that can help get us there. How can we set about making transportation more sustainable? There are three main approaches: inventing new technologies, charging people the complete costs of travel, and planning better so we increase accessibility but not mobility.

3. TRANSPORTATION HEALTH IMPACTS

The policy of transportation and planning decisions can affect health in various ways. How people travel affects physical and mental states, including cancer, disorder, vehicle crashes, and diabetes, four major causes of death. This section discusses the major categories of public health impacts that tend to be significantly affected by transport policies and planning decisions. Travel activity affects public health in several ways. Figure 1 indicates ways in which travel activity affects the ten leading causes of Potential Years of Life Lost (PYLL, which takes under consideration age of death and thus reflects the larger costs to society of risks to younger people). The contribution of pollution in some diseases is noticeable like cancer and congenital anomalies (birth defects) whereas sedentary living (inadequate physical activity) contributes to heart condition and strokes. Transport activity affects five of those health risks, including the three largest, which cause quite 60% of total potential years of life lost.

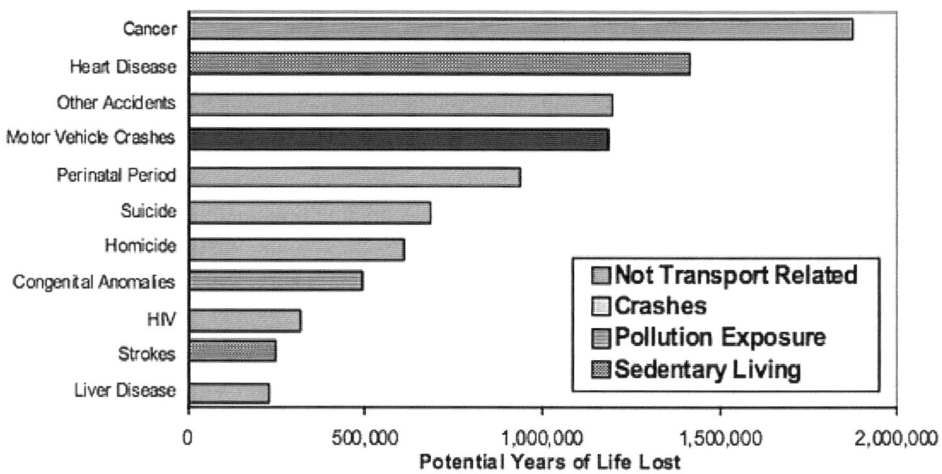

Figure 1. Ten Leading Causes of Potential Years of Life Lost (NCIPC 2009)

Of course, these relationships are complex. There are often several steps between a planning decision and its ultimate health impacts. Transportation activities are only a minor contributor to some of these risks. For example, motor vehicles are only one source of pollution, and pollution is only one contributor to cancer and congenital anomalies, while sedentary living increases some forms of cancer, which are not reflected in this figure.

4. SUSTAINABLE TRANSPORTATION AREA OF IMPACT

4.1 Traffic Accidents

Traffic crashes are a major cause of injuries and deaths (together called casualties), particularly for people aged 4–44 years. This risk can be viewed in different ways, which lead to different conclusions about this danger and the effectiveness of traffic safety strategies. The conventional paradigm assumes that motor vehicle travel is overall safe and that most crashes result from specific high-risk groups and behaviors, such as inexperienced and impaired driving, so safety programs should target these drivers and activities. From this perspective, it is inefficient and unfair to increase safety by reducing overall vehicle travel because this punishes all motorists for problems caused by an irresponsible minority.

Crashes can be measured in different ways, which result in different conclusions about the risk of different modes and activities. Distance-based units, such as fatalities per 100 million vehicle-miles, ignore the additional risk that results from increased vehicle mileage and the safety benefits of travel reductions. Conventional traffic safety analysis tends to measure crash rates per unit of travel (i.e., injuries and fatalities per million vehicle-miles or billion passenger-kilometers). Evaluated this way, US crash rates declined nearly 80% between 1965 and 2010, indicating that conventional safety programs were successful. However, per capita vehicle travel more than doubled during this period, which largely offset declining per-kilometer crash rates (Figure 2). The mileage-based fatality rate declined by more than two thirds during this period, which implies that existing safety programs were effective. However, this was offset by increased mileage. When measured per capita, as with other health risks, there was little improvement despite significant increases in use of safety devices (seatbelts, helmets, airbags, etc.), reductions in intoxicated driving, improved road and vehicle design, faster emergency response, and improved medical care. Considering these factors, much greater casualty reductions should have occurred. For example, seatbelt use grew from virtually zero in 1960 to about 75% in 2000, which alone should have reduced traffic fatalities 33% (seat belt use reduces crash fatality rates about 45%), yet, per capita traffic deaths declined just 25% during this period.

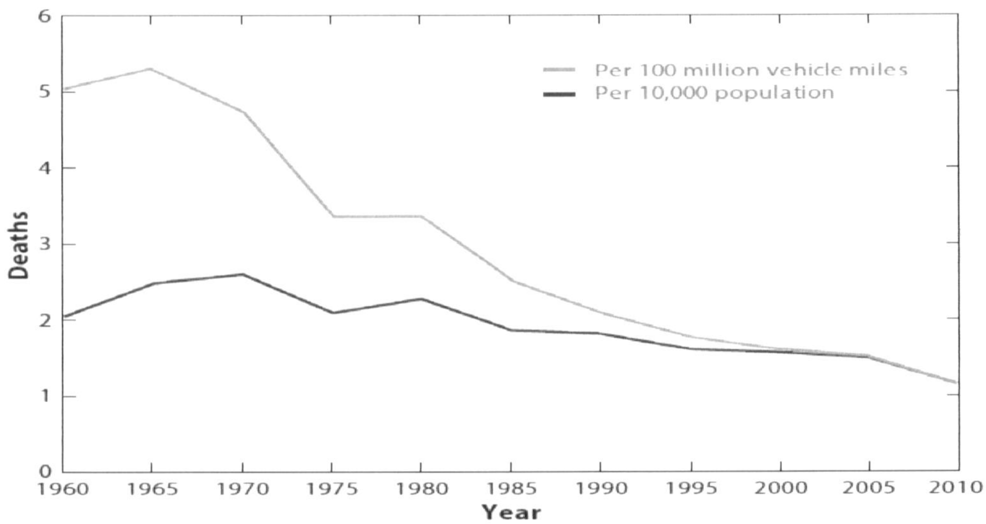

Figure 2. U.S. Traffic Fatalities between 1965 and 2010

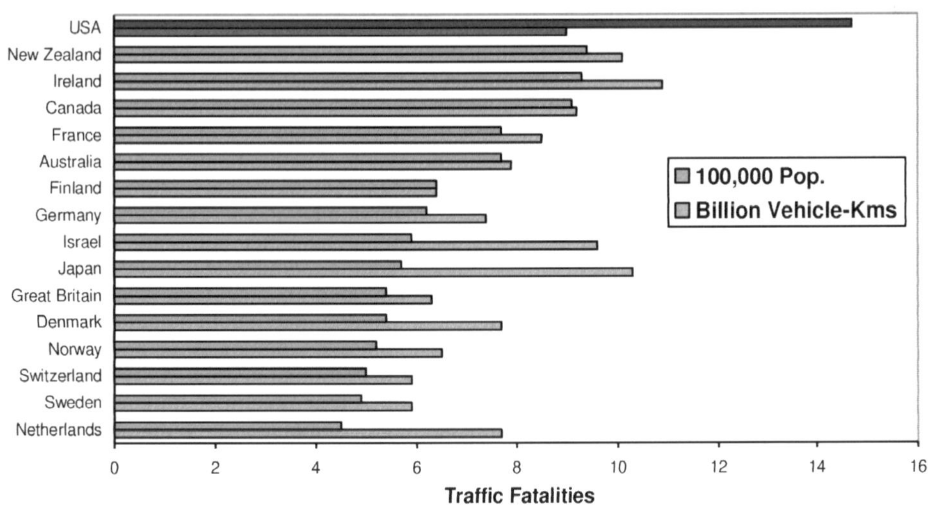

Figure 3. International Traffic Fatalities (Wikipedia 2009; based on WHO and OECD data)

Traffic crashes still be one among the most important causes of deaths and disabilities for people aged 1-44 years. The U.S. has one of the lowest traffic fatality rates per vehicle-mile, it's one among the very high traffic fatality rates per capita, as illustrated in Figure 3, from this attitude, traffic risk continues to be a serious problem, despite high-quality highways and vehicles, and well-established safety programs. From this attitude, traffic crashes still be a serious health risk and new strategies could be justified to realize safety targets. Public transit may be a relatively safe mode, with only about one-twentieth the passenger death rate as automobile travel. Even considering risks to other road users, transit travel tends to possess a lower death rate per passenger-mile than automobile travel under equivalent conditions.

4.2 Pollution Emissions

Transport systems are major emitters of greenhouse gases, liable for 23% of world energy-related GHG emissions in 2004, with about three quarters coming from road vehicles. Currently, 95% of transport energy comes from petroleum. Consumption of energy within the manufacture also because of the use of vehicles and is materialized in transport infrastructure including bridges, railways, and roads.

The first historical attempt of evaluating the Life Cycle environmental impact of the vehicle is due to Theodore Von Karman. After decades during which all the analysis has been focused on emending the Von Karman model, Dewulf and Van Langenhove have introduced a model supported the second law of thermodynamics and exergy analysis. Chester and Orwath, have developed a similar model based on the first law that accounts for the necessary costs for the infrastructure.

Many factors affect vehicle pollutant human health impacts, including per capita vehicle mileage, vehicle emission rates, and exposure (the number of individuals located where emissions are concentrated). The number of premature deaths as traffic crashes is similar to the number of death due to motor vehicle pollution, although pollution victims tend to be older then cause smaller reductions in Potential Years of Life Lost than traffic crashes.

Public transit tends to supply less pollution per passenger-mile, particularly electric-powered and newer diesel vehicles, and as previously described, transit-oriented development tends to scale back per capita vehicle travel and associated emissions. Older diesel buses tend to possess high emission rates and bus transit tends to concentrate activity on the brink of roadways, so under some circumstances increased transit use may rise human exposure to some pollutants such as carbon monoxide and particulates. However, newer and alternative fuel buses produce far fewer emissions. Using fuels of less polluting (like natural gas) increased from just 2.0% in 1992 to 30.4% by 2009, and electric modes (electric trolleybuses and electric rail transit) increased from 29% to 34% of passenger-miles during an equivalent period.

The environmental impacts of transport are often reduced by reducing the load of vehicles, sustainable kinds of driving, reducing the friction of tires, encouraging electric and hybrid vehicles, improving the walking and cycling environment in cities, and by enhancing the role of conveyance, especially electric rail.

4.3 Physical Activity and Fitness

One of the major categories of health impacts concerns the effects that transport-planning decisions have on physical activity and fitness. Public health officials are increasingly concerned about declining fitness, excessive weight, and resulting increases in diseases like diabetes. They recommend that adults average a minimum of 150 weekly minutes (about 22 daily minutes) of moderate-intensity physical activity, and youngsters average about 3 times that quantity. A meta-analysis of 22 cohort studies concluded that, against a reported lack of physical activity, 2.5 hours of moderate activity per week were allegedly reduced by 19% in mortality, and 7 hours per week associated with a 24% decrease. In recent years, public health officials became increasingly alarmed at declining fitness and resulting increases in diseases related to sedentary lifestyles. Inadequate physical activity, and leading to excessive weight, contribute to heart and vascular diseases, strokes, diabetes, hypertensive diseases, osteoporosis, joint and back problems, colon and breast cancers, and depression. Even modest reductions in these illnesses can provide large savings and benefits. The World Health Organization (WHO 2000) states that regular physical activity can provide:

- 50% reduction in the risk of developing coronary heart disease (similar to not smoking).
- 50% reduction in the risk of developing adult diabetes.
- 50% reduction in the risk of becoming obese.
- 30% reduction in the risk of developing hypertension.

- 10/8-mmHg decline in blood pressure in people with hypertension (a similar effect to drugs).
- Reduced osteoporosis and falls in the elderly.
- Relief of symptoms of depression and anxiety.

4.4 Mental Health Impacts

Transport planning decisions also can affect the psychological states in various ways. Improving walking conditions, cycling and the transportation system tend to enhance the psychological state by increasing physical activity and supporting community cohesion, i.e. positive interactions between neighbors. Increased neighborhood walkability is associated with reduced symptoms of depression in older men, and reduced frequency of dementia in women and men. In a study of 299 US older adults (mean age 78 years) Erickson et al. found significantly higher rates of grey matter volume and cognitive ability in those that previously walked quite 72 blocks every week. High-quality public transit services can reduce commute stress compared with driving. Many commuters find a high-quality transportation system travel less stressful than driving. These psychological state benefits are difficult to quantify but potentially large.

4.5 Affordability

Affordability refers to reduced financial burdens, particularly for lower-income households. It generally means transportation expenditures are but 20% of household budgets, and transportation and housing expenditures total but 45% of household budgets. Public transportation and transit-oriented development can increase affordability by reducing the necessity to have and operate personal vehicles, by providing affordable mobility for non-drivers, and by reducing residential parking costs. This supports public health in several ways: it leaves households with extra money to get goods required for health, like adequate shelter, healthy food, and medical aid, and it reduces emotional stresses associated with poverty.

4.6 Basic Mobility

Basic mobility refers to peoples' ability to access services and activities considered essential, like healthcare services, basic shopping, banking, education and employment opportunities, and a specific amount of social and recreational activities. Public transportation and transit-oriented development provide basic mobility and accessibility, particularly for physically and economically disadvantaged people, like people with disabilities and lower-income seniors. This is substantial for public health and can leads to reduce healthcare costs. Inadequate mobility can cause patients to miss appointments, which exacerbates medical problems and wastes medical resources, or forces patients or health care agencies to buy more costly transport, such as taxis.

5. CONCLUSION

Transportation planning decisions can have significant health impacts by influencing traffic crash and pollution emission rates, physical activity, basic access, and psychological state. Conventional planning tends to consider some of these impacts, per-kilometer crash and pollution emission rates in particular, but generally ignore the health problems caused by degraded walking and cycling conditions and therefore the additional crashes and pollution emissions caused by increased vehicle mileage.

Public transportation can provide significant health benefits. People who live or work in communities with high-quality public transportation tend to own fewer vehicles, drive less, and use alternative modes more than they would in more automobile-oriented locations. This can provide large reductions in traffic crashes and pollution emissions, increases in fitness and psychological state, and improved access to healthy food, housing, and medical aid. These health benefits are so useful in magnitude compared with other planning objectives but are often overlooked or undervalued in conventional transport planning.

ACKNOWLEDGEMENT

I am over helmed in all humbleness and gratefulness to acknowledge my depth to all those who have helped me to put these ideas for this paper, well above the level of simplicity and into something concrete. I would like to express my special thanks of gratitude to my wife for her stand with me to complete this paper. Any attempt at any level cannot be satisfactorily completed without the support and guidance of MY parents and friends.

REFERENCES

Berke EM, Gottlieb LM, Moudon AV, Larson EB. 2007. Protective association between neighborhood walkability and depression in older men. *J. Am. Geriatr. Soc.* 5

Chester et al., 2012 *Infrastructure and Automobile Shifts: Positioning Transit to Reduce Life-cycle Environmental Impacts for Urban Sustainability Goals*, Environmental Research Letters 8(1).

Chester M, and Horvath A, 2012, *High-speed Rail with Emerging Automobiles and Aircraft Can Reduce Environmental Impacts in California's Future*, Environmental Research Letters 7(3).

Chester M, and Horvath A, 2009, *Environmental Assessment of Passenger Transportation Should Include Infrastructure and Supply Chains*, Environmental Research Letters 4(2).

Intergovernmental Panel on Climate Change (2007). *IPCC Fourth Assessment Report: Mitigation of Climate Change, chapter 5, Transport and its Infrastructure (PDF).* Intergovernmental Panel on Climate Change. Retrieved 2009-05-26.

Jeon, C M; Amekudzi (March 2005), Addressing Sustainability in Transportation Systems: Definitions, Indicators, and Metrics" (PDF), *Journal of Infrastructure Systems*, 11: 31–50, doi:10.1061/(ASCE)1076-0342(2005)11:1(31)

Larson EB,Wang L, Bowen JD, McCormick WC, Teri L, et al. 2006. Exercise is associated with reduced risk for incident dementia among persons 65 years of age and older. *Ann. Intern. Med.*

Litman T. 2007. Community cohesion as a transport planning objective. Pap. 07–0550. Presented at *Annu.Meet. Transp. Res. Board, Washington, DC*

Murray, et al. (1996). *Global Burden of Disease and Injury. Center for Population and Development Studies*, Harvard School of Public Health (www.hsph.harvard.edu/organizations/bdu).

Ont. Coll. Family Phys. 2005. *The Health Impacts of Urban Sprawl.* Volume Four: Social and Mental Health. An Information Series. Toronto: Ont. Coll. Family Phys. http://www.ocfp.on.ca/docs/committee-documents/urban-sprawl—volume-4—social-and-mental-health.pdf?sfvrsn=5

Racioppi F, Dora C, Krech R, von Ehrenstein O. 2002. *A Physically Active Life Through Everyday Transport: With a Special Focus on Children and Older People and Examples and Approaches from Europe*, ed. A Davis. Rome: WHO, Eur. Reg. Off. http://www.euro.who.int/document/e75662.pdf

Schafer, A. (1998) *The global demand for motorized mobility.* Transportation Research A 32(6).

Subramanian R. 2012. *Motor Vehicle Traffic Crashes as a Leading Cause of Death in the United States*, 2008 and 2009. DOT HS 811 620. Washington, DC: Natl. Highw. Traffic Saf. Inst. (NHTSA). http://www-nrd.nhtsa.dot.gov/Pubs/811620.pdf

Todd Litman (2009). *Sustainable Transportation and TDM.* Online TDM Encyclopedia. Victoria Transport Policy Institute. Retrieved 2009-04-07.

Todd Litman, 15 February 2012, *Evaluating Public Transportation Health Benefits*, Victoria Transport Policy Institute For The American Public Transportation Association

Tom Theis and Jonathan Tomkin, Editors, *PDF generated*: July 5, 2012, Rice University, Houston, Texas

Trancossi, M. (2014). What price of speed? A critical revision through constructal optimization of transport modes. *International Journal of Energy and Environmental Engineering*.

US Dep. Health Hum. Serv., Phys. Act. Guidel. Advis. Comm. 2008. *Physical Activity Guidelines Advisory Committee Report*, 2008. Atlanta: USDHHS. http://www.health.gov/paguidelines/ report/pdf/CommitteeReport.pdf

US Dep. Transp. Fed. Highw. Adm. (FHA). 2010. *Transportation Planner's Safety Desk Reference*. FHWA-HEP-10-001. Washington, DC: USDOT, FHWA. http://tsp.trb.org/assets/ FR1_SafetyDeskReference_FINAL.pdf

U.S. Department of Transportation's Research and Innovative Technology Administration, May 2010, *Helping to Build a Safe and Sustainable Transportation Infrastructure (PDF), U.S.A.*

Woodcock J, Franco OH, Orsini N, Roberts I. 2010. Non-vigorous physical activity and all-cause mortality: systematic review and meta-analysis of cohort studies. *Int. J. Epidemiol.*

THE ADVENT OF SMART CITIES: STATUS QUO AND FUTURE RESEARCH DIRECTIONS

Yusuf Bozkurt, Reiner Braun, Alexander Rossmann and Dieter Hertweck
Department of Computer Science, Reutlingen University,
72762 Reutlingen, Germany

ABSTRACT

The shift of populations to cities is creating challenges in many respects, thus leading to increasing demand for smart solutions of urbanization problems. Smart city applications range from technical and social to economic and ecological. The main focus of this work is to provide a systematic literature review of smart city research to answer two main questions: (1) How is current research on smart cities structured? and (2) What directions are relevant for future research on smart cities? To answer these research questions, a text-mining approach is applied to a large number of publications. This provides an overview and gives insights into relevant dimensions of smart city research. Although the main dimensions of research are already described in the literature, an evaluation of the relevance of such dimensions is missing. Findings suggest that the dimensions of environment and governance are popular, while the dimension of economy has received only limited attention.

KEYWORDS

Smart City, Literature Review, Text-Mining, Environment, Governance, Economy

1. INTRODUCTION

The shift of populations to cities and urban-dense areas is creating challenges in many respects. Cities play a major role in social and economic development worldwide. Therefore, they are key elements for sustainable development in the future (Mori & Christodoulou, 2012). Research on cities has developed rapidly in recent years, and the term "smart city" is often used, but what makes a city smart, and how is it defined?

A review of the literature makes it clear that there is no common definition of what a smart city is. Some definitions focus on information and communication technologies (ICTs) as drivers and enablers of sustainable development, while others focus more on socio-economic, governance, and multi-stakeholder aspects (Albino et al., 2015). Perspectives on smart cities range from technical and social to economic and ecological. Depending on whether the perspective is on urban planning, ICT, energy, mobility, governance, or economy, the definition of a smart city can differ in multiple ways. However, synonyms such as intelligent, virtual, knowledge, sustainable, talented, wired, digital, and eco are often used to describe smart cities (Albino et al., 2015; Catriona et al., 2014). Exploring the concept of a smart city, Lombardi et al. (2012) focused on the production of knowledge and the development of innovations. The main focus of smart city research is on the role of human capital/education, social and relational capital, and environmental issues, all of which are important drivers of urban growth (Lombardi et al., 2012). A precise and general definition of a smart city is still missing, but the main dimensions of research are already visible and described in some literature (Caragliu et al., 2011; Giffinger et al., 2010). With this structure, the main dimensions of smart city research can be classified into six areas: smart governance, smart economy, smart environment, smart people, smart living and smart mobility (Catriona et al., 2014; Giffinger et al., 2010). Despite this raw structure of smart city research, the current state of the art on each of the six dimensions and precise directions for future research on smart city research remains vague. Therefore, future research should investigate how theoretical models can be applied to specific implementation cases. Therefore, this paper focuses on the following two research questions:

RQ1: How is the current research in the area of smart cities structured?
RQ2: What directions for further research are relevant within this structure?

We apply a systematic literature review to answer these questions. Thus, we use text-mining methods to analyze a large number of research articles in a systematic way. This approach leads to the identification of the most relevant publications in the field and gives relevant insights into the state of the art on each research dimension.

This paper is structured as follows: First of all, an overview of existing literature reviews on smart cities is given. After positioning our paper in contrast to existing work, details on the conducted research methodology are presented. This is followed by the results of the text-mining analysis, the mapping of smart city topics to the smart city dimensions, as well as an analysis of the popularity of each dimension in smart city research. Subsequently, the research stream in each smart city dimension is discussed. Finally, this is followed by an aggregated discussion and the presentation of future research directions.

2. RELATED WORK

Different studies on smart city literature reviews are available in the scientific literature. Therefore, we analyzed relevant related work to clarify our position in existing research. Table 1 summarizes the identified literature reviews on smart cities, the used databases and time horizons of reviewed papers, applied methods, search restrictions, and the main focus of the review. We included our paper also in Table 1, to clarify the differences. For instance, Arroub et al. (2016) analyzed research on smart cities in order to provide a description of smart city concepts, thus including the main definitions of the term "smart city", the different dimensions and smart city models. They also discussed smart city challenges and opportunities.

In contrast to existing literature reviews, this research captures a holistic view on the broad research area of smart cities. It presents a high-level summary of smart city research and clusters the topics in well-known and accepted dimensions for smart city research. Although some main dimensions are already described in literature, to date, research has not evaluated the popularity of such dimensions. To do so, we created a ranking for the different dimensions of smart city research. Additionally, further research directions for each smart city dimension are discussed. Moreover, our methodology differs from other literature reviews, as we used text-mining to glean insights from a significantly larger set of papers (e.g. ranking and structure of smart city dimensions).

Table 1. Overview of relevant literature reviews on smart cities

Authors / Database (D) / Time (T)	Method (M) / Restrictions (R) / Focus (F)
Bozkurt et al. (2020) (this paper) ***D*** - Web of Science, ACM, IEEE, EBSCOhost ***T*** - 2009 - 2019	***M*** - Webster and Watson (2002), Creswell (2012), Text-Mining ***R*** - Peer-reviewed articles and proceedings **F** - Holistic view on the broad research area of smart cities and further research directions.
Colding and Barthel (2017) ***D*** - Scopus ***T*** - 1995 - 2017	***M*** - No statement ***R*** - Articles, proceedings, books and doctoral theses **F** - Urban ecology, sociotechnological and biosociotechnical
Purnomo and Prabowo (2016) ***D*** - Science Direct; ACM Digital Library, IEEE Xplore, Google Scholar ***T*** - 2004 - 2015	***M*** - No statement ***R*** - No statement ***F*** - Smart city indicators
Arroub et al. (2016) ***D*** - No statement ***T*** - No statement	**M** - No statement **R** - No statement **F** - Smart city concepts, definitions, models, challenges and opportunities
Ruhlandt (2018) ***D*** - EBSCO, Web of Science, ABI Inform Global ***T*** - 2003 - 2017	***M*** - Webster and Watson (2002) ***R*** - Peer-reviewed journal articles ***F*** - Governance of smart cities.
Trindade et al. (2017) ***D*** - Scopus, Science Direct, and Emerald Insight ***T*** - 2012 - 2017	***M*** - Jesson et al. (2011) ***R*** - No statement ***F*** - Environmental sustainability and smart city concepts.

Bibri and Krogstie (2017) ***D*** - No statement ***T*** - 2005 - 2016	***M*** - Levy and Ellis (2006); Webster and Watson (2002) ***R*** - Articles, books, reports, proceedings, dissertations, theses and policy documents ***F*** - Smart city underlying foundations and assumptions, technological trends and future planning practices
Meijer and Bolívar (2016) ***D*** - Web of Science, Science Direct, Scopus, EBSCOhost ***T*** - 1999 - 2012	***M*** - No statement ***R*** - Proceedings, books, book chapters or doctoral theses ***M***- Smart city governance
Gupta et al. (2019) ***D*** - Scopus ***T*** - 2007 - 2018	***M*** - Kitchenham (2004) ***R*** - Peer-reviewed research papers ***F*** - Business, management, and accounting
Ismagilova et al. (2019) ***D*** - Scopus ***T*** - No statement	***M*** - Filtered based on author experience ***R*** - Journals listed in the 'Information Management' category of the Academic Journal Guide 2018. ***F*** - No statement
Chauhan et al. (2016) ***D*** - IEEEXplore, ProQuest, Sciencedirect, SpringerLink, JSTOR, ACM Digital Library, AIS eLibrary, EBSCO, Informs, Inderscience, Emerald, Sage, Wiley Interscience and Google Scholar. ***T*** - published before February 2016	***M*** - Kitchenham and Charters (2007) ***R*** - Research papers only ***F*** - Smart city and big data

3. RESEARCH METHODOLOGY

This study focuses on a review of extant literature on smart cities to explore the current state of the art and future research directions. We used comprehensive search terms in four databases: Web of Science, ACM, IEEE, and EBSCOhost. Our initial approach was to apply an enhanced review method based on the methodologies of Webster and Watson (2002) and Creswell (2012). Thus, a comprehensive literature review should cover all relevant literature on the topic and is not confined to one research methodology, one set of journals, or one geographic region. When applying the search strings "smart city" OR "smart cities" to the databases, we soon faced the problem of a vast amount of literature dealing with the topics of smart cities. For that reason, we developed an algorithm to identify the most relevant sources for full-text reading. As Figure 1 shows, the research process consists of four phases. The first column shows the phases, the second column the single steps conducted in each phase, and the third column the results after each step.

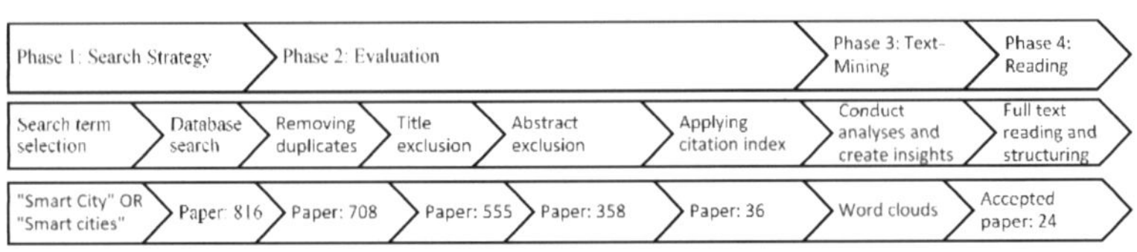

Figure 1. Literature review process

In phase 1, we were able to identify 816 articles. In phase 2, after various steps, we gathered 36 articles. In phase 3, we ran corresponding text-mining analyses. In phase 4, we finally considered 24 articles for the content-related analysis of the six smart city dimensions. The following sections describe each step to give an in-depth look into the methodology of this research.

4. PHASE 1: SEARCH STRATEGY

As noted, for a broad search result, we performed the search in four databases. For consistent results, each database was searched with the same selection criteria. We considered only articles published between 2009 and 2019 and written in English. Furthermore, to ensure a high quality of the sources, we considered only peer-reviewed articles by employing Article (Journal)/Proceedings as the document type. Moreover, we searched the article titles and considered only articles that have been cited more than 10 times. In total, we ended up with 816 documents in a list for the full search results. The results of each database were: Web of Science with 472 articles, IEEE with 208, EBSCOhost with 130, and ACM with 6 articles.

5. PHASE 2: EVALUATION

Removal of duplicate documents reduced the total number of articles from 816 to 708. For the remaining 708 articles, we examined their title and abstract to determine whether the focus on smart cities was clearly visible. Subsequently, we excluded 153 articles with this approach based on the title. Finally, we read the abstracts of these remaining 555 articles, excluded another 197 articles, and ended up with 358 articles in total. The excluded articles either did not clearly focus on smart cities or investigated only technologies and technological implementations. After the exclusion phase, there were still a high number of articles for full-text reading. Therefore, we developed an index to identify the most relevant articles. Such an index needs to consider (a) the total number of citations and (b) the period a specific article is available to other scholars. We created a formula to consider these criteria so that recent articles were not disadvantaged because of their fewer number of citations. Precisely, articles published within the last 12 months received a better ranking. By contrast, articles older than two years received a devaluation for each year. Accordingly, we applied the following formula to the set of 358 articles to determine the most relevant 10 percent of the articles for full-text reading.

$$index = \frac{number\ of\ citations}{wy} \quad (1)$$

where

$$wy = \begin{cases} year - 0.5 & year = 1 \\ year & year = 2 \\ year + \sum_{i=3}^{n=year,max} 0.5 & year > 2 \end{cases} \qquad for\ year: 2019 = 1\ and\ 2009 = 10$$

6. PHASE 3: TEXT-MINING APPROACH

Solely focusing on the 36 most relevant articles (10 percent of 358) would not help answer the research questions of this study. Therefore, we used text-mining to glean insights from both source sets: the full source set with 358 articles and the most relevant source set with 36 articles. With text-mining, we were able to determine the frequency of specific keywords in the abstract of each article and to perform additional analyses. Abstracts have the advantage that they provide the core statement from the perspective of the authors. In addition, the articles are formatted differently and contain sections that can falsify the text-mining analysis, such as related work. Despite the enormous amount of literature, the text-mining approach helped us to cluster the smart city topics in generally accepted smart city dimensions according to Catriona et al. (2014) in order to glean insights about the research structure and popularity.

6.1 Text-Mining Workflow with RapidMiner

For text-mining, we used RapidMiner Studio 9.5 with text processing and R-Script extensions (Hofmann & Klinkenberg, 2014; RapidMiner, 2020). Figure 2 illustrates the implemented text-mining process. Before using RapidMiner, we undertook preparatory work to create the proper data source. Therefore, we created an Excel file as an input file for RapidMiner that contained every article in separate rows, with relevant information such as title, abstract, publishing year, author, and journal or conference in separate columns. The creation of the source file was a straightforward step, as we used the reference management software Citavi 6, which allows to export the whole Citavi project as an Excel file (Swiss Academic Software, 2020).

We divided the workflow in RapidMiner into four core steps. The first step is data access. RapidMiner provides several predefined nodes for accessing various data sources. In this case, the Read Excel node is used. Parameters such as file location, imported cell range, first row as names, and so on, are to be specified within the node configuration. Thus, this node reads the source file, which was created with Citavi. For further text processing, the Data-to-Documents node is required. This predefined node transforms the Excel data set into a collection of documents by generating a document for each instance of the data set. Thus, each row of the imported Excel file is converted into a single document. Step 3 is a predefined node, which provides parameters such as vector creation schema and prune method. In this case, no prune method and the term occurrences schema for vector creation is chosen. The term occurrences schema calculates the number of occurrences of a term in each document, which can also deliver the total number of term occurrences.

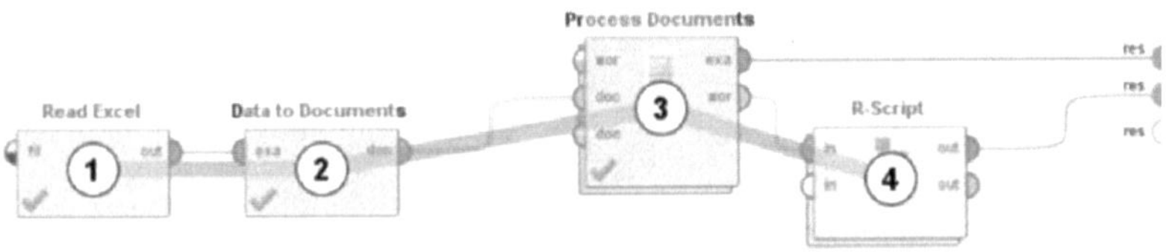

Figure 2. Implemented workflow of the text-mining process in RapidMiner

The node Process Documents consists of two subprocesses. The first subprocess is conducting common text-mining steps. It starts with the tokenization of the text into single tokens. After that, the tokens are filtered by English stop words (e.g. "I", "me", "she") and n-grams in length 2 are created. The node creates terms as a series of consecutive tokens of length 2. For example, the two consecutive tokens "big" and "data" are combined into "big_data". After this subprocess, the second subprocess with our custom rules is conducted. Firstly, it filters the words that are not necessary for our analysis (e.g. "makes", "thanks", "paper"). Secondly, a stemming step transforms the words into their basic form (e.g. "strategies" to "strategy"). Subsequently, the mapping of smart city subtopics in smart city dimensions was conducted. Thus, the step Process Documents is the most extensive in the applied text-mining workflow. Its outputs are the example set and the word list, which is used in the last step. Step 4 takes the created word list as input and then builds a word cloud with a R-script.

6.2 Results

Figure 3 illustrates the results of the text-mining procedure as word clouds.

Figure 3. Word clouds

The left-hand side of Figure 3 is the word cloud based on the whole source set with 358 papers. For better visualization, we restricted the word frequency to at least 10 times. On the right-hand side of Figure 3 is the word cloud based on the most relevant 10 percent of articles (36 in total). We needed to reduce the minimum word frequency to 5 times to gain the best illustration because of the significant smaller word set.

Both word clouds show that keywords such as data, IoT, application and communication appear in the list of the most frequently used words in the source sets. By fading out keywords with a strong focus on IT, we show that energy, sustainability, transport and governance are frequently occurring keywords. Furthermore, several terms such as community, population and buildings are still in the word cloud but are less frequent. To evaluate the popularity of the different areas, we mapped each keyword onto smart city dimensions, following the work of Catriona et al. (2014) which was published by the European parliament. We do not consider ICT keywords such as "communication", "computing", "WSNS" (wireless sensor network), and "sensor" in this mapping, because these are not clearly assigned to a dimension. Table 2 shows the mapping of each keyword as well as the frequency from both source sets. The mapping was also realized with RapidMiner by adding a custom-stemming step in the text-mining workflow.

Table 2. Mapping of words from the world clouds to smart city dimension

Dimension	Word frequency: All articles	Word frequency: 10% articles	Terms/Subtopics
Environment	1472	102	energy, sustainability, architecture, environment, waste, building, light, air, power, road, electricity, grid, consumption, energy_efficiency, pollution, water, emergency, waste_management, street, green, suitable, built, carbon, emissions, heat, nature, ecosystem, solar, temperature, build, place, urbanization, centre, construction, low_power, metropolitan, city_projects
Governance	858	105	service, management, governance, policy, strategy, planning, city_concept, stakeholders, operational, managing, international, authorities, countries, organizations
Mobility	612	34	traffic, parking, transport, vehicle, mobility, car, congestion, transportation_systems, bus, logistics
People	405	47	citizen, innovation, people, human, population, european, inhabitants, residents, personal, university
Living	396	53	privacy, health, social, quality_life, community, live, urban_areas, urban_development, society, social_media, residential
Economy	209	23	economic, sharing, business, knowledge, industry, economy, supply, companies, business_models, facilities

In summary, Table 2 shows the popularity of each dimension from both source sets. The word frequency field shows how often a word for the corresponding dimension occurs in the respective source sets. The table also shows the mapping of individual terms. So, the ranking results in the large source set (358 articles) are as follows: Environment, Governance, Mobility, People, Living, and Economy. In the small source set (36 articles), the ranking is as follows: Governance, Environment, Living, People, Mobility, and Economy. In summary, environment, governance and economy behave similarly in both source sets. However, mobility differs strongly; it is second to last in the small source set and third from the top in the large source set.

7. PHASE 4: RELEVANT RESEARCH STREAMS

This phase provides a content-related list of findings from the identified most relevant articles. The goal is to give insights into relevant research streams and to create a picture of how research is structured around and within each smart city dimension. To achieve this, we analyzed each article in terms of its content. After reading and structuring the 36 papers, we identified 24 sources that suit the smart city dimensions. Table 3 shows the set with 36 articles identified with the formula (described in phase 2). These articles are clustered in the respective dimensions. Some articles are assigned to more than one dimension because they cover more than one dimension, or the topics are overlapping and a separated investigation is not possible. Moreover, there is a cluster for articles that cannot be assigned to at least one dimension. These articles focus on technical issues and implementations (Allam & Dhunny, 2019; Biswas & Muthukkumarasamy, 2016; Centenaro et al., 2016; Cruz et al., 2019; Naranjo et al., 2019; Puiu et al., 2016; Zambom Santana et al., 2018) [1]or do not investigate the smart city dimensions (Albino et al., 2015; Colding & Barthel, 2017; Ferraris et al., 2019; Ismagilova et al., 2019; Kummitha & Crutzen, 2017).

[1] Due to the page limitation these seven paper are not referenced in this paper anymore. Therefore, they are not listed in the reference list. Further information available on demand.

Table 3. Smart city dimension: article overview

Smart City Dimension	Article [Number of citations; Calculated Index]
Environment	Zanella et al. (2014) [1842; 230]; Jin et al. (2014) [462; 57]; Ahvenniemi et al. (2017) [137; 39]; Ejaz et al. (2017) [76; 21]; Qi and Shen (2019) [16; 21]; Batagan (2011) [181; 14]; Sun et al. (2019) [14; 18]
Governance	Chourabi et al. (2012) [551; 50]; Batty et al. (2012) [442; 40]; Angelidou (2014) [170; 21]; Lee and Lee (2014) [158; 19]; Ruhlandt (2018) [50; 25]
Mobility	Menouar et al. (2017) [101; 28]; Djahel et al. (2015) [126; 19]; Gharaibeh et al. (2017) [48; 13]; Qi and Shen (2019) [16; 21]
People	Jin et al. (2014) [462; 57]; Chourabi et al. (2012) [551; 50]; Vanolo (2014) [240; 30]; Schuurman et al. (2012) [224; 20]; Djahel et al. (2015) [126; 19]; Hollands (2015) [124; 19]; Granier and Hiroko (2016) [89; 17]
Living	Solanas et al. (2014) [181; 22]; Zhang et al. (2017) [70; 20]; Al Nuaimi et al. (2015) [124; 19]; Gharaibeh et al. (2017) [48; 13]
Economy	Perera et al. (2014) [328; 41]; Qi and Shen (2019) [16; 21]; Hashem et al. (2016) [126; 25]; Hollands (2015) [124; 19]
Not considered in dimensions	Puiu et al. (2016) [75; 15]; Biswas and Muthukkumarasamy (2016) [82; 16]; Naranjo et al. (2019) [13; 17]; Cruz et al. (2019) [13; 17]; Ferraris et al. (2019) [14; 18]; Zambom Santana et al. (2018) [91; 26]; Centenaro et al. (2016) [198; 39]; Ismagilova et al. (2019) [69; 92]; Kummitha and Crutzen (2017) [53; 15]; Colding and Barthel (2017) [63; 18]; Allam and Dhunny (2019) [40; 53]; Albino et al. (2015) [381; 92]

7.1 Dimension Smart Environment

The reduction of greenhouse gases and the supply with water, energy, and food are some of the primary priorities of cities. ICT can be used to reach these goals (Ahvenniemi et al., 2017; Batagan, 2011). Although the European Commission (2012) defines sustainability, with the help of ICT, as an initial goal for smart cities, the most smart city performance assessment frameworks do not focus enough on the environmental aspects but instead more on economic and social indicators (Ahvenniemi et al., 2017). Some examples of smart environment activities are air quality and noise monitoring (Jin et al., 2014; Zanella et al., 2014), waste management, street lights, and structural health of buildings. All these examples are enabled by ICT (Zanella et al., 2014). With the increasing number of IoT devices, to enable these examples, energy consumption is increasing. Therefore, efficient energy management for IoT in smart cities is a necessity (Ejaz et al., 2017). As in other smart city dimensions, also in the environment dimension, data is an important topic (e.g. probabilistic peak demand estimation with smart meter data) (Sun et al., 2019). Another topic in the smart environment refers to smart buildings. Buildings in cities make up a large part of greenhouse gas emissions. Therefore, Qi and Shen (2019) stress the decarbonization of buildings. To create such emission-light buildings, systems and technologies for energy management, energy efficiency, energy production and storage are required. Another approach in the area of smart buildings is the energy production on-site at buildings (e.g. with photovoltaic systems). Thus, the consumer is a producer as well as a consumer (i.e. “prosumer”). The topic becomes particularly important when surplus energy is fed into the energy market and traded accordingly. Thus, smart buildings have an extreme influence not only on power systems and technologies but also on the energy market and economy.

7.2 Dimension Smart Governance

Smart cities consist of several components that require strong and intelligent coordination. According to Batty et al. (2012), smart governance is the required superior intelligence that connects all smart city components. First, smart governance aims to improve quality of life by engaging various stakeholders (e.g. citizens, service users). To facilitate this goal, ICT solutions are applied to connect relevant stakeholders and to make the city “smarter”. Second, to foster transparency, increasingly more local governments are supplying open data portals to provide public data for interested citizens and professionals. ICT plays a primary role in smart governance (Angelidou, 2014; Batty et al., 2012; Chourabi et al., 2012). According to (Batty et al. 2012), a good decision support solution with real time analysis and several simulations is essential. Furthermore, an integrated database for the whole city, sensing and networks, and social media are at the core of smart governance's ICT applications. Although the use of ICT in governance plays an essential role, it is not sufficient alone. A well-balanced combination of ICT, policies, integration of people, norms and moral makes a governance system smart (Angelidou, 2014; Chourabi et al., 2012).

Another function of governance is to mutually manage diverse smart city projects that are involved with various stakeholders. Political support is necessary to cope with this task. Policy must break the legal and regulatory barriers for easy implementation of smart city initiatives. Thus, policy must be able to cope with the functionality of ICT and enable a means for innovations (Chourabi et al., 2012). The government is also responsible for the smart city strategy. Angelidou (2014) describes an approach for strategy development characterized by four decision types. The first is the distinction between the local and national validation level. The second decision type pertains to the urban development stage in terms of whether to help a city get smarter or develop and create a completely new city based on smart city characteristics. The third decision type pertains to which infrastructure to target from the strategy. Angelidou (2014) distinguishes between hard infrastructure (e.g. transportation, waste management, energy) and soft infrastructure (e.g. human capital, education, social life). The fourth decision type is about the economic sector or geographically based reference area. Economic sector means that the strategy aims for a specific economic sector of the city.

According to Lee and Lee (2014), smart city services are also an important element of smart governance. They especially stress the perspective of users and customers of city services and describe a citizen-centric typology framework for smart city services. The dimension of smart governance is particularly broad, and a systematic understanding of its components is not available. Ruhlandt (2018) stresses the need to better understand the components of smart governance. It is also important to understand how the components can be measured and what their influence are.

7.3 Dimension Smart Mobility

The relevance of smart traffic management systems (TMSs) and mobility services is increasing in the economy as well as in citizens' daily lives. Accordingly, one of the main pillars of smart cities is smart mobility (Gharaibeh et al., 2017). Intelligent transportation systems (ITSs) are enablers of smart mobility (Xiong et al., 2012). ITSs (also known as smart TMSs) aim to solve cities' transportation problems by using ICT. Smart TMSs provide services for citizen and road users so that they can benefit directly. Smart mobility services include, for example, route planning and parking management (Djahel et al., 2015). Intelligent TMSs benefit both individual traffic and public transport (Zhang et al., 2017). Moreover, road authorities can use them for road planning and administration, traffic simulations and emergency monitoring (Djahel et al., 2015). Menouar et al. (2017) describes an approach for ITSs that uses drones as monitoring nodes for detecting emergency situations and traffic offenses. Major challenges of smart TMSs are security and privacy aspects because these systems are a point of malicious attacks (Gharaibeh et al., 2017). Furthermore, smart mobility is often considered along with environmental topics (Djahel et al., 2015; Gharaibeh et al., 2017; Qi & Shen, 2019; Xiong et al., 2012). New mobility concepts are also discussed in the literature. Qi and Shen (2019) discuss the integration of electric vehicles in smart grids and consider their challenges.

7.4 Dimension Smart People

In smart cities, individual citizens, groups and communities are supposed to have the opportunity to participate in and co-design their habitat (Chourabi et al., 2012; Granier & Hiroko, 2016; Hollands, 2015; Schuurman et al., 2012; Vanolo, 2014). Citizen participation ranges from design and implementation to the evaluation and continuous monitoring of diverse entities; as such, it can affect several parts of a city positively, such as policy, social justice and education (Granier & Hiroko, 2016). The research concept of living labs and the usage of ICTs are ways to improve the co-design and innovation process for successful city development (Granier & Hiroko, 2016; Schuurman et al., 2012). Furthermore, scholars seem to agree that successful development of cities depends strongly on citizen participation (Schuurman et al., 2012). Jin et al. (2014) consider participatory sensing part of citizen participation. Thus, data collection and sharing are carried out by voluntary citizens instead of the usual sensing paradigms with deployed sensors. This has the advantage of data being collected in different situations and locations at low cost. However, data quality cannot necessarily be guaranteed (Jin et al., 2014) Although ICT facilitates easy participation (e.g. citizens can use their mobile devices for reporting or feedbacking) (Djahel et al., 2015; Jin et al., 2014), citizen- and participation-oriented smart city projects are more relevant than technology-centric projects.

Most smart city initiatives come from either companies or the government, not from the people who live and work in the cities (Hollands, 2015). According to Hollands (2015), ICT should be used in the service of the citizens and not as high-tech quick solutions with the objective of selling profitable products.

7.5 Dimension Smart Living

Efficient smart city services, realized with ICT and big data, aim to enhance quality of life. Several scholars have stressed the healthcare and privacy and security themes in this context (Al Nuaimi et al., 2015; Gharaibeh et al., 2017; Solanas et al., 2014; Zhang et al., 2017). An often debated topic within smart living is smart health, which considers several facets in healthcare, including fitness, home care, connected hospitals and early diagnosis or spread of disease in the city (Gharaibeh et al., 2017; Solanas et al., 2014; Zhang et al., 2017). For predictive analysis such as spread of disease in a city, consideration of social media data is a possible approach. On the one hand, medical sensors, wearable devices and medical records data keep track of users' health condition in real time. On the other hand, social networks provide information about users' social contact and interactions. However, collaboration on this information is a major challenge because of heterogeneous data sources and sensibility of the data (Gharaibeh et al., 2017; Zhang et al., 2017). Another school of thought is use of a context-aware network and sensing infrastructure of smart cities. Solanas et al. (2014) define smart health as a combination of mobile health services and cities' sensorics and infrastructure. Thus, for example, real-time readings of air pollution and pollination can help inform allergy suffers, or traffic patterns could be controlled for emergency situations. A common challenge, however, of all smart city services is ensuring citizens' privacy. Therefore, to reach broad acceptance, state-of-the-art privacy and security techniques need to be deployed (Gharaibeh et al., 2017; Solanas et al., 2014; Zhang et al., 2017).

7.6 Dimension Smart Economy

Data sources such as consumer-connected electronics or sensors, which are distributed through the whole city, constantly generate data, and thus data collection in smart cities is enormous. According to Hashem et al. (2016), data are at the core of novel and optimized business models. Data can be used to detect new patterns for optimizing existing business models and services or to create new data-driven business models (Hashem et al., 2016). To create value from especially sensor data, Perera et al. (2014) treat the topic sensing as a service model. They describe a four-layer service model that enables business generation, in each layer. Perera et al. (2014) claim that with such a service model, the creation of innovations is easier because the barrier to market entry is lower (e.g. for start-ups). Thus, novel and innovative business models in the whole data life cycle are feasible. According to Hollands (2015) and Hashem et al. (2016), the potential of using data for advertising is enormous. Data can help individualize billboard ads and to create new pricing models (Hollands, 2015; Mulligan & Olsson, 2013). Social media–based business models are another approach in the context of the smart economy (Hashem et al., 2016). The trend towards privatization of public spaces for business is in evidence, and cities are increasingly becoming the places for corporate advertising.

8. DISCUSSION AND FURTHER RESEARCH DIRECTIONS

The main goal of this work was to provide an extensive literature review on smart cities, to answer how relevant research on smart cities is structured and what smart city dimensions are relevant for future research. Although the main dimensions and fields of activity already appear in the literature, there is no analysis on the research popularity of these dimensions. While the environment and governance dimensions are the most popular topics in research in the last decade, the dimension of economy has received less attention from scholars. Furthermore, the analysis of the most relevant 10 percent of articles shows a similar distribution in the upper range of the conducted ranking, but the dimensions of people and living are more in focus than the mobility dimension.

In addition to describing the current state of research, we focus on proposing common ground and further research directions across the different dimensions mentioned in Section 7. This refers to a certain hierarchical structure between the identified research dimensions. A higher-order area for the integration of the different research topics mentioned in Section 7 leads to the discussion of *smart city strategies*. This is usually incorporated in the dimension of *smart governance* (Angelidou, 2014; Ruhlandt, 2018). Therefore, smart governance and the broad discussion around smart city strategies, multidisciplinarity, smart city architecture, and IT governance might be viewed as a starting point and meta model for current research. An important part of this discussion is linked to the demand for *reference architectures* for smart cities. Such architectures are usually divided in the subdomains of 1) technology, 2) data, and 3) services (Hashem et al., 2016; Perera et al., 2014; Ruhlandt, 2018). Moreover, reference architectures describe how different initiatives, e.g. in the context of environment, mobility or living are integrated within a single city or area, strategic context, and data structure.

Adopting this perspective, the subdomain of *technology* is present in multiple research dimensions. For instance, in a smart environment future research might consider energy-efficient mechanisms for software-defined IoT solutions that can provide scalable and context-aware data and services. Furthermore, energy efficiency and complexity of security protocols are crucial aspects for the practical implementation of IoT-based services. An important research stream in the dimension of smart mobility includes active vehicle safety and intelligent vehicles. Core developments in this area are mainly driven by perceptions of the environment, intelligent control, and active collision avoidance. Perceptions of the driving environment entail identifying driving conditions and locations, lanes, traffic lights, vehicles and pedestrians, and so on. Emerging technologies can include security warnings, auxiliary driving, and active collision avoidance (Xiong et al., 2012).

In the subdomain of *data* corresponding strategies need to elaborate in aspects like data integration, data analysis, and data-based simulations. Further research might focus on urban data portals and the integration of data between different dimensions of smart cities. Such an approach is increasingly resulting in complexity, thus leading to the need for statistical mechanics or cognitive systems to simulate smart city solutions. Thus, the science and art of urban simulation will play a major role in future research (Batty et al., 2012). Such a data integration might consider mobility data, environmental data, but also private data in the area of smart living. State-of-the-art security and privacy techniques are essential for intelligent healthcare. Without effective protections, users may not be willing to share their health data with others, leading to challenges in infection analysis (Zhang et al., 2017).

Finally, *services*, business and operating models need further development in the third subdomain of a corresponding reference architecture. This requires a better link among the architectural views of IT, communication networks and the provision of services. Particularly, further research needs to be conducted in the area of smart city business models. It is essential for business models to generate trust in smart city systems. Doing so requires approaches in which the end users have direct control over their data streams, enabling both top-down and bottom-up approaches to civic engagement (Mulligan & Olsson, 2013). Therefore, governance models of the future will be driven by citizens, communities and their collaboration. As such, smart cities need to develop web-based and interactive context that enables a wider range of citizens to understand and contribute to the design of the city (Lee & Lee, 2014).

To sum up, the analysis of the most relevant papers in the area of smart cities shows that integrated ICT solutions play an enabling role in all "smart" solutions in each dimension. Furthermore, the relevance of data is especially stressed in the articles on smart economy, smart environment and smart mobility. We also show the importance of data in the context of smart cities in the word clouds in Figure 3. Another insight is that the dimensions are not completely isolated from one another; in contrast, the different dimensions need to be integrated in a mutual reference architecture.

The results of this review allowed us to establish the status and structure of the smart city research of the last decade, and highlight several research directions in each smart city dimension. We consider that our work provides a form of grounding for further research and practice. The findings enables researchers to understand the research structure of smart cities better and helps focusing their work into existing gaps in specific dimension. Furthermore, practitioners can use our findings to develop strategies and projects purposefully.

REFERENCES

Ahvenniemi, H., Huovila, A., Pinto-Seppa, I., & Airaksinen, M. (2017). What are the differences between sustainable and smart cities? *Cities*, *60*, 234–245.

Al Nuaimi, E., Al Neyadi, H., Mohamed, N., & Al-Jaroodi, J. (2015). Applications of big data to smart cities. *Journal of Internet Services and Applications*, *6*, Article 25.

Albino, V., Berardi, U., & Dangelico, R. M. (2015). Smart Cities: Definitions, Dimensions, Performance, and Initiatives. *Journal of Urban Technology*, *22*(1), 3–21.

Angelidou, M. (2014). Smart city policies: A spatial approach. *Cities*, *41*(1), 3–11.

Arroub, A., Zahi, B., Sabir, E., & Sadik, M. (2016). A literature review on Smart Cities: Paradigms, opportunities and open problems. *IEEE International Conference on Wireless Networks and Mobile Communications (WINCOM)*, 180–186.

Batagan, L. (2011). Smart Cities and Sustainability Models. *Informatica Economica*, *15*(3), 80–87.

Batty, M., Axhausen, K. W., Giannotti, F., Pozdnoukhov, A., Bazzani, A., Wachowicz, M., Ouzounis, G., & Portugali, Y. (2012). Smart cities of the future. *The European Physical Journal Special Topics*, *214*(1), 481–518.

Bibri, S. E., & Krogstie, J. (2017). Smart sustainable cities of the future: An extensive interdisciplinary literature review. *Sustainable Cities and Society*, *31*, 183–212.

Caragliu, A., Del Bo, C., & Nijkamp, P. (2011). Smart Cities in Europe. *Journal of Urban Technology*, *18*(2), 65–82.

Catriona, M., Cochrane, G., Cave, J., Millard, J., Pederson, J. K., Kåre, R., Liebe, A., Wissner, M., Massnik, R., & Kotternik, B. (2014). Mapping Smart cities in the EU: Directorate-General for Internal Policies. Policy Department A: Economic and Scientific Policy. *European Parlament*.

Chauhan, S., Agarwal, N., & Kar, A. K. (2016). Addressing big data challenges in smart cities: a systematic literature review. *Info*, *18*(4), 73–90.

Chourabi, H., Nam, T., Walker, S., Gil-Garcia, J. R., Mellouli, S., Nahon, K., Pardo, T. A., & Scholl, H. J. (Eds.) (2012). *Understanding Smart Cities: An Integrative Framework*. 2012 45th Hawaii International Conference on System Sciences.

Colding, J., & Barthel, S. (2017). An urban ecology critique on the "Smart City" model. *Journal of Cleaner Production*, *164*, 95–101.

Creswell, J. W. (2012). *Educational research: Planning, conducting, and evaluating quantitative and qualitative research* (Fourth Indian edition). PHI Learning Private Limited.

Djahel, S., Doolan, R., Muntean, G., & Murphy, J. (2015). A Communications-Oriented Perspective on Traffic Management Systems for Smart Cities: Challenges and Innovative Approaches. *IEEE Communications Surveys & Tutorials*, *17*(1), 125–151.

Ejaz, W., Naeem, M., Shahid, A., Anpalagan, A., & Jo, M. (2017). Efficient Energy Management for the Internet of Things in Smart Cities. *IEEE Communications Magazine*, *55*(1), 84–91.

European Commission (2012). Smart Cities and Communities - European Innovation Partnership.

Ferraris, A., Erhardt, N., & Bresciani, S. (2019). Ambidextrous work in smart city project alliances: unpacking the role of human resource management systems. *The International Journal of Human Resource Management*, *30*(4), 680–701.

Gharaibeh, A., Salahuddin, M. A., Hussini, S. J., Khreishah, A., Khalil, I., Guizani, M., & Al-Fuqaha, A. (2017). Smart Cities: A Survey on Data Management, Security, and Enabling Technologies. *IEEE Communications Surveys & Tutorials*, *19*(4), 2456–2501.

Giffinger, R., Gudrun, H., Gudrun, & Haindlmaier, G. (2010). Smart cities ranking: An effective instrument for the positioning of the cities. *ACE: Architecture, City and Environment*, *4*(12), 7–26.

Granier, B., & Hiroko, K. (2016). How are citizens involved in smart cities? Analysing citizen participation in Japanese "Smart Communities". *Information Polity: The International Journal of Government & Democracy in the Information Age*, *21*(1), 61–76.

Gupta, P., Chauhan, S., & Jaiswal, M. P. (2019). Classification of Smart City Research - a Descriptive Literature Review and Future Research Agenda. *Information Systems Frontiers*, *21*(3), 661–685.

Hashem, I. A. T., Chang, V., Anuar, N. B., Adewole, K., Yaqoob, I., Gani, A., Ahmed, E., & Chiroma, H. (2016). The role of big data in smart city. *International Journal of Information Management*, *36*(5), 748–758.

Hofmann, M., & Klinkenberg, R. (2014). *Rapidminer: Data mining use cases and business analytics applications. Chapman & Hall / CRC data mining and knowledge discovery series*. CRC Press.

Hollands, R. G. (2015). Critical interventions into the corporate smart city. *Cambridge Journal of Regions, Economy and Society*, *8*(1), 61–77.

Ismagilova, E., Hughes, L., Dwivedi, Y. K., & Raman, K. R. (2019). Smart cities: Advances in research--An information systems perspective. *International Journal of Information Management*, *47*, 88–100.

Jin, J., Gubbi, J., Marusic, S., & Palaniswami, M. (2014). An Information Framework for Creating a Smart City Through Internet of Things. *IEEE Internet of Things Journal*, *1*(2), 112–121.

Kummitha, R. K. R., & Crutzen, N. (2017). How do we understand smart cities? An evolutionary perspective. *Cities*, *67*, 43–52.

Lee, J., & Lee, H. (2014). Developing and validating a citizen-centric typology for smart city services. *Government Information Quarterly*, *31*(1), 93-105.

Lombardi, P., Giordano, S., Farouh, H., & Yousef, W. (2012). Modelling the smart city performance. *Innovation: The European Journal of Social Science Research*, *25*(2), 137–149.

Meijer, A., & Bolívar, M. P. R. (2016). Governing the smart city: a review of the literature on smart urban governance. *International Review of Administrative Sciences*, *82*(2), 392–408.

Menouar, H., Guvenc, I., Akkaya, K., Uluagac, A. S., Kadri, A., & Tuncer, A. (2017). UAV-Enabled Intelligent Transportation Systems for the Smart City: Applications and Challenges. *IEEE Communications Magazine*, *55*(3), 22–28.

Mori, K., & Christodoulou, A. (2012). Review of sustainability indices and indicators: Towards a new City Sustainability Index (CSI). *Environmental Impact Assessment Review*, *32*(1), 94–106.

Mulligan, C. E. A., & Olsson, M. (2013). Architectural Implications of Smart City Business Models: An Evolutionary Perspective. *IEEE Communications Magazine*, *51*(6), 80–85.

Perera, C., Zaslavsky, A., Christen, P., & Georgakopoulos, D. (2014). Sensing as a service model for smart cities supported by Internet of Things. *Transactions on Emerging Telecommunications Technologies*, *25*(1), 81–93.

Purnomo, F., & Prabowo, H. (2016). Smart City Indicators: A Systematic Literature Review. *Journal of Telecommunication, Electronic and Computer Engineering*, *8*(3), 161–164.

Qi, W., & Shen, Z.-J. M. (2019). A Smart-City Scope of Operations Management. *Production & Operations Management*, *28*(2), 393–406.

RapidMiner. (2020). *RapidMiner Studio* (Version 9.5) [Computer software]. RapidMiner.

Ruhlandt, R. W. S. (2018). The governance of smart cities: A systematic literature review. *Cities*, *81*, 1–23.

Schuurman, D., Baccarne, B., Marez, L. de, & Mechant, P. (2012). Smart Ideas for Smart Cities: Investigating Crowdsourcing for Generating and Selecting Ideas for ICT Innovation in a City Context. *Journal of Theoretical & Applied Electronic Commerce Research*, *7*(3), 49–62.

Solanas, A., Patsakis, C., Conti, M., Vlachos, I., Ramos, V., Falcone, F., Postolache, O., Perez-martinez, P., Pietro, R., Perrea, D., & Martinez-Balleste, A. (2014). Smart health: A context-aware health paradigm within smart cities. *IEEE Communications Magazine*, *52*(8), 74–81.

Sun, M., Wang, Y., Strbac, G., & Kang, C. (2019). Probabilistic Peak Load Estimation in Smart Cities Using Smart Meter Data. *IEEE Transactions on Industrial Electronics*, *66*(2), 1608–1618.

Swiss Academic Software. (2020). *Citavi* (Version 6) [Computer software]. Swiss Academic Software.

Trindade, E. P., Hinnig, M. P. F., da Costa, E. M., Marques, J. S., Bastos, R. C., & Yigitcanlar, T. (2017). Sustainable development of smart cities: a systematic review of the literature. *Journal of Open Innovation: Technology, Market, and Complexity*, *3*(1), 234.

Vanolo, A. (2014). Smartmentality: The Smart City as Disciplinary Strategy. *Urban Studies*, *51*(5), 883–898.

Webster, R., & Watson, R. (2002). Analyzing the Past to Prepare for the Future: Writing a Literature Review. *MIS Quarterly*, *26*(2), 13–23.

Xiong, Z., Sheng, H., Rong, W., & Cooper, D. E. (2012). Intelligent transportation systems for smart cities: a progress review. *Science China Information Sciences*, *55*(12), 2908–2914.

Zanella, A., Bui, N., Castellani, A., Vangelista, L., & Zorzi, M. (2014). Internet of Things for Smart Cities. *IEEE Internet of Things Journal*, *1*(1), Article 78, 22–32.

Zhang, K., Ni, J., Yang, K., Liang, X., Ren, J., & Shen, X. (2017). Security and Privacy in Smart City Applications: Challenges and Solutions. *IEEE Communications Magazine*, *55*(1), 122–129.

WHERE TO GO? SMART GUIDANCE BASED ON IOT SENSOR-DATA

Robin Effing[1], Robert J. Brouwer[2], Asen Iliev[2], Thomas Teunissen[2] and Fons Wijnhoven[2]
[1]*Saxion University of Applied Sciences / University of Twente, P.O. Box 70.000, 7500 KB Enschede, The Netherlands*
[2]*University of Twente, P.O. Box 217, 7500 AE Enschede, The Netherlands*

ABSTRACT

There is an increasing interest in indoor occupation and guidance information for business and societal purposes. Scientific literature has paid attention to various ways of detecting occupation using different sensors as data source including various algorithms for estimating occupation rates from this data. Gaining meaningful insights from the data still faces challenges because the potential benefits are not well understood. This study presents a proof-of-concept of an indoor occupation information system, following the design science methodology. We review various types of sensor data that are typically available or easy-to-install in buildings such as offices, classrooms and meeting rooms. This study contributes to current research by incorporating business requirements taken from expert interviews and tackling one of the main barriers for business by designing an affordable system on a common existing infrastructure. We believe that occupation information systems call for further research, in particular also in the context of social distancing because of covid19.

KEYWORDS

Occupation Detection, Occupation Capacity, Internet of Things, Smart Surveillance, WiFi Tracking, Smart City

1. INTRODUCTION

With recent trends of low-cost sensors, miniaturization of computing and wireless communication, it is easier than ever before to obtain real-time data about indoor occupancy. There is a significant interest in smart services for indoor environments as organizations aim to improve energy savings, improve facility utilization (Trivedi and Badarla, 2019), and want to implement social distancing in the context of the recent covid19 pandemic. Due to the pandemic there is an increased interest in crowd control and the smart guidance of people in order to prevent that places get crowded. Smart sensor-technology could help showing people where a lot of room is to make it easier to keep distance from each other. However, for organizations it is still a challenge to obtain sensor data and to develop a model to gain accurate occupancy estimations, mostly due to hardware limitations and cost. While commercial solutions with accuracy levels down to a centimetre are available, they offer a poor business case for most organizations' purposes. At the same time, organizations store readily-available, but unused data, which could be used for this purpose, such as schedules, WiFi logs, and employee/client log-in data. We argue that combining this data with low-cost sensors can also yield a level of accuracy that will match most business needs. In light of this, we suggest a data aggregator information service combining available data with low-cost sensor data to provide an adequate occupancy detection accuracy at the lowest cost. The Smart Campus of the University of Twente (UT) in the Netherlands will be used as a case for this study. The UT is already estimating people count numbers using WiFi Access Points, but not many insights nor applications are based on that. The facility management department is interested in further enrichment of the data in order to provide better insights about the traffic of students and levels of space utilization. At the same time, the data about building-occupation can also be provided to students in order to facilitate their spreading around public study spaces, by recommending the least crowded buildings. This smart routing became high-priority for many campuses given the recent outbreak of the coronavirus and the social distancing measures that followed.

The prototype of our occupation information system is designed for application in a university campus environment. The University of Twente, which serves as a testing environment, includes eleven buildings that house lecture rooms, bookable study rooms and public study spaces available to students. The campus-wide WiFi network is used to estimate lecture attendance and to create occupation heatmaps. A recent project added Passive Infrared (PIR) sensors to bookable study rooms in the library to see if booked rooms are actually used. However, data about public study spaces is still lacking and this could be of value for finding quiet study places and to warrant social distancing in the near future due to the corona virus risk. The main aim of this study is to design a service that could inform students about where space is available to study based on sensor-data.

The paper is structured as follows. First, the methodology is described which explains the three design science cycles in this paper. Second, a semi-structured literature review is carried out to gain better understanding of the current developments of sensors. Expert interviews provide additional feedback on sensors and different aspects of designing a guidance service. Afterwards, the case is presented with the University of Twente as a testbed. Finally, we present our discussion chapter including limitations and a reflection on the value of the findings.

2. METHODOLOGY

The methodology of this study is based upon the design science research approach (Hevner and Chatterjee, 2010), which consists of three different design science research cycles: the relevance cycle, the rigor cycle, and the design science cycle. This chapter describes the three research design science cycles of Hevner and explains how this study complies to the design science approach.

The rigor cycle discusses the already existing knowledge to the research project (Hevner, 2007). This cycle checks artifacts and applications found in the application domain, already existing theories and methods, and expertise and experience on the artifact. The rigor cycle has been applied to this study by performing a literature study on the meta artifacts, existing theories and methods. Afterwards, interviews have been conducted to obtain knowledge in the form of expertise and practical experience. Experts in the field of the research domain have been interviewed: IT, facility management and the University of Twente.

The relevance cycle describes the application domain and the problems together with the opportunities (Hevner, 2007). The problems and opportunities of the research are described in the introduction of the paper. People, organizational systems, and technical systems are part of the application domain and together describe how the newly designed artifact will be implemented in the already existing environment. Therefore, the stakeholders of the artifact are discussed in this chapter. In addition, to properly implement the artifact several user, functional, and quality requirements have been established.

The design cycle generates design alternatives and evaluates these designs against the requirements until a satisfactory design has been achieved (Hevner, 2007). Based on the correspondence of the sensors obtained during the rigor cycle and the requirements established in the relevance cycle, decisions were made on which sensor to use in the design phase. In addition, the prototype has been established to fulfil the requirements in several design iterations.

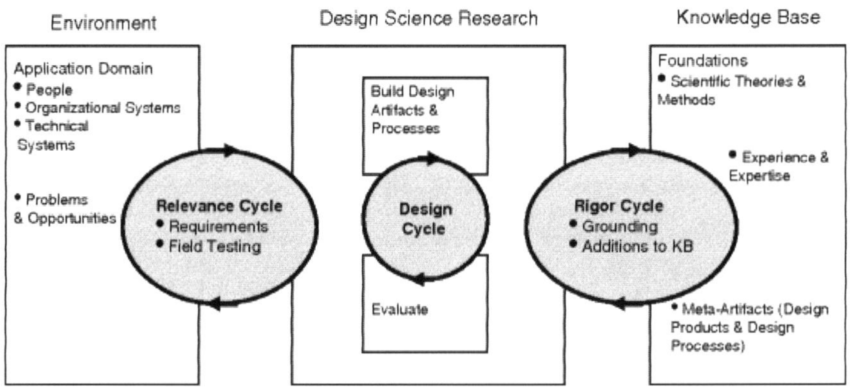

Figure 1. Overall view of the design science research cycle of Hevner (Hevner 2007)

3. THEORETICAL BACKGROUND

We carried out a literature review here with articles from the scientific database Scopus to inspect the current state of sensor research. The search terms "indoor localization" and "occupancy detection" were used to find trends and general information about similar systems. A list of sensor technologies was derived from the initial search that were used subsequently as keywords to find more detailed information for each type of sensor. Below is a summary for each sensor type identified, followed by an overview table.

3.1 WiFi

WiFi Received Signal Strength (RSS) has been a highly attractive method for indoor localization due to the wide deployment of WiFi Access Points (AP) and the fact that nearly no extra technical costs are involved (Guo *et al.*, 2020). However, RSS accuracy is notably low compared to other solutions, and is furthermore very sensitive to changes in dynamic environments. Any object can scatter the WiFi signal in unexpected ways, thus even a small change in the observed indoor space can cause big changes to the received signal, making it unreliable on its own. There are, however, efforts into increasing the accuracy by combining different techniques, such as machine-learning (Guo *et al.*, 2020). Furthermore, the ubiquity of WiFi APs and their ease of use with little extra cost allows this method to be used as a complement to enhance the accuracy of such a system.

3.2 Bluetooth Low Energy

Bluetooth Low Energy (BLE) is a wireless personal area network technology created by the Bluetooth Special Interest Group. This technology has been widely adopted among mobile device manufacturers, where it enables phones to communicate with small task-specific devices, such as Bluetooth headsets. Compared to ordinary Bluetooth, BLE requires considerably less power and is optimized for transferring small data packages (Tekler *et al.*, 2020). Common deployments of BLE for indoor positioning require a number of beacons or tags to be placed in the location of interest. The beacons broadcast a small data package to nearby bluetooth-enabled devices (readers). This is currently used in shopping malls for pushing advertisements to nearby users. Since BLE beacons are one-way communication devices, they can't return information about nearby devices (Borić, Díaz Redondo and Fernández Vilas, 2018). Instead the device uses the received data to estimate its location or sends it to a server. Different locations within the environment will have a different set of RSS, called a fingerprint. The reader collects RSS data from all nearby tags and sends this data to a server. The server has a list of predefined fingerprints, corresponding to specific locations with the associated RSSI received at that spot. The k-nearest neighbour algorithm is often used to establish at which fingerprint the user is located (Tekler *et al.*, 2020). Another method is to have the device estimate its position based on the signals received from beacons, however this is commonly applied for indoor localization systems instead. Researchers state the low price and power consumption as well as the ubiquitous adoption in mobile devices as the main advantages of BLE (Filippoupolitis, Oliff and Loukas, 2016). The user is, however, required to use an app for this method to work.

3.3 Passive Infrared Sensors

Passive Infrared Sensors (PIR) can be used to detect a movement of an individual and to detect the direction of movement. It is able to sense direction because it contains multiple sensing areas which combined output can be used to detect direction. The accuracy of PIR by itself is not always very good. It has the problem of cumulative errors since it cannot correct itself over time. Using the PIR by itself only gives an accuracy of around 27% for estimating room occupation over time. However, this can easily be improved to 90% when combined with other door sensors (Gaonkar *et al.*, 2019). One major drawback of PIR is that it only works in areas with clear doors. Since it works like a door counter it is not possible to deploy it in open areas without clear entrances.

3.4 Video Camera Recognition

Image recognition systems based on video cameras are currently used to determine the availability of parking spaces in car garages and cities. Cameras are used together with an IoT device to monitor the status of a parking spot (Ling *et al.*, 2017). In addition, this system was able to track the shapes and sizes of vehicles (Ling *et al.*, 2017) based on real-time processing of the data. These findings are useful in determining the occupation of seats in public places as well, since a camera can be used to check if a seat is occupied by a person or by, for instance, a bag. Machine learning can be applied to improve the recognition. As a result, the accuracy of using the image detection system is high according to completed experiments (Ling *et al.*, 2017). Hence, using cameras together with an image detection system would be suitable for the research of seat occupancy. Furthermore, real-time face-detection systems are used to identify and authenticate people in a specific picture of video. Statistical pattern recognition methods are used to recognize faces (Kollreider *et al.*, 2007). In addition, algorithms used to determine facial recognition exist, for instance, the Eigenfaces technique building onto the principal component analysis, the Fisherfaces algorithm, and the hidden Markov model (Mitchell, 2010). Currently, advances in technology make it possible to adjust the existing algorithms to achieve significant accuracy like 92% in the study of Pillay (Pillay and Viriri, 2019). Thermal imaging has also been applied to more easily and accurately distinguish between humans and non-living objects.

3.5 Carried Sensor

To locate a person, it is also possible to provide this person with a sensor, like an RFID tag which users use to send their location. This concept has already been tested with cars (Mainetti *et al.*, 2014) . It is also widely adopted in warehouses for tracking the location of goods. But as there is no way for the tag to distinguish between a free and an occupied seat, the only way to use them for occupancy detection is for everyone to wear a tag. Such systems for tracking humans are already used in health monitoring and some localization systems (Trivedi and Badarla, 2019). RFID tags give a high accuracy but this means that users need to wear the tag all the time and have many readers installed, due to their relatively low range. There should also be a thorough debate about the ethics of providing users with this technology. Since the location is determined inside the building this would have to rely on other sensors besides GPS. GPS does not work indoors. Barometers and and compass data or acoustic localization can be used as additional positioning-sensors (Retscher, 2006; Liu *et al.*, 2020).

3.6 Ultra Wide Band (UWB)

UWB is one of the most recent, accurate, and promising technologies for indoor localization (Alarifi *et al.*, 2016). For UWB, Beacons are deployed, similarly to BLE together with some carried receiver. Common methods for positioning are calculating the angle of arrival, time of arrival or time difference of arrival of the signal. Due to having very high bandwidth (100 Mbps) and extremely short wavelength of the signal it offers a high-accuracy positioning, even in the presence of severe multipath (Alarifi *et al.*, 2016). The signals effectively passes through walls, equipment, and any other obstacles. Errors can be brought down to the sub-centimeter range, making it suitable for systems with high accuracy requirements (Alarifi *et al.*, 2016). The main drawback of this technology is the high cost of the sensors and their infrastructure.

3.7 Pressure Sensors

Pressure sensors can measure the force applied to them for detecting an object. They have commonly been used in cars to detect the occupancy of passenger seats to assess if the airbag should deploy (Baur, Huber and Zeeb, 2007). In the case of buildings, the sensors can also be directly built into chairs. This method provides excellent accuracy for a low cost per sensor. However, it cannot distinguish between a student and his bag. A more expensive pressure sensor that uses electric field sensing can be used to achieve this (Tumpold and Satz, 2009). Capacitive pressure sensors sense the difference impedance between two areas of a chair to detect the presence of a person. It has the benefit of being contactless so it can be placed unobtrusively.

Despite its higher cost compared to traditional pressure sensors, it has no wearing parts, which reduces maintenance costs. They provide both rich and accurate tactile data but need to be installed in the seat.

3.8 Acoustic Sensors

Another method which can be used for occupation detection is acoustic sensing (Trivedi and Badarla, 2019). This method consists of a microphone that listens for any sound and optionally speakers that play a constant sound at the border of human hearing to be picked up by the microphone. It is, however, not very suitable for occupation estimations beyond detecting presence, and even then it is rarely used on its own, due to common false-positives and false-negatives (Trivedi and Badarla, 2019). In noisy environments when there is no direct path to the target it is a challenge to select a frequency of the sound for such a system (Liu *et al.*, 2020).

4. EXPERT EVALUATION

In one of the first relevance cycles of the design science approach, we conducted a series of face-to-face semi-structured expert interviews. Table 1 displays the list of experts included in this evaluation. The interviews mostly confirmed our findings from literature, but also provided additional insights into various aspects of the information service design. The most important points have been summarized per category.

Table 1. Expert selection including purpose and background

Interviewee	Purpose	Background
Interviewee A	IoT-Sensor-technology reliability check	Principal consultant at a smart IoT technology company
Interviewee B	IT-infrastructure possibilities overview	Director of a semi-public IT infrastructure company
Interviewee C	University information services control	Information service specialist based on smart WiFi networks
Interviewee D	Potential use and business purposes	Data-driven facility services planning expert

The choice of source data is not only dependent on the organization's budget and required accuracy, but also the type of environment one wants to detect occupation in. For example, fixed static environments allow accurate results using Time-of-Flight or RSS-based technologies, due to low variation of the signal. But if the area has a fixed entrance, it would be much easier and cheaper to use a simple PIR sensor instead. (Interviewee A). The non-sensor data available is also context dependent. In our case study, a roster schedule is available for the lecture rooms around public study spaces as well as booking data about study rooms, giving us an expected number of students that need to be deducted from the total count. The company from Interviewee D is a facility cleaning service supplier, for example, utilizes flight information from airports. Not all non-sensor data can be useful in this regard, though. Interviewee D noted that feedback systems are not reliable in real-time or short-term people counting, as the percentage of people who give feedback fluctuates too much.

4.1 Sensor-Data Review

Device-reliant solutions such as WiFi, Bluetooth and mobile sensors may not accurately account for the number of people. According to Interviewee B, disadvantages of sensing devices, instead of humans are that several devices can be worn by the same person, or the device might be set up to not be discoverable by the beacons or access points, or the device measuring in a different area as expected, all of which skew the results.

Two general types of approaches using mobile devices have been identified both from literature (Trivedi and Badarla, 2019) and Interviewee C device-based and network-based. Network-based approaches are characterized by having an infrastructure of beacons or access points that can listen for nearby devices. When using such an infrastructure, there is no need for the users to install an app, making it more flexible (Interviewee C). On the other hand, you can't count devices that have their WiFi/Bluetooth turned off. This approach can give a good estimation of the number of people nearby. However, it's possible to connect to an AP from another room and deduplication in case of multiple devices is not always accurate. As such, results lack room-level granularity, but can be accurate on floor-level. Device-based approaches require the user to install an app on their mobile device. This method has a higher accuracy compared to network-based WiFi and BLE, due to using additional data sources from the device's sensors to pinpoint the location. In this case the device listens for nearby beacons. The collected data is either used to estimate location using a local database or the information is sent to a server, and the device receives its location back from that server. This approach is more commonly used for localization and navigation systems, however, as you can only see the devices that are actively using the app to navigate at this moment. In light of this, real-time data can't be accurate without a very high adoption level of the app.

Passive infrared sensors are already widely employed in office buildings for controlling automatic lights, blinds, heating and many others. Because of its cheap price and low power consumption, PIR is recommended in solutions where low level of detail is sufficient. For accurate people counting only the use of PIR sensors is not enough. There are also PIR door counters which are quite accurate short-term (95%+, Interviewee D), but they suffer from having an accumulating error over time (Interviewee C). For example, two people walking hand-in-hand are likely to be counted as only one person.

Image recognition is another popular method in practice. Advances in machine learning and AI have led to algorithms that can even recognize faces and objects in less than a second without high computational requirements (Interviewee A). Thermal imaging improves accuracy in distinguishing humans even further. However, while experts consider cameras relatively cheap, such a solution is more costly compared to PIR or using already available WiFi infrastructure (Interviewee B). However, each expert noted that cameras add privacy concerns that need to be addressed. There are ways to circumvent this, for example by analyzing the image offline and sending only the people count and deleting the image (Interviewee B) and installing the camera overhead so that faces are not visible (Interviewee C).

Pressure sensors installed on seats are a very easy way to get accurate occupation information. Such a method is applied for example at a big Airport (Interviewee D). It is a good approach for seat-level accuracy for indoor locations with a relatively small number of fixed seats. The sensors themselves are very cheap, but the total cost of the system in our case exceeds most other options, due to the large quantity of sensors required. The University of Twente, for example, has 10,000 chairs that would need to be equipped with a sensor as well as with a battery and a networking device (Interviewee C).

4.2 Business Value

The experts shared the view that there is a growing demand for indoor occupancy data. Information about the level of utilization of buildings is needed for management decisions aimed at better space management. However, it's important to note the accuracy of the data when taking management decisions.

While there is growing demand for indoor occupation detection, there isn't much demand for high positioning accuracy. Instead organizations are interested in the cheapest solution that will provide a suitable level of accuracy according to their business needs. While a seat-level accuracy can provide better insights, the additional cost usually doesn't warrant the much higher investment required. However, according to interviewee B there is demand for high positioning accuracy in the fire department. The fire department wants to know if there are still people inside of a building and where these people exactly are to rescue them. Students and customers in general demand better information services, but also expect them for free. Furthermore, having an intrusive method of occupancy detection such as cameras is mistrusted, even if the goals of the camera placement are clearly stated by the organization.

4.3 Privacy Concerns

All experts noted the importance of ensuring privacy in such an information system. One of the recommendations was to minimize the personal data stored on the system. Images can be analysed by an AI counting people internally, sending only count estimates over a network, not storing any images. Furthermore, from the point of view of a provider of such an information service, it's not recommended to store data on own servers, but rather create a self-contained system at client's location, using clients' data servers. MAC addresses are also considered personal data, and as such should be anonymized. Interviewee C also notes that MAC addresses should not be traceable for longer than a day. While privacy control is very important, interviewee D noted that the system still should be designed in a way that allows sharing the data between the stakeholders interested in it. As a contractor of the UT, having access to the occupation data can help them provide a better service to the university. Table 2 gives a summary of the literature and expert's evaluations of sensor data technologies.

Table 2. Summary of the sensors identified from literature and interviews

Technology	Advantages	Disadvantages
Device-reliant		
WiFi	Uses existing infrastructure, unobtrusive	Low accuracy, negatively affected by dynamic environments. Device de-duplication challenges
BLE	Low power consumption, high adoption among mobile devices	Needs users to actively use an app, needs beacon infrastructure
Mobile sensors	Available in all modern devices. Combining all sensors provide high accuracy	Needs users to actively use an app and allow permissions to access sensor data
UWB	Very high accuracy positioning, even without direct line of sight.	High cost of UWB equipment, app use, challenge of UWB antenna placement
Self-sufficient		
PIR	Cheap, low energy consumption, proven and widely-used tech	Accumulating error, more useful for detecting presence
Camera	Very high accuracy, high granularity of occupation data	Social obtrusiveness and privacy issues
Acoustic	High location accuracy (2mm-1.2cm depending on setup), low time latency (6-250 ms)	Severe attenuation of aerial acoustic signals, efficiency reduces as distance increases, no counting
Mounted/wearable		
Pressure	Very accurate in 10-100kg range	Needs to be installed on each seat. Needs additional IoT components to send data over a network.
RFID	Cheap tags, low power consumption	Requires people to wear RFID tags, reader needs to be in close proximity to read the tag; tracks people/objects, not occupation

5. CASE STUDY FOR VALIDATION OF THE DESIGN

In this section, we relate our findings to the specifics of our case study. We begin the relevance cycle by describing the case of the University of Twente (UT). Requirements derived from the stakeholder analysis are applied to select the most appropriate scenario out of possibilities identified in the rigor cycle. Finally, we evaluate the feasibility of our idea by carrying out a short feasibility study.

Considering the Students' perspective, they desire to find a free seat in a public study place. They want the proposed information system to appoint them a building, floor of a building, or area of a floor which they are sure of there is an empty seat or a less crowded environment. The application for the students should have an overview of all the buildings and a simple indication system which points out the relative occupancy of seats in public study places. To make the application more friendly and easy-to-use, a filter and recommendationoption should be added.

The second stakeholder in the IS design is the university itself. The facility management department do not have proper information on the occupancy of seats in public study areas. They need this information to determine if there is a need for additional seats in public study areas. Having this data may result in a better utilization of space overall. So, for the university the IS should show a clear overview of the occupancy rates of each building, floor of a building, area of a floor, and in total. Moreover, the users should be able to filter on the building, floor of a building, and area of a floor to give them a more general overview.

The final stakeholder group consist of third parties such as the cleaning service. For third parties it is valuable to obtain the location which currently has the lowest occupancy, so they are able to clean a place without much interference of students studying in a certain place. This IS will give them additional information about public study places. Cleaning services should be able to see the relative occupancy rate of each building, floor of a building, and area of a floor to determine the least busy public study places. Interviewee D argued that the cost optimization is mostly a matter of perception.

Table 3 gives an overview of scores of the different sensors which could be applicable at the UT in public study places together with the quality requirements specified. WiFi is chosen as the baseline and therefore all other sensors are compared to the scores of using just WiFi. A scale of the three levels +, 0 and - has been chosen to keep the overview as clear as possible and to determine the total score of the sensor(s). These levels have the following descriptions: + shows that a requirement is fully met and is thus a positive level, 0 displays that a requirement is partially met and is thus between the positive and negative level, and - describes that a requirement is not met and receives a negative level.

Table 3. An overview of different sensor combinations with their scores on the quality requirements

Sensor type/Quality requirement	Accuracy		Ease of implementation		Legal concerns	Social obtrusive-ness	Implemen-tation costs		Total score of the sensors
	Number of people accurately measured	*Positioning of people accurately measured*	*Low amount of effort to create a system*	*Low amount of effort to obtain devices/equipment*	*Low data privacy concerns*	*Low social obtrusiveness of the sensor*	*Low costs of implementing the system*	*Low costs of obtaining devices/sensors/equipment*	
WiFi (baseline)	-	-	+	+	0	+	+	+	+++
WiFi + BLE	0	+	-	-	0	0	0	-	--
WiFi + Infrared	0	-	+	0	0	0	+	0	+
Cameras	+	+	0	0	-	-	0	0	0

The first scenario considered is using just WiFi to determine the seat occupancy in public study areas. As can be seen in table 3 a significant amount of the requirements is met when WiFi is used. The ease of implementation requirement is met, since the UT already has a system in place and uses it to determine the number of people on a certain floor in a certain building on the UT. In addition, the social obtrusiveness is low, as students' phones are used as a sensor without them knowing this happens. Furthermore, data privacy concerns are low, since the data obtained is only used to create new value for the students and does not harm them in any way. Moreover, the data is not publicly accessible, but only when connected to the WiFi of the UT. As a result of the infrastructure being in place, the costs will be low. Therefore, the cost requirement is met as well. The only downside of using WiFi is the low accuracy. As a result, only a rough estimation of the number of people and their position can be given.

An alternative to the scenario just using WiFi is combining it with BLE. The main advantage of this scenario is the improvement of the accuracy. However, this scenario brings several disadvantages as well.

First, there is no existing system at the UT using BLE. In addition, there are no beacons to track the BLE signals from the mobile phones of students. As a result, the costs of creating a system will be a bit costly and a significant number of Bluetooth beacons have to be bought resulting in a high cost of devices. Third, the accuracy of BLE is high when using the right version, but when using an older version the accuracy depends on if you have your Bluetooth turned on or not. Fourth, the Bluetooth beacons have to be installed and are visible to students which result in a small social obtrusiveness. In conclusion, combining WiFi with BLE will result in a small increase of the accuracy, but add many disadvantages which do not occur when using only WiFi.

The third scenario consists of combining WiFi with infrared sensors. Adding infrared sensors will increase the accuracy of the number of people in a certain study place. However, an infrared sensor might detect the bag on your back as another person. This error cannot be filtered out during the day and will slowly result in a bigger error in the estimation of the number of people. An additional downside of infrared sensors is the utility. Infrared sensors can only be used in public study places where the entries and exits are clear and not in large public areas, since you cannot determine where people are in large areas using infrared sensors. Another small disadvantage is the fact that infrared sensors have to be installed in some areas which students can notice. One major advantage of using infrared sensors is availability in certain buildings of the UT. In addition, the data privacy concerns are low, as only the number of people in a certain public study place are saved. In conclusion, infrared sensors can improve the accuracy without having to deal with additional disadvantages.

The fourth scenario considered uses only cameras. On first sight, using cameras to determine the occupancy of available seats in public places seems favourable, due to the high accuracy of cameras. However, there are a significant number of disadvantages at the ease of implementation, legal, social obtrusiveness and cost side. There are already cameras being used at the UT, but not connected to a system which measures the number of available seats in public study places. Therefore, the system has to be tweaked to work in this study. In addition, cameras have to be bought to install one in every public place. This will result in a social obtrusiveness concern as well, since students are being filmed. The data privacy concerns and social obtrusiveness concerns have to be taken into account when choosing cameras. Since the infrastructure is not fully in place, additional costs have to be made as well. In conclusion, cameras are highly accurate, but add a significant number of disadvantages.

After exploring all four scenarios, we decided to choose the first scenario using WiFi only. According to the literature and experts interviews, this scenario fits the project best. As can be seen in Table 3, WiFi meets the ease of implementation and costs requirements. However, the accuracy requirement is not totally met. As a result, we keep the low accuracy in mind when designing the prototype by not using the exact number and positioning of people. Instead it will give a rough estimation of the number of people and an indication of the positioning of people per floor instead of per table in a public study room.

Figure 2 shows the Archimate 3.1 diagram of a layered high-level architecture of our proposed service. Certain elements are combined, simplified or removed from the model to preserve clarity. Starting from the technology layer, data recorded from WiFi access points and PIR sensors (currently only in the library) is stored on the UT databases, along with Roster data for lecture rooms and Booking data for study rooms. Anonymized data from these sources, limited to just people count, location and time will be drawn into the backend of our app. The backend is also hosted on the UT servers. Aside from the data, the backend also contains two application components. The Occupancy analysis and prediction which takes into account both real-time and historical data. It uses a regression model to predict future occupation. The recommender algorithm uses near real-time data to suggest a ranking of least occupied spaces fitting customer criteria. The backend is accessible via two separate endpoints.

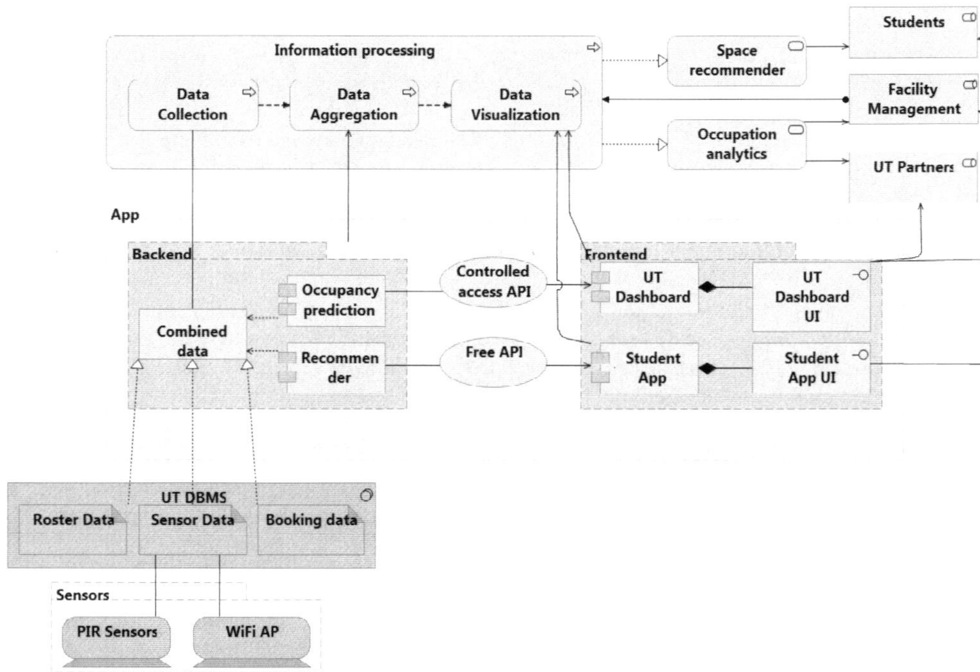

Figure 2. An architecture of an occupation guidance service

The recommender is available to the Student app via a non-restricted API. Historical data from the analytics and prediction component, however, is more sensitive and will only be accessible via a secured login on the UT dashboard page. The backend of the application layer takes care of collecting and aggregating the data, while the front end serves as means of visualization. The processes of collecting, aggregating and visualizing the data realize the two services our system is offering to students and the UT. Third-party contractors may also be allowed access to the dashboard at the UT's discretion. Responsibility for managing the process is assigned to the Facility management.

The occupation information service will be displayed in two separate apps - one for students and one for university staff and they will rely on data already available in the UT's database (WiFi and roster data). The student app will contain a recommender algorithm and a filter to help students find public study spaces faster and easier based on their preferences. The UT app will be a dashboard showing occupation data that can also be filtered based on the user's preferences.

We try to use as much existing infrastructure as possible. Hundreds of WiFi APs are available on campus. Our other stream of input data is the rostering schedule for the rooms around public study spaces. Server and database costs will also be negligible as data is already stored on UT servers and we assume only a minimal amount of additional overhead will be incurred from incorporating our system. The apps that need to be developed will use existing design from the UT app, are not complicated and will be cheap to develop. The system will also have an API developed for it that will facilitate controlled access to the UT databases.

6. DISCUSSION

We reviewed literature on occupation detection systems to gain insights about the current state of the field. Our focus was on the various sensor technologies being used for data generation and the overall design of such a system. What we found was that complete designs for an occupation detection system are hard to find in scientific literature, however each separate sensor was extensively researched. Most papers concerned with design were focused specifically on the algorithms used to extract information from the sensor data to improve the system's accuracy. However, despite the focus on accuracy, it is also difficult to obtain a good understanding of the accuracy one can expect from each sensor. The reported accuracy numbers vary a lot across papers due to different methods and assumptions, and it is hard to generalize from those results. Also, most papers focused on only one data source. Few papers analyse the potential of combining sensors and the benefits of doing so are still not very clear.

Most papers acknowledge the potential insights that can be gained by analysing occupation data such as "energy savings, user comfort and degree of automation" (Trivedi and Badarla, 2019). However, estimating the exact extent of those benefits seems elusive. Our expert interviews also confirmed that companies are interested in occupation insights. However, they noted that businesses don't want to spend a lot of money on this, as justifying the expenditure is difficult. We also identified several gaps between literature and practice. The high accuracy reported in literature doesn't match the estimates of our experts. It remains up for debate whether accuracy is overstated in scientific literature, or if practitioners are not making the most of recent advancements in the field.

We argue that the perceived high cost of the investment, combined with uncertainty in the potential benefits are the main factors preventing faster adoption in a business setting. Research that quantifies potential benefits is needed in our opinion. This is, however, difficult, as the design and therefore cost of such a system depend highly on the business goal and setting. All experts also mentioned data privacy as a challenge for this type of systems.

Future work should expand the occupation information service's information processing. Currently a basic recommender and a general descriptive analytics dashboard are included for simplicity's sake. Designing a recommender that takes into account location proximity would be an important addition for the students for example. Furthermore, user accounts and social contact information can be included in the information processing, allowing user interaction and richer data. Those additions are expensive, however, and require further cost-benefit analysis.

The previous limitation is partly due to the COVID-19 (coronavirus) outbreak which happened in the middle of the study. The coronavirus led to a closure of the whole University of Twente campus, which made the existing infrastructure measuring the number of people in an area based on WiFi useless, as there were no students in the University of Twente buildings. As a result, this is a significant limitation to the study.

Another limitation to the study is the decision to use one central scenario in the designing phase. In this case, the WiFi as a baseline is chosen in the design. However, creating and testing other sensors or combinations of sensors based on data triangulation could have led to different insights which are not explored. It is suggested to, in future work, explore different scenarios where other sensors and combinations of sensors are explored in the same environment. For instance, looking into PIR sensors which the University of Twente uses to estimate the number of people in a specific area as well. Also, we did not include the combination with existing telecom signals such as 5g which are also more convenient using in a outdoor situation.

In this paper we presented a preliminary design of an occupation information service - a potential new niche in the information market but potentially very useful in a social-distancing guidance application. While there seems to be a growing demand for such a service, there are several challenges that a viable business model needs to overcome - cost, unclear benefits and data privacy concerns. We proposed a low-budget solution, showing that the cost of such a can be minimized by a combination of available infrastructure and data sources. We reviewed different source systems for gathering occupation data with their advantages and disadvantages with regards to business requirements. The implications for business are that when high accuracy of occupation data is not necessary, estimations made by matching already available data can fulfil needs at a low cost. The business needs to approach occupation information systems with a clear idea of how to use the information and its value, however, as the benefits are still difficult to quantify or generalize.

REFERENCES

Alarifi, A. *et al.* (2016) 'Ultra wideband indoor positioning technologies: Analysis and recent advances', *Sensors (Switzerland)*, 16(5), pp. 1–36. doi: 10.3390/s16050707.

Baur, R., Huber, H.-P. and Zeeb, E. (2007) '(12) United States Patent'. United States. Available at: https://patentimages.storage.googleapis.com/c1/c6/af/f51bc6e04e48e6/US7162111.pdf.

Borić, M., Díaz Redondo, R. P. and Fernández Vilas, A. (2018) 'Space Occupancy through BLE Dynamic Broadcasting', *Wireless Communications and Mobile Computing*, 2018, pp. 1–17. doi: 10.1155/2018/2182614.

Filippoupolitis, A., Oliff, W. and Loukas, G. (2016) 'Bluetooth Low Energy Based Occupancy Detection for Emergency Management', *Proceedings - 2016 15th International Conference on Ubiquitous Computing and Communications and 2016 8th International Symposium on Cyberspace and Security, IUCC-CSS 2016*, pp. 31–38. doi: 10.1109/IUCC-CSS.2016.013.

Gaonkar, P. *et al.* (2019) 'Occupancy Estimation in Semi-Public Spaces using Sensor Fusion and Context Awareness', *Proceedings of 2019 IEEE Region 10 Symposium, TENSYMP 2019*, 7, pp. 131–136. doi: 10.1109/TENSYMP46218.2019.8971134.

Guo, X. *et al.* (2020) 'Robust WiFi Localization by Fusing Derivative Fingerprints of RSS and Multiple Classifiers', *IEEE Transactions on Industrial Informatics*, 16(5), pp. 3177–3186. doi: 10.1109/TII.2019.2910664.

Hevner, A. and Chatterjee, S. (2010) 'Design Science Research in Information Systems', in *Design Research in Information Systems: Theory and Practice*. Boston, MA: Springer US, pp. 9–22. doi: 10.1007/978-1-4419-5653-8_2.

Hevner, A. R. (2007) 'A Three Cycle View of Design Science Research', *Scandinavian Journal of Information Systems*, 19(2), pp. 87–92. doi: http://aisel.aisnet.org/sjis/vol19/iss2/4.

Kollreider, K. *et al.* (2007) 'Real-time face detection and motion analysis with application in "liveness" assessment', *IEEE Transactions on Information Forensics and Security*, 2(3), pp. 548–558. doi: 10.1109/TIFS.2007.902037.

Ling, X. *et al.* (2017) 'Identifying parking spaces & detecting occupancy using vision-based IoT devices', *GIoTS 2017 - Global Internet of Things Summit, Proceedings*. doi: 10.1109/GIOTS.2017.8016227.

Liu, M. *et al.* (2020) 'Indoor acoustic localization: a survey', *Human-centric Computing and Information Sciences*. Springer Berlin Heidelberg, 10(1). doi: 10.1186/s13673-019-0207-4.

Mainetti, L. *et al.* (2014) 'Integration of RFID and WSN technologies in a Smart Parking System', *2014 22nd International Conference on Software, Telecommunications and Computer Networks, SoftCOM 2014*. FESB, University of Split, pp. 104–110. doi: 10.1109/SOFTCOM.2014.7039099.

Mitchell, C. (Albert N. S. of E. (2010) *Applications of Convolutional Neural Networks to Facial Detection and Recognition for Augmented Reality and Wearable Computing*. Albert Nerken School of Engineering.

Pillay, P. and Viriri, S. (2019) 'Foresight: Real time facial detection and recognition using webassembly and localized deep neural networks', *2019 Conference on Information Communications Technology and Society, ICTAS 2019*. IEEE, pp. 1–6. doi: 10.1109/ICTAS.2019.8703634.

Retscher, G. (2006) 'Location determination in indoor environments for Pedestrian navigation', *Record - IEEE PLANS, Position Location and Navigation Symposium*. IEEE, 2006, pp. 547–555. doi: 10.1109/PLANS.2006.1650643.

Tekler, Z. D. *et al.* (2020) 'A scalable Bluetooth Low Energy approach to identify occupancy patterns and profiles in office spaces', *Building and Environment*. Elsevier Ltd, 171, p. 106681. doi: 10.1016/j.buildenv.2020.106681.

Trivedi, D. and Badarla, V. (2019) 'Occupancy detection systems for indoor environments: A survey of approaches and methods', *Indoor and Built Environment*, 0(0), pp. 1–17. doi: 10.1177/1420326X19875621.

Tumpold, D. and Satz, A. (2009) 'Contactless seat occupation detection system based on electric field sensing', *IECON Proceedings (Industrial Electronics Conference)*, pp. 1823–1828. doi: 10.1109/IECON.2009.5414836.

EVIDENCE-DRIVEN POLICY MAKING USING HETEROGENEOUS SOURCES OF DATA - THE CASE OF A CONTROL PARKING SYSTEM

Anastasios Papazoglou Chalikias[1], Ioannis Tsampoulatidis[1,2], Filareti Tsalakanidou[1],
Spiros Nikolopoulos[1], Ioannis (Yiannis) Kompatsiaris[1], Konstanstinos Doudouliakis[3],
Petros Papafilis[3] and Georgios Papastergios[3]
[1]*CERTH-ITI, Greece*
[2]*Aristotle University of Thessaloniki, School of Architecture, Greece*
[3]*Municipality of Thessaloniki, Greece*

ABSTRACT

Policy making is generally and largely based on intuition and not backed up by evidence. Our goal is to transform the existing paradigm of policy making into an evidence-driven approach enabled by heterogenous sources of data. Methods for data collection, efficient storage and data analysis are implemented to measure the economic activity, assess the environmental impact and evaluate the social consequences of certain policy decisions. The extracted pieces of evidence are used to inform, advise, monitor, evaluate and revise the decisions made by policy planners. In this paper, we examine the use case of Thessaloniki's controlled parking system and its optimization balancing between economic growth, environmental impact and citizen's satisfaction, by harmonizing and visualizing heterogenous sources of data. The case study evaluation consists of a multi–step process that involves user recruitment, user training, formulation of platform-usage scenarios, platform evaluation based on questionnaires, and finally in-depth questionnaire analysis.

KEYWORDS

Policy Making, Big Data, Visualization, Economic Growth, Environmental Impact, Citizen Satisfaction

1. INTRODUCTION

In the past years, interest in the study of policy making has been on the increase. Large multimodal datasets are increasingly available on some facets of policy making and a few useful concepts have been developed, as comprehensibly described in (Dunn, 1981). While some countries have engaged in interesting improvement experiments, no shift for the better in overall policy making has occurred (Dror, 2017). A big issue with the current paradigm of policy making is that there is not enough evidence to justify their creation, thus depending on intuition.

As stated in (Sanderson, 2002) there are two main forms of evidence required in the approach to improve governmental effectiveness. The first is evidence to promote accountability in terms of results – evidence that the government is working effectively. The second is evidence to promote improvement through more effective policies and programmes – evidence of how well such policies and programmes 'work' in different circumstances. These two forms of evidence are different in nature. The first is primarily in the form of information on attributes of performance and is reflected in the growth of performance management in government (Treasury, H. M. S., 2000). The second form of evidence is qualitatively different from the first and is concerned with the knowledge of how policy interventions achieve change in social systems. In the notion of a modern government, evaluation in particular is required to play an enhanced role in providing information on performance to enhance accountability and 'control by results', and in providing evidence of what works to inform policy learning and improvement.

The overall purpose of this article is to explore the notion of evidence-based policy making in the context of policy intervention in increasingly complex social systems and the potential role of piloting and evaluation. Instead of only relying on evaluation during or after the piloting phase after a specific policy is in place, we try to transform the existing paradigm of policy making into an evidence-driven approach aided by the proactive use of heterogeneous sources of data so as to justify every single policy approach. This means that the evaluation of a specific policy can be performed even before a policy is in place.

Our ambition is to differentiate from existing approaches by simultaneously considering environmental, economic and social data, enabling in this way the support of policy design in a holistic manner, taking into account urban resilience. In addition, the proposed approach enables the meaningful cross-correlation of different indicators that can allow shifting from simple observations to short-term predictions. We propose an approach to homogenize the heterogeneous sources of data by using their spatio-temporal properties to interconnect them. In this way, we can support complex queries and facilitate decision making processes that need to simultaneously evaluate the impact of more than one aspects (i.e. environmental, economic and social).

2. METHODOLOGY

2.1 Multi-faceted Approach for Policy Design, Implementation and Evaluation

Our proposed methodology foresees the use of heterogenous data sources to facilitate the decisions required to reach the strategic goals of the city of Thessaloniki. In facilitating this process, we adopted the IAMER (Inform - Advise - Monitor - Evaluate - Revise) approach for developing a multi-faceted dashboard. This dashboard is composed of five different facets that present information and extract insights that are essential to the decision-making process. More specifically: a) **Inform**: Extracts and presents the evidence that are necessary for policy makers to make informed decisions when defining the projects, policies and programs incorporated in their technical program; b) **Advise**: Presents the decision makers with the estimated impact on their planned activities on the resiliency status of their city; c) **Monitor**: Relies on the data obtained from the sensing infrastructures and use the data mining and visualization tools to establish a set of monitoring mechanisms; d) **Evaluate**: Building on the information gathered through the monitoring mechanisms defines a set of KPIs (Key Performance Indicators) that allows quantifying and assessing the impact of the enforced policies. These KPIs serve as the criteria for success or failure of the enforced policies; e) **Revise**: Depending on the value of the KPIs revises the projects, policies and programs for next years' technical program considering also the weaknesses that have caused certain policies to fail. Our main focus in this work lies on the first two facets of the IAMER methodology, Inform and Advise.

2.2 Architecture

Our platform's architecture, consists of seven incremental layers that establish a powerful Software as a Services (SaaS) solution for city data science in the direction of urban development.

Data Layer: There are three main categories of data that are used in our platform: i) *Real-time* data coming from sensors such as vehicle emission measurements, but also historical data found in archives to form time-series data. These data are used in the analytics layer to sense the environmental impact. ii) *Structured data* coming from official sources e.g. GIS-based data on income from a car parking system. These data will be used in the analytics layer to sense the economic activity. iii) *Unstructured data* coming from the open participatory platforms, making engaged citizens to act as living sensors. These data are used in the analytics layer to sense the social consequences.

Collection Layer: The successful collection, integration and analysis of the data classified under the above categories play a significant role. Having in mind the extent of data heterogeneity, our platform integrates the collected data under a common analysis framework. Several pre-processing activities towards data cleaning and harmonization are performed according to (CUTLER Deliverable 3.2). During the data cleaning process, data errors are classified into four types: i) *Pattern violations:* The data are transformed to deal with formatting or attribute value issues. ii) *Rule violations:* Values violating any kind of integrity constraints, for example unique value fields inside data entries. iii) *Duplicates:* Filtering of duplicate entries. iv) *Outliers:* Outlier detection using analytical methods and techniques tailored to each case.

Storage Layer: Our platform's secure large scale storage and processing infrastructure is based on a hybrid cloud based approach. The focus is on the design of a flexible and horizontally scalable architecture that can be easily customized. The solution leverages open source technologies as well as proprietary ones. The architecture takes a security-by-design approach to address any significant threats identified in the threat analysis (CUTLER Deliverable 2.2). The cloud based and network infrastructure, provides a highly scalable bandwidth and capacity that would facilitate the extensive scope of advanced development and use case scenario testing.

Analytics: The purpose of this layer is to translate information into evidence and actionable knowledge by utilizing data analytics. This layer consists of algorithms that operate and aggregate time-series data, interconnect and filter data on a spatio-temporal level, as well as analyze data using machine learning algorithms (e.g. sentiment analysis on textual data provided by citizens in participatory platforms).

Visualization: The platform is designed to act as a multi-tenant, cloud-based, advanced data analytics tool for policy makers and is deployed in a multi-facet dashboard. The visualization widgets allow policy makers to customize the software based on their own needs and requirements. The visualization widgets are coming from economic, environmental and social aspects and builds upon visualization methods such as clustering maps, various charts, tag clouds, and others.

Policies: The outcome and integration of the above layers forms our ecosystem which purpose is to facilitate policy design using heterogenous sources of data towards urban development that effectively balance between economic growth, environmental impact and social consequences. Using this ecosystem the city officials are able to carry out a full cycle of policy development process, including design, implementation and evaluation.

2.3 Data Types and Harmonization

Data harmonization refers to the process of aligning data from heterogeneous sources into a coherent and unambiguous set (CUTLER Deliverable 3.2). Therefore, to deal with various naming and structural differences among diverse data sources, we have relied on the following rules: i) **Time**: Date and time information within have different naming and representations. It was decided to use the following naming conventions where present: Time, Date, DateTime, Timestamp, Year, Month, WeekDay; ii) **Geographical**: Geographic information, is mostly provided as geographical coordinates, but sometimes it is also given at the level of territorial units, e.g. municipalities. It was decided to follow the approach suggested by Nomenclature of territorial units for statistics (NUTS). If geographical coordinates are provided, then it is recommended to use "latitude", "longitude", and "altitude" naming accepting decimal values; iii) **Environmental**: A unified schema was established to model each parameter in terms of naming, units, timezone and usage of spatial information; iv) **Economic**: Most data regarding economic activity are collected by a central statistics office. The collected data then become available to international organizations like the Organization of Economic Cooperation and Development (OECD) and Eurostat among others. Thus, the variables' names, the measurement units and all other reporting indicators are identical across these data sources; v) **Social**: Considering the heterogeneity of social data sources, it is necessary to define a unified data model, so that the data is harmonized before processing. The data model that we have used in our approach is an extension of the SIMMO (Socially Interconnected MultiMedia-enriched Objects) model.

Moreover, the need to take into account different aspects of a certain policy (i.e. economic growth, environmental impact and social consequences) calls for an approach that would enable to query and interact with heterogeneous sources of data in a seamless manner. In this direction, all sources of data need to be tightly interconnected so as to enable their dynamic filtering and interactive interrogation. To this end, we have relied on the spatio-temporal properties of the data to interconnect them. More specifically, we are harmonizing our heterogenous data sources by using various techniques to make sure that each one of them have a spatio-temporal dimension. This way the different datasets can be projected in the same space and we can find correlations between them that impact the envisioned policies. By adding a longitudinal dimension to our datasets that are lacking one, allows us to test new hypotheses about urban structure and dynamics, and by taking into account the specific timeframes that these data belong to, we can predict with certainty specific recurring events.

3. POLICY

3.1 Controlled Parking System

Thessaloniki is a densely inhabited city with limited space available for building new infrastructure. A way of providing solutions to continuing urban problems is to change the use of the existing infrastructure. The area with most different uses is the 1st Municipal District, with people moving towards or away from it during day and night and there is a very high demand for parking spaces. Consequently, the available parking space needs to be controlled.

Since 2017, a new controlled parking system (CPS) has been installed in the 1st and 3rd Municipal Districts of Thessaloniki, which is known as THESi (THESi). The available parking space is divided into white and blue sectors. White sectors are destined for visitors while blue sectors are reserved for permanent residents. More specifically, every visitor must pay a fee per hour in order to park his vehicle in one of the spots of a white sector. At the same time, each resident has to go through an application process, submitting all necessary material/documentation to municipal authorities. This way he can become a holder of a parking card that will allow him to park his vehicle in any spot in a blue sector of his district. In each of the different White or Blue sectors there are multiple parking spots.

The system is supervised by the Municipal Police, which plays a crucial role in the establishment of the CPS. Whenever a new measure is imposed there is always dissatisfaction expressed by part of the population and a social risk needs to be taken into consideration. Visitors that do not pay a parking fee, visitors that park in blue sectors, permanent residents that do not apply for a parking card but persist to park in blue sectors, all have to receive penalty notices. In addition, there were complaints from residents that the parking spots are not enough, so the Municipality Department was confronted with the request to change the characterization of some parking spots from white to blue. Nevertheless, the selection of which parking spots to switch while taking into account economic growth, environmental impact and social consequences is a problem of combined optimization.

3.2 Deciding on the Distribution of Parking Spots

In deciding which parking spots need to be switched, there is a multitude of factors to be taken into account, including: a) **Economic**: Select parking spots that are under performing in terms of occupancy and generating revenue. b) **Environmental**: Select parking spots that are placed on streets exhibiting high levels of emissions. c) **Social**: Select parking spots in streets where there seems to be expressed dissatisfaction from citizens about illegal parking. In addition, select parking spots that exhibit an increased level of penalty notices that impacts both economic (loss of earning due to reduced parking fees) and social (delinquent behavior showing dissatisfaction).

The Municipal Police is providing data coming from daily patrols and data for penalty notices. The goal of using this data is to locate parking sectors with large numbers of penalty notices so as to propose possible changes in use (from visitors to residents) so as to reduce the number of penalty notices and increase citizens' satisfaction.

The Economic Department provides data about the daily income and occupancy of the parking spots. These data are used as evidence upon which changes in policy will be decided. For example, when deciding which sector should be switched from Visitor to Resident, the sector occupancy should be considered so as to minimize profit loss.

The Environmental Department is providing data for air pollution, obtained by existing monitoring stations. The data are processed to obtain values at street level, so there can be an overview of the air pollution footprint of the sectors and what will be the impact of a change in the distribution of sectors. A sector that belongs to a street with increased emissions should be preferred to switch into a residents sector, over a sector belonging to a street with low emissions. We work under the assumption that by changing a sector from visitor to resident, we reduce the associated traffic and thus the generated emissions.

The Improve My City platform (Improve My City) (Tsampoulatidis et al., 2013) is the citizen reporting tool the municipality of Thessaloniki is using to administer citizen issues. Using data from the aforementioned issues we can discover problems that citizens are experiencing in relation to the CPS, by recognizing user sentiment for a specific area and further filtering it down to street level.

3.3 Data Sources

A GeoJSON file (a file format for encoding a variety of geographical data structures) has been provided by the Municipality of Thessaloniki that features information about the entirety of the parking spots like, each sector spot area as a polygon, the address and Municipal District that the spots belong to, and their sector unique identification number. We use this file in conjunction with our data sources to cross correlate information between datasets and find a common dimension between them. More specifically the data sources are comprised of:

Parking scans: The municipal police is patrolling the streets of Thessaloniki, where the CPS is in place. They are equipped with a device that reads the license plate of the scanned vehicle, checks the status of the vehicle and saves a multitude of data for each scan. The data include, a pair of GPS coordinates (latitude and longitude), a date time timestamp, the device id, and the result of the scan. Scan result can be: i) *Legal:* The car owner has paid for the parking spot and the parking duration hasn't exceeded the time limit period that he paid for. ii) *Resident:* The car owner is a resident of the area so he can park legally for free. iii) *Illegal:* The car owner is not a resident neither have paid for the specific spot. We calculate each parking scan entry GPS coordinates distance from each parking spot polygon centroid, using the distance() Turf.js (Turf.js) function that uses the Haversine formula. After we sort the entries based on the minimum distance value in meters we consider as match the first entry that its distance is less than 10 meters. Also we add to each entry additional sector information like its unique sector identification number and the Municipal District that it belongs to.

Parking spot income: From the economic department we have daily income data per spot, collected during the use of the parking system. This dataset includes a sector's address, number of parking spots, spot economic performance, and income per spot. After cleaning up the data we also add sector information for each entry like its identification number, the Municipal District that it belongs to, the street address and the sector type. Additionally for each parking sector we calculate the parking sector centroid and use it as GPS coordinates for location data for each entry.

Vehicle emissions: There are nitrous oxide (NOx) and non-methane volatile organic compound (NMVOC) emission data readings available about a number of major streets in Thessaloniki in 15 minute intervals. To be able to incorporate them into our dataset, we created new entries for each sector, so as to have more values down to sector level. This means that the total number of entries is all emission entries that are tied to a street multiplied with the number of the unique sectors that are inside this street. Moreover, we connected the emission entries to GPS coordinates calculating each sector's centroid and using it as GPS coordinates and added information about the Municipal District that it belongs to, as well as the sector type.

Improve My City data: To incorporate a social aspect into our dataset, we took advantage of the data contributed by citizens in Improve My City. By using this platform citizens submit their everyday issues through a webpage or a mobile application to the Municipality, and get back feedback on the expected resolution. A mechanism has been set up that indexes user issues to our platform, with information like the issue title, description and category that are useful for tag cloud creation, sentiment analysis and category filtering. Sentiment analysis has been performed on the textual description associated with each issue using the algorithm presented in (Tsakalidis et al., 2018). The issues also contain information that connects them to our previous datasets like street address, sector id, Municipal Area and GPS location. To calculate the GPS location coordinates we followed the same approach as in the parking scans. We calculated each issue's GPS coordinates distance from each parking spot polygon centroid, using the distance() Turf.js (Turf.js) function that uses the Haversine formula. After we sorted the entries based on the minimum distance value in meters we considered as match the first entry that its distance was less than 10 meters.

4. USE CASE

4.1 Dashboard

We have used Elasticsearch (Elasticsearch) to store and query our data, and Kibana (Kibana) to visualize them into charts inside a Dashboard. The Dashboard (CUTLER Thessaloniki pilot) that we have created has been set up and populated with charts from economic, social and environmental data. In this dashboard we focused on creating charts that contribute to easy decision making, when trying to decide which Visitor sector should change into a Resident one, minimizing economic turnover losses and vehicle emissions per street, while maximizing citizen satisfaction. Inside the dashboard a user can select a date range and since all sources of data are time bound, all charts update their content accordingly. The user can also select an area on any of the map charts that are available, performing a special query. Charts with the parking scans clustered all around the city, exist to give a quick overview on which sectors or streets are more frequently visited by the Municipal Police. The user can also see the vehicle emission data for a number of large streets and decide on which sector to select based on the emission street levels. Information about the economic performance of a specific sector and the distribution of scan types per sector, can also be observed so as to draw some conclusions on sector spots income. Extracted social data from the Improve My City platform, namely the description the users leave when they submit an issue to a specific street, are included in our dataset in the form of user sentiment using sentiment analysis. This way the user of the dashboard can recognize the citizen sentiment about a street or sector, and further analyze if it has any ties to the parking system or it is totally unrelated.

4.2 Usage Scenario

A usage scenario was created as a starting point for decision makers to use our dashboard as a policy making tool. In this concrete scenario, the Municipality of Thessaloniki is receiving complaints from residents about the insufficient number of parking spots and our platform is intended to help the decision makers to select the optimal sector for changing its use.

As we access the dashboard, in the chart shown in Figure 1.A there is a clustered view of the total parking scans performed to give an overview of how the administration patrols the sectors. Bigger circles denote larger scan frequency. In Figure 1.B, the user can click on a Municipal Area to select it and filter the data that belong only to this area. In our case, we want to see data only from the first Municipal Area, so we can click on Municipal Area '**A**'. We can see that the changes reflect on all charts, so the dashboard is now refreshed to show only data from Municipal Area A.

Next we can see in the chart of Figure 1.C the Nitrous Oxide emissions for a number of large streets. Some streets have higher emissions than others, so hypothetically we can lower emissions if we focus our attention in sectors that are included in these streets. From the Street Selector component as shown in Figure 1.D we can select only the streets that have high Nitrous Oxide emissions to filter the dashboard accordingly, namely 'DRAGOUMI I.', 'VENIZELOU EL' and 'MITROPOLEOS'.

In Figure 1.E we can see the chart for the revenue / performance data for each sector. We can filter through the sectors that are located inside certain streets that are performing better than others. Thus, we can safely exclude streets we included in the previous step from our list of options since we want the sectors that are generating a high amount of revenue to remain intact. In our case we exclude the 'MITROPOLEOS' street, so we are left with 'DRAGOUMI I.' and 'VENIZELOU EL'.

Next we go to the social data charts illustrated in Figure 2.A, that are populated with data from the Improve My City platform, cross referenced with street addresses. There is a heatmap that depicts how many issues the residents of Thessaloniki submitted in this area, a Pie chart that shows a percentage for the categories of these issues, and a dropdown where you can filter the category that you want to further investigate. We select the illegal parking category from the dropdown so we can only see citizen issues that are related to parking. In the sentiment stacked bar chart as seen in Figure 2.B we can see the sentiment of the people extracted from the submitted issues. This way we can identify through the social aspect of the dataset, in which sectors the citizens have negative feelings on issues related to parking. So we can safely exclude streets that users are less negative about than others from the Street Selector dropdown chart that we used before to end up with one street. In our case we exclude street 'VENIZELOU EL.' and end up with 'DRAGOUMI I.'.

Going further down on the charts of the dashboard to the 'Economic - Performance per sector' chart illustrated in Figure 2.C, we can see all sectors that belong to the 'DRAGOUMI I.' street. This chart features the economic performance of a sector, which is shown as a percentage on the Y axis, and the yearly income for each sector, depicted as a disk with variable size. Right next to this chart there is another chart that shows the number of parking spots per sector. We can see that two sectors, namely 21.324 and 21.184 have the lowest performance and also low yearly incomes while spanning a low number of spaces. Comparing the two sectors we can safely assume that sector 21.324 can be switched to a Resident type, minimizing the loss of income and parking spaces while also tackling with the negative comments of the citizens about parking. The entire process can be repeated if there is a need to allocate more parking spots on residents, or vice versa.

4.3 Evaluation Study

A number of 27 end-users from the Municipality of Thessaloniki used the aforementioned scenario to test and evaluate the platform. As a result of the evaluation workshops, a great deal of information was gathered on the usability and practicalities of the dashboard. The difficulties that users experienced were recorded as part of their responses questionnaires.

More specifically, our platform was evaluated positively on its usefulness and on allowing faster decisions, assisting to the accomplishment of new tasks and encouraging the combination of different types of data (economic, environmental and social) for decision making. The contribution of the platform that was evaluated most positively by the users was the fact that more parameters than before are now considered before making a decision. Most of the users think that the visualizations of the platform are helpful in extracting the information they need for decision making. Many users think that the use of effective filtering is absolutely necessary to make the features easier to understand and to use.

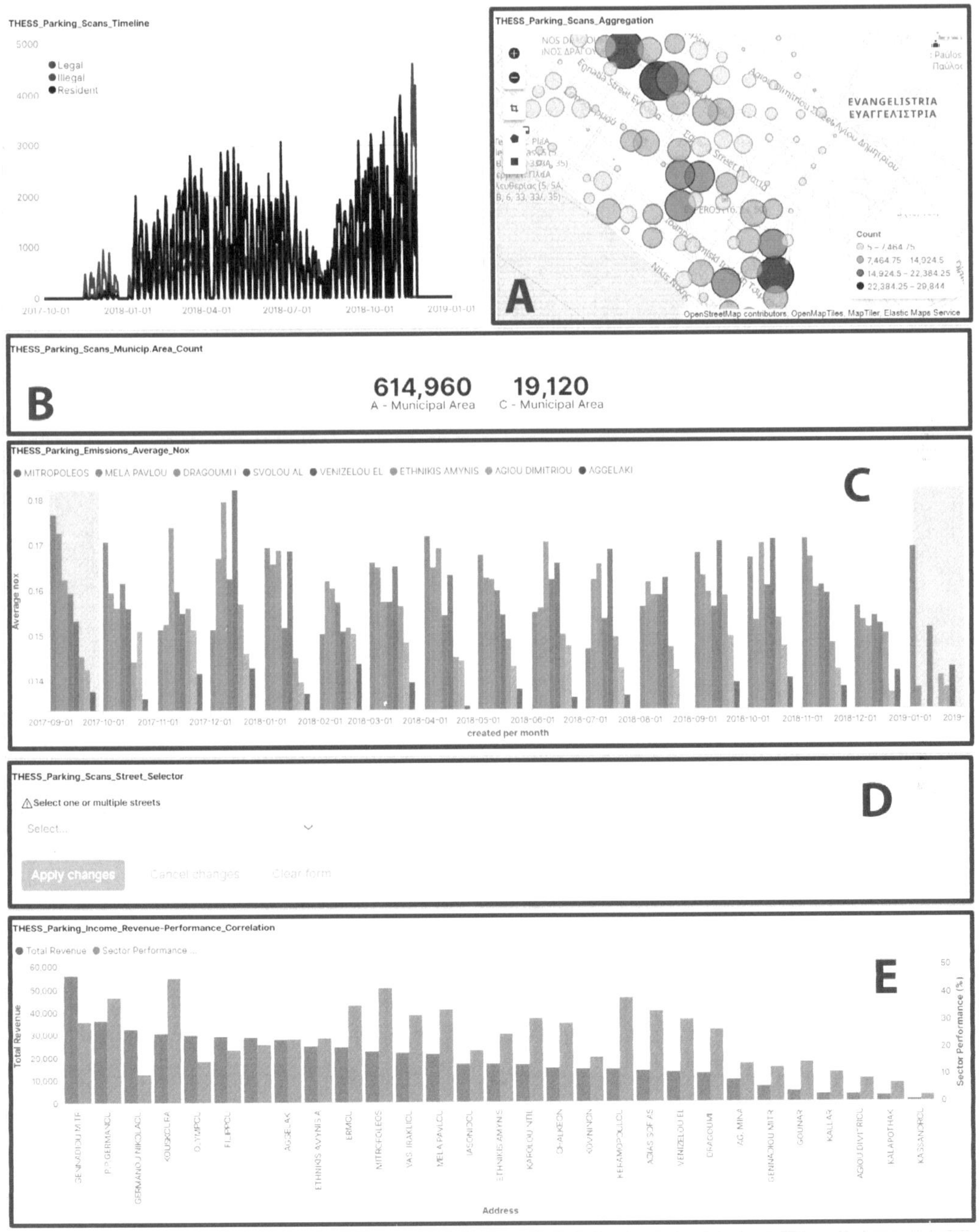

Figure 1. Dashboard showing: A) Parking Scans aggregation clustering, B) Parking Scans Municipality Area Count, C) Emission Data, D) Street Selector component, E) Parking Income Revenue/Performance correlation

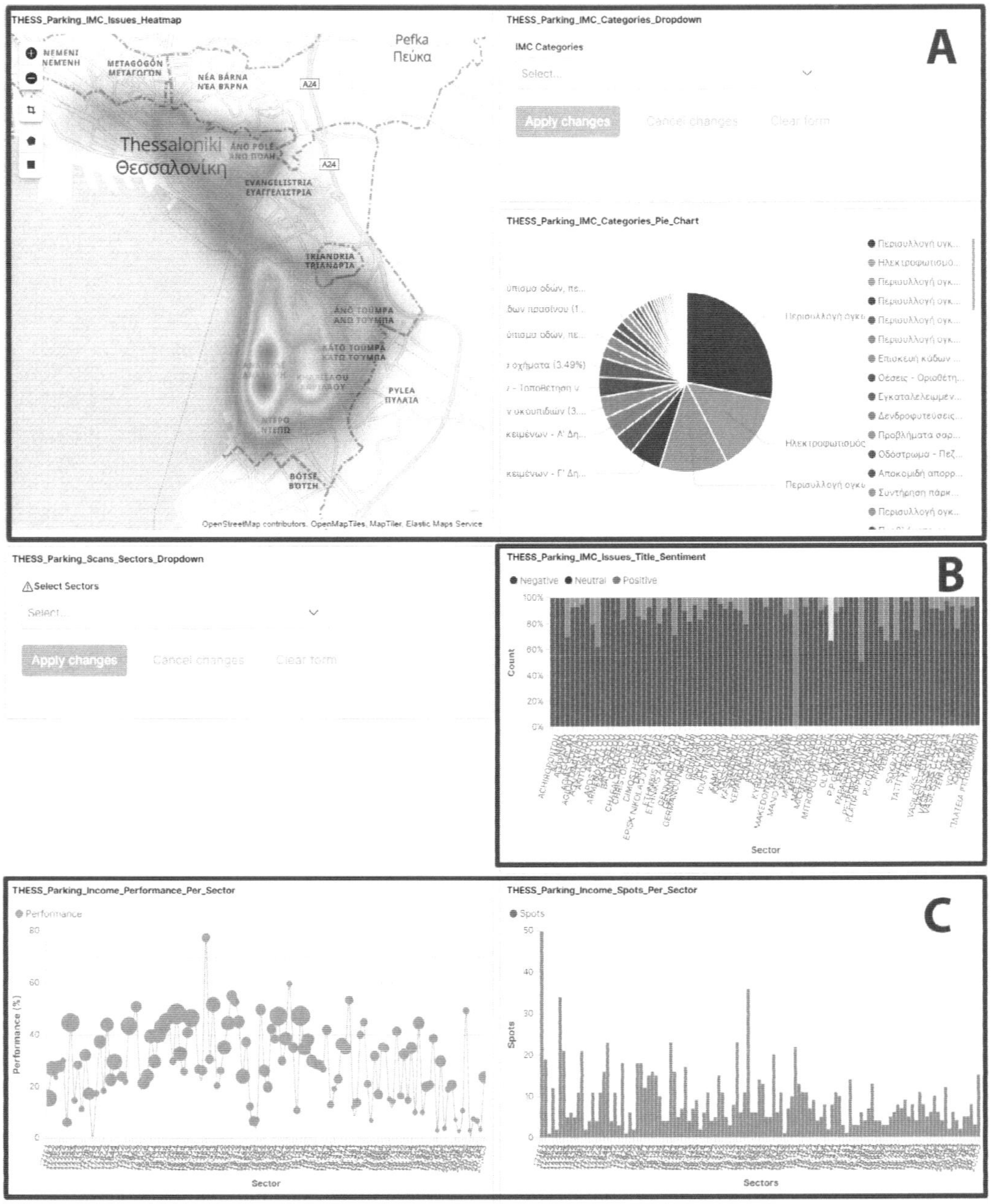

Figure 2. Dashboard showing: A) ImproveMyCity charts, B) Sentiment bar chart, C) Parking Income/Performance and Spots per Sector charts

Concerning the dataset included in the current version of the dashboard the users evaluated positively the quality and quantity of the visualized data but also made a series of suggestions. Many users would like more charts to be included in the environmental section, and specifically more data on air quality. They also suggested that the maps should include more GIS data on land use, concerning all aspects of economic life like tourism and commerce, and cover more policy fields. They would find useful information of how busy a street is commercial-wise, whether there are hospitals or public service buildings close to specific sectors, or if they knew the number of residential buildings of a street. Other users would like more social data (complaints/suggestions) coming from the permanent residents to be included. A few users would find it useful to visualize data on the duration of the parking sessions. Finally, regularly updated or live data would also be useful for optimal patrol calculation and improvement of supervision.

5. CONCLUSIONS

In the use case of Thessaloniki's controlled parking system, our work has helped to balance between economic growth, environmental impact and citizen's satisfaction, by harmonizing and visualizing heterogenous sources of data, effectively shifting the paradigm of policy making from intuition-based to evidence-driven. In evaluating our work a multi–step process was designed that involved user recruitment, user training, formulation of platform-usage scenarios, platform evaluation based on questionnaires, and finally in-depth questionnaire analysis. Most of the end-users found useful the dashboards and recognized their potential in supporting informed decisions and enabling evidence-based policy making. The use of heterogeneous data sources and the visualization of environmental, social and economic evidence in the same dashboard were considered important contributions of the platform, which have the potential to lead in more effective and accurate decisions combining and balancing different information, which is the cardinal objective of our work.

ACKNOWLEDGEMENT

The research leading to these results has received funding from the European Community's Horizon 2020 - Research and Innovation Framework Programme under grant agreement no 770469, CUTLER.

REFERENCES

CUTLER Deliverable 2.2. *Threat analysis for policy-supporting hybrid cloud infrastructure.* Currently not available for retrieval.

CUTLER Deliverable 3.2. *First version of the framework for the collection, cleaning, integration and anonymization of big data.* Retrieved from https://www.cutler-h2020.eu/download/520

CUTLER Thessaloniki Pilot, Kibana Dashboard. Retrieved 20 March 2020, from https://pilots.cutler-h2020.eu:5603/

Dror, Y. (2017). Public policy making reexamined. Routledge.

Dunn, W. N. (1981). Public Policy Analysis Englewood Cliffs. N.].: Prentice-Hall.

Elasticsearch, The heart of the Elastic Stack. Retrieved 20 March 2020, from https://www.elastic.co/elasticsearch

Improve My City - Municipality of Thessaloniki, Direct citizen-government communication & collaboration. Retrieved 20 March 2020, from https://imc.thessaloniki.gr/imc

Kibana, Your window into the Elastic Stack. Retrieved 20 March 2020, from https://www.elastic.co/kibana

Sanderson, I. (2002). Evaluation, policy learning and evidence-based policy making. Public administration, 80(1), 1-22.

THESi, Municipality of Thessaloniki Controlled Parking System. Retrieved 20 March 2020, from https://www.thesi.gr

Treasury, H. M. S. (2000). Spending review: public service agreements.

Tsakalidis, A., Papadopoulos, S., Voskaki, R., Ioannidou, K., Boididou, C., Cristea, A. I., ... & Kompatsiaris, Y. (2018). Building and evaluating resources for sentiment analysis in the Greek language. Language resources and evaluation, 52(4), 1021-1044.

Tsampoulatidis, I., Ververidis, D., Tsarchopoulos, P., Nikolopoulos, S., Kompatsiaris, I., & Komninos, N. (2013, October). ImproveMyCity: an open source platform for direct citizen-government communication. In Proceedings of the 21st ACM international conference on Multimedia (pp. 839-842).

Turf.js, Advanced geospatial analysis for browsers and Node.js. Retrieved 20 March 2020, from https://turfjs.org/

MEXICO CITY'S AIRBNB LISTING PRICE ANALYSIS USING REGRESSION

Daniela A. Gomez-Cravioto, Ramon E. Diaz-Ramos, Virginia I. Contreras-Miranda and Francisco J. Cantu-Ortiz
School of Engineering and Science, Tecnológico de Monterrey, Monterrey, México

ABSTRACT

The AirBnb platform provides users with the option of renting their vacant spaces as tourist accommodations and competing with traditional accommodation enterprises. However, since AirBnb gives the user the freedom to establish the price of their listing, a challenge is placed on the owner to determine the most appropriate number. This study analyses the information from listings in Mexico City to determine how the listing attributes can be used as predictors for a new listing's price. The study uses statistical methods and machine learning techniques to analyze the information scraped from AirBnb's website, which is publicly available at the Inside AirBnb webpage. In this work, an experiment was made to compare a quantile regression, logistic regression, and a generalized additive model to find the most suitable technique for predicting an AirBnb listing's price. The models were compared based on the residual standard error, R squared, and AIC. The results show that the generalized additive model provides the best fit for the dataset explaining 60% of the variance.

KEYWORDS

AirBnb, Mexico, CRISP-DM, Logistic Regression, GAM, Quantile Regression

1. INTRODUCTION

The sharing economy has created a great number of opportunities for Smart Cities and communities around the world to create a better and smarter working and living environment (Tedjasaputra and Sari, 2016). The smart city concept covers a variety of industries, one of these is the tourism industry. Bringing smartness into tourism destinations requires the destinations to facilitate information exchange amongst stakeholders to enhance the decision-making process. This is helping the tourism service providers provide new improved services to tourists (Jasrotia and Gangotia, 2018). An example of this is the AirBnb business.

Since its creation in 2007, the company has experienced explosive growth, from being an online bed and breakfast company to a leading peer-to-peer hospitality corporation. The company now offers its services in over eighty thousand cities worldwide and it is continuously growing. This expansion is considered a part of a large rise in the sharing economy which has represented an inordinate source of strategic disruption and business successes over the last decade (Aaker, 2019). The service offers people with a free-living space a new source of income and for guests an affordable option.

One challenge that hosts in AirBnb experience is determining their optimal nightly price for their listings. This is a problem that can be approached with the use of machine learning techniques. There is existing literature focused on price predictions. We analyze six works that are the most pertinent to this study. First, Mason and Quigley (1996) analyzed the decline in condominium house values in downtown Los Angeles with the use of a generalized additive model (GAM). Secondly, Zietz et al. (2008) determined the relationship of a particular housing characteristic with selling price with quantile regression. Raymond et al. (2016) defined three types of neighborhood housing markets in the Atlanta region based on the zip code level, their levels of volatility, and stability before, during, and after the housing crisis with Multinomial Logistic Regression. Yu and Wu (2016) also used Multinomial Logistic Regression to predict house prices given explanatory variables that cover many aspects of residential houses. Finally, a study performed by Perez-Sanchez et al. (2018) identified the determinants of AirBnb accommodation prices by estimating a hedonic price model that adopted quantile regression methods.

We consider this study adds to the current literature by focusing on regression techniques and comparing these in a dataset from Mexico City since we did not find previous related work performed in this country. The main objective of this paper is to build and evaluate several regression models to suggest the most convenient pricing for a new AirBnb host's listing taking into account the listing features. The goal is to allow hosts to understand which features are the most important for price assignment and understand how the price changes based on seasonality and holidays in Mexico. Specifically, the research questions that we are trying to solve are the following: (1) What are the most common AirBnb property types in Mexico City available for renting?; (2) What is the average price of the properties?; (3) What is the most expensive location in Mexico City?; (4) What time of the year are AirBnb's most popular in Mexico City? Is there any holiday that spikes pricing?; (5) What are the most important features of a listing in Mexico city, and how does this affect the price?; (6) Can the selected features be used to create a data-based model that can predict the price of a new listing? The machine learning techniques used in this paper are the following: quantile regression, logistic regression, and generalized additive model.

2. RELATED WORK

In this section, we present related studies focused on house pricing; these are shown in Table 1. Firstly, Perez-Sanchez et al. (2018) identified the determinants of AirBnb accommodation prices by evaluating housing characteristics (advertisement, features, and location) which adopted quantile regression methods. Secondly, Zietz et al. (2008) determined the relationship of particular housing characteristics (physical, geographic, and neighborhood characteristics) with selling price with Quantile Regression. Mason and Quigley (1996) analyzed the decline in condominium house values in downtown Los Angeles with the use of a GAM model. The dataset contained a sample of 843 condominium sales recorded for 12 years. Finally, Raymond et al. (2016) defined three types of neighborhood housing markets in the Atlanta region based on the zip code level, their levels of volatility and stability before, during, and after the housing crisis with Multinomial Logistic Regression.

Table 1. Evaluation of the related works models

Source	Variables	Model	Results
Affuso et al. (2019)	Noise levels, property, and neighborhood characteristics.	GAM	AIC = 14,066
Perez-Sanchez et al. (2018)	Price and characteristics of the accommodation, advertisement, host features, environmental and location characteristics.	Quantile Regression	Pseudo R2 Q.10=.479, Q.25=.415, Q.50=.378 Q.75=.378, Q.90 = .397
Yu and Wu (2016)	79 features such as areas of the houses, types of floors, and the number of bathrooms.	Multinomial Logistic Regression	RMSE = .5587
Zietz et al. (2008)	33 attributes that include physical, geographic, and neighborhood characteristics of each house.	Quantile Regression	Pseudo R2 Q.10=.523, Q.20=.531, Q.30=.543 Q.40=.548, Q.50=.554, Q.60=.565 Q.70=.568, Q.80=.569, Q.90=.549
Mason and Quigley (1996)	Condominium sales.	GAM	R^2 = .759
Raymond et al. (2016)	Housing market and demographic variables of 137 zip codes.	Multinomial Logistic Regression	Pseudo R2=.679

3. METHODS AND METHODOLOGY

This study uses the CRISP-DM methodology as a standard approach to perform data mining analysis. CRISP-DM stands for "Cross-Industry Standard Process for Data Mining" (Chapman et al., 2000). It consists of a six-step process, including Business Understanding, Data Understanding, Data Preparation, Modelling,

Evaluation, and Deployment. Each phase consists of second-level tasks which aim to cover all the data mining applications. The initial intention of this methodology was to develop modeling techniques for industry. In this study, we will illustrate the CRISP-DM process and apply it to the problem of predicting new listings in the Mexico AirBnb dataset.

3.1 Quantile Regression

The advantage of using the quantile regression technique is that it aids in understanding the relationship between variables outside of the mean of the data, making it useful for understanding outcomes that are non-normally distributed and which do not have linear relationships with the predictor variables (Koenker 2012).

Quantile regression methods offer a mechanism for estimating models for the conditional median function, as well as other conditional quantile functions. It is highly used in econometrics studies, for wage determinants, discrimination effects, as well as trends in income inequality. Due to the nature of the outcome variable, there have been previous studies that have used quantile regression to predict the price of AirBnb listings for other cities (Perez-Sanchez et al., 2018) (Wang and Nicolau, 2017). This study uses quantile regression to predict the price of a new AirBnb listing in Mexico City because it provides a more comprehensive description of the conditional distribution and measures the effects of individual explanatory variables on the whole distribution (Wang and Nicolau, 2017).

3.2 Logistic Regression

The method of logistic regression can be used both as a classification technique and a regression technique, it depends on the scenario in which it is used (Dutt et al., 2019). For logistic regression, the dependent variable can be binary (1,0) or multinomial (more than 2 labels) and the independent variables can be either nominal or numerical. This machine learning technique uses the sigmoid function (Figure 1) and obtains the values of the coefficients (β) by using the maximum likelihood. The function outputs a value between 0 and 1, which corresponds to the probability of a Bernoulli random variable X (Deisenroth et al., 2020).

$$p(X) = \frac{e^{\beta_0+\beta_1 X}}{1 + e^{\beta_0+\beta_1 X}} \quad (1)$$

3.3 Generalized Additive Model

The generalized additive model (GAM) provides the advantages of allowing a non-linear relation function of independent variables. It can be used with both numeric and nominal dependent variables, however only the numeric can be replaced with a nonlinear function (smooth) which gives it more flexibility to fit the data. The limitation of GAMs is that the model is restricted to be additive, so some variable interactions can be missed. The model can be represented as Function 2, where the $f_j(x_{ij})$ represents the nonlinear function or smoothing term (James et al., 2013).

$$y_i = \beta_0 + \sum_{j=1}^{p} f_j(x_{ij}) + \epsilon_i \quad (2)$$

4. DATA UNDERSTANDING AND PREPARATION

The goal of this research is to make a predicting model to suggest the most convenient pricing for AirBnb host's listing with respect to the attributes of accommodation obtained from the Mexico City dataset. More specifically, the research questions that we are trying to solve in this study are the following:(1) What are the most common AirBnb property types in Mexico City available for renting?; (2) What is the average price of the properties?; (3) What is the most expensive location in Mexico City?; (4) What time of the year are AirBnb's listings most popular in Mexico City? Is there any holiday that spikes pricing?; (5) What are the most important features of a listing in Mexico city, and how does this affect the price?; (6) Can the selected features be used to create a data-based model that can predict the price of a new listing?

4.1 The Dataset

This study analyzes the information from the Mexico City AirBnb dataset. The data was scraped from AirBnb's website and publicly available from the Inside AirBnb website (Cox, 2017). Two datasets were collected: "listing.csv", which contains demographic information from the AirBnb listings and the "calendar.csv", that contains the dates and prices of each listing. The listing data is a snapshot of searchable listings from November 25 of 2019. The Mexico City original listing file contains 20,571 AirBnb listings and 106 features.

It was identified that some of the attributes did not contain relevant information for our prediction model, in those cases the feature was eliminated. The 29 features that were selected for the final dataset are shown in Table 2.

Table 2. Features

Feature	Feature Type
host_since, last_review	date
host_response_time, neighbourhood_cleansed, property_type, room_type, bed_type, cancellation_policy	factorial
host_response_rate, latitude, longitude, accommodates, bathrooms, bedrooms ,beds, price, guests_included, extra_people, minimum_nights, maximum_nights, availability_365, number_of_reviews, review_scores_rating, calculated_host_list, review_per_month	numerical
host_is_superhost, host_has_profile_pic, host_identity_verified, instant_bookable	logical

4.2 Data Cleaning

There were missing values present in some of the attributes, those attributes with more than 50% of their total data being missing values were removed from the data set, and the rest were replaced by using an imputation method. Imputation works by calculating the mean/median/mode of the non-missing values of an attribute and then replacing the missing values with this value. The mean was used for numeric data, the median for the numeric data with extreme values, and the mode for nominal data. The attributes "host response time", "host response rate", "reviews score rating", and "reviews per month" had 16%, 16%, 21%, and 21% of missing values respectively. The mean was used to fill out missing values for the variable "review per month"; the median, which is a more robust statistic for variables with extreme values, was used to replace the missing values of "host response rate" and "review score rating"; and for the categorical attribute, "host response time", the mode was used.

It was observed, through a boxplot (Figure 1.a) that the target variable "Price" contained outliers. These values can influence negatively in our model. For this reason, we performed the method of winsorization. This method involves the replacement of the outlier values with the most extreme retained values (Wilcox, 2005). In this study, we used the quantiles 3 and 97 to define the limits of the extreme values and those outside these limits were replaced (Figure 1.b).

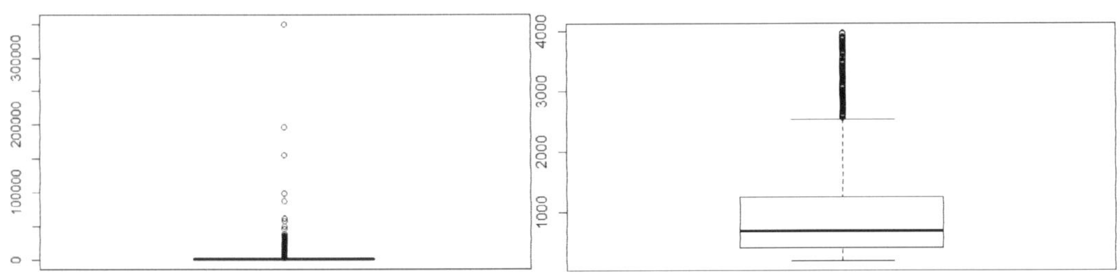

Figure 1. Price boxplot left (a) with outliers and right (b) without outliers

4.3 Data Exploration

This section will seek to answer the first five research questions through the use of an exploratory data analysis performed on Mexico city's AirBnb listing dataset obtained in November of 2019.

4.3.1 What are the Most Common AirBnb Property Types in Mexico City Available for Renting?

An interesting attribute is the number of room types in Mexico City. To answer the question of what are the most common AirBnb property types available for rent, we plotted the number of accommodations (Figure 2.a) The frequency of room types varies between 349 and 9,238. Also, we can observe that the amount of shared rooms and hotel rooms is rare and the entire home apartments dominate the listing. Additionally, (Figure 2.b) shows that besides hotel rooms, the room types are affected by extreme values in the listings. Private rooms and shared rooms are both below the mean, while entire-home apartments and hotel rooms are around the mean or higher.

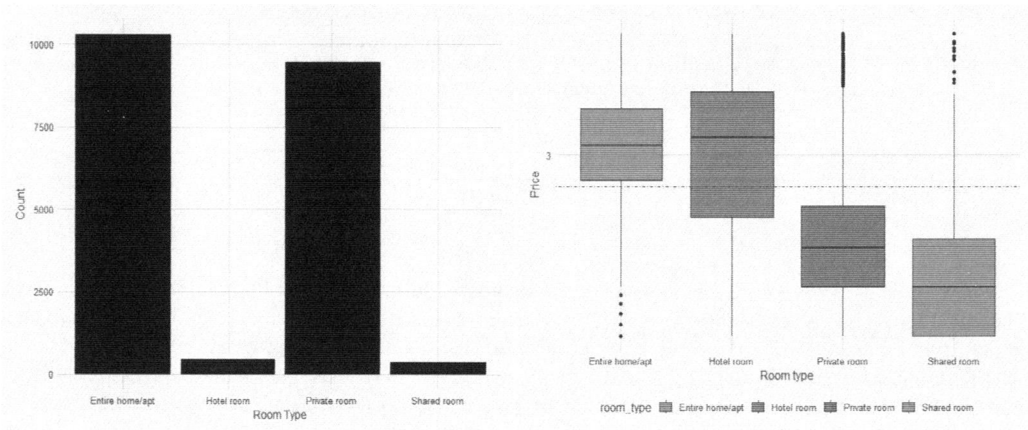

Figure 2. (a) Count of room types in left and (b) price by type room in right

4.3.2 What is the Average Price of the Properties?

To answer the question of what is the average price of the properties, we plotted the price distribution (Figure 3) The average price of a property in Mexico City is MXN $991.80. Due to the skewness observed in the plot, and the violation that the data reflects when performing residual analysis of normality, we can conclude that the distribution is not normal, therefore we perform a logarithmic transformation to transform the dependent variable "Price" into a more symmetric distribution and reduce the negative effect of the skewness when performing the regression models.

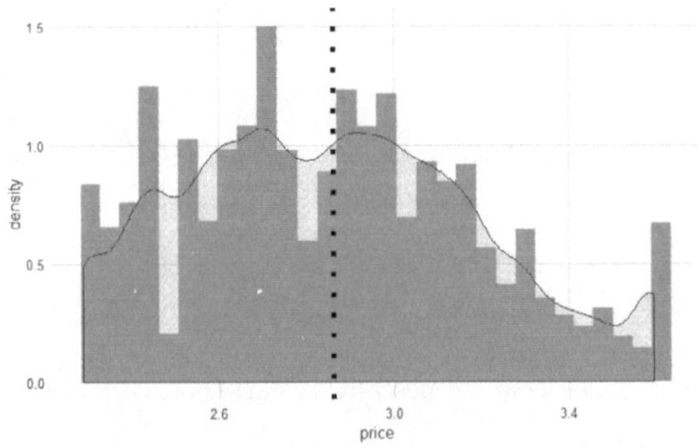

Figure 3. Price distribution logarithm scale

4.3.3 What is the Most Expensive Location in Mexico City?

To visualize the most expensive locations in Mexico City, we created a plot showing the density of the price per neighborhood attribute. From the plot (Figure 4) we concluded that the neighborhood "Miguel Hidalgo" has the highest AirBnb average price in the city.

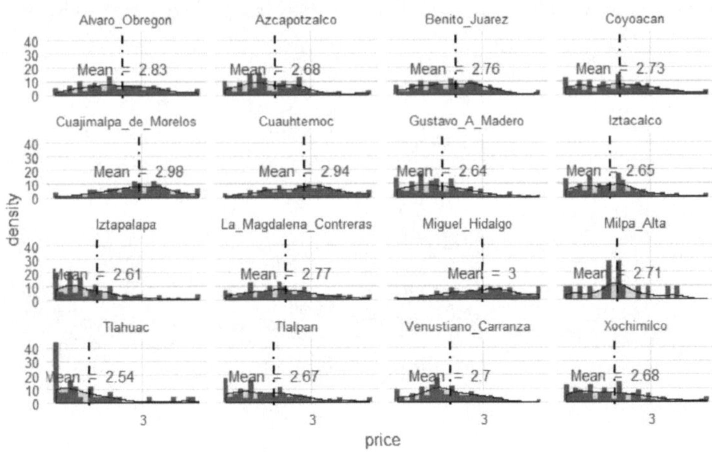

Figure 4. Price distribution by neighborhood log10

4.3.4 What Time of the Year are AirBnb's Listings Most Popular in Mexico City? Is there any Holiday that Spikes Pricing?

When exploring the calendar data, an interesting trend is a price in comparison to the days of the week. (Figure 5.a) shows a peak on Friday and remains stable until a fall on Sunday. This reflects how the weekends suffer from higher prices in the AirBnb listings of Mexico City. Calendar data are not used to train the predictive model, the prices of the listings are taken from November AirBnb listing prices of 2019.

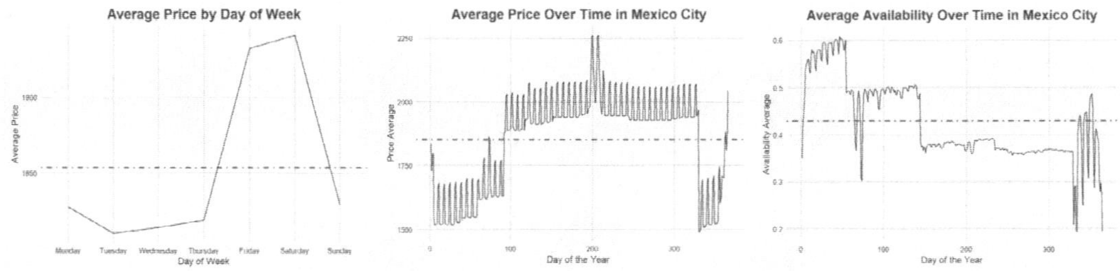

Figure 5. (a) Average price by day of the week in left, (b) average price over time in Mexico City in middle, and (c) Average availability over time in Mexico City in right

4.3.5. What are the Most Important Features of a Listing in Mexico City, and how does this Affect the Price?

To inspect the correlation between all variables, we built a Spearman correlation matrix (Figure 6). From the results of this matrix, we can conclude that the feature "accommodates" is strongly correlated with the price ($>$ 0.5 Spearman correlation), and there are other features which are slightly positively correlated with the following features of the listing, these are: "bedrooms" (0.47), "beds" (0.44), "guests_included" (0.33), "bathrooms" (0.35), and "latitude" (0.21); on the other hand "longitude" (-0.23) is slightly negatively correlated. The "latitude" and "longitude" attributes indicate the coordinates where the listings are situated in Mexico City. As the latitude is positively correlated and the longitude is the other way, those listings located in the northwestern part are more expensive than those in the southeastern part of Mexico City.

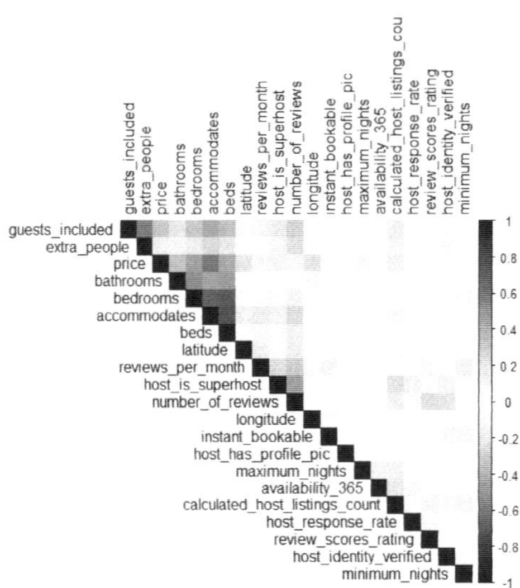

Figure 6. Spearman correlation matrix plot

4.4 Data Transformation

The dependent variable was transformed to a logarithmic scale to deal with skewed data. Another transformation done was feature scaling. We can observe that the data contains features with varying magnitudes, when this occurs the distance measure can overweight the features with larger values than the others. To solve this issue, we scale the data to a specific range. In this study, we use the Min-max normalization technique to obtain a distribution of values between [0,1].

5. DATA MODELING

This phase is the fourth of the CRISP-DM process and consists of the selection of the appropriate modeling technique.

5.1 Quantile Regression Model

To calculate the results of the quantile regression model, each regression model quantile is accounted for independently from each other by its percentage. In this study, we obtained a model for each of the following quantiles: 0.10, 0.25, 0.50, 0.75, and 0.90. The complete list of coefficients for each quantile is not presented due to its length and the requirement of this paper's limit, however, the first 3 most representative coefficients for each quantile are shown in Table 3, the rest are available upon request.

Table 3. Quantile regression coefficients summary

		minimum_nights	accommodations	bedrooms	bathroom	(Intercept)
	Estimate	-6.0845	1.7513	1.4722	1.1932	0.2343
Quantile .10	Std. Error	0.7454	0.0941	0.1771	0.1807	0.7533
	P-value	0.0000	0.0000	0.0000	0.0000	0.0019
	Estimate	-9.4427	1.9119	1.4041	1.5446	0.2223
Quantile .25	Std. Error	0.7251	0.0628	0.1594	0.1371	0.0296
	P-value	0.0000	0.0000	0.0000	0.0000	0.0000
	Estimate	-10.5326	1.9574	1.2156	2.1234	0.3293
Quantile .50	Std. Error	1.0884	0.0723	0.1544	0.1475	0.0646
	P-value	0.0000	0.0000	0.0000	0.0000	0.0000
	Estimate	-12.9230	1.8742	1.0397	2.8419	0.6096
Quantile .75	Std. Error	1.2729	0.0817	0.1967	0.1557	0.6795
	P-value	0.0000	0.0000	0.0000	0.0000	0.3696
	Estimate	-13.4145	1.6431	1.1637	2.5852	0.9595
Quantile .90	Std. Error	1.9573	0.1412	0.3135	0.2695	0.1242
	P-value	0.0000	0.0000	0.0002	0.0000	0.0000

The quantile regression graphs in Figure 7 provide a visualization of the difference in coefficients across the quantiles with their confidence intervals.

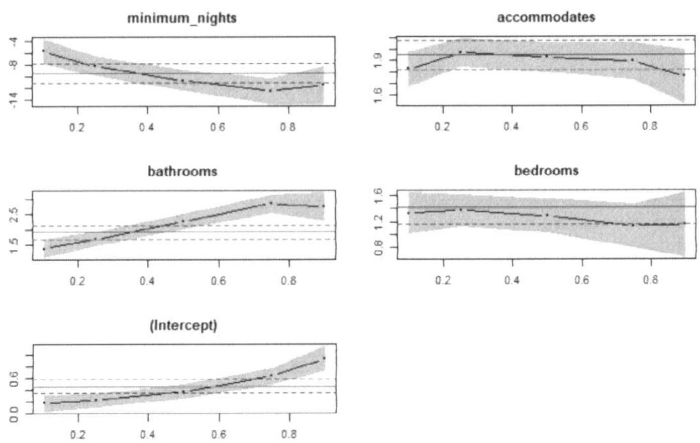

Figure 7. Quantile plot

5.2 Multinomial Logistic Regression Model

Some levels can be grouped to simplify the interpretation of the model and reduce categories that contain few observations. The grouping of the attributes is as follows: the cancellation policy (3 levels) variable as flexible (10223), moderate (6013), strict (4335); host_response_time (3 levels) as within an hour (15482), within a few hours (2470), a_day_or_more(2619); the neighbourhood_cleansed (3 levels) variable as center_sector (16504), south_sector (1200), north_sector (2867); the room_type variable is left as it is and the bed_type attribute is eliminated as there are 20,411 observations with Real Bed level that represents the 99% of the bed_type category.

Before fitting the model, a one-hot encoding of the categorical variables was required. Then, the response variable column that discretizes the price of the listings was created with 3 thresholds and obtained the labels: low, medium, and the high price of listings. The low level contains prices from \$194 to \$407 MXN, the medium level contains listing prices from \$426 to \$1,259 and the high level contains listing prices from \$1,278 to \$3,971. Table 4 shows the results obtained from the multinomial logistic regression model. The model obtained an accuracy of 0.67 of correctly classified instances and an AUC of 0.84. The results of the confusion matrix are shown in Table 5.

Table 4. Logistic regression models performance summary

			Logistic Regression		
Model	AIC	Pseudo R2	RMSE	Accuracy	AUC
Binomial	13571.00	.49	.36	.82	.89
Ordinal	24641.34	.29	257.21	.65	.83
Multinomial	23969.99	.31	1.34	.67	.84

Table 5. Confusion matrix of the multinomial logistic regression model

		Predict_mlog_price	
	Low	Medium	High
Low	800	328	17
Medium	372	1402	205
High	40	418	531

The resulting coefficients are shown in Table 6, only the three most significant are shown in this paper, but the complete model can be shared upon request.

Table 6. Quantile regression coefficients summary

Coefficients	Dependent Variable	Estimate	Std. Error	P-value
minimum_nights	Medium	-112.7035	16.48	7.96E-12
	High	-178.3325	23.3	1.95E-14
accommodates	Medium	25.8465	1.52	< 2E-16
	High	35.4447	1.76	< 2E-16
beds	Medium	-17.4296	2.03	< 2E-16
	High	-19.4665	2.33	< 2E-16
(Intercept)	Medium	-0.4706	0.29	1.06E-01
	High	-2.7296	0.39	2.57E-12

5.3 Generalized Additive Model

With the GAM, we obtained the relationship between the dependent variable (AirBnb listing price) and the independent variables. For this model, the same target labels, as in logistic regression, were used. Table 7 shows the three most important parametric coefficients of the GAM model and Table 8 shows the numerical smooth terms of the effective degrees of freedom that showed less complexity and were statistically significant for the model. Finally, Table 9 shows the evaluation results of this model.

Table 7. GAM Parametric Coefficient Summary

Coefficients	Estimate	Std. Error	P-value
room_type Private Room	-0.1750	0.00	< 2 E-16
Room_type Shared Room	-0.2452	0.01	< 2 E-16
Neighbourhood Center_sector	0.0381	0.00	5.12 E-10
(Intercept)	0.5096	0.03	< 2 E-16

Table 8. GAM Smooth Terms Summary

Coefficients	edf	Ref.df	P-value
s(maximum_nights)	1.784	2.016	7.20 E-8
s(minimum_nights)	3.760	4.481	5.95 E-15
s(host_response_rate)	5.015	4.826	7.51 E-6

6. EVALUATION

To identify the ability of the independent variables in explaining the price we use pseudo-R-square for logistic regression comparison and R2 for the regression models. In the quantile regression models, we found that the value in R squared recorded the highest value in quantile 0.5 (R square = 0.55), which means that the independent variables can explain up to 55% of the variation of the listing's price. The best performing model was the GAM with an R2 of 0.60 and an AIC of -13,750.50. The GAM gave the best results because it captures the nonlinear relationship between the variables. However, the multinomial logistic regression model also proved to be a good prediction model for this study, with an accuracy of 0.66 and an AUC of 0.835. Table 9 shows the model performance summary of the constructed models.

Table 9. Models performance summary

		Logistic Regression		
Model	Quantile	AIC	R2	RMSE
Quantile Regression	.10	-8273.15	.52	.27
	.25	-11997.89	.54	.21
	.50	-12125.63	.55	.18
	.75	-7370.15	.54	.19
	.90	329.44	.51	.28
GAM		-13750.5	.60	.16

7. CONCLUSIONS

This paper mainly concentrates on the application of machine learning models to the prediction of Mexico city's AirBnb listing prices. It performs exploratory data analysis and compares regression models (Quantile Regression, Logistic Regression, and GAM) for price prediction. Additionally, it shows how to do a proper use of the CRISP-DM methodology for analyzing housing data and obtaining insights.

The exploratory data analysis phase of the study was able to respond to several of the research questions established in the business understanding of the Mexico AirBnb data. We obtained information regarding the highest amount of accommodation type, the most expensive neighborhood, and the average price of the properties. Additionally, with the use of visualization, we were able to get insight regarding the days of the week in which the prices rise, and the months that have lower availability and its relation with the price. Finally, we identified with the use of statistics the positive correlation between the price of a listing and its attributes.

From the results obtained from the modeling phase, the GAM obtained a better fitness score for the data when compared to the rest of the models. The most important features to predict the price obtained from this model were: 'room type', 'neighborhood', 'maximum nights', 'minimum nights', and the 'host response state'.

Additionally, we were able to obtain better results in the quantile regression model in comparison to previous studies, which we recommend to obtain a complete picture for the observations of AirBnb listings through a number of quantile regression lines.

In comparison to the related studies, we can see that our results for the best model (GAM) obtained a lower R2 than that of Mason and Quigley (Mason and Quigley, 1996) which considered variables such as historical prices. However, since our results only consider the characteristics of the housing, we consider the results of R2 = 0.6 as a good baseline score for future analysis. Additionally, when comparing the multinomial model in the housing study from Raymond (Raymond et al., 2016), we can see that we could improve our results by integrating neighborhood characteristics such as race and poverty rates into the model. The future work for this study can include integrating these variables and exploring tree-based methods and deep learning techniques to improve the performance of the classifier. We consider this analysis as a good contribution to the existing literature about hospitality analytics introducing business methodologies and machine learning techniques that can be used in accommodation sharing platforms like AirBnb.

ACKNOWLEDGEMENT

This study was supported by the School of Engineering and Science, Tecnológico de Monterrey, Monterrey, México, and by the PNPC CONACYT program with its financial support for studying our master's degree.

REFERENCES

Aaker, D., 2019. Winning in the sharing economy: Six keys to airbnb's success, Journal of Brand Strategy, vol. 7, no. 4, pp. 310–317, 2019.

Affuso, E. et al, 2019. Is Airport Proximity an Amenity or Disamenity? An Empirical Investigation Based on House Prices. Land Economics, 95(3), 391-408.

Chapman, P. et al, 2000. CRISP-DM 1.0: Step-by-step data mining guide. SPSS inc, 9, 13.

Cox, M., 2017. Inside Airbnb: Adding data to the debate. Inside Airbnb [Internet].

Deisenroth, M. P., Faisal, A. A., & Ong, C. S., 2020. Mathematics for machine learning. Cambridge University Press.

Dutt, S. et al, 2019. Machine Learning, 1st ed. Uttar Pradesh, India: Pearson India Education Services Pvt. Ltd.

James, G. et al, R., 2013. An introduction to statistical learning Vol. 102 New York: springer.

Jasrotia, A., & Gangotia, A., 2018. Smart cities to smart tourism destinations: a review paper. Journal of Tourism Intelligence and Smartness, Volume 1, pp. 47-56.

Koenker, R., 2012. Quantile regression in R: A vignette. Retrieved November.

Mason, C., & Quigley, J. M., 1996. Non-parametric hedonic housing prices. Housing studies, 11(3), 373-385.

Perez-Sanchez, V. et al, 2018. The what, where, and why of Airbnb price determinants. Sustainability, 10(12), 4596.

Raymond, E. et al, 2016. Race and uneven recovery: Neighborhood home value trajectories in Atlanta before and after the housing crisis. Housing Studies, 31(3), 324-339.

Tedjasaputra, A., & Sari, E., 2016. Sharing economy in smart city transportation services. In Proceedings of the SEACHI 2016 on Smart Cities for Better Living with HCI and UX (pp. 32-35).

Wang, D., & Nicolau, J. L., 2017. Price determinants of sharing economy-based accommodation rental: A study of listings from 33 cities on Airbnb. com. International Journal of Hospitality Management, 62, 120-131.

Wilcox, R., 2005. Trimming and winsorization. Encyclopedia of biostatistics, 8.

Yu, H., & Wu, J., 2016. Real estate price prediction with regression and classification. CS229 (Machine Learning) Final Project Reports.

Zietz, J. et al, 2008. Determinants of house prices: a quantile regression approach. The Journal of Real Estate Finance and Economics, 37(4), 317-333.

VIRTUAL BRAND COMMUNITY INFLUENCE ON BRAND LOYALTY: CUSTOMER RELATIONSHIPS AND TRUST MEDIATORS

Joshua Doe
Central University, Ghana
PO Box DS 2310, Dansoman, Accra

ABSTRACT

This study examines whether online brand community affects brand loyalty through mediators such as customer-product relationship, customer-brand relationship, customer-company relationship, and trust. Data was randomly collected from 720 members of an online brand community page using an online questionnaire and analysed with Structural Equations Modelling (SEM). The study found that online brand community activities influenced customer-product relationships, and not customer-brand nor customer-company relationships. None of the customer relationships mediate the link between online brand community and trust. Trust, however partially mediates between customer-product relationships and brand loyalty, as well as between customer-company relationships and brand loyalty. Trust of the online community was confirmed to lead to loyalty. For industry practitioners, these findings support the need to ensure favourable customer/product related activities, experience and word of mouth within the online community. It also demonstrates the possibility of brand extension and brand trust at lower costs. The paper contributes to industrial and academic knowledge of virtual brand community and its effects.

KEYWORDS

Virtual Brand Community, Customer Relationships, Brand Loyalty, Brand Trust

1. INTRODUCTION

Social media such as Facebook, Twitter, MySpace and LinkedIn, have become popular online attraction sites for consumer interactions (Alharthey, 2020). These social media create online communities that allow more dynamic roles in consumer to firm interaction and virtual presence. Individuals, professional groups, governments, and businesses alike are currently experimenting with social media marketing strategies, in what appears to be an exceptionally viral way to get messages (Saji, Chauhan, & Pillai, 2013; Sohail, Hasan, & Sohail, 2020). In this regard, researchers on social media have found that brand loyalty is enhanced through brand experiences and emotional connections, particularly through the use of social media brand community activities (Iglesias, Singh, & Batista-Foguet, 2011). These virtual brand community activities such as entertainment, interaction, and customization (Sohail et al., 2020) invariably build upon trust (Alharthey, 2020) that can yield loyalty. The horizon of marketing therefore has been broadened.

Within the context of a sub-Saharan developing country such as Ghana, a few companies seem to have engaged customers on facebook sites over the last couple of years. As part of their marketing drive to maintain brand communities, these firms developed social media campaigns as a strategic tool to engage customers.

Given this increasing use and popularity of these social media as brand communities in Ghana, studies that seek to examine brand loyalty (Barnet & Ferris, 2016), trust on social media (Alharthey, 2020), social media marketing (Sohail, Hasan, & Sohail, 2020) are worth doing. However, there is a paucity of research on how social media brand communities affect the brand within the context of sub-Saharan Africa. There is also limited research on the contribution of the social media brand community in the achievement of brands in Ghana. In this regard, this study is positioned to fill the research gap of examining a) whether brand community (Facebook) affects its relationship with customers, and b) the extent to which the online community affects brand loyalty.

2. LITERATURE REVIEW

2.1 Social Media

Kaplan and Haenlein (2010) define social media as a group of internet based applications propelled by Web 2.0, allowing the creation and exchange of user generated content, in a sharing and collaborative way. In this way, users now create and consume content, thereby adding value to the site (Campbell et al., 2011). This has progressed from simple information recovery to interactivity, interoperability, and collaboration (Campbell et al., 2011), enabling brands to listen to consumers and respond (Fournier & Avery, 2011). This has resulted in a fundamental marketing strategy shift in how organizations and customers relate to each other (Angel & Sexsmith, 2009). Social media marketing therefore is the connection between brands and consumers, that offer personal channels and currency for user-centred networking and social interaction (Chi, 2011). The phrases, social networking and social media are often used interchangeably. Social media is the online interactive environment in which social networking takes place and has altered the way in which consumers gather information and make buying decisions. Popular social media sites that are accessible in Ghana include social networks (Facebook, Myspace, and LinkedIn), micro-blogs (Twitter, Plurk, and Friend Feed), reviews and ratings (Yelp, Amazon, and Trip Advisor), video (YouTube and Vimeo), messengers (WhatsApp, imo, Snapchat, Telegram, Wechat, Viber etc.), photo sharing (Instagram, Snapchat, Pinterest etc.), and more.

2.2 Virtual Brand Community

Virtual Brand Communities (VBCs) can be described as aggregations of consumers that occur on a virtual space due to their interest in a brand or product (Georgi & Mink, 2012), or the site[s] of complex brand meaning creation and consumption efforts (Muñiz & Schau, 2007). The essence of VBC therefore is to generate loyalty to the brand through the creation of brand experiences, based on common interest.

In the discussion of what makes a virtual brand community (VBC) cohesive and loyal to a brand, Casaló, Favián, and Guinalíu (2008) found that trust for a VBC leads to increased participation, and positive VBC participation experience leads to more loyalty of the brand. Trust itself is influenced by security *(*Cha, 2009), individual users' participation, group unity and awareness (Casaló, Favián, & Guinalíu, 2008). Habibi, Laroche, and Richard (2014) emphasised four types of customer relationships open to virtual brand community participants: customer-product, customer-brand, customer-company and customer-other customer relationships.

Group norms represent the set of shared goals, beliefs, and values that group members follow. The nature and culture of social media group norms affect the way its members interpret and attach meaning to brands and products (Muñiz & Schau, 2007). Thus community members within a strong social group are more likely to have group intentions to accept the organization's offer in online communities or not (Zeng, Huang, & Dou, 2009).

2.3 Brand

"A 'brand' is a name, term, sign, symbol or design, or a combination of them intended to identify the goods and services of one seller or group of sellers and to differentiate them from those of competitors" (Keller, 1998). Brands may be represented by a personality and a signature tune to capture the hearts of consumers and keep them loyal (Batra, Ahuvia, & Bagozzi, 2012). Strong brands therefore enable the consumer to identify products, evaluate their quality, and make it easier for the customers to develop attitudes and expectations. Brands also make shopping more efficient as it tends to reduce perceived risks of purchase (Keller, 1998). Well-known brands are capable of developing favourable attitudes and perceptions more easily, leading to loyalty (Kapferer, 2008).

2.4 Brand Trust

Gaining the trust of a brand audience is essential to building brand loyalty (Lau & Lee, 1999). While Lau and Lee (1999) viewed brand trust as the willingness to rely on the brand, Moorman et al. (1992) described trust as the willingness to rely on an exchange partner confidently. Thus brand trust is the willingness and keenness to depend on another party in the face of risk. In relationship-marketing literature, trust has been viewed as a determinant of the loyalty (Berry, 1983), and has been recognised in recent studies as a key variable in long-term relationships with customers, which in turn positively affects brand loyalty (Ming et al., 2011; Bowen and Bowen, 2020). Chaudhuri and Holbrook (2001) summarises this phenomenon that brand trust strongly influences the customer's attitude and repurchase loyalty.

2.5 Brand Loyalty

Brand loyalty has been widely discussed within the offline brand loyalty literature, giving prominence to two dimensions of the concept. These are behavioural and attitudinal loyalty (Balginger and Rubinson, 1996). Oliver (1997) defines loyalty as capturing its multi dimensionality as "a deeply held commitment to rebuy or patronise a preferred product/service consistently in the future, thereby causing repetitive same-brand or same brand-set purchase, despite the situational influences and marketing efforts having the potential to cause switching behaviour". Aaker's (1991) description of brands as the measure of attachment that a customer has towards a brand conceptualises brand loyalty as a pyramid with five tiers: the switchers; satisfied, but habitual buyers; satisfied buyers with switching cost; brand likers; and committed buyers.

2.6 Hypothesis Development

Consumer engagement on social media can be measured by consumers' propensity to invest the resources of themselves in activities in the social media group activity such as value co-creation, social interaction, knowledge sharing/storing, and word of mouth (WOM) (Liu, Lee, Liu and Chen, 2018). While this has been found to moderate between the various customer-virtual brand relationships (product, brand, company) and trust (Habibi et al., 2014), Stokburger-Sauer (2010), however, suggests a significant relationship between online brand community engagement and consumer personal relationships with product, brand, and company. This study examines whether the social media brand community engagement leads to enhanced consumer-product relationship, consumer-brand relationship, and consumer-company relationship. It is therefore hypothesised that:

H1:Online brand community engagement influences customer/product relationship.

H2:Online brand community engagement influences customer/brand relationship

H3:Online brand community engagement influences customer/company relationship

Habibi et al. (2014) developed and tested a model on how consumers' relationships with the elements of a brand community based on social media (brand, product, company, and other consumers) influences brand trust. Apart from customer relationship with other customers, Habibi et al. (2014) reported a significant relationship between the other three constructs and brand trust among the online brand community participants. This study tests these hypotheses under the current contexts, and therefore hypothesise the following:

H4: Customer/product relationship influences trust among customers

H5: Customer/company relationship influences trust among customers.

H6: Customer/brand relationship influences trust among customers.

Brand trust resulting from online community engagement has been reported to lead to brand loyalty (Laroche, Habibi, & Richard, 2013). This study therefore hypothesise that:

H7: Brand trust leads to brand brand loyalty

3. METHODOLOGY

Items for the measurement of customer-product relation, customer-brand relation, and customer-company relation were all adapted from Habibi, Laroche, and Richard (2014) and Casalo, Flavian, and Guinali (2010). Question items for trust were adapted from Habibi et al. (2014), brand loyalty were adapted from Casalo, Flavian, and Guinali (2010) and the social media engagement construct was adapted from Liu, Lee, Liu, and Chen (2018). Data was conveniently collected with questionnaires conducted in a central shopping mall in Ghana. A sample size of 740 useable responses were received from users of various brand communities. The data was analysed with Structural Equations Modelling (SEM) in SmartPLS software (Ringle, Wende, & Smith, 2005).

4. DATA ANALYSIS

In order to run structural equation modelling analysis in SmartPLS, the data must first meet conditions of data validity and reliability as outlined by Chin (1998). Reliability refers to the extent to which the data collection instrument produces consistent results if replicated in another study (Saunders et al., 2006). Composite Reliability (CR) and Cronbach's Alpha (α) tests were used to assess reliability of the research the instrument consistency. Chin (1998) recommended that an instrument indicated acceptable reliability if the Composite Reliability (CR) and Cronbach's Alpha (α) were greater than 0.70.

Convergent validity tested the extent to which two or more indicators measure the same variable/construct. For example, customer/product relation was measured with four (4) indicators; hence it was important to test whether all these four indicators measure the concept of customer/product relation well or not. Chin (1998) recommended that a construct exhibited acceptable validity of the items if the Average Variance Extracted (AVE) value was above 0.50.

Table 1 below shows the results for the test for reliability and validity of the constructs/variables used in the study. The CR values were between 0.75 and 1.00, well above the recommended threshold of 0.70. This implied that the items used to measure the variables/constructs showed high reliability and would produce consistent results if replicated on another sample. The AVE values were between 0.58 and 1.00, again showing acceptable convergent validity of measures since they were well above the recommended 0.50 value.

Table 1. Construct Reliability and Validity

	Composite Reliability (CR)	Average Variance Extracted (AVE)
Brand Loyalty	0.75	0.61
Customer/Brand Relation	0.95	0.90
Customer/Company Relation	1.00	1.00
Customer/Product Relation	0.85	0.66
Online Brand Community	0.89	0.73
Trust	0.80	0.58

Discriminant validity tested whether the items selected to measure a variable actually do so. This was tested in two ways: first, with the Fornell-Larcker criterion, the diagonal values were greater than the off-diagonal values (the pair-wise correlation between factors) as shown in Table 2 and cross loadings were higher on their respective construct (i.e. above 0.60) than on other constructs as shown in Table 3: both depicted acceptable discriminant validity.

Table 2. Discriminant Validity of Variables/Constructs

Brand Loyalty	Customer/Brand Relation	Customer/Company Relation	Customer/Product Relation	Online Brand Community	Trust
Brand Loyalty	0.782				
Customer/Brand Relation	-0.054	0.948			
Customer/Company Relation	0.339	0.088	1		
Customer/Product Relation	0.547	0.073	0.295	0.813	
Online Brand Community	0.009	0.201	-0.016	0.227	0.857
Trust	0.562	-0.125	0.335	0.496	-0.06

Three (3) items with a loading of below 0.60 on their respective constructs were removed to attain acceptable discriminant validity. These were one item each from Brand Loyalty (BLOYAL2), Customer/Brand Relation (BRND3) and Customer/Company Relation (COMP1).

Table 3. Cross Loadings of Items/Indicators on Variables

	Brand Loyalty	Customer/ Brand Relation	Customer/ Company Relation	Customer/ Product Relation	Online Brand Community	Trust
BCOM1	0.111	-0.007	0.016	0.217	0.845	0.052
BCOM2	0.095	0.012	0.025	0.211	0.848	0.046
BCOM3	-0.079	0.328	-0.045	0.178	0.877	-0.144
BLOYAL1	0.906	-0.059	0.362	0.559	0.019	0.543
BLOYAL3	0.634	-0.016	0.115	0.231	-0.015	0.296
BRND1	-0.044	0.932	0.07	0.048	0.160	-0.097
BRND2	-0.057	0.963	0.093	0.085	0.213	-0.134
BTRUST1	0.386	-0.131	0.22	0.429	0.017	0.753
BTRUST2	0.371	-0.105	0.268	0.26	-0.169	0.670
BTRUST3	0.514	-0.057	0.281	0.425	-0.011	0.849
COMP2	0.339	0.088	1.000	0.295	-0.016	0.335
PROD1	0.415	0.087	0.391	0.840	0.213	0.433
PROD2	0.480	-0.001	0.200	0.814	0.174	0.350
PROD4	0.446	0.082	0.113	0.786	0.162	0.418

PLS Structural Model Results

First, the bootstrap method in SmartPLS 3 (Ringle, Wende, & Becker, 2015) was run to determine the significance of the hypothesized relations in the research model. It was evident that three (3) path relationships were statistically non-significant, namely: Customer/Brand Relation -> Trust; Online Brand Community -> Customer/Brand Relation and Online Brand Community -> Customer/Company Relation. Overall, four (4) path relationships showed statistical significance: Customer/Company Relation -> Trust and Online Brand Community -> Customer/Product Relation was at 95% significance level whilst Customer/Product Relation -> Trust and Trust -> Brand Loyalty was at 99% significance level. The results and further details are shown in Table 4 below.

Table 4. Path Significance

	Original Sample (O)	T Statistics (|O/STDEV|)	P Values	Remark
Customer/Brand Relation -> Trust	-0.176	0.883	0.378	n.s
Customer/Company Relation -> Trust	0.219	2.198	0.028	$p \leq 0.05$
Customer/Product Relation -> Trust	0.444	4.022	0.000	$p \leq 0.01$
Online Brand Community -> Customer/Brand Relation	0.201	0.922	0.357	n.s
Online Brand Community -> Customer/Company Relation	-0.016	0.129	0.897	n.s
Online Brand Community -> Customer/Product Relation	0.227	2.291	0.022	$p \leq 0.05$
Trust -> Brand Loyalty	0.562	9.601	0.000	$p \leq 0.01$

Test for Mediation

The study assessed the following: (i) whether the type of relationships established mediates the relationship between online brand community and trust; and (ii) whether trust mediates the relations between the types of customer relationships and brand loyalty. To assess mediation, guidelines by Hair et al. (2013) were followed. First, the model was made with only the exogenous and the endogenous constructs. Then the model was run with the introduction of the mediating constructs. If the relationship is not statistically significant, then there is no mediation, however, if there exists a significant relationship, then there is mediation. This mediation is full if the mediator makes the original relationship between the independent and dependent variables non-significant. Otherwise, only partial mediation is established.

5. FINDINGS

Online Brand Community and Customer Relations- Overall, the results revealed that online brand community led positively and significantly to customer/product relation (β=0.201, n.s.). This showed that online brand community improved customers' consumption of the product. In this case, customer purchase of roduct increased due to the organisations online community activities. Online brand community also led positively to customer/brand relation (β=0.227, sig. $p \leq 0.05$), however, the relationship was statistically non-significant. Online brand community was once more found to exhibit a non-significant negative relationship with customer/company relation (β=-0.016, n.s.). In effect, therefore, online community improved customers' relations mainly with the product, but not the company nor brand. This implies that online brand community can cause the increased consumption of a product as a group activity and not necessarily as a preference for the brand, nor the company. Overall, online brand community explained only a small percentage of the variance for the three types of relations tested, customer/product relation (R2=0.051%), customer/brand relation (R^2=0.040), and customer/company relation (R2=0.00). This implies that the online brand community is not necessarily the main reason why customers relate well with the product, brand or company.

Customer Relations and Trust- The study tested the impact of customers' relationships with the product, brand and company through online communities on their level of trust. Results showed that customer-product relation (β=0.444, $p \leq 0.01$), as well as customer-company relation (β=0.219, $p \leq 0.05$) significantly helped build trust among customers. However, customer/brand relations (β=0.176, n.s.), which negatively related to the level of trust among customers, was not statistically significant. This means that customer-product relationship could mediate between online brand community and brand trust. This mediation effect implies that an online brand community can lead to brand trust only through the experience with the product. Even though customer-company relationship leads to brand trust directly, it however does not mediate between online community and brand trust. Customer-brand relationship neither led to brand trust, nor mediated between online community and brand trust. Overall, the three types of customers' relation with the product, brand and company on online brand communities (in this case the online brand community of firms studied) explained about 30% of the variance for customers' trust (R^2=0.303).

Trust and Brand Loyalty- The results showed that the trust-loyalty relationship is strong (β=0.562, $p \leq 0.01$) and trust accounts for about 30% of why customers are loyal to the brand. This means that it is important for brands to work towards winning the trust of customers of the online community, as this greatly led to brand loyalty, which is found to spur repurchase and generate increased performance.

Result of Mediating Relationships- Results reveal that the types of relations do not mediate the link between online brand community and trust. For example, the direct relationship between online brand communication and trust (β = -0.232, n.s.) was not statistically significant. Hence, there could not be a mediating effect by customer/product, customer/brand and customer/company relations. On the other hand, trust seems to have some mediating effect on some of the relationships and brand loyalty. For instance, the strength of the direct relationship between customer/product relations and brand loyalty (β = 0.562, $p \leq 0.01$) reduced, but maintained statistical significance with the introduction of the mediating construct, trust (β = 0.494, $p \leq 0.0$). This shows that trust only partially mediates the relationship. Similarly, trust only partially mediates the relationship between customer/company relations and brand loyalty as the strength of the direct relationship reduced but was still statistically significant with the inclusion of trust (i.e. from β = 0.355, $p \leq 0.0$ to β = 0.335, $p \leq 0.0$). Nonetheless, trust does not mediate the relationship between customer/brand relations and brand loyalty (β = -0.058, n.s) due to the non-significant nature of the direct relationship.

6. DISCUSSION

The data revealed that online brand community activities caused the increased consumption of the product as a group activity and not necessarily as a preference for the brand, nor the company. Customer-product relationship was the only significant consumer relationship resulting from virtual brand community engagement. The result confirms some findings from earlier studies (Muñiz & Schau, 2007; Mangold

& Faulds, 2009; Barnet & Ferris, 2016) as well as come current studies (Alharthey, 2020) that online brand community interaction between consumers results in opinion leadership and group consumption decisions.
Even thouth customer-product relationship did not mediate between virtual brand community and trust, it led to brand trust. This implies that online brand community can only lead to brand trust through experience with the product, and not the brand image nor company relationship. This result partly confirms Habibi, Laroche, and Richard's (2014) report that customer-product and customer-company relationships influenced trust, while customer-brand relationship did not influence brand trust.

Even though the customer-company relationship leads to brand trust directly, it is not significantly affected by online brand community engagement and therefore does not mediate between online community and brand trust. This partly supports Habibi, Laroche, and Richard's (2014) contention that customer-company relationship influences brand trust.
Customer-brand relationship neither led to brand trust, nor mediated between online community and brand trust. This result supports Habibi, Laroche, and Richard (2014), but differs from that of Casaló, Flavián and Miguel (2008) who reported that virtual community has a positive influence on consumer commitment to customer-brand relationship.

Trust of the online community was confirmed to lead to loyalty. The finding supports the report of Casaló, Favián, and Guinalíu (2008) as well as Bowen and Bowen (2020) that brand trust influences loyalty to the brand.

7. MANAGERIAL IMPLICATIONS

Managerial implications of the findings above include the following:

Organizations using online community as a marketing communications tool need to ensure favourable customer/product related activities, experience and word of mouth within the community. This can influence more purchase of the brand through opinion leadership.

Awareness creation of brand extensions can be done at very reduced marketing cost, as the brand community increased its purchases as a community activity even if they dislike the company or other elements of the brand.

Offline programs pertaining to brands need to be promoted as part of the online brand community activities to enhance the personal interaction with customers. This personal interaction can improve the customer/company relationship, thereby enhancing trust.

It is important for organisations to work towards winning the trust of customers of the online community, as this greatly leads to brand loyalty, which is found to spur repurchase behaviour and generate increased performance.

8. LIMITATIONS AND RECOMMENDATIONS

This study was a cross sectional survey, which does not examine the effect the online brand community on individual consumers before and after the engagement with a online virtual brand community. Therefore a longitudinal survey of individual virtual brand engagement is recommended with qualitative explanations of the various constructs like trust and loyalty are developed over time withing the community. This can unravel or decompose the composition of online trust and online loyalty. Further studies could introduce customer-other customer relationships. A comparative study could also be done between product related virtual brand communities and service related virtual brand communities. This can throw more light on which sector (product or service) performs better with the use of virtual community.

REFERENCES

Aaker, D. A., 1991. *Managing Brand Equity: Capitalizing on the Value of a Brand Name*, NY: The Free Press.

Alharthey, B., 2020. The Role of Online Trust in Forming Online Shopping Intentions. *International Journal of Online Marketing (IJOM)*, *10*(1), 32-57.

Angel, R., and Sexsmith, J., 2009. Social networking: the view from the C-suite. *Ivey Business Journal*, *73*(4), 5.

Baldinger, A. L., and Rubinson, J., 1996. Brand loyalty: the link between attitude and behavior. *Journal of Advertising Research*, *36*(6), 22-35.

Batra, R. et al, 2012. Brand love. *Journal of Marketing*, *76*(2), 1-16.

Barnet, K., and Ferris, S. P., 2016. Brand Loyalty and Online Brand Communities: Is Brand Loyalty Being Strengthened Through Social Media? *International Journal of Online Marketing (IJOM)*, *6*(3), 50-61.

Bowen, G., and Bowen, R., 2020. Differences and Similarities: Brand Trust Offline and Online. In *Global Branding: Breakthroughs in Research and Practice* (pp. 466-498). IGI Global.

Campbell, C., Pitt, L. F., Parent, M., and Berthon, P. R., 2011. Understanding consumer conversations around ads in a Web 2.0 world. *Journal of Advertising*, *40*(1), 87-102.

Casaló, L. V., Flavián, C., and Miguel, G., 2008. Promoting Consumer's Participation in Virtual Brand Communities: A New Paradigm in Branding Strategy. *Journal of Marketing Communications, 14*, 19-36.

Casalo, L. V., Flavian, C. and Guinaliu, M., 2010. Some antecedents and effects of participation in Spanish virtual brand communities. *International Journal of Web Based Communities, 6*(1), 25.

Cha, J., 2009. Shopping on Social Networking Websites: Attitudes towards real versus virtual items. *Journal of Interactive Advertising, 10*, 77-93.

Chaudhuri, A., and Holbrook, M. B., 2001. The chain of effects from brand trust and brand affect to brand performance: The role of brand loyalty. *Journal of Marketing, 65*, 81-93.

Chi, H. H., 2011. Interactive digital advertising vs. virtual brand community: Exploratory study of user motivation and social media marketing responses in Taiwan. *Journal of Interactive Advertising*, *12*(1), 44-61.

Chin, W. W., 1998. The partial least squares approach to structural equation modeling. *Modern Methods for Business Research*, *295*(2), 295-336.

Fournier, S., and Avery, J., 2011. The uninvited brand. *Business Horizons*, *54*(3), 193-207.

Georgi, D., & Mink, M., 2013. eCCIq: The quality of electronic customer-to-customer interaction. *Journal of Retailing and Consumer Services*, *20*(1), 11-19.

Habibi, M. R., Laroche, M., and Richard, M. O., 2014. The roles of brand community and community engagement in building brand trust on social media. *Computers in Human Behavior*, *37*, 152-161.

Howe, J. (2006). The rise of crowdsourcing. *Wired Magazine*, *14*(6), 1-4.

Iglesias, O., Singh, J. J., and Batista-Foguet, J. M., 2011. The role of brand experience and affective commitment in determining brand loyalty. *Journal of Brand Management*, *18*(8), 570-582.

Kapferer, J.-N., 2008. *The New Strategic Brand Management: Creating and Sustaining Brand Equity Long Term*. London: Kogan Page Ltd.

Kaplan, A. M., and Haenlein, M., 2010. Users of the world, unite! The challenges and opportunities of Social Media. *Business Horizons*, *53*(1), 59-68.

Keller, K. L., 1998. *Strategic Brand Management*, Prentice Hall, Upper Saddle River, New Jersey.

Lau, G. T., and Lee, S. H., 1999. Consumers' Trust in Brand and their link to Brand Loyalty. *Journal of Market Focused Management, 4*, 341 370.

Liu, L., Lee, M. K., Liu, R., and Chen, J., 2018. Trust transfer in social media brand communities: The role of consumer engagement. *International Journal of Information Management*, *41*, 1-13.

Ming, T.T., Ismail, H.B., and Rasiah, D., 2011. Hierarchical Chain of Consumer-Based Brand Equity: Review From The Fast Food Industry. *International Business & Economics Research Journal, 10*(9), 67–80.

Muñiz, Jr, A. M., and Schau, H. J., 2007. Vigilante marketing and consumer-created communications. *Journal of Advertising*, *36*(3), 35-50.

Nielsen.com, 2012. State of The Media - The Social Media Report 2012. Retrieved December 2019, from http://www.nielsen.com/us/en/insights/reports/2012/state-of-the-media-the-social-media-report-2012.html

Oliver, R. L.,1997. *Satisfaction: A behavioral perspective on the consumer*. New York: McGraw-Hill.

Ringle, C. M., Wende, S., and Becker, J. M. (2015). SmartPLS 3. SmartPLS GmbH, Boenningstedt. *Journal of Service, Science and Managment*, *10*(3).

Saunders, M., Lewis, P., & Thornhill, A., 2012. Research methods for business students, 696. *Essex: Pearson Education Limited.*

Sohail, M. S., Hasan, M. and Sohail, A. F., 2020. The Impact of Social Media Marketing on Brand Trust and Brand Loyalty: An Arab Perspective. *International Journal of Online Marketing (IJOM)*, *10*(1), 15-31.

Stokburger-Sauer, N., 2010. Brand community: Drivers and outcomes. *Psychology & Marketing*, *27*(4), 347-368.

Zeng, F., Huang, L., and Dou, W., 2009. Social factors in user perceptions and responses to advertising in online social networking communities. *Journal of Interactive Advertising*, *10*(1), 1-13.

HOW DO FAKE NEWS PROPAGATORS EXPLOIT SOCIAL ALGORITHMS TO PROMOTE THEIR CONTENTS?

Ittipon Rassameeroj[1] and Shyhtsun Felix Wu[2]
[1]*Faculty of ICT, Mahidol University, Nakhon Pathom, Thailand*
[2]*Department of Computer Science, UC Davis, Davis, CA, USA*

ABSTRACT

Social media has currently become a primary platform to consume and exchange information. Instead of browsing through media source websites we are interested, we have enabled social media to deliver related contents to us. As a black box, social algorithms were designed and trained to pick up, filter, and rank the most relevant and desired contents to be delivered to each individual one of us. In addition, social media allows us to add more contents as a comment on an original post, which we call user-created content. Unfortunately, a lot of fake news contents have been created and disseminated in Facebook fan pages. Many of them could draw many attentions from users. Our research question is how do fake news propagators successfully make their contents be more visible and disseminate it to many users through social algorithms? In this work, we explored behavior and activities of fake news propagators and their trapped recipient to understand how social algorithms widely delivered those contents to many users on Facebook fan pages. From our SINCERE data, we extracted top 300 fake news comments that got the highest number of participants as our data set. We statistically analyzed the data set based on our hypotheses, which were mainly from our previous work of reverse-engineering for content delivery algorithms in social media and from what we observed from the SINCERE data. Our main contribution for this work is to understand behaviors, activities, and strategies of fake news propagators who successfully disseminated their contents to many users through social algorithms on Facebook.

KEYWORDS

Fake News, Misinformation, Social Algorithms, Social Media, Facebook Fan Pages, Online Public Communities

1. INTRODUCTION

In past decade, online content consumption behavior has been changed. We had to browse through websites of media source that we are interested or use online search engine tools to search and bring us to the online content we desired. On the contrary, social media has currently become a primary platform to consume and exchange information. We have enabled social media to deliver online contents to us. In addition, social media platforms allow us to add contents by creating comments on an original content, which we call user-created content. For Facebook, many users not only focus on the original posts, but also consume other user comments nowadays. Like online search engine tools, social media systems have some mechanisms to pick up, filter, and rank the most relevant and desired contents, included both original posts and user comments, to be delivered to each individual one of us, which we call social algorithms. Conceptually, social algorithms are usually designed and trained by usually using social network data, personalization, and online activities. However, as a black box, we do not really know how social algorithms work. It is obvious that even we have more and more online contents, but we cannot control and customize our content delivery algorithms much in social media systems.

A user-created content (or a user comment) could be opinion, more related information, other aspects of information, or even misinformation. Unfortunately, a lot of misinformation contents, like fake news, have been created and disseminated in social media. Many of them could successfully draw attentions from many users more than even other good contents, such as fact-checking contents. For example, on Facebook, those fake news contents got many likes or reactions. Initially, our simple question is many users were interested in those contents, or social algorithms made those contents to be more visible to them? We strongly believe that social algorithms play an important role in that. If so, our main research question is how do fake news propagators make use of social algorithms to make their contents to be more visible to many users?

In this work, we explored social algorithms for fake news contents in Facebook fan pages and public communities. Also, we tried to find main factors or behavioral patterns that fake news propagators made their fake news contents to be more visible and be delivered to many other users via social algorithms. We empirically defined hypotheses, which mainly were from what we have observed from our SINCERE data and from our previous work of reverse-engineering for content delivery algorithms in social media, based on behaviors and activities of fake news propagators. We statistically analyzed our data set based on our hypotheses to find main factors that fake news contents could be widely delivered to many users though social algorithms on Facebook fan pages.

The remainder of this paper is organized as follows. We motivated our study with additional related work and backgrounds in Section 2. In Section 3, we briefed our conceptual approach. In Section 4, we introduced our SINCERE data and the data set we used in this work. Also, we showed top 5 fake news URLs we found in the SINCERE data and top 10 Facebook fan pages that had the largest number of fake news comments. In Section 5, we presented our hypotheses and experimental results of data analysis. Finally, in we discussed our limitations for this work, and we summarized this paper in Section 6.

2. RELATED WORKS

Lazer (2015) presented some ideas, overview, and brief definition of social algorithms. The author also gave some examples to show how social algorithm had an impact on choosing and ranking all content on the Internet for users. On the other hand, Yang (2017) presented social algorithms in terms of computational algorithms, which is a special class of algorithms for solving optimization problems. The author showed the algorithms that did not focus on only social media systems, but they could be applied for general context, mainly nature-inspired, population-based algorithm for optimization.

Social media systems, like Facebook and Twitter, have become one of the main channels to diffuse information rapidly. Basic techniques that have been used for their content delivery algorithms include personalization, interests, and online activities. In addition, the strength of weak ties theory (Granovetter, 1973) is one of the most popular techniques applied to content delivery algorithm in most of social media providers. Gilbert and Karahalios (2009) presented a predictive model that maps social media data to tie strength in online social networks. For example, contents that were created from friends whom we frequently interacted with should be picked and shown first. Bakshy (2012) presented how strong and weak ties had influences in terms of information propagation in social networks.

A very challenging research question is how can we evaluate that contents filtered by social algorithms are the most desired we would like to see? There are existing researches investigating bias in social algorithms. Pariser (2011) presented filter bubble, which personalization made people see different viewpoints of content. In addition, since we all do not really know how social algorithms work, there are some concerns about bias of algorithmically selected content. Furthermore, ideological diverse issue is another concern for social algorithms. Flaxman, Goel, and Rao (2016) pointed out that both search engines and social media systems may use ideological distance as a factor to pick a content up and push it to users. Also, those systems are associated with an increase in the mean ideological distance between individuals.

We did reverse engineering of social algorithms on Facebook fan page. They have focused on top posts that had a largest number of comments in news media pages (Rassameeroj and Wu, 2019). However, they did not investigate misinformation contents and did not analyze behaviors and activities of comment authors.

Del Vicario et al (2016) did governing misinformation spreading through a thorough quantitative analysis and focused on how Facebook users consume information related to two distinct narratives: scientific and conspiracy news. In (Shao et al, 2017), the authors analyzed 14 million messages spreading 400 thousand claims on Twitter during and following the 2016 U.S. presidential campaign and election. They found that accounts that actively spread misinformation are significantly more likely to be bots. In (Del Vicario et al, 2019), they analyzed Italian Facebook dataset to identify topics that are susceptible to misinformation. Vosoughi, Roy, and Aral (2018) investigated the differential diffusion all of the verified true and false news stories distributed on Twitter from 2006 to 2017. They found that false news was more novel than true news, which suggested that people were more likely to share novel information. Hu et al (2013) did modeling the messages and pathway propagation in a social network based on social network users and structures.

3. CONCEPTUAL APPROACH

Basically, our goal is to explore how fake news propagators exploit social algorithms to make their contents be more visible to many users based on their behavior and activities. In this work, we considered user comments, which contained fake news URLs or domains, in posts in Facebook fan pages and communities, as fake news contents. We focused on Facebook fan pages because they are popular targets for fake news. Since all users can interact with anyone as long as they are members in the same communities regardless of relationship, it is very easy to disseminate malicious contents on there. In order to work towards that, we analyzed behaviors or activities of fake news propagators and their recipients based on our hypotheses. We assume that users, who liked, reacted, or replied to the fake news comments, are the recipients. Our hypotheses empirically were from our previous work (Rassameeroj and Wu, 2019), what we have noticed in Facebook features, and what we observed in our data set. From the data set, we statistically analyzed each fake news comment in each original post independently.

4. DATA

We used our Social Interactive Networking and Conversation Entropy Ranking Engine (SINCERE) data (Erlandsson et al, 2015). It was crawled via Facebook API from public interaction data on almost all Facebook fan pages and public communities from 2008 to early 2018. The SINCERE data is composed of almost all posts, comments, likes, reactions (love, haha, wow, anger, sad), and shares. Table 1 presents total amount of the SINCERE data we have.

Table 1. Total amount of data on SINCERE

Data type	Amount of data
Facebook fan pages	4,706,324
Posts	342,998,071
Comments	6,432,081,954
Likes and reactions	132,876,481,459
Replies	1,110,940,833
Shares	163,301,864

To get all fake news contents (comments) from the SINCERE data, we firstly used a list of fake news URLs and domains mainly collected from Shao et al (2017) and fact-checking websites, such as snopes.com, factcheck.org, politifact.com, washingtonpost.com, mediabiasfactcheck.com, and truthorfiction.com. From the SINCERE data, Table 2 shows some samples of our fake news URLs or domains, which is the top five of fake news URLs that were attached in comments in Facebook fan pages.

Table 2. Top five Fake News URLs or domains attached in comments in Facebook fan pages

No.	Fake news URLs/domains	The number of comments contained the URL	The number of fan pages
1	infowars.com	73,610	4,061
2	thegatewaypundit.com	59,724	2,970
3	globalresearch.ca	41,632	3,593
4	naturalnews.com	37,934	3,892
5	beforeitsnews.com	27,459	2,644

From the SINCERE data we have in Table 1, we extracted top 300 comments contained fake news URLs, which got the highest number of reactions from users, to be our data set. In addition, the total number of fake news comments on our SINCERE data is 533,973 comments. The total number of reactions of those fake news comments is 361,758, which we could imply that is the number of infected users from fake news contents.

As we analyzed behavior of both fake news propagators and their participants, we would like to make sure that their participants naturally received the fake news contents from social algorithms only, not from other techniques of fake news propagators, such as likebait. Thus, we investigated whether all fake news comments in our data set got reactions from normal users, not from bot accounts or users who only participated in those fake news comments for some other reasons. For example, if most participants of a fake news comments did not participate in other comments, or they did not have other activities, it is most likely that fake news comment might be promoted by using fake news propagators' techniques (such as generating likebait from bot accounts), not by social algorithms.

Hence, for each of top 300 fake news comments from our data set, we would like to see how many participants reacted to other comments. Figure 1 shows percentage of participants who reacted to other comments (on y-axis) for each of top 300 fake news comments (on x-axis). Please ignore comments number 62 and 184 in the figure because we have lost some data for these comments. In the figure, we could imply that all fake news comments from our data set did not generate from any bot accounts because most of participants also interacted with other comments as usual, not only with the fake news comments.

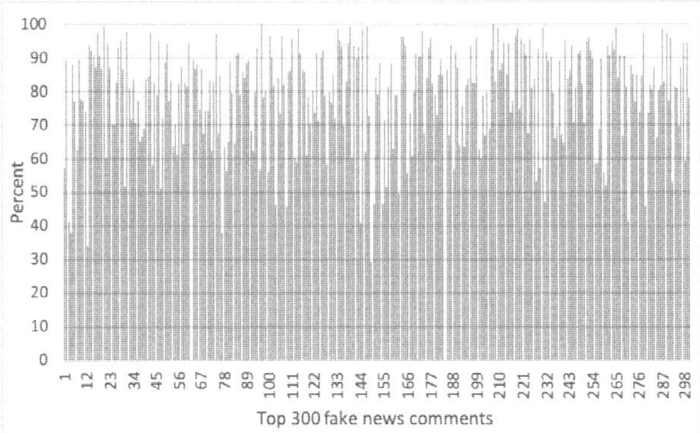

Figure 1. Percentage of reaction users who reacted to other comments for each of top 300 fake news comments

Before we investigated fake news propagators behavior, we would like to present top 10 targets of Facebook fan pages that have the largest number of fake news contents from the whole SINCERE data in Table 3. We also show the number of reactions for those comments in the last column in the table, which we simply imply the total number of users who might be trapped by a fake news.

Table 3. Top 10 Facebook fan pages with the largest number of fake news comments

No.	Facebook fan pages	The number of fake news URL comments	The number of reactions
1	Fox News	40,811	19,069
2	Hillary Clinton	26,281	6,649
3	The White House	21,232	7,046
4	Barack Obama	20,017	7,004
5	Donald J. Trump	15,490	5,279
6	MSNBC	12,031	4,661
7	CNN	11,529	6,307
8	Alex Jones	6,649	19,455
9	Ted Cruz	5,645	1,883
10	RT	5,472	8,015

5. HYPOTHESES AND EXPERIMENTS

In this section, we present hypotheses of fake news propagator strategies and behavior. Then, we present experimental results from statistically analyze the data set based on interaction, activities, and behavior of fake news propagators (Section 5.1 and 5.2) and their recipients (Section 5.3).

5.1 Creation Time

Our first hypothesis is that if a fake news comment is created very early right after an original post is published, social algorithms will probably choose that comment to be the top comment for the posts, which means most users will see that comment first. Hence, we analyze the data set to see how early fake news comments were created after their original posts, and the result is presented in Figure 2. From the result, we have found that many fake news comments were created very early. 26% of them were created within two minutes after their posts, 19% and 17% of them were created in first five and 10 minutes after the posts respectively. It is obvious fake news content creator use this strategy to try to get a lot of attention from users.

In addition to the times when the fake news contents were created, we are also interested in their position or chronological order in that post. Even we have just shown the comments, that were created very early after the posts, were apparently seen by many users, we believe those comments might not be the first comment in their posts. From (Rassameeroj and Wu, 2019), the authors shown that users who create comments earlier in a post will very likely see other comments created later because of Facebook notification features. For this reason, our next hypothesis is a fake news comment might be created after a few of other comments were created in the same post. Thus, users who made comments before the fake news comment may see it, and they very likely reacted, such as liking, to it if they were still online, so the fake news comment seems credible because of getting a few likes early.

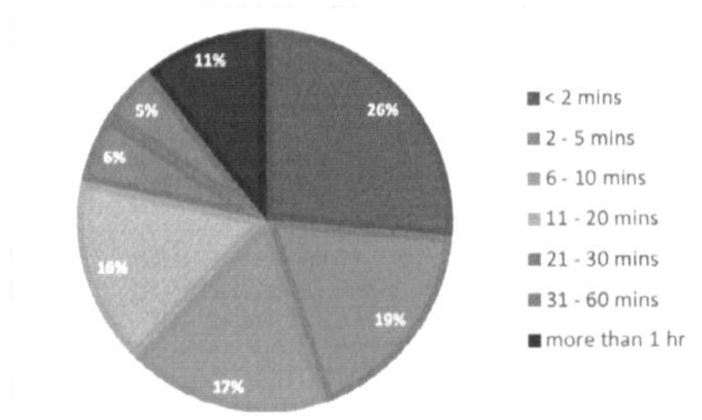

Figure 2. How early top fake news comments had been created after original posts were created

Figure 3 presents chronological order of the top 150 fake news comments (on x-axis) from the data set. Since we have found their orders very vary, we simply scale them as 0 to 100 in Figure 3 (on y-axis), which 0 represents the first comment while 100 represents the last comment in a post. From the result, most of top fake news comments were not created as the first comment in their post.

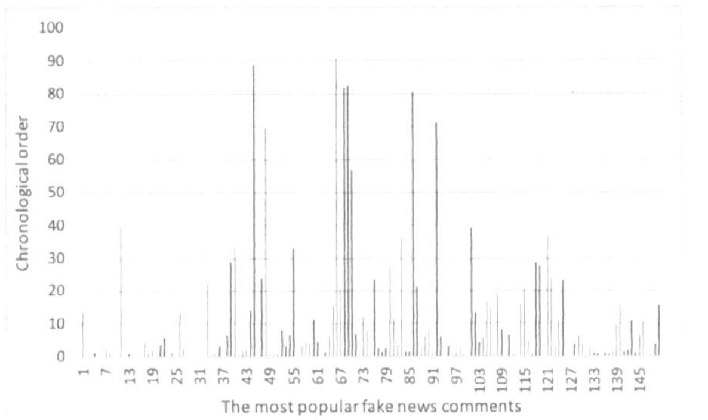

Figure 3. Chronological order of top 150 fake news comments in its post

5.2 Interaction Behavior in a Post

In this section, we tried to see interaction behavior of fake news propagators from our data set. Our hypothesis is that they might have some interactions to make social algorithms to understand that they are very active users so that their contents will be promoted to be more visible. We have initially listed all possible interaction behavior then have analyzed our data set to see their activities pattern.

5.2.1 Did they Like or React the Posts?

Rassameeroj and Wu (2019) has been stated that if two users react to a post, and one of them makes a comment, then another user probably see that comment. We believe that reaction a post may be a factor to promote the content. From the data set, there are 93 of 300 fake news authors (31%). Thus, based on our result and (Rassameeroj and Wu, 2019), reacting a post might be a good factor to promote contents.

5.2.2 Did they make other Comments before and after their Fake News Comment in the Post?

There are 25 of 300 fake news propagators (8.33%) created other comments before their fake news comments. The average number of comments they created is 1.44 comments. Also, 64 of them (21.33%) made more comments after the fake news comments, and the average number of comments they created is 2 comments per author. Hence, creating more comments might not be a good strategy to exploit social algorithms.

5.2.3 Did they Click Like or Reaction on other Comments?

93 of 300 fake news authors (31%) liked or reacted other comments that were made before their fake news contents, and the average number of comments they reacted is 28. However, 180 of 300 authors (60%) liked or reacted other comments that were created after their fake news comments, and the average number of comments they reacted is 22. That is their obvious behaviors, and it might be a strategy to promote their fake news contents be more visible to many users.

As a result, we have analyzed the data set more to see how they make use of social algorithms in that case. For each of fake news comments, we have investigated the reactions they got to see how many of them were from users who got liked or reacted from the fake news propagator. For example, suppose user a and b create comments in a post, and user x likes comments of user a and b. Then, user x creates a fake news comment. We would like to see whether x will get likes from a and b. From the result, unfortunately, most of fake news comments got small reactions from users who got reactions from fake news authors. The average percentage of reactions from users who got likes from the fake news authors is 1.04%, which is very small. As a result, recipients of fake news comments did not come from users who got reactions from fake news propagators, but the recipients might from users who did not make any comment. Accordingly, reactions to other comments may be still a good strategy to exploit social algorithms to cause users to see the their contents somehow based on the behavior of fake news propagators.

5.2.4 Did they Reply to Other Comments?

From the data set, 17 fake news propagators (5.67%) replied to other comments made before their fake news comments, and the average number of replies is 1.7. In addition, 29 of 300 fake news propagators (9.67%) replied to other comments that were created after their fake news comments, and the average number of replies for that is 1.9. Consequently, we conclude that replying other comments is not a good way to promote contents.

5.3 Exploring Reaction Users

We have just done reverse engineering of how fake news propagators make use of social algorithms to promote the contents from their activities and interactions so far. In order to understand all aspects, in this section, we would like to shift from the author side to recipient side or users who saw reacted to those fake news contents. We believe if we see activities and behaviors of reaction users, we may correlate their patterns to understand where reactions were from. That is, we may understand why fake news comments were delivered to them. In this section, when we mention reaction users, that means users who liked, reacted, or replied to the fake news comments in the data set.

5.3.1 Reactions from Users who Reacted to the Post

We have found that many recipients, who reacted to the fake news comments, are from users who liked or reacted the original post of that comment. Figure 4 shows percentage of users, who reacted the post, from all reaction users of the top 150 fake news comment, which is on x-axis. That could imply that the top fake news comments were visible around the same time when users saw the post.

5.3.2 Reactions from Users who made Comments in the Post

In (Rassameeroj and Wu, 2019), the authors have presented a hypothesis saying that users who made a comment in a post may see other comments in the same post. Accordingly, we would like to see comment activities of users who had reactions to the fake news comments. Figure 5 presents percentage of reaction users who also made comments in the same post. Y-axis is represented the number of top fake news comments from 300 comments in the data set, and x-axis is represented ranges of percentage of reaction users who made comment(s) in the same post. Most reaction users usually made 1 - 1.63 comments per post in average.

5.3.3 Did Reaction users also React to other Comments?

From all reaction users of 300 fake news comments in the data set, Figure 6 presents the number of other comments that reaction users liked in each post. They mostly liked about 1 - 5 comments in a post. From Figure 6, we could imply that if the number of likes is small, we might assume that social algorithms deliver a few contents with the fake news comments at that time. In addition, since the number of likes is quite small, most reaction users should not be like clicker users.

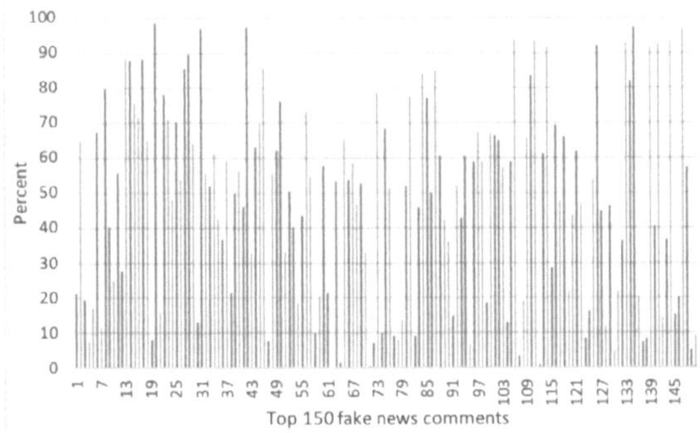

Figure 4. Percentage of users who participate in top 150 fake news comments and reacted to the post

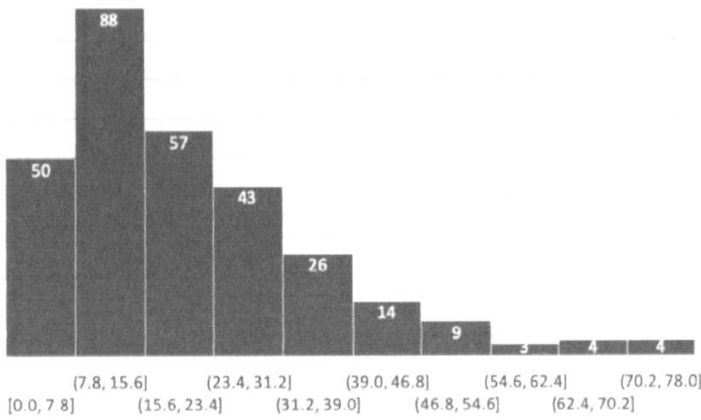

Figure 5. Percentage of fake news reaction users who made comments in the same post

6. CONCLUSION

We analyzed activities and behaviors of fake news propagators to understand how they make use of social algorithms to make their contents be more visible to users. We expected to see some participation patterns of authors to promote their contents. One apparent factor to make their contents to be seen by many users is to post early after the original posts. Besides, we also analyzed behavior of users who reacted to all fake news comments to understand how reactions of the fake news contents were from. We figured out that reactions of fake news comments were from users who reacted the posts and comments the posts.

Furthermore, we explored interaction and activities history of fake news propagators across different posts in the same page for one week and one month before. Unfortunately, we have not found any behavior that can be influence factors for them to promote the contents. Our main contribution for this work is to understand behaviors, activities, and strategies of fake news propagators who successfully disseminated their contents to many users through social algorithms on Facebook. We strongly believe our contribution could support other researches to understand fake news propagators in social media systems.

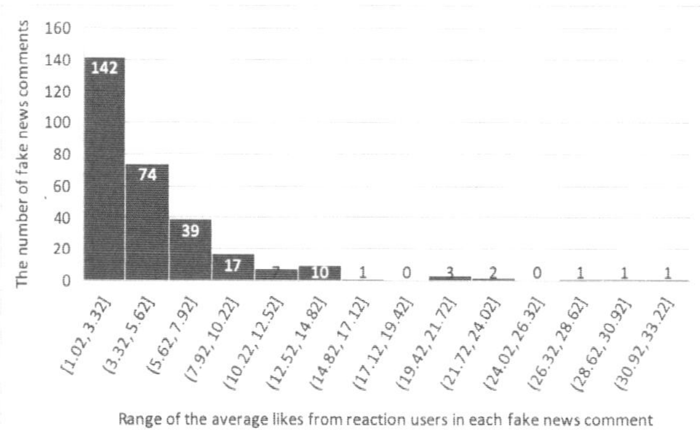

Figure 6. Percentage range of reaction users who reacted to other comments for each of 300 fake news comments

REFERENCES

Bakshy, E. et al, 2012. The role of social networks in information diffusion. *Proceedings of The 21st International Conference on World Wide Web*. New York, NY, USA, pp. 519 – 528.

Del Vicario, M. et al, 2016. The spreading of misinformation online. *Proceedings of the National Academy of Sciences*, 113(3), pp. 554 – 559.

Del Vicario, M. et al, 2019. Polarization and fake news: Early warning of potential misinformation targets. *ACM Transactions on the Web*, 13(2).

Erlandsson, F. et al, 2015. Crawling online social networks. *Proceedings of 2nd European Network Intelligence Conference*, pp. 9 – 16.

Flaxman, S., Goel, S., Rao, J.M., 2016. Filter bubbles, echo chambers, and online news consumption. *Public Opinion Quarterly*, 80(S1), pp. 298 – 320.

Gilbert, E., Karahalios, 2009. Predicting Tie Strength with Social Media. *Proceedings of the SIGCHI Conference on Human Factors in Computing Systems*, New York, NY, USA, pp. 211 – 220.

Granovetter, M.S., 1973. The Strength of Weak Ties. *American Journal of Sociology*, 78(6), pp. 1360 – 1380.

Hu, X. et al, 2013. Social Spammer Detection in Microblogging. *Proceedings of IJCAI International Joint Conference on Artificial Intelligence*, pp. 2633 – 2639.

Lazer, D., 2015. The Rise of The Social Algorithm. *Science*, 348(6239), pp. 1090 – 1091.

Pariser, E., 2011. The Filter Bubble: What the Internet Is Hiding from You. *Penguin Group*.

Rassameeroj, I., Wu, S.F., 2019. Reverse Engineering of Content Delivery Algorithms for Social Media Systems. *Proceedings of 2019 6th International Conference on Social Network Analysis, Management*, and Security, Granada, Spain, pp. 196 – 203.

Shao, C. et al, 2017. A Platform for Tracking Online Misinformation. *Association for Computing Machinery*, pp. 745-750.

Shao, C. et al, 2017. The Spread of Fake News by Social Bots, *Nature Communication*.

Vosoughi, S., Roy, D., Aral, S., 2018. The Spread of True and False News Online, *Science*, pp. 1146 – 1151.

Yang, X.S., 2017. Social Algorithms, Springer Berlin Heidelberg, pp. 1 – 15.

USING THE NETWORKED KNOWLEDGE ACTIVITIES FRAMEWORK TO EXAMINE LEARNING ON SOCIAL NETWORKING SITES

Vanessa P. Dennen, Kari Word, Dawn Adolfson, Victor Arechavaleta, Dan He,
Chia-Wei Hsu, Jaesung Hur, Daeun Jung, Heather Kent, Annemarie Russell and Korinna Toth
Florida State University, Tallahassee, FL, USA

ABSTRACT

This study uses the Networked Knowledge Activities (NKA) framework to examine social media archival data for evidence of learning-related actions across six major social networking sites (SNS). Findings show that while the NKAs are present on and fostered by the tools available on most SNS, most non-verbal indicators of NKAs provide insufficient reliable evidence of a networked knowledge activity. User intent, which is not detectable unless articulated in a message by a user, must be known to accurately use SNS archives to measure networked knowledge activities. We recommend combining this approach with user surveys or interviews within the studied knowledge network to improve accuracy and better understand social media knowledge activities.

KEYWORDS

Informal Learning, Knowledge Activities, Knowledge Networks, Learning, Sharing

1. INTRODUCTION

Learning is one of many functions that can be supported via interactions on social networking sites. Although popular social networking sites (SNS) like Facebook and Twitter were not originally designed as learning tools, they have quickly been drafted into service in a variety of learning contexts. For example, Facebook groups have been used as an alternative to learning management systems for university classes (Meishar-Tal, Kurtz et al. 2012, Wang, Woo et al. 2012) as well as to support informal learning (Adalberon and Säljö 2017) and provide a space where students might blend social interaction and schoolwork (Aaen and Dalsgaard 2016). YouTube is a frequent content provider for students when they study (Moghavvemi, Sulaiman et al. 2018), but also hosts communities such as beauty bloggers through which informal learning is supported (Choi and Behm-Morawitz 2017). Twitter can swiftly unite groups of people with shared interests through hashtags to engage in professional development discourse (Greenhalgh and Koehler 2017). Although SNS are frequently discussed as relationship (Chambers 2013) and political spaces (Bond and Messing 2015), their function as learning spaces that support knowledge networks is equally robust even if less frequently considered.

In this study, we examine how different SNS support knowledge networks through their various features and tools, and consider how readily one can find evidence of these networked knowledge activities through an analysis of archived user actions and interactions. This knowledge has implications for educators seeking ways of assessing social media learning processes as well as researchers seeking ways of making meaning from social media archival data.

2. NETWORKED KNOWLEDGE ACTIVITIES FRAMEWORK

The Networked Knowledge Activities (NKA) Framework (Dennen 2019) articulates and describes the six discrete knowledge activities that people use in networked online contexts (e.g., online classes, social media, virtual communities of practice). These activities were identified through an examination of the complex ways that people naturally interact with knowledge objects and members of their online networks in the service of learning.

The six networked knowledge activities are summarized in Table 1. Although each can be uniquely described, the NKAs tend to not occur in isolation. In other words, they are likely to co-occur in the midst of an individual's learning process, or to flow from one to another. For example, collecting can lead to curating, and curated collections may be shared with one's network. Or, in response to a query within one's network, a resource might be brokered between networks, resulting in a discussion where meaning is negotiated. Should multiple network members offer resources, a collection may be formed.

The NKAs support three main knowledge functions: management, communication, and creation (Dennen 2019). Collecting and curating are both forms of knowledge management, whereas sharing, brokering, and negotiating are acts of communication. Curating and constructing both are forms of creation. When looking at this broader level, there are parallels to the 4C framework (Milligan, Littlejohn et al. 2014), which focuses on consuming, creating, connecting, and contributing. However, the NKA do not account for idle consumption, instead focusing on more purposeful knowledge management activities which are an extension of consumption. Additionally, the NKA framework groups the share, broker and negotiate activities as communication functions, whereas the 4C framework splits these into two areas, connect and contribute. Essentially, the NKA framework pulls out negotiate (the discursive process of collaboratively exploring ideas and making meaning) as an activity that stands alone.

Table 1. Overview of networked knowledge activities

Activity	Description
Collect	To save a copy of or link to an item so it can be found or retrieved at a later time.
Curate	Creating organized, annotated collections of online artifacts. More purposeful and selective than collecting, and often follows the collection process.
Share	To take something has been collected, curated, or constructed and make it available online.
Broker	The act of connecting online and offline groups or networks via knowledge transmission. The broker acts as a purposeful intermediary agent between groups.
Negotiate	A collaborative, discursive process in which learners work together to agree upon meaning.
Construct	The act of making something new or combining existing things in a new manner. Often an outcome of knowledge negotiation. Results in a product that can be shared with others.

The NKA framework's initial purpose was to guide the design and development of social media-based learning activities in formal learning contexts. To that end, the different activities could be used in conjunction with Bloom's Taxonomy (Bloom 1956, Krathwohl and Anderson 2009) or Gagne's domains of learning (Gagne 1984) to help instructors design lessons supported by social networking sites and related online tools. By aligning activities with desired learning outcomes, learners can be guided toward purposeful online interactions.

While this framework is useful for supporting instructional design processes, its ability to guide assessment and measurement has previously been unexamined. Of particular interest is whether there are visible indicators of NKAs in social media archives, and what these indicators might be. The ability to easy identify NKAs in archival data could be helpful for instructors who are assessing student work, especially work processes. It would also be useful for researchers seeking evidence of knowledge and learning activities among different online networks and spaces.

3. METHODS

The research questions that guided this study are:

1. Which networked knowledge activities are readily visible through user actions on popular SNS?
2. What user actions on SNS indicate different networked knowledge activities?
3. How do the tool features and norms enable or prohibit the ability to perform and identify NKA?
4. How do NKA flow across or connect different SNS?

To investigate our research questions, we reviewed authentic user posts and interactions in spaces and contexts where people were known to be engaged in classroom, informal, and professional learning.

We focused on six SNS (Facebook, Instagram, Twitter, Pinterest, LinkedIn, YouTube). These were selected based on their broad popularity with teens (Anderson and Jiang 2018) and adults (Anderson and Perrin 2017, Perrin and Anderson 2019), and for their prior research connections to classroom learning (Salomon 2013, Lapolla 2014), informal learning (Greenhow and Lewin 2016, Bagdy, Dennen et al. 2018, Brown Jarreau, Dahmen et al. 2019), or professional development (Carpenter and Krutka 2015, Hu, Torphy et al. 2018, Bridgstock 2019) activities. Our primary data sources were groups and hashtags where informal learning and professional development activities occurred. We did not focus on formal learning contexts because an instructor-led context is a bit different, and instructors may provide specific guidance related to how they want students to share, tag, like, and comment. Most data sources involved English language messages, but our multi-linguistic research team also incorporated data sources posted in Chinese and Korean.

Sub-groups of 2-3 researchers on the larger research team chose individual SNS to focus on. In these sub-groups, the researchers looked across interactions in different group and network contexts to find evidence of different NKAs. Contextual cues in comments were relied on to confirm non-verbal NKA evidence, noting that in many instances of the same NKA the corresponding comments may be absent. When evidence was found, they considered whether the same evidence would be present in each instance of the NKA, or if it was user dependent. For example, one indicator of brokering might be to state in a message something similar to "This item came from this other group to which I belong, and I am sharing it here because it relates to the question you are asking." However, a person could broker knowledge in this way without formally acknowledging the act, making it difficult to distinguish sharing from its more purposeful counterpart, brokering. When clear or unambiguous evidence of a particular NKA was not found, the researchers considered whether the NKA was likely supported by that SNS, and the various means through which the NKA might occur. Throughout this investigation, the manner in which specific tool features facilitated NKAs was documented, and group members tested features to see how well they would support different NKAs. Once each sub-group completed their individual investigation of NKAs on a specific SNS, they shared their findings with the larger research group. Through whole group discussion, these findings were refined, and comparisons made across the SNS.

4. RESULTS

4.1 Facebook

Collection is difficult to see on Facebook, although users may save or bookmark individual posts. Some users may use the emoji function to like a post, or post a comment (e.g., "F" or "follow") to ensure they can find and later review or collect the responses to that post. However, these are not reliable indicators; there are many reasons why a person may like a post or want to follow a post. Similarly, curation is difficult to see unless a user deliberately curates and shares resources within a post or across multiple posts. Alternately, a photo album may be evidence of curated visual materials on Facebook.

Sharing and brokering are facilitated via the sharing tools and the ability to tag other individuals and call their attention to a particular item. Both may also be invisible acts, with post shared from public pages to private messages or within closed or secret groups. Share counts show how many times the share function has been used, but tracking the locations of shares is difficult given varying privacy settings.

Facebook has a high degree of posting and commenting, with knowledge negotiation frequently visible in the comment-based dialogues. Again, privacy settings and shifting dialogues to messenger can obscure access to knowledge negotiation. Additionally, high rates of posting and commenting are not necessarily indicators of knowledge negotiation. It is necessary to examine the content of comments in order to make that determination.

Finally, knowledge construction may occur directly on Facebook through posts of varying types. Co-constructed knowledge often occurs in Facebook groups as an outgrowth of sharing and negotiation, or a focused curation effort. Additionally, media constructed in other tools are frequently shared on Facebook. Facebook is designed to support the flow of information in from other platforms. While this is useful for sharing purposes, the way that shared items on pages, timelines, and groups function make it poorly suited for collecting and then curating knowledge objects from other platforms.

4.2 Twitter

Much like on Facebook, it is difficult to see collection on Twitter, although users can save and return to tweets through three Twitter-based functions, favorites, bookmarks, and retweets. Each of these actions ties the original tweet back to the collector's Twitter account. However, it is difficult to say with certainty when favorites and retweets are used in this manner versus for another purpose. Twitter makes analytic data about tweets available, but like and retweet counts, while indicators of message visibility and amplification, do not reliably demonstrate collection. Bookmarks are only visible to the individual who did the bookmarking. Similarly, curation has limited visibility on Twitter. The moments feature, which was infrequently seen, can help connect a set of tweets in a curation-like manner. What remains unknown is how many people click through content on Twitter and then proceed to collect or curate the shared content on another platform.

Sharing is at the heart of Twitter use in a networked knowledge context. Sharing does not mean hosting knowledge on Twitter, but rather pointing to knowledge objects that are hosted elsewhere. Sharing may co-occur with negotiation when a person shares a knowledge item and others proceed to comment on and discuss it. occurs on Twitter in the form of an initial tweet with the intended purpose of sharing knowledge. Twitter shares that originate on another site (e.g., sharing from a news source) tend to carry over not only a link to shared content but an @mention that tags the original source on Twitter. People who share items can also add their own @mentions to draw a specific person's attention to a tweet, which would them be demonstrative of knowledge brokering. Although sharing is a high frequency activity on Twitter, deciphering the intent of a share is complex without clear verbal indicators. Additionally sharing, brokering, and negotiation may occur that is not visible when private messaging is used or tweets are linked or embedded and potentially discussed on other platforms.

When knowledge negotiation occurs on Twitter, it takes the form of a conversation among individuals responding to each other. The @reply function helps continuously tag people into the conversation and organize it in threads. Of course, not every reply is an act of negotiation. Some are purely social, entertaining, or may be offered as acknowledgements or answers to brief questions. It is necessary to view the content of a twitter thread to know whether knowledge negotiation actually took place.

Hashtags also can be used to support multiple knowledge activities on Twitter. Hashtags serve as aggregators, and can help unite a larger network in discussion, as in the case of Twitter chats; share a resource with likeminded others; or mark and collect tweets in a personally meaningful way. However, hashtags have also been used as performative expressions of attitude (e.g., #dontcare), and may not be meant to aggregate tweets topically or by network, or to support knowledge activities.

Finally, although some people regularly use Twitter as a means of sharing the pictures, videos, blogs, and other content they have created outside of Twitter, it is not a platform where that construction is likely to occur. This is probably due to Twitter's character and content hosting limitations. That said, there have been instances where Twitter has been used as a form of writing, and a novel artefact has been constructed primarily on Twitter. While intriguing, this is not how most people use Twitter in their knowledge networks.

4.3 Instagram

Instagram is a heavily visual platform, with supporting tools that facilitate liking, commenting, sharing, and tagging. On Instagram, similar to the other platforms, the bookmark and like functions potentially support collection activities. Through bookmarking, images posted by others can be stored in personal "collection" that is not shared with others. The like button, triggered by clicking on a heart, has been a controversial features and the platform is experimenting with its removal of public likes (Al-Heeti 2019), which will likely have minimal effect on networked knowledge activities. Liking is not a useful means of marking Instagram posts for collection because the interface makes it difficult to compile liked items.

An Instagram user can also curate information from their own collections. After bookmarking posts, a user can make new folders into which the posts can be saved and organized. Individual posts can be hidden from a user's feed as well, to ensure that the feed itself has a curated look and feel. Feed curation is an important activity for many Instagram users. Instagram also has a story feature that supports temporary sharing of images. After a day, story posts are no longer visible unless they have been otherwise saved.

As seen on other SNS, Instagram supports hashtags which can be used to aggregate posts on a topic. This feature may be used to support curation activities when users consistently tag images they wish to search and access together or share to others as an intentionally grouped collection. It also can support a collaborative form of collection. For example, co-learners or events may use a hashtag to pool together their images. Hashtags also may be used to direct a specific post toward an affinity group, whether that group contains people who are within the individual's network or are simply people who are likely to search that hashtag.

Users share information on Instagram through both posts and comments. Instagram posts may videos, photos, or other images. Text may be incorporated directly onto a shared photo or image, or added as a caption to an image. or image with text information. Images can be constructed (i.e., captured and edited) directly on the SNS, or items constructed using other tools can be uploaded. Many third-party tools have been developed to facilitate the construction of attractive graphics, including text, that meet the image dimensions on Instagram.

Unlike other platforms, Instagram does not have a dedicated function for sharing another user's posts, although these posts can be added to one's Instagram story. Third-party apps like can be used to integrate this functionality, called regramming, as desired. Additionally, although Instagram has a commenting feature, comments are not commonly used to support the level of discourse necessary to see knowledge negotiation. Perhaps this is because Instagram is typically associated with visuals, which are the centerpiece of every post, and the app space that is devoted to comments is small.

On the surface, Instagram may appear to have similarities to Facebook and Twitter, and when a user creates Instagram posts they can readily share those posts to their accounts on the other platforms. However, Instagram appears to foster NKAs in a much more limited manner than Facebook and Twitter. The sharing and negotiation tools are far less robust. Individuals may be searching Instagram for visual content to be used for knowledge purposes, but SNS like Pinterest, better serve the interests of people looking to collect, curate, and share visual knowledge.

4.4 LinkedIn

LinkedIn is a social networking site primarily used by professionals and organizations. In addition to hosting online profiles of one's work experiences, LinkedIn allows users to post content in the form of text, images, and videos. Each post allows users to react (e.g., like) or share. Not all NKAs may be visible on LinkedIn, but they are all likely to occur on LinkedIn.

Collection, which may lead to curation, occurs on LinkedIn through the "save links for later" option. Items saved for later are privately saved, which means that collection is not visible to third parties. One clue to items of interest are the reactions feature that offers five visual comments that can be quickly applied to posts. LinkedIn provides a resource to indicate their intended meaning although that does not guarantee their use in this manner. The two that seem most closely related to networked knowledge activities, the insightful and curious reactions, were rarely applied to posts. In contrast, like, love, and celebrate were heavily used.

Through posts, LinkedIn users can share their own written content and other knowledge objects (e.g., images, videos, slides, PDFs). Much of the knowledge objects that are shared are constructed outside of LinkedIn, which only supports the construction of articles within the platform. It is likely due to LinkedIn's focus on professional interactions that posts explicitly share knowledge in an informal or professional development context. Points of sharing occasionally turn into negotiation via conversation within comments. It should be noted that LinkedIn also contains many posts of a professional-social or broadcast announcement nature, such as statements about recent accomplishments, job transitions, or events and opportunities.

4.5 Pinterest

Pinterest supports users as they search, collect, and organize interesting knowledge objects on the internet. These objects can be images, websites, videos, documents, and more, and are represented on Pinterest with images that link through to more extensive content. User can take the knowledge objects that they have found and pin them to boards organized around specific topics. Boards can be constructed individually or collaboratively. then post, or pin, these items to a board that's organized around a specific topic. Similarly, boards can be searched and followed. Users can add other people to their networks to receive alerts about new pins that have been added.

The Pinterest platform is clearly focused on four of the NKAs: collect, curate, share, and construct. The collecting is done by saving pins onto boards. Boards can be general, open collections, or they may contain intentionally curated ones, with pinned items annotated by the person who pinned them. Pin collections may be kept private, or they can be shared with others. Pins frequently are shared to other sites, such as Facebook and Twitter. Additionally, many bloggers will curate and share pins on their blogs or websites. Pinterest also has a feature that allows users to email or text pins or boards to other users.

Finally, users can construct their own pins to share on Pinterest. Pins are created by using a Pinterest share link on another website or by posting the site URL on Pinterest to create a new pin. Pinterest will ask the user to select a display image for the pin and then the user can also annotate the pin and post it to one of their boards. If the pin was created publicly, then other users can re-pin that object to their own boards.

Some activities are not visible on Pinterest but could be happening, such as brokering. Pinterest's sharing tools do not provide clear indicators of sharing pathways and purposefulness. However, much of the outward flow of sharing, which may occur at the pin or board level, may be related to brokering activities. Negotiating is also unlikely to occur on Pinterest. Pinterest supports commenting, but this feature is infrequently used and likely reflects the network-dependent but still fairly solitary nature of collecting and curating items.

4.6 YouTube

YouTube hosts a vast expanse of videos, and the relative amount of NKA occurring on the platform is low. People can collect videos on YouTube by subscribing to them, saving playlists, liking videos, or downloading them. These acts allow an individual user to easily find their favorite videos. Curation occurs as users generate playlists, often facilitated by the YouTube recommender algorithm. Sharing and brokering videos are both facilitated through various means. A creator can upload and share to YouTube, and a consumer can use the built-in sharing tools to alert others to specific videos. Sharing can occur in video description fields, and in the comments, although in practice there relatively little discussion occurs in comments unless a channel community has been developed (e.g., popular youtubers). Finally, construction is possible through embedded video creation tools.

Playlists are a feature unique to YouTube, and merit discussion on their own. The playlist feature enables users to collect videos and revisit them. Within a playlist, a user can give a name to it, add any description, and reorder the videos to be played. A playlist can be set to be public, private, or unlisted (i.e., only people who know the direct link can view). Users can save videos to their YouTube library.

The playlist feature may lead to a curation if users intentionally make new playlists and organize videos for certain topics or purposes. For example, someone who is trying to study statistics can collect statistics lecture videos and make a new playlist, ordering the videos from basics to advanced. This playlist can be made public and shared so it benefits others. Furthermore, the playlist feature can be used for knowledge construction. For example, a history teacher who wants to teach students about a particular era can assemble video sources that share news, movies, songs, and other key details about the era, creating a comprehensive learning resource.

On YouTube the flow of video media onto the platform occurs via a user upload. Several video recording and editing tools have embedded sharing tools that connect direction to YouTube, facilitating the process of sharing one's personal creations. In a SNS NKA context, YouTube most often serves as a hosting platform for videos that are embedded into web pages and other platforms. In other words, there is a high degree of content flowing out of YouTube to support NKA.

Despite these findings that YouTube can support the NKA, many users continue to use YouTube in a passive sense, making their intent and potential use of NKA largely invisible. Video play counts greatly outnumber comments, saves, and appearances on playlists. Likes and dislikes are not clearly related to any knowledge activities. The play counts and likes/dislikes make clear that many users are present, but they do not appear to be heavily interacting with each other or building networks.

5. DISCUSSION AND CONCLUSION

The NKA framework was useful to identify different types of knowledge activities that occur on SNS and separate them out from other SNS functions like social conversation, identity performance, and message broadcasting. At the same time, the NKA framework alone applied to a social media archive, while useful for identifying general user knowledge actions, may not be sufficient to fully identify and count all of these actions accurately. It is easiest to identify the presence of NKAs when people state their purpose (e.g., 'Thank you! I am saving this to review later.' or 'Another group I belong to created this resource and I think you might find it useful.'). However, it can be difficult to interpret user intent when tools such as like buttons, share buttons, and tags are used. For example, collect and curate use the same tools (bookmarks, downloads, likes), but with different ends; individuals who curate are more purposeful in their selection and organization processes.

Across all six SNS, collecting and curating tended to be individual activities, often done without leaving a meaningful indicator in archival data sets. Collaborative efforts to collect or curate were evident when networks shared group spaces or hashtags for the purpose of building knowledge bases. The norms that a network upholds for saving and organizing items determines whether the product would be considered a simple collection or a curated collection.

Sharing and brokering involve multiple participants, and can be directed at specific people or groups via tags and comments, but unless a visible acknowledgement of receipt is provided (e.g., a like, download, or comment) it is difficult to know if they have had any more effect on networked knowledge than shouting into an empty room. In contrast, negotiation inherently involves two or more active participants. With that noted, we did see instances in which people shared items while writing commentary that appeared to be an act of knowledge negotiation with the original author of the shared item. Although the author was unlikely to be tagged, and many of these shared items we saw were formally published articles and news stories, there is potential for tagging in the author of a knowledge object to try to engage them in further discourse.

Several SNS tools enable users to collect and share. Likes, favorites, and other forms of paralinguistic digital affordances (PDA) are perhaps the most interesting to explore, because the simple action of clicking a button can have multiple meanings (Hayes, Carr et al. 2016), especially in a knowledge activity context. It is less likely in this context that individuals use PDAs to provide social support as they do in other contexts (Wohn, Carr et al. 2016), although supporting network relationships and social capital may still be a concern (Fish 2018). Distinguishing among users who click on these indicators to say "I saw this," "I like this," and "I want to save this so I can find it later," can be difficult if there are not corresponding linguistic cues in a comment that explain the user's intent. On SNS like Twitter, likes can be easily revisited and reviewed. Although there is also a bookmark feature, it can be simpler to click a like to mark a tweet while scrolling past. Alternately, these indicators can be used as a shortcut way of saying "I saw this item." From there it is difficult to interpret whether the indicator is a marker of acknowledgement, agreement, or something else altogether. On SNS platforms with multiple PDA indicators (e.g., Facebook), interpreting a PDA click remains complicated. For example, we saw verbal comments where people clarified they had chosen the angry emoticon response not because they were angry at the person who posted, but rather at the message in the item being shared. Similarly, the wow emoticon response is vague with regards to whether it offers a positive or negative sentiment.

In terms of flow, the tools all freely facilitate sharing of knowledge objects. Platforms that heavily focused on verbal message exchange and sharing (e.g., Facebook, Twitter) more robustly support flow in. Tools where creation occurs or creations are hosted (e.g., YouTube), more robustly support flow out.

Through our analysis, we have seen how challenging it is to definitively identify different NKA through analysis of social media archives. The challenge is not in finding indicators, but in knowing that those indicators are always present to mark a networked knowledge activity and reliably indicate that activity. Although this may seem to be a disheartening finding, it is not surprising and does not render NKA useless as an analytic framework. However, it once again affirms what has been learned via many studies in the field of learning analytics: Evidence of user actions in a data archive cannot be accurately interpreted for user intent.

This work is not yet complete. Next steps include surveys, which will be used to confirm findings from this initial analysis and ascertain frequency of the NKAs from the user perspective. Through this continued work, we can better learn how to identify learning indicators on social networking sites and offer both meaningful ways of assessing whether knowledge activities have occurred from data archives.

REFERENCES

Aaen, J. and C. Dalsgaard (2016). "Student Facebook groups as a third space: Between social life and schoolwork." Learning, Media and Technology 41(1): 160-186.

Adalberon, E. and R. Säljö (2017). "Informal use of social media in higher education: A case study of Facebook groups." Nordic Journal of Digital Literacy 12(04): 114-128.

Al-Heeti, A. (2019) "For Facebook and Instagram, axing likes may not be about mental health after all." cnet news.

Anderson, M. and J. Jiang (2018). Teens, social media & technology 2018. Washington, D.C., Pew Research.

Anderson, M. and A. Perrin (2017). Tech adoption climbs among older adults. Washington, D.C., Pew Research Center.

Bagdy, L. M., V. P. Dennen, S. A. Rutledge, J. T. Rowlett and S. Burnick (2018). Teens and social media: A case study of high school students' informal learning practices and trajectories. Proceedings of the 9th International Conference on Social Media and Society. New York, NY, ACM: 241-245.

Bloom, B. S. (1956). Taxonomy of educational objectives. Vol. 1: Cognitive domain. New York, NY, McKay.

Bond, R. and S. Messing (2015). "Quantifying social media's political space: Estimating ideology from publicly revealed preferences on Facebook." American Political Science Review 109(1): 62-78.

Bridgstock, R. (2019). Employability and career development learning through social media: Exploring the potential of LinkedIn. Challenging future practice possibilities, Brill Sense: 143-152.

Brown Jarreau, P., N. S. Dahmen and E. Jones (2019). "Instagram and the science museum: A missed opportunity for public engagement." Journal of Science Communication 18(2): A06.

Carpenter, J. P. and D. G. Krutka (2015). "Engagement through microblogging: Educator professional development via Twitter." Professional Development in Education 41(4): 707-728.

Chambers, D. (2013). Social media and personal relationships: Online intimacies and networked friendship. London, Palgrave Macmillan.

Choi, G. Y. and E. Behm-Morawitz (2017). "Giving a new makeover to STEAM: Establishing YouTube beauty gurus as digital literacy educators through messages and effects on viewers." Computers in Human Behavior 73: 80-91.

Dennen, V. P. (2019). Activity interactions in online courses. Handbook of Distance Education. M. G. Moore and W. Diehl. New York, NY, Routledge.

Fish, L. (2018). Exploring the motivations underlying the use of paralinguistic digital affordances on Facebook, University of Tasmania.

Gagne, R. M. (1984). "Learning outcomes and their effects: Useful categories of human performance." American Psychologist 39(4): 377-385.

Greenhalgh, S. P. and M. J. Koehler (2017). "28 Days Later: Twitter Hashtags as "Just in Time" Teacher Professional Development." TechTrends 61(3): 273-281.

Greenhow, C. and C. Lewin (2016). "Social media and education: Reconceptualizing the boundaries of formal and informal learning." Learning, Media and Technology 41(1): 6-30.

Hayes, R. A., C. T. Carr and D. Y. Wohn (2016). "One click, many meanings: Interpreting paralinguistic digital affordances in social media." Journal of Broadcasting & Electronic Media 60(1): 171-187.

Hu, S., K. T. Torphy, A. Opperman, K. Jansen and Y.-J. Lo (2018). "What do teachers share within socialized knowledge communities: A case of Pinterest." Journal of Professional Capital Community.

Krathwohl, D. R. and L. W. Anderson (2009). A taxonomy for learning, teaching, and assessing: A revision of Bloom's taxonomy of educational objectives. New York, NY, Longman.

Lapolla, K. (2014). "The Pinterest project: Using social media in an undergraduate second year fashion design course at a United States University." Art, Design & Communication in Higher Education 13(2): 175-187.

Meishar-Tal, H., G. Kurtz and E. Pieterse (2012). "Facebook groups as LMS: A case study." The International Review of Research in Open & Distributed Learning 13(4): 33-48.

Milligan, C., A. Littlejohn and A. Margaryan (2014). "Workplace learning in informal networks." Journal of Interactive Media in Education 1(6).

Moghavvemi, S., A. Sulaiman, N. I. Jaafar and N. Kasem (2018). "Social media as a complementary learning tool for teaching and learning: The case of YouTube." The International Journal of Management Education 16(1): 37-42.

Perrin, A. and M. Anderson (2019). Share of U.S. adults using social media, including Facebook, is mostly unchanged since 2018. Washington, D.C., Pew Research Center.

Salomon, D. (2013). "Moving on from Facebook: Using Instagram to connect with undergraduates and engage in teaching and learning." College & Research Libraries News 74(8): 408-412.

Wang, Q., H. L. Woo, C. L. Quek, Y. Yang and M. Liu (2012). "Using the Facebook group as a learning management system: An exploratory study." British Journal of Educational Technology 43(3): 428-438.

Wohn, D. Y., C. T. Carr and R. A. Hayes (2016). "How Affective Is a "Like"?: The Effect of Paralinguistic Digital Affordances on Perceived Social Support." Cyberpsychology, Behavior, and Social Networking 19(9): 562-566.

INFLUENCING FOLLOWERSHIP: UNDERSTANDING THE PERSPECTIVE OF THOSE LEADING ACTIVE DISCUSSIONS ON QUORA

Martin C. Nwadiugwu
University of Nebraska at Omaha, 2626 PKI, University of Nebraska Omaha, Omaha, NE 68182, USA

ABSTRACT

As social media influence becomes popular, having an understanding of why some posts are more highly followed than others as viewed from the perspective of those leading the post allows us to gain insight on how followership is being influenced. A qualitative study of eight participants leading active discussions on Quora was conducted using semi-structured in-depth interviews, followed by thematic analysis. The open coding method was used to iteratively code related answers to develop themes. Results suggest that copyright tactics, controversial answers and sharing new information are some of the mechanisms for influencing followership. These mechanisms are built overtime through strong engagement and self-awareness by writing a consistently well-thought-out answer. The motivation for leading and writing answers on Quora were more intrinsic than extrinsic. Most participants believed influencing followership should not be a concern if one has the right message.

KEYWORDS

Followership, Influence, Leadership, Online Communities

1. INTRODUCTION

Quora is a social media online platform that brings together people with diverse perspective to understand each other in a culture of knowledge sharing (Quora 2020). It is a popular question and answer site that differs from others because it integrates social network into its basic structure (Maity et al. 2017; Wang et al. 2013) and a platform where users write and answer questions; the best answers are seemingly identified by upvotes and downvotes (Patil and Lee 2016). It has been previously reported that Quora and draws about 200 million visitors monthly and over 13 million questions have been asked as at 2017 (D'Angelo 2017; Quora 2017). Interestingly, while there are many questions and answers on the platform, it is not widely known why some answers are more influential than others (Paul et al. 2012). It is pertinent to understand the experiences and perspectives of those writing answers and leading discussions on Quora to gain understanding into how followership is being influenced.

Assessment of Quora shows it follows the principles for online community design as suggested by Kim (2003). The platform has a defined purpose that understands the intended users and services to be delivered in the "Why Quora Exist" section of the home page that also highlights the mission statement of the community which simply is: "to share and grow the world's knowledge" (Quora 2020). An overview of the site content is shown in a simple and usable way for visitors allowing them to navigate the design of member profiles that evolve over time, and to be made aware of their rights and responsibilities in the community that is seen in the "conduct policy" link at the bottom of the home page. While there is a clear code of conduct, controversy, debate and allowing members to be different in a way that is not disruptive can be seen in the online community and this creates the fun (Kim 2003). Ranking of members and level of completed membership profile is also visible to the user so that more accurate information can be updated. As a Q&A online platform, discussion areas exist engaging the community with effective leadership (Kim 2003). New members are allowed to lead discussions and answer questions which is in line with the principles of creating a balance that accommodates new members without alienating those that are active (Kim 2003). The focus of this study is on effective leadership within discussion areas on Quora. It aims to gain insight into understanding why some answers are highly followed; specifically, to understand if those leading active discussions are self-aware and if they play a role in influencing followership, comments and upvotes. The social mechanisms and decision-making processes that help them judge if an answer would be trending is a focus of the study. For example, 1) What do social media influencers hope to gain from writing answers or leading a discussion? 2) What influences active discussion on Quora? In other words, which scenarios will encourage a post to trend and 3) how does the topic affect user experience and followership on Quora?

A closer observation of the platform showed that each user has a profile history that keeps track of all answers and questions an individual had posted, the number of shares and followers they have. The Technology space within Quora (observed from February 6 to March 15 2020) was selected for the study and the activities of people who had posted answers that consistently received considerable activity with about 50 or more comments, upvotes and shares were observed. While some users on the platform could be identified with pseudonyms, only those who used supposedly real identities were further observed and selected as potential participants because real identities build perception of trust for high quality answers (Paul et. al 2012; Kollock 1998). Although popularity based on real identities may be biased due to the fact that users may in general have an attachment and preferential treatment to some notoriety which can influence the voting and promotion of answers that may not be novel (Barabási & Albert 1999); the social voting is still considered as a way of identifying quality answers (Paul et. al 2012) and was used in this study as the criteria for selecting participants leading active discussions on Quora.

The remaining sections of the study will highlight the purpose and the methodology used. Next, a weaving of the in-depth interview from the participants will be synthesized to answer the study question of how followership is being influenced. Answers to questions about the participant's understanding of leadership, motives for leading online discussions, self-awareness of user behavior, cherry-picking discussion topics, mechanisms for influencing followership and how unrelated questions affect user experience will be sought. The study will conclude with a summary of the narration and how users of online communities may benefit from future design improvements.

1.1 Purpose of the Study

Although every member in an online community can exhibit leadership behavior, some are more effective in influencing others (Zhu et al. 2012). According to Weeks et al. (2017) opinion leaders and highly active users in online communities can be influential in persuading their peers and believe they are both indirectly and directly able to persuade others. In a study on the effectiveness of shared leadership in online communities, Zhu et al. (2012) found that person-focused leaders are more effective in influencing others to contribute, while legitimate leaders are the more influential. However, leadership can only exist when there is a followership, and the advent of the internet has given rise to global followership allowing leaders and followers to be united in a partnering process (Tolstikov-Mast and Yulia. 2016). It is therefore important to know the mechanisms that influences followership and why some answers and discussion posts in online communities have more participation than others especially given the theory that leadership is founded on the desire for control over others (Ford and Harding 2018).

2. METHODOLOGY

The study was conducted using a semi-structured, in-depth interview. Eight participants were selected for the study comprising of six males and two females as seen in Table 1. All participants were above 18 years of age. A pilot test ensured adequate refinement of the interview questions according to the interview guide (Creswell 2007). The interviews were conducted via Zoom and were audio-recorded except for one that was text-based. The interviews lasted from 15 to 30 minutes.

Table 1. Characteristics of Selected Participant

Participants	Gender	Country	Followers	Answers	Content views	Job Highlight
P01	Male	USA	245	129	932,400	College Student
P02	Male	USA	510	120	807300	Online Writer
P02	Male	Nigeria	504	3923	7,600,000	Blogger
P04	Female	USA	4310	2787	5,600,000	Patreon Analyst
P05	Male	USA	1075	4436	13,300,000	Business Adviser/Writer
P06	Male	France	74532	387	29,600,000	Stand-up Comedian
P07	Male	USA	6558	566	7,100,000	College Student
P08	Female	USA	3828	319	2,900,000	Borderline Advocate

The terms of confidentiality were addressed and the participants gave recorded consent to use the transcript of the interview in the study. Participant names were de-identified as seen in Table 1. This is in line with suggestions that pseudonyms, and disguising person names are recommended for protecting confidentiality of research subjects (Bruckman 2006). The participants were sent the initial transcript at the end of the interview to allow them make clarifications on possible errors in the transcription process. The following open-ended questions were asked:

1. Tell me about your understanding of being a leader on Quora?
2. What do you hope to gain from leading a discussion on Quora?
3. Tell me about any concern you have in leading an online discussion?
4. What scenarios will make a post trending on Quora?
5. Do people look up to suggestions on Quora in making their decisions?
6. How do unrelated questions affect user experience/behavior?
7. Anything else you would like to share?

The data was analyzed using was a thematic methodology that incorporated an inductive approach to generate explanations from the data (IER 2014). The rationale for using this method was because the aim of the interview follows a strategy that seeks an explanation of a substantive theory (IER 2014) and the thematic analysis provides a well-structured approach in explaining the data (Nowell et al. 2017).

2.1 Participants Interview

Table 2 shows the thematic analytic approach used to code the interview transcripts and to iteratively develop themes related to the interview questions as suggested by Strauss and Corbin (1990) and Vollstedt and Rezat (2019)

Table 2. Coding Interview Data

Interview Extract	Codes
"I would categorize being a leader as one who has lots of followership" - P01 "I have been influenced by post made on Quora." - P03 "I write and interact a lot but don't think of myself as a special leader" - P04 "Some people are more successful than others, it depends on topics they write" - P05 "you can accrue a following based on merit" - P06 "a person with a lot of followers on Quora" – P07 "I am diagnosed with Borderline Personality Disorder, I created my own page. When Quora introduced spaces, I was invited to be an admin for three pages" – P08	Followership as a criteria for influential leadership
"People on Quora take a little bit more time to write answers unlike in Reddit" – P01 "I never seek it out. " – P02 "I try to have well founded argument and express my bias" – P04 "After you've established yourself.. you can broadcast your own message " –P05 "do something commercial do…sell your product"-P06 "start first by giving answers that people enjoy and getting their attention."-P07	Followership is built not made
"a post I made surprisingly ended out getting sent to about two million people" – P01 "I sometimes post funny answers to create humor for those reading my post" – P03 "I would not write answers that are inimical to societal values or on things" –P05 "I use copywriting tactics to make my answers…there are topics I wouldn't lead" – P06 "First, you have to capture the audience's attention,.. with a controversial post" P07 "I started writing to see if my understanding of my disorder was accurate."- P08	Leaders cherry-pick topics
"One answer could be seen by a million people and another seen by five."-P01 "You have to respect your readers and not to give them an error-filled answers" – P02" "Quora audience is more reflective of people on the internet and like Tiktok" - P06 "After you capture their attention, you keep it by writing interesting answers"- P07	Self-awareness of user behavior
"to just share what I knew for whoever would listen".-P01 "I do not want to gain anything. I enjoy answering questions" – P02 "no monetary motives.. to seek approval with up-votes and top-writer ranks"-P03 "I have a patreon (crowdfund) – I actually get paid by people to write on Quora"-P04 "for knowledge and sharing your experience" – P05 "I hope to connect with other people on Quora"-P06 "I try to influence public perception about overlooked topics I care about" –P07 "is to remove the stigma that is attached to my disorder."-P08	Motivation for leading

2.1.1 Followership is the Criteria for Determining Influential Leadership

Studies have posited that the experience of leadership roles varies in relation to how followers differ in acting out their roles (Carsten et al. 2017). Followership role orientation co-produces leadership outcome of influence, motivation, and perceived follower support (Carsten et al. 2017). In other words, influential leadership is hinged on the perception of follower's support which motivates the leader. The ability to influence participation on Quora was highlighted by 7 participants as a feature of leadership. One participant said: "I would agree and categorize being a leader as one who has lots of followership. I also think being a leader is being one with integrity and that's what is kind of falls down to"–P01. Apart from having a lot of followership, the ability to have strong engagement in a culture of sharing was considered a criterion for leading and six participants alluded to this. For example, a participant mentioned: "In Quora there are a lot of people who would post [comment on a post] but won't write a post. The silent majority are probably people who read and don't interact at all"- P04. There was an agreement that most users on Quora were passive rather than active which necessitate that discussion leaders would strategize for a stronger participation. Moreover, user participation is vital to sustain the platform as a "third place" for Q&A where regular discussion leaders makes it lively without which it would be an empty space (Oldenberg 1999).

The focus topic was suggested as the reason for the differences and success of influential people leading discussion post on Quora. According to the fifth participant: "Everybody is different on Quora with different perspectives. Some people are more successful than others and it depends on the topics they write about. Some topics I have written about got only about 500 views. After you've established yourself in some select topics that is more followed, you can broadcast your own message very effectively" The focus topic is usually what the participant cares about. Two participants agreed that taking up discussion leader roles on topics have attracted some attention; one of them stated: "I am diagnosed with Borderline Personality Disorder. I started writing to see if my own understanding of my disorder was accurate. I have no ability to perceive myself. It's part of the disorder. I have no identity. We can, without treatment, become emotional remoras. What I discovered was this…to show what I write makes sense to many people. And my voice has a way of healing or helping others on their journey. I created my own page, Invisible Lines, mostly to blog my day to day frustrations. My own page did not take off, but when Quora introduced spaces, I was invited to be an admin for three pages."- P08. The number of followers an individual has is able to determine their influence on Quora, and because the Ask-to-Answer design of the platform allows users to tag other Quora members, highly active users are promoted as they would be tagged in most questions increasing their influence (Paul et al. 2012). Five participants alluded to this and one particularly stated: "I try to influence public perception about topics I care about that are being overlooked and people don't have much information about it. I try to give my answers, make them popular so some people will learn about it for the first time and others who know about it will have complete information."-P07.

2.1.2 Followership is Built not Made

The process of influencing followership and participation on Quora requires expertise and experience that builds up overtime. The fifth participant explicitly revealed that this building process is shrouded in mystery: "Sometimes you write answers that don't get any readership. I have noticed that if you focus on what you really know and what you can help people with, eventually your articles would start getting attention. This is very hard in the beginning. When I started on Quora and wrote an answer, I would be lucky if 100 or 200 people read it. Everybody that seems to be doing well on Quora in terms of readership, tend to write in the same subject and have a good broad knowledge and a certain message in the way they write." One way Quora can support newcomers sharing great ideas and leading discussions to increase their audience base could be by making their feeds visible in order to encourage other members pay more attention to them (Burke et al. 2009).

Leadership is built on the theory of followership, and leaders have been reported to compare followers to their ideal expectation of followership, and judge them against this model sometimes without considering the actual behavior of the follower (Ford and Harding 2018). Determining what scenarios would make a post trending on Quora, five participants agreed that this process takes time; P07 stated: "First, you have to capture the audience's attention, let's say If you have an intriguing picture or a controversial post or something like the corona virus. After you capture their attention, you have to keep it by writing answers that are interesting and easy to understand. Popularity of answers on Quora boils down to talking about things that are interesting where you have a unique perspective that keeps the audience's attention." While this may be true, some people are necessarily convinced that you don't need to worry about followership if you have the right motivation as the fourth participant posited: "I don't worry about trending, but on writing good stuff and that is the reward. My post on coronavirus is just an example. Sharing answers on topics that have not been shared is a motivation. On Quora, I can trust the audience to choose what they want and don't want to absorb. I am very widely read and that is what makes my post trending."

2.1.3 Leaders of Online Discussion Cherry-Pick Topics

People in active leadership roles could improve the relationship with followers by advancing connections that elevates, stimulates, and transform both followers and leaders into confident leaders and moral agents respectively (Burns 1978). This perhaps could be the rationale why active leaders of a discussion post in online communities cherry-pick their topics to influence conversation. Answering the question on what will make a post trending on Quora the sixth participant stated: "I use copywriting tactics to make my answers. I post about sex usually on first headline, because people are naturally gravitating towards that. Things like sex, racism, and something controversial generally elicits more comments. Although I would not like to do those things, sometimes when I have written answers of great value, they got almost no traction. Sometimes you have to do something commercials do such as the use of sex, cars to sell your product and then once they are inside you give better forms of advice." Another participant [P03] was also in agreement saying: "You want to make sure your answers are flawless and free of errors when you lead a discussion post... when people see that your answers are impeccable, they would know you are competent and want to follow you." On the other hand, there were other contrasting views; participant one and two mentioned not seeking to influence followership, the first participant who was particularly surprised at the traction gotten by a recent post said: "I have been surprised a couple of times. There was a post I made that was a little bit technical and I did not imagine it would elicit much interest. It ended out getting sent to about two million people because they have an email where they broadcast messages to people, and it was a little bit surprising, I really don't know what causes them to be successful". An overview of the answers given showed that six participants alluded to the fact that what made an answer on Quora trending involved a strategic process and that if one is an expert in a range of topic and had a wealth of experience on advising, they would not be concerned with scenarios that makes a post trending. This agrees with the study by Meindl (1995) who stated that charisma is influenced by discussions among followers and it arises from the minds of followers who concludes that a leader is charismatic.

2.1.4 Leaders of Online Discussion are Self-Aware of User Behavior

Emerging studies in leadership have been focused on followership that assumes that there is a common purpose for both leaders and followers and a mutually beneficial relationship (Shamir et al. 2007; Challef 1998; Ciulla 1998). Those who lead discussions and write answers on Quora are self-aware of their audience. A participant [P03] on being asked for additional comment on experience writing answers on Quora mentioned: "Being a writer means that you are sometimes "naked" [revealing secrets] just in a bid to convince people that you are sure of what you are talking about. Many secrets about countries, government and people are being exposed in a bid to get up-votes." Apart from knowing their audience, they are also aware of the designs of online communities and how they affect user behavior. A participant [P05] said: "In standard media you could get one answer, one article, one perspective unlike in Quora where you could get fifty articles if it's a popular question. Also, there are people on Quora who have not written anything but come there to get knowledge." Participant six also shared similar opinion: "I think one of the good things about Quora is that you could get answers to a question you really didn't know you needed an answer to. I think that the randomness of that makes the user experience more exciting because for example, a big problem with Instagram which is a completely controlled platform [i.e. you are not seeing anything except things you want to see] therefore you are getting a very myopic sense of the world and there is a level of non-randomness which gets boring and stale. The Quora stream is more similar to Tiktok where you get what you want. Those algorithms tend to heighten user experience".

Accordingly, there are similarities in the opinion of the participants that influential leaders of online discussion write answers using tactics that increases participation because they are aware of their audience, their content and the design of the online community. This self-awareness makes them reconsider feedback from their readers to keep the followership they have been able to acquire overtime. The eight-participant said: "For a while I used to write some trashy answers. I used to write answers with underlined italics to capture attention, but people were of the opinion that "this isn't cool" and that it looks like am hunting for attention and not providing as much value as I could, which made me rethink how am writing. Yes, I will change it if people point how badly am writing."

2.1.5 The Motivation for Leading is Mixed

According to Mamykina (2011) intrinsic rewards such as the desire for learning, altruism or extrinsic benefits such as social or material rewards have been highlighted as the motivations for participating in online question and answer sites. Some sites such as YouTube have a reward mechanism for active users with rich content, while other have point based reward system (Mamykina 2011). However, Quora is devoid of point-based reward system (Paul et al. 2012). Therefore, to understand the intrinsic or extrinsic motivations for leading discussions, participants were asked what they hoped to gain from leading a discussion on Quora. Seven out of eight participants mentioned intrinsic rewards such as altruistic actions (helping people with advice, direction, spreading knowledge), social interaction and building social capital as the main motivations. Providing further information on the motivations for writing answers on Quora [P03] stated: "*Some people have come to Nigeria to meet me and learn more about the country and what I have written. Some of my followers who are in a dating relationship with a Nigerian call me to know about the country and verify the authenticity of the locations and its safety. Quora is a place where people build relationship and trust one another based on the answers and suggestions they are reading. It is one of the most visited sites in the world and I think people take post there seriously.*"

In addition, others have seized the networking opportunity provided by the online platform to create awareness to remove stigma attached to a disorder. P08 said: "*My primary goal for writing on Quora is to remove the stigma that is attached to my disorder. Borderlines have a particularly brutal stigma attached to their disease. A whole lot of support are subjective and very few facts. Clinicians hate to treat us. We burn through people and their emotions like a woodchopper and it takes years of multidisciplined help to get anywhere near better. I have done a lot of work but still more to do. I also managed to create a community of both Borderlines, and former partners, who are willing to put aside their anger to get to a place of acceptance, radical acceptance. It feels very validating, that I have accomplished through real hard work, the ability to bridge the communication gap that is so frustrating about BPD*." Furthermore, social appraisal is the popular reward mechanism that exists on Quora, and while some participants have leveraged on their popularity on Quora for extrinsic benefit from external sources, others have called on the designers of Quora to recognize and reward creative contributions. P06 said: "*I think that Quora should add 'tip features' where people can give creators money. There is an immense amount of value being created on the internet, and the people that are creating it for the first time in human history are not getting access to profit from it. Am not saying that platforms should pay people, but, if someone writes an answer that changes your life [like benefits from YouTube] we can create a line between consumer of their content and the creators bank account. I think with this, we would get a better content; and this is the reason why YouTube has better videos than a lot of NetFlix documentaries.*"

The motivation to offer these services is aided by the design of Quora platform. It was suggested that the design algorithms on Quora frequently engineers related notifications to a user as unrelated feeds would discourage participation. On how an unrelated post would affect the user experience the seventh participant stated: "*I think Quora does a good job with its algorithms about giving you things you would be interested in. At some point I once interacted with a topic (conjoined twins) that I cared very little about but I enjoyed it and kept on getting questions and answers [scientific] about it and there's no way for me to indicate that am uninterested in it. And this causes more unrelated things to pop up in my feed and notification which drives me away from Quora.*"

3. DISCUSSION/CONCLUSION

An in-depth study to understand the perspectives of those writing answers and leading discussions on Quora was conducted to comprehend mechanisms that influences comments, posts or suggestions and how discussion topics affect user experience and followership on Quora. It was found that the motivation to lead discussions were mostly intrinsic (altruism, knowledge sharing) than extrinsic (material reward) suggesting that providing balanced argument and reducing bias is highly valuable. The mechanisms that influences followership and participation in a discussion requires expertise and experience and this happens over time. It includes the ability to engage strongly and to improve relationship with followers by advancing connections that excites both parties (Burn 1978). This greater knowledge of deliberative etiquette is needed to resist targeted incivility (Gervais 2015). A well-thought-out answer were largely considered as a means of reaching a targeted audience and increasing participation, while biased and error-prone messages could lead to distrust. It can be suggested from the study that those who lead discussions and write answers on Quora are self-aware of their audience; and perhaps use tactics that increases participation. Copyright tactics, controversial answers and sharing new information were some of the highlighted mechanisms for influencing followership.

Exploring the concept of building leadership on the theory of followership, most participants were of the opinion that followership should not be a concern if one has the right message. However, it has been reported that leaders have an ideal expectation of followership that differs from reality (Ford and Harding 2018). The study by Paul et al. (2012) to understand reputation mechanisms on Quora found that influential users get more votes than are deserving for their answers. This is further supported by Lerman and Galstyan (2008) who studying social voting on Digg noticed that some users on the site had their topics promoted in the front page of the platform because of their notoriety in large social networking sites. Although it has been reported that Quora uses an algorithm called PeopleRank to rank answers based on some select criteria, it has also been suggested that this could potentially lead to undue influence because it highly ranks the answers of popular users even when their answers are not catchy (Paul et al. 2012). This study suggests that active users influences follower perception, and the platform design of Quora promotes this influence by allowing users tag other members to a particular answer.

In summary, findings from the study provides important insight on the mechanisms influencing followership. This information would be paramount in understanding the design implications for knowledge-building in online communities. Further studies may be carried out to investigate preferential attachments that influences social voting from the perspective of the follower. Also, understanding the way information is produced and circulated on Quora in relation to the PeopleRank algorithm is another interesting area for future studies.

4. COMPLIANCE WITH ETHICAL STATEMENTS

(a) Ethical Approval: This article was approved by the IRB
(b) Funding: The author declares no research funding for this study.
(c) Conflict of Interest: The author declares no conflict of interest
(d) Availability of Data and Material: Tables and data used are duly provided.
(e) Authors' Contribution: M.N. developed the study question, designed the research and typed the manuscript.

ACKNOWLEDGEMENT

I would like to acknowledge Briana Morrison (PhD), Assistant Professor, University of Nebraska at Omaha for reviewing the manuscript.

REFERENCES

Barabási, A.-L.; R. Albert. Emergence of scaling in random networks" Science 286, 5439 (1999), 509–512.

Burke, M., Lento, T. and Marlow, C. (2009) Feed Me: Motivating Newcomer Contribution in Social Network Sites. http://www.thoughtcrumbs.com/publications/paper0778-burke.pdf [Accessed: January 16 2020]

Burns J. 1978. Leadership. New York, NY: Harper and Row.

Bruckman, A. (2006) Teaching students to study online communities ethically. *Journal of Information Ethics*, 3(11), p.82-95.

Carsten, M. K., Uhl-Bien, M. and Huang, L. (2018) 'Leader perceptions and motivation as outcomes of followership role orientation and behavior'. Leadership, 14(6), pp. 731–756. doi: 10.1177/1742715017720306.

Challeff, I (1998) The Courageous Follower: Standing Up To and For Our Leaders, San Francisco: Berrett-Koehler Pub.

Ciulla, J (1998) Ethics: The Heart of Leadership, London: Praeger.

Creswell, J.W. (2007) Qualitative Inquiry and Research Design: Choosing Among Five Approaches: International Student Edition. Thousand Oaks, California: Sage Publications.

D'Angelo, A. (2017) How many people use Quora. Available: https://www.quora.com/How-many-people-use-Quora-3

Ford, J., Harding, N. (2018) Followers in leadership theory: Fiction, fantasy and illusion. Leadership, 14(1), 3–24. Doi: https://doi.org/10.1177/1742715015621372

Gervais, B. (2015) Incivility Online: Affective Behavioral Reaction to Uncivil Political Posts in a Web-based Experiment. *Journal of Information Technology and Politics.* 12(2), pp. 167-185.

Kollock, P. (1998) Design Principles for Online Communities. *Harvard Conference on the Internet and Society*, 15(5), 58-60.

Kim, A. (2003) Nine Principles of Community Design. Available: https://people.apache.org/~jim/NewArchitect/webtech/1998/01/kim/index.html [Accessed: January 21, 2020]

Lerman, K. and Galstyan, A. (2008) Analysis of social voting patterns on Digg. *Proc. WOSN*, ACM Press, 7-12.

Maity, S.K., Kharb, A., Mukherjee, A. (2017). Language Use Matters: Analysis of the Linguistic Structure of Question Texts Can Characterize Answerability in Quora. Proceedings of the Eleventh International AAAI Conference on Web and Social Media. Available: https://www.aaai.org/ocs/index.php/ICWSM/ICWSM17/paper/view/15647/14866

Mamykina, L., Manoim, B., Mittal, M., Hripcsak, G., Hartmann, B. Design lessons from the fastest Q&A site in the West. *Proc. CHI 2011*, ACM Press, 2857-2866.

Meindl, JR (1995) The romance of leadership as a follower-centric theory: A social constructionist approach. The Leadership Quarterly 6: 329–341.

Nowell, L. S., Norris, J. M., White, D. E., and Moules, N. J. (2017) Thematic Analysis: Striving to Meet the Trustworthiness Criteria. *International Journal of Qualitative Methods*. https://doi.org/10.1177/1609406917733847

Oldenberg, R. (1999). The Great Good Place. Available: https://www.mnsSu.edu/voices/greatgoodplace.pdf

Patil, S., Lee, K. (2016) Detecting experts on Quora: by their activity, quality of answers, linguistic characteristics and temporal behaviors. Soc. Netw. Anal. Min. 6, 5. https://doi.org/10.1007/s13278-015-0313-x

Paul, S.A., Hong, L., Chi. E.H. (2012). Who is authoritative? Understanding reputation mechanisms in quora. Available: https://www.researchgate.net/publication/224053714

Peh, J. (2017) How many questions have been asked on Quora. Available: https://www.quora.com/How-many-questions-have-been-asked-on-Quora-1/answers/19190364

Quora (2020) Why Quora Exist. Available https://www.quora.com/about

Shamir, B, Pillai, R, Bligh, M (2007) Follower-Centered Perspectives on Leadership: A Tribute to the Memory of James R. Meindl, Greenwich, CT: Information Age Publishing.

Strauss, A., and Corbin, J. (1990) Basics of Qualitative Research: Grounded Theory Procedures and Techniques. Sage Publications, Newbury Park, CA, USA.

Tolstikov-Mast, Yulia. (2016) Global Followership: The Launch of the Scholarly Journey. Advances in Global Leadership, pp. 107-150. Doi: 10.1108/S1535-120320160000009013.

Vollstedt, M., Rezat, S. (2019) An Introduction to Grounded Theory with a Special Focus on Axial Coding and the Coding Paradigm. Compendium for Early Career Researchers in Mathematics Education,13, pp. 81- 100. Doi: https://doi.org/10.1007/978-3-030-15636-7_4

Wang, G., Gill, K., Mohanlal, M., Zheng, H., and Zhao, B.Y. (2013). Wisdom in the Social Crowd: an Analysis of Quora. IW3C2. ACM 978-1-4503-2035-1/13/05.

Warwick Institute for Employment Research (IER) (2014) Analyzing Interview Data. University of Warwick. Available: https://warwick.ac.uk/fac/cross_fac/esrcdtc/researchandtraining/ct201314/quals/analysing_interview_data_2014_wk3_for_web.pdf [Accessed: March 23 2020].

Weeks, B.E., Ardèvol-Abreu, A., de Zúñiga, G.H. (2017) Online Influence? Social Media Use, Opinion Leadership, and Persuasion. *International Journal of Public Opinion Research*, 29(2), pp. 214–239.https://doi.org/10.1093/ijpor/edv050

Zhu, Haiyi & Kraut, Robert & Kittur, Aniket. (2012) Effectiveness of Shared Leadership in Online Communities. Proceedings of the ACM Conference on Computer Supported Cooperative Work, CSCW. 407-416. 10.1145/2145204.2145269.

EMOTION ANALYSIS USING SELF-TRAINING ON MALAYSIAN CODE-MIXED TWITTER DATA

Kathleen Swee Neo Tan, Tong Ming Lim and Yee Mei Lim
Department of Computer Science and Embedded Systems, Faculty of Computing and Information Technology, Tunku Abdul Rahman University College, Kuala Lumpur, Malaysia

ABSTRACT

Microblogs such as Twitter has made available a vast resource of User Generated Content (UGC) on which emotion analysis may be performed. Organizations increasingly value the opinions obtained from emotion analysis. These insights help to drive decision-making activities and provide constructive inputs to engage their customers and services. In a multiracial country such as Malaysia, it is common to find that tweets are written in mixed languages of Malay, Malaysian slang and English. These tweets increase the complexity of the emotion analysis task, especially considering that there is a serious lack of labeled data available in order to make use of supervised learning techniques. This paper explores the use of self-training, a semi-supervised technique that only requires a small initial labeled dataset to conduct emotion analysis of Malaysian code-mixed Twitter data. The results are promising as the accuracy achieved is higher compared to the baseline models.

KEYWORDS

Emotion Analysis, Code-Mixed, Twitter, Self-Training, Sentiment Analysis

1. INTRODUCTION

There has been an increasing use of microblogs. People express their sentiments towards a certain object, be it a product, an organization, a person, an event or a policy on microblogs. Various organizations have adopted microblogs as a means of branding, marketing and maintaining customer relations. Among the microblog platforms, Facebook and Twitter are the most popular microblog sites in Malaysia (Statcounter, 2020) and have emerged as platforms that enable not only rapid dissemination of information but also has the ability to influence other people's sentiments on a topic that was written about.

Another development that has been observed recently is the growing interest in the area of sentiment and emotion analysis on microblog text. The aim of sentiment analysis is to identify positive and negative polarity expressed in the text. Emotion analysis, on the other hand, identifies the specific emotion (such as joy, sadness or anger) that is being expressed in the text. Organizations such as commercial companies, governments, political parties and non-governmental organizations (NGOs) realize that there is a vast amount of data available from which they can obtain useful insights regarding the sentiments and emotions of their customers, citizens and people in general. This allows organizations to arrive at better decisions and timely actions.

Malaysians are generally able to speak in at least two different languages due to the multi-racial composition of its society. This unique characteristic has made it very natural for Malaysians to speak and write using mixed languages. For example, it is quite common to tweet using a mix of Malay and English, a phenomenon known as *code-mixing*. An example of a code-mixed tweet is "*Stress tu adalah apabila barang dah sold out and kau kene marah dengan customers???? Hmmmmmm murung hari aku*", which means "*Stress is when your products are sold out and you're scolded by your customers???? Hmmmmmm my day is sad*". These code-mixed tweets impose a number of challenges when trying to perform emotion analysis. Firstly, the language used is a mix of formal as well as informal single-word terms and Multi-Word Expressions (MWE). Secondly, non-standard sentence structures are used due to the fact that the constituent languages of the code-mixed text have different vocabulary and grammatical characteristics (Lo et al., 2016). Thirdly, there are limited available labeled code-mixed datasets to serve as training datasets (Aghababaei and

Makrehchi, 2017). Fourthly, there is a lack of sentiment and emotion resources for languages other than English and even more so for code-mixed languages (Dashtipour et al., 2016).

In view of the above-mentioned problems, semi-supervised learning has become a viable technique to be utilized (Hemmatian and Sohrabi, 2019). Although its performance is usually not as good as supervised learning techniques, it has the important benefit that it does not require a large labeled dataset for training (Da Silva et al., 2016). This paper explores the use of self-training, a semi-supervised technique that only requires a small initial labeled dataset, to conduct emotion analysis of Malaysian code-mixed Twitter data. Specifically, experiments to evaluate the accuracy of self-training with different confidence thresholds and n-gram features are carried out on Malaysia Twitter data. In the experiments conducted, emotion analysis is treated as a multi-label classification problem with six categories which correspond to the basic emotions *happy*, *sadness*, *love*, *fear*, *anger* and *surprise*.

2. RELATED WORK

He and Zhou (2011) proposed a self-training approach that used labeled features to classify positive and negative sentiments. The labeled features contained words with prior sentiment orientation obtained from the MPQA subjectivity lexicon (Wilson et al., 2005) . The lexicon was used to build an initial classifier using generalized expectation (GE) criteria (Mann and McCallum, 2010), to perform predictions on an unlabeled dataset. The samples labeled with high confidence were then collected to form a labeled dataset. Their framework was evaluated on the movie review dataset (Pang and Lee, 2005), which comprised 1000 positive and 1000 negative movie reviews, and a multi-domain sentiment dataset (Blitzer et al., 2007). Their results showed a better accuracy (75.10%) compared to the baseline model. However, this approach does not address multi-label classification and is difficult to implement for languages which do not have available sentiment lexicons.

Haimovitch et al. (2012) used AROW (Crammer et al., 2013), an online algorithm based on confidence weighted learning, to build a sentiment analysis model. Their model was evaluated on datasets comprising Amazon product reviews from 8 domains that were labeled as positive or negative based on the number of stars accompanying their review. From each dataset, 1000 examples were randomly selected to form the initial dataset. They reported that for all domains, the test error was 40% lower compared to the test error of the baseline. They also found that since AROW is an online algorithm, the order and rate of using the data affects the performance of the final classifier. As the metrics used in their paper was test error, it is not possible to compare against the performance in other work which typically uses either accuracy or F1-score.

Han et al. (2019) proposed a self-training model that comprised two stages. First, the model utilized dynamic thresholds for the confidence scores, with higher threshold values for the initial iterations and lower threshold values for the later iterations to cater for the declining confidence scores of the predicted labels in later iterations. Next, multiple Support Vector Machine (SVM) classifiers based on the bagging algorithm were used in order to avoid overfitting and reduce the impact of misclassification errors. A weighted voting strategy was then applied to combine the results from the multiple classifiers and determine the final prediction. They evaluated their model using different initial labeled training dataset sizes ranging from 500 to 1000 and reported that their proposed model achieved F1-scores ranging between 79.96% and 82.69%, outperforming the baseline methods. The higher F1-scores were achieved when the larger initial labeled datasets were used.

The self-training model built by Iosifidis and Ntoutsi (2019) used Multinomial Naïve Bayes (MNB) as the base learner with unigrams as features to classify tweets as positive, negative or neutral. They experimented with different confidence thresholds in the range 65-100% with 5 iterations and reported that the accuracy obtained for the iterations was lower than that of the initial model, which is an expected outcome as the training set is progressively expanded through predictions. The final accuracy achieved in their experiments ranged between approximately 89.5% and 93.5%. They concluded that tweets are far different from comments or reviews as the character limitations may cause the structure of a tweet to vary significantly compared to other texts. In addition, the different spanning periods may result in changes in the words and their relevance to different classes.

Most of the previous work used self-training to classify text into positive and negative sentiments (Da Silva et al., 2016) and there is very limited work that utilized the self-training approach for multi-label emotion classification on code-mixed text.

3. EXPERIMENTAL DESIGN

In this paper, emotion analysis was treated as a multi-label classification problem with six categories which correspond to the basic emotions: *happy*, *sadness*, *love*, *fear*, *anger* and *surprise*.

Self-training is a wrapper-based semi-supervised approach (Da Silva et al., 2016) whereby a supervised learning classifier is used as a base learner which is "wrapped" within an algorithm which iteratively (1) trains a classifier using a small labeled dataset, (2) carries out prediction on a much larger unlabeled dataset, and (3) transfers the predicted examples with high confidence scores from the unlabeled dataset to the labeled dataset. The confidence score for a given example is considered high if its value exceeds a set threshold value. These three steps are repeated either for a pre-determined number of iterations or until the unlabeled dataset is exhausted.

In this study, SVM was used as the base learner. The feature set used was Term Frequency-Inverse Document Frequency (TF-IDF) and n-grams. TF-IDF is a statistical score that indicates the importance of a term in a dataset. It is obtained by multiplying the normalized frequency of the term in the tweet with the log-scaled inverse frequency of the term in the entire dataset. For the initial labeled dataset, it was ensured that there was a balanced representation of each emotion. Experiments were conducted to investigate the effect of using different confidence thresholds and the various n-gram features.

The dataset used for the experiments was the publicly available Malaya emotion dataset (Husein, 2018) which is a collection of Twitter data organized into six files according to the emotions *happy*, *sadness*, *love*, *fear*, *anger* and *surprise*. The tweets in this dataset are mostly in Malay and Malaysian slang, as well as code-mixed Malay-English text. A few examples of the tweets in the dataset with their labels are provided in Table 1. Details of the dataset's composition according to the different emotion classes are shown in Table 2.

Table 1. Samples of tweets in the Malaya emotion dataset

Sample tweet	Emotion label
Awek cantik, high maintenance. Takut kita	fear
Why is it internet like siput babi when I want to do something important	anger
ohh itu your mommy, not mine dah kenapa dia voice note? rindu barang kali	love
at least aku siap 2 assigment dah lega weh	happy
Same here Allahu sedih but life goes on	sadness
Sy tlmpau sakit hati tengok muka dia nai... hahaha like im speechless tkjut sis	surprise

Table 2. Malaya emotion dataset composition by emotion

Emotion label	Number of tweets
fear	18,895
anger	51,745
love	59,242
happy	48,924
sadness	79,233
surprise	37,778
Total tweets	295,817

In order to evaluate the overall performance of self-training on the code-mixed Twitter data, accuracy was use as the evaluation metric. Additionally, F1-score was used to compare the performance of self-training in terms of the individual emotion labels. The baseline model used in this study was the traditional SVM trained on the initial labeled dataset of 600 examples alone as the training set.

4. EXPERIMENTS

4.1 Data Preprocessing

Basic text preprocessing was carried out and this included the removal of tokens such as stopwords, mentions (@), URLs, emails and telephone numbers, as these tokens do not reflect any emotion. The stopword list was built by merging the English stopwords obtained from nltk with the Malay stopword list published by The Proteus Project (2004). In addition, the words were converted to lowercase.

As can be observed in Table 2, the subset of tweets categorized with the emotion *fear* had the lowest number (18,895) of tweets. To avoid bias due to imbalanced representation of classes in the training dataset, a balanced dataset was created by first randomly extracting 18,895 tweets from each emotion subset of tweets. From each subset, 30% was set aside to make up the test set for validation. Table 3 shows the distribution of tweets for the six emotion classes in the training and test datasets that were used in the experiments.

Table 3. Number of tweets in the training and test datasets

Emotion	Training	Test
anger	13, 226	5, 669
fear	13, 226	5, 669
happy	13, 226	5, 669
love	13, 226	5, 669
sadness	13, 226	5, 669
surprise	13, 226	5, 669
Total Tweets	**79, 356**	**34, 014**

4.2 Experimental Settings

The experiments were conducted on the code-mixed dataset using SVM as the base learner, as described in Section 3. The initial labeled dataset was created by randomly extracting 100 tweets from each emotion class of the training set, thus yielding a total of 600 tweets which were than shuffled to ensure a randomized distribution of emotion labels within the initial labeled dataset. To create the unlabeled dataset, the emotion labels of the remaining 78,756 tweets in the training set were removed and then shuffling was performed.

A total of 10 iterations were carried out. At the end of each iteration, the data with predicted labels that had confidence scores that met the threshold were removed from the unlabeled dataset and added to the labeled dataset to create a new training set for the next iteration. In the experiments, the following aspects of self-training were explored.

- *Self-training with different confidence thresholds.* To study the effect of using different confidence thresholds, different threshold values ranging from 0.65 to 1.00 with increments of 0.05 (i.e., 0.65, 0.70, 0.75, etc.) were used. The initial labeled dataset comprised of 600 tweets. The features comprised of unigrams with TF-IDF set to a max_df of 0.7, which meant that 70% of the most frequently used terms were excluded as these terms appeared with high frequency among the tweets in the training set and were therefore not able to provide much discriminative value of the different emotions.
- *Self-training with different n-gram feature sets.* Experiments using three different features sets – unigrams, bigrams and trigrams – with TF-IDF were carried out. The initial labeled dataset consisted of 600 tweets and the confidence threshold was set at 0.80.

5. RESULTS

The performances of the models were evaluated using the balanced hold-out set comprising a total of 34,014 tweets as shown in Table 3. The results of the self-training approach with different confidence thresholds are shown in Table 4 and Figure 1. The accuracy of the self-trained classifier reached a plateau after the second or third iterations. This was consistent with the growth in the labeled dataset size depicted in Figure 2 which increased greatly in the second or third iterations before reaching a plateau as well. The accuracy achieved when using lower confidence thresholds were much lower compared to higher thresholds as adding labeled data with lower prediction confidence scores to the training set for the subsequent iterations would result in lower accuracy (Iosifidis and Ntoutsi, 2019). However, the final accuracies obtained by self-training with the various thresholds were still higher than the baseline SVM model which achieved an accuracy of 84%.

The ability to enlarge the labeled training set by adding data with high confidence predicted labels throughout the iterations is important as a means to supplement the limited labeled data, considering that it is very expensive to produce manually labeled datasets. Moreover, to ensure good accuracy when predicting the emotion labels of new (previously unseen) tweets, there is a need for classifiers to be trained using a substantially large dataset (Mishne, 2005).

Table 4. Accuracy per iteration for self-training with various thresholds

	Iterations									
Threshold	**1**	**2**	**3**	**4**	**5**	**6**	**7**	**8**	**9**	**10**
0.65	0.84	0.87	0.87	0.87	0.87	0.87	0.87	0.87	0.87	0.87
0.70	0.84	0.87	0.88	0.88	0.88	0.88	0.88	0.88	0.88	0.88
0.75	0.84	0.87	0.88	0.88	0.88	0.88	0.88	0.88	0.88	0.88
0.80	0.84	0.87	0.88	0.88	0.89	0.89	0.89	0.89	0.89	0.89
0.85	0.84	0.87	0.87	0.88	0.88	0.88	0.88	0.88	0.88	0.88
0.90	0.84	0.87	0.88	0.88	0.89	0.89	0.89	0.89	0.89	0.89
0.95	0.84	0.86	0.87	0.87	0.88	0.88	0.88	0.88	0.88	0.89

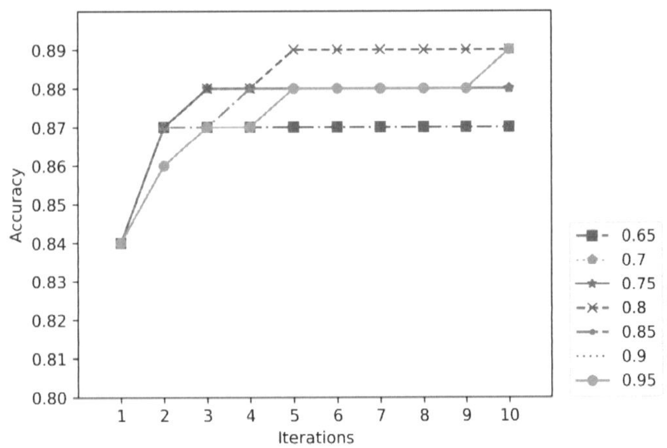

Figure 1. Accuracy of self-training with unigram features and different confidence thresholds

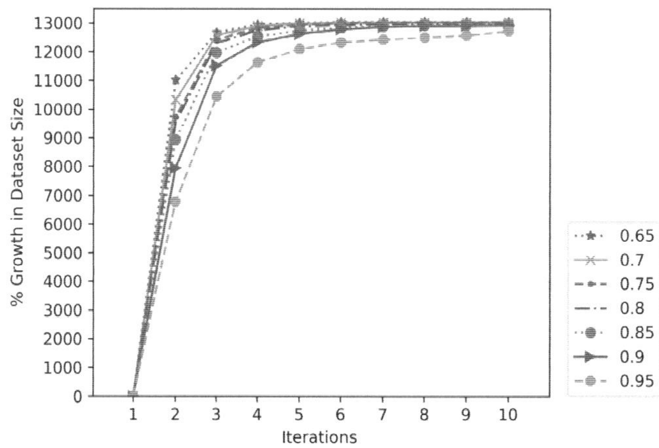

Figure 2. Labeled dataset growth of self-training with unigram features and different confidence thresholds

Self-training with n-gram features also outperformed the baseline SVM models, as shown in Figure 3. Among the n-gram features, unigrams provided the best performance compared to bigrams and trigrams. As the predicted labels are able to achieve confidence scores exceeding the threshold of 0.8, the accuracy obtained are higher compared to that of the baseline model. This is promising as it shows the potential of using self-training in situations where there is limited labeled code-mixed microblog datasets available for training. It was observed that the accuracy achieved by using unigram features achieved a higher accuracy compared to bigram and trigram. This is most likely due to the fact that for $n > 1$, the constituent individual terms in the n-gram would appear as separate parallel features together with the n-gram itself in the feature vector resulting in some duplication of features (Tang et al., 2015). For example, if the trigram "*best day ever*" appeared in a tweet, the list of features for the tweet would include the terms "*best day ever*", "*best day*", "*day ever*", "*best*", "*day*" and "*ever*". To address this problem, the n-grams have to be filtered such that only multiword expressions (MWE) would be retained and their constituent terms are removed from the feature vector of the tweet concerned. However, this would require the availability of an appropriate code-mixed MWE lexicon.

All three n-gram features used were able to expand the labeled dataset and had the largest growth rate during the second and third iterations as shown in Figure 4.

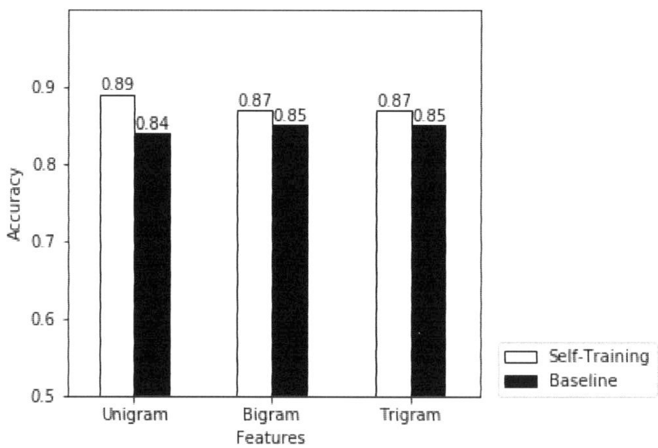

Figure 3. Accuracy of self-training with various n-gram features

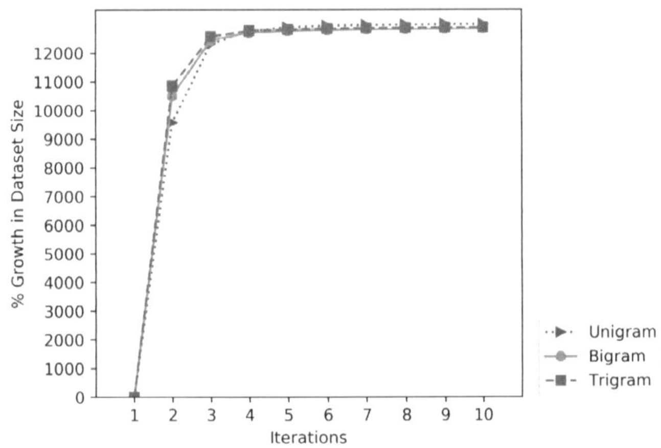

Figure 4. Labeled set growth per iteration for self-training with various n-gram features

The comparison of individual F1-scores for each emotion in Table 5 showed that the self-training classifiers were able to achieve a better performance compared to the baseline models. The emotion labels that achieved the best results with F1-scores above 0.90 were *anger*, *fear* and *happy*. This is probably attributed to the consistent way in which people expressed these emotions in the tweets that they write. On the other hand, the emotion that obtained the lowest F1-score was *sadness*. This could be due to either the implicit expression of this emotion and the use of sarcasm or irony which is difficult to detect in tweets.

Table 5. F1-score by emotion label for various n-gram features

n-gram	unigram		bigram		trigram	
Emotion	baseline	self-training	baseline	self-training	baseline	self-training
anger	0.90	**0.94**	**0.91**	**0.91**	0.91	**0.92**
fear	0.95	**0.98**	0.94	**0.97**	0.94	**0.95**
happy	0.92	**0.93**	0.92	**0.93**	0.92	**0.93**
love	0.84	**0.91**	0.84	**0.86**	0.84	**0.85**
sadness	0.70	**0.75**	0.71	**0.75**	0.71	**0.75**
surprise	0.75	**0.80**	0.76	**0.80**	0.76	**0.81**
average	0.84	**0.89**	0.85	**0.87**	0.85	**0.87**

6. CONCLUSION

Code-mixed microblog text presents challenges to emotion analysis due to its use of informal language and mixture of languages, as well as its lack of proper structure. In this paper, self-training with SVM was used to carry out emotion analysis of Malaysian code-mixed Twitter data. The experiments carried out evaluated the use of different confidence thresholds as well as various n-gram features. The results are promising as a relatively high accuracy was achieved even with a small initial labeled dataset, which is ideal for situations where labeled datasets for emotion analysis is very limited.

For future work, the use of other classifiers as the base learners should be investigated. There is also a need to explore the effect of using other type of features including syntactic language features such as part-of-speech (POS), emoticons, and emotion-bearing terms. In addition, the importance of ensuring that the resulting enlarged labeled dataset generated at the end of each iteration has a balanced representation of each emotion should also be studied.

REFERENCES

Aghababaei, S. and Makrehchi, M., 2017. Interpolative self-training approach for sentiment analysis. *IEEE/ACM BESC 2016 - Proceedings of 2016 International Conference on Behavioral, Economic, Socio - Cultural Computing*, pp.1–6.

Blitzer, J., Dredze, M. and Pereira, F., 2007. Biographies, bollywood, boom-boxes and blenders: Domain adaptation for sentiment classification. *ACL 2007 - Proceedings of the 45th Annual Meeting of the Association for Computational Linguistics*, pp.440–447.

Crammer, K., Kulesza, A. and Dredze, M., 2013. Adaptive regularization of weight vectors. *Machine Learning*, 91(2), pp.155–187.

Dashtipour, K. et al., 2016. Multilingual Sentiment Analysis: State of the Art and Independent Comparison of Techniques. *Cognitive Computation*, 8(4), pp.757–771.

Haimovitch, Y., Crammer, K. and Mannor, S., 2012. More is better: Large scale partially-supervised sentiment classification. *Journal of Machine Learning Research*, 25, pp.175–190.

Han, Y., Liu, Y. and Jin, Z., 2019. Sentiment analysis via semi-supervised learning: a model based on dynamic threshold and multi-classifiers. *Neural Computing and Applications*, 32(9), pp.5117–5129. Available at: https://doi.org/10.1007/s00521-018-3958-3.

He, Y. and Zhou, D., 2011. Self-training from labeled features for sentiment analysis. *Information Processing and Management*, 47(4), pp.606–616. Available at: http://dx.doi.org/10.1016/j.ipm.2010.11.003.

Hemmatian, F. and Sohrabi, M.K., 2019. A survey on classification techniques for opinion mining and sentiment analysis. *Artificial Intelligence Review*, 52(3), pp.1495–1545. Available at: https://doi.org/10.1007/s10462-017-9599-6.

Husein, Z., 2018. Malay-Dataset. Available at: https://github.com/huseinzol05/Malay-Dataset.

Iosifidis, V. and Ntoutsi, E., 2019. Sentiment analysis on big sparse data streams with limited labels. *Knowledge and Information Systems*. Available at: https://doi.org/10.1007/s10115-019-01392-9.

Lo, S.L., Cambria, E., Chiong, R. and Cornforth, D., 2016. A multilingual semi-supervised approach in deriving Singlish sentic patterns for polarity detection. *Knowledge-Based Systems*, 105, pp.236–247.

Mann, G.S. and McCallum, A., 2010. Generalized expectation criteria for semi-supervised learning with weakly labeled data. *Journal of Machine Learning Research*, 11, pp.955–984.

Mishne, G., 2005. Experiments with mood classification in blog posts. *Proceedings of ACM SIGIR 2005 workshop on stylistic ...*. Available at: http://citeseerx.ist.psu.edu/viewdoc/download?doi=10.1.1.111.2693&rep=rep1&type=pdf.

Pang, B. and Lee, L., 2005. Seeing Stars: Exploiting class relationships for sentiment categorization with respect to rating scales. *Proceedings of ACL 2005*. 2005 pp. 33–40.

Da Silva, N.F.F., Coletta, L.F.S. and Hruschka, E.R., 2016. A survey and comparative study of tweet sentiment analysis via semi-supervised learning. *ACM Computing Surveys*, 49(1), pp.1–26.

Statcounter, 2020. Social Media Stats Malaysia - April 2019 - April 2020. Available at: https://gs.statcounter.com/social-media-stats/all/malaysia.

Tang, D. et al., 2015. A Joint Segmentation and Classification Framework for Sentence Level Sentiment Classification. *IEEE Transactions on Audio, Speech and Language Processing*, 23(11), pp.1750–1761.

The Proteus Project, 2004. The Proteus Project. Available at: https://nlp.cs.nyu.edu/GMA_files/resources/malay.stoplist.

Wilson, T., Wiebe, J. and Hoffmann, P., 2005. Recognizing contextual polarity in phrase-level sentiment analysis. *HLT/EMNLP 2005 - Human Language Technology Conference and Conference on Empirical Methods in Natural Language Processing, Proceedings of the Conference*, pp.347–354.

CREDIBILITY MEASURE IN TWEET RETRIEVAL BASED ON TEXTUAL CONSISTENCY

Ibtissem Mejbri and Lobna Hlaoua
Mars Research Lab, Isitcom, University of Sousse, Hammam Sousse, Tunisia

ABSTRACT

Nowadays, social media is a space where information can be shared concerning any type of event. These networks have become a mass of social information that is accumulated day by day. This accumulation can even be doubled in a time of sudden crisis or even within the spread of a pandemic as the example of the famous COVID-19 virus. This social information can, without a doubt, impact, not only the internet surfer, but also the others who have no relationship with the social networks. The major problem here is based on the credibility of information, since the users have the ability of sharing any kind of information. This, in its way, explains why the credibility of social information presents an important challenge. Consequently, in this paper, we are particularly interested in the social media Twitter, where our primary goal is to evaluate the credibility score of a tweet. More precisely, we have presented a hybrid system that takes into consideration, on one hand, the content and the author of the tweet, and on the other hand, includes the notion of textual coherence between the tweet and its comments. In order to validate our proposed approach, we performed our work on a database based on the tweets concerning the COVID-19. Experimental study shows the efficiency of our system, since it's able to reach the same level of judgment as a human. The advantage of our approach based on adapting to changes, where each comment added can also influence credibility, unlike most of the work which is based on machine learning.

KEYWORDS

Credibility, Tweet Retrieval, Comments, Textual Consistency

1. INTRODUCTION

The search of information has grown since the appearance of Web 2.0, more precisely since the emerge of the social media (Facebook, Twitter, LinkedIn...). This new innovation is viewed as the most useful and rich new source of information. As the days go by, the number of users increases in an exceptional manner. According to the latest statistics[1], we found 3.484 million users in 2019. Social media evaluates the information retrieval permitting each surfer to share, in an instant manner, millions of information tackling different subjects. The famous example, Twitter, the microblogging media, today presents an excellent information radiator tool in real time, since it aims to shed light on the potential of this social research. In fact, the main goal of this media consists of perfectly responding to the needs of the users based on the diversity of information that it possesses with approximately 500 million tweets sent per day. Evidently, in phase of this growth of information shared each day, the information retrieval problem does no longer exist. Nevertheless, the main problem revolves around the quality of information. In other words, the majority of times rumors possess strong impact that can in certain cases affect the public opinion and especially when it tackles sensitive subjects (Scientific, meteorological, political etc.). As an example, the millions of tweets shared concerning the disease provoked by the coronavirus, the virus that terrified humanity, without knowing whether they are reliable or not. In that matter, today we talk about a massive quantity of brilliant data and also filled with rumors. According to the study of (Zhao *et al.*, 2015), most microblogging sites are filled with one third of false information. In this order the social media have become, unfortunately, in a certain manner, a field for rumors (Azri *et al.,2019*). For this reason, the credibility presents a subject of interest and actuality. So, it is evident before sharing any information, the system has to be able to measure its credibility. As a matter of fact, many works are situated in the detection of rumors field in Twitter and a

[1] https://www.smartinsights.com/social-media-marketing/social-media-strategy/new-global-social-media-research/

very good part of the approach is interested in the score calculation of credibility, but it still always non-sufficient since at any given moment anyone, behind their little screen, can say whatever they feel like saying according to any event (Froissart *et al.*, 2002). In order to fill the gaps and define the credibility score to obtain an optimal score and precise each tweet a user issues, in this paper, we have the opportunity to propose a hybrid approach. This approach is based partly on the aggregation of three levels of credibility, well explain thereafter, and partly on the analysis of comments with the notion of " Textual consistency", since our definition of credibility in this paper, is strongly related with the reasoning of the human being based, on the comments associated with each tweet.

This paper is organized as follows: Starting with section 2, we presented related credibility estimation works. Moving on to section 3 and 4 with the different levels of our approach as well as the different evaluations results. Finally, we conclude this paper with a conclusion and our future work.

2. RELATED WORKS

In order to enhance the performances and to obtain a credible optimal score, according to literature, there is a number of works that evaluate the credibility of the tweet. (Alrubaian et al., 2018) (Nagy et al., 2012) classify the credibility into big levels: "Post Level", "User Level", "Topic Level" and "Hybrid-Level" which combine the three levels at the same time, where each level has their own priorities, characteristics, advantages and disadvantages.

- **Post-Level**

The principle of this level is founded essentially on the analysis of the attributes of the tweet's content. In other words, this level is not interested neither in the writer nor the subjects tackled by the tweet. But on the opposite, it sheds light only on the content of the post, which means the length of the tweet, the number of words, if it contains pictures and videos (Boididou *et al.*, 2015). So, the more the tweet contains these attributes, the more it has a more important and elevated value of credibility. Based on these functionalities, (Sharf *et al.*, 2013) have proposed an android application dedicated to measure the credibility of current information on Twitter that provide the user with a graphic representation that expresses the credibility rate.

- **User-Level**

Other researchers supposed that the credibility of the tweet is strongly related to the credibility of the contained source. In that order, many works are interested in knowing the influential users and relying on the reputation of the social media. To attend this goal, it is important to extract the characteristics from the account (Alrubaian *et al., 2018)* in order to identify the importance of the user following their number of followers and followed accounts, their picture, if the account is verified or not... (Westerman *et al.*, 2012) have elaborated a study only available information elements that can influence and impact the credibility of the source.

- **Topic-Level**

The works of (Damak et al., 2013) have announced the record of 500 million tweets published per day. This quantity can be doubled when a trending subject or an important topic spread (Al-Qurishi *et al.,* 2017). In fact, when users begin to comment and share their opinions, at times being totally different, it can either confirm or deny the topic. For this reason, an acceptable number of approaches have taken the occasion to estimate the efficiency and flexibility of information carrying topics with strong impact.

- **Hybrid-Level**

Certain researchers have adapted hybrid approach by using the two or even three levels together and their features. The aggregation of the three levels then to assemble the functionalities and the strong sides of each level (Canini *et al.*, 2010). In a general manner, the hybrid approaches provide powerful results and performances compared to the others. As a result, many researchers work on this level since it solves the obstacles that prevent the analysis of the credibility. (Lorek et al., 2015) proposed a combined approach using both content and feature analysis. This approach achieves an accuracy of 89% (the accuracy increases between 8% and 10%).

Each level possesses advantages and disadvantages. Indeed, it is difficult to judge credibility only from a tweet of 280 characters or from the user reputation, since from Twitter follower markets users can obtain followers.

In a general manner, the hybrid level is able to combine all the advantages and can produce better results.

However, in this level the comments were not taken into consideration although they may be a new source of evidence.

3. CREDIBILITY ASSESSMENT BASED ON THE CONSISTENCY OF REPLAY

3.1 Motivation

Firstly, the idea of using comments is presented among the most dominant factors in this strategy to test the importance of the blog. Secondly, the comments in the e-commerce domain it obtains a preponderant effect on the reputation of the products. According to these facts, in this paper, we have chosen to highlight this notion. We are particularly interested in the combined levels of credibility and shedding light on the different opinions of the users throughout the comments that are most of the time ignored in related works. This choice is not random, but very well studied because of its advantages precisely in the degree of impact of the comments on news, decisions, products... Also, the comments can without a doubt clarify the ideas and opinions. But, it still to be known if a tweet is credible or not by observing the coherence of its comments?

3.2 Description of the Approach

To perfectly respond to the previous question, we have proposed an approach that is mainly based on the consistency of the comments, in order to well define its impact on the credibility measure. To make the access fast and effective, our first step is based on the representation of the tweet. Said differently, this task consists in extracting the most important information in creating two vectors; The first one being a logical view of the tweet, while the second one indicates another logical view dedicated for the author that designates its position in the social network. The tweet's table is defined throughout different fields such as "tweet author", "content", "number of shares" " number of responses "... When it comes to the author's table, it consists of fundamental fields for example "user name ", "number of followers", "number of the following accounts"... The main goal of our approach, is to obtain a vague score of credibility not only throughout the level of the tweet content and the author level but also throughout the comments. That's why, it's important to extract and represent the comments. So, this step possesses the same objective, but it needs the addition of another specific field permitting to identify the associated tweet "parent tweet" with a given tweet. Our approach is based on 4 steps as presented in figure 1 and explained below.

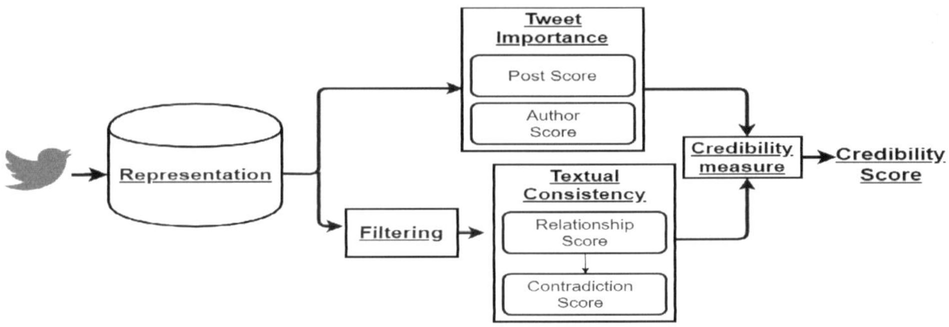

Figure 1. Process for calculating the credibility of a tweet

3.3 Filtering

As a side note, it is important to mention that in our case, we are only interested in the English language. To obtain a tweet with relevant and precise comments it is essential to go through the filter comments step in order to reduce the noise and only show the high-quality comments. It means, in this step, we are partly interested in eliminating all the comments that have different languages than English. And also, we are only keeping the comments that carry a clear idea. So, we will erase all the comments with grammatical, syntax or autographic mistakes that can without a doubt trouble the relevant credibility.

3.4 Tweet Importance

In a general manner, a tweet is defined as important, in the first place, if its content is rich and possess a number of acceptable interactions. And as second place, if it is written by an author with a good social reputation. In order to calculate this score, our proposition goes through two levels. The first being interested in the importance of score in the level of the post, the second being interested in the score in the level of the author as it shows in the formula below:

$$TweetImportanceScore(t,u) = AuthorScore(u) * PostScore(t) \tag{3.1}$$

As a start, we begin with the first level, where the calculation is based on the analysis of the content of the attributes as well as the volume of the shares, the responses, the likes...The more these characteristics are presented, the more the importance of the score is increased.

$$PostScore(t) = \frac{(length(t) + retweet(t) + replay(t) \ + like(t) + \ Url(t) + Hashtag(t) + Mention(}{7} \tag{3.2}$$

$$Url(t) = \begin{cases} 1 & if\ t\ contains\ URL \\ 0 & Otherwise \end{cases} \tag{3.3}$$

$$Hashtag(t) = \begin{cases} 1 & if\ t\ contains\ \ Hashtag \\ 0 & Otherwise \end{cases} \tag{3.4}$$

$$Mention(t) = \begin{cases} 1 & if\ t\ contains\ Mention \\ 0 & Otherwise \end{cases} \tag{3.5}$$

The calculation of the second level is founded upon the extracted characteristics from the author's account (u), which reflects its reputation in the social network. Our proposed formula is calculated as follows:

$$AuthorScore(u) = \frac{(\ followers(u) + following(u) + likesCount(u) + +verifiedAccount(u))}{4} \tag{3.6}$$

$$verifiedAccount(u) = \begin{cases} 1 & if\ Account\ is\ verified\ by\ Twitter \\ 0 & Otherwise \end{cases} \tag{3.7}$$

3.5 Textual Consistency

This step is the heart of our process, the textual coherence or consistency notion (Bergeron *et al.*, 2003) where we will know if there is a chain of information between the tweet and its comments. (Charolles 1978) consider that the textual coherence is assured throughout 4 main rules (**Progression**, **Non-contradiction**, **Repetition** and **Relation**). It is true that these four rules granite the redaction in a well coherent text, but in our case, we are interested in the coherence of the comments. Meaning, it is useless to apply these four rules in our process. In other words, we will only be interested in the "**Relation**" and "**Non-contradiction**". That we can define as follows:

- **Relation**: This rule focuses on the congruence of information (the events, the actions, and the facts) (Carbonneau *et al.*, 2005). Put differently, to produce a sequence or a coherent text, the sentences brought must establish a meaningful relationship between them and must belong to the same universe (domain).
- **Non-contradiction**: This rule is among the most essential rules for the construction of the textual coherence. In a general manner the existence of contradictory information in a text does not only disturb the coherence but also the comprehension, the readability and the credibility. In order to avoid these problems, the principle of this rule requires that the succession of information does not suffer from any contradiction with those which proceed.

In that order, the coherence score of each comment is calculated thanks to this following equation:

$$\text{TextConsistencyScore}(t,r) = \begin{cases} Contradiction\text{Score}(t,r) + \text{RelationshipScore}(t,r) & if\ Contradiction\text{Score} = 1 \\ Contradiction\text{Score}(t,r) - \text{RelationshipScore}(t,r) & if\ Contradiction\text{Score} = -1 \end{cases} \tag{3.8}$$

Relationship score

Before applying our calculation algorithm of the relationship score, we first begin with eliminating of all the empty words (the, this, so...) in the tweet and its comments. Since these empty words have no influence but can disturb the calculations. Our proposed algorithm to calculate the relationship score is based on the calculation of semantic similarities between the tweet (t) and the comment (r). Differently put, with the help of an online thesaurus we will calculate the number of words in relation. The more this number increases the more the comment is in relation to the tweet. (See algorithm table 1).

Table 1. Relationship Score Calculation Algorithm

```
Input: TweetList Tl: List of original Tweet, ReplayList Rl: List of Replay
Output:  SR: relationship Score
Begin
        Count ← 0
        ReplayListSynonyms R' ← List of Synonyms (Rl)

        For each word w ∈ Tl do
            If (w ∈ Rl) Then
                Count ++    // Direct Synonym
            Else
                If (w ∈ R') Then
                    Count ++    // From ReplayListSynonyms
                Else
                    TweetListSynonyms T'← List of Synonyms (word)
                    For each word' w' ∈ T' do
                        If (w' ∈ Rl') || (w' ∈ R') Then
                            Count ++    // From TweetListSynonyms
                        EndIf
                    EndForEach
                EndIf
            EndIf
            SR ← Count / Tl.size()
        EndForEach
End.
```

Contradiction score

The notion of contradiction is the second aspect of our approach. In a general manner, the comments can be divided into two groups. The first group is dedicated to the comments that support and confirm the tweet's idea. The second group concern the opposing comments that contradicts in any manner the tweet. To simplify the idea, we take this example of a tweet T with two comments C1 and C2 below:

- **T**: Covid-19 is a deadly virus.
- **C1**: It's wrong, covid-19 is a simple virus, it's not deadly.
- **C2**: Exactly, one of the most dangerous viruses killing humanity.

In this regard, in order to strictly understand the ownership of each comment, we need the collected indicators which are detailed in section 4.1, where through them we can discover the positioning of the comments. In that order, the contradiction score is calculated as follows:

$$ContradictionScore(t,r) = \begin{cases} -1 & if\ r\ contains\ expressions\ \ contradict\ t \\ 1 & if\ r\ \ contains\ expressions\ \ confirm\ t \end{cases} \qquad (3.9)$$

In the intention of ameliorating our approach and obtain a hybrid system, the integration of a commentary author score can be considered as a predominant factor that can without a doubt influence the calculation. In this context, our idea consists of multiplying the coherence score with the commentary author score as it is indicated in the following formula:

$$ReplayScore(t,r,u) = \text{TextConsistencyScore}(t,r) * AuthorScore(u) \qquad (3.10)$$

The **ReplayScore** needs to be recalculated for each comment. In other words, each score obtained is classified whether in the list of comments that support the idea of the tweet named **ReplayForScore**, or in the list of comments that contradicts the tweet named **ReplayedAgainstScore**. To further explain, the list of scores that belongs to **ReplayForScore** are scores strictly positive, on the other hand the list of **ReplayAgainstScore** is dedicated for the negative scores. At this point, it is important to have a final consistency score which is a combination of the **ReplayFor** and the **ReplayAgainst**. The main foal of this score is to assess, in a global manner, to what extent different users are convinced by the credibility of the tweet.

$$ReplayConsistencyScore(t,r) = \frac{\sum ReplayForScore(t,r)}{|\sum ReplayForScore(t,r)| + |\sum ReplayAgaistScore(t,r)|} \quad (3.11)$$

3.6 Credibility Measure

The goal of this final step is founded on the aggregation of notions in order to obtain a hybrid approach that causes to refine the credibility score that is mainly based on the comments (r), the content of the Tweet (t) and the author (u). To obtain this objective, the final calculation of the credibility score is the result of the sum of Tweet's importance score with the final Replay consistency score obtained with the following formula:

$$\text{CredibilityScore}(t,r,u) = TweetImportanceScore(t,u) + ReplayConsistencyScore(t,r) \quad (3.12)$$

4. EXPERIMENTAL EVALUATION

4.1 Data Collection

Tweet collection: In order to validate our proposed solution, in this section, we have focused on solving the major problem of many approaches, we are concerned with the task of collecting real data. Since there is no standard database for the detection of the tweets credibility. So, the majority of works used synthetic data (Stattner, 2012) as a cause of the complexity and difficulty of this task. The importance of our work lies in the choice of tweets. In other words, the selected tweets must belong to the subject of strong impact precisely being on the COVID-19 virus. For this reason, in our case the task of selecting tweets must be manual. Therefore, we used data representing actual tweets, were our test sample established from the official API offered by Twitter and thanks to the Java library Twitter4J. We have collected 200 tweets. Each tweet is associated with its author, it's comments, and the authors of the comments. In this case, in our database we have 4850 comments and 4900 authors. As a consequence, we notice that an author, of our collection, and not only comment numerous times but also write multiple tweets. In order to test if our system is able to detect the credibility as a user (section 4.2), it is crucial for us to create a well-organized form containing all the tweets and necessary information for the tweets and send it to a group of users (200 researchers) to vote which, according to them, the tweets that are credible and which are non-credible.

Adverbs of affirmation and doubts: Taking into consideration the different views of numerous users from the comments is the added aspect to our approach. In which, we are in need of a collection of expressions of approval and disapproval. In fact, we have allocated a first file that contains nearly the majority of the most used expressions that express the approval in Twitter. For example, "It's very true"," That's so true"... And a second file is reserved for the collected expressions of disapproval. For example, "It's fake", "It's a lie"...

4.2 Experiments and Results

The main goal of this section is to show the performance of our system, and also to well determine if the idea of aggregating the different levels of credibility, already explained in the section 2, with the notion of textual consistency can refine the credibility of the tweet. The evolution of our system is performed by the three evaluative metrics (Recall, Precision, F-Measure). To put it differently, in order for our approach to be performant, it is necessary for it to be able to ameliorate not only the Precision but also the Recall. Our evaluation strategy is composed of different versions of credibility measure well explained in the following. To well validate our system, it is highly important to compare the scores obtained with the reality (the exact results). Taking it from this point of view, we have chosen to follow the topics of COVID-19 in order to verify its truth, which will allow us to obtain truthful results to exercise the comparison to.

4.2.1 Impact of Textual Consistency

In the first version of credibility measure "Tweet importance", we have precisely focused on the Tweet importance score expressed in formula 3.1. In the second version "Textual consistency credibility", we are particularly interested in the textual coherence score between the tweet and its comments expressed in formula 3.8. The main objective of this version, is to study the impact of this notion that adapts the "Relation" factor and the "Non-contradiction" factor to distinguish between the credible and the non-credible tweets. While, in "User consistency credibility", we did not only shed light on the textual coherence but also on the author of each comment expressed in formula 3.10. The concept of this version is based on a simple idea: having a comment coherent with the tweet but written by an author with a mediocre reputation can certainly affect the credibility degree. As the goal is to push the limits, the fundamental aim of the "Credibility assessment system" is to test the impact of our hybrid approach expressed in formula 3.12. Our approach combines, on one hand, the tweet important score, that adapts the publication level with the user level, and on the other hand, the textual coherence score, which takes into consideration the author of the comment.

Table 2. Obtained Results for the credibility measure

	Credible			Non-Credible		
	Recall	**Precision**	**F-Measure**	**Recall**	**Precision**	**F-Measure**
Tweet importance	61%	67%	58%	28%	33%	30%
Textual consistency credibility	84%	73%	78%	42%	50%	49%
User consistency credibility	76%	76%	76%	57%	57%	57%
Credibility assessment system	**76%**	**83%**	**79%**	**71%**	**62%**	**66%**

The evaluation results demonstrated in table 2 show the impact of each version of credibility measure. The first result show very well the imperfection of "Tweet importance" to detect "credibility" and "non-credibility. Using only the textual consistency to measure credibility allows to obtain remarkable results, but it's unable to distinguishing the non-credible tweets (F-Measure= 49%). On the other hand, when it comes to "User consistency credibility", we noticed that it has a decent, but still mediocre, improvement when detecting the non-credible tweets. This poor improvement can confirm that the reputation of the comment's author is able to influence the calculations. Concerning the results obtained by "Credibility assessment system", shows that our proposed hybrid system ensures a significant improvement, since it positively affects not only the Recall but also the Precision to detect "credibility" and "non-credibility". This improvement shows the efficiency and performance of our hybrid system.

4.2.2 Comparison between our Results and the User Judgments

After evaluating our system in the previous versions with certain and verified information, at this stage, it is important to find out if our proposed approach is able to evaluate and detect the credibility such as the user's judgment. Afterwards, we compared their results with the results obtained with our system. Table 3 shows the obtained evaluation outcome. These results have clearly shown that our hybrid system functions nearly as the judgment of users, that being referring to the ion of the Tweet's credibility (F-Measure = 86%) and even the detection of the non-credible tweets (F- Measure =80%).

Table 3. Evaluation according user judgments

	Credible			Non-Credible		
	Recall	**Precision**	**F-Measure**	**Recall**	**Precision**	**F-Measure**
Credibility assessment system	**90%**	**83%**	**86%**	**77%**	**85%**	**80%**

Finally, we can see that our system is able to detect credibility compared to the user judgments better than the reality. Consequently, in general, it can be confirmed that a hybrid system based on the notion of the textual consistency between the tweet and its comments can detect the credibility of tweet.

5. CONCLUSION

The concept of the credibility of social information has become essential. In this paper, we have proposed a hybrid information credibility system in the social network Twitter. The added aspect in our system is that it adapts to change, or in some cases, a new comment added can easily change the result. Our approach depends, on one hand, on the hybridization of different levels and on the other hand, on the addition of the textual coherence notion between the comments and the tweet. The experimental evaluation shows that our system is able to distinguishing the credible tweets and also the non-credible tweets, that while being compared to the judgment of the users and the reality. At this point, it is safe to say that these results successfully show the efficiency of our proposed approach. Consequently, we can confirm that comments may be a new source of evidence able to detect credibility. But in order to ameliorate the results, in our future work we will be adapting the other two factors of the textual coherence notion "Progression" and "Repetition", and also, we will be testing our approach on other datasets to compare it with other approaches.

REFERENCES

Al-Qurishi, M., Hossain, M.S., Alrubaian, M., Rahman, S.M.M. and Alamri, A., 2017. Leveraging analysis of user behavior to identify malicious activities in large-scale social networks. *IEEE Transactions on Industrial Informatics*, *14*(2), pp.799-813.

Alrubaian, M., Al-Qurishi, M., Alamri, A., Al-Rakhami, M., Hassan, M.M. and Fortino, G., 2018. Credibility in online social networks: A survey. *IEEE Access*, *7*, pp.2828-2855.

Azri, A., Favre, C., Harbi, N. and Darmont, J., 2019, October. Vers une analyse des rumeurs dans les réseaux sociaux basée sur la véracité des images : état de l'art.

Bergeron, R., and Blain, R., 2003. La cohérence textuelle. *Québec français*, vol. 128, pp. 47-47.

Boididou, C., Andreadou, K., Papadopoulos, S., Dang-Nguyen, D.T., Boato, G., Riegler, M. and Kompatsiaris, Y., 2015. Verifying Multimedia Use at MediaEval 2015. *MediaEval*, *3*(3), p.7.

Canini, K.R., Suh, B. and Pirolli, P., 2010. Finding relevant sources in twitter based on content and social structure. In *NIPS Workshop*.

Carbonneau, C. and Préfontaine, C., 2005. Enseigner et évaluer la cohérence textuelle. *Québec français*, (138), pp.78-81.

Charolles, M., 1978. Introduction aux problemes de la coherence des textes:(Approche théorique et étude des pratiques pédagogiques). *Langue française*, (38), pp.7-41.

Damak, F., Pinel-Sauvagnat, K., Boughanem, M. and Cabanac, G., 2013, March. Effectiveness of state-of-the-art features for microblog search. In *Proceedings of the 28th Annual ACM Symposium on Applied Computing* (pp. 914-919).

Froissart, P., 2002. Rumeurs sur Internet. *Les cahiers de médiologie, 13 (premier semestre)*. Gallimard, Paris, pp. 205-208.

Lorek, K., Suehiro-Wiciński, J., Jankowski-Lorek, M. and Gupta, A., 2015. Automated credibility assessment on Twitter. *Computer Science*, *16*(2)), pp.157-168.

Nagy, A. and Stamberger, J., 2012. Credo: A framework for semi-supervised credibility assessment for social networks. In *Proceedings of the International Conference on Data Mining (DMIN)* (p. 1). The Steering Committee of The World Congress in Computer Science, Computer Engineering and Applied Computing (WorldComp).

Sharf, Z. and Saeed, A.U., 2013. Twitter news credibility meter. *International Journal of Computer Applications*, *83*(6).

Westerman, D., Spence, P.R. and Van Der Heide, B., 2012. A social network as information: The effect of system generated reports of connectedness on credibility on Twitter. *Computers in Human Behavior*, *28*(1), pp.199-206.

Zhao, Z., Resnick, P. and Mei, Q., 2015, May. Enquiring minds: Early detection of rumors in social media from enquiry posts. In *Proceedings of the 24th international conference on world wide web* (pp. 1395-1405).

COVID 19: WORKING FROM HOME: TWITTER REVEALS WHY WE'RE EMBRACING IT

Fiona Carroll, Mohamed Mostafa and Simon Thorne
Cardiff Metropolitan School of Technologies, Llandaff Campus, Western Avenue, Cardiff, CF5 2YB, UK

ABSTRACT

As more than a third of the world's population is now in lock-down, we see COVID-19 not only having severe implications on people's health but also having a significant knock-on effect on their livelihoods. A recent YouGov report highlights that one in twenty people in the UK lost their job due to coronavirus and that 52% of those studied expect the British economy to be in recession within a year (Sparkes, 2020). In this paper we aim to investigate the online social response to the working from home WFH concept, by analysis the twitter activity around the coronavirus and WFH, initial findings suggest, 70.6% positive tweets before the lock-down, on the other hand, 78.6% positive tweets after the lock-down around the WFH.

KEYWORDS

Working from Home, Coronavirus, Online Social Response, WFH, COVID-19, Remote Working, Post-Coronavirus

1. INTRODUCTION

In all this uncertainty, the authors of this article feel that it is essential to highlight some positives especially as technology is, yet again, proving its worth by enabling many of us to keep our jobs and work from home. As PwC research (Teow, 2020) suggests up to half the UK workforce can work from home; technology is enabling as much as 80% of UK finance and insurance industry workers to work remotely. There are, indeed, a lot of people around the world who are suddenly experiencing the full value that digital technology affords for remote working. Technology is enabling us to run our businesses from home, to deliver lectures and classes from our sitting rooms and to undertake other essential work duties while still maintaining efficiency and productivity.

2. WORK AND TECHNOLOGY: THE 'NEW' NORMAL

For many of us, technologies are shaping a 'new' typical workplace which is influencing and often improving how we work and communicate with colleagues. However, the debate over, what technology does to work, jobs, and wages has been going on for many years and in not such a positive light. In the eighties, the Nobel Prize-winning economist Wassily Leontief talked about how horses became unnecessary with the advent of new technologies such as tractors, automobiles and trucks. He drew a parallel between human labor and horses: 'a farmer couldn't keep his horses and postpone the change to tractors by feeding them fewer oats. So he got rid of the horses and used the more productive tractor' (Leontief, 1983). In truth, for over two hundred years, people have been worried about what technology will do to their jobs. More recently, Cascio and Montealegre (2016) have considered the disruptive effects of emerging information and communication technologies. In the last few years, there has been a slight 'negative' emphasis on robotics stealing our jobs with several big headlines announcing the future of jobs as robot-shaped (Elliott, 2018).

In the light of COVID-19, the prospect of robot doctors treating patients, drones transporting supplies and vaccines to infected areas and 3D printers producing quick and cheap face masks does not seem a strange or frightening thing. In many ways, technology has become essential for us; we realize how, 'Yes', robots can make effective support staff enabling doctors to communicate with contagious patients remotely, saving time and saving lives. We can also see how technology is enabling a remote workforce, so we can minimize the effects of the coronavirus on both our personal and work lives. As Evangelista et al. (2014) highlighted digitization has the potential to drive productivity and employment growth; for many of us, today, it is just about keeping the jobs we have, and technological innovations are enabling us to do so. During a COVID-19 pandemic, we are finding ourselves with no other options but to embrace and use technology to undertake our work and maintain our social lives. Interestingly, we seem to be understanding things for the way that they are, and despite some concerns about the safety of videoconferencing applications (Lyons, 2020), we are generally quite cheerful in this #WFH (work from home) 'new' normal.

3. WHAT IS THE ONLINE SOCIAL RESPONSE TO #WFH?

On the 14th of March 2020, we started a Twitter collection streaming service around 'Coronavirus, COVID-19' as an observation for the social network reaction to the pandemic. We collected more than 60 million tweets until the 6th of April 2020. After pre-processing the dataset to remove RT retweets, the data-set was queried for the keyword #WFH, taking it to only 6500 tweets and restricted to the UK area. In general, the majority of collected tweets reported a positive sentiment towards the #WFH concept with 70.6%, as shown in figure 1. The data collected after the lock-down suggested the majority of community still had a positive reaction to the working from concept with a rise in the positive feedback sentiment to 78.6% as shown in figure 2.

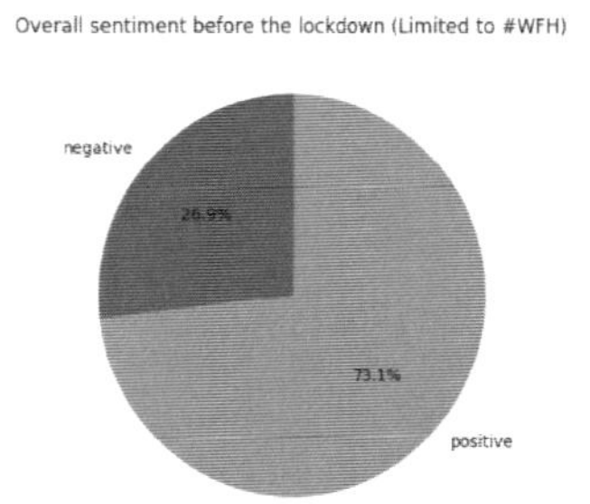

Figure 1. Overall sentiment before lock-down - limited to #WFH

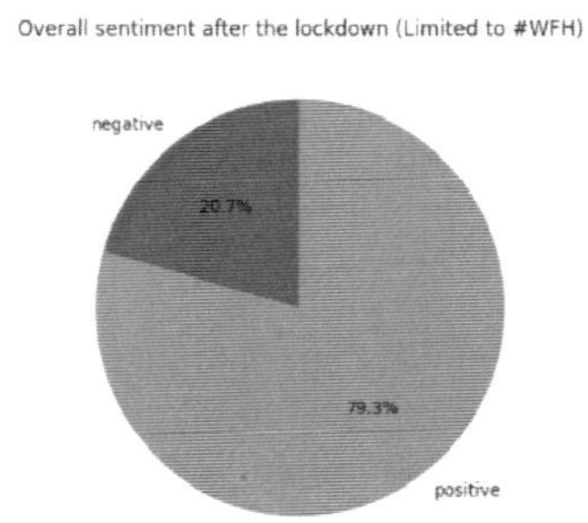

Figure 2. Overall sentiment after lock-down (till 6th of April 2020) - limited to #WFH

In an attempt to explain the main topics emerging of Twitter conversations, we gathered all tweets before and after the lock-down and demonstrated a word-cloud figure to present the frequency of the words in the tweets (as shown in figure 3). A similarity, it is noticeable that before the lock-down, the rise a mix of words such as working, employee, home, social distance. The population were talking about working from home even before the lock-down to achieve the social distance enforced. Furthermore, similar words are appearing after the lock-down with the new addition of words such as challenges and cyber-security aligning with the challenges some business faced while their employees worked from home.

(a) Combined word-cloud after lock down (limited to #WFH)

(b) Combined word-cloud before lock down (limited to #WFH)

Figure 3. Word-clouds from before and after lock-down

3.1 Topic Modelling

Social Networks have been a vital resource in highlighting the main topics and trends locally and globally (Chapman et al., 2018). Twitter, in particular, is where people connect with their passions, share their thoughts and feelings, and find out what is happening in the world. In Crisis management, Twitter was a significant player in detecting the sentiment of public reactions to events (Chapman et al., 2018) and the feedback received from Twitter had helped decision-makers to make decisions on significant issues. To probe the Twitter data further, we apply topic modelling and consider the techniques of Latent Dirichlet Allocation (LDA), which is a generative probabilistic model for a collection of discrete data (Ostrowski, 2015). We used LDA to generate the topics from the tweets, and then we divided the tweets into two central part (Before the lockdown) and (After the lockdown).

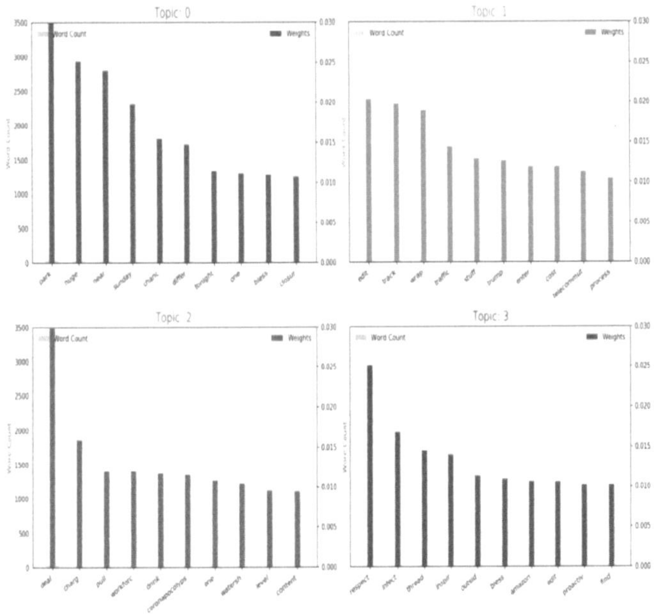

Figure 4. Before lock-down - Topic modelling (Word Count and Importance of Topic Keywords) #WFH

In line with this, figure 4 highlights keywords like Park, Deal and Respect as being most significant to peoples' experiences before the COVID-19 lockdown. In addition, words like process, edit, track, charge, deal and find give us the strong impression that people are thinking about the practicalities of working from home. There is also a strong positive feeling, with words like respect, inspire, bless, proactive and chance showing that people are embracing the concept of working from home in the time of COVID-19. In contrast, words featuring in the tweets after the lockdown, highlight a slightly different tone. Keywords such as kill, mild and privacy are featuring most frequently in the Twitter #WFH conversations. There is a stronger emphasis on the impact of the actual virus with words such as treatment, disease, cancer, medicine, accept and lockdown. Also, from the tweets, we sense more concerns around the far-reaching impacts on jobs, with frequently tweeted words such as director, hire, Morgan Philips and unemployment.

3.2 Drilling into the Data

Moreover, figure 5 shows the sentiment (emotions) generated from the tweets per day before the lock-down in the UK. It is very noticeable that the line-plot is not continuous every day, and the reason is, most of the tweets before the lock-down were not about the #WFH. However, on 15th of March 2020, 16th of March 2020 and 22nd of March 2020 there is an increase in the mentioning of #WFH. One possible explanation for this is that the United States' Centre for Disease Control advised against gatherings of more than 50 people (Abbruzzese, 2020).

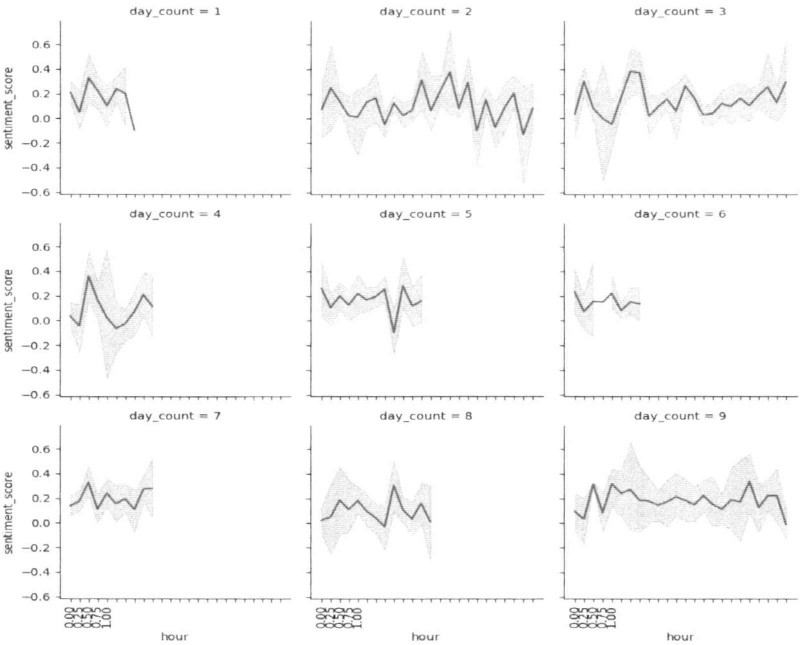

Figure 5. Sentiment in Twitter before the UK lock-down #WFH[1]

On the 15th of March and the 16th of March, the United States Schools close for nearly 30 million children of the 56.6 million students (only 53%) (Kristof & Thompson, 2020). On the 22nd of March, the talking around #WFH rapidly increased with the majority of positive sentiment towards the concept. The sentiment of the tweets per day after the lock-down in the UK, days 24th of March 2020, 25th of March 2020, 26th of March 2020 show a noticeable rise in the overall sentiment being shared, in line with the increase of reported global coronavirus cases (see figure 7). We believe that the #WFH boosted the sentiment for a big portion of the community. However, at the end of the day 14 there was a steep drop which lasted for three days, we investigated these three days, generating a word-cloud to observe the frequency of the words appearing in the tweets during this period. It is clear that some concern started to be raised regarding the kids well-being, Cyber-security and Zoom which is aligned with the news reported around Zoom's software security (Baker and Shaw, 2020).

Figure 6. Word-cloud from 27th of March 2020 to 30th of March 2020) #WFH

Generally, the overall sentiment of the social response to the #WFH is positive with a clear sense of productivity as shown in 6 and words such as team, tips, office, business, staff, employee, satisfaction, service, remote, support, good, normal, internet.

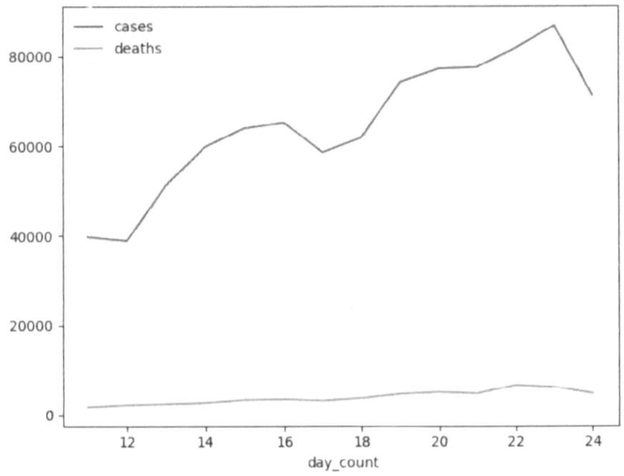

Figure 7. After the lock-down - reported COVID-19 cases globally) #WFH

4. CONCLUSION

This is a preliminary study to observe the online social response to the #WFH. Although 'work from home' is not a new concept, this pandemic has forced the #WFH practice out to a broader sector of our workforce. Furthermore, despite natural concerns about the coronavirus, the main findings from our study show that most of the online responses seem positive, as shown in figure 2. This raises the question, what will happen after the lock-down lifted? Will businesses start to widen this practice to allow more flexibility to their employees? Or we will go back to our 'old' normal?

REFERENCES

Abbruzzese, J., 2020. CDC recommends canceling all events of 50 people or more until early may. Retrieved from https://www.nbcnews.com/health/health-news/cdc\-recommends\-canceling\-all\-events\-50\-people\-or\-more\-until\-n1159771.

Baker, M. & Shaw, N., 2020. Fears over security of popular video conference chat app zoom. Retrieved from https://www.walesonline.co.uk/news/uk-news/fears-over-security-popular-video-18004433

Cascio, W.F & Montealegre, R., 2016. How Technology Is Changing Work and Organizations. *Annual Review of Organizational Psychology and Organizational Behavior,* Vol.3, No.1, Pp. 349-375.

Chapman, L., Resch, B., Sadler,J., Zimmer, S., Roberts, H. and Petutschnig, A., 2018. Investigating the emotional responses of individuals to urban green space using twitter data: A critical comparison of three different methods of sentiment analysis. *Urban Planning*, Vol.3, No.1, pp. 21-33.

Elliott, L. 2018. Robots will take our jobs. We'd better plan now, before it's too late. Retrieved from https://www.theguardian.com/commentisfree/2018/feb/01/robots-take-our-jobs-amazon-go-seattle

Evangelista, R., Guerrieri, P., and Meliciani., V., 2014. The economic impact of digital technologies in Europe. *Economics of Innovation and New Technology*. Doi: 10.1080/10438599.2014.918438.

Kristof, N. & Thompson, S.A., 2020. How much worse the coronavirus could get, in charts. Retrieved from https://www.nytimes.com/interactive/2020/03/13/opinion/ coronavirus\-trump\-response.html

Leontief, W., 1983. Technological advance, economic growth, and the distribution of income. *Population & Development Review*, Vol.9, No. 3, pp. 403 -410.

Lyons, K., 2020. Zoom vulnerability would have allowed hackers to eavesdrop on calls - The Verge. Retrieved from https://www.theverge.com/2020/1/28/21082331/zoom-vulnerability-hacker-eavesdrop-security-google-hangouts-skype-checkpoint.

Ostrowski, D.A., 2015. Using latent dirichlet allocation for topic modelling in twitter. In *Proceedings of the 2015 IEEE 9th International Conference on Semantic Computing (IEEE ICSC 2015),* pp 493-497.

Sparkes, M., 2020. More than half of Britons expect a recession within a year. Retrieved from https://yougov.co.uk/topics/economy/articles-reports/2020/03/30/ more\-half\-britons\-expect\-recession\-within\-year

Teow. J., 2020. Responding to the UK business impacts of COVID19. PwC UK. Retrieved from https://www.pwc.co.uk/issues/crisis\-and\-resilience/covid\-19.html

ADOPTION OF AI IN AGRICULTURE: THE GAME-CHANGER FOR INDIAN FARMERS

Tapan Kumar[1] and Nupur Prakash[2]
[1]Research Scholar, University School of ICT, GGSIP University, Delhi, India
[2]Professor, University School of ICT, GGSIP University, Delhi, India

ABSTRACT

This paper presents a study of various AI-powered ICT applications to numerous challenges related to the agriculture life cycle and its positive impact on the well-being of Indian farmers. Technology-driven solutions to various problems, such as soil fertility, inadequate irrigation, pest control, weed management and yield prediction have been discussed, along with, affirmative actions taken by the Indian government to promote smart agriculture. The agricultural life cycle faces many impediments, such as disease, weeds, pest infestation, improper soil conditions, outdated irrigation methods, unpredictable weather conditions, etc. These lead to severe crop failure, food shortage and increasing environmental hazards, driving the farmers to poverty. Extensive research has been done to address these problems in the past few decades. Further, due to the outbreak of pandemic COVID 19, certain restrictions have been imposed by the Indian Government in the farming sector to ensure the safety of farmers from getting infected with the deadly virus. This has resulted in an acute shortage of farmworkers. The use of ICT in agriculture becomes even more important at this crucial time, when, the pandemic has spread across the globe. The ICT based solutions reduce the dependence of farmers on farm-workers and enable them to maintain stable income levels and farm yield, despite the shortage of farm labourers. Various agro-intelligent practices adopted in the last 15 years, worldwide, have also been surveyed, in this paper. Some of the tools and platforms developed by Indian Start-ups to implement smart agriculture and to deal with the shortage of manpower and supply chain disruption due to lockdown during pandemic, have also been discussed.

KEYWORDS

Artificial Intelligence, Smart Agriculture, Yield Prediction, Biomagnification

1. INTRODUCTION

The agricultural activities across the world continue to shift towards ICT enabled automated systems that perform real-time predictions. Farmers are increasingly using the latest technologies, from intelligent irrigation systems, to drones taking aerial photos of arable fields and using drones/robots to spray pesticides. The impact of the adoption of smart agriculture in improving the lifestyle and prosperity of Indian farmers has been phenomenal. The rapid growth of the population in India demands a ramp up in food production. According to the Food and Agriculture Organization of the United Nations, with a population of 1.3 billion, India is the world's second-most populous country. It is also an agrarian society, being the seventh-largest country in the world in terms of area, with 67% of it's population dependent of agriculture (FAO, 2020). Traditional agriculture methods are not enough to meet the present needs, as they are obsolete and facing huge challenges ranging from sowing to harvesting. Major challenges are weed control, irrigation, yield prediction, excessive use of pesticides, climatic conditions, soil conditions, and overuse of chemical fertilizers (Bannerjee, et.al., 2018). In addition to these problems, to combat the sudden outbreak of COVID 19, several restrictions have been imposed in the farming sector during lockdown, resulting in a huge shortage of migrant farm-workers. In the present scenario, the adoption of ICT in the farm sector can mitigate these challenges and reduce the distress level of farmers to a great extent. Few AI-inspired ICT solutions in farming are discussed in the following sections of this paper.

2. ICT IN SOIL TREATMENT

India is the land of diversity. According to the Indian Council of Agriculture Research, Indian agriculture land has different types of soil such as, alluvial soil (43%), red soil (18.5%), black /regur soil (15%), other soil (23.5%). Presently, 661 soil-testing centres established by the government of India are in place, where the soil samples are taken to laboratories and tested for essential nutrients against the crop grown in that region. It is a time-consuming process with low accuracy.

With the adoption of ICT and AI in agriculture, the Indian landscape has undergone a major transformation. Artificial Neural Network (ANN) based model can be effectively used to test the Indian soil using three parameters (texture, color, moisture) for on-site soil testing (Zhai et al., 2006). The data can be collected through a wireless sensor network (WSN) which measures soil moisture of the field in real-time and connects to the farmer's mobile phone through Zigbee, wifi, or cellular network, depending on the area of the farm land. It is observed that this AI-based on-line solution gives more accurate results over traditional soil testing methods done in the labs offline. Moreover, the traditional method of soil testing requires huge manpower, whereas, ICT based soil testing requires less manpower and useful in such unprecedented times during pandemic, when human movement is minimal and restricted.

3. ICT IN IRRIGATION

Indian irrigation system uses traditional methods such as irrigation through the river, pond, canal using water pumps. Presently, two-third of farmers in India use traditional methods of irrigation. Inadequate rainfall and outdated irrigation methods lead to a huge loss in crop yield. The latest developments in the field of automation in irrigation using artificial intelligence is discussed in this section.

Various wireless technologies (Kumar, 2014) and ANN-based models were proposed for drip irrigation through Automatic plant irrigators and rainfall prediction using climate variables during year 2010 to 2019 (Yadav and Sagar, 2019). Using various parameters like soil moisture, precipitation level, wetting pattern, ANN-based models are developed for Indian farmers. The simulation shows, that the cost of irrigation is likely to be reduced up to 50% over traditional irrigation methods along with improved yield. With the adoption of ICT and AI in irrigation the prediction of total monsoon rainfall would be possible a few weeks and days in advance.

4. ICT IN PEST CONTROL

Pest control is one of the most challenging activities in agriculture, that leads to severe health issues and biomagnification. The traditional agriculture life cycle in India involves indiscriminate usage of pesticides, such as Insecticides (61%), Fungicides (19%), Herbicides (17%), and other pesticides (3%). An integrated pest management system using a fuzzy expert system has been deployed in Malaysia, to monitor the pest activity in rice crop (Siraj and Arbaiy, 2006). A pesticide spraying system has been deployed in China, where variable spraying technique has been adopted based on fuzzy control and sensor networks (Shi et. al., 2007). The same has been extended to include geographic information and geolocation for pest control for olive culture in Portugal (Jesus and Panagopoulos, 2008). A Bayesian Network-based Expert System in Pest Management has been proposed in India (Singh and Gupta, 2020). A model combining image capturing using camera and ANN is under trial, which identifies the exact location of pests and minimizes the use of pesticides in rice, wheat, and cotton crops, through targeted spraying. A LoRa Wide Area Network is used to connect a wireless sensor network in the fields with the farmer's mobile for live updates.

5. ICT IN WEED CONTROL

Traditional weed control methods include the application of hoses, cultivators, mulch, and chemical control such as herbicides. The excessive application of herbicides directly impacts human health and the environment due to the phenomena of Bio-magnification. The usage of ICT in weed control is gaining momentum and various AI approaches are being applied to minimize the application of herbicides.

John Deere, an agricultural and forestry equipment company, acquired Blue River Technology, which uses AI based algorithms to plan targeted herbicide spraying for crops. The program selects for spraying only those parts of the field that require it. This solution minimizes the wastage by reducing the amount of herbicide needed for spraying. The image analysis using ANN is commonly used for real-time weed identification and control to minimize the usage of herbicides/weedicides. A smart sprayer for precision weed control using deep learning frameworks, distinguishes target weeds from non-target objects (e.g. vegetable/crops) and precisely sprays on the desired target/location (Partel et.al., 2019). A novel computer vision-based robotic weeding control system is highly effective in weed identification and control (Wu et.al., 2020) and also reduces health hazards for farmers by spraying the right amount of herbicides only on desired spots. A deep learning framework using computer vision is to be trained on the images of various Indian crops like rice, wheat, and cotton, to identify the unrecognized images of weeds and spray them with herbicides using drones and robots. This technique not only reduces the consumption of herbicides, but also, reduces agrochemical residues on food products and protects the environment from bio-magnification.

6. ICT IN YIELD PREDICTION

The crop yield prediction is very important for determining the minimum support prices (MSP) and crop cost estimation. Further, the analysis of relevant factors, that directly affect the yield can also be done through predictive modelling. To predict yield, growth, and water consumption in a greenhouse environment, a neural network-based predictive model integrated with GIS was used in 2011(Thongboonnak and Sarapirome, 2011). The energy output has been used as a means of yield prediction for basil plants in a greenhouse in 2012 (Pahlavan et. al., 2012). Later on, a CNN-RNN based framework has been applied for yield prediction of corn and soybean crops (Khaki et.al., 2020).

A similar model is proposed for yield prediction for the Indian farm sector which uses soil parameters, compost, fertilizers, and climate conditions as input to a neural network that is trained on known dataset of the past 20 years.

7. INITIATIVES IN SMART AGRICULTURE

The Indian government is promoting and funding projects and start-ups for innovations in the farm sector.

7.1 Project on Weather Prediction & Soil Moisture Analysis

The agriculture ministry of India has initiated a pilot project on climate prediction and soil moisture analysis in three regions of India namely, Bhopal, Rajkot, and Nanded for the Kharif crop of 2019. IBM's Watson Decision Support System has been used to provide weather forecast and soil moisture information on a pro bono basis to help farmers in taking decisions regarding water and crop management. This has resulted in achieving bumper rice crops in these regions.

7.2 Sowing App

The pilot project, to experiment with an innovative sowing procedure, was launched in 2016 for Indian farmers. The Sowing App was developed to assist farmers to attain best groundnut harvests by sending the notification to the farmers their mobile phones about the most suitable time to sow depending upon climate conditions. The sowing app inputs data provided by farmers and the International Crops Research Institute for the Semi-Arid Tropics (ICRISAT) regarding soil and climate conditions for different crops. AI and Machine Learning based data-driven weather forecasting models are applied to this data to predict a suitable sowing date. The Microsoft Power Business Intelligence (BI) platform was used to develop this model which sends an SMS to farmers about the appropriate sowing dates in their local language. This pilot project was implemented in the Indian province of Andhra Pradesh, which resulted in a 30% higher average in yield per hectare. A bumper harvest resulted despite irregular and insufficient rainfall. This, ICT enabled solution resulted in better financial returns to Indian farmers by improving their income and quality of life.

7.3 Agri-Intelligent Solutions offered by Indian Start-ups

The government of India has introduced a new AGRI-UDAAN program to mentor start-ups innovating in the field of smart agriculture and to connect them with potential investors. Some of the tools and Apps launched by Indian start-ups for smart agriculture are as follows:

7.3.1 Intello Labs

This start-up has developed an AI platform using a deep learning algorithm on which intelligent solutions are developed for various applications in smart agriculture, e-commerce, advertising, manufacturing, etc. Intello Labs also provides automated grading of fresh products by quality analysis of images and helps farmers get a better price for their produce. Their solution uses deep learning algorithms integrated with image processing to recognize any disease or pest infestation in the farm produce.

7.3.2 Smartfarm

CropIn is a start-up, which, has developed Smart-farm an intuitive, intelligent, self-evolving system that addresses future-ready farming solutions to the entire agricultural sector of India. The system supports decision-making tools that bring consistency, dependability, and sustainability to agri-businesses by providing cloud-based solutions for smart farming based on local/regional conditions and connects the farmer through his mobile phone using the cellular network.

7.3.3 Gobasco

The Intelligent Agri supply chain based start-up in India uses an AI platform for their operations. It deals with commodity flow maps, customer preference maps, credit rating systems, GoProcure AI tools, and price prediction modules. It helps in the transport of grains from farmers to vendors at Minimum Support Price (MSP) set by the government of India, making farmer's life easy and stress-free.

7.3.4 Gramophone (Agstack Technologies)

This Indian start-up offers a decision support system and an IoT based hardware integrated with mobile phones of the farmers to carry out agricultural activities, such as seed selection, crop protection, irrigation, etc. It also provides customized IoT based hardware for smart agriculture to Indian farmers at their doorstep.

8. CONCLUSION

The AI-based ICT solutions have been a game-changer for Indian farmers in terms of improving the quality of their produce and yield, thereby, enhancing their income levels, lifestyle, and happiness quotient. Indian agriculture activities are gradually shifting towards automated systems that perform real-time predictions and actions. Usage of AI technology not only optimizes the work on farms, using less resources, but also automates many activities, thereby reducing human involvement (and especially the number of farm worker). In this paper, various AI-powered ICT solutions applied to the agricultural domain have been presented. Numerous technology initiatives are taken by the Indian government to promote smart agriculture which increases farmer's income and reduces their dependence on soil and climatic conditions are also discussed. In the last decade, the use of hybrid systems, which, combine image processing with trainable ANNs, integrated with Mobile IoT and Sensor networks is predominant in smart agriculture. The farmers get alerts on their mobile phones and control various farming activities remotely using WSN connected to Zigbee, wifi, LoRa WAN, or 3G/4G mobile networks. Due to the COVID outbreak, there is an acute shortage of farmworkers in the villages of India. Usage of drones and mobile robots reduces manpower requirements in various farming activities and minimizes health hazards experienced by farmers during spray of pesticides.

With ICT interventions, the economic and health condition of the farmers improves and their distress level is reduced. Accordingly, each country can adopt a model based on its soil and climate condition to improve the quality of harvest and yield of farming land by at least 30%-50%. Ultimately, it results in a higher yield per hectare, poverty alleviation, better health, cleaner environment and good quality of life, among farmers. Further, studies are being conducted in India using AI and Machine learning so that conventional farming can shift towards ICT enabled smart farming at an affordable cost.

REFERENCES

Bannerjee, G., Sarkar, U., Das, S., & Ghosh, I. (2018). Artificial Intelligence in Agriculture: A Literature Survey. International Journal of Scientific Research in Computer Science Applications and Management Studies, 7(3), 1-6.

FAO: India at a Glance, by Food and Agriculture organization of United Nation, http://www.fao.org/india/fao-in-india/india-at-a-glance/en/,

Jesus, J. O. R. G. E., Panagopoulos, T. H. O. M. A. S., & Neves, A. L. C. I. N. D. A. (2008, June). Fuzzy logic and geographic information systems for pest control in olive culture. In 4th IASME/WSEAS International Conference on Energy, Environment, Ecosystems & Sustainable Development, Algarve, Portugal.

Jha, K., Doshi, A., Patel, P., & Shah, M. (2019). A comprehensive review on automation in agriculture using artificial intelligence. Artificial Intelligence in Agriculture.

Khaki, S., Wang, L., & Archontoulis, S. V. (2020). A cnn-rnn framework for crop yield prediction. Frontiers in Plant Science, 10, 1750.

Kumar, G. (2014). Research paper on water irrigation by using wireless sensor network. International Journal of Scientific Research Engineering & Technology (IJSRET), 3-4.

Pahlavan, R., Omid, M., & Akram, A. (2012). Energy input–output analysis and application of artificial neural networks for predicting greenhouse basil production. Energy, 37(1), 171-176.

Partel, V., Kim, J., Costa, L., Pardalos, P., & Ampatzidis, Y. (2019). Smart Sprayer for Precision Weed Control Using Artificial Intelligence: Comparison of Deep Learning Frameworks.

Shi, Y., Zhang, C., Liang, A., & Yuan, H. (2007, August). Fuzzy control of the spraying medicine control system. In International Conference on Computer and Computing Technologies in Agriculture (pp. 1087-1094). Springer, Boston,

Singh, N., & Gupta, N. (2020). Bayesian Network for Development of Expert System in Pest Management. In Internet of Things and Analytics for Agriculture, Volume 2 (pp. 45-65). Springer, Singapore.

Siraj, F., & Arbaiy, N. (2006). Integrated pest management system using fuzzy expert system. In Proc. KMICE-2006, University of Malayasia, Sintok.

Thongboonnak, K., & Sarapirome, S. (2011). Integration of Artificial Neural Network and Geographic Information System for Agricultural Yield Prediction. Suranaree Journal of Science & Technology, 18(1).

Wu, X., Aravecchia, S., Lottes, P., Stachniss, C., & Pradalier, C. (2020). Robotic weed control using automated weed and crop classification. Journal of Field Robotics, 37(2), 322-340.

Yadav, P., & Sagar, A. (2019). Rainfall Prediction Using Artificial Neural Network (ANN) for tarai Region of Uttarakhand. Current Journal of Applied Science and Technology, 1-7.

Zhai, Y., Thomasson, J. A., Boggess III, J. E., & Sui, R. (2006). Soil texture classification with artificial neural networks operating on remote sensing data. Computers and Electronics in Agriculture, 54(2), 53-68.

GAMIFICATION AND INTERDISCIPLINARY SCIENTIFIC RESEARCH: SCIENTIFIC TEXT MINING

Olga Kononova[1], Dmitry Prokudin[1,2], and Angelina Timofeeva[1]
[1] *ITMO University 197101, St. Petersburg, Russia*
[2]*St. Petersburg State University 199034, St. Petersburg, Russia*

ABSTRACT

This study investigates the issues of forming the terminological base of interdisciplinary areas of scientific research to discover new knowledge, to make the prediction, such as to identify the public discourse effects on the dynamics of scientific interests. The goals of this paper are to highlight gamification as interdisciplinary area and to represent the complex approach to contextual knowledge research with scientific text mining on the example of "The gamification in the main spheres of digital society" topic. In the work, we use the capabilities of contextual search and extraction of metadata from texts, describing the use of gamification in various fields of activity, followed by quantitative and qualitative processing of the textual arrays obtained. The knowledge gained was used to expand the capabilities of the synthetic method in the part of the text mining analysis as well as the construction and interpretation technique of subject-specific trends. The conclusion of the research consists in the establishment of the sustainable dependence amongst scientific and public discourse: socio-political initiatives form the modern public life which term-concepts identify not only applying technologies in the life of society as such but the scientific discourse directions.

KEYWORDS

Contextual Knowledge, Contextual Search, Digital Society, Interdisciplinary Scientific Research, Synthetic Technique, Scientific Text Mining, Subject-Specific Trends, Terminological Landscape

1. INTRODUCTION

In modern scientific studies, the task of analyzing promising interdisciplinary scientific areas is being actualized, which allows us to predict the relevance of research results in these areas (knowledge) in various fields of social life. There is a lag in the development of scientometric and scientific disciplines from the growth rate of the terminological and categorical base of interdisciplinary scientific fields, which is uncontrollably formed by scientific schools, groups, and individual researchers. The ambiguity of terminology and unstructured information, even with free access, makes it impossible to quickly monitor emerging trends and relationships.

One of the significant trends in modern scientific research is the identification (explication) of contextual knowledge by applying methods, approaches, technologies and tools of Digital Humanities as well as the text mining analysis. Contextual knowledge is usually understood as the ability to "read" the context correctly, to extract and interpret professionally significant information regardless of the origin source. The extraction of relevant information is performed through a contextual search. Contextual search is a method of sequentially searching for fragments of text entries relevant to a user's query and the desired context. In this case, the context is a part of the text, the verbal environment of the selected text element (term-concept) for analysis. The context concept used in this study is interpreted by us as an independent conceptual unit of the categorical apparatus, which can be used as the basis for the classification of scientific texts, visualization of hierarchical and associative relations between terms.

Reinterpretation the role of interdisciplinary disciplines and the applicability of traditional scientific methods in interdisciplinary research is widely covered in scientific publications. Interdisciplinary areas (in fact contexts) are believed to be identified through a thematic search and described quantitatively and qualitatively through various kinds of measurements and procedures. Thus, for instance, K. Okamura, focusing on clusters of highly cited papers widely known as research fronts (RFs), has suggested that interdisciplinarity is statistically significantly and positively associated with research impact by focusing on highly cited paper clusters [Okamura K., 2019]. C. Carusi and G. Bianchi have applied the quantifying of journals' interdisciplinarity by exploiting relation between scholars and journals where such scholars do publish [Carusi C., Bianchi G., 2020]. J. Raimbault has offered a measurement methodology that combines the analysis of citation networks and semantic analysis, studying the qualitative laws of relations between endogenous disciplines [Raimbault J., 2019]. The scientists G. Abramo, C. A. D'Angelo, and L. Zhang have used two bibliometric approaches to the measurement of interdisciplinary research at the same time: the analysis of disciplinary diversity in the reference list of publications; the disciplinary diversity of authors of publications [Abramo G., et al., 2018]. C. Piciocchi and L. Martinelli have conducted research on the development of categorical-conceptual apparatuses of various scientific areas, where Digital Humanities methods and approaches are used [Piciocchi C. and Martinelli L., 2016]. The paper on the cultural initiatives and the mapping process of governance and participation dynamics involve an abductive reasoning as a pragmatic approach to advancing the social sciences through a process of "systematic combining" both the analytical framework and the case studies in order to expand the theoretical and empirical understanding of results [Biondia L., et al., 2020]. The methodology of research groups [Pejic-Bacha M., et al., 2020; Jimenez-Marquez, et al., 2019] consists of data extraction, analytical approach (descriptive analysis and text mining), and machine-learning analysis. G. Paré, M. C. Trudel, M. Jaana, S. Kitsiou focus the researchers on the preparation as well as analysis of reviews, and develop their own typology of reviews, encouraging authors to use this typology to position their contribution [Paré G., Trudel M. C., Jaana M., Kitsiou S., 2015]. Gamification studies constitute a significant part of such studies. For instance, Finnish researchers practice intellectual search and analysis of scientific texts in their study, preferring manual data processing [Hamari J., Koivisto J., et al., 2014, 2018, 2019]. The search strategy of Indonesian authors described in their paper "The Approach to the Meta-description of the Interdisciplinary Research Terminological Landscape" consists of "sorting digital libraries, determining keywords, using existing tools in digital libraries to facilitate the search, and taking primary studies obtained for processing" [Purwandari B., et al., 2018].

We propose to use the Synthetic technique in this kind of research, which involves the use of ICT at all stages of the research: from searching and collecting information to its quantitative and qualitative processing. The scientific text mining is based on the technologies of contextual search, explication and mapping of contextual knowledge (contexts). We show the effectiveness of this method to achieve the main goal of the study.

2. RESEARCH METHODOLOGY

The general approach to conducting research is to apply the synthetic method in interdisciplinary research to analyze contexts, build and interpret subject-specific trends. The Synthetic technique used is aimed at extracting and processing contextual knowledge from unstructured or semi-structured information resources. Moreover, it allows, through explication and mapping, forming collections of fragments (thematic contexts) that are thematically relevant to the interdisciplinary direction. In the frames of the research, the theoretical and practical results of applying science-research methods for extracting, processing and analyzing contextual knowledge have been analyzed [Kononova O., Prokudin D., 2018]. Thus, the research agenda consists in identifying semantic groups and contexts, revealing patterns and building trends that reflect the development dynamics of topics in the scientific and public discourse. The proposed approach was applied to various interdisciplinary scientific areas for identification and analysis of contextual knowledge in practice (Figure 1). It takes no account of the programs and environment used, the language, and the presentation format of information resources. To demonstrate the general approach, ScienceDirect, the full-text and abstract databases of scientific publications, have been selected as text source. The heterogeneity of the source material led to the choice of information platforms and the environment for the explication of contextual knowledge. Selecting tools, the authors have adhered to the principle of source accessibility to a wide circle of researchers.

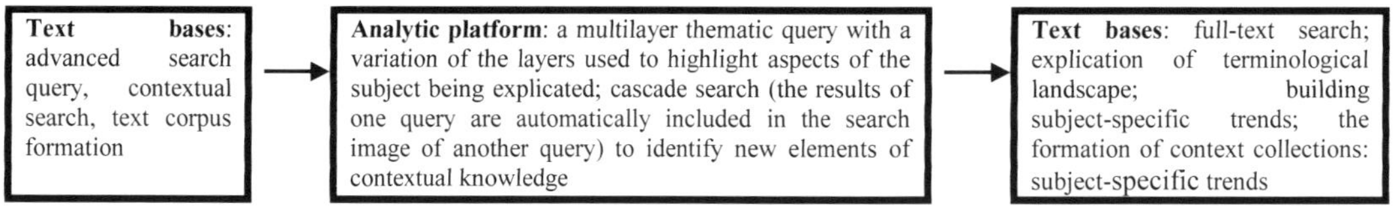

Figure 1. Phases of identifying and analyzing contextual knowledge in practice

The first phase of the approach involves the formation of search queries, the terminological core and collections of text materials (thematic collections) relevant to the interdisciplinary direction of scientific research. Thematic collections are formed by performing a sequential iteration of search queries. The second and the third phases of the approach reflect the sequence of steps from the allocation and explication of primary contexts to the construction of subject-thematic trends as a result of repeated thematic queries in previously explicated arrays of text materials.

In parallel with the main process, the identification and formation of a qualitatively new type of contextual knowledge (namely thematic collections of full-text queries) take place. Collections can simultaneously be used both as ready-made thematic knowledge (context), expanding the composition of the information resources of the electronic library, and as a user tool for creating and developing similar collections. In conducting the study and presentation of the results of "The gamification in the main spheres of digital society" pilot study, the full range of the above-mentioned information sources and Voyant-Tools research information environment was used.

3. GAMIFICATION PILOT STUDY

To assess the dynamics of research interest in gamification technology, the authors searched and selected scientific publications from the information resources ScienceDirect, Google Scholar (for English), and CyberLeninka, Google Scholar, eLibrary (for Russian sources). The scientific papers corpus obtained were found by the "gamification" search query, and then selected by the expert method according to the attribute "relevance of the subject area of research."

The dynamics study of the terminological landscape development has allowed us to identify trends and connections which are inherent in the contextual knowledge in the interdisciplinary scientific area considered. To track the use of term-concepts close to the term-concept 'gamification' and to construct subject-specific trends, the identification task has required the contextual search of relevant publications in each year separately. The search has been carried out based on the materials published from 2010 to 2019. On the whole, our results have confirmed the conclusions of the previous research that scientific articles on gamification have appeared in the scientific discourse since 2010 [Hamari, et al., 2014; Vanolo A., 2018; Harviainen J. T., Hassan L., 2019; Koivisto, J, Hamari, J., 2019]. The search results for the period previous to 2013 are characterized by single publications in both Russian and World scientific spaces and disaffect the overall view. The number of papers for the period from 2010 to 2012 is insignificant, therefore, the data were not included in the general statistics. The Media search results (via Integrum) from 2013 to 2019 have also demonstrated an annual increase of "The gamification in the main spheres of digital society" topic interest.

The analysis of the data allowed us to make the following conclusions: the number of scientific publications on gamification in the world has been increasing annually since 2010; the dynamics of growth in the number of Russian scientific publications on this topic shows a two-year delay. However, in general, the dynamics correspond to global scientific trends. Based on the application of Phase 3 (Fig. 1), the evolution of the terminology base being formed was predicted. Methods implement text mining analysis on the unstructured or semi-structured data processing and handling to construct subject-specific trends "by identifying relevant words and relationships in order to categorize or draw conclusions" [Pejic-Bacha, M., et al., 2020].

The text mining analysis of English scientific gamification discourse was executed, using Voyant-Tools software (https://voyant-tools.org/). The first pre-processing step was to collect the text array extracted from the full-text database of scientific information Science Direct, 2013-2019, (Fig. 1, Phase 1). The second step was to search, assess, exclude, and explicate the papers relevant to "The gamification in the main spheres of digital society" topic followed by analytic processing to extract relative term-concepts (Fig. 1, Phase 2). There were 275 text sets obtained. To analyze the text sets, a search of collocations with Voyant-Tools has been applied on the base of 'gamification' term-concept with the text context size limited by 11 words at the left and at the right from the key term. The limitation selected allows taking into account and considering as a solid context at least neighboring sentences into texts. As a result of the collocation analyses, semantic groups and relative term-concepts have been obtained. Semantic groups are Economy, Education / Science, Technology, Game Mechanisms, City, and others. The most significant relative term-concepts identified are indicated in descending order of the absolute frequency of collocation occurrences for all text set.

In addition, term-concepts: 'health', 'business', 'engineering', 'participation', 'industry 4.0', 'computing', 'energy', 'transport' have been extracted. These terms were found only in the last two- or three-years papers' sets. However, the appearance of that key words' cluster let us draw a conclusion gradual gamification invasion in different branches of social and business human activity. The analysis has identified the main subject areas and spheres of application of gamification as rule on the base of digital technologies. This fact could be unambiguously interpreted as interdisciplinarity. The list of subject areas is stable throughout the studied time interval. The leaders in the frequency of publications are Education, Economics, Organization and Management, Sociology. Depending on the year, the rest occupy different positions in the frequency list. With regard to the contexts of using gamification, the analysis has revealed four directions, in which the growth of not only scientific, but also media discourse, both in the world and in Russia, is especially noticeable. They are urban planning, e-government, e-participation, and e-learning. The construction of subject-specific trends demonstrates the methods suggested on the base of three term-concepts – 'motivation', 'engagement', and 'communication' included in the "Game mechanisms" semantic group in corresponding with Phase 2 (Fig. 1). To compare the common and particular dynamics, the graph of research interest in the gamification topic (the gamification graph) has been added (Figure 2).

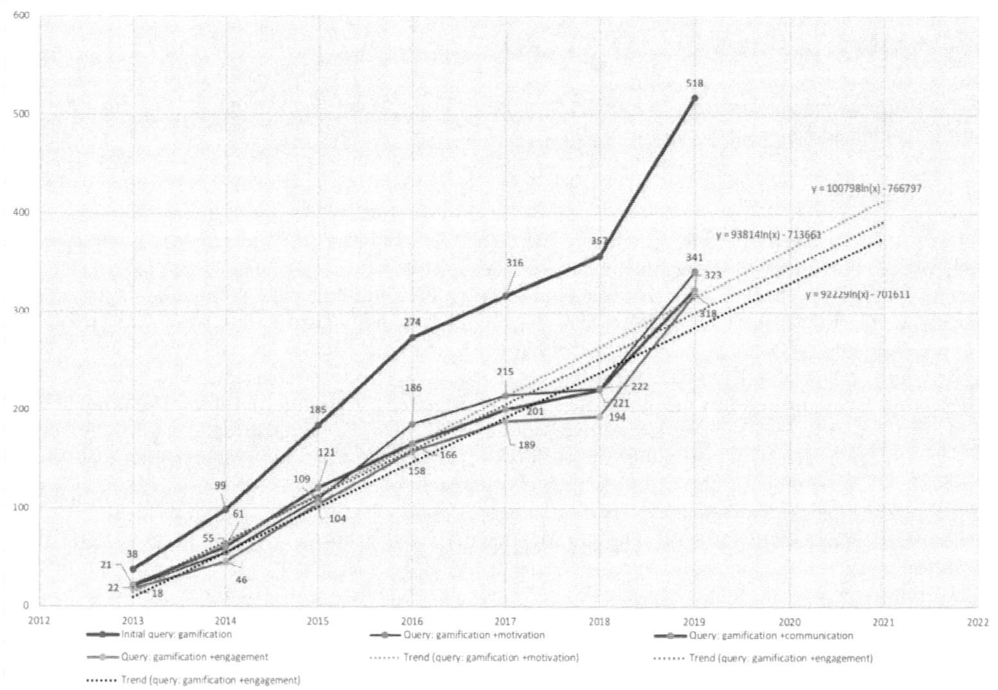

Figure 2. Trends on three relative term-concepts in comparison with the dynamics of 'gamification' as such

Trends on the three identified relative term-concepts ('motivation', 'engagement', 'communication') related to the "Game mechanisms" semantic group have been proving that the study of the mechanics of gamification will continue to be of scientific interest. Moreover, the "gamification as the motivational mechanisms" topic will not lose its significance, the interest in the "gamification as engagement mechanisms" as well as "gamification as communicational mechanisms" topics are expected to continue increasing. Testing the thesaurus of the gamification interdisciplinary area on the updated data of 2019 and data of 2020 will confirm or refute the previously obtained prediction and, consequently, the stability of the results of the proposed approach.

4. CONCLUSIONS

To sum up, the study demonstrates the following results: the use of the Synthetic technique allowed us to identify the interdisciplinarity of the direction of scientific research "gamification"; the correlation amongst the dynamics of research interest in topics related to gamification in Russian and World discourse has been found; reference-term concepts of a terminological base of "The gamification in the main spheres of digital society" interdisciplinary research area has been identified; Russian scientific discourse depends on the official state environment - the subject of scientific publications reflects the emergence of various governance initiatives; the main contexts have been identified; trends reflected the dynamics of the development of the interdisciplinary area have been constructed. Further research involves the construction of interdisciplinary thesaurus as ontology with semantic characteristics that define the relationship (synonymy, hierarchy, association) among term-concepts, as well as, attributes of term-concepts.

ACKNOWLEDGEMENT

The reported study is funded by RFBR according to the research project "The integrated approach elaboration to the analysis of the terminological base of the developing interdisciplinary research in distributed network environment" № 18-011-00923, 2018-2020.

REFERENCES

Abramo, G., D'Angelo, C.A., Zhang, L., 2018. A comparison of two approaches for measuring interdisciplinary research output: The disciplinary diversity of authors vs the disciplinary diversity of the reference list. *In Journal of Informetrics*, Vol. 12, No. 4, pp. 1182-1193. DOI: 10.1016/j.joi.2018.09.001

Biondia, L., Demartinia, P., Marchegiania, L., Marchioria, M., Piberb, M., 2020. Understanding orchestrated participatory cultural initiatives: Mapping the dynamics of governance and participation. *In Cities*, Vol. 96, 102459. DOI: 10.1016/j.cities.2019.102459

Carusi, C., Bianchi, G., 2020. A look at interdisciplinarity using bipartite scholar/journal networks. I*n Scientometrics*, No. 122, pp. 867–894. DOI:10.1007/s11192-019-03309-3

Hamari, J., Hassan, L., Dias, A. 2018. Gamification, quantied-self or social net- working? Matching users' goals with motivational technology. *In User Modeling and User-Adapted Interaction*, Vol. 28, No. 1, pp. 35–74. DOI:10.1007/s11257-018-9200-2

Hamari, J., Koivisto, J., Sarsa, H., 2014. Does Gamification Work? — A Literature Review of Empirical Studies on Gamification. *Proceedings of the 2014 47th Hawaii International Conference on System Sciences (HICSS '14)*. IEEE Computer Society, Washington, DC, USA, pp. 3025-3034. DOI: 10.1109/HICSS.2014.377

Harviainen, J. T., Hassan, L., 2019. Governmental Service Gamification: Central Principles. *In International Journal of Innovation in the Digital Economy*, Vol. 10, No. 3, pp. 1-12. DOI: 10.4018/IJIDE.2019070101

Hassan, L., Hamari, J., 2019. Gamification of E-Participation: A Literature Review. *Proceedings of 52nd Hawaii International Conference on System Sciences (HICSS'52)*. At Maui HI, USA, pp. 3077-3086.

Jimenez-Marquez, J. L., Gonzalez-Carrasco, I., Lopez-Cuadrado, J. L., Ruiz-Mezcua, B., 2019. Towards a big data framework for analyzing social media contente. *In International Journal of Information Management*, Vol. 44, pp. 1–12. DOI: 10.1016/j.ijinfomgt.2018.09.003.

Koivisto, J, Hamari, J., 2019. The rise of motivational information systems: A review of gamification research. *In International Journal of Information Management*, Vol. 45, pp. 191-210. DOI: 10.1016/j.ijinfomgt.2018.10.013

Kononova, O., Prokudin, D., 2018. Synthetic Method in Interdisciplinary Terminological Landscape Research of Digital Economy. *In SHS Web Conf.*, Vol. 507, 01082. DOI: 10.1051/shsconf/20185001082

Okamura, K., 2019. Interdisciplinarity revisited: evidence for research impact and dynamism. *In Palgrave Communication*, Vol. 5, 141. DOI: 10.1057/s41599-019-0352-4

Paré, G., Trudel, M. C., Jaana, M., Kitsiou, S., 2015. Synthesizing information systems knowledge: A typology of literature reviews. *In Information & Management*, Vol. 52, No. 2, pp. 183–199. DOI: 10.1016/j.im.2014.08.008

Pejic-Bacha, M., Bertoncelb, T., Meškob, M., Krstićc, Ž, 2020. Text mining of industry 4 job advertisements *in International Journal of Information Management*, Vol. 50, pp. 416–431. DOI: 10.1016/j.ijinfomgt.2019.07.014

Piciocchi, C, Martinelli, L., 2016. The change of definitions in a multidisciplinary landscape: the case of human embryo and preembryo identification. *In Croatian Medical Journal*, Vol. 57, No. 5, pp. 510-515. DOI:10.3325/cmj.2016.57.510

Purwandari, B., Sutoyo, M.A.H., Mishbah, M., Dzulfikar, M.F., 2019. Gamification in e-Government: A Systematic Literature Review. *Fourth International Conference on Informatics and Computing (ICIC)*. Semarang, Indonesia, pp. 1-5. DOI: 10.1109/ICIC47613.2019.8985769

Raimbault, J., 2019. Exploration of an interdisciplinary scientific landscape. *In Scientometrics*, Vol. 119, No. 2, pp. 617-641. DOI: 10.1007/s11192-019-03090-3

Vanolo, A., 2018. Cities and the politics of Gamification. *In Cities*, Vol. 74, pp. 20-326. DOI: 10.1016/j.cities.2017.12.021

ESTIMATING THE MONETARY BENEFITS OF TELEREHABILITATION IN THE COUNTRYSIDE – CASE OF INTRODUCTION OF TELE-HOMECARE

Päivi Kekkonen[1], Arto Reiman[1], Pirjo Lappalainen[2], Marika Tuiskunen[2] and Kirsi Jokinen[2]
[1]*Industrial Engineering and Management, University of Oulu, P.O. Box 4610, 90014 University of Oulu, Finland*
[2]*Social Services and Rehabilitation, Oulu University of Applied Sciences, P.O. Box 222, 90101 Oulu, Finland*

ABSTRACT

Digitalization provides new solutions for health and welfare services. In cases where the customer has a long distance to reach the face-to-face services or has other limitations related to mobility, telerehabilitation can be used to provide the needed services for the customer. This study presents a tele-homecare service introduced in a municipal health and welfare services provider for the elderly. The cost saving potential of tele-homecare service as compared to traditional homecare service is a key interest. A categorization of costs in cases of traditional and tele-homecare is presented and further effects of tele-homecare in terms of costs are discussed. The case study is a part of an on-going project, the aim of which is to provide information that can be utilized in making well-grounded decisions on introducing telerehabilitation services that take into account the special needs and characteristics of rural areas.

KEYWORDS

Demographic Change, Cost Accounting, Digitalization of Services, Tele-Homecare, Telerehabilitation

1. INTRODUCTION

Global megatrends, such as digitalization, aging population and the current economic situation throughout Europe have forced the nations to develop cost-efficient solutions and practices in healthcare. Different telemedicine practices have been introduced through the development of information and communication technologies (ICT) during the 2000s', yet until recent years the mobilization of such solutions has been rather modest. (Dorsey & Topol, 2020) However, the utilization of ICT in facilitating remote work has expanded in 2020 due to the global crisis as a consequence to the COVID -19 virus (see e.g. Heymann and Shindo, 2020; Hollander and Carr, 2020).

In this study we focus telerehabilitation in the countryside in northern Finland. Our case studies on telerehabilitation are performed in sparsely populated areas where long distances and aging population are typical. In practice, our target groups fit well to a more general definition by Selzler et al (2018) who bring out in their review that there are people living in such rural areas who need rehabilitation services but who have either physical or social limitations, or both, related to mobility. In our cases, examples of such people are elderly living on their own, disabled people, and others, both young and old, who are at risk of exclusion socially and from the job market. Both practitioners and decision makers at our focus areas have expressed the need for low threshold rehabilitation services among these target groups.

Telerehabilitation means providing rehabilitation with the use of different telecommunication networks and ICT solutions. Telerehabilitation that can be called or referred as to e-rehabilitation, virtual rehabilitation, telehealth, telepractice or teletreatment is meant to facilitate rehabilitation through technology (Tousignant et al., 2015). Telerehabilitation is a process that provides equal access to the necessary services for the inhabitants of sparsely populated areas, thus responding not only to the social and health care needs, but also on those related to wider societal perspective (Tousignant et al., 2015).

In our ongoing research and development project, the aim is to introduce new telerehabilitation practices in a municipal target organization and test these practices in real-life rehabilitation contexts (Kekkonen et al. 2019). Telerehabilitation practices are examined from the viewpoints of an individual taking part in the rehabilitation, the rehabilitation service provider and their employees, and the municipalities responsible for offering rehabilitation services. Testing of new telerehabilitation practices include an examination focusing on their costs and benefits on monetary terms, contributing thus to an ongoing scientific debate on the economic aspects related to healthcare (Hill, 2010, Tousignant et al., 2015). Our economic analysis is based on the cost-benefit analysis method presented by Oxenburgh and Marlow (2005) and in this article we present the categorization of the costs related to telerehabilitation and calculate different scenarios for those cost elements in which we consider variation exists.

The article continues with a presentation of a study setting involving tele-homecare service. The results section consists of a calculation comparing the costs of the tele-homecare and traditional homecare. The approximations used in the calculation, its validity and limitations of the study are presented in the discussion section together with future research interests on the theme. In the conclusions the results are wrapped up with notions related to the wider perspective of the role and increase of tele-healthcare solutions in the future.

2. STUDY SETTING

Target organization of this study is a municipal health and welfare services provider for the elderly. The organization operates in North-Eastern Finland and offers services to a population of approximately 15 000. According to an internal population forecast by the municipality the amount of the elderly people (aged 75 years and above) in the population of the municipality is estimated to increase from the current approximately 1900 individuals to 2700 by the year 2030 and further to 3200 by the year 2040. Characteristic to the area are also long distances and a minor share of the population living in remote locations of up to 60 kilometers from the center of the municipality.

In this study, tele-homecare services provided by the target organization are examined as an example of introducing remote health and welfare service for the elderly. In the year 2018 homecare services were provided for 240 customers in total. The introduction of tele-homecare services was initiated in the target organization in 2019. The data used in the following calculations is based on an interview carried out with the homecare service manager of the target organization and further updates carried out by e-mail concerning the figures used for calculation. Approximations by the researchers are used to supplement the data provided the target organization as described in the following section.

3. RESULTS

A calculation of costs in cases of traditional and tele-homecare services is presented in Table 1. The table includes columns for costs targeted for both the municipal service provider and the customer. The rows include different categories of costs identified earlier in this project together with the representatives of target organizations (Kekkonen et al. 2019). The calculation is carried out with following estimates:

The service in the target organization was initiated by recruiting and training three employees to provide the tele-homecare service. If their daily work time is not filled by tele-home visits, they also do traditional homecare work. In daily work the actual work time of traditional and tele-homecare visits was estimated to be the same and thus the direct work costs similar. The tele-homecare was not viewed to call for more planning or preparation on behalf of the employee and this also does not produce a difference between the work costs of traditional and tele-mediated method.

In the calculation of costs in following categories, an amount of 25 customers was used. This amount of customers was estimated to fill the daily work time of tele-homecare service employee. The Daily amount of visits for the traditional home-care used in the calculation is three visits. The amount of 25 customers could not be cared for with the same employee work costs in traditional home care with this amount of visits, although this is assumed in this calculation. Three daily visits for each of the 25 customers in the traditional homecare during one month would add up to 2250 visits in total.

The biggest difference, in terms of the costs between traditional and tele homecare, is the travel costs. These are highly affected by the location of the homes of the customers. In case of our target organization, the distance between the customer and the homecare services can span between 0 km to 60 km. Here an average distance of 1 kilometer for the home of the customer was used, since most of the customers live in the center of the municipality. A two-way trip to the home of the customer and back to the workplace was assumed, although in reality the routing is something else based on the locations of the customers. With a short average distance this should not contribute to a major error. The travel costs are dependent on the transportation method of the employee. In this case the travel costs were calculated using the current national mileage allowance. In addition to actual cost of travelling, also the work time used for the travelling needs to be considered. This was estimated by using the average travel speed corresponding to city area (40 km/h) for the short distances used in the calculation. An additional time of 6 minutes for the transitions from/to the vehicle to/from inside of the building for each travel leg was added.

In terms of customer fees the target organization had made a decision of offering the tele-homecare service for the customers for a price that is 10% lower than the traditional homecare service customer fee. The actual individual customer fee is determined based on the income of the customer, and the value of 200 euros per month for each individual customer used in the calculation is a mean value based on the information from the target organization.

The costs related to ICT of tele-mediated solution can be divided to equipment and telecommunications costs. In the studied case, the telecommunications costs are included in the leasing price of the ICT equipment, which are the monthly fees of the customer terminals and the employee license for the software.

The calculation also aims to take into account the ICT costs related to the needed equipment and telecommunications start up, and costs related to the introduction of telerehabilitation practices. The calculation includes one-time purchase costs of the system and additional equipment such as needed headsets and web-cameras for the employees. Also training of the employees through user orientation to the ICT system used in the service is taken into account. The maintenance and support costs of the customer terminals are included in the leasing costs of the equipment and thus the maintenance and support costs include only the IT maintenance and support of target organization for the employee terminal.

The total cost of both methods based of the aforementioned data is presented on the bottom line of Table 1. The customer fees can be treated as an income for the municipality. With the aforementioned figures the calculation of costs already for one month favors the tele-homecare instead of traditional homecare. If the daily amount of visits in case of traditional homecare is decreased from the three visits used in the calculation to two visits, tele-homecare becomes profitable after two months.

Table 1. Calculation of costs related to traditional and tele-homecare. The figures are monthly costs, except for those that are marked with an asterisk (*), which are one-time purchases. The figures are presented in euros

Cost categories	Traditional homecare		Tele-homecare	
	Municipality	Customer	Municipality	Customer
Work costs	6469		6469	
Travel costs				
- direct	1935			
- work time used for travelling	7824			
Client fees		5000		4500
ICT costs			1285	
Costs related to introduction of tele-homecare				
- purchases and technical realization			455*	
- introduction			5208*	
- user orientation			647*	
- maintenance and support			67	
Total cost	16228	5000	14130	4500
Total cost for municipality	11228		9630	

4. DISCUSSION

As a limitation for the above presented calculation it must be noticed that it is based on a single case in a single organization and thus the results are not necessarily generalizable to other contexts. In addition, approximations were used in several cost categories, due to the fact that not all figures were not obtainable at the time of the calculation. Most noticeable limitations of the presented calculation according to authors are following:

The costs related to the introduction of telerehabilitation practices are often hard to estimate, and thus are often omitted in calculations (McLean et al., 2013, Tousignant et al., 2015). These costs include definition and design, purchases and technical realization, introduction, user orientation and maintenance and support. In this case the definition of the need and design of the introduced system was realized over a longer time period as a part of normal development activities of the organization and the services it offers for its customers, and was thus not considered in the calculation. However, it can be estimated to constitute a significant figure. The calculation takes into account the purchases and technical realization, introduction, user orientation and maintenance of the ICT system. The considered user orientation, however, only covers the one-time initial user orientation at the start-up of the service and not the familiarization for upcoming employees.

In addition, the introduction of a new service takes time and the amount of customers is likely to increase gradually through the marketing and information shared by the organization to potential customers. The gradual increase of the amount of customers was not included in the calculation but instead an assumption of introduction of the service to 25 customers straight away was made. In reality finding the suitable customers calls for work on behalf of the employees in informing and advertising the service to potential customers as well as assessing their suitability for the service in terms of the evaluation of their performance ability.

As seen in the calculation, the travel costs in the traditional service are a dominant source of costs. These are highly dependent on the locations of the homes of the customers at one time and the routing of the employees visiting the customers. This therefore constitutes a significant source of uncertainty in the calculation through the used approximations. An additional bonus in favor of the introduction of telerehabilitation practices is that it also contributes to environmental sustainability by reducing carbon dioxide emissions through decreased need for travelling. Especially in today's situation that calls for actions that can have an effect on climate change this can be viewed as an important benefit.

The need for assistance in using the telerehabilitation equipment was also identified in earlier work (Kekkonen et al. 2019). An e-assistant that aids the client with the remote technology could be an employee of homecare or technical services, or even a family member. In our case, there was no identified need to an e-assistant other than the homecare service employee. Also identified in possible sources cost categories related to traditional rehabilitation is the loss of earnings on behalf of the customer in using the service due to the time reserved by the use. However, for the elderly customers the loss of earnings due to the use of health and welfare services is also not applicable.

The effectiveness of telerehabilitation as compared to traditional rehabilitation is an important issue to be considered. Obviously, the decision on choosing the appropriate service for each individual customer is important. This calls for the expertise of the rehabilitation professionals in terms of evaluating the performance ability of the potential customer. Also, in reality it might be that a hybrid solution including both tele- and traditional rehabilitation could be a suitable solution for many customers. In addition to the abilities and condition of the elderly customer, also the motivation of the customer to use the equipment (Early et al., 2017, McLean et al., 2013) and the needs for customer support and employee attitudes should be taken into consideration and studied further (McLean et al., 2013). These are aspects are considered in the on-going part of this project though the collection of experiences of both the customers and the employees during the introduction and early phases of telerehabilitation pilots, which will be reported later on.

The case studied in this article focuses on tele-homecare. Homecare cannot necessarily be considered rehabilitation, but it is an essential factor that has an effect on the performance ability of the elderly. Providing tele-homecare to those individuals that have the abilities that are needed for independent living, can aid them in retaining their performance ability in everyday life with a suitable amount of support through tele-homecare. This can be seen as a sign of social sustainability from the municipality to their inhabitants.

5. CONCLUSION

During this project we aim to develop both cost-effective and high-quality telerehabilitation services for rural areas. Our aim is to provide analyses that could be used as community level information when decisions are to be made on rehabilitation and telerehabilitation practices at countryside. The results of the calculation presented in this article speak for the economic viability of introduction of tele-homecare solution. Next steps include further calculations and sensitivity analyses to the data as well as similar cost analyses for smaller-scale telerehabilitation practices. Qualitative data on the experiences of both customers and homecare employees is also gathered and analysed during the project to study the functionality and usability of the solution considering both the perspectives of customers and employees. These results are expected to shed light in the discussion of the quality and effectiveness of tele-homecare solution.

ACKNOWLEDGEMENT

The project is funded by the European Agricultural Fund for Rural Development.

REFERENCES

Dorsey, E. R. and Topol, E. J., 2020. Digital medicine - Telemedicine 2020 and the next decade. *In The Lancet,* Vol. 395, No. 10227, pp. 859.

Early, F. et al, 2017. A Case Series of an Off-the-Shelf Online Health Resource with Integrated Nurse Coaching to Support Self-Management in COPD. *InInternational Journal of COPD*, Vol. 12, pp. 2955–2967.

Heymann, D.L. and Shindo, N., 2020. COVID-19: what is next for public health? *In The Lancet*, Vol. 395, No. 10224, pp. 542-545.

Hill, A., 2010. Telerehabilitation in Scotland: Current Initiatives and Recommendations for Future Development. *In International Journal of Telerehabilitation*, Vol. 2, No. 1, pp. 7–14.

Hollander, J.E. and Carr, B.G., 2020. Virtually perfcet? Telemedicine for Covid-19. *In New England Journal of Medicine*, DOI: 10.1056/NEJMp2003539.

Kekkonen, P. et al, 2019. Considerations on the Benefits of Using Telerehabilitation Practices in the Countryside. *In: Patrone Cotrim, T., Serranheira, F., Sousa, P., Hignett, S., Albolino, S. & Tartaglia, R. (eds). Building health and social care systems for the future: Demographic changes, digital age and human factors. 6th edition of the International Conference Healthcare Ergonomics and Patient Safety*, 3-5 July 2019, Lisbon, Portugal, pp. 59-63.

McLean, S. et al, 2013. The Impact of Telehealthcare on the Quality and Safety of Care: A Systematic Overview. *In PLoS ONE,* Vol. 8, No. 8 pp. e71238.

Oxenburgh, M., and Marlow, P., 2005. The Productivity Assessment Tool: Computer-Based Cost Benefit Analysis Model for the Economic Assessment of Occupational Health and Safety Interventions in the Workplace. *In Journal of Safety Research,* Vol. 36, No. 3, pp. 209–214.

Selzler, A.-M. et al, 2018. Telehealth Pulmonary Rehabilitation: A Review of the Literature and an Example of a Nationwide Initiative to Improve the Accessibility of Pulmonary Rehabilitation. *In Chronic Respiratory Disease*, Vol. 15, No. 1, pp. 41-47.

Tousignant, M. et al, 2015. Cost Analysis of In-Home Telerehabilitation for Post-Knee Arthroplasty. *In Journal of Medical Internet Research*, Vol. 17, No. 3, pp. e83.

DIGITAL PLATFORMS, AFFORDANCE, AND PUBLIC GOVERNABILITY

Leonid Smorgunov
St. Petersburg State University, 7/9 Universitetskaya emb., St. Petersburg, 199034, Russia

ABSTRACT

Public governability on digital platform is an affordance effect arising in network structures with a wide participation of citizens. Network platforms provide collaboration based on an institutional form of interaction that is more effective than competitive representation. The digital institutional platform provides principles of equality, indifference, reciprocity and autonomy. A participatory public administration based on cooperation assumes an appropriate technical platform, which should have some qualities of affordance, i.e. the ability to act as a mediator for this type of interaction. The technological component, expressed in the idea of the state as a platform, is characterized by the presence of affordances for cooperation. The technology of blockchain is studied as the example. Blockchain is oriented towards procedural justice, which expresses the technological affordances of cooperation. Procedural justice is ensured by the affordability of technology that is created by blockchain algorithms. The paper compares the corresponding problems of affordance.

KEYWORDS

Digital Platforms, Public Governability, Collaboration, Affordance, Blockchain

1. INTRODUCTION

The use of network forms of coordination in economics and politics, based on digital technologies, has questioned the traditional forms of governability associated with centralization, representation, feedback and maintaining equilibrium with the environment. It is possible to believe that digitalization generates a new form of governability by increasing the number of governance participants organized into network platforms, and that a governability is a network effect based on the ability of the digital system to afford procedural fair norms. Affordance is an essential feature of technical systems that guide people to use them (Neff et al., 2012).

In the scientific literature, the objective function of participatory governability has been fixed. Firstly, participatory public governance is used not just as a form of democracy development, but is a response to the need for governability arising in the conditions of differentiation of interests and growing conflict in society (Kübler et al., 2019). Secondly, participatory public administration in the form of networks arises as the need to ensure governability in the context of increasing the role of innovations in the public sphere (Gil-Garcia et al., 2018). Thirdly, governance networks that attach greater importance to citizen participation tend to create an affordance policy, the concept of which is more comprehensive, and emphasize aspects of technical usability (Santos, Faure, 2018). Participatory governability is formed in certain technoecology and is expressed in reaching consensus based on a set of affordances. The main theoretical question of this article is that public governability in the context of digitalization, along with other factors, is determined by the system of affordances, which make digital platforms relevant to the network idea of their use. The article describes the system of affordances and considers their manifestation based on the study of the digital platform "Active Citizen" (Moscow).

2. GOVERNMENT PLATFORM AND PARTICIPATORY GOVERNABILITY: TECHNOLOGY AND AFFORDANCE

In the first decade of the existence of electronic governments in the world (conditionally 1995-2005) they were organized into Internet portals. The portals are less democratic, than Internet platforms based on interactive Web 2.0 technology and relational affordances. If bureaucratic administration uses technology, then they contribute to the affordances of information by passing the signal from top to bottom. Public management is incentive-oriented, and technology provides effective resource savings. Public governance, focused on interaction and co-governance, requires participatory affordances, ensuring coordination and reciprocity.

2.1 Citizen Oriented Government Platforms

Currently, the functioning of e-government is only partially organized in Internet portals, i.e. complex electronic means that provide for the implementation of a number of government functions and services for citizens. Internet portals provide search and information acquisition, interaction of citizens and organizations with state authorities, holding events for citizens and organizations, and providing public services. Internet platforms are complex electronic tools that provide not only services, but the participation of citizens in the choice of public services and influencing the decision-making process (O'Reilly, 2010). If we use the direct meaning of the concept of platform as an aggregate of ICT 2.0, oriented to the use of a web application system on one server for interactivity and personal participation, modern public governance includes such technologies under the flag of "ability for collaboration". In this respect, electronic platforms are an open and technical means of accordance for interrelations.

E-government now has characteristics that promote democracy in the broadest sense of the word, including civic participation virtually in the day-to-day activities of the state and in the processes of providing public services. In this respect, e-government becomes the basis for the network interaction of citizens, associations of civil society and business with the state in various areas of public activity. At this stage, the importance of assessing the electronic participation of citizens through the diverse sites of such e-government. As Kay Erickson and Henry Vogt rightly write, new digital forms of policy and management include network-based inputs for organizing all government information and public services in accordance with the needs and interests of certain segments of the population. This approach from the standpoint of "one window" is built on the concept of self-service with the requirement for users to become more active and self-governing (Eriksson, Vogt, 2013). There are three main areas for studying platform-based public administration. One of them puts emphasis on the formation of a special ecology of interaction between platforms and human agents in the public administration system (Van Dijck et al., 2018). Here affordances are the relational characteristics of the emerging technoecology. The second direction indicates the significant role of algorithms and artificial intelligence in platform control processes (Gillespie, 2010). Considering algorithms as a specific system of norms, researchers pay attention to the coordinating function of algorithmic control. Accordingly, affordances are considered by them as properties of the structure and architecture of algorithmic control. The third area of research includes the role of companies producing digital public administration technologies in the scope of digital public administration (Gorwa, 2019).

Although the theme of affordances is subordinate to the political role of information companies, here too, the possibility of a democratic or authoritarian structural filling of algorithms and interfaces takes on its significance. Describing platforms and affordances, we will follow some integrated research strategy, emphasizing that the affordances of participatory governability are determined by all three conditions of digital public administration - technoecology, algorithms, and digitalization policies.

Platforms are technical and information conditions for increasing the self-organization of communities formed in networks. However, their quality is determined by certain conditions related to the orientation of the algorithms for the admission of interaction in the form of collaboration, i.e. the affordances of technology as a mediator, not as an intermediary. The difference between intermediaries and mediators, made by Bruno Latour with respect to mediating things [Latour, 2005], is that intermediaries are simple transfer structures between action agents, while mediators have their own agent binding policies, introducing a transformation into this connection. In this regard, platforms are mediators, manifesting their agent qualities through their performative functions. To perform these functions, they must possess some relational qualities that create a sociotechnical interaction ecology. To select the performance functions of digital technologies for public administration, we used the data obtained on the basis of the study of works that describe platform functions [Janowskia, 2019]. Analysis of different types of affordances allows you to correlate these functions, affordances and their location. The latter is conceptualized on the basis of two types of understanding of affordances: (1) as the qualities of technology; (2) as relational characteristics inherent in technoecology. A mixed source suggests that affordances are the result of both the qualities of technology and its involvement in the interaction of various socio-technical assemblies.

Table 1. The affordances of citizen oriented government platform

Performative functions	Affordances	Location
administer	normalize ability	algorithm
steer	programmability	algorithm
regulate	standardization	algorithm
serve	interoperability	mixed
engage	availability	technoecology
transform	ability to choose	technoecology
legitimize	identifiability	mixed
disclose	multimediality	mixed
monitor	persistence	mixed
participate	association ability	technoecology
empower	voice ability	mixed
learn	ability to share knowledge	mixed
coordinate	ability to stair a link	algorithm
create	ability to perceive new	mixed
collaborate	reciprocity	technoecology

In the table. 1 you can see the results of a conceptual analysis of the relationship between the performative functions of digital platforms, affordances and the space of their appearance. It is clear that the functions of administering, general management (steering) and regulation with the corresponding affordances appear as a result of the introduction of the necessary algorithms into digital public governance. Whereas the functions of engagement, transformation, participation and collaboration involve the formation of such assemblages of human and technological agents that give rise to the corresponding technoecology as a space for the formation of relational affordances. Other functions and affordances suggest a mixed co-way of appearance and perception.

2.2 Institutions of Affordance for Participatory Governability

Digitization of public administration is a process of transformation of culture, organization and relations of public authorities with business and society through the use of new digital technologies (big data, internet things, artificial intelligence). Understanding the digitalization process as a way to transform the public governance space is determined not only by an orientation towards greater sensitivity and accountability, but also by a citizen-oriented government organization.

Digitization of public administration is often understood as the process of using new ICTs and, in particular, electronic technologies to organize and ensure the effective functioning of the public sphere. Moreover, it is emphasized that digitalization in the political sense is a way to expand the political forms of interaction between society and the state, making public governance collaborative. At the same time, it is important to note that citizen participation contributes to the development of "liquid democracy" in local communities - when political actors choose and vote on important issues - and this indicates that this issue is beginning to be on the political agenda. This type of democracy allows not only direct participation in decision-making processes, but also creates the conditions under which the representation of interests takes on the character of "tied reputation" secured by participation in the co-production of political decisions.

The value of digitalization goes far beyond simple control engineering. The regulatory framework used by digital technology allows us to solve a number of problems arising from the crisis of representative democracy, accountability and control. Analysis of the blockchain technology shows that it creates the affordances for a pure procedural justice, providing the possibility of an honest solution of public issues (Smorgunov, 2018). This example demonstrates the enormous possibilities of digitization of governance processes for the formation of its new organization. The previous choice was based on minimizing the costs of interdependence (external costs and transaction costs), while public governability was based on the affordances of the system to ensure security and be sensitive to basic interests. Digitalization does not diminish these requirements, but goes further, providing governability as mediator through a technological algorithm and collaborative technoecology. Governability as a network effect of digitalization of public administration is based both on the number of possibilities to interact and on the inclination to just public communication. It is supported by a procedure of fair consensus based on the affordance capacities of blockchain algorithm for the institutions of reciprocity, equality, indifference and autonomous organization.

3. BLOCKCHAIN AFFORDANCES AND COLLABORATIVE GOVERNABILITY

Distributed data technology is gaining popularity in the economy and public policy. In the latter, it is used in the processes of voting, making decisions, determining agenda, policy evaluating, and other areas. The general belief of researchers is that the blockchain is not just a technology that increases the effects of economic production and political interaction, but is an institution that creates new affordances for the coordination of interactions.

3.1 Blockchain Protocols and Rules of Justice

As an example, confirming the presence in the protocols of digital technology norm, providing a fair consensus, we give the blockchain protocols. Currently, the important conditions for the technical support of fairness of interactions and decisions in the networks of the distributed register are the various algorithms included in the protocols and ensure the normal operation of mining. We turn here to some of them. Mining is the procedure for selecting a leader who has solved the task of agreeing the entries to the network in the form of another block that is recognized as valid for continuing the blockchain. Primary research on ontological questions of blockchain (philosophical, political, sociological) formed the idea of a transition from an institutional governance architecture with representation and hierarchy (centralism), to a procedural one, based on a humanitarian and technical platform of networked cooperation with free identification organized by anarchy, and distributed knowledge. In this respect, the question was raised whether the blockchain system is a complex system with nonlinear constraints that create affordances for the algorithmization of control and operation within it, or if we can speak about a complex but algorithmic blockchain-governance.

For this, certain validation procedures are formed. In the Bitcoin system, such a confirmation procedure was the Proof of Work, which was based on the principle of choosing a leader by the criterion of the speed of solving the task of forming the next block. For the formation of the next block leader (miner) received a reward in the form of cryptocurrency. Since the formation task was voluminous, it required the use of large computer capacities and, consequently, a lot of electricity. This system has a number of problems of economic, environmental and procedural properties. One of the procedural problems is related to the possibility of forming a monopoly (51% of the combined miners) within a distributed network, which makes decisions in its favor. Although this is unlikely due to the possibility of confronting a monopoly on the output of honest users, it is not impossible. Therefore, other proof systems arose on other grounds. Proof on the basis of the rate (Proof of Stake) is constructed in proportion to the rate that everyone owns in accordance with the current blockchain register (Ethereum, Cardano). The main problem on the basis of PoS is the ability to imitate the process of choosing leaders in favor of one side. According to the developers of the improved Ourobokos blockchain proof protocol of the Cardano type, their addition to the protocol contributes to the viability and persistence of honest transactions (Kiayias, 2017). Often, this system is supplemented by methods for ensuring resiliency based on solving the Byzantine problem (EOSIO, BOScoin): security is achieved if two thirds of validators in the system are honest.

The question arises: what does the blockchain technology provide for relationships between people? Partnership or collaboration? Of course, at first glance, partnership is a collaboration. Often these terms are used interchangeably. Meanwhile, the practice of partnership and collaboration allows us to divide the content of these forms of interaction and find their distinctive features. Differences between these terms should be considered when comparing contexts in which these relationships occur. Somewhere the main dividing line is the difference between "being together" (being partners) and "acting together" (collaborating) (Carnwell, Carson, 2008). For a clearer separation of these concepts, we can probably say that a partnership is a joint activity based on distributed (often equal) rights and duties aimed at achieving common goals, whereas collaboration is a joint activity that proceeds from the unconditional desire of the interacting parties to work together to achieve common interests. The partnership is loaded with external legal conditions for joint activities, and collaboration implies an internal willingness to act together, subject to mutual assistance and responsibility.

3.2 Affordances of "Active Citizen" Platform

One of the important areas of use of the blockchain is the "Active Citizen" platform, which was initiated in Moscow (Russia) to involve citizens in the choice of prioritized areas for the development of urban life in the capital, and to address topical current issues. This platform is part of the system of interaction between the city authorities and citizens, called system of joint decisions "Together". The joint decision system, formed by the mayor of Moscow for citizens' participation in the affairs of the city, includes a number of platforms related to the open government, open data, government services, as well as platforms for organizing the direct participation of citizens in public policy.

The "Active Citizen" is a platform for conducting open referendums in electronic form, created on the initiative of the Moscow Government in 2014. The project allows people to conduct citywide and local voting on a wide range of topics. Every week, Muscovites are invited to discuss important issues for the city. On the platform, a habitant needs to register, and to participate in a local vote, and must specify his address. For the passage of each vote, the participant is awarded points. Having gained 1000 points, he attains the status of "Active Citizen" and the opportunity to exchange them for city services (parking hours, visits to theaters and museums) or useful souvenirs. Bonus points can be earned also if he visits the application more often, invites friends, and shares information about the passed votes in social networks.

To solve the task of ensuring the transparency of the project, a number of tools have been implemented that allow users to monitor the progress of voting and monitor the reliability of the results obtained. In particular, each user who participated in the voting can: check the correctness of recording their vote; in online mode, monitor the overall dynamics of voting results. For these purposes, anyone can install a special program based on the system of the Ethereum, that is, everyone can become a member of the network of blockchain. This program allows network participants to see in real time those questions which have passed, or are still being voted on, as well as the appearance of new votes. The system allows anyone to become a member of the blockchain network not only as a resident of Moscow, but also as an organization. Blockchain, as indicated by the organizers of the program, affords for a number of additional performative functions: check the chronology of the appearance of votes and confirm their uniqueness; control the distribution of votes on issues; see the voices of real people (personal data is encrypted).

In 2018, this system in Moscow offered the use of multi-apartment housing blocks for citizens to vote. For this purpose, the "Electronic House" project is being implemented. This project is based on the affordance of Ethereum to form the decentralized autonomous organizations (DAO). In these last two cases of using blockchain technology to monitor the progress of voting and to make decisions, a number of characteristics of distributed network affordances that are related to the problem of procedural justice are seen. First of all, this is the honesty of the conditions of the emerging consensus, determined by the technological characteristics of distributed networks, and a small degree of identification in connection with the cryptographic protocols of recording and presenting users. Secondly, it is the acceptance of the terms of interaction that ensure the implementation of reciprocity affordance for the exchange of goods, decisions, knowledge and supervision. In this respect, the blockchain is a platform of collaboration for reciprocal benefits, whether it concerns finances, things, norms or regulation. Fair interaction affordances, together with a reciprocity, create a form of procedural justice in which incentives for genuine collaboration arise.

4. CONCLUSION

Recently, the concept of "co-creation" and "co-production" has been actively used in political science, public administration, and sociology as an innovation. Initially, this concept established a new attitude to the provision of public services and was directed against the market approach to the organization of this activity (Gil-Garcia, 2018). New breath she acquired in the development of the movement for digital governance. The concept of "co-production" is common in the study of public policy in general. Co-production is a new position for democratic public policy in conditions of uncertainty and complexity.

Some researchers focused on presenting research materials related to "governing through collaboration", "co-creation" and "co-production" of public policy not only on the above aspects of the topic, but also on the impact of collaboration in public policy that would correspond to sustainable and inclusive development (Krenjova, Raudla, 2017). In this respect, a distinction is made between co-production based on technological intermediaries and co-production based on a technological affordance for partnership and collaboration. The latter takes the form of participation on the basis of identification with the objectives of public programs and responsibility for their implementation (O'Brien et al., 2017).

New digital public administration platforms ensure co-production in public policy with such basic norms that make citizen participation open, fair and reasonable. On this basis, participatory governability will mean joint action to develop society, when the network effect of collaboration generates the value of participation. In this case, the participatory governance is the higher, the more technology affords communication. Of course, there are many challenges and threats in this way of introducing digital affordances into the public sphere. However, they are rather temporary inconsistencies in the process of formation of modern culture, organization and forms of interaction provided by digitalization.

ACKNOWLEDGEMENT

This work was supported with a grant from the Russian Science Foundation (grant 19-18-00210 "Political ontology of digitalization: Study of institutional bases for digital forms of governability").

REFERENCES

Carnwell, R. and Carson A., 2008. The Concepts of Partnership and Collaboration. *Effective Practice in Health, Social Care and Criminal Justice: A Partnership Approach.* 2nd ed. Ed. by R. Carnwell, J. Buchanan. Open Universities Press, Maidenhead, USA, pp. 3-21.

Eriksson, K. and Vogt, H., 2013. On self-service democracy: Configurations of individualizing governance and self-directed citizenship. *European Journal of Social Theory*, Vol. 16, No 2, pp. 153-173.

Gil-Garcia, R. et al., 2018. Digital government and public management research: finding the crossroads. *Public Management Review*, Vol. 20, No 5, pp. 633-646.

Gillespie, T. 2010. The politics of "platforms". *New Media & Society*, Vol. 12, No 3, pp. 347–364.

Gorwa, R., 2019. What is platform governance? *Information, Communication & Society*, Vol. 22, No 6, pp. 854-871.

Janowskia, T. et al, 2019. Platform governance for sustainable development: Reshaping citizen administration relationships in the digital age. *Government Information Quarterly* [online], 1-49.

Kiayias, A. et al, 2017. Ouroboros: A Provably Secure Proof-of-Stake Blockchain Protocol. *Criptography ePrint Archive*, pp. 1-52.

Krenjova, J. and Raudla, R., 2017. Policy Diffusion at the Local Level: Participatory Budgeting in Estonia. *Urban Affairs Review*, Vol. 3, No 4, pp. 1-29.

Kübler, D. et al, 2019. Strengthen governability rather than deepen democracy: why local governments introduce participatory governance. *International Review of Administrative Sciences*, Vol. 0, No 0, 2019, pp. 1-18.

Neff, G. et al, 2012. Affordances, Technical Agency, and the Politics of Technologies of Cultural Production. *Journal of Broadcasting & Electronic Media*, Vol. 56, No 2, pp. 299-313.

O'Brien, D. et al, 2017. Uncharted Territoriality in Coproduction: The Motivations for 311 Reporting. *Journal of Public Administration Research and Theory*, Vol. 27, No 2, pp. 320-335.

O'Reilly, T., 2010. Government as a Platform. *Open Government: Collaboration, Transparency, and Participation in Practice.* O'Reilly Media, Sebastopol, Calif., USA, pp. 11-40.

Santos, M. and Faure, A., 2018. Affordance is Power: Contradictions Between Communicational and Technical Dimensions of WhatsApp's End-to-End Encryption. *Social Media & Society,* July-September, [online], pp. 1–16.

Smorgunov, L., 2018. Blockchain and a Problem of Procedural Justice of Public Choice. *Digital Transformation and Global Society. Third International Conference, DTGS 2018, St. Petersburg, Russia, May 30 – June 2, 2018, Revised Selected Papers, Part I.* Springer International Publishing, Ham, Swizerland, p. 13-23.

Van Dijck, J. et al, 2018. The Platform Society: Public Values in a Connective World. Oxford University Press, New York, USA.

INDIVIDUAL'S INTENTION TO SUBSCRIBE TO FREEMIUM MUSIC STREAMING SERVICES: A CONCEPTUAL FRAMEWORK

Norshidah Mohamed[1] and Hanif Haghshenas[2]
[1]College of Business Administration, Prince Sultan University, P.O. Box 53073 Riyadh 11586, Kingdom of Saudi Arabia.
[2]Azman Hashim International Business School, Universiti Teknologi Malaysia, Jalan Sultan Yahya Petra, 54100 Kuala Lumpur, Malaysia

ABSTRACT

While the music industry continues to undergo through significant revolution, the last few years show that growth in freemium music streaming services continue to be noteworthy, in particular, in the American music industry. The research aspires to gain insights into individual's intention to subscribe to freemium music streaming services. This paper reports a research in progress. The research integrates the Theory of Reasoned Action, Dual Mediation Hypothesis, Motivation Theory, and Social Identity Theory to develop a conceptual framework toward explaining individual's intention to subscribe to freemium music streaming services.

KEYWORDS

Music Streaming, Freemium Music, Free Music, Purchase Intention, Attitude

1. INTRODUCTION

The Internet has brought about innovation that spans many information technological advances. It has shaped many industries. The music industry is one example that has experienced phenomenal transformation as a result of the Internet. To date, the industry is still going through a revolution. Despite notable music piracy issues, the Recording Industry Association of America recently reported that the American music industry's 2019 retail revenue was about $11.1 billion. This is an increase from $9.8 billion in 2018 and $8.8 billion in 2017. Streaming consumption surged from 75 percent in 2018 to 79 percent in 2019.

The notion of offering individuals with free music streaming services stems from the need of the industry to curtail music piracy, lowered sales attributable to piracy and decreased music rights holder revenue (Aguiar, 2017). Freemium business model is grounded on offering consumers with basic services as providers earn their revenue through advertisements. This is in anticipation that over time consumers will develop needs for advanced features and therefore turn to freemium services (Wagner et al. 2014).

While explaining digital music purchase intention, researchers in the past, have focused on determinants such as unauthorized downloading (Hampton-Sosa, 2017) and attitudes toward digital music services (Dörr et al. 2013; Wagner et al. 2014; Fernandes, T. Guerra, 2019). Anecdotal evidence shows that among theories that have been adopted in digital music services research include Theory of Planned Behavior (Dörr et al., 2013). Dual Mediation Hypothesis, (Wagner et al. 2014), and Technology Acceptance Model (Hampton-Sosa, 2017).

This research is different from past researches in that it builds on and integrates the Theory of Reasoned Action, Dual Mediation Hypothesis, Motivation Theory, and Social Identity Theory, to explain individual's intention to stream free music. The research significantly contributes to the literature through development of this new framework. From practical contributions standpoint, findings can aid music service provider in shaping their services to encourage potential subscription and discourage piracy. Hence, the research question sets out in this research: ***What are the determinants of individual's intention to subscribe to freemium music streaming services?***

This paper is organized into four sections. This section has introduced the research area. Section two discusses the literature review and related theories. The third section the paper presents the research propositions and conceptual framework. The last section concludes the paper.

2. LITERATURE REVIEW AND RELATED THEORIES

2.1 Theory of Reasoned Action

The Theory of Reasoned Action (TRA) (Fishbein & Ajzen, 1975; Ajzen & Fishbein, 1980) has been used to explain individual's behavior. The TRA (Figure 1) has been widely applied in various researches. More recently, it is evident in green IT (Mishra et. al. 2014) and water conservation for a lodging study (Untaru, 2016). Accordingly, the theory specifies that intention induces individual's behavior while his/her attitudes (affective reaction) and subjective norms determine the intention.

Subjective norm refers to an individual's perception of what his/her referent think he/she should engage in a behavior (Ajzen, 1991; Fishbein and Ajzen, 1975). Subjective norms have been theorized in several behavioral models from cognitive psychology including TRA (Fishbein and Ajzen, 1975) and the Theory of Planned Behaviour (TPB) in Ajzen (1991).

The phenomenon of interest in the present research is individual's intention to stream freemium music. In freemium music, individuals pay subscription to enjoy additional features of the music. In free music, individuals enjoy basic services with advertisements. The research proposes that the intention to stream freemium music is dependent on individual's attitude to stream free music and freemium music; free services is a precursor to freemium.

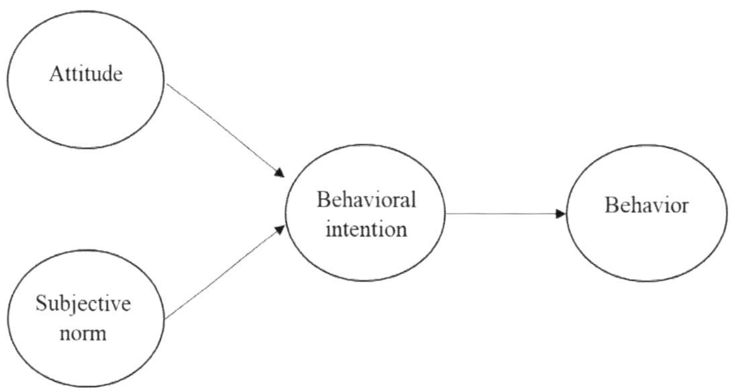

Figure 1. Theory of Reasoned Action

2.2 Dual Mediation Hypothesis Theory

The Dual Mediation Hypothesis (DMH) theory is traced to advertising literature (MacKenzie, Lutz, and Belch, 1986). The theory suggests a direct and indirect influence of attitude toward advertisement (A_{ad}) on attitude toward brand (A_b). The indirect influence is through brand cognition (C_b or perception). Further, attitude toward advertisement has indirect influence on purchase intentions (PI) through attitude toward brand.

Notably, the DMH has been used in investigating return to a website (Karson and Fisher, 2005a), online advertisement (Karson and Fisher, 2005b), website effectiveness (López and Ruiz, 2011), and purchase and use of games (Davis et al. 2013). Figure 2 shows the conceptual framework of the DMH.

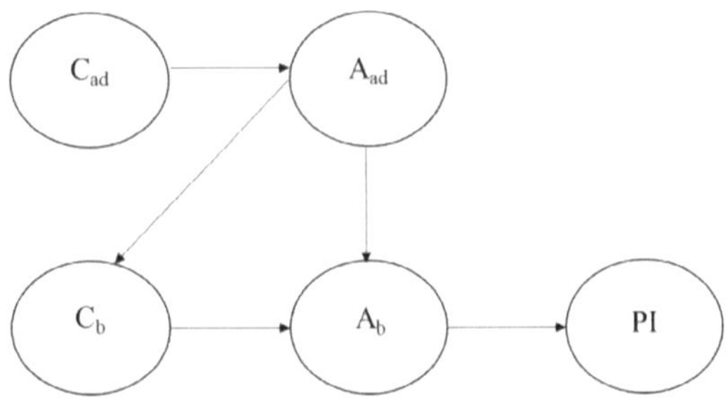

Figure 2. Dual Mediation Hypothesis

2.3 Motivation Theory

The present research builds on the hedonic motivation and utilitarian motivation theories. These theories are discussed further in this section.

Hedonic motivation is defined by Holbrook (1994) as intrinsic value which is derived from "appreciation of an experience for its own sake, apart from any other consequence that may result". Hedonic information systems concern leisure activities and fun aspect about the use. The context of hedonic information systems is home and personal rather than organization and job context (van der Heijden, 2004). Accordingly, in attaining a pleasurable experience, individuals often seek sensations on multiple sensory channels (Holbrook and Hirschman 1982). Therefore, hedonic motivation relates to sound, color, aesthetically appeal, visual layout, animated images etc.

This definition is not similar to perceived usefulness which is commonly identified as "the degree to which a person believes that using a particular system would enhance his or her job performance" (Davis, 1989). Hedonic motivation is also different from task completion concept because fun and playfulness are personal and subjective sources of perception about an intrinsic value (Babin, 1994). Hedonic motivation relates to psychological or emotional values (affective features of technology or intrinsic values).

Utilitarian motivation is formed as value, believed to be a driver of consumer's choice and preferences (Chiu et al., 2005). Value was initially and dominantly considered as unidimensional and economic-based consumer utilitarianism. Value in this regard was defined as a cognitive trade-off between benefits or performance (quality) and sacrifices as costs (or price) (Zeithaml, 1988). Mathwick et al. (2001) further divided utilitarian or extrinsic values into two dimensions: (i) efficiency/customer ROI (extrinsic-active value) and (ii) excellent/quality appeal (extrinsic -reactive value). This conceptualization has been confirmed in the context of online book and CD retailing (Wetzels, et al., 2009). Excellence was defined as service excellence and customer return on investment (ROI) were conceptualized as efficiency and economic values. In the context of mobile games, efficiency (convenience) of a game has been captured through communication characteristics such as game speed and accessibility, while the quality of a game has been captured through attractive characteristics such as sound quality, goal setting, and game options (Kim, et al., 2010).

In recent years, the application of hedonic and utilitarian motivation is evident in shopping goals (Chiu, et al., 2014) and in a shopping website López and Ruiz (2011).

2.4 Social Identity Theory

Social Identity Theory (SIT) suggests that individuals emphasize more on a shared social identity rather than a personal identity (O'Fallon and Butterfield, 2012). Individuals identify themselves in relation to their social groups in projecting a positive social identity (e.g. Tajfel, 1978; Tajfel and Turner, 1985).

SIT could also be specified as perceived fit with group identity (O'Fallon and Butterfield, 2012). SIT has been applied in fashion patronage behavior; people who keep up with fashion follow herding behavior (Evans, 1964; Gurel et al., 1972) and are prone to peer influence (McKintyre and Miller, 1992). More recently, SIT is evident in in application of digital data about veganism (Davis et al. 2019) and among online gamers (Liao, 2020). This research posits that individuals identify themselves with the image consistent with the group they belong to in regard to streaming music.

3. PROPOSITIONS AND CONCEPTUAL FRAMEWORK

Against this backdrop, the present research proposes that individual's attitude toward free music services is determined by cognition about free music. This comprises the hedonic, utilitarian and social identity factors. Subjective norm is also proposed to determine attitude toward free music services. Consequently, individual's attitude toward free music services and brand cognition about freemium services are posited to determine attitude toward freemium music services. However, this brand cognition is proposed to be determined by the brand price value. Individual's attitude toward freemium service determines the intention to purchase the services.

Thus, we postulate the following propositions and conceptual framework (Figure 3) in determining individual's intention to subscribe to freemium music services:

P1: Individual's attitude toward freemium music services is positively and significantly correlated to intention to subscribe to freemium music services.
P2: Individual's attitude toward free music services is positively and significantly correlated to attitude toward freemium music services.
P3: Individual's cognition about freemium music services is positively and significantly correlated to attitude toward freemium music services.
P4: Individual's perceived price value is positively and significantly correlated to freemium music services.
P5: Individual's need for escapism is positively and significantly correlated to his attitude toward free music services.
P6: Individual's need for enjoyment is positively and significantly correlated to his attitude toward free music services.
P7: Individual's need for entertainment is positively and significantly correlated to his attitude toward free music services.
P8: Individual's need for safe music streaming services is positively and significantly correlated to his attitude toward free music services.
P9: Individual's need for quality sound of music streaming services is positively and significantly correlated to his attitude toward free music services.
P10: Individual's need for accessible of streaming music services is positively and significantly correlated to his attitude toward free music services.
P11: Individual's subjective norm is positively and significantly correlated to his attitude toward free music services.
P12: Individual's need for perceived fit with his group is positively and significantly correlated to his attitude toward free music services.

4. CONCLUSION

The music industry continues to undergo through significant revolution. Despite this phenomenon, the American music industry, in particular, exhibits growth in freemium music streaming services over the last few years. The research aspires to gain insights into individual's intention to subscribe to freemium music streaming services. It aims at making a significant theoretical contribution to knowledge and practical contribution to knowledge application. This paper reports a research in progress. It demonstrates the integration of the Theory of Reasoned Action, Dual Mediation Hypothesis, Motivation Theory, and Social Identity Theory to develop a conceptual framework toward explaining individual's intention to subscribe to freemium music streaming services. The research aspires to make significant theoretical contributions by the development and testing of a model that explains individual's intention to subscribe to freemium music streaming services. From practical contribution standpoint, the research anticipates that findings could offer guidelines in aligning administrative and business policies to factors that determine intention to subscribe to freemium music streaming services.

The next stage of the framework is developing and testing a theoretical model toward operationalizing the constructs. Plans are underway to collect data using online survey questionnaire. Data are planned to be analyzed using structural equation model.

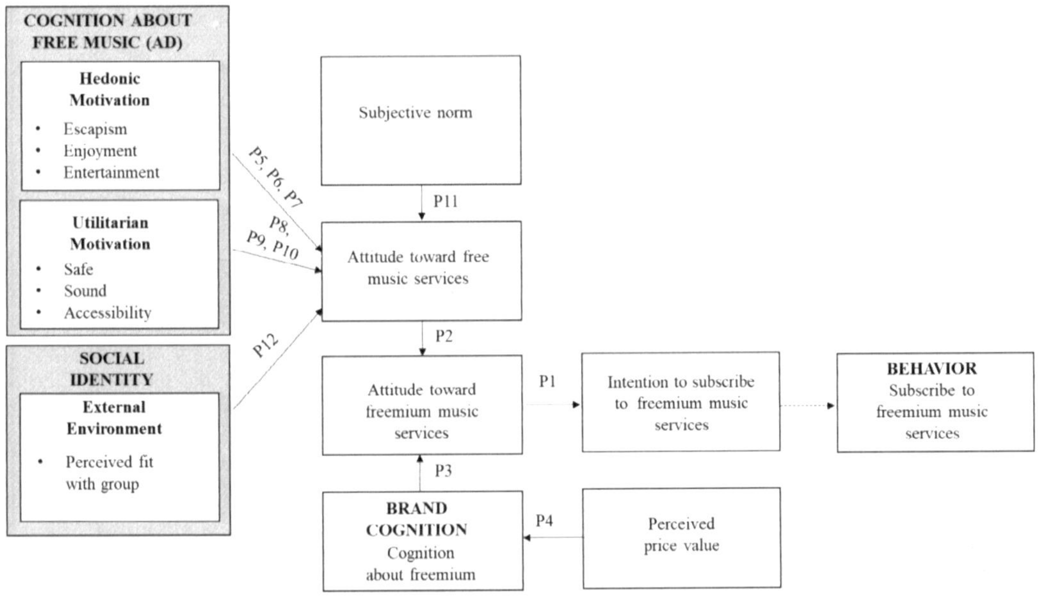

Figure 3. Conceptual Framework

REFERENCES

Aguiar, L. 2017. Let the music play? Free streaming and its effects on digital music consumption. *Information Economics and Policy*, Vol. 41, pp. 1-14.

Ajzen, I. and Fishbein, M. 1980. *Understanding Attitudes and Predicting Social Behavior*. Prentice-Hall, Englewood Cliffs, NJ.

Babin, B. J., Darden, W. R. and Griffin, M. 1994. Work and/or fun: measuring hedonic and utilitarian shopping value. *Journal of Consumer Research*, Vol. 20, No. 4, pp. 644-656.

Chiu, H.-C., Hsieh, Y.-C., Li, Y.-C. and Lee, M. (2005). Relationship Marketing and Consumer Switching Behavior. *Journal of Business Research*, Vol. 58, No. 12, pp. 1681–1689.

Davis, F. D. 1989. Perceived usefulness, perceived ease of use, and user acceptance of information technology. *MIS Quarterly*, Vol. 13, No. 3, pp. 319-339.

Davis, R. Lang, B. and Gautam, N. 2013. Modeling utilitarian-hedonic dual mediation (UHDM) in the purchase and use of games. *Internet Research*, Vol. 23, No. 2, pp. 229-256.

Davis, J. L., Love, T. P. and Phoenicia Fares, P. 2019. Collective social identity: Synthesizing identity theory and social identity theory using digital data. *Social Psychology Quarterly*, Vol. 00, No. 0, pp. 1–20.

Dörr, J., W., Benlian, T. M., A. and Hess, T. 2013. Music as a service: an alternative to music piracy? An empirical investigation of the intention to use music streaming services. *Business & Information Systems Engineering*, Vol. 5, No. 6, pp. 383–396.

Evans, S. E. 1964. Motivations underlying clothing selection and wearing. *Journal of Home Economics*, Vol. 56, September, pp. 739-743.

Fernandes, T. Guerra, J. 2019. Drivers and deterrents of music streaming services purchase intention, *International Journal of Electronic Business*, Vol.15, No. 1, pp.21 – 42.

Fishbein, M. and Ajzen, I. 1975. *Belief, Attitude, Intention and Behavior: An Introduction to Theory and Research*. Addison-Wesley, Reading, MA.

Gurel, L.M., Wilbur, J.C. and Gurel, L. 1972. Personality correlates of adolescent clothing styles. *Journal of Home Economics*, Vol. 64, No. 3, pp. 42-47.

Hampton-Sosa, W. 2017. An exploration of essential factors that influence music streaming adoption and the intention to engage in digital piracy. *International Journal of Electronic Commerce Studies*, Vol. 8, No.1, pp. 97-134.

Holbrook, M. B. 1994. The nature of customer value: An axiology of services in the consumption experience. In Rust, R. T. and Oliver, R. L. (ed.), *Service Quality: New Directions in Theory and Practice*, Thousand Oaks, California, pp. 21-71.

Holbrook, M. B., and Hirschman, E. C. 1982. The experiential aspects of consumption: consumer fantasies, feelings, and fun. *Journal of Consumer Research*, Vol. 9, No. 2, pp. 132-140.

Karson, E. J. and Fisher, R. J. 2005a. Predicting intentions to return to the web site: extending the dual mediation hypothesis. *Journal of Interactive Marketing*, Vol. 19, No. 3, pp. 2-14.

Karson, E. J. and Fisher, R. J. 2005b. Reexamining and extending the dual mediation hypothesis in an on-line advertising context, *Psychology & Marketing*, Vol. 22, No. 4, pp. 333–351.

Kim, C-S., Oh, E-H., Yang, K. H. and Kim, J. K. 2010. The appealing characteristics of download type mobile games. Service Business, Vol. 4, No. 3-4, pp. 253-269.

Liao, G-Y., Pham, T.T. L., Cheng, T.C.E., Ching-I Teng, C-I. 2020. How online gamers' participation fosters their team commitment: Perspective of social identity theory. *International Journal of Information Management*, Vol. 52, pp. 1-12.

López, I. and Ruiz, S. 2011. Explaining website effectiveness: The hedonic–utilitarian dual mediation hypothesis. *Electronic Commerce Research and Applications*, Vo. 10, pp. 49–58.

Mathwick, C., Malhotra, N. and Rigdon, E. 2001. Experiential value: conceptualization, measurement and application in the catalog and Internet shopping environment. *Journal of Retailing*, Vol. 77, No. 1, pp. 39-56.

MacKenzie, S. B., Lutz, R. J., and Belch, G. E. 1986. The role of attitude toward the ad as a mediator of advertising effectiveness: A test of competing explanations. *Journal of Marketing Research*, Vol. 13, pp. 130–143.

McKintyre, S.H. and Miller, M. C. 1992. Social utility and fashion behavior. *Marketing Letters*, Vol. 3, No. 4, pp. 371-382.

Mishra, D., Akman, I and Mishra, A. 2014. Theory of Reasoned Action application for Green Information Technology. *Computers in Human Behavior*, Vol. 36, pp. 29-40.

O'Fallon, M. J. and Butterfield, K. D. 2012. The influence of unethical peer behavior on observers' unethical behavior: A social cognitive perspective. *Journal of Business Ethics*, Vol. 109, No. 2, pp. 117-131.

Tajfel. H. (1978) The achievement of group differentiation. In *Differentiation Between Social Groups: Studies in the Social Psychology of Intergroup Relations*, Tajfel, H. (ed.), Academic Press, London, pp. 77-98.

Tajfel, H. and J.C. Turner, J. C. 1985. The social identity theory of intergroup behavior, in *Psychology of Intergroup Relations*, Worchel S. and Austin, W.G. (ed), Nelson Hall, Chicago, pp. 7-24.

Untaru, E-N., Ispas, A., Candrea, A. N., Marcela Luca and M. Epuran, G. 2016. Predictors of individuals' intention to conserve water in a lodging context: the application of an extended Theory of Reasoned Action. *International Journal of Hospitality Management*, Vol. 59, pp. 50-59.

van der Heijden, H. 2004. User acceptance of hedonic information systems. *MIS Quarterly*, Vol. 28, No. 4, pp. 695-703.

Wagner, T. M., Benlian, A. and Hess, T. 2014. Converting freemium customers from free to premium—the role of the perceived premium fit in the case of music as a service. *Electronic Markets*, Vol. 24, pp. 259–268.

Wetzels, M., Odekerken-Schroder, G. and Van Oppen, C. 2009. Using PLS path modeling for assessing hierarchical construct models: guidelines and empirical illustration. *MIS Quarterly*, Vol, 33, No. 1, pp. 177-195.

Zeithaml, V. A. 1988. Consumer perceptions of price, quality, and value: A means-end model and synthesis of evidence. *Journal of Marketing*, Vol. 52, No. 3, pp. 2-22.

DESIGN POINT. AN INTEGRATED E-LEARNING & INDUSTRY 4.0 FASHION PLATFORM FROM ITALY TO ZAMBIA

Dalia Gallico
Università San Raffaele, Roma, Italy

ABSTRACT

The project focuses on a standard of sustainability and multiculturalism applied to the fashion industry 4.0. Culture has a major impact on reducing poverty and contributes to a development, which is primarily human, inclusive and fair.
The result of the construction of a cultural and educational bridge, through E-learning platform between Italian design and the artisans of developing countries at each different season, or low income ones, such as Zambia and others in South America, Africa and Asia.
Design Point (the name of the project) goes in the field on mission, and after a first period of meeting and research of the various indigenous skills, many of which are dying out, it studies together with local artisans and contact persons, how to develop a product fashion-textile-accessory combining the host country's traditional craftsmanship with the well known Italian design and savoir-faire on E-learning platform to study and Industry 4.0 skills to create and sell new collections.
A cooperation very functional to bilateral development, that can count on a partner which in this dynamic at the end turns into an instrument: Technology. Acknowledging fashion's potential, as cultural activity, to provide significant opportunities for decent work for men and women around the world. Now it is possible thanks to remote education and work, to recover a research difference gap of decades of years. Nothing about them without them, an exchange of know-how and know-why, whose reactivation generates in the local populations a sense of self sufficiency, deriving from the direct employment creation, business and training related to these recovered competencies and cultural resources. In addition to the inducement, generated by the international promotion of a positive image of the country that attracts investment and triggers tourism therefore commercial interest, compared to remote geographical areas mostly unknown or maybe known for the wrong reasons.
Moreover, to overcome the lack of trade opportunities, the access to the international market is facilitated by a special agreement which allows the sale of ethical products resulting from this project, through one of the world's first e-commerce platform, which ensures a transparent business process management.
This activity has objective to oppose a welfarism that has proved so far to be inefficient. A goal of integrationial contamination, which promotes a cultural crossover, in which no identity is ever negotiated. Not charity, but serious work and cooperation with distance e-learning, the creation of an industry 4.0 fashion laboratory in Lusaka, the sale on e-commerce international platform.
To promote custom-made fabrics, exclusive samples are created by locals and subsequently presented at the international Milan Fashion week, where orders are collected within a quantity compatible with the local production capacity and commissioned to the communities, to finally return to Italy, and be finished manually by Italian seam stresses. An ideal Laboratory of Nations, which permeates the dignity of work, as an indispensable element at any latitude, thanks to ICT. This mission statement is a voluntary declaration, whose uniqueness is revealed as a reflection of the designer's personal multicultural DNA, translated into her signature style, as well as into a business model of sustainable technological development. These missions are officially supported from time to time by the various entities such as: Ministries of Foreign Affairs, Ministry of Culture and Trade, Embassy cooperating with the coordination of the United Nations.
The projects are structured by University San Raffaele Roma in consultation with local authorities and Foundations, so that there is always transparency and unity of purpose in achieving common and shared promotion and development objectives. A new business model and sustainable development on E-learning and Industry 4.0 platform made with collaborative innovation from Italy to Zambia in seven steps:
Craftship recovery; Cultural Heritage as enabler and a driver of sustainable Development; Enhancing opportunities through knowledge transfer and exchanges on E-learning platform; Enterprise creation with Fashion Industry 4.0; Promotion, as Tourism and Commerce developer; Enduring International Trade Development with E-commerce Platform; Integrationist contamination by technology.

KEYWORDS

Collaborative Innovation, Design of Societal Systems – rethinking, Managed Learning Environments (MLEs), Learning Theories and Approaches, E-Learning Models, E-commerce

1. INTRODUCTION

Fashion design occupies in present-day reality a role that involves sharp relief - directly or indirectly - a number of areas and types of professions. The project Design Point aims to encourage an increasing development and a greater appreciation of the excellence of the production system in Zambia. This will raise the degree of development / Zambia internationalization of production using the Milan Fashion design education (product, packaging, marketing, management, communication, etc.) as a driver of competitiveness / growth opportunity for exchange of local products with foreign markets is the focal point from which begins the project implementation.

Actually, the proposal, based on expertise gained from the reality of Milan, is just part of the value that design plays in that area and that - if properly developed and promoted to practical applications - is able to generate value for the companies involved. The project in particular promotes the establishment of a "Design Point" in Zambia that could become a platform for exchange and concrete support to the innovation of small/medium Zambia artisans through a strong focus on the value of design and new technology.

2. DESIGN POINT

The Design Point is an E-learning and Co-working Area where the designers from zambian companies are facing every day, developing a capacity to interpret and identify potential opportunities still untapped by local system: developing a new product and / or improve an existing business decisions, using the new address / new adaptation of existing materials (new ideas and products, prototypes, etc.) or enhancing the image of their products and presentation / packaging of their products (suitable for creating a brand, develop new packaging, etc.) are some examples and real cases that the design point -along with other measures- face on a daily basis in the interest of local companies. The Centre also designs the task and the role of promoting and building -together with partners- more and more ambitious planning and development paths, capable of enhancing the promotion and the outlet of the companies involved in Zambia, developing a constructive synergy with Milan / Lombardy on E-commerce platform that will increase international appreciation Zambia handicraft offering new opportunities for development and growth.

This program satisfies the general objective of education for university degree in training of human resource of fashion engineering, which partly upgrades people's intellectual level, carries out researches and tech-trans those can create scholars, new products to develop the economy, national defense and security and international integration. The curriculum trains an engineering of good political perspective, morality, knowledge, professional practical skills, researching and practical scientific and technological developing abilities corresponding degrees awarded; bachelors possess good health; originality and professional responsibility, new environment adaptability; awareness of people serving.

Graduates from this program have a scientific education and a complete professionalism which allow them to gain success in engineering career generally, and fashion engineering particularly.

Specific objectives:

- Have fundamental engineering and major knowledge: processing procedures from textile to fashion finishing and technical textile products, production and maintenance systems, abilities in new product design and development which helps to detect and solve problems related to design and manufacture in fashion production systems, to solve technical aspects thanks to knowledge and modern IT tools.
- Have individual skills, professional morality, good conversation and team-work skills enabling to join a multidisciplinary, multi-cultural and international working environment.
- Have knowledge of technical international language, so to improve him-/herself and exchange knowledge with others.
- Have understanding in economy, politics, fundamentals in social sciences, and humanity which are appropriate to usefully contribute to the sustainable development of the society and community.

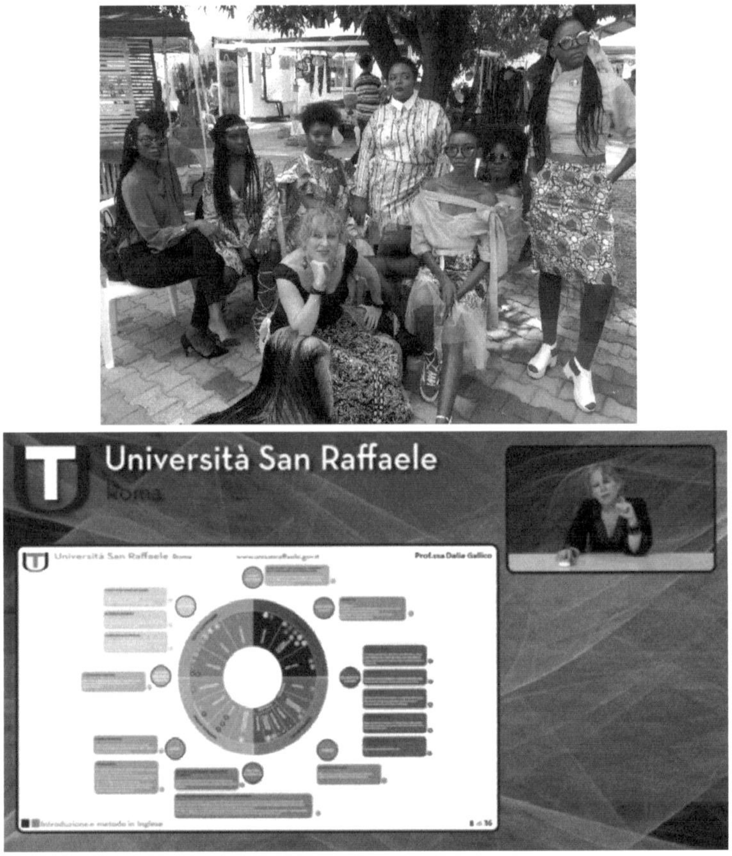

Figures 1. Zambian Designer's meeting with Director at "Design Point" in Lusaka, Zambia with Prof. Dalia Gallico. Screenshots. E-learning Design & Business lessons

3. TECHNOLOGICAL APPLICATIONS AND CHARACTERISTICS

As part of the project devoted to the dissemination of high quality material in Design, University San Raffaele Roma with the portal https://design.uniroma5.it/ is designed to allow easy and flexible access to a big potential user arena. In this sense, the portal is based on some of the most widely used, reliable and functional tools in the field of content management, electronic commerce, and technology training. Inside the portal, the Joomla and VirtueMart platform is integrated in conjunction with Moodle for the sale and use of online courses. The implementation of the online sales system for the https://design.uniroma5.it/ site is concerned with the Moodle, Joomla and VirtueMart platforms. The latter is an add-on for Joomla cms that allows you to extend its capabilities to create and manage an e-commerce portal. This tool, in conjunction with an API implementation, enables the integration of Moodle courses with the sale and purchase auto-subscription.

The basic component of VirtueMart covers the basic features of an on-line shop (online catalog submission, file download, cart), but add-ons that implement additional functionality such as product search or preview in. The shop management allows you to modify the seller and related product information by entering basic information (name, identifier), advanced (weight, unit of measure, size, related products) and images (Picture of the article).

Streaming video with Vimeo provider. To increase the portability of the contributions and to exploit the potential offered by streaming video, it has been chosen to use a professional broadcast service.

4. DESIGN POINT: FASHION INDUSTRY 4.0 TO ZAMBIA

The Fashion Design Point Laboratory set up in Lusaka is unique and available to all designers who need it. A trained instructor is always there available. Design point automates the entire personalization process, from order reception and product development to the final cutting stages. Resulting from a four-year research-and-development process, the digital solution for on-demand production was developed based on Industry 4.0 principles.

The project Design Point allows Zambian designers to produce personalized clothing at the same speed as ready-to-wear and avoid overstocking by producing in precise quantities.

It is available in the form of two packages, one dedicated to made to measure, with pattern adjustments, and the other to customization, with product characteristic alterations. This turnkey solution automates on-demand production right from order reception to production development stages and the cutting room. Companies can define their desired product personalization criteria for each item depending on the package, and launch production processes right from the get-go, without interfering with their standard workflows.

This innovative cloud-based platform solution ensures efficient made-to-measure and customization production processes and facilitates nearshoring for companies that offer individualized products. This technology is up and running and can be used by the fashion industry on a plug-and-play basis.

Born at the confluence of two worlds, fashion and software, Design Point converted iconic Italian luxury brands to computer assisted design (CAD). The software: Kaledo for textile design and creation, Modaris for product development and 3D prototyping, Diamino for marker making, Kubix Link and Fashion PLM for collaborative management of collection life cycles.

Equipment in automated cutting, cutting room equipment too. The solutions —integrated machines and software— are adapted to each market, as well as to the broad diversity of materials processed: fabrics, leather, and textiles. All the cutting solutions are compatible with Industry 4.0 principles.

Design Point Services are deployed in three areas: support, training and consulting. Support and preventive and predictive maintenance services assist our customers remotely and on-site, ensure the availability of cutting equipment and make the latest versions of our software available. Training provides a continuous transfer of skills to empower the users of solutions throughout their customer journey. Finally, consulting services enable to fully benefit from o solutions and to take an optimization approach.

We cross-reference and analyze it to better understand the processes and to propose new services and applications, such as driving our customers' performance based on their own objectives or the best indicators from their sector.

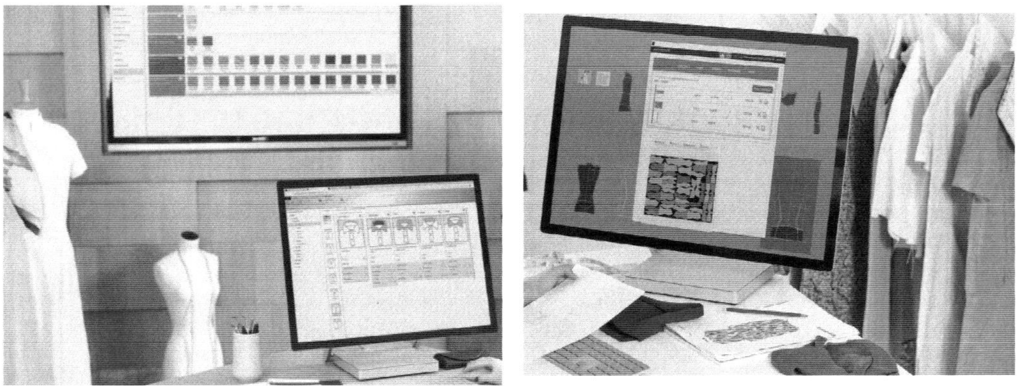

Figures 2. Design Point Cad instruments for Fashion

5. CONCLUSION

Fashion design as a cross-operative clot? An industrial design not only as a product but also as communication and as an image? A focus on product innovation as a complex reality built by the continuous transfer of the outcomes and results? These are the objectives that the Design Point aims to achieve with the leadership of Director Dalia Gallico and the Steering Committee.

Design point aims to strengthen, deepen, expand, promote and help implement the appropriate conditions for the enhancement of design, with technology support, from the territory of Milan, Italy to the world.

Its purpose is to promote and help implementing the appropriate conditions for the design of goods and services, through the cultural debate, the intervention in the institutions, the provision of services and technology. It is involved in the design of products, services, visual communication, packaging, interior architecture, and environmental design.

Design Point is exploitation of research and industrial skills and excellences. Skills development involves, among the others, the next fields:

- Advanced communication media, based on Web 2.0 technologies, suitable to support B2C sale for fashion design, jewellery and trinkets.
- Analytical instruments able to produce channels analysis and customer segmentation in automatic way;
- Logistic organizational models with high performance driven to offer a worldwide service at top level, also flexible and affordable.

New technologies allow to create global communities with a lot of users sharing contents. This proves that management technologies can do more and more. The project aims to use these technologies for the marketplace development to build an international community on the Italian design know.

Related to growth of ICT technologies, the project allows the development and joining of innovative technologies Web 2.0, able to:

1. Create a place where all designers are connected, both Italian and Zambian, could develop ideas, contents, events, opinions, all related to fashion design. Advanced technologies Web 2.0 join potential of companies, designers, students, interested people and keen on fashion design.
2. Translate the characteristics of products in a way that a user/buyer can exactly understand and feel the additional value of the product just through the web (experience on E-commerce platform).
3. Use buyer's profile and location data to increase the offer and create return information flows which could be translated into marketing information available for vendors;
4. Create data exchange with the industry 4.0 platform able to assure the quality of logistic performance expected from the market

The key factors for this are the increased implementation of the Internet of Things (IoT) and the digitalization of the industry. As products are usually at the heart of manufacturing business, data and analytics are often aimed at refining product development rather than the end-to-end production process. Due to constantly increasing expenses, companies in the sector are always looking to:

- Reduce the cost of manufacturing
- Increase production efficiency
- Minimize waste, optimize the use of energy and other resources

The final product is unique, and knowledge, concepts and system support developed can be used later in other contexts to support innovation trough design. At least the Design Point's model is in line with 6 of the 17 United Nations Sustainable Development Goals (SDGs): No Poverty, Gender Equality, Decent Work and Economic Growth, Reducing Inequality, Responsible consumption and production Partnerships for the Goals.

REFERENCES

Bentley, T. (1998). *Learning beyond the classroom: Education for a changing world.* London: Routledge.

D'Andrea A., Ferri F., Fortunati De Luca L., Guzzo T (2009). *"Mobile Devices to support advanced forms of e-Learning"* Handbook of Research on Multimodal Human Computer Interaction and Pervasive Services: Evolutionary Techniques for Improving Accessibility. Editor: Patrizia Grifoni, IGI Global

Dillenbourg, P., Baker, M., Blaye, A., & O'Malley, C. (1996). The evolution of research on collaborative learning. In E. Spada & P. Reiman (Eds.), *Learning in humans and machine: Towards an interdisciplinary learning science*. Oxford, UK:

Gallico D (2013). *Contam-Innovation Cinquecento icone tra design, cultura e innovazione.* Bologna:Logo Fausto Lupetti editore

Gallico D, (2016). *Rapporto nazionale sul Design nelle imprese italiane (dalla A alla Z)* isbn 9788868741518 Logo Fausto Lupetti editore

Gallico D, (2020). *Moda in Formazione* Bologna:Logo Fausto Lupetti editore Isbn 9788868742072

Grew, P., & Pagani, E. (2005). Towards a wireless architecture for mobile ubiquitous e-learning. *Workshop on Learning Communities in the Era of Ubiquitous Computing*, Milan, Italy.

THE SMART CITY AS A SOCIAL POLICY ACTOR

Diogo Miguel Mendes Correia[1] and José Eduardo Silva Abreu Lopes Feio[2]
[1]*Department of Economics, Management, Industrial Engineering and Tourism (DEGEIT)*
University of Aveiro, Portugal
[2]*Department of Social Policy and Intervention, University of Oxford, United Kingdom*

ABSTRACT

Smart City literature has started focusing on new technologies that are being developed to improve cities' inner processes. Nowadays, it moved into considerations of the role of citizens in these improvements and ways to adapt new technologies to fit their needs. Smart Cities are, therefore expanding. It can be noted both in numbers and in scope. For the former, investment and interest in the topic has been growing as more and more cities aim to be considered "smart". For the latter, with more and more technological developments, the possibilities for the areas in which cities can be "smart" has increased. This has led to Smart Cities increase in the scope of action. Social participation and inclusion are taken in consideration, creating the Smart Inclusive City. Moreover, this article argues that Smart Cities are emerging as new social policy actors. Concepts from the social policy literature such as welfare regimes, intersectionality, and gender mainstreaming become relevant to Smart City scholars.

KEYWORDS

"Smart Inclusive Cities", "Social Policy", "Citizens", "Inclusion", "Intersectionality", "Welfare Regimes"

1. INTRODUCTION

Smart Cities, and especially Smart Cities technologies, are seen as the solution to create new ways to solve these emerging problems such as urban pressure, air pollution, congestion, waste management, and human health (Ahvenniemi *et al.*, 2017). However, it is difficult to find ways to finance a Smart City initiative if it is not possible to monetize its benefits, which happens, for example, in social impact projects. Which lead them not to be a priority to policymakers. There are huge disparities within cities. While some authors discuss for how long we will continue living without the autonomous vehicles, there are still cities that are not even coherent in obliging buildings to have access for disabled people.

Nowadays, we are witnessed a change in how decision-makers include citizens in the co-creation and co-designing processes. We are in the Smart Cities 3.0 stage (Cohen, 2015). Smart Cities are more and more seen as cities for people, created and designed with the citizens instead of focusing on the technological approach. However, we must ensure that all voices are heard, not letting the most needed out of the equation.

A real change in paradigm is still to come, and the literature on Smart Cities still lags. In the next chapters, it is argued that in the next phase of its development, the concept of Smart Cities should embrace the language of inclusion. Moreover, elements of the literature of social policy that can inform this move are outlined.

2. TIME OF CHANGING THE PARADIGM

The latest technological advances in the field of Information and Communication Technology (ICTs) supporting a citizen-centric urban development for cities can have a tremendous effect on future cities. ICTs can be a fundamental help to cities in every stage: in diagnosing problems, devising solutions, and the analysing results.

After Hollands (Hollands, 2008) criticized the fact that the focus should not be on the technological side, the concept evolved from the technical point of view and has been hardly discussed. Technological companies were the ones to push for innovation and the quick implementation of solutions. These were most of the times not prepared to install in the urban furniture. Cities started to understand the benefits of implementing ICTs to gather real time data to increase the awareness of the cities' problems and act quickly. During the last years, the focus changed from the technology and economy, where the citizens were had a passive role to a focus on people, governance, and policy where citizens act as co-creators and contributors for the citizen (Trencher, 2019). We are now in the time of the "Smart City 3.0" (Cohen, 2015), where citizens now have an active roll in the establishment of the strategy and associated policies. Smart Cities are now seen as the final stage of urban development, representing a conceptual urban development model, using human, collective and technological capital (Angelidou, 2015), where the adoption of technology is not an end. Still, a more vital thing is the management and policies behind the use of the technology (Nam and Pardo, 2011).

3. SMART INCLUSIVE CITY

Smart Cities face the challenge of dealing with the issue of widening inequality and social polarization (Hollands, 2008). Special attention has started to be noted in the literature of having policies that shall promote the inclusion of citizens in cities by including them in the process of decision making as one of the interested parties (Oliveira, 2015).

Cities of the future are seen as sustainable cities where all residents (with no exception) live well and the attraction of cities is preserved (Thuzar, 2011). Cities will have to provide conditions for a healthy and happy community under the challenging conditions that global, environmental, economic and social trends may bring. Cities encompass an efficient, technologically advanced, sustainable, and socially inclusive city (Pereira *et al.*, 2017).

Smart Inclusive City is a city that puts innovation available and working to everyone and whose policies are made with and to improve the quality of life of every citizen, not letting aside the disadvantaged. Moreover, it is a city whose aim is to reduce social learning restrictions and social participation barriers (Silva, Khan and Han, 2018).

The role of citizens in Smart Cities, passed from a passive role to one where they are seen as a "source of data". Nowadays, they are much more than that, and citizens now understand that it does not make sense to build a city without including the main stakeholder in the equation (Healey and Gonza, 2005; Cossetta and Palumbo, 2016), helping on the planning and design (Cowley *et al.*, 2018; Sadoway and Univerisity, 2018). Moreover social innovation can be understood as a 'design– by-doing' process (Brown *et al.*, 2012). Citizens are more and more the center of cities. However, cities of today are not seen as inclusive as they should be since there still a lot to do in this matter to accomplish the basic needs of every citizen, as identified above.

Smart Cities must consider a global vision to develop and implement a set of policy-mechanisms through an alternative institutional governance model to change this scenario (Lee, Hancock and Hu, 2014). Inclusion is something that should be promoted by city policymakers. A City can no longer be smart without being inclusive.

Therefore, several points must be taken into account by cities. First, cities must incentive companies to develop technologies to everyone or dedicated to solving a specific problem dictated by citizens. Second, cities must consider previously implemented technologies and best-practices and make the match between these and the needs of the city.

4. SMART CITIES AS SOCIAL POLICY ACTORS

We argue that Smart Cities have the potential to be social policy actors that embrace inclusivity at the foreground of its agenda. This changing in the way one conceptualises Smart Cities will lead to two main consequences. First, a whole set of areas of action will be open for Smart Cities. In other words, changing how we conceptualise Smart Cities will enable us to ask different questions about what they can and should do. Second, changing conceptualisations will open a whole tool kit of concepts that have been developed in the social policy literature, which can be now served Smart City scholars.

Changing conceptualisations are often implicit in policy actors (Bacchi and Goodwin, 2016). These happen as practitioners realise via lived experience that the potential for a concept to evolve exists in practice. When it comes to conceptualising Smart Cities as social policy actors, this can be noted in local authorities' work in various cities such as Vienna, Rio de Janeiro, Ljubljana and London.

Over the past few decades, Vienna has integrated gender considerations into how they plan the development of the urban space. For example, through evaluating commuting patterns, it was made clear that women and girls use footways more than men, who tend to reduce more using vehicles. The city then used this knowledge to invest in public lightning in areas used predominantly by women and girls (Vienna, 2019). In the same line of investment, in Rio de Janeiro, local authorities have used technologies such as Safetipin to gather data on violence and harassment against women and girls. (Women, 2013). Women and girls are then able to record the areas of the city where they feel less safe. This has allowed local authorities to shape their urban development towards addressing these specific areas of the city.

The capital of Slovenia, Ljubljana, has implemented a solution for its citizens by providing electric vehicles that are available for everyone to request them by phone or online, to take them from home to the city center (Wedam, 2019).

Homelessness in London is a significant problem as the number of people living in the street has been rising for the past few years. To address this, the Mayor of London has put contactless points across the city to people donate money to various NGOs and created a GoFundMe page. Through this, they were able to raise more than £74.000 in less than two weeks (London, 2018).

The above can be seen as evidence for greater care from local authorities towards implementing various technologies to improve the inclusion of their cities. This is often not done as an explicit change in the way Smart Cities are understood but rather as an implicit change in goals. A policy change of this type is referred to in the literature as social learning (Bennett and Howlett, 1992). This can involve changes in "the social construction of policy problems, the scope of the policy, or policy goal" (May, 1992). What the examples above show is a shift in the policy goals of these cities. These cities are changing the purposes for which they use technologies towards the promotion of inclusion. In this way, we argue that even if implicitly, they are conceptualizing Smart Cities as social policy actors. This is, actors concerned with promoting inclusion and social wellbeing of their populations through the use of technologies.

How one conceptualises policy issues and policy actors change the expectations and questions asked about them (Lancaster, Duke and Ritter, 2015). In the early 20th century, changing conceptualisations about the role of the state led to changes in expectations towards (Castles, 2012). Foucault called bio-politics to the development of ways in which the state has become concerned with wellbeing and the life of its citizens (Nadesan, 2008). Conceptualising Smart Cities as social policy actors can be seen as a parallel transformation to this. It means seeing the goal of Smart Cities not just in terms of technologies but also the inclusivity and well-being of its citizens. It means asking different questions about the role that the technologies developed can play. For example, besides questioning how they can impact effectiveness and costs, it means asking how they affect inclusivity.

5. WELFARE REGIME TYPES AND THE "SMART CITY 3.0"

With a move towards a view of Smart Cities as social policy actors and an increasing attempt to include citizens and stakeholders at various levels, a whole literature from the discipline of social policy becomes relevant.

One of the pivots works in the field of social policy is that of (Esping-Andersen, 1990). Esping-Anderson (1990), divides high-income countries into three ideal types. These typical types, which he calls welfare regimes, correspond to different ways of combining the market, family, and the state in the provision of goods and services. The United Kingdom, for example, is considered as a liberal welfare regime (Wincott, 2006). Liberal welfare regimes are characterised by liberalised labour markets that lead to high levels of commodification. In other words, too high degrees of market influence on the provision of goods and services. The social democratic welfare regime is exemplified by countries such as Sweden. There are high decommodification levels and heavy reliance on the state for the provision of goods and services over the family and the market. Conservative welfare regimes type countries such as Germany and Italy are countries can be seen as in between liberal and welfare regime, with a higher reliance on family and social structures than any of the other two.

The relation between welfare regimes and specific policies is sometimes hard to discern. While some policies might follow the commodifying tendency of the welfare regime, other policies might act in a decommodifying way in order to counteract some of the undesirable trends of the welfare regime's general commodifying effect (Stephens and Fitzpatrick, 2007). Nevertheless, policy choices will always be influenced by the wider context in which they are inserted, one way or the other. When it comes to homelessness policy, Stephens and Fitzpatrick (2007) give the example of housing policy in which the UK's safety net for under risk homelessness people can be seen as having a decommodifying effect. This, in response to the undesirable effects of commodification in this field created by the UK's welfare regime types. However, other homelessness policies, such as the specific reliance on charities and volunteering organizations can be seen as following the welfare regime's commodifying tendency.

Any attempt to pursue more inclusive and stakeholder aware Smart Cities need to consider this wider context. If Smart Cities are to get out of their bubble, they must be mindful of what is out of it. More specifically, they must be mindful of the structures and relations between stakeholders who attempt to provide welfare to citizens and how these vary from country to country. The literature on welfare regimes can provide an entry point to this.

6. NON-TOKENISTIC PARTICIPATION AND INTERSECTIONALITY

Various early attempts to promote gender equality suffered from the fact that they were based on tokenistic approaches (Cornwall, 2003). In other words, programs and policies were designed including specific women, assuming that they would represent the views of other women. However, it has been realised that there is a need not to assume that one individual just because they are members of a group, such as women, will automatically represent this group. Moreover, just because someone is present that does not mean that their interests will be represented. Cornwall reviews various attempts to promote gender equality in countries of the Global South. She outlines how many of these while they aim to include women, they do so in a tokenistic way. Individual women are present, but they are often either not given the opportunity to express their interests or do not represent the interests of women more broadly. Groups such as women are not homogeneous, the struggles they face are shaped by factors beyond gender, such as income and race.

If Smart Cities should aim to be inclusive, they need not start from zero. Insights from previous failed attempts to address issues of inclusivity should be taken into consideration.

7. CONCLUSION

In conclusion, digitalisation inequalities will be growing in the future. Without considering inclusion, the barrier between those who are able to access the benefits of Smart Cities and those who are not will keep growing.

This article has argued that with the evolution of Smart Cities, one can start to conceptualise them as social policy actors who should care about its own inclusivity. Some of the consequences of conceptualising Smart Cities in such a way have been discussed. It has been argued that literature from social policy becomes relevant once this conceptualisation is accepted. Notions such as welfare regimes and intersectionality become suitable for scholars of Smart Cities. Smart Cities have the potential to become inclusive if they embrace citizens at all stages. Doing so will lead to better Smart Cities that genuinely fit with the needs of its people.

Aligned with the evolution of the Smart Cities concept, the methodology that a city must follow to become smart must acknowledge the role of the citizen over the several steps, and with the aim of promoting the inclusion of every citizen. There is still plenty of work to do in this field. There is more and more discussion about participatory approaches and what may be the designing tools citizens can help from. However, it is still missing KPIs focused on inclusion and a definition of an index capable of quantifying the inclusiveness in a city, guaranteeing that the promoted policies are aligned with inclusion goals.

REFERENCES

Ahvenniemi, H. *et al.* (2017) 'What are the differences between sustainable and smart cities?', *Cities*. Elsevier B.V., 60, pp. 234–245. doi: 10.1016/j.cities.2016.09.009.

Angelidou, M. (2015) 'Smart cities: A conjuncture of four forces', *Cities*. Elsevier Ltd, 47, pp. 95–106. doi: 10.1016/j.cities.2015.05.004.

Bacchi, C. and Goodwin, S. (2016) *Poststructural policy analysis: A guide to practice*.

Bennett, C. J. and Howlett, M. (1992) 'The lessons of learning: Reconciling theories of policy learning and policy change', *Policy Sciences*, 25(3), pp. 275–294. doi: 10.1007/BF00138786.

Brown, T. *et al.* (2012) 'Design Things and Design Thinking : Contemporary Participatory Design Challenges Erling Bjögvinsson , Pelle Ehn , Per-Anders Hillgren', 28(3), pp. 101–116.

Castles, F. G. (2012) 'The Oxford handbook of the welfare state'. Oxford: Oxford University Press.

Cohen, B. (2015) *No Title*. Available at: https://www.fastcompany.com/3047795/the-3-generations-of-smart-cities.

Cornwall, A. (2003) 'Whose Voices ? Whose Choices ? Reflections on Gender and Participatory Development', 31(8), pp. 1325–1342. doi: 10.1016/S0305-750X(03)00086-X.

Cossetta, A. and Palumbo, M. (2016) 'The Co-production of Social Innovation Social innovation : The Case of Living Lab Living Lab', (July). doi: 10.1007/978-3-319-06160-3.

Cowley, R. *et al.* (2018) 'The smart city and its publics : insights from across six UK cities', *Urban Research & Practice*. Routledge, 11(1), pp. 53–77. doi: 10.1080/17535069.2017.1293150.

Esping-Andersen, G. (1990) 'The three worlds of welfare capitalism'. Princeton, N.J.: Princeton University Press.

Healey, P. and Gonza, S. (2005) 'A Sociological Institutionalist Approach to the Study of Innovation in Governance Capacity', 42(11), pp. 2055–2069.

Hollands, R. G. (2008) 'Will the real smart city please stand up? Intelligent, progressive or entrepreneurial?', *City*, 12(3), pp. 303–320. doi: 10.1080/13604810802479126.

Lancaster, K., Duke, K. and Ritter, A. (2015) 'Producing the "problem of drugs": A cross national-comparison of "recovery" discourse in two Australian and British reports', *International Journal of Drug Policy*. Elsevier B.V., 26(7), pp. 617–625. doi: 10.1016/j.drugpo.2015.04.006.

Lee, J. H., Hancock, M. G. and Hu, M. C. (2014) 'Towards an effective framework for building smart cities: Lessons from Seoul and San Francisco', *Technological Forecasting and Social Change*. Elsevier Inc., 89, pp. 80–99. doi: 10.1016/j.techfore.2013.08.033.

London, M. of (2018) *Mayor's rough sleeping campaign raises over £78,000 in first fortnight*. Available at: https://www.london.gov.uk/press-releases/mayoral/all-funds-going-to-vital-charities (Accessed: 18 April 2019).

May, P. J. (1992) 'Policy Learning and Failure', *Journal of Public Policy*, 12(4), pp. 331–354. doi: 10.1017/S0143814X00005602.

Nadesan, M. H. (2008) *Governmentality biopower and everyday life*, *Governmentality Biopower and Everyday Life*. doi: 10.4324/9780203894620.

Nam, T. and Pardo, T. A. (2011) 'Conceptualizing smart city with dimensions of technology, people, and institutions', in *ACM International Conference Proceeding Series*, pp. 282–291. doi: 10.1145/2037556.2037602.

Oliveira, Á. (2015) 'From Smart Cities to Human Smart Cities'. doi: 10.1109/HICSS.2015.281.

Pereira, G. V. *et al.* (2017) 'Delivering public value through open government data initiatives in a Smart City context', *Information Systems Frontiers*. Information Systems Frontiers, 19(2), pp. 213–229. doi: 10.1007/s10796-016-9673-7.

Sadoway, D. and Univerisity, C. (2018) '(Re) prioritizing Citizens in Smart Cities Governance : Examples of Smart Citizenship from Urban India', 324953632(May).

Silva, B. N., Khan, M. and Han, K. (2018) 'Towards sustainable smart cities: A review of trends, architectures, components, and open challenges in smart cities', *Sustainable Cities and Society*. Elsevier, 38(January), pp. 697–713. doi: 10.1016/j.scs.2018.01.053.

Stephens, M. and Fitzpatrick, S. (2007) 'Welfare Regimes, Housing Systems and Homelessness: How are they Linked?', *European Journal of Homelessness*, 1(December), pp. 201–212.

Thuzar, M. (2011) 'Urbanization in Southeast Asia: Developing Smart Cities for the Future?', *Regional Outlook*, pp. 96–100. doi: 10.1355/9789814311694-022.

Trencher, G. (2019) 'Technological Forecasting & Social Change Towards the smart city 2 . 0 : Empirical evidence of using smartness as a tool for tackling social challenges', *Technological Forecasting & Social Change*. Elsevier, 142(October 2017), pp. 117–128. doi: 10.1016/j.techfore.2018.07.033.

Vienna, C. of (2019) *Gender mainstreaming in Vienna*.

Wedam, D. (2019) *Kavalir: getting around the city centre by electric car*. Available at: https://www.visitljubljana.com/en/visitors/travel-information/getting-around/kavalir-getting-around-the-city-centre-by-electric-car/ (Accessed: 20 April 2019).

Wincott, D. (2006) 'Paradoxes of new labour social policy: Toward universal child care in Europe's "most liberal" welfare regime?', *Social Politics*, 13(2), pp. 286–312. doi: 10.1093/sp/jxj011.

Women, U. (2013) *In Rio de Janeiro's favelas, a new online tool tackles violence against women and girls*. Available at: http://www.unwomen.org/en/news/stories/2013/6/rio-de-janeiro-apps-to-endviolence-%0Ain-favelas (Accessed: 17 April 2019).

A HOLISTIC SOCIAL COMMERCE FRAMEWORK FOR SAUDI ARABIA

Mohammed Aljaafari
Curtin University, WA, Australia

ABSTRACT

The evolution of social networking and the significant growth of e-commerce has changed the nature of e-commerce interaction between customers and organizations. This evolution has produced a new form of e-commerce known as named "social commerce" (SC). In Saudi Arabia, social networking usage has increased rapidly and has begun to be an indispensable part of everyday life. The current literature indicates that social commerce has not been studied extensively and the majority of the studies on social commerce have focused mainly on the investigation of specific factors. However, in this study, the researcher intends to investigate a comprehensive range of factors including Organization Characteristics factors, HCI factors, Social factors, Psychological factors and Cultural factors. Hence, the purpose of this study is to identify the major factors that influence the customers' attitude to the adoption of s-commerce in Saudi Arabia. A new initial holistic framework will be developed for s-commerce in Saudi Arabia based on an extensive literature review. A mixed methods approach suggested for this research. This study will provide a holistic framework that will benefit stakeholders such as companies, organizations and governments by suggesting ways to encourage customers to adopt SC and find practical solutions to improve the use of SC in Kingdom Saudi Arabia (KSA) as well as those in developing countries, especially the Gulf Cooperation Council countries.

KEYWORDS

Social Commerce, Social Networking, E-commerce, Online Shopping, Consumers' Attitude

1. INTRODUCTION

Electronic commerce, commonly known as e-commerce is the process of online buying and selling of goods and services (Khan, 2016). According to numerous statistical data study (99firms, 2019, Law, 2019, Statista, 2019c, Webalive, 2019), there are a growing number of consumers use the internet to gather data regarding the online goods and services as well as buying goods and services (Gatautis and Medziausiene, 2014). An almost 1.8 billion population of the entire world purchase the online goods in the year 2018 (Statista, 2019b). Many businesses consider e-commerce as an essentially element to hold their place in the competitive markets; it is also consider as a significant economic growth factor (Makki and Chang, 2015). In 2019, Saudi Arabia e-commerce purchases grow gradually to US$7,141 million (Statista, 2019a). According to statistics, in 2019 there are around 23 million users on different social networking in Saudi Arabia (Gmi_Blogger, 2019). The popularity of social networking along with the significant growth of e-commerce is having a massive effect on the world economy. The change in the users' shopping behaviour has evolved a new form of e-commerce, named "social commerce" (Busalim and Hussin, 2016). This recent concept can be the future interest for researchers (Liang and Turban, 2011). Social commerce (s-commerce) is a phenomenon that has continued to evolve since its initial emergence in 2005 (Wang and Zhang, 2012). The first paper to discuss the concept of s-commerce was published in 2006 (Beisel, 2006, Han et al., 2018). In practice, the first formal beginning of SC was in 2009 with the opening of the flowers.com Facebook store (Busalim and Hussin, 2016). Numerous researchers consider the SC as an extended part of traditional e-commerce or a new development of it (Han et al., 2018). S-commerce is actually a subset of e-commerce, that uses the social networking platforms as a bridge to e-commerce to facilitate the online buying and selling of products and services via Internet technologies (Noh et al., 2013).

2. LITERATURE REVIEW

This section reviews the current literature relating to the factors relevant to the proposed s-commerce framework for Saudi Arabia (see Figure 1).

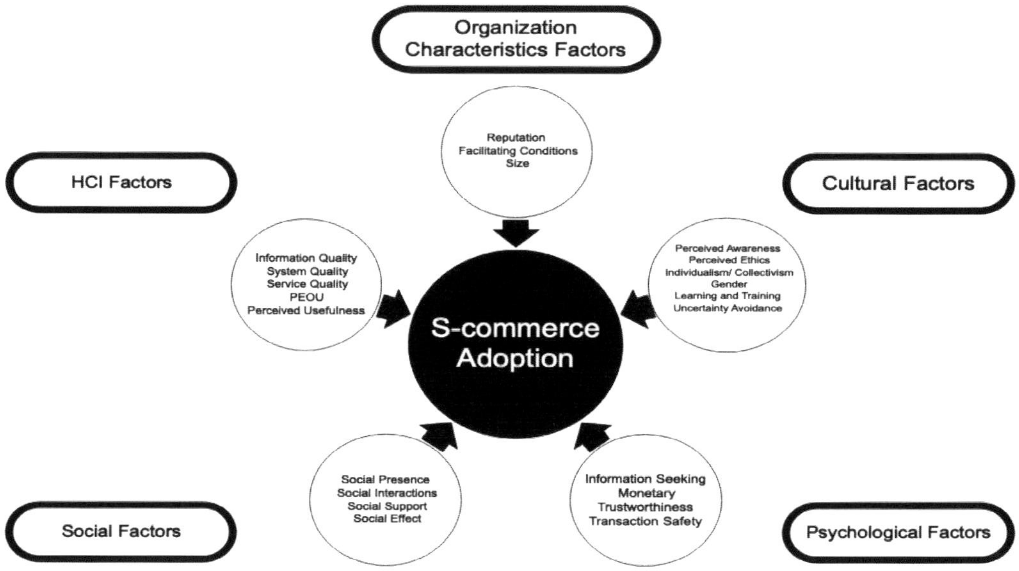

Figure 1. Initial holistic s-commerce framework for users in Saudi Arabia

2.1 Organization's Characteristics Factors

In terms of the factors relating to an organization's characteristics, the first factor is the organization's reputation which is the degree to which consumers' perceive that an organization is reliable and concerned about its clients (Li et al., 2018). Many e-retailers believe that excellent reputation is a significant factor that inspires trust in consumers (Li et al., 2018). The next dimension is facilitating conditions which refers to the extent to which a person's perception that an organizational structure and technical infrastructure are available to facilitate system use. This dimension examines the extent to which a customer believes that the social networks, as a workplace, support the usage of social commerce (Choi, 2019). The size of an s-commerce organization is the last variable, since the user might consider the size of the social commerce organization in terms of its share of the market. The large size of online organizations that offer online transactions will increase users' confidence because they expect to encounter only minor risks from their operations (Kim and Park, 2013).

2.2 Human Computer Interaction Factors

The quality of a website is a significant factor in determining the success of a social networking site (SNS) and usage behaviour. S-commerce includes using an SNS for commercial transactions. The quality of a website can be measured by three factors: information quality, system quality, and service quality. The system quality is associated with the desired and essential capabilities of a website such as its reliability, availability and response time (Hsu et al., 2017). On the other hand, information quality determines the accuracy, completeness, and timeliness of the website content (Abed, 2016). The final factor is service quality, which indicates the timeliness of responses when a consumer accesses supports and services provided through the website by the service provider (Hsu et al., 2017). The excellent quality of a social networking site will encourage consumers to believe that the platform is a valuable avenue for social interactions, and it could encourage users to continue using the platform for the exchange of information (Ahn et al., 2007, Teo et al., 2008).

Another HCI factor is perceived usefulness which is the degree to which consumers perceive that a new technology could improve performance (Davis, 1989). In term of s-commerce, Al-Adwan (2019), Bounkhong (2017) claimed that perceived usefulness has a positive impact on consumers' behavioural intention to adopt social commerce.

Like the perceived usefulness factor, the perceived ease of use (PEOU) is considered to be another vital factor in a variety of innovative technology researches where TAM theory was applied. PEOU refers to the extent to which an individual perceives that using a specific system will require little effort (Davis, 1989). The positive influence of this PEOU on behavioural intention has been proven by numerous studies related to the new technologies (Hajli et al., 2017b, Lu, 2017).

2.3 Social Factors

Social commerce mainly concerns the usage of social networks. Thus, a person's behaviour is influenced by the social factors that encourage collaboration and communication between individuals (Lal, 2017). In this study, social presence, social interactions, social support and social effect, have been identified as the major contributing factors that influence a person's decision regarding the use of SC. The first variable of social factors is social presence, which is associated with the ability of a website to elicit a feeling of warmth and sociability (Al-Adwan and Kokash, 2019). Social presence is considered as a prime concept in SC sites (Hajli et al., 2017a). The second factor is social interactions. The ease of interaction between buyers and sellers, without any constraints being imposed due to time or space, is considered to be a unique aspect of online shopping (Kim and Joo, 2001). The consumers who interact socially more with each other on the social networking platforms, have stronger feelings of closeness and familiarity with each other. Thus, there is more likelihood of the user's purchasing intention being influenced by the social networks community (Ng, 2013). The third social factors variable is social support that is explained by Cobb (1976) as being perceived love, care, and support obtained from individuals within a group. In one community, it is likely that an individual will receive support from peers and friends (Hajli, 2019). When community members realize that their participation in online communities will strengthen their reputation, they will like to participate by their experiences and information (Hajli and Sims, 2015). Several studies (Hajli and Sims, 2015, Liang et al., 2011) indicated that users' SC intentions are influenced by online social support. The last social factor is social effect. Shin (2013) claimed that online customers' behaviour is strongly affected by those individuals whom they know and trust. This implies that social effect is a vital behavioural antecedent to the adoption of SC (Akman and Mishra, 2017).

2.4 Psychological Factors

In this study, information seeking, monetary considerations, trustworthiness, and transaction safety, have been identified as psychological factors that influence the adoption of SC. Firstly, seeking information related to s-commerce refers to an individual's efforts to acquire information related to any product or online sellers on SNSs such as ratings, reviews, and recommendations to facilitate purchasing decisions (Hajli et al., 2017a). A consumer's knowledge about a product can be enhanced by seeking and acquiring SC information from a plethora of sources available online. Subsequently, this additional knowledge about a specific product facilitates the customer's decision-making and increases the individual's purchase intentions (Chiou et al., 2002, Turcotte et al., 2015). Moreover, one of the most important factors influencing an individual's purchasing decisions is the monetary issue (Kim and Park, 2012). Maia et al. (2019) have mentioned that one of the significant advantages of online shopping is the offering of low-priced services or products, which can improve the level of customer trust in online organizations. The third psychological factor is trustworthiness. Trust is considered to be the key to the successful establishment of a long-term relationship and it becomes even more important in the context of online platforms because much uncertainty surrounds the online environment (Lin et al., 2018). In s-commerce, the users seek advice and reliable information from SNSs and members whom they can trust regarding their online experiences of purchasing a product or using service (Chen and Shen, 2015). Thus, in this study, Community Commitment, Trust in Marketplace, Trust towards Members and Trust in Sellers have been identified as the trustworthiness factor that could influence an individual's decision to use SC. The last psychological factor is the transaction safety that refers to the degree to which SC consumers perceive that SC supports a high level of security related to both transactions and transaction-related information (Maia et al., 2019). According to previous researches, transaction safety is a significant factor that determines the users' trust in e-commerce organizations (Cheung and Lee, 2006, Kim et al., 2008).

2.5 Cultural Factors

Globalization in the business world has increased dramatically; therefore, culture now plays a considerable role in all the business operations (Straub et al., 1997) and it directly impacts upon the consumers' adoption of technologies (Sheikh et al., 2017). As suggested by (Biucky et al., 2017), the acceptance and adoption of information technologies are influenced by cultural factors. This study focuses on five dimensions of culture: perceived awareness, perceived ethics, individualism / collectivism, gender and learning and training, which are the most relevant to this study.

3. RESEARCH METHODOLOGY

In the field of information systems, mixed methods design can provide a wider range of data that enable IS researchers to deal with such issues (Venkatesh et al., 2013). Moreover, the mixed methods approach provides a more in-depth comprehension of the research issue and questions than does a single method (Creswell and Clark, 2017). One type of mixed methods strategy known as "sequential explanatory research design" suggested in this study. This strategy involves two phases of data collection and analysis: a quantitative phase, followed by a qualitative phase (Saunders, 2016). In this study, the quantitative data should be collected first via an online survey to assist the researcher to identify the factors which should be added to the initial social commerce adoption framework. After that, the qualitative method should be applied by conducting semi-structured interviews to validate the improve of the social commerce adoption framework and to ensure that it is represented in a comprehensive manner.

The target population for the online survey can include any social network users in Saudi Arabia who have at least one social networking account.

A pilot survey questionnaire can be distributed before the online survey is conducted in order to ensure the survey questions' reliability and validity. A pilot test helps to refine the questionnaire and gives the researcher some indication of the validity and the likely reliability of the survey questions (Saunders, 2016).

After that, the researcher can conduct semi-structured interviews with e-commerce experts or proprietors to gather the data required for the purpose of achieving the research objectives and supporting the data obtained from the online survey results.

4. CONCLUSION

As a conclusion, the main purpose of this research is to makes new theoretical and academic contributions to the current literature on the significant factors required for the successful implementation of social commerce in Saudi Arabia. The study will contribute to the researches on social commerce adoption by adding information about the factors that affect consumer behavior in terms of using social commerce in the KSA. To the best of this researcher's knowledge, none of the previous researches has reviewed all these factors comprehensively. Thus, there is a need for a better understanding of the major factors that affect the consumers' online behavior.

In addition, in terms of practical application, it is anticipated that the study's outcomes will benefit stakeholders such as companies, organizations and governments as they will provide guidance on how to encourage customers to adopt social commerce and find practical solutions to improve the use of s-commerce in KSA. Furthermore, this research is aligned with the objectives of Saudi Vision 2030, a project map for strengthening the Saudi economy by diversifying income resources. One of the goals of Saudi Vision 2030 is to promote economic growth by empowering Saudi entrepreneurs (VISION). Hence, this research contributes to the Vision and has practical implications for Saudi internet entrepreneurs by offering recommendations that will encourage consumers to adopt SC in Saudi Arabia. Furthermore, this holistic framework could be applied in the Gulf Cooperation Council (GCC) countries as they have many factors in common such as culture, religion, social, languages, and economic and financial systems.

Finally, although the proposed holistic framework offers practical and theoretical contributions, its factors and relationships need to be empirically tested. In future work, we plan to extend the current research by examine the proposed framework by using a mixed-methods to determine the factors that influence customers' behaviour toward SC in KSA. Finally, this paper is part of a broader research project that we will publish in the future.

REFERENCES

99FIRMS. 2019. General Stats & Facts [Online]. Available: https://99firms.com/blog/ecommerce-statistics [Accessed Sep 20, 2019].

Abed, S. S. 2016. Exploring factors influencing consumer intention to use social commerce. 27811745 Ph.D., Swansea University (United Kingdom).

Ahn, T., Ryu, S. & Han, I. 2007. The impact of Web quality and playfulness on user acceptance of online retailing. Information & management, 44, 263-275.

Akman, I. & Mishra, A. 2017. Factors influencing consumer intention in social commerce adoption. Information Technology & People, 30, 356-370.

Al-Adwan, A. S. 2019. Revealing the influential factors driving social commerce adoption. Interdisciplinary Journal of Information, Knowledge, and Management, 14, 295-324.

Al-Adwan, A. S. & Kokash, H. 2019. The Driving Forces of Facebook Social Commerce. Journal of Theoretical and Applied Electronic Commerce Research, 14, 15-32.

Beisel, D. 2006. The emerging field of social commerce and social shopping. Genuine VC.

Biucky, S. T., Abdolvand, N. & Harandi, S. R. 2017. The Effects of Perceived Risk on Social Commerce Adoption Based on the TAM Model. International Journal of Electronic Commerce Studies, 8, 173-196.

Bounkhong, T. 2017. Factors Affecting Intentions to Use Social Commerce in Shopping for Fashion Products. 10275567 M.S., University of Arkansas.

Busalim, A. H. & Hussin, A. R. C. 2016. Understanding social commerce: A systematic literature review and directions for further research. International Journal of Information Management, 36, 1075-1088.

Chen, J. & Shen, X.-L. 2015. Consumers' decisions in social commerce context: An empirical investigation. Decision Support Systems, 79, 55-64.

Cheung, C. M. & Lee, M. K. 2006. Understanding consumer trust in Internet shopping: A multidisciplinary approach. Journal of the American society for Information Science and Technology, 57, 479-492.

Chiou, J.-S., Droge, C. & Hanvanich, S. 2002. Does customer knowledge affect how loyalty is formed? Journal of Service Research, 5, 113-124.

Choi, Y. 2019. The study of antecedents of aesthetic experience and consumer purchase intention in social commerce. International Journal of E-Services and Mobile Applications, 11, 67-78.

Cobb, S. 1976. Social support as a moderator of life stress. Psychosomatic medicine.

Creswell, J. W. & Clark, V. L. P. 2017. Designing and conducting mixed methods research, Sage publications.

Davis, F. D. 1989. Perceived usefulness, perceived ease of use, and user acceptance of information technology. MIS quarterly, 319-340.

Gatautis, R. & Medziausiene, A. 2014. Factors Affecting Social Commerce Acceptance in Lithuania. Procedia - Social and Behavioral Sciences, 110, 1235-1242.

GMI_BLOGGER. 2019. Saudi Arabia Social Media Statistics 2019 [Online]. Available: https://www.globalmediainsight.com/blog/saudi-arabia-social-media-statistics/ [Accessed Oct 12, 2019].

Hajli, N. 2019. The impact of positive valence and negative valence on social commerce purchase intention. Information Technology & People, 33, 774-791.

Hajli, N. & Sims, J. 2015. Social commerce: The transfer of power from sellers to buyers. Technological Forecasting and Social Change, 94, 350-358.

Hajli, N., Sims, J., Zadeh, A. H. & Richard, M.-O. 2017a. A social commerce investigation of the role of trust in a social networking site on purchase intentions. Journal of Business Research, 71, 133-141.

Hajli, N., Wang, Y., Tajvidi, M. & Hajli, M. S. 2017b. People, Technologies, and Organizations Interactions in a Social Commerce Era. IEEE Transactions on Engineering Management, 64, 594-604.

Han, H., Xu, H. & Chen, H. 2018. Social commerce: A systematic review and data synthesis. Electronic Commerce Research and Applications, 30, 38-50.

Hsu, C. L., Chang, K. C., Kuo, N. T. & Cheng, Y. S. 2017. The mediating effect of flow experience on social shopping behavior. Information Development, 33, 243-256.

Khan, A. G. 2016. Electronic commerce: A study on benefits and challenges in an emerging economy. Global Journal of Management and Business Research.

Kim, D. J., Ferrin, D. L. & Rao, H. R. 2008. A trust-based consumer decision-making model in electronic commerce: The role of trust, perceived risk, and their antecedents. Decision support systems, 44, 544-564.

Kim, S. & Park, H. 2012. Effects of various characteristics of social commerce (s-commerce) on consumers' trust and trust performance. International Journal of Information Management.

Kim, S. & Park, H. 2013. Effects of various characteristics of social commerce (s-commerce) on consumers' trust and trust performance. International Journal of Information Management, 33, 318-332.

Kim, S. Y. & Joo, Y. H. 2001. Perceived Interactivity and Web site Loyalty/On the Role of Flow as a Mediating Variable. Journal of Consumer Studies, 12, 185-208.

Lal, P. 2017. Analyzing determinants influencing an individual′ s intention to use social commerce website. Future Business Journal, 3, 70-85.

Law, T. J. 2019. 19 Powerful Ecommerce Statistics That Will Guide Your Strategy in 2019 [Online]. Available: https://www.oberlo.com/blog/ecommerce-statistics-guide-your-strategy [Accessed Oct 3, 2019].

Li, Q., Ni, L. & Li, E. Y. 2018. Does friendship quality matter in social commerce? An experimental study of its effect on purchase intention. Electronic Commerce Research, 18, 693-717.

Liang, T.-P., Ho, Y.-T., Li, Y.-W. & Turban, E. 2011. What drives social commerce: The role of social support and relationship quality. International journal of electronic commerce, 16, 69-90.

Liang, T.-P. & Turban, E. 2011. Introduction to the Special Issue Social Commerce: A Research Framework for Social Commerce. International Journal of Electronic Commerce, 16, 5-14.

Lin, J., Li, L., Yan, Y. & Turel, O. 2018. Understanding Chinese consumer engagement in social commerce. Internet Research, 28, 2-22.

Lu, W. 2017. An Examination of Social Online Shopping Attitudes of Undergraduate Students Enrolled in the Department of Agricultural Leadership, Education, and Communications at Texas A&M University. 10662557 Ph.D., Texas A&M University.

Maia, C. R., Lunardi, G. L., Dolci, D. & D'avila, L. C. 2019. Competitive Price and Trust as Determinants of Purchase Intention in Social Commerce. Brazilian Administration Review, 16, 1-24.

Makki, E. & Chang, L.-C. 2015. Understanding the effects of social media and mobile usage on e-commerce: an exploratory study in Saudi Arabia. International management review, 11, 98.

NG, C. S.-P. 2013. Intention to purchase on social commerce websites across cultures: A cross-regional study. Information & Management, 50, 609-620.

Noh, M., Lee, K., Kim, S. & Garrison, G. 2013. Effects of collectivism on actual s-commerce use and the moderating effect of price consciousness. Journal of Electronic Commerce Research, 14, 244.

Saunders, M. A. 2016. Research methods for business students / Mark Saunders, Philip Lewis, Adrian Thornhill, Harlow Pearson Education.

Sheikh, Z., Islam, T., Rana, S., Hameed, Z. & Saeed, U. 2017. Acceptance of social commerce framework in Saudi Arabia. Telematics and Informatics, 34, 1693-1708.

Shin, D.-H. 2013. User experience in social commerce: in friends we trust. Behaviour & information technology, 32, 52-67.

STATISTA. 2019a. E-commerce in Saudi Arabia [Online]. Available: https://www.statista.com/outlook/243/110/ecommerce/saudi-arabia [Accessed Oct 10, 2019].

STATISTA. 2019b. E-commerce worldwide - Statistics & Facts [Online]. Available: https://www.statista.com/statistics/534123/e-commerce-share-of-retail-sales-worldwide/ [Accessed Dec 19, 2019].

STATISTA. 2019c. Number of digital buyers worldwide from 2014 to 2021 [Online]. Available: https://www.statista.com/statistics/251666/number-of-digital-buyers-worldwide/ [Accessed Sep 18, 2019].

Straub, D., Keil, M. & Brenner, W. 1997. Testing the technology acceptance model across cultures: A three country study. Information & management, 33, 1-11.

Teo, T. S., Srivastava, S. C. & Jiang, L. 2008. Trust and electronic government success: An empirical study. Journal of management information systems, 25, 99-132.

Turcotte, J., York, C., Irving, J., Scholl, R. M. & Pingree, R. J. 2015. News recommendations from social media opinion leaders: Effects on media trust and information seeking. Journal of Computer-Mediated Communication, 20, 520-535.

Venkatesh, V., Brown, S. A. & Bala, H. 2013. Bridging the qualitative-quantitative divide: Guidelines for conducting mixed methods research in information systems. MIS quarterly, 21-54.

Wang, C. & Zhang, P. 2012. The evolution of social commerce: The people, management, technology, and information dimensions. Communications of the Association for Information Systems, 31, 105-127.

WEBALIVE. 2019. The State of Australia's Ecommerce in 2019 [Online]. Available: https://www.webalive.com.au/ecommerce-statistics-australia/ [Accessed Sep 25, 2019].

INTERACTIVE POTENTIAL OF NEWS NARRATIVES IN COMMUNITIES FORMED AROUND NEWS MEDIA

Artem Zakharchenko
Taras Shevchenko National University of Kyiv, 17a, Biloruska Street, #16, Kyiv 04119, Ukraine

ABSTRACT

The paper describes how the narrative features of highly shared news publications allow predicting the strength of their influence on social media communities. The Interactive potential was used as an indicator for measuring the strength of influence of news, which were classified on four levels of inner and external narrative structure. News stories published by popular Ukrainian media were taken as examples to show that the share of publications with inner narrative is low among high-influential articles, and the same holds for the share of publications that are parts of long or short media stories. In contrast, the articles, which could be embedded into the national narrative, and publications with certain issues of media agenda more often have high influence.

KEYWORDS

Media Influence, Interactive Potential, News Narrative, Social Action, Agenda-Setting

1. INTRODUCTION

Measurement of the influence of media publications on different groups and communities in social media is a complex issue, widely discussed in social (Bagozzi and Lee, 2002) and communication research papers (Gerbaudo, 2016), as well as in the information science investigations (Even-Dar and Shapira, 2011). Even more complicated is the issue of revealing the drivers of influence. Most of the papers that measure influence quantitatively do not go into mechanisms of influence. And vice versa, communicative researchers that analyze content do not use measurements or apply a simple parameter: the total number of article shares.

Researchers tried to reveal the interconnection between the number of shares and characteristics of shared content. In part, it is determined, that fake news usually is shared better than truthful because of their higher perceived novelty (Vosoughi et al., 2018). Negative news usually spread better than positive (Yan and Jiang, 2018). But in some situations reverse is true (You and Ju, 2018). (Nikolinakou and King, 2018) summarize that mobilizing emotions, both negative and positive, usually prompt sharing better than demobilizing ones. (Zengin Alp and Gündüz Öğüdücü, 2018) propose a mathematical model of different topics sharing.

But the number of shares is not the only indicator of influence. Interactive potential (IP) introduced in (Zakharchenko, 2017a) shows how strong was the influence of a media publication on the users of some social network community. This indicator shows how many interactions of news with users (in this research – 'likes', shares, or comments on Facebook) are, on average, caused by one previous interaction. If this value is >1, spreading is accelerated as a power function, but if <1, it gradually fades out. In a case of some particular number of interactions, for example, 10 000, IP shows whether this number is due to the strong influence of this publication on 10 000 readers or weak influence on 1 000 000 readers. It is calculated as a slope factor (on logarithmic scale) of the line of dependence of publication interactions number on the so-called 'audience time' (substitute of the time, the number of page views of a sample of Ukrainian media) in the specific period of sharing (so called specific period, on which the network topology has no big influence).

This indicator was used in (Zakharchenko, 2019) to reveal how the strength of influence depends on the type of social action implied by sharing. Five types of sharing were detected. Four of them are Weber`s types of social actions: goal-rational, value-rational, affective, and traditional. The fifth, goal-rational (internalization), is singled out of the first-mentioned type, and means sharing just to inform followers, instead of other goal-rational shares aimed at actions outside the social networks. The media publications implying goal rational spreading have the highest IP, and therefore the strongest influence on the audience. Instead, the news intended for emotional actions, as a rule, are less influential, even if they have a high number of shares.

2. BODY OF PAPER

Thus, our research question is such: is there any substantial interrelationship between the narrative features of news media publications and the strength of their influence on the news consumers' communities?

To answer this question the sample of the data used in (Zakharchenko, 2019) was taken and a narrative analysis of publications in it was provided. This dataset includes 827 publications of news website Ukrainska Pravda published from January 2016 to June 2017 and having at least 600 Facebook shares, likes, or comments. They dwelled on different topics: from politics and economics to sport and culture. The collected publications were divided into four ranges according to its IP value: 0-0.3; 0.3-1.0; 1.0-1.7 and over 1.7. Distribution of news according to the value of interactive potential corresponds to the normal distribution; the mode is 0.55.

Ukrainska Pravda is one of the most visited Ukrainian news websites. It has a mild patriotic bias and one of the largest audience cores in Ukraine, so, there is a community of people who share its content.

The narrative analysis dealt with four narrative indicators detected in the news publications. Two trained coders detected four parameters applying different approaches of narrative analysis:

1. The first indicator is an inner narrative of publication. The categorical-form type of narrative analysis was applied. Here coders looked for stories in common, not strictly scientific sense. It is known that the persuasive ability of narrative is determined by the narrative structure (Busselle and Bilandzic, 2008, p. 266). Most of the typical news made by an 'inverted pyramid' scheme doesn`t have the narrative structure, as well as some long articles based only on facts and its analysis. In contrast, all publications applying the narrative style in all text or its parts like quotations were marked as publications with inner narrative as well as publications with clear 'Hollywood' structure (inciting incident, rising action, climax, resolution) or just publications that describe the temporal course of events, not just separate facts.

2. Belonging to 'short' or 'long' external narratives or appearance as a single publication. The holistic-content type of narrative analysis was applied. As determined in (Zakharchenko, 2017b), whole media narrative consists of plot lines with different lengths, and of separate single publications. In this paper the term 'long plot lines' was used for topics covered by the news media sample, which duration is more than 2 weeks without substantial decrease of coverage intensity and with more than 10 newsworthy events. Topics that had at least 2 newsworthy events and lasted up to 2 weeks were called 'short plot lines'. And other news publications were considered single. It was concluded that the weekly fluctuations in attendance of online-media were primarily due to fluctuations in the number of news stories of long plot lines. So, the audience usually follows long plotlines like a kind of TV series. In this paper, the same approach was used for coding.

3. Belonging to the national narrative. The holistic-content type of narrative analysis was applied. The national narrative as a comprehensive story about the origins of the nation, its development, justify the rules for its representatives and their relations with foreigners, is widely discussed (Khaldarova and Pantti, 2016; Krasodomski-Jones et al., 2019; Szostek, 2017). The feature of the Ukrainian nation is that it has no unified national narrative, instead, it has five different narratives (Korostelina, 2014). Taking into account the patriotic bias of Ukrainska Pravda, it was assumed that most of its readers agree with two patriotic narratives (according to Korostelina): 'Recognition of Ukrainian Ethnic Identity' and 'Fight for a Ukrainian ethnic identity'. So, in this section publications which could be embedded in one or both mentioned narratives were marked.

4. Agenda of publications. Social issues covered by media and called media agenda could be considered parts of the media narrative. The coding was based on the division of (Comparative Agendas Project, n.d.); its categories were amalgamated considering the Ukrainian realities. Seven categories were derived: Civil rights; Crime and corruption; Domestic commerce; Government operations and internal politics; Humanitarian (health, education, religion, culture); Social welfare and householding; War (foreign policy, defense).

Intercoder reliability was 87.3%, disagreements were resolved by the author of the paper.

Distribution of all coded parameters showed a strong dependence on IP value. Specifically, the share of publications with an inner narrative decreased with the rise of the IP. (See Figure 1.) Publications with inner narrative usually induced emotional or goal-rational (internalization) shares which usually had low IP value. The sharing message could be formulated as 'Let`s read this story'. Conversely, value-rational and goal-rational shares usually were caused by crude facts.

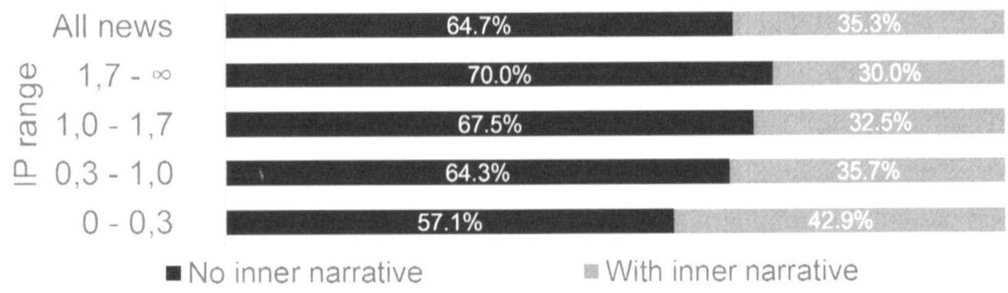

Figure 1. Share of publications with inner narrative and without it depended on the IP range

A similar pattern can be established regarding the external narratives and its length. (See Figure 2.) Publications that are parts of long and, especially, short stories rarely attained high IP values. High-intensity goal-rational and value-rational shares usually were caused by single stories. In contrast, short stories predominantly provoked emotional shares.

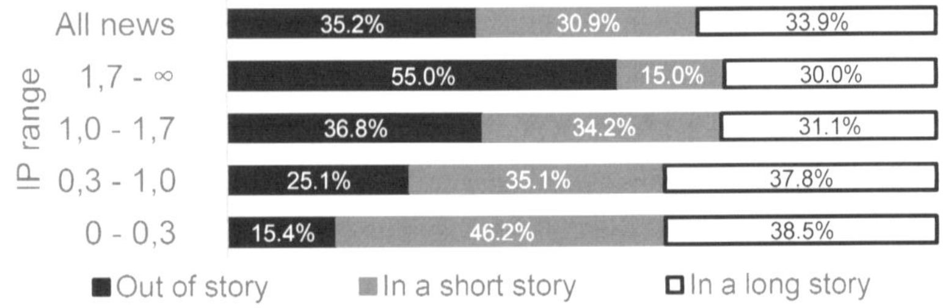

Figure 2. Share of publications embedded in short, long news narratives, and of single stories depended on the IP range

News embedding into the national narrative showed the opposite effect. (See Figure 3.) A higher share of publications that could be embedded into the national narrative is in the highest IP range. This is due to the value-rational type of news sharing with this narrative and, to a lesser extent, by goal-rational sharing; indeed, national narratives usually do not employ a simple emotional mood of sharing.

Figure 3. Share of publications embedded in the national narrative depended on the IP range

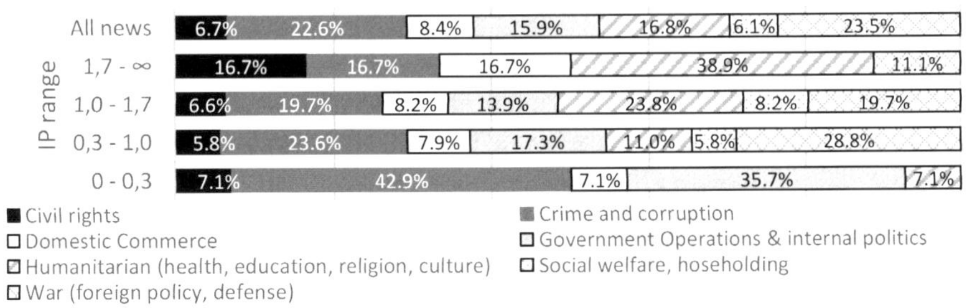

Figure 4. Share of publications with different agendas, depending on the IP range

The dependence of agenda on IP is a bit more complicated. (See Figure 4.) Some issues which share decreases with the growth of IP may be singled out. These are Crime and corruption, Government operations and internal politics, and War. They all were predominantly shared in an emotional mood, even stories about war that usually could be embedded into the national narrative. The share of other issues grew with the increase of IP, including Civil rights, Humanitarian (health, education, religion, culture) and Domestic commerce. This corresponds to the predominant type of shares: value-rational for the Civil rights and Humanitarian issues, and goal-rational (internalization) for Domestic commerce and Social welfare and householding issues.

3. CONCLUSION

The research shows that the Interactive potential and correspondingly the strength of influence depends on the narrative features of shared news content. Some narrative indicators are more common for news with high IP, while others for low. In each case it can be attributed to the type of sharing as social action which is predominant for this indicator value. So, there is a three-level dependence. The narrative features with other content parameters like sentiment, topic, lexicon, etc. determine the type of sharing and the strength of influence. Meanwhile, these two parameters are not completely independent: the type of sharing usually corresponds with particular IP diapason, as it is shown in (Zakharchenko, 2019).

No doubt, the mechanism of this determination could be different in different audiences. Though the question requires further study with different datasets, even now the findings of this paper may be used to create messages with a higher influence on particular parts of the media audience.

REFERENCES

Bagozzi, R.P., Lee, K.-H., 2002. Multiple Routes for Social Influence: The Role of Compliance, Internalization, and Social Identity. *Social Psychology Quarterly*. Vol. 65, Is. 3, pp. 226.

Busselle, R., Bilandzic, H., 2008. Fictionality and perceived realism in experiencing stories: A model of narrative comprehension and engagement. *Communication Theory,* Vol. 18, Is. 2, pp. 255–280.

Comparative Agendas Project, n.d. CAP Topics [WWW Document]. URL https://www.comparativeagendas.net/pages/master-codebook

Even-Dar, E., Shapira, A., 2011. A note on maximizing the spread of influence in social networks. *Information Processing Letters*, Vol. 111, Is. 4, pp. 184–187.

Gerbaudo, P., 2016. Rousing the Facebook Crowd: Digital Enthusiasm and Emotional Contagion in the 2011 Protests in Egypt and Spain. *International Journal of Communication*. Vol. 10, pp. 254–273.

Khaldarova, I., Pantti, M., 2016. Fake news. The narrative battle over the Ukrainian conflict. *Journalism Practice*. Vol. 10, Is. 7, pp. 891–901.

Korostelina, K.V., 2014. *Constructing the narratives of identity and power: Self-imagination in a young Ukrainian nation.* Lexington Books, Lanham.

Krasodomski-Jones, A. et al, 2019. *Warring Songs: Information Operations in the Digital Age*. London: Demos.

Nikolinakou, A., King, K.W., 2018. Viral video ads: Emotional triggers and social media virality. *Psychology and Marketing*. Vol. 35, pp. 715–726.

Szostek, J., 2017. The Power and Limits of Russia's Strategic Narrative in Ukraine: The Role of Linkage. *Perspectives on Politics*. Vol. 15, Is. 2, pp. 379–395.

Vosoughi, S. et al, 2018. The spread of true and false news online. *Science*. Vol. 359, pp. 1146–1151.

Yan, X., Jiang, P., 2018. Effect of the dynamics of human behavior on the competitive spreading of information. *Computers in Human Behavior*. Vol. 89, pp. 1–7.

You, M., Ju, Y., 2018. Preferring negative or positive news? A closer examination of journalistic negativity in a health crisis. *Atlantic Journal of Communication*. Vol. 26, Is. 5, pp. 318–329.

Zakharchenko, A., 2019. Social Actions of Social Networks Users Triggered By Media Posts Content. *Social Welfare: Interdisciplinary Approach*, Vol. 2, Is. 8, pp. 53–65.

Zakharchenko, A., 2017a. Evaluating the social influence of internet media news. *Civitas et Lex*, Vol. 3 (15), pp. 7–21.

Zakharchenko, A., 2017b. Serial structure of the online media narrative. Studia Methodologica, Is. 45, pp. 103–112.

Zengin Alp, Z., Gündüz Öğüdücü, Ş., 2018. Identifying topical influencers on twitter based on user behavior and network topology. *Knowledge-Based Systems*. Vol. 141, pp. 211–221.

INITIATING AND ASSESSING AN E-NUDGING MODEL FOR HIGHER EDUCATION IN SAUDI ARABIA

Salihah Alotaibi
Curtin University, WA, Australia

ABSTRACT

Decisions related to education are complex and have long-term consequences. For higher education students, particularly first-year students, most of these decisions are made when students are young and with little academic experience; these decisions can potentially influence students' futures. This study aims to propose an e-nudging model for higher education that offers an early and low-cost support for universities to encourage better education decision-making for students in a digital environment (i.e. learning systems). The empirical study will be conducted in the Kingdom of Saudi Arabia (KSA) using a mixed-methods approach to assess the effectiveness of the proposed model derived from the literature review. Also, the study will examine the current factors (behavioral, cognitive, and environmental barriers) that influence the effectiveness of the e-nudging model. The research will enhance the understanding of behavioral and cognitive barriers in a digital environment, and how these influence students' decisions. The research will contribute by establishing a relationship between digital nudging, the field of Information Systems (IS) and Human Computer Interaction (HCI), in particular by assisting designers to understand student behaviors and guide users to make the most desirable choice. Lastly, the proposed e-nudging model will improve our understanding of the concept of digital nudging and its application in the learning and teaching field in the KSA and generally in the Gulf Cooperation Council (GCC) countries.

KEYWORDS

Digital Nudging, Educational Decision, Behavioral, Cognitive and Environmental Barriers, HCI

1. INTRODUCTION

Universities play a significant role in the human development process. Universities provide a high level of academic knowledge, educational skills, and learning experience to students, allowing them to make a more positive impact on society and the economy. Despite the importance of universities and their benefits, many students perform poorly or decide to drop out of university. In fact, the dropout rate from universities and colleges in Saudi Arabia is 30% (Sulphey & Alkahtani, 2018). This high rate is attributed to several factors such as lack of student interest, poor attendance, and a social structure that has made the younger generation more immature and more dependent on family and society (Sulphey & Alkahtani, 2018). In addition, some studies found that Saudi students are negatively influenced by scheduling issues (Khan, 2011) and lack time management skills resulting in overdue assignment submissions (Sulphey & Alkahtani, 2018) These factors are more common among first-year students and have more detrimental consequences(Brock, 2010).

In the context of education decisions, students, face a series of complex decisions. Most of these decisions, which can potentially influence the students' futures, are made when students are young and have limited academic experience (Damgaard & Nielsen, 2018). This complex situation may cause some students to postpone the completion of academic tasks, to make unwise or wrong decisions, miss key deadlines or lose confidence (Castleman & Meyer, 2016). Furthermore, many studies indicate that adolescents are particularly likely to be impacted by self-control problems (Bettinger & Slonim, 2007; Green, Fry, & Myerson, 1994). In an online environment, sometimes the system's complexity or behavioral factors might affect the students' commitment, while interventions such as reminders may significantly increase student commitment to complete academic tasks and improve outcomes (Patterson, 2018). Therefore, understanding the cognitive, behavioral economics (Castleman & Meyer, 2016) and environmental (Mirsch, Lehrer, & Jung, 2017) barriers are essential when designing motivational interventions that reduce the detrimental impact of such barriers, because they secure the person's attention and possibly prevent unwise decision making.

This paper is organized as follows: section 2 provides a brief introduction to the education decision barriers including (behavioral economics, cognitive and environment). Section three (3) is the core of the research and presents the notion of nudging and proposed model. Section 4 describe of the research methodology. Finally, section 5 describe the research conclusion.

2. LITERATURE REVIEW

This section reviews the current literature relating to the factors that influence the effectiveness of the proposed e-nudging model for higher education in Saudi Arabia.

2.1 Behavioral Economic Barriers

The behavioral economic field is one that studies and describes economic decision-making. Behavioral economic insights become interesting topic to inform intervention design in education (Andor, Fels, Renz, & Rzepka, 2018; Damgaard & Nielsen, 2018; Hortal, 2019). One of the behavioral barriers is known as bounded rationality (Hortal, 2019; Patterson, 2018; Sulphey & Alkahtani, 2018). Thaler and Sunstein (2008) state that irrational decisions are likely to occur in four situations. The first is when a person prefers to have immediate gratification and is prepared to deal with its cost in the future. The second situation is when no immediate feedback is given. Finally, there are situations which are unfamiliar, or which rarely occur. Unfortunately, in regard to education, many decisions are made by people who are young and therefore susceptible to making unwise or neon-optimal decisions (Damgaard & Nielsen, 2018). In addition, some education decisions are difficult, complex, unfamiliar, and rare, because the university's environment is new. Students might not understand some academic practices, making it difficult for them to make decisions. Moreover, some situations may be unfamiliar and may rarely occur, so students cannot make decisions based on past experience. For example, choosing a college is usually a once-in-a-lifetime occurrence (Damgaard & Nielsen, 2018; Thaler & Sunstein, 2008). Another behavioral barrier that affects students' outcomes is lack of self-control. Thaler and Sunstein (2008) mention that, generally, a series of bad outcomes eventuate when people have self-control issues combined with mindless choices. During their study journey at university, students are required to make a sustained effort and stay motivated. Therefore, students need a gentle nudge to improve their outcomes and help them make better decisions.

2.2 Cognitive Barriers

Cognitive biases play an important role in the decision-making process. These biases occur because the human brain tends to simplify information processing by using different techniques such as heuristics. One important type of cognitive bias is attentional limitation. When student face a complex choice, they are more likely to pay attention to some information and (intentionally or unintentionally) ignoring other information, which leads to poor decisions. For instance, many researches have revealed that students have poor information about education policies such as administration, course withdraw, changing major policies, although the information is available (Damgaard & Nielsen, 2018). Sometimes, the limited attention issue may cause students to forget to do tasks (Patterson, 2018). Moreover, optimism and over-confidence bias leads students to believe that their abilities are better than those of their peers (Damgaard & Nielsen, 2018). Unrealistic optimism influences students' decisions which in turn impact on their academic performance. If the students face one or more of these cognitive biases, they are more likely to benefit from nudges.

2.3 Environmental Barriers

The environment and how information is presented strongly influence a person's choices and decisions. In a digital environment, people are more likely to make imperfect decisions. On screen, they make a quick and automated decision or choice as a result of the massive amount of information available on the Internet that make it difficult to process relevant details in order to make the best decision (Mirsch et al., 2017). Hovdhaugen and Aamodt (2009) found that dissatisfaction with the learning environment and problems related to academic achievements and motivation are reasons why students abandon higher education. Hence, some universities are now using electronic learning systems such as Blackboard and Angel/LMS Learning Management System (LMS) to enhance the education environment and make learning more convenient. These learning systems focus on providing efficient techniques to improve students' learning (Landry, Griffeth, & Hartman, 2006; Talebian, Mohammadi, & Rezvanfar, 2014). Nevertheless, many students found it hard to use, particularly those students who had less academic and computational experiences (Bradford, Porciello, Balkon, & Backus, 2007). On other hand, Zhang, Almeroth, Knight, Bulger, and Mayer (2007) designed a learning system, similar to Moodle, that provides feedback and reminders to students via email. They found that the students become more interested in viewing course materials. Therefore, the creation of a learning environment that is easy to deal with and improves student motivation would influence students to make better decisions and improve their outcomes. To sum up, these barriers and limitations impede the learning process. They are predictable (Bradbury, McGimpsey, & Santori, 2013; Thaler & Sunstein, 2008), so decision-making can be framed in specific ways to nudge students to choose better in order to produce optimum outcomes.

3. DIGITAL NUDGING

Digital nudging is a concept that emerged in 2016. It transferred the nudge theory to the digital environment. Digital nudging "is the use of user-interface design elements to guide people's behavior in digital choice environments" (Weinmann, Schneider, & vom Brocke, 2016). The authors argue that the concept of digital nudging is based on insights from behavioral economics. It deals with the user interface design elements to steer user behavior toward specific decision-making in a digital environment. In addition, there are several advantages of digital nudging: the implementation is easier, faster and cheaper; moreover, the Internet allows designers to tailor nudges for particular users, which makes them more effective (Mirsch et al., 2017). In addition, digital nudging can be easily generated and modified for a digital environment. Hence, the effectiveness of the nudging can be tested quickly by means of an online experiment (Schneider, Weinmann, & vom Brocke, 2018).

3.1 Digital Nudging Model

This subsection reviews the current literature relating to nudging models. Currently there are five proposed models for nudging. One particular model for design nudging was proposed by (Ly, Mazar, Zhao, & Soman, 2013). The authors proposed a general approach to nudge-development. They provided a sequential structure that makes the process more accessible. Weinmann et al. (2016) designed the first model for the digital nudging process, which comprise five phases for online decision environments. The second model proposed by Meske and Potthoff (2017), consists of a cyclical three-phase process for the design of digital nudges, called "digital nudging process model" (DINU). The third model proposed by Schneider et al. (2018), also developed a cyclical model to design digital nudges which contains four phases (identify the goals, understand the users, design the nudge, and test the nudge). The fourth model proposed by Bertheim (2018). In his model, he considered the ethics factor for the entire process, not just for design nudging phases .The last model modified the Schneider et al. (2018) model by considering timing as a critical factor for the success of digital nudges (Purohit & Holzer, 2019).

However, after comparing these models, some of the processing steps and factors were found to be missing in some models, and none of these models consider the HCI and usability when designing digital nudging. According to Issa and Isaias (2015), the aim of Human Computer Interaction (HCI) is to design a user interface (UI) that meet users' needs and requirements. UI design aims at maximizing the usability and user experience (UX). The usability refers to the ease of use and efficiency. As mentioned above, there is no general way to design choices due to the changes in the environment and the ways in which humans interact with technologies (Mirsch et al., 2017; Weinmann et al., 2016). Digital nudging is an emergent concept that can potentially inspire HCI research (Mirsch et al., 2017). Furthermore, all the models assess the effectiveness of the digital nudging at the end of the entire process in the test phase. Evaluation is a critical step in developing new technology in order to ensure that the new technology meets the user's requirements (Issa & Isaias, 2015). Furthermore, no digital nudging model appropriately identifies the environmental barriers as factors that affect the user's behavior. Although the environment is mentioned as a possible influencing factor, no details are given. Digital choice environments are included in the user interface. The ways in which a system is organized and presented in the digital environment is more likely to influence the user's decisions (Issa & Isaias, 2015; Weinmann et al., 2016). This is central to the design of nudges. (Dimitrova, Mitrovic, Piotrkowicz, Lau, & Weerasinghe, 2017). Therefore, it is important to understand the behavioral effects of interface design elements on the user's decisions, and to ensure that digital nudging is properly conducted and does not occur at random. Finally, ethics must be taken into account when designing a nudge. It is unethical to nudge people towards decisions that could harm them or compromise their welfare (Hortal, 2019). Also, it is important to not use individuals' behavioral barriers such as inertia or inattention against them (Sunstein, 2016).

3.1.1 The Study Proposed Model

The study proposed e-nudge model in the digital environment comprises three phases. The first phase involves analysing user behaviour which consists of two stages: planning and analysis. The second phase concerns nudging or designing user behaviour which also consists of two stages: design and implementation. The last phase is evaluating user behaviour which includes the testing stage. All three phases include a feedback loop to enhance the development process. The e-Nudging model architecture is illustrated in Figure1.

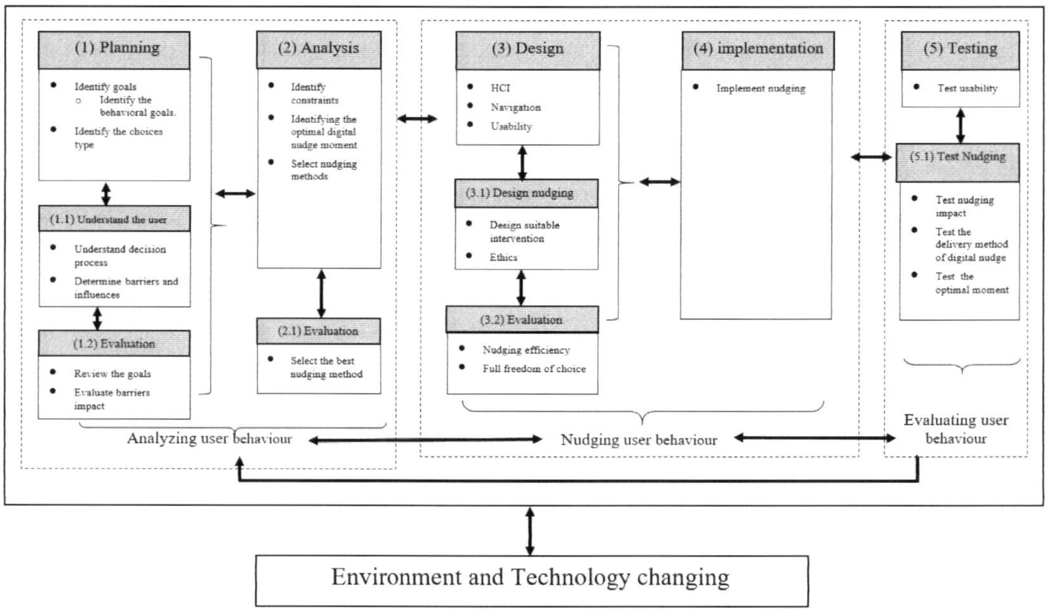

Figure 1. Proposed e-Nudging Model for higher education in KSA

However, in the education field, a few studies applied nudging in a digital environment. Dimitrova et al. (2017) applied personalized nudges to encourage students to engage with video content by rating and adding comments in an active video watching system (AVW). Smith, White, Kuzyk, and Tierney (2018) also designed a "grade nudge" sent to students via e-mail after each assignment. The findings indicated that the homework performance improved by about four percentage points. Andor et al. (2018) tested nudging as a prompt which was embedded in the course interface as a pop-up rather than an external website to reduce the drop-out rate in MOOCs. The nudging prompt increased the course completion rate by 19%. This study did not apply to students, schools, or universities.

4. RESEARCH METHODOLOGY

This study concerns the intersection of three streams: digital nudging, HCI and the education system. In fact, Information Systems (IS) researchers frequently face challenges in that research findings often do not provide enough explanations about a phenomenon of interest. Therefore, in this study, the mixed-methods research design can be used as a powerful tool that enables IS researchers to deal with such conditions and achieve a better understanding of the research problem (Venkatesh, Brown, & Bala, 2013). The mixed-methods research approach can be defined as a procedure for collecting, analyzing, and integrating the findings from both quantitative and qualitative data within a single study (Doyle, Brady, & Byrne, 2009; Johnson, Onwuegbuzie, & Turner, 2007).

The study will apply an approach called "Explanatory Sequential Design" which is a type of mixed-methods research design in order to achieve research objectives and answer the research questions. The approach consists of two phases: a quantitative phase, followed by a qualitative phase. This means the data will be collected equally from each phase: quantitative data via online survey in order to obtain students' academics and technology staff's opinions, to identify any new factors that may influence the impact of the e-nudging model. In the next phase, the qualitative method will use semi-structured interviews to obtain expert academics' opinions about the use of the e-nudging model, and to obtain a better understanding of these constructed factors.

5. CONCLUSION

This study will contribute a new theoretical perspective to the growing literature on the relationship between HCI and digital nudging. The concept of digital nudging is likely to add a new aspect to UI and user experience (UX) design. A clear understanding of the behavioral and cognitive effects on the human decision-making process will assist UI designers to improve their design and determine whether or not the digital environment nudges the users as intended. Also, this study aims to provide academic knowledge about important behavioral, cognitive and environmental factors in the education field, facilitating the design of successful digital nudging in learning systems.

In the context of education in the KSA, this study will make a contribution in terms of practical application. Until recently, to the best of the researcher's knowledge, no study has been conducted on the initiation and assessment of the effectiveness of digital nudging in Saudi Arabian universities. This study aims to assess the proposed e-nudging model, the relevant factors and how they influence the effectiveness of digital nudging in a learning system. Given the Saudi Arabian government's vison for the development of the higher education sector, the research findings will assist stakeholders such as universities, education departments and governments to make more informed decisions about applying digital nudging successfully in the education system and reap the benefits of this emerging concept. The main outcome of this study will be an e-nudging model for higher education in the KSA. This model will provide the foundation for stakeholders to effectively establish and implement the e-nudging model in the Saudi education system. Moreover, this model can be applied in the Gulf Cooperation Council (GCC) countries as they share many common factors and characteristics such as culture, religion, social, languages, and economic and financial system.

Finally, the proposed model factors and relationships need to be empirically tested. In future work, this reserarch will extend by examining our e-nudge model using a mixed-methods approach to determine the factors that influence the effectiveness of the proposed e-nudging model for higher education in Saudi Arabia. At the end, this paper is portion of a large research project that the approach results and reserch findings will be published in future.

REFERENCES

Andor, M. A., Fels, K. M., Renz, J., & Rzepka, S. (2018). *Do planning prompts increase educational success? Evidence from randomized controlled trials in MOOCs*: Ruhr Economic Papers.

Bertheim, J. (2018). Designing Digital Nudges to Encourage Sustainable Decisions: Developing and Testing a Framework. In.

Bettinger, E., & Slonim, R. (2007). Patience among children. *Journal of Public Economics, 91*(1-2), 343-363.

Bradbury, A., McGimpsey, I., & Santori, D. (2013). Revising rationality: the use of 'Nudge'approaches in neoliberal education policy. *Journal of Education Policy, 28*(2), 247-267.

Bradford, P., Porciello, M., Balkon, N., & Backus, D. (2007). The Blackboard learning system: The be all and end all in educational instruction? *Journal of Educational Technology Systems, 35*(3), 301-314.

Brock, T. (2010). Young adults and higher education: Barriers and breakthroughs to success. *The future of children*, 109-132.

Castleman, B. L., & Meyer, K. (2016). Can text message nudges improve academic outcomes in college? Evidence from a west virginia initiative. *Center for Education Policy and Workforce Competitiveness Working Paper, 43*.

Damgaard, M. T., & Nielsen, H. S. (2018). Nudging in education. *Economics of Education Review, 64*, 313-342.

Dimitrova, V., Mitrovic, A., Piotrkowicz, A., Lau, L., & Weerasinghe, A. (2017). *Using learning analytics to devise interactive personalised nudges for active video watching.* Paper presented at the Proceedings of the 25th Conference on User Modeling, Adaptation and Personalization.

Doyle, L., Brady, A.-M., & Byrne, G. (2009). An overview of mixed methods research. *Journal of research in nursing, 14*(2), 175-185.

Green, L., Fry, A. F., & Myerson, J. (1994). Discounting of delayed rewards: A life-span comparison. *Psychological science, 5*(1), 33-36.

Hortal, A. (2019). Nudging and educating: bounded axiological rationality in behavioral insights. *Behavioural Public Policy*, 1-24.

Hovdhaugen, E., & Aamodt, P. O. (2009). Learning environment: Relevant or not to students' decision to leave university? *Quality in higher education, 15*(2), 177-189.

Issa, T., & Isaias, P. (2015). Color, Prototyping and Navigation, Principles and Guidelines Design, Evaluation and Testing; Task Analysis. In *Sustainable Design* (pp. 71-86): Springer.

Johnson, R. B., Onwuegbuzie, A. J., & Turner, L. A. (2007). Toward a definition of mixed methods research. *Journal of mixed methods research, 1*(2), 112-133.

Khan, I. A. (2011). An analysis of learning barriers: The Saudi Arabian context. *International Education Studies, 4*(1), 242-247.

Landry, B. J., Griffeth, R., & Hartman, S. (2006). Measuring student perceptions of blackboard using the technology acceptance model. *Decision Sciences Journal of Innovative Education, 4*(1), 87-99.

Ly, K., Mazar, N., Zhao, M., & Soman, D. (2013). A practitioner's guide to nudging. *Rotman School of Management Working Paper*(2609347).

Meske, C., & Potthoff, T. (2017). The DINU-model–a process model for the design of nudges.

Mirsch, T., Lehrer, C., & Jung, R. (2017). Digital nudging: Altering user behavior in digital environments. *Proceedings der 13. Internationalen Tagung Wirtschaftsinformatik (WI 2017)*, 634-648.

Patterson, R. W. (2018). Can behavioral tools improve online student outcomes? Experimental evidence from a massive open online course. *Journal of Economic Behavior & Organization, 153*, 293-321.

Purohit, A. K., & Holzer, A. (2019). *Functional Digital Nudges: Identifying Optimal Timing for Effective Behavior Change.* Paper presented at the Extended Abstracts of the 2019 CHI Conference on Human Factors in Computing Systems.

Schneider, C., Weinmann, M., & vom Brocke, J. (2018). Digital Nudging-Influencing Choices by Using Interface Design. *Communications of the ACM, 61*(7), 67-73.

Smith, White, D., Kuzyk, P., & Tierney, J. (2018). Improved grade outcomes with an e-mailed "grade nudge". *The Journal of Economic Education, 49*(1), 1-7.

Sulphey, M., & Alkahtani, N. S. (2018). Academic excellences of business graduates through nudging: prospects in Saudi Arabia. *International Journal of Innovation and Learning, 24*(1), 98-114.

Sunstein, C. R. (2016). Do people like nudges. *Admin. L. Rev., 68*, 177.

Talebian, S., Mohammadi, H. M., & Rezvanfar, A. (2014). Information and communication technology (ICT) in higher education: advantages, disadvantages, conveniences and limitations of applying e-learning to agricultural students in Iran. *Procedia-Social and Behavioral Sciences, 152*, 300-305.

Thaler, R. H., & Sunstein, C. R. (2008). *Nudge: Improving decisions about health, wealth, and happiness*: Penguin.

Venkatesh, V., Brown, S. A., & Bala, H. (2013). Bridging the qualitative-quantitative divide: Guidelines for conducting mixed methods research in information systems. *MIS quarterly*, 21-54.

Weinmann, M., Schneider, C., & vom Brocke, J. (2016). Digital Nudging *Business & Information Systems Engineering, 58*(6), 433-436.

Zhang, H., Almeroth, K., Knight, A., Bulger, M., & Mayer, R. (2007). *Moodog: Tracking students' online learning activities.* Paper presented at the EdMedia+ Innovate Learning.

TWITTER SENTIMENT ANALYSIS: FAN ENGAGEMENT IN ESPORTS MATCHES

Sarah Anne Yan and Peter Mawhorter
Wellesley College, United States

ABSTRACT

Sentiment analysis is used to gain an understanding of the opinions, emotions, and subjectivity of text. Twitter is a social networking service where millions of users post and interact with messages. For multiplayer video game competitions, known as esports, many fans use Twitter as a platform to react to the match progress and results. In this study, we utilize the Twitter API and analyze tweets relating to Overwatch League matches using TextBlob to compute the sentiment polarity based on POS tagging. Each tweet will be assigned a score in the range of -1 to +1. We hypothesized that tweets mentioning winning teams would include more positive sentiments on average than tweets mentioning losing teams, but our preliminary analysis (with limited data) indicates that the relationship between sentiment and match outcomes may be more complicated.

KEYWORDS

Esports, Twitter, Sentiment Analysis, Polarity Analysis, Flashbulb Memory, Python

1. INTRODUCTION

Multiplayer online battle arena games, such as Dota 2, real-time strategy games, such as Clash Royale, and first-person shooter games, such as Overwatch, all have active esports scenes: virtual leagues where professional players compete in a manner similar to physical sports, often sponsored by the developer of the game. Esports have seen a steady growth in both viewership and participation in the past few years. In 2017, 33% of U.S. esports fans are younger millennial consumers (ages 18~24) (The Nielsen Company, 2018). With fan data from channels like Twitter, Twitch, and YouTube, we have an ability to look at their aggregated expectations and opinions of the team's performance. In the 2019 season of the Overwatch League, known as OWL (Blizzard 2020), the stage 2 finals were the best performing esports broadcast across ESPN and ABC (Activision 2019). In this paper, we will focus on Overwatch League fan data gathered from Twitter.

Public opinion about teams changes based on their match performance. In a study that looked at fans of winning and losing teams, Talarico and Moore found that the two groups of fans remembered the same game differently (Talarico and Moore 2012). Winning teams' fans found the game to be more emotional and remembered the factual details more accurately. The other fans' memories had decreased vividness. These memories can be classified as flashbulb memories, which is a subset of autobiographical memory (Brown and Kulik 1977). They are recalled with distinct vividness, sense of reliving the memory, and confidence. According to several studies, when relating memories of an event, participants who viewed the event as positive were more vocal than those who viewed it as negative (Berntsen 2009). If fans of the winning team were generally more vocal, we would expect the overall balance of sentiment to be more positive for winning teams. We investigate this hypothesis by looking at the public statements about two opposing teams on Twitter in a given Overwatch match using sentiment analysis.

Sentiment analysis is a text analysis method used to understand the opinions, emotions, and subjectivity of text. This can be done at document, phrase, and sentence levels, and often assigns a simple polarity score to text, measuring the degree to which the text conveys positive or negative sentiment. The Natural Language ToolKit, NLTK, is a platform that was developed by Loper and Bird for natural language processing education (Loper and Bird 2002), which includes sentiment analysis tools. Previous works have algorithmically analyzed categories of fan engagement from tweets based on Part Of Speech (POS) tagging and per-word sentiment scores (Bhangle and Krishnan 2017). In order to understand the effectiveness of this technique in our target corpus, our initial hypothesis is quite simple: in a given Overwatch League match, we expect tweets mentioning the winning team to have more positive average polarity than tweets mentioning the losing team.

2. METHODOLOGY

There are four major steps in our study, starting with data collection. We used the Twitter Standard Search API (via the Tweepy Python library) to collect the data. Twitter's standard search API deletes data after 5~7 days, so after each Overwatch League (OWL) weekend of matches was completed, we downloaded the data immediately. For each OWL team, there are official and unofficial Twitter hashtags that are used as well as official team Twitter accounts. For the Twitter API call, we used these hashtags and official account IDs to search for a team in a specific match. For ease of filtering, we only included tweets in English. The example below shows how we utilized the API's query parameter to look at tweets about the Boston Uprising OWL team during the match between Boston Uprising and LA Valiant.

query = "BostonUprising OR #BostonUp -filter:retweets -ShanghaiDragons AND -#Breakthrough AND -Charge AND -Hunt AND -spark AND -TorontoDefiant AND -#RiseTogether AND -ParisEternal AND -Spitfire AND -NYXL AND -#EverUpward AND -Reign AND -Mayhem AND -Justice AND -SFShock AND -#Winnable AND -LAGladiators AND -SeoulDynasty AND -TigerNation AND -DallasFuel AND -#BurnBlue AND -#PlayWithFire"

For this string, we included any tweets that contain Boston Uprising's Twitter account ID or their official hashtag, while excluding any tweets that were retweets or which contained any Twitter account IDs or official hashtags from teams not in the match. We used searches to collect two different datasets per team per match. The first search was for pre-match fan engagement, starting 2 hours prior to and ending 10 minutes after the start of a match. The second search aimed to measure engagement during and after the match. Given that the same team played twice during a weekend (Saturday and Sunday), tweets about both matches would overlap if the search extended past the 12-hour mark. We shall refer to pre-match fan engagement as the Prior-Match Period and the 12-hour search period as the Match Period. To avoid potential biases, only the first set of matches in any given OWL weekend was collected.

After gathering the raw data, the next step is post-filtering. Post-filtering is necessary since some OWL teams utilize account IDs and hashtags that are also used in other contexts. Common non-related words are "military", "army", "virus", "college", and "law". These words were generated by adding non-related topics from 10 random tweets in each category (positive, negative, and neutral) to the filter array. We continued to add to the filter array until there were no unrelated tweets for any of the 3 categories of tweets. For each tweet, if they contained any of the filtered words, they would be excluded from the final tweet collection. From a single match between Team A and B, for example, the same post-filtering was applied to all 4 datasets: Team A's Prior-Match Period, Team B's Prior-Match Period, Team A's Match Period, and Team B's Match Period. While this post-filtering may have excluded some tweets that are about OWL, our initial observations confirmed that the tweets filtered out were overwhelmingly unrelated.

The third step in our procedure is analyzing the tweets using sentiment analysis. We utilized TextBlob, which is a Python library for processing textual data built on top of NLTK. TextBlob provides an easy-to-use API for diving into common natural language processing (NLP) tasks (Loria 2020). For sentiment analysis, TextBlob uses a Movies Reviews dataset, which has already been hand-labeled as positive or negative. We passed the post-filtered datasets through TextBlob and measured the average polarity of the tweets in each dataset, ignoring neutral tweets (tweets with 0 polarity).

The final step in our analysis is determining statistical significance. To test our hypothesis, we compared the average polarities for tweets associated with different teams in both winning and losing matches. To compare the two groups of datasets (Match Period datasets from winning vs. losing matches) we ran the Student's t-test by using the t-test function in Google Sheets.

3. ANALYSIS AND RESULTS

We collected and analyzed tweets during the Overwatch League 2020 Season. For the 25 matches that we collected, there were 16,649 tweets and after the post-filter was applied, there were 15,653 remaining tweets, or an average of 626.12 tweets per match.

3.1 Data Collection

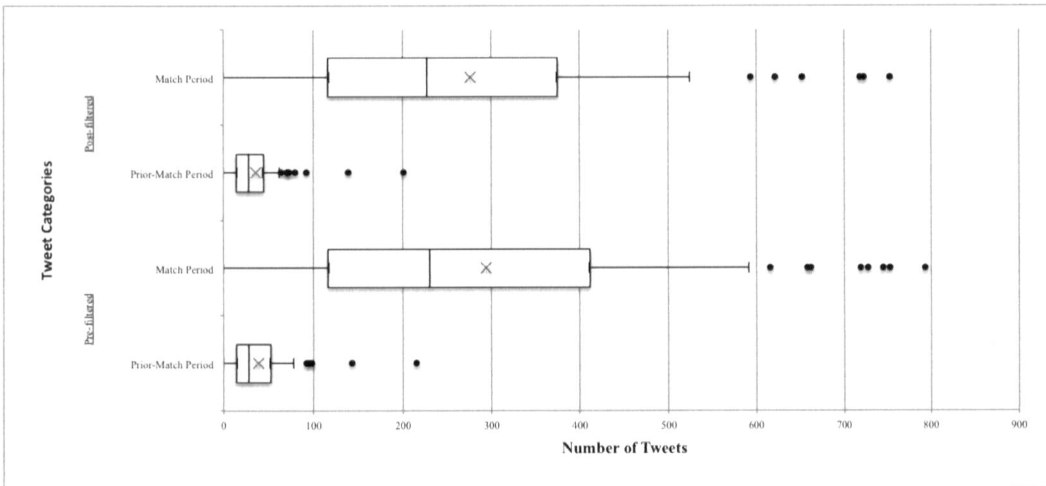

Figure 1. Prior-match period and match period tweets collected

These 25 matches were from weeks 11, 13, 14, and 15. Out of 25 matches, 16 required post filtering. Figure 1 shows the number of tweets we gathered across all of our Prior-Match Period and Match Period datasets. There were an average of 38.7 tweets in the Prior-Match Period (minimum 0, maximum 201, with an average of 36.3 after filtering) and an average of 294.28 tweets in the Match Period (minimum 26, maximum 754, with an average of 276.16 after filtering).

3.2 Sentiment Analysis

Table 1. Examples of collected tweets with polarities

Tweet	Polarity
@BostonUprising it was hard fought but I know you will keep improving and surprising everyone.	0.204166667
@Closer @SFShock Nah. Y'all did good https://t.co/YDeoVeGHAp	0.7
@Crimzo @SFShock You guys popped off	0
This game is kind of sad. Numbani sucks to attack on anyway, rip Outlaws.	-0.15
@Outlaws Hey outlaws, a tip of advice. Fire that sorry sack of crap you call a coach. Sincerely, a former fan	-0.433333333
I BELIEVED. I BELIEVED THEY CAN WIN WAHOOOOOOOO https://t.co/aGChgT4Kex	0.8
watching seoul dynasty is such a rollercoaster of emotions #TigerNation https://t.co/g9MRqJ0pWd	0

After we applied TextBlob to our data, we calculated the average polarity for tweets with non-zero polarity for every team in every match by using just the Match Period tweets. Table 1 lists some examples of the collected tweets plus TextBlob's calculated polarity. The third tweet is an example of misclassification: it is labeled as 0 for polarity, but in the context of gaming, saying that a player "popped off" indicates they played well. Out of 25 matches, 17 had higher average polarity for the winning team, as shown in Figure 2. We ran a paired two-sample two-tailed Student's t-test to determine whether the mean difference in polarity between the winning and losing side of each match was different from zero (our hypothesis was that the mean difference would be positive, indicating that the winner of each match was mentioned in overall more positive tweets than the loser). Although our results did not reach statistical significance, Table 2 shows that as we have been able to collect more and more data, the p-value for our t-test has steadily decreased.

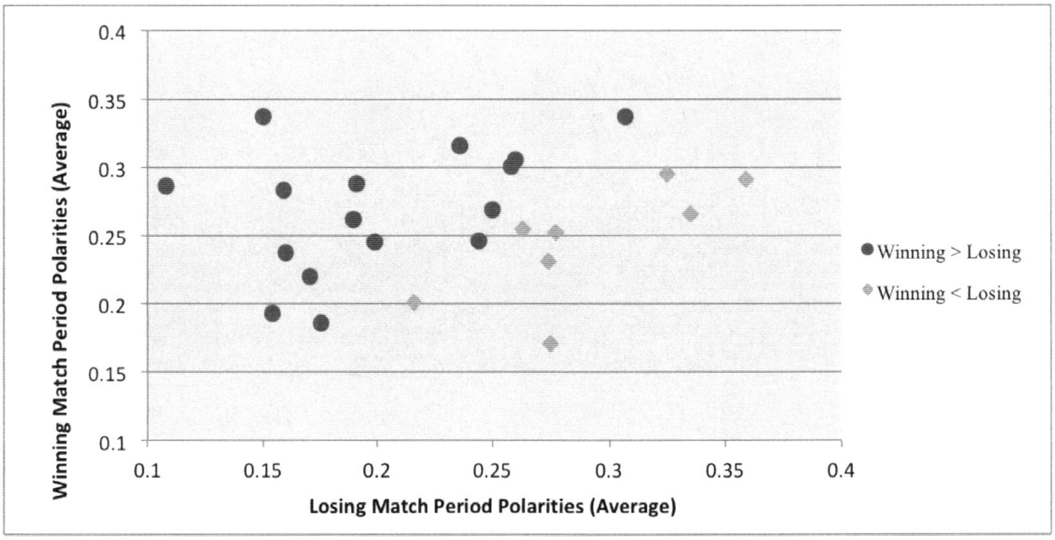

Figure 2. Comparing winning team and losing team average polarities

Table 2. T-test p-values for the mean difference in average polarities for winning and losing sides of each match as more data points are added

Week	end of week 11	end of week 13	end of week 14	end of week 15
P-value	0.658	0.471	0.274	0.158

3.3 Limitations

Fan engagement overall has recently decreased due to OWL moving from the Twitch streaming platform to YouTube. For this season, the average number of viewers at a time was around 44,000 whereas the 2019 season had an average of at least 100,000 viewers. Those games were available to watch in person at homestead arenas, but due to COVID-19 circumstances, matches were postponed during the middle of the current season and subsequent matches (including those we collected data for) were only viewable online.

Furthermore, some teams simply were not mentioned in many of the tweets collected by the search parameters, and most of these are teams that have predominantly Asian players. Given this, their supporters may also be predominantly Asian and would therefore be tweeting in their respective languages and not in English. Also, the classification of tweets is not perfect. The high percentage of neutral tweets might be explained by the classifier not picking up positive or negative language in the context of a video game.

4. CONCLUSION

4.1 Implications

With the data we were able to gather for this study, the p-value for our hypothesis is 0.158, which is not significant, indicating that the relationship between tweet polarity and match outcomes may be subtler than our initial hypothesis proposes. We are hopeful that our originally proposed relationship may be confirmed with more data, but the fact that it is not confirmed given the data we have collected so far suggests that the relationship is not a straightforward one. If we do achieve statistical significance, it would imply that the public opinion on Twitter is more favorable to the winning team than the losing team, but the effect size might be small. Our analysis so far seems to indicate that sentiment analysis can be productively applied to look for patterns in Twitter responses to OWL matches, but we may need to develop a more sophisticated theory about what kinds of relationships might exist.

4.2 Future Work

Aside from collecting more data to potentially confirm our hypothesis, future work could go in a few different directions. We could try to identify teams' fan accounts and more directly explore our hypothesis in the context of fan engagement by looking at tweets from those specific accounts. With enough data, we could also look at how the public opinion and fan base opinion change based on the closeness of a match, such as comparing the polarities between 3-2 matches and 3-0 matches. As for the sentiment analysis part of future research, changing how the tweets' polarities are calculated such that they account for gaming linguistics as pointed out in Section 3.2 could be productive. There are other Python libraries for sentiment analysis such as SpaCy, Stanford CoreNLP, and Gensim; one of these libraries might yield more accurate results for polarity.

REFERENCES

Activision Blizzard CEO says 2019 season of Overwatch League breaking records. (2019, August 8). The Fly. https://link-gale-com.ezproxy.wellesley.edu/apps/doc/A595916939/ITOF?u=mlin_m_wellcol&sid=ITOF&xid =3a564133'

Berntsen, D. (2009). Flashbulb memory and social identity. In O. Luminet, & A. Curci (Eds.), Flashbulb memories: New issues and new perspectives (pp. 187–205). New York, NY: Psychology Press.

Bhangle R.S. and Sornalakshmi K. (2018) Twitter Sentimental Analysis on Fan Engagement. In: Rajsingh E., Veerasamy J., Alavi A., Peter J. (eds) Advances in Big Data and Cloud Computing. Advances in Intelligent Systems and Computing, vol 645. Springer, Singapore

Blizzard Entertainment, INC. (2020). Overwatch League. https://overwatchleague.com/en-us

Brown, R., & Kulik, J. (1977). Flashbulb memories. Cognition, 5(1), 73–99. https://doi.org/10.1016/0010-0277(77) 90018-X

Loper, E. and Bird, S. (2002). NLTK: the Natural Language Toolkit. In Proceedings of the ACL-02 Workshop on Effective tools and methodologies for teaching natural language processing and computational linguistics - Volume 1 (ETMTNLP '02). Association for Computational Linguistics, USA, 63–70. https://doi.org/10.3115/1118108.1118117

Loria, S. et al. (2020). TextBlob: Simplified Text Processing. TextBlob. https://textblob.readthedocs.io/en/dev/

The Nielsen Company (2018). Distribution of eSports fans in the United States in 2017, by age group. In Statista: The Statistics Portal. https://www.statista.com/statistics/532322/esports-viewers-by-age-usa/

Talarico, J.M. and Moore, K.M. (2012). Memories of 'The Rivalry': Differences in How Fans of the Winning and Losing Teams Remember the Same Game. Appl. Cognit. Psychol., 26: 746-756. doi:10.1002/acp.2855

HUMAN-CENTRIC TECHNOLOGY FOR URBAN PLANNING

Vaijayanthi Iyengar[1] and Paul Chavez[2]
[1]*7 Eleven, Director/UX, 1 3200 Hackberry Rd, Irving, TX 75063,, USA*
[2]*Arup, Associate Technology/UX,. 900 Wilshire Boulevard, Los Angeles, California, USA*

ABSTRACT

When people gather, the space in which they meet has the potential to form bonds and create lasting communities. Successful urban spaces evolve structurally based on these communities, societal models, and the ability to coexist. With the evolution of smart and ubiquitous computing, spaces have a new variable that impacts social perception — technology. In the past two decades, humans have evolved an intimate and everyday relation with digital technology. This article infers from studies on these performative relationships between humans and technology, it's behavioral manifestation and applies it to the current practices in urban development. The article also refers to a phase in the history of urban design where behavior-based people-oriented design gained momentum. The inferences from these two topics are used for making a case to formalize the process of inclusive technology in urban development so as to create a sustainable and resilient environment for urban denizens.

KEYWORDS

Citizen Engagement, Urban Perspective, Socio-Technical Challenges, Smart City Interaction

1. INTRODUCTION

This article is a collective output of exploratory discussions between a User Experience Designer and a Spatial Strategist. The discussion specifically focuses on two aspects: the 3rd paradigm of Human-computer interaction (Harrison, Tatar & Sengers, 2007) and the impact of 1960s Behaviorism on urban development. While seemingly disparate, these two topics were explored together because they both fundamentally address the cultural and emotional aspects of considering humans in the design process. The 3rd paradigm of human-computer interaction, or: The Situated Paradigm, acknowledges the social, cultural, and physical situatedness of users in the context of digital technology. This helps to understand the behavioral aspirations of technology in humans and consequently in urban society. Historically, a similar momentum existed during the 1960s and 70s between behavior and spaces. During this era, the citizens and few urban designers questioned the monofunctional approach to architecture. A call for urban inclusion was made because the gap between the goals of urban residents and urban designers was widening. We discuss the manifestation of this historic movement into today's urban development processes and extrapolate some inferences into the future. The overarching goal of this effort is to identify the framework and theories that can be juxtaposed between urban planning and technology and therefore serve as the catalyst for a holistic design process for smart city planning.

2. SITUATEDNESS IN HUMAN-COMPUTER INTERACTION

Human-Computer Interaction could be informally classified in three paradigms: Human-Factors based, Classical Cognitivism/Information-Processing based, and the Third/Phenomenological-Situated paradigm based (Frauenberger, 2019). The third classification, which is an evidence-based developmental paradigm was of particular interest to our discussion since it elaborates on the concept of meaning-making. A comparable thought in urban design is termed "placemaking" (Thomas, 2016). Both concepts beseech the designers to create contextual artifacts based on the situation, collaborative inputs, socio-economic and psychological needs, and diversity in user/citizen requirements. In contemporary cities where political opinions are polarized, religion is an influencer, migration is debated, racial friction is heightened and the current pandemic is isolating, technology needs to be situational and emotional. This situatedness will encourage technologists to evolve operational algorithms for connected cities with non-tangible elements such as citizen psychology and other socio-tech factors. The ad hoc nature of digital networks is capable of supporting an adaptive urban space. The emerging technologies that are being applied for smart cities of the future should have the ability to respond to a fluid context. New modalities in technology like gestures, AR/VR, tangible/ non-tangible interfaces, and pervasive technology are often designed and applied in isolation (Bødker, 2006). The adaptive context of a space could be reflected in the modality of the chosen technology. For example, smart streetlights could be used to communicate the general health of a district using color-coded illumination.

3. BEHAVIORISM OF THE 60S

"The job of buildings is to improve human relations; architecture must ease them, not make them worse." - Ralph Erskine

Around the early 60s as rapid urbanization happened across the major cities in the world, the modernist movement was gaining a lot of popularity among urban designers. 'Functionalism' is often characterized as the driving force for creating simplified, minimal spaces. This popular notion also emphasized creating negative spaces that often led to a "no man's land." While popular among urban designers for multiple decades from a human settlement perspective there was often a gap in addressing realities like social disparity, diversity and economic inclusivity (Forlano, 2009). Designers and urban inhabitants, with arguments that favored inclusion of people-centricity in urban design, later questioned these monofunctional approaches in design. They encouraged collective participation of citizens and designers to reinvent the definition of spaces, especially with focus on creating sustainable communities and shared values.

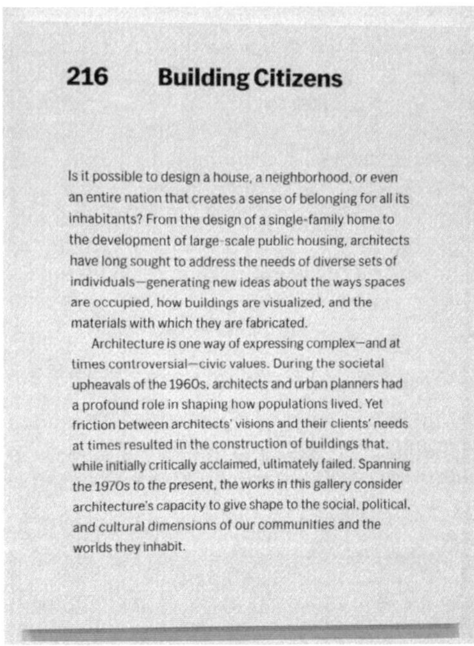
216 Building Citizens

Is it possible to design a house, a neighborhood, or even an entire nation that creates a sense of belonging for all its inhabitants? From the design of a single-family home to the development of large-scale public housing, architects have long sought to address the needs of diverse sets of individuals—generating new ideas about the ways spaces are occupied, how buildings are visualized, and the materials with which they are fabricated.

Architecture is one way of expressing complex—and at times controversial—civic values. During the societal upheavals of the 1960s, architects and urban planners had a profound role in shaping how populations lived. Yet friction between architects' visions and their clients' needs at times resulted in the construction of buildings that, while initially critically acclaimed, ultimately failed. Spanning the 1970s to the present, the works in this gallery consider architecture's capacity to give shape to the social, political, and cultural dimensions of our communities and the worlds they inhabit.

Figure 1. Exhibit 216 MoMA

There was a demand for a platform to be heard and for their voices to be included in design decisions. The series of exhibits in the Museum of Modern Arts (MoMA), titled "Building Citizens" (Figure 1), one can view the struggle of social disruption in cities, gaps in layout, occupation of spaces, and even the visual language of buildings. This critical thinking invoked a sense of belonging while designing a home, neighborhood, or an entire nation.

The urban landscapes created during the 60s and 70s were labeled by some urban designers as "Behaviorism". The scholarly publications and urban design communities of this period often called out that urban settlements were failing owing to a gap between planners and residents. In her famous book, 'The Death and Life of Great American Cities', Jane Jacobs mentions the perils of modernist city planning, the rigidness of Functionalism, or rather the lack of people-sensitive insights (Sim, 2019). These observations were fueled by the ambiguities in pubic versus private space and the needs of its inhabitants. These gaps could be attributed to the fact that urban planners were designing with little, if any, input from the citizens. The changing viewpoints and perspectives led to a movement where the interaction between these factors were given greater importance and hence these decades marked the beginning of a very different phase of urban development.

4. CURRENT SOCIO-TECHNICAL RELATIONSHIPS IN URBAN SPACES

The systems that build a city are all not just physical entities. In fact, in his talk 'The Happy City Experiment', Charles Montgomery talks about how the parks, the roadways, the buildings, and the water bodies all contribute to the emotional infrastructure of a city. Similarly, the digital proliferation in transportation, commerce, waste disposal, communication, sheltering, health, and civic systems is also influencing this emotional infrastructure. Current technology trends are surpassing the needs of an individual and lending support for more connected community spaces. The networked nature of technology provisions liaising between the citizens, public infrastructure and urban developers. From the recent gatherings and conferences on emerging design systems (RSD8 Symposium, 2019), it is observed that dynamic ecosystems come together for an instance of time, contextual to an event or message, and peer produced through social media. To design for future cities grounded in the principles of resilience, collaboration and inclusion, the complexity of these systems should be considered in building solutions for 'connected' cities.

The proliferation of technology in the past twenty years has enabled citizens to be vocal about their needs in urban evolution. Ranging from casual park gatherings to the #BLM movement, we can see how emotion through social media, texting, tweeting, etc. made its way to the streets and reflected the pulse of the time. The tweets, vlogging and multiple social media channels were associated with zip codes, demographics, and law and order infrastructure. While the digital technology enabled transmission of citizen emotions, this was a reactive platform. If the cities can be proactively prepared to facilitate citizen participation in an organized approach, it can help create meaningful collaborations that could lead to accountability.

The following table outlines some contemporary examples of how technology and urban spaces have reactively and proactively come together to define new experiences.

Table 1. Contemporary examples of technology in urban spaces

Technology	Human Experience
Wayfinding in Airports	Rideshare like Uber or Lyft - digital interaction within an app is defining the parking needs, pedestrian circulation, and signage in a space. For example, most urban airports now have designated zones to accommodate rideshare users. The introduction of this new pick-up zone resulted in an additional requirement: guidance to get there. Hence the traditional physical signage is being overlaid with digital counterparts like GPS aps and AR-based guidance apps for aiding circulation. In addition, the circulations paths of pedestrians, traffic flow of pick up and drop vehicles, etc. have changed based on these popular digital applications (Kim, Wang & Han, 2015)

Digital physical retail stores	Amazon Go retail - The rating and review in a web application transcend into a brick-and-mortar store. These stores carry a highly curated selection of products from the top categories across Amazon.com. Strategically based beacons & sensors, app-based POS systems and integration with biometrics all work to make this experience seamless (and with little human services intervention).
The wireless scooter	Uber is developing robotic versions of the ubiquitous electric scooter to support micro-mobility. This will have an impact on urban planning, road traffic control, safety hazard and support, docking and charging requirements and correlation with pedestrian circulation. This is an example of a new transport ecosystem enabled by IoT that in turn impacts other infrastructures within a city. The layout of roads, dimensions for circulation, anthropometric considerations are all possibly going to get modified by these digitized vehicles.
City as a platform (CaaS)	London is working with tech companies to tackle urban challenges. Widely addressed topics included homelessness, social care, cyber-security, diversity, and inclusion. Tech companies are developing the City as a platform strategy to create a more modular and sustainable approach to smart cities. This approach will help to address the layers of complexity in a city and aims to identify drivers necessary for change

5. AREAS TO EXPLORE AND IMPROVE

Based on the hypothesis drawn from an important phase of urban development and emerging paradigms in the HCI community, we conclude that technology can play an immersive role in the future of city planning. The gaps identified from urban development movements of the 60s and 70s reflect that built forms need to consider individual and societal needs including diversity, inclusivity and resiliency. Leading architectural journals like World Health Design, Environment Behavior, and HERD, have voiced that consciously designed spaces can influence behavior. Technology can facilitate emotional liaising between city planners and its dwellers on subjects that lend social, political, and cultural dimensions to space. Here are suggestions for Human-Centered Technology in urban planning

- Identification of tangible and intangible drivers that impact spatial aspirations
- Utilize big data to create metrics based on public trust, user acceptance, and citizen engagement in smart services. Intangibles like societal conflicts, fear, compatibility, well-being, hopefulness, empathy and tangibles like air quality, proximity, waste management
- Track behavior changes led by the daily usage of smart city services and facilities
- Trace and correlate emotional quotient and well-being related to an event or incident impacting the community
- Document socio-technical and systemic design industry challenges that impact the development and deployment of smart infrastructure in cities like smart mobility and waste management
- Provide dynamic and real-time channels to maintain transparency with citizens
- Identify touch points between technology and transitional environments — Transitions from home to vehicular environment, to a productive environment or commuting for leisure, the transition from work to recreation area
- Creating balances the automation systems that is tailored based on social context and real-time demographics

Today technology mostly exists in execution and realization capacity. In execution modes, technology often focuses on efficiency and productivity. This task-based process usually results in a capsule solution overlaid on traditional elements of urban architecture (e.g. buildings, streets, signage, lights, etc.).

In contemporary smart city solutions, the success is measured in terms of productivity and efficiency. But we fail to evaluate intangible factors, for example trust, fear and timelessness. To elaborate the impact of trust and fear in a smart city project we can take the example of the City of San Diego's Smart Streetlight program: While this program addresses energy efficiency, traffic congestion issues, IoT based crime tracking, it has also caused unrest in terms of unrestricted data mining triggering a fear of panopticism and prompting the question, "How can the data being acquired be more transparent and visible to citizens?" the artifacts installed and maintained by civic and urban development bodies can have a perception based context (Hargrove, 2019). These designs may have missed to consider that with passage of time citizens will interact with these urban elements in their everyday lives. And everyday interactions include political and emotional opinions.

This correlation technology, emotions and politics was observed early by Winner where he wrote that technical artifacts have political properties and in turn can embody forms of authority and subordination (Winner, 1980). Timelessness is another intangible factor for technology-based design consideration. Networked devices, digital displays, and audio systems do not have life spans that compare with street signs and lampposts. This requires planners and technologists to plan cities together in ways that allow for a high level of infrastructure flexibility where technologies may be added or updated. The mode of technology is merely a delivery system; however, the messaging is eternal. Inferences drawn from history (section 2 of this reflection) reflect that the concerns of citizens are more or less similar. Fifty years later, there are still divides, tensions and conflicts that great cities have to face and resolve. Through immersive technology, the citizen concerns get a collaborative platform, an amplified medium and an effective way of documenting actions and emotions.

6. CONCLUSION

Technology has been an important part of city planning of the past decade and modern cities have taken many steps to integrate technology. Urban planners are drifting from rigid guidelines of zoning into creating a human-centered urban design. Appointing CTOs, CIOs and CXOs of cities, partnering with innovative tech companies, and creating digital touch points for citizen engagement and participation are some examples.

Urban development and design are historically associated with architecture and hence have deep rooted connections with aesthetic theories of design and ingrained design practices. For the principles of human computer interaction design to be adopted for urban development, it is important to acknowledge the pockets of ad-hoc ecosystems that technology helps to create. Similarly, technologists designing for 'smart cities' also need to look beyond efficiency and productivity and take accountability to address the socio-economic and psychological aspirations of citizens. A technology solution to a human problem requires that human considerations are at the forefront of any technology application.

Cities outlive technology, so while the mode of technology might keep changing, the citizen's voices change slowly. In this information age of vloggers, bloggers, tweeters, and YouTubers, we have numerous channels to amplify their voice and the designers better be listening.

REFERENCES

Bødker, Susanne. (2006). When second wave HCI meets third wave challenges. ACM International Conference Proceeding Series. 189. 1-8. 10.1145/1182475.1182476.

Forlano, Laura. (2016). "Decentering the Human in the Design of Collaborative Cities." Design Issues 32, no. 3: 42-54.

Frauenberger C. (2019). "Entanglement HCI The Next Wave?" ACM Transactions on Computer-Human Interaction (TOCHI) 27: 2.

Hargrove Dorian. (2019, December 13). City Is Hiding Data From Smart Street Lights, https://www.nbcsandiego.com/news/local/city-is-hiding-data-from-smart-street-lights-lawsuit-claims/2230490/

Harrison, S. Tatar, D. and Sengers, P. (2007) The three paradigms of HCI. Ext. Abstracts CHI 2007, ACM Press

Kim, M., Wang, X., Han, S. et al. (2015). Implementing an augmented reality-enabled wayfinding system through studying user experience and requirements in complex environments. Vis. in Eng. 3, 14 https://doi.org/10.1186/s40327-015-0026-2

RSD8 Symposium. (2019, October 13-15). IIT Institute of Design, Chicago

Sim, David. (2019). Soft City: Building Density for Everyday Life, Island Press

Thomas, D. (2016). Placemaking: An Urban Design Methodology. Routledge.

Winner, Langdon. (1980). "Do Artifacts Have Politics?" www.jstor.org/stable/20024652.

THE EFFECT OF THREE DIFFERENT POSTURE COMPUTER WORKSTATION ON WORKING PERFORMANCE

Takeshi Sato[1], Mizuki Nakajima Macky Kato[1], Ryota Murano[2] and Hiroshi Morikawa[2]
[1]Jissen Women's University, 4-1-1, Osakaue Hino Tokyo, Japan
[2]Waseda University, Tokorozawa Saitama, Japan

ABSTRACT

This study aimed to investigate the effect of active workstation designs on sitting, standing and walking during simple typing and pad pointing, and combined tasks for office job. The gradual shift from manufacturing to service industries, combined with technological advanced has resulted in increasing number of people employed in sedentary occupations. It was well known that prolonged sitting was to associate with an increased risk of premature mortality and high levels of sitting cannot be compensated for leisure-time physical activity. Sedentary behavior as sitting computer operation should not be viewed as simply the absence of physical activity or as the extreme lower muscles of lacing physical activity. 13 females performed 20-min office work as typing and searching tasks in each posture, siting, standing desk and standing desk with walking while Oxygen uptake data and HR values was recorded. On the first occasion, a brief description of the test procedures and apparat us was repeated both orally and in writing. They performed on a treadmill to determine their individual oxygen uptake (VO2) and office work like several tasks. Mainly finding showed that walking had significantly higher VO2 than sitting and standing. Moreover, studies have found no effect of Changes in working posture like sitting and standing on computer work performance. Insufficient physical activity is a major threat to health and productivity of office workers. The study confirmed that the difference in energy expenditure of tasks carried out in sitting compared to standing is negligible. Therefore, it is considered that providing exercise habits such as standing and walking while performing office work is an opportunity to eliminate lack of exercise by employees. Rather than sitting all the time, sometimes changing postures and working was considered as one of the health management of employees.

KEYWORDS

Working Posture, Oxygen Uptake, Office Work, Sedentary Worker

1. INTRODUCTION

Prolonged sedentary behavior is associated with increased cardiovascular disease risk and decreased energy expenditure due to lacking physical activity. Time spent sedentary is increasing both in the workplace and during everyday life and work. Physical inactivity has long been recognized as detrimental for cardiovascular and metabolic health, however previous studies has remained sedentary behavior as one of the independent health risk factors (Dunstan, et al., 2012). It was well known prolonged sitting is associated with decreased metabolic health, cardiovascular disease and increased mortality. It means that low energy expenditure with sitting is to implicate in the increased prevalence of overweight and obesity, making sedentary behavior an expanding research filed within work-based ICT environment. Therefore, standing computer work is increasingly popular. Standing posture is generally less muscularly demanding than the sitting computer work, neck/shoulder musculature responds evaluated electromyography in each posture during typing tasks. There was not enough data to measure the directory energy expenditure as VO_2 during three different working posture. The purpose of this study was to investigate the computer operation tasks and compare the VO_2 and heart rate (HR) responses during sitting, standing and walking.

2. METHODS

Thirteen females with no smoking, no cardiovascular and metabolic disease participated in this study. It was performed 20 min pseudo office work test as typing and searching tasks operating computer in three difference posture, siting, standing desk and standing desk with optimum walking recording VO_2 (VO2000, MGC, USA) and HR. It was performed on three different same level computer tasks during three working posture (Figure 1). Data were analyzed during three different posture performance, were compare using ANOVA. When a significant main effect or interaction effect was identified, differences were delineated using a paired Student's t-test. For all comparisons, significance was set at $P < 0.05$. All data are presented as means ± SD. Statically analyses were performed using SAS University edition.

Figure 1. Experimental settings with measurement devices, sitting(left), standing(middle), walking(right)

3. RESULTS

There were significantly different between sitting (7.8±6.3 ml/kg/min) and standing (10.9±9.4 ml/kg/min), and walking (27.6±17.8 ml/kg/min) in VO_2 (Figure 2). It was normalize performance adjusted standard deviation score as pseudo office work with using personal computer in three conditions. There was no significantly difference performance tasks during 20 min several personal computer operation tests. Moreover, there was no significant difference HR response (Figure 3) for sitting (76.0±5.3 beat/min) and standing (86.2±9.1 beat/min), and walking (89.2±10.4 beat/min).

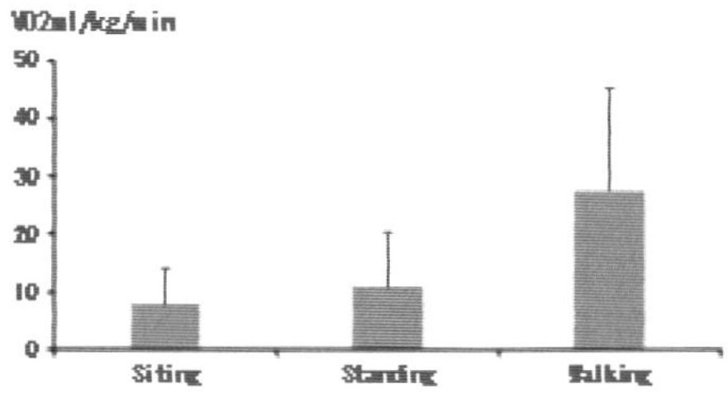

Figure 2. VO_2 response in three different working posture

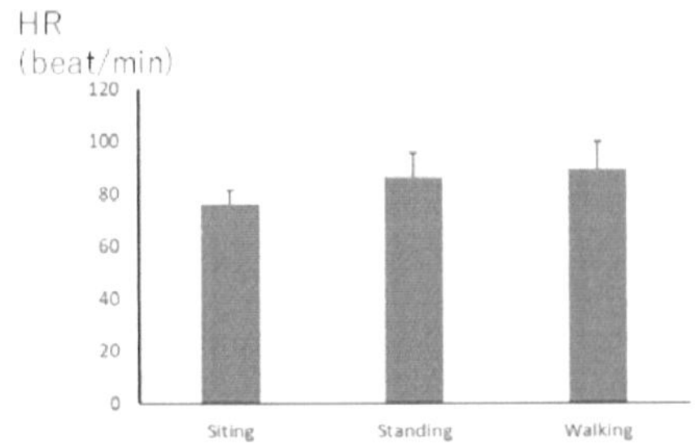

Figure 3. Heart Rate response in three different working posture

4. DISCUSSION

This study investigated three different working posture as an alternative intervention choice which could be utilized to interrupt sedentary time. It was important the current definition of sedentary behavior by measuring the energy expenditure of office-based tasks in three different posture. During this experimental task, participants were required to repetitively scroll pages and perform mouse pad operations due to notebook station as well as type texts and simply drawing. Previous study performed the definition of sedentary work behavior using METs as calorimetry (Mansoubi et al., 2015) but included tasks were watching television, just typing, playing PlayStation Portable and Wii that were different from office-work tasks. Therefore, it was performed to walk optimized each other, walking speed was very slowly at around 1.4 km/h. Then, it was not change in HR responses between standing task and walking task with keeping sedentary physical level. This study found the task of personal computer had a greater effect on VO2 energy expended than the three different posture. This finding would suggest that to increase the energy cost of office activity with personal computer, to perform office-activity on the standing and walking in acceptable conclusion range.

5. CONCLUSION

This study demonstrates standing posture are a time efficient method to break up sedentary time, which has the practical potential to be employed in workplaces.

HEADING

Working posture with walking, standing, sitting.

ACKNOWLEDGEMENT

We wish to thank the daily help given by Miss. Mana Yoshioka in analyzing the experimental data.

REFERENCES

Dunstan DW, Howard B, Healy GN, Owen N, 2012. Too much sitting - a health hazard. *Diabetes Res Clin Pract*, Vol 97, pp. 368-376.

Mansoubi M. Pearson N, Clemes S, Yates T, 2015. Enegy expenditure during common sitting and standing tasks: Examining the 1.5MET definition od sedentary behavior. BMC Public Health, Vol 15, pp.515, doi:10.1186/s12889-015-1851-x.

INFORMATION SYSTEMS FOR ENVIRONMENTAL SUSTAINABILITY. HOW CAN COMPANIES CREATE A SUSTAINABLE AQUACULTURE INDUSTRY?

Carolina Costabile
Norwegian School of Economics, Helleveien 30, 5045 Bergen, Norway

ABSTRACT

Environmental sustainability is among the main global challenges of the 21st century. Although information systems that can provide data and insights about the status of the environment are considered valuable to better handle sustainability concerns, their potential is still not fully realized. Moreover, information systems research for sustainability is proceeding at a slow pace in relation to the real needs of our society. Therefore, this doctoral paper aims at embracing the urgent call for studies about sustainability from an Information Systems perspective. Through a case study in the Norwegian aquaculture industry, my work will contribute in understanding how companies can address environmental challenges by relying on digital technologies and their (IS-enabled) sensing, seizing, and recombining capabilities.

KEYWORDS

Information Systems, Environmental Sustainability, Dynamic Capabilities, Aquaculture

1. INTRODUCTION

Sustainability is internationally receiving increasingly attention from governments, consumers, organizations, and the whole society (Ziegler et al, 2013), which are all concerned in playing their role for a better world (Malhotra et al, 2013). Indeed, resources are currently being overused compared to what the nature can offer. And the way resources are being utilized is affecting the environment, often going towards a point of no return (Sarkis et al, 2013). The current environmental deterioration makes it clear why environmental sustainability initiatives are considerably popular across the world (Chen et al, 2009).

Information systems can be of pivotal importance in addressing environmental issues (Olson, 2008; Elliot, 2011; Malhotra et al, 2013; Seidel et al, 2017), and in affecting the success of these initiatives, especially because they can assess the status of the environment, and provide data and insights on which to make informed and appropriate decisions (Gholami et al, 2016). However, despite technology potential is broadly acknowledged, it is not fully exploited nor realized.

Therefore, I want to embrace the urgent call for solution-oriented studies directed towards information systems for sustainability (Gholami et al, 2016), and I want to give my contribution in solving environmental concerns in the aquaculture industry that is one of the sectors where challenges are extremely severe. Through a qualitative case study about a data lake initiative, I want to explore how companies can significantly address and progress towards environmental sustainability by relying on digital technologies and (IS-enabled) dynamic capabilities.

2. BACKGROUND

The World Commission on Environment and Development defined sustainability as the "*development that meets the needs of the present without compromising the ability of the future generations to meet their own needs*" (WECD, 1987, p.43). The concept involves environmental, social, and economic aspects.

Environmental sustainability has been studied for decades in the field of operations, marketing and management, but not as much as needed as in the Information Systems field (Melville, 2010). Here, some studies have addressed the minimization of technology impacts on the environment (Green IT) and some others the enabling greening power of technology (Green IS) (vom Brocke et al., 2013), which is stronger when technology provides actionable knowledge (Gholami et al, 2016) about environment and business operations.

2.1 Sustainability Challenges in the Norwegian Aquaculture Industry

Aquaculture industry has pulled the Norwegian seafood industry (norwayexports.no, 2008) but has also raised concerns (Ziegler et al, 2013; Tveterås, 2002).

Indeed, after a decade of fast growth, aquaculture production volume has stagnated since 2012 because of, among other reasons, lice breakouts. Sea lice represents a big threat to wild salmon life and welfare together with escaped farmed salmon, which spreads diseases and parasites, and causes crossbreeds (Olaussen, 2018).

Another challenge that affects biological sustainability is pollution due to the high fish density in the cages, which results in faeces and undigested feed, and to the chemical treatments used to fight parasites (Olaussen, 2018). The whole industry must find a solution to the several and current challenges to stay competitive and to achieve a sustainable production of 5 million tons of salmon and trout by 2050.

2.2 Digital Technologies for Sustainability in the Aquaculture Industry

Automation will play a key role for sustainability in the aquaculture industry.

Useful technologies are drones which may detect sea lice, monitor feeding process, maintain and repair net damages to prevent fish escapes (sintef.no, 2017), as well as IoT and Big Data analytics to collect, extract and analyze the massive daily amount of data that the industry produces.

The value extracted from data must not be considered as a source of competitive advantage for a single company, but something beneficial to the whole industry, since companies should jointly act to address the width of environmental sustainability that is far beyond a single organization (Watson et al, 2010).

It has been estimated that 85% of the aquaculture industry leaders is willing to invest in new technologies thanks to decreasing costs and time-to-market (PwC, 2017), showing times are ripe for leveraging on the technological transformative power in facing environmental issues.

3. THE THEORETICAL FRAME

Dynamic Capability theory gained popularity after the seminal article by Teece et al (1997) where dynamic capabilities were defined as the firm's ability to face evolving environments by integrating, building, and reconfiguring competencies.

Dynamic capabilities, as the name suggests, are not static as in the Resource-based view theory, and are essentially of three kinds: 1) *sensing* (and shaping) that refers to scan, create, and interpret new opportunities; 2) *seizing* that means addressing these opportunities; 3) *reconfiguring* that is related to assets recombination to face the changes in the environment and not to be constrained by well-known routines (i.e. *path dependencies*, Teece et al, 1997) (Teece, 2007). The theory highlights the role of managers who are supposed to find new and valuable combinations of resources both within and across the borders of their firm (Teece, 2007) in order to make its asset base not imitable (Teece, n.d.).

4. METHOD

I will start my research with a literature review in order to gain an understanding of what has been discovered so far about my topic of interest.

Aiming at investigating how aquaculture companies choose and implement technologies (sensors, AI, Big Data Analytics), build and organize practices and processes to face environmental sustainability, I will study the AquaCloud platform which daily calculates the number of sea lice per fish in order to reduce sea lice infestations to environmentally sustainable levels (seafoodinnovation.no, 2017). I will study this data lake initiative from its launch in 2017 up to date by giving specific focus on how companies organize around and use technology within and across their borders to solve environmental sustainability issues.

A qualitative and longitudinal case study will allow me to comprehend how this initiative has emerged and developed over time, as well as to contribute to the development of a theory in its initial stage as Dynamic Capability (Helfat and Peteraf, 2009).

4.1 Data Collection

Data collection will be mainly based on semi-structured interviews.

In order to gather rich and quality data, I plan to interview different companies, and especially managerial and technical figures who are directly involved in AquaCloud development, architecture and governance, and who are key deciders about technology and sustainability.

Based on my theoretical lens, which will act as a guideline to access the empirical setting (Dubois and Gadde, 2002), I will design an interview protocol. I plan to collect information about environmental issues that need to be dealt with, motives that made companies join AquaCloud, technologies which have been put in place, and sharing attitude among the industry. On this last point, attention will be put on path dependencies (Teece et al, 1997), which may constrain the willingness to share data and collaborate among companies, and which may prevent the achievement of data harmonization and quality, important for the success of the whole initiative (seafoodinnovation.no, 2017). With the aim of uncovering sensing, seizing, and reconfiguring capabilities, I may ask about: how new opportunities are identified and technologies for environmental sustainability are chosen; how the identified opportunities are selected and executed, and how knowledge is shared; how changes in the environment are managed and to what extent data can improve the way sustainability is being addressed.

I will also try to investigate if new capabilities arise thank to the usage of technology (Singh et al, 2011). Data will be also collected through more objective sources as observations and archival data which will allow me to triangulate data coming from interviews.

4.2 Data Analysis

I plan to analyze data by using an abductive approach.

By going back and forth between theory, empirical world and case analysis, my first goal will be to discover core and recurrent themes in the data which refer to sensing, seizing and reconfiguring capabilities to address environmental sustainability with the use of technology. At first, the coding will reflect the participants' language as much as possible, so to ground my interpretation in the empirical context (Gioia et al, 2013). Then, a more abstract level will be reached, by combining the 1st round findings with theory.

5. CONCLUSION

With my research, I am willing to contribute to a real problem and to help businesses tackle environmental sustainability by means of technology.

I plan to develop a framework with best practices and give practical examples of dynamic capabilities. Dynamic capabilities have not been fully well explained so far, and I may contribute by identifying the capabilities needed to exploit technology, how these capabilities are created, and what supports (e.g. technology) or hinders their development.

Limitations and personal biases, as well as ethical aspects will be taken into consideration.

REFERENCES

Chen, A. et al, 2009. Organizational Adoption of Green IS & IT: An Institutional Perspective. *ICIS 2009 Proceedings*, 142.

Dubois, A. and Gadde, L.E., 2002. Systematic combining: an abductive approach to case research. *Journal of business research*, 55(7), pp.553-560.

Elliot, S., 2011. Transdisciplinary perspectives on environmental sustainability: a resource base and framework for IT-enabled business transformation. *MIS quarterly*, 35(1), pp.197-236.

Gholami, R. et al, 2016. Information systems solutions for environmental sustainability: How can we do more?. *Journal of the Association for Information Systems*, 17(8), pp.521-536.

Gioia, D.A. et al, 2013. Seeking qualitative rigor in inductive research: Notes on the Gioia methodology. *Organizational research methods*, 16(1), pp.15-31.

Helfat, C.E. and Peteraf, M.A., 2009. Understanding dynamic capabilities: progress along a developmental path. *Strategic Organization*, 7 (1), pp.91-102.

Malhotra, A. et al, 2013. Spurring impactful research on information systems for environmental sustainability. *MIS quarterly*, 37(4), pp.1265-1274.

Melville, N.P., 2010. Information systems innovation for environmental sustainability. *MIS quarterly*, 34(1), pp.1-21.

Norwayexport.no, 2008. *Norway's Fisheries: Healthy, Productive & Sustainable*. [online] Available at: <https://www.norwayexports.no/norways-fisheries-healthy-productive-sustainable/> [Accessed 10 December 2019].

Olaussen, J.O., 2018. Environmental problems and regulation in the aquaculture industry. Insights from Norway. *Marine Policy*, 98, pp.158-163.

Olson, E.G., 2008. Creating an enterprise-level "green" strategy. *Journal of business strategy*, 29(2), pp.22-30.

PwC, 2017. *Sustainable growth towards 2050. PwC Seafood Barometer.* [pdf] Available at: <https://www.pwc.no/no/publikasjoner/pwc-seafood-barometer-2017.pdf> [Accessed 20 March 2020].

Sarkis, J. et al, 2013. Green information systems & technologies – this generation and beyond: Introduction to the special issue. *Information Systems Frontiers*, 15 (5), pp.695-704.

Seafoodinnovation.no, 2017. *AquaCloud – The use of artificial intelligence in sea lice management*. [online] Available at: <http://www.seafoodinnovation.no/article/213/AquaCloud_The_use_of_artificial_intelligence_in_sea_lice_management> [Accessed 10 December 2019].

Seidel, S. et al, 2017. The sustainability Imperative in Information Systems Research. *Communications of the Association for Information Systems*, 40 (3), pp.40-52.

Singh, R. et al, 2011. Dynamic capabilities in home health: IT-enabled transformation of post-acute care. *Journal of the Association for Information Systems*, 12 (2), pp.163-188.

Sintef, 2017. *Tomorrow's fish farms will be unmanned.* [online] Available at: https://www.sintef.no/en/latest-news/tomorrows-fish-farms-will-be-unmanned/ [Accessed 10 December 2019].

Teece, D.J., 2007. Explicating dynamic capabilities: the nature and microfoundations of (sustainable) enterprise performance. *Strategic management Journal*, 28(13), pp.1319-1350.

Teece, D.J., n.d. *Dynamic Capabilities*. [online] Available at: https://www.davidjteece.com/dynamic-capabilities [Accessed 20 March 2020].

Teece, D.J. et al, 1997. Dynamic capabilities and strategic management. *Strategic management Journal*, 18(7), pp.509-533.

Tveterås, S., 2002. Norwegian salmon aquaculture and sustainability: the relationship between environmental quality and industry growth. *Marine Resource Economics*, 17(2), pp.121-132.

vom Brocke, J. et al, 2013. Green Information Systems: Directives for the IS Discipline. *Communication of the Association for the Information Systems*, 33 (30), pp.509-520.

Watson, R.T. et al, 2010. Information systems and environmentally sustainable development: Energy informatics and new directions for the IS community. *MIS quarterly*, 34(1), pp.23-38.

World Commission on Environment and Development (WECD), 1987. Our Common Future: Report of the World Commission on Environment and Development.

Ziegler, F. et al, 2013. The carbon footprint of Norwegian seafood products on the global seafood market. *Journal of Industrial Ecology*, 17(1), pp.103-116.

AUTHOR INDEX

International Association for Development of the Information Society (IADIS)
Rua Sao Sebastiao Da Pedreira
No. 100, 30, 1050-209
Lisbon, Portugal

ISBN 978-1-7138-2276-9

CURRAN ASSOCIATES INC.
proceedings.com